THE KILLING SEASON

It is mid–October 1914, and British artillery approaches Ypres through a still-tranquil Belgian land-scape. The photographer was Paul Maze, the French post-Impressionist painter, who had volunteered to work as an interpreter for the British staff. (Imperial War Museum, London)

THE KILLING SEASON

THE AUTUMN OF 1914, YPRES,
AND THE AFTERNOON THAT
COST GERMANY A WAR

ROBERT COWLEY

RANDOM HOUSE
NEW YORK

Random House
An imprint and division of Penguin Random House LLC
1745 Broadway, New York, NY 10019
randomhousebooks.com
penguinrandomhouse.com

LIBRARY OF CONGRESS CATALOGING–IN–PUBLICATION DATA
Names: Cowley, Robert, author.
Title: The killing season: the autumn of 1914, Ypres, and the afternoon that cost
Germany a war / Robert Cowley.
Other titles: Autumn of 1914, Ypres, and the afternoon that cost Germany a war
Description: First edition. | New York: Random House, [2025] | Includes
bibliographical references and index.
Identifiers: LCCN 2023009505 (print) | LCCN 2023009506 (ebook) |
ISBN 9781400068524 (hardback) | ISBN 9780812988628 (ebook)
Subjects: LCSH: Ypres, 1st Battle of, Ieper, Belgium, 1914. | World War, 1914–1918—
Campaigns—Belgium—Ieper. | Ieper (Belgium)—History, Military—20th century. |
Command of troops.
Classification: LCC D542.Y6 C68 2025 (print) | LCC D542.Y6 (ebook) |
DDC 940.4/21—dc23/eng/20230909
LC record available at https://lccn.loc.gov/2023009505
LC ebook record available at https://lccn.loc.gov/2023009506

Printed in Canada on acid-free paper

randomhousebooks.com

2 4 6 8 9 7 5 3 1

First Edition

BOOK TEAM: Production editor: Ted Allen • Managing editor: Rebecca Berlant •
Production manager: Jenn Backe • Copy editor: Rachelle Mandik •
Proofreaders: Claire Maby, Deborah Bader, Al Madocs • Indexer: Ina Gravitz

Book design by Susan Turner

The authorized representative in the EU for product safety and compliance is
Penguin Random House Ireland, Morrison Chambers, 32 Nassau Street,
Dublin D02 YH68, Ireland. https://eu-contact.penguin.ie

For Didi
who has made growing old a joy
with great love

Remember the beginning of the war, those never-to-be-forgot days when something truly great had happened, which none thought still possible! We hadn't believed in the war; our political thinking was incapable of recognizing the need for a European catastrophe. As moral beings, though, we had seen the affliction coming—more than that, we even longed for it in some way. Deep in our hearts we felt that the world, our world, could no longer go on as it had. . . .

War! It felt like a purification, a liberation, and a tremendous hope.

—THOMAS MANN,
"Thoughts in Wartime" (1914),
translated by Mark Lilla and Cosima Mattner

We arrived in Paris
Just as the mobilisation posters were going up
We understood my buddy and I
That the little car had taken us into a New epoch
And although we were both grown men
We had just been born.

—GUILLAUME APOLLINAIRE,
"The Little Car," from *Zone: Selected Poems*,
translated by Ron Padgett

We'd line up for the privilege of getting killed.

—LOUIS-FERDINAND CÉLINE,
Journey to the End of the Night,
translated by Ralph Manheim

Turning points do often originate . . . below historians' radars. That only imagination evokes them doesn't diminish their significance, for what documents could show a great army losing its confidence overnight?

—JOHN LEWIS GADDIS,
On Grand Strategy

CONTENTS

IV

NE PLUS ULTRA

INTRODUCTION

THERE IS A GOOD REASON FOR THE TITLE OF THIS BOOK, *THE KILLING SEASON*. More men died in the first four months of the Great War on the Western Front than in any comparable interval in the four-year struggle. "The enormous losses in August and September 1914," writes historian Alan Kramer, "were never equalled at any other time, not even by Verdun." On a single day, August 22, 1914, the French attained the lethal summit of the war, with 27,000 killed, a figure that exceeded by 8,000 the number of Englishmen killed on a more famous date, July 1, 1916, the first day of the Battle of the Somme.

During the four days of the Battle of the Frontiers, August 20–23, the French had 40,000 killed. (The Germans suffered a mere 15,000 deaths in the same brief interval.) The Great War had been going on for less than three weeks. That August the number of French dead approximated between 75,000 and 84,500. September, the month of the Marne, was worse: 99,000. The corpse fields diminished after that vast battle: 46,000 (October), a still-monstrous 38,300 (November), with a Christmas bonus of only 33,300. By the end of the year, French combat deaths totaled 301,100: roughly one Frenchman killed every forty-three seconds—2,007 per day.

Let us take the number of Germans killed from the beginning of August to the end of November 1914. The most reliable compilation, undoubtedly, was that reported by the *Sänitätsberichte*, the German Army Medical Service, early in the 1930s: 18,662 (August); 25,894 (September); 17,720 (October); 14,265 (November)—a total of 76,541 killed in action. In *The World Crisis*, Winston Churchill raises the figure to 116,750 German Western Front deaths in the same period, a considerable difference. Were the losses of the attacking Germans that much less than those of the French? It seems improbable, but there you are.

The truth is that we will never know to a certainty the ultimate arithmetic of annihilation for both sides. Even today, after more than a century has passed since the end of the Great War, the fields of crosses and headstones, the enclosures and the head-high marble boxes that conceal the prodigal boneheaps of the unidentified, or the thousands of names on memorial walls defy comprehension. Enough time has passed for the statistics of mass grief to turn into metaphor. But whatever estimates of mortality we accept, one circumstance is undeniable: The massacres of autumn produced the earliest chapter in the continuing saga of demographic catastrophe in the twentieth century. We can do no more than speculate on the damage done to our genetic heritage.

"The casualties of the First World War," writes the late George Steiner, one of our most perceptive public intellectuals, "were not only enormous, they were cruelly selective." The butcheries that began with the Killing Season "gutted a generation of English moral and intellectual talent, and they eliminated many of the best from the European future." As the historian Alan Kramer notes, as many as 29.3 percent of those men who entered Oxford between 1905 and 1914 and who served in the military perished, as compared to 12 percent of all men mobilized. Entire pages of magazines like the *Tatler* or *L'Illustration* would be thronged with handsome, mustached upper-class faces, those dance cards of the dead. They were the young men who normally would have been groomed to lead and innovate, to administer the colonies that made Europe powerful. In the short term, that would prove a disaster. The voices of division, discord, and revenge, the ham actors of tyranny, the thugocracy of fascism and communism, would before long take center stage.

"We cannot think about the crises of Western culture," Steiner continues, "about the origins and forms of totalitarian movements in the European heartland and the recurrence of world war, without bearing sharply in mind that Europe . . . was damaged in its centers of life. . . . The satiric conceits of Brecht and George Grosz, of children murdered because never to be born has its special genetic meaning." Estimates have, in fact, been made. In France, writes Professor Alexandre Lafon of the University of Toulouse, "It is possible to calculate an approximate population deficit of about 1,500,000 births resulting from the premature death, and absence during the war, of young men who were of marrying and reproductive age."

WHY WAS THE RATE OF killing for those early months of the Western Front so inordinately high? There is a simple answer. Open warfare is far more murderous than fighting from prepared defensive positions. The trenches actually saved lives. During much of that summer and fall, the opponents clashed aboveground in exposed and unprotected country, in one of the most domesticated, but for soldiers dangerously open, landscapes on Earth, amply patterned with fields and well-regulated woodlands, like lethal deer parks that too often offered unobstructed avenues of fire. They did so amid gunfire of all kinds and calibers that continued almost nonstop. Places to hide were scarce.

Artillery, the greatest killer throughout the war, limited only by intermittent shell shortages and tube fatigue of cannon fired too often, thrived in the open. Rifles and machine guns did their share. A single battalion, supposed to number a thousand men but more likely to have been reduced to six or seven hundred, might even fire off a hundred thousand rounds per day—which meant that all up and down the line, millions of bullets were expended every twenty-four hours. In the open, the fraction that collided with flesh may have been small, but was sufficient to kill a few thousand daily.

The killing was only accentuated by the enthusiasm of men going to war for the first time, primed with the bitterness and patriotic misconceptions that governments deliberately ramped up. Nor should we underestimate the effect of the close-order tactics favored early on in the war that, far from overwhelming defenders, more often resulted in close-order slaughters of the attackers. Generals on both sides believed that the defense could best be served by massing troops up front, even in the open. That might have increased firepower, but it also made them ready targets for enemy artillery. The vast numbers of men available asked for vast casualties. Density ruled, but did not always dominate.

The leadership of those early months, which veered from the stolid and the timorous to the foolhardy and the blindly overoptimistic, bore a large share of the blame. Too many generals on both sides had made it to the top more through political deftness and a dogged determination to outlast their competitors than an innate gift for making war. Age, especially in the German Army, prevailed over imagination and energy. The generals of 1914 were still fighting the battles of the nineteenth century, the Franco-Prussian War especially. The double-envelopment of Sedan, echoing Cannae, Hannibal's triumph over Rome in 216 BCE, was forever in the thoughts of German generals, as well as those of the majors and colonels who aspired to High Command.

Though it soon became apparent that new ways and means of killing had overwhelmed the doctrines and fixations of the past, generals on all sides resisted change. Small minds were incapable of managing big human numbers. The German commander in chief, Erich von Falkenhayn, estimated that by the middle of October 1914, 4 million men, Allied and German, were arrayed against one another on the Western Front. The events of that autumn would take the combatants, in the words of that fine historian Robert T. Foley, "into poorly charted and largely unknown territory."

Operational brilliance, let alone strategic, was in short supply that season. Both sides were, however, blessed with exceptional soldiers in the middle ranges of command, most of whom are forgotten now. They shouldn't be. Men like Rear Admiral Pierre Ronarc'h, who led the French marine brigade at Dixmude, or inspired commanders like the German Johann Zwehl, the British Edward Bulfin, or Brigadier Charles Fitz-Clarence, V.C., are the real heroes of this narrative. Only three individuals in positions of influence—you will meet them in these pages—approached that standard of genuine excellence, a Frenchman, a Belgian, and a German: Ferdinand Foch, King Albert, and Fritz von Lossberg (whose most notable achievements as the defensive genius of the Western Front would come later). Besides their fine minds and their capacity to lead and motivate, they had one attribute in common. Before August 1914, not one of them had ever been under fire.

Once stationary trench systems replaced the war of movement, the death rate leveled off. For all its miseries and lurking hazards, its clever expedients of extinction, trench warfare was measurably safer than naked brawling aboveground.

WE TEND TO FORGET HOW fluid those first two and a half months of the Great War were. The opposing armies advanced or retreated over hundreds of miles before the lines finally congealed. The increasingly intricate trench systems left their mark almost as an afterthought. As the killing headed north (and south) that fall, the first trenches followed. I focus on their relentless spread as part of the story, largely untold, of the so-called Race to the Sea. In the words of Hew Strachan, in his masterful *To Arms,* the opening volume of his projected history of the First World War, trenches made it possible for "ground to be defended with fewer troops, so allowing tired men to recuperate and—above all—permitting the creation of new formations for mobile operations elsewhere. Bitterest of ironies, trench warfare was adopted to enable mobile warfare to take place."

The Race to the Sea could not have taken on the renewed strength and intensity, which it did, if the two sides had lacked open stretches to digest. As they ran out of open space in which to maneuver, the trenches caught up to them, becoming the dominant fact of the war in the west. We can even identify the days and the places on both sides of the line where they closed for good.

The action of those first months of war was practically nonstop, a "perpetuity of crisis," to borrow Steiner's apt phrase. The Western world had experienced nothing like that frenzied interval since the French Revolution and the Napoleonic Wars—again to quote Steiner—that "literally quickened the pace of felt time." (I would add the American Civil War.) It was a phenomenon that can happen only when events are in the saddle, as they were that summer and autumn. Time, like any other psychological essence, reacts to the stimulus of overload. The course of its fabled arrow may be direct and straight—the eminent French historian

Marc Bloch, himself a Great War veteran, called historical time "a concrete and living reality with an irreversible onward rush"—but the speed of that flight is rarely constant. That may be one of its great puzzles. History, time's servant, has a mind of its own.

IN 1914, TWO TRULY CONSEQUENTIAL—I shy from the word "decisive"—land battles took place in the west.* Both did fundamentally alter the historical landscape of the Great War on the Western Front, which was never the same after them. The first, undeniably, was the Marne, which saw German military expansion briefly reach its outermost limits. It lasted six days—nine if you count the final pursuit of the Germans to the heights of the Aisne—and spread over almost two hundred miles of northern France—roughly from Soissons to just beyond Nancy. What began as a seemingly unstoppable German advance ended with their armies retiring and reluctantly digging in. The battle saved Paris, and perhaps France itself. For the French, there would be no repetition of the humiliation of the Franco-Prussian War forty-three years earlier, no Sedan, with its capture of an emperor.

Indeed, in just less than a week, the initiative on the Western Front passed from the Germans to the Allies (or from the Central Powers to the Entente, to use names that now seem unfamiliar, if not a bit musty). The scythelike sweep of the legendary Schlieffen Plan proved only as effective as the generals who orchestrated it. Not for the last time in that war, German nerve failed—the nerve of commanders, not that of the common soldiers.

The other major land battle in the west took place around the old Belgian town of Ypres. I would argue, and it is the premise of this book, that its results were even more considerable, more far-reaching, than those of the Marne. That is not the accepted view. Indeed, before I started researching and writing *The Killing Season,* it wasn't mine. I was once

---

* I have come to regard the phrase "decisive battle" with a certain suspicion. Too rarely do "decisive battles" actually decide. I once heard that fine military historian, the late Russell F. Weigley, say that the only decisive battle in a war is the last battle. I will go with that.

quoted as calling the Marne "the most important military event of the last century." I now have reservations about my own assertion (though not about the superb book commented on). Momentous the Marne was, but it did not signal eventual defeat for Germany. Ypres did.*

The strategic stakes were high, and plainly in view. They were the Channel ports: Dunkirk, Calais, and Boulogne. For one side, their capture, or, for the other, their saving, remained the ever-present reason for the battle. Their loss would, at the very least, have compelled a wholesale Allied retreat, and a potential reopening of the way to the French capital. It might have interrupted the hitherto secure flow of men and armaments from England—or, worst-case scenario, knocked Great Britain out of the war. For a couple of days before the Marne, that seemed altogether possible. In late August or early September, moreover, the Germans could have walked into the Channel ports. They missed the opportunity. They were too preoccupied with Paris.

A decision can have a ripple effect. So can the failure to make one.

Ypres, a little under thirty miles from Dunkirk, was the key that could unlock the way to the Channel ports. The principal encounters—battles within the great battle—were scattered along a fifty-mile crescent that swept from the Lys River flatlands past Ypres, up to the market town of Dixmude, and then west along the tiny Yser River to the North Sea. The Germans attacked everywhere, practically without letup. The crises lasted close to a month. Each nation seemed to come up with a different day of termination.

The geometry of movement from all directions, a collision of grosser arrows, representing four armies, French, British, Belgian, and German, assured the pivotal position of Ypres. This account traces that collision, and its outcome on a single October afternoon.

When the events recorded here occurred, the struggle for Flanders was thought of, simply, as the Battle of Ypres or the Defense of the Channel Ports. The notion that it might be just the *First* Ypres was unthinkable. Both sides still hoped, and were convinced, that the war, already too

* The book in question is Holger H. Herwig's *The Marne 1914,* Random House, New York, 2009.

costly, would be settled before 1914 was done and there were still leaves left to fall.

YOU HAVE TO REGARD THE Great War as one of the rare dividing lines of history: the dissolution of empires, fascism, communism, the worldwide Depression, the "American Century," the loosening of the White Man's grip on Asia, the never-ending turmoil in the Near East, the Second World War, the Cold War—all, and so much more, can be traced back to those four years.

What would have happened if Germany had defeated the Allied armies, as it nearly did two times in 1914? Would its victory early on have forestalled, or at least delayed, such dramatic changes?

In *The Killing Season* I examine—re-examine might be a more precise word—one of the neglected episodes of a struggle now more than a century behind us. The early months of the Western Front in France and Belgium have never really surrendered their full importance to historians. Except for events surrounding the Battle of the Marne—and even it has only produced a relative handful of substantial works—this interval is still overlooked and all but forgotten.

The best-known text describing this period of the Great War, Barbara Tuchman's *The Guns of August,* ends where the main part of my narrative begins. Combat in these months was totally unlike the abiding image we have of what followed, the stagnant siege warfare of the trenches. This was, rather, a time of constant movement, constant battle, and constant loss of life. Cavalry still mattered. So did the bayonet, a weapon that proved impractical in the narrow confines of the trench. The grenade, on the other hand, hardly used when the war broke out, soon found itself the infantryman's weapon of choice. Another nuisance, the officer's sword, disappeared, except for ceremonial occasions. Barbed wire, first popularized by American homesteaders, spread across no-man's-land, another new feature of a war without motion.

There is much about this early period of the Great War that has escaped notice. Facts can't be changed, of course, but explanations, speculations, and deductions can. Certain events that I shall discuss in these pages have never been fully accounted for. Many records no longer exist. Air raids destroyed critical papers in the Second World War. Sons burned the papers of their fathers, leaders in that earlier war, afraid that they would fall into the not-indifferent hands of advancing Soviet legions. Though the total picture of those months will forever remain incomplete, a great deal can be surmised by what you might describe as historical triangulation. We can do a lot with what we do have.

As I followed the relentless progress northward of the so-called Race to the Sea—those futile alternating attempts by the French and then by the Germans to turn a flank and break into the open in a potentially war-winning maneuver—I began to question long-held assumptions. They mainly concerned the primacy of the Battle of the Marne—that, and the rarely examined Race itself. I would suggest a reason for that month that has practically dropped out of the calendar of annihilation. The British were almost entirely absent until the end. Their normally tireless chroniclers chose to ignore an affair that was mainly French and German. The British prefer to read about themselves and their exploits. That changed early in October 1914, once British battalions, surreptitiously transferred from the Marne front, began to filter into Flanders, the area that straddles the border between France and Belgium. British troops occupied the big and venerable Belgian town called Ypres and began to dig rudimentary trenches around its outskirts. The French Channel ports, Dunkirk, Calais, Boulogne, and the Channel passage itself, were all plainly menaced. My estimation of the importance of events changed, too, as the battle grew in size and duration. I came to recognize that I was dealing with something bigger than what I had originally imagined. The four-nation brawl was as consequential as the Marne, perhaps more so. The final decision would matter. That became the central premise of this book.

History can't be changed. Interpretations can.

NOTE: I HAVE ATTEMPTED TO follow the spellings of local place names that were standard on French and British military maps of the Great War. For example, I use "Eessen" and not the current Flemish "Esen," or "Gheluvelt" and not "Gheluveld." Such spelling changes can be minor. "Nieuport" for "Nieuwpoort," "St. Eloi" for "Sint–Elooi," or "Dixmude" for "Diksmuide" are more extreme, if not by much. But "Ypres," and not the Flemish "Ieper," has become practically embedded in our historical subconscious. The same is true of the ever-unreachable "Roulers" instead of the present "Roeselare."

I have made this choice not from lack of respect for the Flemish majority in the area but as a matter of historical convenience. I make one exception. In cases I have used names for geographical features that were not local designations but ones that British soldiers gave them: Black Watch Corner, Shrewsbury Forest, Sanctuary Wood, FitzClarence Farm, or Plugstreet.

The Flemish population has many legitimate bones to pick with the French-speaking Walloon establishment that once dominated life in Belgium. This is not the proper forum to address issues that have long divided them, and indeed they play only a small part in this narrative of events now more than a century old.

I

THE SHADOW OF SCHLIEFFEN

Alfred von Schlieffen, Chief of the German General Staff, masterminded the bold 1905 plan to sweep through Belgium and down into France. (Bridgeman Images)

PROLOGUE:

August 20, 1914

NEAR CHARLEROI, BELGIUM

"THERE WAS A MOMENT IN THE EXPERIENCE OF EVERY MAN IN THE WAR, WHEN he realized suddenly the magnitude of the forces he was pitted against. It might come soon or it might come late, it might be screamed out with the distraught voice of a frenzied imagination, or whispered with the ashen lips of fear, but inevitably the time came when a cold hand gripped each man's heart."

For Edward L. Spears, a twenty-eight-year-old lieutenant in the 11th Hussars, that moment came early, on a summer evening in 1914. Spears was something of an exotic bird in his own army: He spoke fluent French. He had been born in France and had lived there until his Anglo-Irish parents divorced. He was then raised in Ireland; at sixteen and a half, he joined the British cavalry. Army intelligence made use of the young officer's language skills. He devised and compiled an Anglo-French codebook and translated French tactical handbooks. His fellow officers regarded him as too brainy for his own good—and, indeed, as Max Egremont, his biographer, writes, Spears was "an outsider in both countries: not quite English and certainly not French." Late in the spring of 1914, the British War Office sent him to Paris to work with the French in the Ministry of War, posing as a civilian; he also ran agents in Belgium. He packed a uniform, just in case.

By the beginning of August, Great Britain found itself swept up in a continental war, which soon became a world one. London chose Spears to serve as a liaison officer with Gen. Charles Lanrezac's Fifth Army. Spears's appointment was crucial because he would also act as the principal connection with the British Expeditionary Force (BEF) that would take up position to the left of the Fifth. Soon he was on his way to Rethel, Lanrezac's headquarters in the forest of the Ardennes. Spears always claimed that he was the first British officer to reach the Western Front and to see action of any kind. During one of his first days at Rethel, German cavalry scouts chased, and nearly caught, the car in which he was riding. Only a chauffeur's quick-thinking U-turn and a high-speed dash away from the galloping horsemen saved him from capture.

On the evening of August 20, a Thursday, Spears sat with a French officer on a grassy hillside just below the River Sambre. The two looked north across the dark, polluted stream to the sprawling grid that defined the mining center of Charleroi. Streetlights were coming on. Beyond, the plain of Belgium widened into a gray distance in which mist and fumes from collieries and the home-fire smoke of miners' rude villages seemed to merge in a featureless, darkening blemish. This was the region known locally as the "Borinage" (coal country) or "Le Pays Noir" (the black land). In his late twenties, Vincent van Gogh had spent time here as a Protestant missionary—miners seemed to belong to another race—and also worked in the mines.

Spears and his companion speculated about "how great armies could possibly fight amid those streets, those endless houses," as though the mazes of the Industrial Revolution could confound and defy the massed thousands of approaching invaders. By what sign could they recognize that the Germans had actually arrived? "We imagined the endless columns of grey-clad men with spiked helmets, rolling forward, flattening out poor little Belgium in their overwhelming advance."

The Germans were, in fact, already deploying their vaunted artillery siege train in the fields opposite Namur, that fortress on the long buttelike rock overlooking the confluence of the Sambre and the Meuse, just twenty-odd miles to the east. And that same evening, not many more miles away, up to 300,000 men of Generaloberst Alexander von Kluck's German First Army had begun their passage down the broad avenues of Brussels, Belgium's capital, bands playing martial anthems and marchers' voices raised in patriotic song. The procession of conquerors would continue into that night and through the next two.

Spears, meanwhile, would remember those last minutes of twilight as "still and wonderfully peaceful. The ominous rumble of guns from the direction of Namur, which had been going on all afternoon, had ceased. A dog was barking at some sheep. A girl was singing as she walked down the lane behind us. From a little farm away on the right came the voices and laughter of some soldiers cooking their evening meal."

How many of them would still be alive a couple of nights later?

The light began to fail. Then it happened. They had their sign, their premonition.

Without a moment's warning, with a suddenness that made us start and strain our eyes to see what our minds could not realize, we saw the whole horizon burst into flames. To the north, outlined against the sky, countless fires were burning. It was as if hordes of fiends had suddenly been released, and dropping on the distant plain, were burning every town and every village. A chill of horror came over us.

To Spears, the meaning of that aurora-like vision, sinister and manmade, was inescapable:

It suddenly became clear that to survive it would be necessary to go on beyond exhaustion, to march when the body clamored to be allowed to drop and die, to shoot when eyes were too tired to see, to remain awake when a man would have given his salvation to sleep. And we realized also that to drive the body beyond physical powers, to force the mind to act long after it had surrendered its power of thought, only despair and the strength of despair could furnish the motive force.

"The strength of despair." That was the essence of what was to come. "It was quite dark now. The distant fires glowed red against a violet black sky."

1

"The Virtuosity of Sheer Audacity"

DECEMBER 1905—AUGUST 1914

"NO STRATEGIC PLAN GOES WITH ANY CERTAINTY BEYOND THE FIRST EN-counter with the enemy's main forces," warned Helmuth von Moltke the Elder, Germany's greatest military leader of the nineteenth century, victor over Denmark, Austria-Hungary, and France. "Only the layman believes he can see in the course of a campaign the carrying through of an initial idea, thought out in advance, considered in every detail, and adhered to right to the end." Wars have a way of taking unlikely turns. Single seasons lengthen into years. Evasions don't evade. Destinations come as a surprise; armies collide in the least convenient of places. Early losers mature into late winners. Beginnings may be predictable; endings are invariably unexpected. Lofty intentions sink into the mud.

Despite Moltke's epigrammatic caution, no group in Europe was more proficient at plan-making than the German military. The nation it served felt hemmed in and pressured by the competitors who surrounded it—by a surging Russia, which had, since 1894, a secret mutual defensive agreement with France, by Great Britain and its mighty fleet, and by France, still bitter from defeat in 1871 and a never-quenched desire to regain the lost provinces of Alsace and Lorraine. At the same time Germany's strident push for supremacy on the Continent was beginning to frighten those same neighbors. And there were, of course, increasingly bitter rivalries over markets and colonies, the trophies that established a nation as a great power. The ingredients for a European civil war were brewing. The lid was ready to blow on the overheated boiler that was the Continent: the animosities, the frustrations, the pent-up rage, the societal dissatisfactions, the unresolved bondage of class, the ennui, and the suppressed longings of an entire century were about to explode beyond repair or peaceful resolution.

Of all the German planning documents of the time, none is more legendary than the December 1905 *Denkschrift*—memorandum—of the retiring chief of the general staff, Count Alfred von Schlieffen, to his successor, Helmuth von Moltke the Younger. Those few pages would shape the course of the as-yet-unfought war and, indeed, of a century that was still young.

Schlieffen had commanded the German Army for fourteen years. Almost from the beginning of his tenure, he had faced the prospect of a two-front war, the French menacing Germany from one direction, the Russians from the other. But by the time he set down his thoughts as he prepared to retire, the threat from Russia had, for the moment, diminished. The Japanese had defeated Russia on land in the Far East, had sunk most of its navy, and, to further neutralize its potential for war, revolution, barely suppressed, had swept the nation. For the first time in years, Germany would not have to watch its back. It could concentrate almost all of its army in the west, against France.

Schlieffen dictated his *Denkschrift* to his devoted son-in-law, Maj. Wilhelm von Hahnke. It outlined his thoughts on how best to destroy France quickly and without an outrageous cost in German lives or wealth. Schlieffen's plan had inherent political risks, which he dismissed. He proposed to take out France and its armies by means of a gigantic armed envelopment. "To accomplish this," the count said, "the neutrality of Luxembourg, Belgium, and the Netherlands has to be violated."

A couple of his divisions could practically walk through the Grand Duchy of Luxembourg, but taking advantage of its small and efficient rail network was more to the point. The dangers of Schlieffen's gamble mounted as his proposed invasion approached the Dutch border, in the form of an inconvenient geographical feature known as the Appendix of Maastricht—a narrow bit of national membrane that dangled down on either side of the Meuse (at this point the name changes to Maas) River. Here was the shortest route to Antwerp, Belgium's great port, which he could not allow to remain in the hands of a potential adversary. Meanwhile his key drive would also cross the Appendix, heading over the plains of Belgium, passing through the capital, Brussels, and then wheeling southward in a scythelike sweep, to barge virtually unannounced into northern France.

Here was the great political risk of Schlieffen's proposal: when Belgium had gained independence in 1830, Great Britain had agreed to back it in the event of an attack. The identity of the invader didn't matter. The real possibility of involving England, the count decided, could not be avoided. The British had refrained from getting involved in the Franco-Prussian War; perhaps they would do so again. How would Belgium react? The ailing king, Leopold II, was probably more preoccupied with pleasing his mistress, a former Parisian prostitute, and presiding over the wealth derived from his genocidal rule of his Congo colony, to care. Millions had died to enrich one of the genuine monsters of recent history. Leopold II commanded an army of six weak divisions. "It can be assumed," Schlieffen reassured his successor, "that the deployment of the German Army will be completed undisturbed."

The benefits of Schlieffen's plan seemed to outweigh its potential costs. Paris beckoned and would be reached by passing through the relatively unfortified country between Verdun and Lille. Schlieffen concentrated the principal weight of his drive on his right wing: the tip of the scythe always cuts the most hay. He calculated that the offensive right wing had to be seven times as strong as his defensive left—to begin with, that would be mainly a holding operation. The invasion of France would end in a battle of annihilation, though the German word for it, *Vernichtung*, meant not "extermination" in the sense of mass killing but the breaking of an opponent's will to resist, a total psychological defeat.

The main army of the right wing would circle Paris from the west, pass the underbelly of the city, and then turn upward. Other armies would advance from the north, resulting in a double envelopment and the final, and decisive, entrapment. (Schlieffen was obsessed with Cannae, for two millennia the signal example of the double envelopment.) Where would the battle that settled the fate of France have been fought? The maps drawn by the faithful Hahnke suggest that it might have taken place in the Seine Valley, perhaps in the gently wooded region around Fontainebleau, so favored by generations of French artists. The scenic oils this time would have been painted by Germans.

Schlieffen did leave Moltke a warning: do not under any circumstances let the French retreat behind the Marne and the Seine. "If one allows them to proceed in this direction, it will lead to an endless war."

THE MYTHOLOGY SURROUNDING SCHLIEFFEN OVERSHADOWED his slight but determined figure, a mustached man forever twisting his monocle on his index finger. Memorable sayings were attributed to him, as though he had the touch of a military poet: "If you march into France," he supposedly said toward the end of his life, "see to it that the man on the utmost right brushes the Channel coast with his sleeve." Much to the chagrin of his heirs of 1914, it never happened that way.

He also had a touch of the unpoet about him. He belonged to an emerging breed of German army chief. They were, in the words of a historian of the German general staff, Gordon A. Craig, "apt to be professionals of a new kind, technicians of power, intent on the problems of their métier, but with little or no interest in anything that lay outside the confines of the garrison. As this kind of professionalism increased, political awareness and responsibility tended to shrivel and disappear." These were men who had no "appreciation of the subtle inter-connection of war and politics."

This could be a perfect description of Alfred Graf von Schlieffen, an obsessed and lonely figure, as single-minded as he was joyless, as reticent as he was given to sarcasm, icy and damning. If a subject lay outside his immediate interest, he denied that it had importance. Once, on a staff journey in Prussia, his adjutant exclaimed about the lovely valley through which their train was passing. "An unimportant obstacle," Schlieffen muttered, and returned to his characteristic silence.

Though the German commander in chief had been around for years, he was almost invisible to the public. He was rarely photographed. There was no real mystery about his obscurity: This joyless man was neither colorful nor truly interesting. Workaholic obsessives rarely are. The graf (or "count") courted obscurity. A widower, his only break from his ceaseless labor in his Berlin laboratory of war was the hour of each day he spent with his two daughters. He was laconic, aloof, and given to secrecy; his subordinates called him "the sphinx." His shortsighted eyes were heavy-lidded; smiles rarely creased his dyspeptic countenance. His mantis-like frame was concealed in an elaborately braided uniform that seemed to wear him and not the other way round.

IN ITS BROAD OUTLINES, SCHLIEFFEN'S 1905 memorandum reached for the rafters, a trapeze act in armor that required a sure-handed sense of balance—and, most of all, nerve. Touched with brilliance, it was also a little mad. I am not the first writer to use that word. For all its reasonable arguments, the count's grand design remained something of a fantasy, complete with dream outcome: total victory and the humbling of the French state. But then, the most plausible fantasies are founded on, and constructed with, realistic building blocks. Schlieffen's scheme was bold, and not a little immoral, a formula for quick victory that exhibited what military historian B. H. Liddell Hart called "a gambler's belief in the virtuosity of sheer audacity." By way of emphasis, he added, "Its magic is a myth."

It was a myth that, before its course was run, had seduced a nation and its leaders. The flaws of this spider's symphony, never resolved, go to the heart of why a short war was unlikely, if not impossible.

Nothing, however, now seems more striking about the plan outlined in the *Denkschrift* than what Schlieffen overlooked or omitted. He devoted little time or serious thought to the unglamorous subject of logistics. The farther the German armies removed themselves from their original bases, the more difficult supplying them would become. It would be important to get any portions of the Belgian and French railway system that had been deliberately damaged working again as quickly as possible. Schlieffen barely concerned himself with such problems or with how to feed the legions that were to pour down on France. They could live off the land, he suggested, and in the late summer of 1914, many of the invaders had to do just that.

There were surprising loose ends. Schlieffen gave too little thought to what Carl von Clausewitz, the military philosopher (and himself a Prussian) called "friction," chance and contingency. He believed, for example, that Great Britain's army was too small and too scattered over the globe to make a difference. He would beat France long before it arrived. He was only prepared to seize the Channel ports if the British started to land troops in their harbors. Should that happen—which he doubted—the Germans would "detach a sufficient number of corps to defeat the English, and then continue the operations against the French. . . ." He actually paid scant attention to that dampened sleeve of the man on the farthest right, and it would turn out to be one of his worst misjudgments. Schlieffen assumed that he could make use of the efficient Belgian and French railway systems but ignored the possibility that his retreating enemies would tear up rails, dynamite bridges, and block tunnels. Though such deliberate destruction was not totally effective in August 1914, it did help to slow the German advance. By that time, Belgium was no longer the country of the dim, rapacious Leopold II but of Albert I, a different kind of monarch and military leader.

The war that Schlieffen imagined was mainly a war fought on foot, as would still be the case in 1914, nine years later. The army on the far right, the one that would have to swing around Paris, could not avoid traveling four hundred miles, or more, with predictable intermissions to fight and recover. Let us say that the average march per day would be up to fifteen miles, each man carrying a load of more than fifty pounds, including rifles and knapsacks—in, most likely, the heat of midsummer. No one seemed to have contemplated the movement of troops by motorized transport. Schlieffen apparently didn't (though he did spend as many as nine hours a day in the saddle). By 1906, the year Schlieffen retired, the army was beginning to use lorries to carry supplies and ammunition—but not men. Men marched. Lorries could average an unimpeded seventy-five miles a day, five times the average rate of infantry on foot. Even with the inevitable traffic jams, think of how many unturnable flanks might have been turned.

Schlieffen, that frail technician of military might, apparently never considered what would happen if his plan miscarried, or fell short of its objectives. Failure was not an option.

TO REPLACE THE AGING AND increasingly infirm Schlieffen, the kaiser chose Helmuth von Moltke, nephew and namesake of the legendary warlord who, reinforced by the Iron Chancellor, Bismarck, had unified Germany. The elder Moltke was not an easy act to follow, and Helmuth the Younger was the first to admit that. When he learned that the kaiser was about to offer him Schlieffen's position, he expressed immediate, and barely disguised, doubts. Early one morning in January 1905, he was out riding in the Tiergarten in Berlin with Prince Bernhard von Bülow, the imperial chancellor. Bülow brought up the possibility of Moltke's elevation. Moltke's answer, which Bülow recorded in his journal, was a lacerating moment of self-perception.

"I lack the power of rapid decision," the general said. "I am too reflective, too scrupulous, and, if you like, too conscientious for such a post. I lack the capacity for risking all on a single throw, that capacity which made the greatness of such born commanders as Napoleon, or our own Frederick II, or my uncle."

Word of Moltke's reluctance got back to the kaiser, who made light of his qualms. Moltke had been his aide-de-camp; the two were close. The kaiser had nicknamed him "Julius" and addressed Moltke with the familiar "Du." In the end, at a dinner meeting, "Julius" gave in.

The kaiser and Moltke may have had an easy relationship, but not Moltke and Schlieffen. They were never close. They argued. On one matter they agreed: the inevitability of a war—specifically, a war with France. They agreed, too, on the way it should be fought. Schlieffen may have offered his not-so-casual plan as a suggestion; Moltke did not hesitate to appropriate his vision. He would spend the next years giving operational flesh to its strategic bones. Schlieffen's envelopment scheme became his, a fixation that possessed German military thinking in those years before the war.

There is no tyranny like the tyranny of an idea.

Helmuth von Moltke—"the nervous nephew," as he has been characterized—is one of the overlooked movers of history. Few have done so much to change our world. No person in charge was more responsible for starting the Great War. Someone had to give the order to begin, and on a total scale, involving the manipulation of hundreds of thousands in a crusade of annihilation. That man was Moltke. He did so for what he saw as the best and most noble of reasons: to save his country. He helped to bring its downfall instead, unleashing furies that would undermine his once-secure world forever. Surely Schlieffen, too, deserves a share of the blame. But the good fortune of mortality allowed his reputation to ascend to the realm of legend and remain there unblemished.*

Moltke had everything going for him, perhaps too much. Tall and lithe as a young man, and sporting a small, dapper mustache that emphasized his sharp good looks, he had distinguished himself under fire and as his uncle's adjutant. He had inherited his great relative's bent for Humanism, though he gave it his own special mystical twist. He translated poetry and carried Goethe on his travels. He was a tolerable cellist and spoke several languages. His inclinations stood out among the parochial technocrats who surrounded him. Under the urging of his wife, he dabbled in theosophy and was an intimate of that secular religion's self-appointed pope, Rudolf Steiner. He believed in the afterlife and in reincarnation. His friend the All Highest, Wilhelm, advised him to put his beliefs on hold.

Forty years of peace had exacted a toll. Moltke had partaken too liberally from the tables of Wilhelmine plenty. The dashing young officer of the 1870s had grown into a mountain of a man, an Alp of flesh, with loose skin and a blotchy complexion. He took repeated cures. He developed an embarrassing tendency to fall off his horse during public occasions. He could be a deep pessimist. Picking up on the nickname bestowed on him by the kaiser, his officers referred to him behind his back as "Gloomy Julius."

Moltke was fifty-eight when he took over, rather on the young side for men in his position. (German generals tended to be in their sixties: to have reached the top of the ladder was often evidence less of wisdom,

---

* Only one biography has done justice to Moltke, and it is a remarkable example of what scholarship should be, Annika Mombauer's *Helmuth von Moltke and the Origins of the First World War*.

Kaiser Wilhelm II, foreground, observes the 1911 army maneuvers with Schlieffen's successor, Helmuth von Moltke, nephew of the man with the same name and victor in the 1870–71 war with France. Moltke, "the Younger," was never easy in the saddle or in command. (Alamy Stock Photo)

imagination, or energy than of venerable sharp elbows.) In the early years of his ascendancy, Moltke made hardly a change in Schlieffen's scheme. But by 1909, Moltke and his chief aide, Erich Ludendorff, were beginning to consider improvements that would make the plan his as much as Schlieffen's.

The first came a couple of years later when the nephew elected to forgo the invasion of Netherlands territory that the original plan advocated. As Moltke wrote in a memorandum that year, "It will be very important to have in Holland a country whose neutrality allows us to have imports and supplies. She must be the windpipe that enables us to breathe."

To avoid violating the neutrality of the Netherlands presented a hitherto unforeseen problem: Between a fortress-ringed Belgian city of Liège and the Dutch frontier, the corridor was a mere twelve miles wide, a potential bottleneck. How could upward of 300,000 men of the far-right wing, the First Army, along with its bulky garland of cavalry, artillery, and wagons and lorries, thread the eye of that needle? That had to be accomplished before the First could burst into the open country beyond and head for Brussels. The answer, which Moltke's staff had been working on since 1908, was a coup de main, a lightning surprise attack on Liège and its forts that would be mounted at the same moment Germany was declaring war on Belgium, if not before. Moltke came to regard the gap to be opened not as an obstacle but as his ace in a meager hole. His developing coup de main was a secret that only a chosen few were privy to. He did not inform the loose-lipped kaiser until German troops were actually storming the easternmost forts of Liège. This had to be the single truly major departure from the original Schlieffen proposal, a gamble within a gamble, and a bit of unaccustomed daring on Moltke's part.

In response to the French buildup in the sectors facing Alsace and Lorraine, the provinces lost in the Franco-Prussian War—they were now called Oberlsass, Unterelsass, and Lothringen—Moltke shifted divisions from the right to the far left, opposite Nancy. The final big change that he made had to do with his second, and mostly ignored, front, the eastern. No longer beleaguered by defeat and revolution, Russia had developed into the threat it had not been when Schlieffen formulated his plan. Moltke took an educated risk. The chances were that Russia's armies would need weeks or more to mobilize, allowing him to dispense with France before his foes to the east got it together. Better simply to leave one 200,000-man army in East Prussia, charged with the difficult, but not impossible, task of "securing our eastern provinces against a Russian invasion." Let Austria-Hungary deal with the major threats in that quarter. In April 1913, Moltke dropped an elaborate, multi-army deployment plan that had been in the unenthusiastic works for years. Before long, he would regret this absence of an Eastern Front alternative. For the moment, though, most of his as-yet-unscrambled eggs were in the Western Front basket. He was determined to keep them there.

Moltke's critics have roasted him endlessly for those changes, blaming him for nothing less than the loss of the war. The true wonder is how little of Schlieffen's scenario he did revise. In the eight years of his command, balances beyond Germany's borders were constantly shifting, new threats and new doctrines emerging. The fast-developing technology of war was elbowing its way into the driver's seat. The new emphasis of the French Army on the all-out attack—the vogue for *offense à outrance*, attack to the limits—would have to be dealt with. So would Russia's unexpectedly swift bounce back from the disasters of the early 1900s.

One question resists explanation—and since the bulk of Moltke's papers have not survived, it may never be answered: Why, in spite of a relationship that was at best strained, did Moltke cling to Schlieffen's rough blueprint for so long, until it was too late to substitute one of his own? To conceive anything as original—or as unhinged in its high hopes—was beyond him. Flights of fancy were not in his makeup. The plan that he adopted and made his own had been the creation of a solitary and sardonic neurotic, a man who had spent too much time in a martial vacuum. His words were a command posing as a suggestion. That may be the answer. Schlieffen was a man who could not be refused, and Moltke lacked both the nerve and the energy to take him on. He was, by instinct, an obeyer, whether it was his uncle or the kaiser giving the orders, or Schlieffen.

Schlieffen's final memorandum, dated December 28, 1912, reiterated the need to send troops through Belgium. "It will be adviseable," said the old soldier, by now a field marshal, "to confront the Belgian Government with the choice of a bombardment of its fortified towns . . . as well as a considerable levy—or of handing over all fortresses, railways, and troops." To the end of his life Alfred von Schlieffen remained a near-sighted visionary, forever twisting his monocle on his index finger.

Hours after he finished dictating to his son-in-law, the count lapsed into a terminal coma. He died a week later. His last words were reputed to be: "It must come to a fight. Only make the right wing strong." The sentences have a made-up feel. Still, he probably would have agreed with them. You have to give the Impresario of Envelopment his due.

IT IS TEMPTING TO COMPARE the German and French war plans in terms of their originators. They couldn't have been more different. The two Germans were both aristocrats who shared a single dark vision—what could be described as a panzer thrust without the panzers. And then there was Joseph Jacques Césaire Joffre, a commander who came from the solid middle class. His greatest military talent was a sense of when—and where—to react. An initiator of bold schemes he was not.

In the summer of 1914, Joffre had been chief of the general staff for just three years. Edward L. Spears described his first sight of him. Joffre, Spears wrote, was "a bulky, slow-moving, loosely-built man, in clothes that would have been the despair of Savile Row, yet unmistakably a soldier." Spears was struck by how "the whiteness of his hair, the lightness of his almost colorless blue eyes, which looked out from under big eyebrows the color of salt and pepper, white predominating, and the tonelessness of his voice coming through the sieve of his big whitish mustache, all gave the impression of an albino." He had few friends and numerous enemies. Joffre would have made "a perfectly good stationmaster," one of his detractors said. Among his most tenacious critics was the British military historian B. H. Liddell Hart, who called him "the modern Delphic Oracle," whose "qualifications outwardly seemed to be that he had none."

Joffre came from a town in the foothills of the Pyrenees close to the Mediterranean; his father was a barrel maker—a cooper—and a wine merchant. The boy was something of a math prodigy, the youngest in his class at the École Polytechnique, France's most prestigious scientific and engineering school, and an accepted stepping-stone to an army commission. During the Franco–Prussian War, he had served as a junior officer in a Paris fort but apparently never came under fire. Joffre discovered a talent for military engineering. He spent much of his career in Asia and Africa, and made a name for himself as a builder of railroads and the enormous harbor forts of Madagascar. In 1894, he led a relief expedition to Timbuktu. Joffre related how volleys from a lead platoon stopped a rush by local tribesmen, his one experience of combat: "In less than a quarter of an hour the enemy was in flight, leaving a hundred dead on the field." Even in describing a moment of peril, he could not shake his monotone.

Joffre returned to France. A career that had seemed stalled suddenly took flight. He made general, commanding first a division and then a corps. He had never led infantry before. For most of those years the French Army was in a deplorable state. The Dreyfus affair, with its trumped-up conviction of a Jewish officer based on the testimony of a man who was secretly dealing with the Germans, had left wounds that were still not closed. Fear of military coups d'état had long prevented the appointment of one person to head the army, even if war broke out. Command was divided between a chief of staff, who dealt mainly with administrative matters, and the so-called commander in chief, who would take charge in the field in combat emergencies but had no permanent staff.

It took the Moroccan crisis of 1911 to produce reform of the army, from top to bottom. After the French occupied Morocco that year, a German gunboat appeared in the harbor of Agadir to challenge them. What began as an exercise in saber rattling nearly got out of hand. Britain supported France, an unwelcome surprise to the Germans—who backed away, humiliated. They never forgave the British. The French, meanwhile, were becoming steadily more frightened of the menace of Germany and took measures to strengthen their army.

Adolphe Messimy, then the minister of war, decided that the army must at last have a single commander, one with absolute control. A compromise choice emerged on top: Joffre. He was relatively young, fifty-nine. He was a card-carrying Republican. Military and political leaders were still fighting the French Revolution. Joffre openly admitted that he had no experience in strategic planning. For the moment he left that to his right-hand man, the Catholic aristocrat Édouard de Castelnau.

The announcement of his appointment came on July 28, 1911. Generals are mostly remembered for their battles, but many of Joffre's major contributions to an eventual victory were made before the war began. In his three years as commander in chief, he took an army that was all but broken and repaired it. He may not have been a fighting general, but he was a superb organizer, a natural-born facilitator. He was a leader of what you might call the military branch of the Age of Efficiency, years that saw the emergence of what became known as "scientific management." Stopwatches and diagrams in hand, men measured industrial processes long taken for granted, shaving seconds or minutes from their manufacture. "Scientific management" was in the air. Joffre translated the new techniques of production to the systematic organization of armed men. He was the ultimate pragmatist of his trade. The onetime fort builder saw that the great defensive chain that fronted the border with Germany was already obsolete, unable to withstand the pounding of the newest heavy artillery. There was a simple and efficient answer: let offense replace defense.

Joffre soon came to wield, in the words of Robert A. Doughty, "more power over the French Army than anyone had possessed since the time of Napoleon." A man who had the figure of a sugar beet, he was too bulky to go unnoticed in a roomful of ordinarily diminutive types, a bit ponderous of thought as of body, but his few words had the power to overawe and convince. At that moment, the French Army needed nothing so much as an efficiency expert, and efficiency was the vision that the engineer Joffre imposed.

Joffre had much to do, and little time, less even than anyone imagined. The stinginess and suspicion of politicians never let up. But he was surprisingly effective at pressing his case. Largely through his unflappable prodding, the Chamber of Deputies took up a bill upping mandatory military service from two to three years. The debate lasted five months through the spring and summer of 1913. Protest riots broke out. The bill passed in July, adding as many as 200,000 men to the French Army, at a time when the German Army was also expanding. Joffre used the passage of the law to increase the number of junior officers and NCOs; he raised their pay. He established officer training schools. He promoted training manuals, which spelled out the way the French Army should wage war—what we now call "doctrine." The essence of that doctrine was *offensive à outrance*. As one of the manuals explained, "Only the offensive yields positive results." The new regulations were a warning to Joffre's generals: "An energetic commander-in-chief" will, at the beginning of a war, "launch operations of such violence and fury that the enemy, weakened in its morale and paralyzed in its action, will be reduced, perhaps, to remaining on the defensive."

Such words may have offered bracing medicine for an army in reform, although their longer-term consequences would prove less than a magic cure.

Joffre's remedial prescriptions weren't always successful. The army lacked the barracks to accommodate the influx of new men, and training facilities remained primitive and antiquated. Many camps were too small for artillery practice. Indeed, artillery played a secondary role—an order of importance that would soon be reversed. For the common soldier, life was brutish and unpleasant. No wonder so many men had protested the extra year of service. His woolen uniform was hot in summer, itchy in all seasons. His red pantaloons made ideal targets. He carried a pack that was too heavy. Food was atrocious, the wine sour. Medical services were rudimentary. Joffre observed that, in too many cases, "our officers were not prepared to meet the conditions of modern war."

Bulky in body and plodding of mind, the French commander in chief, Joseph Joffre, was an organizer and engineer who had only been under fire once, during a skirmish in Africa. But his prewar reforms of the Army may have contributed as much to his country as any battle won. (Getty Images)

Still, what Joffre's reforms of the army accomplished in the three years before the war, imperfect as the results were, may have done as much to save France as the Battle of the Marne.

AS ABLE A BUILDER, ORGANIZER, and logistician as he was, Joffre had never led men in battle. Few continental generals, except those with the experience of colonial dustups, knew the need for improvisation, instant decision, or, indeed, the terror of being under fire. Some, French and German, had served in the Franco–Prussian War, but they were in their sixties now, and that experience had dimmed with the passing of more than four decades. It would take time for leaders with a genuine gift for making war to emerge. For the time being nations had no choice but to put their trust in men like Joffre or Helmuth von Moltke.

Joffre did eventually devise a plan of his own, one that has been ridiculed as the "notorious" or the "infamous" Plan XVII. If the grandiose Schlieffen/Moltke Plan had something of a Wagnerian opera about it, Plan XVII was more a simple variation on a theme for an orchestra, a mere prelude, and a tentative one at that. It was plainly its master's handiwork, methodical and solid, but lacking flash or inspiration, constrained by the limits of geography, political oversight, and its originator's imagination.

The basic idea of Plan XVII was to concentrate five armies, from the Swiss border to just opposite the southeastern corner of Belgium. The four forward armies would be held back ten meters—about six miles—from the German and Belgian frontiers. That was to prevent an accidental clash of arms or unplanned violation of neutrality. Even at this late date, there was still a fear that the ever-touchy Belgians might veer to the German side, which would leave the French left flank largely uncovered. A fifth army, "the army of maneuver," was stationed in the rear, ready to move in whatever direction seemed most threatened, or where an advance seemed promising. Joffre kept his intentions to himself, judging it "dangerous to disclose in advance the various movements I had in mind." He was determined to prevent politicians from meddling in military matters. Orders were verbal, not written. If he didn't reveal his offensive scheme, there was a simple reason. He hadn't decided where to attack. He would wait until the Germans committed themselves. Then he would pounce.

Plan XVII was his plan, and his alone; it has long been misunderstood. To call it the "virtual incarnation of the *offensive à outrance*" is wrong. Some excellent military historians have been misled about its true function, which was mainly the concentration of the armies of France. Offensive action would only come as the fighting took shape and German intentions became clear.

Plan XVII was actually a plan within a plan. The French worked in concert with the Russian military, the object being to squeeze Germany from two directions, preferably at once. The two nations had begun talks on a general alliance to be secret in 1891, and had added a military convention the following year, also secret. But, after numerous delays and revisions, the agreement only came into formal being on January 4, 1894.*

The French poured money into the Russian rail network, building new lines and converting single tracks into double ones. They paid particular attention to the so-called Polish Salient, which thrust itself forward like a thumb gouging the eye of Berlin, less than two hundred miles away, too close for German comfort. A wireless telegraph connected the two Allies, its main line running directly from northwestern Russia to Paris, and a backup one through the Black Sea to Tunisia, and then north to the French capital. Messages passed back and forth daily. Military and political leaders made regular inspection trips, usually on alternating summers. Joffre sailed for St. Petersburg in August 1913, to confer with his Russian counterparts. He observed maneuvers and was not always pleased with what he saw. "The realities of war," he said, "were not sufficiently taken into account." Of the Russian Minister of War, he commented, "He promised everything we asked but kept his word on nothing."

As events began to heat up the following July, Joffre had a tense meeting with a reciprocating visitor, the Russian chief of the general staff, Gen. Yakov Zhilinsky, who showed plans for an invasion of East Prussia.

---

* No historian has described the Russian connection and its effects better than Robert A. Doughty, in his landmark study of French strategy in the Great War, *Pyrrhic Victory*.

An onlooker, the Russian military attaché, related how "Joffre, waving his pudgy hand over the outspread map of our western borders"—the Polish Salient—"instead of approving the plan of attack, tried to convince Zhilinsky of the dangers of an invasion of East Prussia." Joffre kept repeating, "This direction is for us the least favorable. C'est un quet-apens." It is a trap.

Joffre's instincts were right, as it would soon turn out. Though he might question the details of execution, this was no time to disown the treaty itself. As the hours ticked away to a war that seemed ever more inevitable, he swallowed his apprehensions and prepared for joint facing offensives. That meant broad attacks into Alsace and Lorraine, and then on the center of the German line. These attacks had less to do with recovering lost provinces than with relieving pressure on a distant ally. "It is at the very heart of Germany that we must strike," Tsar Nicholas told a French military representative. "The objective of both of us ought to be Berlin." That was, as it were, the party line. The French, in fact, never did convince the Russians to throw the main weight of their forces against Germany. Russia placed 1.2 million men against the Austrians in Galicia but just half that number, 600,000, against the Germans in East Prussia. A Hapsburg Empire rendered impotent was even more in its interest than a defeat of Germany. (It also needed French—and possibly British—support in a long-range project, the dismemberment of the Ottoman Empire.) Who was using whom? In the words of historian Sean McMeekin, "the metaphor which best describes the strategic landscape of August 1914 is clearly that of France falling on its sword for Russia, and not the other way round." Russian promises, unkept, would lead France into disasters, and ones that nearly tipped the balances of 1914. The secret alliance with St. Petersburg, and not Plan XVII, was to blame.

For both France and Russia, grand strategy had outsmarted itself.

IN THE GATHERING EUROPEAN CONFRONTATION, Great Britain played an uncertain role right to the end. Should the Continent finally erupt, France thought that it could count on the island kingdom's large navy and small but efficient army. But British involvement was never a sure thing. That the two nations, enemies for centuries, were even on friendly terms was a new development in the ever-shifting power balance of Europe. It had been barely ten years since the French ambassador had gone to the office of the British foreign secretary on April 8, 1904, and signed the treaty of cooperation that came to be known as the Entente Cordiale. A mutual fear of the growing German menace on land and sea had brought about this unforeseen union. Though the document mainly dealt with the resolution of long-standing colonial differences, military matters would before long become inescapable, including the possibility that British troops might one day be needed on the Continent.

If the British had not developed a grand war plan like those of the Germans and French, it was largely because they lacked a conscript army that could summon millions of men within days. The British regular army had been deliberately kept small. "Britain in 1914," military historian John Terraine writes, "was primarily a sea-power, the greatest in the world, reposing upon a century of supremacy that was only now being challenged." That challenge came from the kaiser and his belated push for naval supremacy.

Britain had its navy, France its army. The British Army was mainly a colonial police force. It had been much criticized for its performance, both brutal and lackluster, in the Boer War at the turn of the century. The name Richard Burdon Haldane (later Lord) will appear, briefly but importantly: the secretary of state for war was the man who did so much to create the best small army in the world, a tightly knit, rigorously trained, and immaculately drilled force, distinguished by its ability to handle a rifle—fifteen rounds a minute, as the saying went. The men in the ranks were all volunteers, many having escaped the slums of the industrial Midlands or the coal mines of Wales. They often just met a basic medical standard: five feet three inches tall, a thirty-three-inch chest, and weighing 112 pounds. But they did lend a touch of democracy to the martial mix. The middle range of officers, a head taller, could be superb. They tended to be the second and third sons of landed gentry, the ones who would not inherit their fathers' big land holdings and the responsibilities that went with them. They had been brought up as hunters and horsemen. For them, a private income was a necessity, which, in marriage, often meant sacrificing love for wealth. With the cost of uniforms, mess contributions, servants' outfits, and social obligations, officering in 1914 was not cheap, as much as £400 a year in an elite Guards regiment (close to £50,000 in the U.K. currency of today). There was an almost unbridgeable gap between officers and men. Class counted.

IN LONDON, THE CABINET OF Herbert Asquith's ruling Liberal Party let matters of strategic coordination between the two militaries drift. For most of the first decade of the twentieth century, war was a distant concern. Politicians and military men did not mix easily. They hardly spoke the same language. A Parliament inclined to the dovish argued about the cost of a standing army: there were constant demands for a reduction in its size. Both cabinet and Parliament regarded with particular suspicion the Anglo-French military discussions, afraid that workable proposals might actually emerge from them, which would lead England into dangerous Continental commitments. The military talks went on anyway.

No talker was more persistent than Brig. Gen. Henry Hughes Wilson, then commandant of the Staff College, the British officer who became the cement of the Entente Cordiale. Wilson was a curious, even tricky, individual, not without charm or influence, who preferred to operate in the shadows, dispensing a covert opinion here, a gently humorous but devastating bit of condemnation or quiet warning there, at all times making a sage assessment of who was on top, who in disfavor. A mischief-maker and an intriguer, Wilson had a knack for finagling himself out of plum assignments. The men who controlled advancement didn't always trust him. To judge by the tart-tongued and rashly intemperate journal he kept, they had ample reasons for their qualms. He will turn up often in these pages.

Wilson came from the landed Irish Protestant gentry, a knobbly-faced personage with a long nose and elephantlike ears, along with the standard officer's mustache. He called himself "the ugliest man in the British Army." His looks were not enhanced by the scar running beside his left eye, the lasting imprint of a dah slash by a Burmese insurrectionist in the 1880s. Wilson was six feet four inches tall, ten inches taller than the man he would soon serve under, Sir John French. "Always a glutton for exercise," as one biographer put it, Wilson bicycled over much of the French and Belgian landscape that he would soon be defending, making mental notes: those sightseeing jaunts convinced him that the Germans were bound to make a dive through Belgium. As early as 1910 he was already wondering whether British regimental officers should take interest in "the topography of a funny little country like Belgium, although most of them may be buried there before they are much older."

To Henry Wilson's credit, he could be an exceptional logistical organizer who was better at arranging at short notice for the transportation of large numbers of troops than he was at leading them in battle. He possessed one other gift that few other British commanders shared: he spoke excellent French. That, as much as any leadership qualification, was to boost his importance in the coming war—and, occasionally, to save his ungainly skin. (By the same token, few French military men spoke English.) French generals became his greatest champions, and he returned their admiration in equal measure.

An inspiration that came to Wilson in 1909 would change the direction of his career. He was then the commandant of the British Army Staff College, and he decided to visit his French opposite, Gen. Ferdinand Foch, who headed L'École supérieure de guerre in Paris. Foch was well known for his writings on military subjects; Wilson felt he might have much to learn from listening to him and observing his teaching methods. Foch agreed to see Wilson, but with a marked lack of enthusiasm. The British brigadier sat in on a couple of lectures on the morning of December 2. When it came time for a break, Foch said goodbye "with a cordiality," Liddell Hart wrote, "that conveyed relief." He didn't invite Wilson to join him in a midday meal. But they did have afternoon tea together; their conversation stretched on for a couple of hours. Foch invited Wilson for a second day of classes and more talk, mainly about the possibility of combined action between the French and British Armies. In his diary that night, Wilson noted: "His appreciation of the German move through Belgium is exactly the same as mine, the important line being between Verdun and Namur"—though both men misjudged how wide-sweeping the thrust would turn out to be or how much of Belgium the Germans were prepared to swallow.

Wilson and Foch were becoming friends. The Irish brigadier returned to Paris that January. Foch visited England in May, his first Channel crossing. It was probably that visit when Wilson asked him, "What would you say was the smallest British military force that would be of any practical assistance to you in the event of a contest such as we have been considering?"

"One single private soldier, and we would take good care that he was killed."

It was Foch's way of making clear that if the British Army crossed the Channel, it would be coming to stay.

The man was accustomed to speaking in riddles. Wilson seemed to understand them.*

THE MOROCCAN CRISIS LEFT NERVES all over Europe jumpy. The universal fear was that the next such eruption would defy solution—or, just as likely, the fatigue of constant crisis would have dulled the will to reach a solution. Would the words "inevitable war" become a self-fulfilling prophecy?

Meetings between British and French staff members were now held regularly. The Asquith cabinet grew increasingly nervous about where those talks were headed. In November 1911, a showdown erupted in Downing Street. Tempers flared. Moderates who were opposed to military involvement of any sort talked openly of resigning. Asquith and his foreign secretary, Sir Edward Grey, barely averted a rupture that might have led to the dissolution of the cabinet, and even to a new election. "It

---

* Foch called his new friend Henri, or sometimes simply "Doubleh-Vay," the French pronunciation of the letter *w*. French staff officers came to adopt the single letter *w* as a blanket designation for the British, both in messages, or, later, in the sixty-eight volumes of the Official History of what they called La Grande Guerre. So, the British Army became "l'Armée W" or, say, the British I Corps, the Ier C.A.W. (Premier Corps Armée W). Regard that Doubleh-Vay as a tip of the kepi to Wilson, the most enthusiastic original backer of a military alliance with the French.

was agreed," Margaret MacMillan writes, "that there should be no exchanges between the British and French general staffs that amounted to a commitment on the part of Britain of military or naval intervention in a war."

Still, the talks went on. No one worked harder than Henry Wilson, the behind-the-scenes enabler of the Entente Cordiale. He took it upon himself to reassure the French that Great Britain would not abandon them. He was now director of military operations (DMO), and rising in the military hierarchy. During 1913, the last full year of peace, Wilson made seven visits to France. He was promoted to major general.

Months before the gunshots at Sarajevo, Wilson had begun arranging for a Channel crossing of a BEF—as the British Expeditionary Force would soon be called. He made sure that ships were available to ferry more than 70,000 men to France. He found hundreds of fresh horses, scrounged for extra supplies of ammunition and petrol. He purchased reconnaissance aircraft, an innovation. He made plans for coordinating the movement of troops by rail, setting exact times of departure from army bases and arrivals at ports. In the first days of the conjectured con-

It took a mutual fear of mounting German power for France and England to turn their backs on a millennium of strife. No men were more responsible for cementing their armies than the three conversing in this c.1914 photo: the British Director of Military Operations, Sir Henry Wilson (left), towering over his friend, Ferdinard Foch (center), onetime head of the École Supérieure de Guerre, and the French military attaché to London, Colonel Victor Huguet. (Photo by Hulton Archives/Getty Images)

flict, four divisions and a cavalry corps would land at Rouen, Le Havre, and Boulogne. Trains would rush the entire force to staging areas below the Belgian border, at the far left of the French line.

A force to himself, Henry Wilson was both a necessary man and a dynamo gone haywire. He accomplished exactly what the Asquith cabinet didn't want: his preparations amounted to a commitment. He had over-planned. He had not only arranged for the BEF to cross the Channel, but his machinations had set its destination, in what proved to be a precarious forward position. One man, who was not even in command, had decreed the manner and direction in which the land power of Great Britain was to be employed. He left the army he represented no alternatives.

He already had enemies. He made more.

On the final day of the year, 1913, Wilson fairly gloated in his journal: "Enormous preparations for war, except with us, and great and unusual unrest, interior and exterior, in all parts of the world."

AS 1914 BEGAN, THE INDIVIDUAL who seemed most likely to lead Great Britain in any continental battle was Field Marshal Sir John French. He was one of the few recognizable heroes to emerge from the Boer War, and had since then steadily climbed the leadership ladder, relying on impor-tant friendships to camouflage occasional missteps. In the next months, however, one would nearly put an end to his career.

History has not been kind to French. He lacked a wide-sweeping view of strategic potential; he thought small. He had a tendency to waffle, to veer from overenthusiasm and hyperactivity to near paralysis produced by unrestrained despair, sometimes within hours. French tried to placate everyone, and often ended by satisfying no one. He was a man who had difficulty making up his mind, and frequently had to have it made up for him. "Weathercock" was B. H. Liddell Hart's description of him; his sentiments seemed to spin in whatever direction the prevailing winds of attitude or persuasion blew him. He was called "the little Field Marshal," but in fact he was five feet six inches tall, the height in 1900 of the average British man. French was only "little" by the standards of the landed gen-try to which he was born and the cavalry officers with whom he served.

Edward L. Spears, the literary liaison officer, described John Denton Pinkstone French as being "ruddy-faced, his white mustache drooping over the corners of his mouth," with "clear penetrating blue eyes. His face, with its heavy underlip, seemed set in a perpetual scowl." At sixty-two, his figure was still trim, though with a noticeable thickening around the waist. He moved purposefully with a cavalryman's bowlegged strut, taking long, brisk strides out of proportion to his size. In the years leading up to the war, his biographer Richard Holmes wrote, "He graced the house parties of Liberal political hostesses with his bulldog swagger and roving eye."

Winston Churchill, an admirer, saw French as "a natural soldier." French had earned a deserved reputation as a cavalry leader—"perhaps the most distinguished since Cromwell," one biographer noted, without exaggerating. His men took risks to please him. In the Boer War he had evidenced a talent for luck. Military luck can be the ability to spot, and take advantage of, the moment when an opponent has his guard down. It requires discipline, preparation, a sixth sense for opportunity in the confusion of battle. You have to be in the right place at the right time: all the clichés have to come together. Though it may seem like chance, luck doesn't happen by accident. Consider the well-informed risk French took when he raced his cavalry division down a dust-choked valley to Kimberley, the besieged hub of the De Beers diamond mining empire, and rescued its head, Cecil Rhodes, the most powerful man in Africa. Douglas Haig and Edmund Allenby, like French future field marshals, served under him that day in February 1900. London music-hall minstrels at last had a Boer War hero to shower with demotic adulation:

> *'E's a daisy, 'e's a brick,*
> *An 'e's up to every trick,*
> *And 'e moves amazin' quick,*
> *Don't yer, French?*

In that war, French had almost more luck than he could handle. To be consistently lucky requires preparation. You have to acquire what historian John Lewis Gaddis describes, in a slightly different context, as "the capacity to make the most of an opportunity." Luck may seem like an accident; it has to become an instinct, the automatic ability to recognize your best chance, and to seize it. Luck takes practice.

By 1914, luck had abandoned Sir John French—except, perhaps in the bedrooms of upper-class London. Or perhaps he had abandoned it.

Still, there was hardly a high post in the army that he hadn't held. It didn't seem to matter that he had never commanded a unit larger than a division, and a cavalry division at that.* Like his fellow British generals, he had known only colonial wars. French had shown himself to be a skilled motivator; he was less successful as a manager. He did not belong to the new breed of military technocrats or understand the increasingly advanced tools of war. (He did, though, appreciate the potential of aircraft, especially for reconnaissance purposes.) French's heart still belonged to the horse. "The sphere of action of cavalry is steadily widening," he wrote in 1910. To the most distinguished cavalry leader since Cromwell, the shock of the massed charge by men on horseback, wielding lances and sabers, had an awesome pride of place. The reign of the arme blanche—cutting or thrusting weapons such as the bayonet or the sword—seemed to remain secure.

As peerless a horseman as he was, French was never able to master a bicycle.

What, then, are we to make of the Little Field Marshal? Brave he certainly was, but determined is another matter. Determination is not a quality we associate with a weathercock. His eye was rarely fastened on a single prize; he was easily distracted. His personal relationships were forever unpredictable. French, writes Richard Holmes, "could be a good friend, but could be an equally good hater, and the motives for friendship or dislike were not always clearly comprehensible." His private life was messy. He was constantly in debt, and suffered, you might say, from the Midas touch in reverse. In 1899, at the beginning of the Boer War, he asked his friend and subordinate, Douglas Haig, for a loan of £2,500; he was on the verge of bankruptcy, which would have forced him from the army. Haig gave him the loan. French never repaid it.

* A British infantry division numbered 18,000; a cavalry division, 9,269.

In June 1913, French would grasp a field marshal's baton. Few in the army then doubted that, in the unlikely event of a European explosion (and the even more unlikely one of British involvement), he would be the man to lead an expeditionary force to the Continent. As the New Year arrived, Ireland, and the issue of Irish home rule, preoccupied the nation. Would the six counties of Protestant Ulster, the north of Ireland, tolerate domination by a Catholic Parliament in Dublin? Ulster, Henry Wilson wrote in his journal, was "rapidly becoming the sole & governing & immediate factor in the national life." Volunteer militias were forming, especially in Ulster. In army camps, Protestant officer groups held clandestine protest meetings. A confrontation between Protestants and Catholics was taking shape, one that would endure for most of the century. Call it the last war of the Reformation.

Sir John French would find himself caught in the Irish maelstrom that spring, and nearly sucked under by it. March was the month of greatest crisis. Would the Army be ordered into Ulster to enforce home rule? Civil War loomed. Winston Churchill, the First Lord of the Admiralty, told French that if Belfast, the principal city in Ulster, showed fight, the navy would leave it in flames. In one cavalry brigade quartered at the camp southwest of Dublin called Curragh Barracks, the commander of the 3rd Cavalry Brigade, Hubert Gough, and sixty of his officers threatened a mass resignation if ordered north to put down a Protestant uprising. French feared that if this happened and others followed the example of Gough's brigade, the entire army might disintegrate. What if war broke out in Europe while this happened? That was French's greatest worry, and given the Continental tinderbox, it was not an idle fear.

French and the secretary of state for war, Col. John Seely, recognized that they had to calm the rebellious officers and put a quick end to the Curragh affair. But Gough and his followers demanded that French and Seely promise in writing that the army would not be ordered north. French and Seely gave in. The pro–home rule Asquith government disavowed their pledge. French and Seely resigned: "The future," Churchill wrote, "now seemed completely closed to French." Even if a Continental war broke out, he would be "on the shelf." (His friend Churchill's phrase.) In July, the First Lord of the Admiralty invited French to watch naval

In July 1914, as Europe careened into war, the Irish Home Rule crisis consumed Great Britain. It had already forced one of its most conspicuous soldiers, Field Marshal Sir John French, to resign. His friend, Winston Churchill, First Lord of the Admiralty, invited him to come along on an inspection tour. Here, at a naval base in Scotland, Churchill (center) leads French to a waiting launch. He described the "Little Field Marshal" as a "heart-broken man." (Fremantle/Alamy Stock Photo)

maneuvers. The two rode in picket boats and took long walks along the Esplanade in Deal. "My impression of French, for all his composure," Churchill wrote, "was that he was a heart-broken man."

Two weeks later, Europe was hurtling toward war, a runaway carousel whose eccentric spins no one could control, or perhaps wanted to: the riders were too busy reaching out for gold rings to think of their predicament or of consequences. One who did grasp a prize was Sir John French. In a matter of days his fortunes turned. On July 30, a Thursday, as Germany mobilized, the new chief of the imperial general staff (CIGS), a post that French had once held, sent for him and, as he later wrote, he "was given private intimation that, if an expeditionary force was sent to France, I was to command it."

Had he been elevated beyond his capacity? His old friend Douglas Haig, who had a festering unease about his former mentor, thought so. He knew he would be serving under French as a corps commander. He had, he confided to his diary on August 11, "grave doubts . . . whether his temper was sufficiently even or his military knowledge sufficiently thorough to enable him to discharge properly the very difficult duties which will devolve upon him. . . . In my own heart, I know that French is quite unfit for this great command at a time of crisis in our nation's history."

Haig never mentioned the unpaid debt.

Sir John French had experienced his ultimate piece of good luck, the luck of the last man standing. For all his flaws, and they were legion, French was probably the best, the only, man to take the BEF to the Continent. That says much about the leadership vacuum in the British Army of 1914. There was really no one else available.

2

The Man Who Willed a War

JULY 1914

THE STRUGGLE FOR SUPREMACY IN EUROPE AND THE WORLD INTENSIFIED. Schlieffen campaigned for the war he saw as inevitable; so did Moltke. Neither was especially discreet in his advocacy. They served a nation with a chip on its shoulder; the fear of encirclement had become a peculiarly German phobia. Neighbors in Europe viewed the accelerated growth of the kaiser's navy as a threat to their security—none more so than Great Britain. Crisis followed crisis: Morocco, the Balkan Wars, Morocco again. The prickly Germans, especially their leaders, could see nothing good in their future. Russia had not only regained strength but also seemed ready to overtake and pass Germany as an industrial and military power: commanders like Moltke the Younger reckoned that the balance might shift as early as 1916 or 1917. The German military leadership began to talk of preventive war. Nobody seemed to heed Bismarck's scornful observation: "Preventive war is like committing suicide out of fear of death."

Moltke led the charge; political decision-makers withered before it. His voice, insistent, assured, refusing to budge in its conviction, rose above, and drowned out, the opposition. The kaiser vacillated until the end. What Moltke never let on were his private doubts and fears about the war he advocated. He was not even certain that Germany could win. He predicted that war "would destroy the culture of almost the whole of Europe for decades to come." Why, in spite of these dark reservations, did he continue to push an armed solution? Did he feel that Germany had no choice? Moltke let himself be swept along by events, never taking steps to head off disaster before he ushered Germany over the edge. Worse, his great secret, the coup de main, effectively blocked any last-minute diplomatic efforts to head off war. Once troops crossed beyond national boundaries in a preemptive strike, they could not be recalled. Peace was out of the question.*

Many men—and remember, this was still a man's world—were responsible for the Great War. But only one, Generaloberst Helmuth von Moltke the Younger, could give the final order that would empty the barracks, fill the troop trains, and set them rolling. He was the man who would, as it were, pull the switch.

The assassination of the archduke merely provided the excuse.

Field Marshal Helmuth von Moltke, who posed for this formal photograph about 1910, was not shy about proclaiming that "war was unavoidable, and the sooner the better." Privately, though, he feared that it would devastate vanquished and victor alike. Still, when the time came, he was more than ready to pull the switch. (Getty Images)

"ALL SIDES ARE PREPARING FOR a European War, which all sides expect sooner or later," Moltke told the German head of government, Chancel-

---

* On questions of motive, we can only speculate. Moltke's eldest son, Wilhelm, burned all his father's papers, including a diary, as the Soviets were about to overrun Berlin in the spring of 1945.

lor Theobald von Bethmann Hollweg, on December 2, 1912. Eight days later, at a Berlin meeting of the kaiser and high-ranking army and navy officers, the chief of the German general staff said what everyone was already thinking. One admiral present recorded in his diary: "Gen. v. Moltke: 'I consider a war unavoidable, and the sooner the better.'" Moltke's words, "the sooner the better," repeated mantra-like, became a ceaseless refrain during the months that followed. It was as if Moltke were willing a war.

The sooner the better. Moltke may have had another reason for those words. The longer a secret is kept, the less likely it is to remain a secret. Had the Schlieffen/Moltke plan exceeded its shelf life? Moltke worried openly that it had. What he failed to admit at the meeting was that he had nothing, no grand scheme of his own, to replace it.

The French certainly suspected that the Germans intended to make some sort of sweep through Belgium, though they placed the point of initial contact closer to the lower Meuse or the Ardennes Forest, both in the southeastern corner of the country. And they didn't anticipate the size of the invasion. The British, too, were wary. As early as August 23, 1911, Winston Churchill attended a special meeting of the Committee of Imperial Defense. There, the new director of military operations, Gen. Henry Wilson, stood by an enormous map and explained, Churchill remembered, "with what proved afterwards to be extreme accuracy, the German plan for attacking France."

Did Moltke give away his intentions when he met with King Albert of Belgium on November 6, 1913? Albert and his queen had been staying with the kaiser at his Potsdam palace, and his visit had apparently been an uneasy one. Wilhelm remarked in his perfect French that he considered war with France "inevitable and near." (Though the young queen of Belgium was German, Albert's command of the language of his neighbor was hesitant.) At a court ball, the kaiser had also pointed out a general— his name was Alexander von Kluck—commenting to the young king that he would be the man "to lead the march on Paris." He left it to Moltke to spell out the implications the following day. An alliance with Germany, Moltke recognized, was probably out of the question, but he at least hoped for an assurance that his troops could pass through Belgium unchallenged. There would be no territorial exactions, he promised: when the brief war was over, Belgium would retain its original size and shape.

Once it became clear that the tall, handsome, bespectacled monarch would meet none of Moltke's demands, the bulky Prussian turned to intimidation. "Modern war," he said, "involved terrible destructions, and small nations such as Belgium would be wise to join the victor if they wished to retain their independence." The resistance of Albert's six infantry divisions clearly didn't worry him: they were, as his officers quipped, mere "chocolate soldiers." To Moltke, war with France was certain. He could not refrain from remarking, "the sooner the better." And, he added with an ominous flourish, "We are certain of victory."

Albert left the meeting "profoundly alarmed." Had Moltke let the Schlieffen cat out of the bag? He had certainly more than hinted at a German invasion of Belgium. Albert returned to Brussels determined to build up his little army and strengthen his defensive systems while there was still time.

THE ICY FOGS OF A Berlin winter took a toll on Moltke's health. In the spring he traveled to the famous Bohemian spa at Carlsbad, spending a month there. His doctors diagnosed bronchitis. At the end of his stay, his Austro-Hungarian counterpart, Franz Graf Conrad von Hötzendorf, came to consult with him. On the night of May 14, 1914, Conrad noted in his journal that the two men "took a simple supper." Before Conrad left, he asked Moltke "his view of how soon, in a general war against Russia and France, Germany would be able to turn its full strength against Russia.

"M[oltke]. We hope that, six weeks after the start of operations against France, to be ready, or at least nearly ready, to be able to send our main forces to the east." The conquest of France, Moltke estimated, would take forty-two days.

Back in Berlin not long after, Moltke spoke with the German foreign minister, Gottlieb von Jagow. He voiced his apprehensions about the growing strength of Germany's enemies—by the spring of 1914, "enemies" was a term that fairly tripped off the Generaloberst's tongue. Jagow recorded the gist of the conversation. "Today we are still a match for them," Moltke said. "In his opinion there was no alternative to making preventive war in order to defeat the enemy while we still have a chance for victory. The Chief of the General Staff therefore proposed that I should conduct a policy with the aim of provoking a war in the near future." Moltke was not the only German leader overcome by apprehension. Chancellor Bethmann Hollweg, who had lost his wife that same spring, called Russia "an increasingly heavy nightmare." Convinced that before long Russian hordes would trample his country holdings east of the capital, this perpetually fearful man refrained from planting trees on his estate.

Once again, Moltke's health broke down, this time from an acute but unspecified liver ailment, at the time an endemic complaint of the affluent and the overfed. He arrived back in Carlsbad on June 28, a man burdened by the constant illnesses that he seemed unable to slough off. For the entire summer of 1914—one of the crucial periods in human history—the chief of the German general staff was a sick man, a man in pain and discomfort. Surely that must have affected his ability to cope with the kind of constant, often split-second, decisions a commander must make to sort out from the confusing and contradictory inflow of information what is accurate and truly matters. Over and again those three summer months, he teetered on the edge of collapse. Even the high of going to war, hardly unalloyed for him, was a tonic too soon expended.

June 28 was, of course, the day that, half a thousand miles to the south, Gavrilo Princip assassinated Archduke Franz Ferdinand, the future ruler of the Austro-Hungarian Empire, and the archduke's wife. The excuse that Moltke and his pro-war faction had been hoping for now presented itself. They were fortunate that so many political decision-makers were already on, or about to leave for, their summer vacations. July 28 was also the day when the Vienna "Season" officially ended, and everyone of wealth and importance headed for the hills. Diplomacy, too, took a holiday. At Carlsbad, Moltke settled in amid the curative mineral waters and waited for the ache in his considerable belly to ease. If the war he so desired did come, he needed to be fit to run it. Such an ideal opportunity might not present itself again.

All this invites a question. How could Germany venture into a summer of peril with an army commanded by a sick man? That no one had the nerve to speak out against a trusted friend of the kaiser was a measure of the weakness at the top. On June 28, perhaps, it didn't matter. A month later, it did.

THE KAISER WAS INDISCRETION PERSONIFIED. As T. G. Otte, author of that model history, *July Crisis*, writes of Wilhelm II: "Tone-deaf to nuances and color-blind to the shades of grey that dominate political life, he was given to exuberant outbursts." He had a tendency to act before he thought. On July 5, he was preparing to take his annual North Sea cruise on his 390-foot-long yacht, *Hohenzollern*, but not before a hasty luncheon meeting with the Austro-Hungarian ambassador, who had come to discuss what to do about the murder of the archduke. The kaiser told him that, subject to approval by the chancellor, as far as he (and Germany) were concerned, Austria-Hungary could do anything it wanted to Serbia and to the government that had no doubt planned the assassination of his friend. Germany would endorse any and all initiatives, including war. The kaiser's impetuous declaration became the infamous "blank check" that the Austrians could fill in when and as they pleased.

That afternoon, in the anodyne precincts of the kaiser's Potsdam rose garden, he obtained the blessing of the minister of war, Gen. Erich von Falkenhayn, and that of the chancellor. (Berlin courtiers nicknamed Bethmann Hollweg "the dancing bear" because of his habit of shifting from foot to foot when speaking to the kaiser.) Though Austria was making savage noises in Serbia's direction, Falkenhayn didn't think much would come of them. He also expected threats from Russia. To call Moltke back from his sick leave might only cause needless alarm. "Certainly in no circumstances will the coming weeks bring any decision," he wrote Moltke that night. The kaiser left for his cruise believing that he had signed a check that would never be cashed. They were all wrong. The kaiser had given Vienna permission to make mischief, and the empire proceeded to do just that. Loose lips can sink ships—especially ships of state. As Otte writes, "The blank check would determine not only the course of events during July 1914 but, arguably the shape of the twentieth century."

The inevitable still required a switch-puller.

IN THIS MONTH OF CRISIS, it comes as a surprise to discover how little seemed genuinely menacing until its final days. Then, events not only ganged up on the participants but also overwhelmed them.

By the time Moltke returned to Berlin on the night of July 25, Vienna had delivered an ultimatum to Serbia packed with demands no sovereign nation could accept: under the guise of joining the investigation of the archduke's murder, it would have allowed Austria to meddle in Serbia's government. Serbia went far to accept the demands, but it probably never could have gone far enough. The Austrians asserted that the Serbian reply was unsatisfactory. The next day, the twenty-sixth, Moltke did advance work on an ultimatum of his own, to the Belgian government. It requested that Albert's kingdom permit German armies to march across Belgian territory. The rationale of Moltke's draft was that "reliable news" suggested that France was preparing to enter Belgium from the south, in a kind of Schlieffen sweep in reverse, and Germany had to meet that phantom invasion—in Belgium. Fake news was as good as real news. The document concluded with a threat: "Should Belgium oppose the German troops . . . Germany will, to her regret, be compelled to consider Belgium as an enemy." The ultimatum made no attempt to justify its demands; Serbia or the Balkan crisis were never mentioned. It demanded an answer within twenty-four hours.

Moltke sent the document to the foreign minister for his approval, which Jagow gave. The German diplomats in Brussels were ordered not to present the ultimatum to their Belgian counterparts until Berlin gave the word. The timing of Moltke's composition made it clear that the Generaloberst—and official Germany—were already contemplating war.

On July 27, the kaiser arrived at Wildpark Station in Potsdam. The sudden rush of events had persuaded him to cut short his cruise. A delegation led by Moltke and the chancellor greeted him. The kaiser, that congenital waverer, unexpectedly counseled peace: Moltke's nightmarish roller-coaster ride was about to begin. It took only a day for the kaiser's mood to change. Now he announced to his generals that war was inevitable. "His Majesty," Falkenhayn recorded in his journal, "claims, as he says, that the ball that is rolling can no longer be stopped." That same day, July 28, Austria-Hungary declared war on Serbia. Then, in the early hours of the twenty-ninth, Austro-Hungarian river gunboats on the Danube, and artillery dug in on the opposite bank, began lobbing shells into Belgrade, Serbia's capital. Vienna had cashed the blank check.

Russia, determined to protect its small Slav ally, began to mobilize, depending on its great conscripted pool of manpower. France's secret treaty obligations to Russia compelled it to follow suit. Germany's turn would come next. And once Germany invaded Belgium, Great Britain and its empire, which had pledged to protect the Lowlands kingdom, was bound to follow. Where, and when, would the dominoes stop falling? Never had irresistibly wise statesmen been more needed. No such personage existed. Mediocrity ruled.

The time for diplomacy was rapidly passing. Moltke advocated a general mobilization—and general mobilization meant war. The time had come to spring his coup de main, the secret leaven in his offensive recipe. As Annika Mombauer, Moltke's careful biographer, points out: "Germany could not afford to wait until her enemies mobilized—military concerns were now beginning to dictate political measures." At a meeting of military and political leaders on July 29, the cautious Bethmann resisted mobilization: wait, he maintained, and let Germany's opponents attack first, putting them in the wrong. The meeting broke up with nothing resolved.

The following night, the same leaders met again. Bethmann Hollweg still held back. Falkenhayn's journal recorded the July 30 confrontation, which dragged on into the small hours. "Late in the evening an argument between him [the chancellor] and Moltke over who would carry the responsibility for a possible war. . . . Moltke declares himself decidedly in favor of war *sans phrase* [without mincing matters]." Bethmann Hollweg reluctantly backed down, bending to the demand of the generals that "a state of imminent war" be immediately proclaimed. He left the gathering, an observer reported, "red-faced." A Rubicon had been crossed. From this moment on, the German military, and not civilian politicos, would determine the country's future—calling the shots, you might say.

Moltke, too, was feeling the heat. His wife, Eliza, later complained that he was "overworked day and night." His personal adjutant could tell that his boss was under serious psychological pressure. That he continued to advocate war to anyone who would listen did not square with his deeper anxieties about the hideous form it might take, one in which there would be only losers. And yet, for all of Moltke's apprehensions, expressed only to intimates, he still allowed blind patriotism and imagined duty to transcend considerations of what might be best for Europe in particular and humankind in general. He refused, most of all, to risk his precious coup de main. The long view—of an endless conflict—frightened him, as well it might, and in public he pushed it from mind and mouth. He remained to the end a short-term man.

The July 31 drama continued to gather. Some eight hundred miles away in St. Petersburg, Russia did just what Moltke, Falkenhayn, and Bethmann Hollweg had been hoping for: the tsar responded to the Austrian shelling of Belgrade by announcing a general mobilization of his armed forces. The Wilhelmstrasse, the center of government in Berlin, got wind of the tsar's decision that night. If true, it was precisely the opening Moltke sought, and a century later, historians are at last beginning to grasp what happened. In *Europe's Last Summer*, the late historian David Fromkin detected the military sleight of hand that the German general staff pulled off. Russia's mobilization allowed it to substitute one war for another, replacing Austria's ineffectual retaliation against Belgrade with a Continental-sized explosion. The Germans had, in effect, hijacked a war. Moltke, the military grifter, had played, Fromkin writes, "a sort of confidence trick that kept generations afterwards in the dark as to who caused what."

So far Moltke's scheme was playing to perfection. France now would have to come to the aid of Russia—the Germans were apparently aware of the mutual defense pact and were ready to take advantage of it. Russia's mobilization would happen within hours, leaving Germany free to attack, and destroy, its real target, France.

AS THE SUN ROSE ON July 31, official Berlin sought absolute confirmation of the Russian mobilization and whether it was indeed a general one. The one thing certain was that the day would be hot and clear. Hoping to find a definite answer, Moltke, a confirmed user of the telephone, placed a call to a corps commander in East Prussia, on the Russian border.* Was Russia indeed mobilizing? the Generaloberst asked. The corps commander replied that he was reasonably sure that it was a fait accompli. The frontier was sealed; no one could cross it from either direction. The Russians were burning their frontier guardhouses. Red-lettered mobilization posters had apparently been plastered on conspicuous walls in public places.

It is early evening on August 1, and a crowd gathers at the *Berliner Schloss,* the German royal palace, to cheer the kaiser, a distant figure on a balcony (top center). Little did the multitudes realize that this had to be one of the worst days in history, as nations mobilized, declared war, and entered a killing season never equaled. (Imperial War Museum, London)

* In 1914, Poland still belonged to the Russian Empire.

Moltke asked the general to get him one. He reported back that he had the evidence in hand.

Moltke next sent a telegram to Conrad in Vienna, advising Austria to mobilize. Normally such a suggestion would have gone through civilian decision-makers. It was a certain sign that the military was taking charge in both nations. "Who rules in Berlin," the Austro-Hungarian foreign minister remarked to Conrad, "Moltke or Bethmann?" He needn't have asked.

At 5 P.M. that afternoon, the kaiser signed the "imminent danger of war" decree, in Germany the mandated step before general mobilization, to be followed within hours by a formal declaration of war. The nation was now under martial law. A flourish of the pen had put the military officially in the driver's seat.

IN THE LONG HISTORY OF humankind, few dates can be less auspicious than Friday, August 1, 1914. A Socialist leader, Philipp Scheidemann, returned to a Berlin where "there was only one topic of conversation—war." That first day of August, the kaiser, wearing an eagle helmet and the uniform of the Cuirassiers of the Guard, the empress at his side in a claret gown, drove past cheering throngs from Potsdam to his Berlin palace. He was dressed for the occasion. Moltke and Falkenhayn were waiting for him. They insisted that mobilization could not be delayed a moment longer. The kaiser knew nothing of Moltke's hidden reason, the coup de main. At 5 P.M. the kaiser had signed a general mobilization order. Moltke left, "his face bathed in perspiration," determined to transmit the mobilization order to his armies before any unforeseen event delayed it. The war, his war, would go on, and it would start with the coup de main.

Then the unforeseen did happen. Just minutes after the signing, a telegram from Prince Lichnowsky, the German ambassador to London, arrived. The kaiser read it. Lichnowsky said that Sir Edward Grey, the British foreign secretary, had told him not only that England would remain neutral but also that it would guarantee French neutrality. Everyone in the room agreed that, bluff or not, they could not turn down such an offer. Now Germany would have to face not opponents on two fronts but one only, Russia. The kaiser suggested an immediate change of deployment: the trains, carrying their thousands of troops, would simply change direction. A call went out for Moltke to return.

Moltke found the kaiser and his chancellor—who had long been pushing for a détente with Great Britain—in a jubilant mood. "Well, now we simply march the entire army to the east," the kaiser told Moltke. That was impossible, the chief of staff replied. It was too late to stop the deployment. Germany had to attack the French. The argument grew heated. Moltke, his lips trembling, refused to back down. Seven-eighths of his forces would soon be headed west—to attempt to turn them around would cause chaos, possibly irreparable. And, he added, troops had already entered Luxembourg; a full division was on their heels. To do what the kaiser suggested would leave "a mass of disorderly armed men without provisions."

"Your uncle would have given me a different answer," the kaiser replied. And then he added, "It must be possible if I order it." For Moltke, no verbal thrust could have been more wounding.

He had been caught in a trap of his own devising. Three years earlier he had made the decision to leave only a token army in East Prussia. Beyond that, he had no plan. He had allowed for no alternative to the deployment in the west, for his coup de main.

Falkenhayn, no real friend of Moltke, pulled the distraught chief of staff away and tried to calm him. The generals reached a compromise with the kaiser: Germany would continue mobilizing, but the division poised to enter Luxembourg would halt its advance short of the border. A telegram went out to Lichnowsky: Germany would accept the British proposal, with the understanding that France would remain neutral for the length of the Russo-German war, a treaty-breaking impossibility; no German troops would cross the border into France. The telegram said nothing about Belgium.

Another telegram arrived from Lichnowsky. The time was now 7 P.M. Once again the message seemed to promise British neutrality, even in the event of a Continental war. The kaiser could not contain his joy. He ordered champagne. Amid the popping of corks, Moltke made a hasty, and no doubt almost unnoticed, exit. "I want to wage war against the French and Russians, but not against such a Kaiser," he said to an aide. "He was dark red in the face," another aide observed when Moltke arrived at the general staff building. "It appeared as if he might suffer a stroke at any moment." Frau von Moltke feared the same; in her opinion her husband had already suffered a light seizure. As she later remarked, "I had a desperate man in front of me."

Later that night Moltke returned to the Schloss—as the Berlin palace was called—in a final attempt to persuade the kaiser to change his mind. How that shattered man made the brief trip we shall never know. In the interim, unknown to Moltke, a final telegram had arrived from Lichnowsky, bad news. There had been "no positive English proposal" after all. When Grey made his original suggestions, he hadn't known that France had already mobilized. He had added new conditions that the Germans couldn't accept. This was followed by a telegram from the kaiser's friend, King George V ("Nicky"): "I THINK THERE MUST BE SOME MISUNDERSTANDING . . ."

Paris, early August: shouldering her loved one's Lebel M1886 rifle, a woman dressed in black waits for him to retrieve his weapon and, after a presumed final embrace, to join the marchers bound for trains to the front. (Imperial War Museum Q 81765, London)

The kaiser, who was in bed by now, told Moltke that he was free to go ahead and occupy Luxembourg. "Lichnowsky's telegram was based on a misunderstanding," he said. He rolled over, his back to Moltke.

"Now do as you please, I don't care either way."

Moltke left, to give the final order. Many men may have been responsible for the war. Only one pulled the switch.

THE FLANDERS CONVERGENCE

Corpses litter a field somewhere in northern France. These happened to be German and merited a full gravure spread in the Paris predecessor to *Life*, the picture weekly *L'Illustration*. In the entire Great War, no months saw more battlefield carnage than August and September 1914. On the Western Front, that carnage was most likely to have been French—who suffered the most awesome casualties of all the combatants. (*L'illustration*)

3

"The Strength of Despair"

AUGUST 4—SEPTEMBER 1

The last warrior king: Throughout the war, Albert I of Belgium, posing here in uniform, remained commander in chief of his little army, not just in name but in fact. Though only holding an average of ten miles of line (out of a Western Front total of around 470), he became a powerful symbol of Allied resistance. (Hulton Archive/Getty Images)

HE IS AMONG THE HANDFUL OF GENUINELY ATTRACTIVE PUBLIC FIGURES IN the last century, a tall, wavy-haired man with a long, handsome face, spectacles, and a mustache that always seemed too wispy for his personality. If a single individual occasionally does have the power to shape destiny—if a leader's character really can influence his nation's fate—then Albert I of Belgium has to be counted in that select number.

Of all the presidents, prime ministers, and emperors who presided over the Great War, Albert was the only one who actually commanded his army, even overseeing its day-to-day operations. He was the only one who regularly showed up in frontline trenches. That army was, to be sure, small, but its symbolic importance was far out of proportion to its size and the tiny stretch of line it would end up holding—twenty-odd miles, about 4 percent of the Allied side of the Western Front. Belgium, and its violated neutrality, provided the Allies with the ready-made patina of morality the war otherwise lacked. And Albert, the man who chose against all odds to resist, became, despite a distaste for killing, the world's last warrior king.

Neither the isolation nor the ordinary ceremonial preoccupations of kingship were for Albert. He had a collection of automobiles, which he repaired himself. He experimented with wireless radios, made balloon ascensions, and descended into coal mines. An autodidact whose formal education had been pretty much limited to some nondescript palace tutoring and training as an officer in military school, he became a man obsessed with, but not bowed down by, information. Albert's appetite for books was voracious—Barbara Tuchman rightly used the word "gluttony" in this connection—and he read an average of two a day, in several languages. (Curiously, his German was shaky, though his wife, Queen Elisabeth, was a German.) He never left a waking moment unfilled. "Boredom," the king once remarked, "is a sure sign of a mediocre mind. Such people are weary because, when alone, they are with themselves." He kept a rowing machine beside his desk.

Albert was a pioneer environmentalist who would later worry about the effects of wartime deforestation. Unlike his royal contemporaries, who, as if participating in some ancient blood rite, slaughtered game by the hundreds and thousands, he refused to hunt. His passion, rather, was for mountains, and he collected rock faces and summits the way Theodore Roosevelt or the kaiser collected trophy heads; he might be heard casually discussing botany as he went up the Jungfrau. "He would have discovered a pretext for scaling something in the flattest and most monotonous stretch of land," one biographer commented. The maritime plain of Flanders, to which his patriotism condemned him for the four years of the Great War, strains even that hyperbole.

ALBERT HAD BEEN KING FIVE years when the kaiser's armies breached the Belgian frontier on August 4, 1914. He automatically became commander in chief of his army, and would direct its operations for the next fifty-two months of the war, from beginning to end. He was not quite forty, the youngest of the rulers of Europe. Almost until that moment, his general staff had been uncertain about whom the violators of the neutrality of their small nation were likely to be, the French or the Germans. So they selected what seemed to be the best place to parry both threats, concentrating their 117,000-man field army along the Petite Gette, a river that lay halfway between Brussels and Liège, the manufacturing center of the nation and a railroad hub.

It took the German ultimatum, the one that Moltke had concocted at the end of July, demanding that its armies be allowed to pass through Belgian territory on their way to France, to clear up any residue of confusion. That was on the evening of August 2; the Germans had carefully designed a document that would be rejected. They asked for an "unequivocal answer" within twelve hours, eight of them night hours. The ultimatum was written in German; the translation process ate up one of those hours. In the end, time didn't matter. With the firm backing of Albert, the Belgian government did what the Germans expected it to do: turn down their demands. Moltke had already unleashed his coup de main—or *Handstreich,* to use the German word for the phrase. Even before Germany declared war on Belgium, troops had crossed the frontier and were beginning to execute civilians whom they believed had resisted their progress. Now Great Britain, protesting the violation of Belgian territory, prepared to mobilize. An extraordinary council of war issued a formal declaration of war on the afternoon of the fifth; it announced the dispatch of British troops to the Continent.*

THE WORLD HAD NEVER WITNESSED anything like the movement of armies those first days of August. Just consider the German effort, the early

---

* Because Belgium never officially declared war on Germany, it still technically remained neutral, not an Allied power but an associated one.

preponderance of it in the West. The historian Holger H. Herwig has put together an accounting of the call to arms. "The Military Telegraph Section of the German General Staff mobilized 3,822,450 men and 119,754 officers as well as 600,000 horses. This gigantic force was transported to the front in 312 hours by 11,000 trains. More than 2,150 54-car trains crossed the Rhine River over the Hohenzollern Bridge at Cologne in 10-minute intervals between August 2 and 18. The west army, consisting of 1.6 million men organized into 23 active and 11 reserve corps (or 950 infantry battalions and 498 cavalry squadrons), thundered across the various Rhine bridges at a rate of 560 trains per day . . ." Belgium was the destination of a sizeable portion of this huge force.

Liège, that river valley city on the Meuse and a natural target, was the key. Its quick capture would unlock the narrow corridor through which the German First Army would pour, gathering momentum for its descent on France. Moltke estimated that, relying on shock and surprise, he could take Liège, with its ring of twelve forts, in two days; he needed ten. (Should the siege have lasted a couple of days longer, German planners recognized, the need to make up for lost time would have forced them to violate Dutch territory.) Moltke, who had devoted so much energy overseeing his coup, proved to be an inept tactician: forty-four years had passed since he had made his last appearance on a battlefield, and it showed. He approved the sending of long columns down roads that were the most obvious approaches to the city. He intended to break through the spaces between the Belgian forts on the right bank. Those supposedly empty spaces turned out to be jammed with enemy riflemen. He placed commanders at the heads of the attacking columns, where they were conspicuous targets: a major general, who commanded a brigade, died, along with fourteen colonels and majors, leaders of regiments and battaltions. He neglected to provide sufficient guides or skirmishers. To gain a supposed edge of surprise, he ordered a night attack, which was promptly swamped in a summer rainstorm. As one officer put it, "We've been washed so that we will arrive upstairs clean."

Troops, brimming with patriotic enthusiasm, reckless bravery, and inexperience, left windrows of eager corpses, marking the limits of their rush to oblivion. For at least a thousand men, Moltke's cherished fancy was a death sentence. German casualties on the night of August 5–6 totaled about 4,000—not the sort of news the home front wanted to hear. Those in charge made sure it didn't. As the minister of war, Erich von Falkenhayn remarked, "It is critical that we use the prevailing euphoria before it goes up in smoke."

Too soon Moltke's coup de main was threatening to do just that.

Moltke's former chief of operations, Gen. Erich Ludendorff, rescued the coup de main—and, temporarily, Moltke. The never-smiling military technician, that chunky von-less upstart from a background of small landowners and merchants, had joined one of the attacking brigades as a "spectator." When Belgian gunfire killed the brigade commander, Ludendorff took over. The brigade was the only one that broke through. He reached the Meuse and crossed, leading his troops into the center of town. The Belgian defenders had already retreated, leaving the bridges unprotected.

That same day, August 6, a silvery cigar shape appeared in the sky:

At Liège, artillery conquered, infantry occupied. German guns methodically reduced the forts that ringed the city, which were not built to withstand the pounding of advanced ordinance. A single giant Krupp howitzer shell penetrated a powder magazine of Fort Loncin, the explosion killing 250 men and destroying all the fort's gun turrets, including the one shown here, tossed around like a child's toy. (*L'Illustration*)

Liège earned the unhappy distinction of being the first European city to be bombed from the air, by a Zeppelin, the Z–6; nine civilians died.

One further exploit made Ludendorff the hero of the moment, as if he weren't one already. At dawn the following morning, a commandeered automobile drove him to the citadel of Liège, which stood on a height overlooking the city. He got out and pounded on the entrance gate with (it is said) the hilt of his sword, demanding to be admitted. Several hundred Belgian soldiers proceeded to surrender to him.

What infantry couldn't finish off, artillery did, and with a ruthless efficiency that, Zuber writes, stood "in stark contrast with Moltke's amateurish insistence that Liège be taken by a risky and politically and militarily foolish coup de main." The Germans never attempted another on such a scale. A week passed while the invaders waited for a siege train to come up.* Two of the twelve forts surrounding the city fell during that interval, the other ten in just four days, beginning on August 12. The gunners battered each one into submission in a matter of hours, and then turned to the next. Banks of widemouthed 21cm (8.3-inch) siege mortars did most of the damage; the giant 42cm (16.5-inch) Krupp howitzers got the lion's share of the publicity and the credit, even though they took out just a single fort. The misinformation was deliberate: for propaganda purposes, bigger was not only better but spread more alarm, bolstering the myth of German irresistibility.

Artillery conquers; infantry occupies. Rarely had that conceit, allegedly coined by Philipe Pétain, been more appropriate than in the second, and final, phase of the siege of Liège.

Artillery had caused the most severe damage, helped by outmoded design and poor construction of the forts: they were not built to stand up to the kind of heavy high explosives the Germans hurled at them. A single giant 42cm mortar shell with a delayed-action fuse penetrated the concrete roof of Fort Loncin, exploding in a magazine containing twelve metric tons of powder and sending a fireball up two hundred feet, along

---

* The siege train (as it was called), that ponderous line of artillery behemoths, then mostly horse-drawn, crept along, tractor-treaded wheels chewing up the cobbled and metaled Low Country roads. It was a "train" in the sense that it was a long line of moving weapons. But at this time a siege train was rarely transported on an actual railroad.

Redeemed by the outbreak of war and by the need for his services, Sir John French was elevated from the possible ash heap of history to head of the British Expeditionary Force (BEF). This photo catches the moment when the field marshal arrived in the Channel port of Boulogne. It is August 14, at 5 P.M. Following him is Huguet, the French military attaché. (*L'Illustration*)

That same afternoon the townspeople of Boulogne presented flowers to the first contingent of British troops in France, men just loaded into a waiting procession of lorries and cars, soon to be headed north. (*L'Illustration*)

with a 39-ton steel turret, which cartwheeled in the air and landed upside down. Ceilings fell, corridors became fiery deathtraps. Two hundred and fifty men died.

Crowds of Belgian locals came out to watch the spectacle of demise; German military police had to keep them under control. The bombardment doomed the forts outside and in. General Gérard Leman, the captured commander of the Liège fortress system, later told his German interrogators that the principal cause of the surrender of eight of twelve was the danger of asphyxiation from the gas released by exploding shells and, even more intolerable, the ordurous fumes from burst or backed up latrine pipes and shattered cesspools. The Belgian garrisons may have been undone by their own waste.

Kluck's First Army streamed through the gap in columns thirty to forty-five miles long. Think of that valedictory storm of steel as the real coup de main, the only one that could, and did, succeed. Calculations made after the war indicate that the siege had cost Germany little or no time in its advance west. Moltke's coup de main had gone for nothing. The last two Liège forts surrendered on the morning of August 16. The armies of Kluck and Bülow did not even cross the border until the next day.

THE FORTS OF LIÈGE WERE still holding out when the first contingents of Sir John French's British Expeditionary Force, the BEF, landed in France on August 14. French himself arrived with his staff on the cruiser *Sentinel* at Boulogne late that afternoon, to be greeted by enthusiastic crowds. The crossing, he remembered, had been "dark, dull and gloomy, and rather chilly for August." But later the sun had broken through, flooding with light the khaki lines marching inland.

The fourteenth was the day, too, that two French armies began to cross the border into Lorraine, one of the two provinces annexed from France after the Franco-Prussian War. As military bands struck up "La Marseillaise," the troops in the van tore down the striped barriers that marked the frontier and set out on their presumed way to the Rhine. The Germans—Bavarians in this case—made a deliberate retreat, trying to lure the French into the fatal sack mandated by the Schlieffen Plan. To the world, the French move seemed predictable, preordained: to erase the humiliation of 1871. But as Robert A. Doughty has reminded us in *Pyrrhic Victory*, there was more to the summer invasion. France was living up to its two-decades-old agreement with Russia. It would invade Germany from the west even as Russia was doing so from the east. All that remained was to tighten the strategic vise.

Sir John French, meanwhile, found his next days taken up with meetings, not combat. On August 15, he went to Paris to meet with the French president, Raymond Poincaré, and Adolphe Messimy, the minister of war. Poincaré took an immediate dislike to the field marshal, remarking that "one would take him rather for a plodding engineer than a dashing soldier." He noted that French "speaks our tongue with great difficulty."

French had always had trouble with languages. When he served in India in the early 1890s, he found himself barely able to give orders to indigenous troops. Sir John French's vocabulary was limited, and his pronunciations barbarous. "Brutal," was Winston Churchill's word. As Sir John's good friend put it, "He used to speak of 'Compiayny' at the junction of the 'Iny' and the 'Weeze' "—Compiègne, the Aisne, and the Oise.

When French showed up at Joffre's Vitry-le-François headquarters at noon the following day, language proved no hindrance. Interpreters were in plentiful supply—though it is a fact that few French officers could speak English, and their British counterparts could muster little besides half-forgotten schoolboy French. Joffre and his staff were elaborately courteous and considerate. "There was a complete absence of fuss, and a calm, deliberate confidence was manifest everywhere." The two men impressed each other. When Sir John said the BEF would not be able to start operations before August 24, Joffre asked him to try to speed up his advance to the front—wherever that might be. French said he would do so. Joffre admitted that he was puzzled by the intentions of the Germans: the last thing he still expected was a great right hook through Belgium.

As rosy and full of good feeling as French's interval with Joffre had been, his next meeting was a textbook example of military miscommunication, and it came close to having dire consequences. Joffre had heaped praise on Gen. Charles Lanrezac, who headed the French Fifth Army: Joffre called him "the best commander in the French Army."

General Charles Lanrezac, the portly, sarcastic commander of the French Fifth Army, met Sir John on Monday, August 17. Ever paranoid, the two closeted themselves alone, and without interpreters, though neither spoke the other's language. They emerged, with nothing accomplished except for the forming of an instant dislike, one that explained much of what happened on the Allied side in the next two weeks. (Tallandier/ Bridgeman Images)

Sir John would visit Lanrezac the next morning, August 17, at his headquarters in the Aisne River town of Rethel. This was an urgent meeting: the BEF would take its place in line to the left of the Fifth, adding about 70,000 men to Lanrezac's 254,000; more than 20,000, the IV Corps of the BEF, destined from Antwerp, had already landed at Zeebrugge, on the Belgian coast. French showed up promptly at 10 A.M., looking (in the words of E. L. Spears) "very spic and span." Lanrezac's chief of staff, a major general named Alexis Hély d'Oissel, remarked sourly to Col. Charles Huguet, the chief French representative to the British Army, who had accompanied French's party: "Well, here you are—it's about time. If we are beaten, it will be thanks to you."

The downhill drift of the morning continued. Lanrezac came out to greet French, speaking in a deep, loud voice. He dwarfed the compact field marshal. Spears described the army commander as "a big flabby man with an emphatic corporation. . . . His face was weatherbeaten and dark, and his cheeks and lower lip hung rather loosely. . . . I was struck by the fact that his eyeglasses were hitched over his right ear, a trick he much favored." Lanrezac seemed to be in a perpetual bad temper. He spoke no English.

"The two men walked into Lanrezac's sanctum together," Spears continued, "the one short, brisk, taking long strides out of proportion to his size, the other big, bulky, heavy, moving with short steps as if his body was too heavy for his legs. No interpreter or interpreters accompanied them." Why were none present? Spears blamed what he called "the fetish of secrecy." The two generals, neither of whom could speak the other's language, remained alone together in Lanrezac's office. French apparently did get across to Lanrezac that his three corps could not possibly take their places in line before August 24, a delayed arrival that the Fifth Army commander regarded as "dangerous." But as he later wrote, "I judged that it was useless to insist."

Outside the closed door, staff members of both armies wondered what was happening. Nothing good, it soon became apparent. The exchange that did take place after the two generals emerged was later described to Spears by a British officer, who was there, and gives a fair indication of what must have gone on behind that closed door.

Sir John, the witness related, stepped up to a map on the wall, "took out his glasses, located a place with his finger, and said to Lanrezac:

"Mon Général, est-ce que—" His French then gave out, and turning to one of his staff, he asked: "How do you say 'to cross the river' in French?" He was told, and proceeded: *"Est-ce les Allemands vont traverser la Meuse—à—à—"* Then he fumbled over the pronunciation of the name. "Huy" was the place, unfortunately one of the most difficult words imaginable to pronounce, the "u" having practically to be whistled. It was quite beyond Sir John. "Hoy," he said at last, triumphantly.

Sir John wanted to know what the Germans were doing there, and what they were likely to do next. Would they cross the river?

French failed to grasp Lanrezac's answer, and asked the question

On August 20, the German first Army reached Brussels, capital of Belgium, and began to march unresisted down its broad avenues. For three days and nights, as many as 250,000 men poured through the city in a theatrical show of force designed to intimidate. This photo was probably taken by one of the spectators and smuggled across still-porous borders to Paris. (*L'Illustration*)

again. Lanrezac was growing impatient. *"Pour pêcher dans la rivière!"* he said with a dismissive shrug of the shoulders. To fish in the river. "What does he say, what does he say?" Sir John demanded of Sir Henry Wilson, who was present. "He says they're going to cross the river, sir," replied Wilson. The conference broke up, Wilson reported, "with the usual compliments and bowings and hand-shaking."

GERMANY PILED TRIUMPH ON TRIUMPH in the next days. On August 20, the irrepressible siege train began to make sport with another Meuse fortress complex, Namur. Brussels fell without a struggle: King Albert had already fled north to Antwerp. The Germans used the occasion to make a grand display of military might. As many as a quarter of a million men—Kluck's entire First Army—marched along the avenues of the Belgian capital and then wheeled south. The parade lasted three days and nights, magnificently ominous theatre. The show of force, designed to strike terror, seemed well worth whatever time might have been wasted.

The same day another German army, Prince Rupprecht of Bavaria's Sixth, routed the French striking toward the heights around Morhange (or Mörchingen, to use the name by which the Germans had rechristened the town). It was a morning of thick fog, and as French troops were assembling in the open, wave after long wave of Bavarian infantry swept down the steep sides of a long bluff, striking them in a preemptive attack. They hurled back two French armies. Passages from a German history of 1929 captured wild and chaotic scenes that ranged over a wide front for the next four days. "The fight in the wood had cost" one German regiment "significant casualties. Snipers in the trees fired on stretcher bearers, and many wounded could not be saved. . . . The uncoordinated French resistance appeared as a withdrawal. This was reinforced by the standing grain, which hid French movements and casualties and produced an empty battlefield. Nevertheless, the French had suffered a serious defeat. . . . Overzealous leaders committed all their troops to the firing line: soon they lay shoulder-to-shoulder and one behind the other. Every French bullet had to find a mark: there were painfully heavy casualties. Farmer's barbed wire fences disrupted movement. Nevertheless by 0800 hrs the high ground had been taken and the French were running away, to be cut down by the pursuit fire."

The sun eventually burned off the fog, uncovering, said a French major standing on a hillside, "a sorry spectacle." On the main road moved a long procession of flatbed carts carrying limp and bloody forms stretched out on beds of straw, walking wounded, units of fleeing infantry, and columns of horse-drawn artillery impatient to get to the rear, wherever that was. The broken remnants passed below him "with a heavy step under the broiling sun of August, all heading in the same direction, back to France, like a great river flowing without end." Only Ferdinand Foch, commander of the XX Corps, the former professor of military science, a soldier who had never seen action, held firm in the center of the line, like a Gallic Rock of Chickamauga; he helped to buy his side time to escape and dig in, back beyond the border. Joffre rewarded him with the command of an army, one that was only then being formed, the Ninth.

For the French, worse was to come. Joffre now switched attention to the long, isolated, and mainly forested stretch above Metz, an ill-omened city considered impregnable, and, hence, to be bypassed. There, in 1870, the Germans had encircled an entire French Army and starved it into surrender. Two of Joffre's armies struck in the Ardennes, crossing the border into Belgium for the first time. But few on either side were prepared for the size of the clash, which came as something of a surprise to both. The French advance began on August 21, the day after the Morhange disaster. The Ardennes Forest, which dominates the eastern, Walloon extremities of Belgium and sprawls into Luxembourg and what was then Germany, hardly seemed a promising place in which to launch an offensive. "A great forest of small trees," it has been called, with hills and ravines submerged under a tangle of mixed hardwoods and evergreens and crisscrossed by a few narrow dirt roads that made troop movement and supply trying and risky. Towns and villages were few. This could be pleasant country, with wide, well-cultivated valleys rising into the enveloping woodlands. For a rare American visitor, it could have the feel of Vermont in those years—hilly, rural, and seldom visited. Wolves, wild boars, lynx, and elaborately antlered stags roamed the deciduous jungle of the Ardennes. This was ambushland.

Joffre had forbidden reconnaissance: he wanted his attack to be a surprise. Some of his regiments had only rough tourist maps of the area— a scattering of quaint villages was one of its few attractions—or pages torn from railroad timetables to guide them. German cavalry, on the other hand, had already thoroughly explored the area and had assessed both its danger points as well as potential places to block and destroy an enemy advance. The great forest of the Ardennes has long been regarded as an unfashionable and overlooked backwoods region, mainly of eastern Belgium, but including smaller chunks of France, Luxembourg, and, after its annexation of Lorraine as a result of the Franco-Prussian War, Germany. One economic feature redeemed these dogpatch confines, and we shall examine this source of wealth in a moment. It was a major explanation for what would come to be known as the Battle of the Frontiers.

Intelligence was about to let the French down. Untrustworthy knowledge of the enemy would increasingly become a stumbling block for both sides in those early months of the war, but nothing matched the horrendous results of this failure. Joffre believed that the enemy had drastically reduced numbers on the Ardennes front, where he was concentrating his next blow, in order to strengthen Rupprecht's pursuit of the French armies retreating from their disaster in Lorraine. As he crossed into Belgium, the French commander in chief was confident that he held a sizeable numerical advantage. Instead, two of his armies would collide with two German armies that were equal in size or larger than his, both waiting to join the Schlieffen/Moltke wheel into France.

The sun was still high and insufferably hot, especially for those sweaty new legions in their heavy wool uniforms, throwing up choking clouds of dust as they trudged along roads that were as yet largely unpaved. In his neglected classic of military history, *The Campaign of the Marne*, an American lawyer-historian, Sewell Tyng, described the vast encounter battle taking shape, expected on the German side, unexpected on the French:

> It was in fact not one battle, nor even two, but a series of engagements, fought simultaneously—by army corps, divisions, brigades, and even battalions, for the most part independently of the conduct of adjacent units. The character of the terrain rendered liaison between forces fighting almost side by side difficult, if not impossible.*

The Germans arrived first. Though the eastern extremity of Belgium was unfamiliar to them, they did have time to reconnoiter and set up defensive positions. Their two armies, the Fourth and Fifth, carved trenches at the edge of the forest and, since big guns could not be moved in dense woods, dug artillery emplacements wherever they found hills shorn of timber or given over to pasture. The trenches were mainly temporary precautions that troops expected to abandon once they began their swing

---

* A recent French authority on the Great War, Jean-Claude Delhez, in his *La Bataille des Frontières*, has counted fifteen engagements on a single day, August 22, that he regards as separate battles—though the title of his book treats them as one.

into France in the next few days. Then reconnaissance aircraft and cavalry sweeps began to report columns of the enemy advancing in their direction. They waited, perhaps surprised at the size of the French advance but not unprepared for it. On the night of August 21, after a fatiguing day of marching and countermarching, and directions of advance repeatedly changed in this country of few maps, heavy rain fell, which, by sunrise, had turned into a thick, humid fog. French infantry, groping forward, would literally stumble on German trenches.

The fighting that day, August 22, took place in scrubby timber, freshly mown clearings studded with haystacks and upright sheaves of wheat neatly bound and, intermittently rising above the forest, naked ridges, logged over and ideal for the siting of guns and howitzers. In much of the Ardennes, though, artillery could not maneuver or find a decent field of fire. More often it was a war of infantry, in which men blundered and clubbed their way through a close confusion of trees and fought hand to hand. Here the rifle ruled, a weapon that the well-trained Germans handled with more accuracy and efficiency than they were ordinarily given credit for.

The fog lifted, revealing massed thousands of French attackers in their rain-sodden blue overcoats and red pantaloons. August 22 was a day on which men died in damp uniforms. They were easy targets for German rifles, machine guns, and field pieces firing over open sights. Shellfire from the forest but mainly from the high-angle fire of howitzers parked on cleared hills and ridges killed not just men but obliterated large numbers of the vaunted enemy 75mm guns even before they had a chance to unlimber. "Suddenly deprived of their artillery support," Tyng wrote, "panic seized the French infantry." Confusion grew as the morning progressed; up and down the long line, whole units began to bolt.

In the muggy August heat, men drenched in sweat and assailed by biting insects dodged from trunk to trunk and cowered in potholes, "dazed by the Thunderclaps that followed them from clearing to clearing," a French diarist wrote. Except for those commanders on both sides who found themselves close to the action, few in charge had much idea of what was happening up front. There can be no better example than General Pierre Ruffey, who led the French Third Army: he operated from a headquarters in Verdun, just under forty miles from Longwy, the closest point of contention for his troops. It could take hours for a message to go back and forth. Only the men who actually did the fighting could sense the debacle approaching. "The battle is lost," a French artilleryman wrote. "I knew neither why nor how. I saw nothing."

The French threw in more men; the Germans kept killing them. The most intense slaughter occurred around a village called Rossignol. It involved the elite Colonial Corps, comprised of the 2nd and 3rd Colonial Divisions, regular army men who (despite the name "Colonial") were native Frenchmen. Their distinction was that they had volunteered for special duty abroad, damping down the small wars of Indochina and Africa; they were among the only French troops to have been under fire—the Foreign Legion would have qualified, but didn't see action until the day after Christmas. The 3rd Colonial waited for the fog to lift and then sent forward wave after wave of bayonet charges, five battalions, worth on a front perhaps half a mile wide. The Germans brought down 5,000 that morning. The division, much depleted, did reach Rossignol, and occupied it. Those who did penetrate the trees ran into a virtual wall of lead. Here, some of the worst slaughter occurred. Two regiments, one French and the other German, engaged in a stand-up rifle battle. The Colonials may have been fine soldiers, but the Germans rifles and machine guns nearly destroyed them. It was, Terence Zuber writes, testimony "to the effectiveness of German small arms fire." At this point, as fighting men, their soldiers were simply better.

For the Colonials, chaos and death reigned. The road to Rossignol was jammed with advancing and retreating artillery wagons, dead or dying horses, downed trees and severed branches, horse-drawn ambulances filled with moaning and shrieking wounded that sometimes seemed to dissolve in the blast of a single shell, soldiers stampeding for the rear, and everywhere, fresh corpses. One regiment fighting to save Rossignol began the morning with 3,200 men: by the time the day ended, it had lost 88 percent of that number. (If that seems an unimaginable figure, compare it with the casualty rate, only a bit lower, of a regiment at Bertrix, some miles to the north: 82 percent. Other regiments reported casualties of up to 70 percent.) The 3rd Colonial Division and the 2nd Colonial between them lost 11,153, more than a third of whom were dead.

Not even commanding officers were immune. A burst from a German machine gun cut down all three battalion chiefs, majors, as they conferred on a roadside. Léon Raffenel, commander of the 3rd Colonial Division, a general who had made his reputation overseas, abruptly wandered off, dazed and alone. Abulia, it was later said, the pathological inability to make decisions, had overwhelmed him.

That may have been the kindest psychological explanation of his disfunction as a leader. He had sent battalions into the woods, where the Germans ambushed them—and then sent in more battalions. Before he disappeared, his chief of staff noted his disintegration:

> At one stage the general looked me in the eye for a long time without speaking. His face was convulsed. . . . I believe I could read in his eyes what he was thinking. The unfortunate man had had revealed to him his incapacity [for command] and at the same time the irredeemable disaster [facing his division].

Raffenel was seen once in the late afternoon. He had apparently swum across a winding tributary of the Meuse called the Semois and appeared at the rear area command post, covered with mud and carrying a rifle. He told an officer who tried to stop him that the battle was lost: he vanished again. Retreating soldiers came on Raffenel's body that evening. No one stuck around long enough to determine whether he had shot himself or had been killed by a German bullet.

Surrenders began. By evening, the Germans had retaken Rossignol. They entered the village with drums beating and were met by French soldiers with hands raised. They bagged three generals, 2,600 men, and 39 cannons. One regiment of the 3rd Colonial Division, about to be swept over, buried its colors; survivors recovered the banner after the war. One soldier wrapped the colors of his regiment around his waist and was able to slip away. But an officer felt that only he could take proper charge of the medals attached to them; he also escaped. Though as many as a thousand did reach the French lines, fleeing for safety through the perilous woods, the 12,000-man 3rd Colonial Division had ceased to exist.

Fernand de Langle de Cary, who led the Fourth Army, reported to Joffre that night, "All corps engaged today. On the whole results hardly satisfactory." Those words had to be one of the great understatements of 1914.

The following day was mainly a time of regrouping and retreat. Most units were soon back across the French border. Report upon report of battlefield disasters flooded into Joffre's Vitry-le-François headquarters on the upper Marne.* At 9:35 on the morning of August 24, he sent a message full of uncharacteristic gloom to the minister of war, Adolphe Messimy. Joffre announced, in as many words, that *offensive à outrance*, offensive to the limit, was, after just three weeks of war, done for. The French Army, he said, had everywhere "suffered checks" that had "forced it to retire":

> One must face the facts. Our army corps . . . have not shown on the battlefield those offensive qualities which we had hoped for. . . .
>
> We are therefore compelled to resort to the defensive, using our fortresses and great topographical obstacles to enable us to yield as little ground as possible.
>
> Our object must be to last out as long as possible, trying to wear the enemy out, and to resume the offensive when the time comes.
>
> —"J. Joffre."

"The real state of affairs in all its relentless grimness was revealed to him," Edward Spears wrote. "There is a note of hopelessness in his report to the Minister."

---

* Always the engineer, Joffre originally chose Vitry-le-François because it was equidistant from each of the five French armies. He was, however, forced to vacate his early GQG (Grand Quartier Général) when the Germans overran the town in the first days of September 1914. By November, he had permanently relocated in Chantilly, north of Paris.

———

NO PREVIOUS ARMED CONFRONTATION IN history could approximate the scale of the Frontiers. The battles lasted four days, from August 20–23: though they were more or less continuous, the plural is in order. They began in Lorraine with Morhange and another losing French effort, Sarrebourg, jumped over the impregnable Metz and the iron smelter center, Thionville, passed through the Ardennes, and then took a turn west across the Meuse at Namur, to the *Borinage* of Charleroi and the soggy industrial low country around Mons. Well over a million men faced off along a front of 150–170 constantly changing miles, that more or less followed France's borders with Germany, Luxembourg, and Belgium. Like so much else that happened in those first weeks, precise details of the Frontiers have been distorted, forgotten, or were never recorded. Men were more involved in making history—or in trying to keep it from being made—than in documenting it. The greatest battle in the history of humankind until that time has almost dropped from view. Greater ones would soon erase that distinction. With its constant shifting of scene from dry plain to deep forest to coal field, this was not the stationary Great War of entrenched siege lines that have practically become an historical cliché. Open warfare can be death's moveable feast, and so it proved in the last five months of 1914. The Battles of the Frontiers was the kind of disaster from which few nations at war can recover. Just short of twenty-six years later, France didn't, and with a fraction of the casualties of August 1914.*

---

* You can argue that the Battles of the Frontiers lasted three more days, actually ending on August 26, with the fall of Longwy, an important town across the border from Luxembourg that was not only an iron-smelter center but was dominated by a Vauban-designed fortress. The German XIII Corps, which played a large part in the siege, was commanded by General Max von Fabeck; its chief of staff was Lieutenant Colonel Fritz von Lossberg. Both men will figure in this book. Lieutenant Erwin Rommel, the famous "Desert Fox" of another World War, also took part in the siege, and, in what amounted to a duel between riflemen, killed his first man in combat.

On August 24 and 25, to the east of Verdun, the French and Germans fought a two-day battle at a place called Étain. Two exceptional writers took part, Alain-Fournier *(Le Grand Meaulnes)* and Louis-Ferdinand Céline *(Voyage au Bout de la Nuit)*. The combined casualties for the two sides approached 14,000, hardly a minor confrontation. Both

The Frontiers may well have been Germany's major victory in the west that year. Some at German headquarters, still two hundred miles away from the Western Front in Coblenz but soon to move closer to the action, celebrated as if the war in the west was all but won. For the next week or so it must have seemed that way, as Moltke's remorseless columns swept into northern France. The good news continued to pour in. Eager to top one another on the triumphal bandwagon, Hew Strachan writes, German generals "were sending back reports that exaggerated their own achievements. In truth, neither their headquarters nor that of Moltke had the means to gather sufficient intelligence to confirm or deny the claims."

If they had based their jubilation on body counts alone, preliminary indications of unusually high enemy losses might have excused their premature abandon. That first month of war had exacted a fearful toll on France, less on its present, perhaps, than on its future, a sequel that would take months and years to reveal its true dimensions. By August 29, casualties had soared to 206,515, of whom 128,047, more than half, were now corpses or missing. (Ordinarily, that proportion is about a quarter.) Some 40,000 Frenchmen, 10,000 per day, died in the first four days of the Battles of the Frontiers. (In 1914, by way of comparison, the average daily peacetime death rate in France was 2,000.) On a single day, August 22, 27,000 of Joffre's soldiers perished. The combined casualties for both sides were 81,000 killed, wounded, or missing—52,000 of them French and 29,000, German. That 27,000 has to include the estimated 6,000–7,000 killed the same day at Charleroi. It established a record of lethality for the Western Front, and, indeed, for the entire war, exceeding, as already pointed out, by almost 8,000 the more famous number of British dead, 19,240, on July 1, 1916, the first day of Douglas Haig's "Big Push" on the Somme.

The various frontier battles cost France some 140,000 casualties. The

---

men survived, though. Alain-Fournier would be killed in a forest ambush in the same area a month later. The large square hole where French archaeologists discovered the twenty-two skeletons of the writer amid his platoon, and carefully marked their positions, in 1991, can still be seen under a glass canopy. They were able to identify Alain-Fournier himself because of his bad teeth.

deaths of trained leaders, especially at the lower levels of command, captains, lieutenants, and sergeants, created an immediate handicap. Officers, wearing white gloves and kepis with gold stripes or shakos sporting defiant white plumes, practically asking to be targets, were slaughtered in droves. They included Foch's only son, Officer Germain Foch, and a son-in-law, Captain Paul Bécourt, both killed on August 22. It was not until mid-September that Foch, now commanding the newly created Ninth Army, heard the news: Bécourt was dead and his son was missing. He knew what that probably meant. Germain's name had not turned up on any prisoner list. The general asked his staff to leave him alone in his office. After an hour he summoned them. "Now," he said, "let's get on with our work."

The Frontiers battles could have been a war-deciding event. They weren't. The Schlieffen/Moltke scythe had begun its downward sweep, reaching northern France. But the Germans had so far failed to destroy the French Army. They had not come close to doing so. They had underestimated French resilience, the growing ability to learn from mistakes, however grievous, the improving quality of the French soldier as he became accustomed to an advanced and fast-evolving style of warfare, and the emergence during the next weeks of a new breed of commander, men who seemed to come from nowhere to replace the time-servers who weren't up to fighting this different kind of war. But as profligate as its leadership had been with life, the French army still had more than enough manpower to survive, and even thrive. Only forty-eight out of ninety-six Allied divisions had seen action during the reverses of the Frontiers. "France was able to make up its losses," Strachan writes. "By not having used all its reserves from the outset, and by falling back on its lines of communications, it could bring over 100,000 men . . . to fill its depleted ranks. By 6 September"—the day when Joffre struck back on the Marne—"most French units were up to 80 to 85 per cent of their establishment." The quick declaration of neutrality by Italy released another five divisions. And the coming of the British, with their small but highly professional army, would bolster the Allied cause at what might have been its lowest low point.

The Germans could claim a collective victory for which no individual stood out as deserving of special credit, though many of their mid-level commanders on the scene performed with distinction. So far it had been a soldiers' war. The men who headed armies and their chiefs of staff were too far removed from the action to exert determining control. Age had sapped too many of innovative energy. No leader on either side was as yet equipped to manage an operation so large or so complex, certainly not the valetudinarian Moltke nor Joffre, whose calm was at times almost pathological. He may have had a knack for organization and efficiency but he lacked a masterful, even eccentric, imagination, coupled with an attention to detail that is a mark of military genius. He was too predictable. Direction of a war machine, in its developing industrial sense, would come later and not to him. Meanwhile, the common soldier and his leaders at the divisional and regimental level would have to slug away, and gradually take charge of, immense brawls like the Battles of the Frontiers. Running a war as big as this one promised to become still had to be learned.

ONCE AGAIN THE FRENCH ADVANCE was designed to coordinate with the Russians, who had by this time breached the borders of East Prussia, their part of the opening squeeze of the Second Reich. The early days of the Russian incursion seemed full of promise as the German Eighth Army retreated; there was much initial panic in Berlin. The Russians won an early battle on the Eastern Front, at Gumbinnen. Moltke immediately fired the dithering commander of the Eighth and replaced him with Paul von Hindenburg, a solid but unspectacular figure, recalled from retirement. "First weigh the cost and then dare": that quote was the man in essence. Ludendorff, fresh from his flashy adventures at Liège, joined Hindenburg en route to forward headquarters as his new chief of staff. The two, who would become the Siamese twins of the Great War, had never met before. In a matter of days they turned around the war in the east. At Tannenberg, between August 27 and 30, the Germans trapped the Russian invaders in an East Prussian forest; two whole corps, 120,000 men, surrendered. The Russian commander, Samsonov, disappeared into the wooded darkness and shot himself. "Few victories in history," wrote Oxford historian C.R.M.F. Cruttwell, "have been so crushingly complete." Tannenberg, as General Doughty points out, erased "all hopes of a dramatic change in the strategic situation" that the Russians and French had hoped to parlay into a big, and ever-tightening, squeeze of Germany.

The Russians later complained that the French weren't pulling their weight—that if only the French had applied more pressure, Tannenberg never would have happened. If only. Can there be a sadder phrase in any language? The Convention of 1892 was beginning to prove exemplary only as a strategic misfire of epic proportions.

That strategic nightmare that the two-decades-old convention with Russia had become was compounded with another. The one major source of wealth in the Ardennes came from the iron mines and smelters around Briey and Longwy. The Germans had gobbled them up in the first days of August, with hardly a shot being fired, a loss to France that has never been adequately explained; they then surrounded the smelting center, Longwy. Its surrender marked the practical end of the Battles of the Frontiers. More important, these were the richest ore deposits in Europe. They stretched for more than fifty miles, from the two Lorraines, French and German, north to Luxembourg and a small corner of Belgium, four nations. By the time August was over, the German Army had deprived France of nearly three-quarters of its annual iron ore output. The French were now obliged to import that shortfall to maintain its war effort. Night after night in the next four years French troops cowering in the trenches and shell holes of Verdun could see a red glare in the dark sky from the blast furnaces of Briey and Longwy just thirty-odd miles to the east, blast furnaces that were feeding the German guns that killed and maimed them. Only the Armistice of 1918 stilled the storms of steel they generated.

The worth to Germany of those deep, open pits at Briey was another sign that this was a different kind of war. Economic strategy had gained a place along with military. Fortresses and national capitals were still great prizes, but so were rail lines and junctions, ports, industrial centers, and mineral deposits. Tactics, weaponry, operational goals, doctrines, and the architectural adaptations to warmaking, like trenches and, soon, pill-boxes, were changing by the day. The French received a harsh initiation to that new reality at Morhange and the Frontiers; the Germans would stumble into a similar experience a couple of months later at Ypres. The lessons of the nineteenth century, so slavishly followed in those first days, were already proving invalid. The shock and awe of line after line of visible numbers clad in gaudy uniforms and wielding bayonets no longer worked martial magic. Nor did the charge of cavalry. Offense was no longer the best form of defense. The past was no sure prologue to the future.

Some French officers in charge had grasped the nettle, and were making the changes they viewed as necessary, indeed urgent. One was a recently elevated brigadier, Philippe Pétain. When a fellow officer complained about the lack of direction from above, Pétain shot back, "What do you want? Everything we've learned has become false. We have to relearn our calling from top to bottom."

With that, a then-obscure brigadier defenestrated the military tradition of a nation and a century.

THE GERMANS WERE NOT DONE. Joffre became their unwitting ally. He was finally ready to invade Belgium. His plan was to have Lanrezac's Fifth Army link with Sir John French's BEF on his left flank and, on the right, the Belgians garrisoning the forts of Namur, where the Sambre River joins the Meuse, thus creating a solid line against attack from the north. He vastly underestimated the size and potency of the German onslaught. The spectacle at Brussels should have been warning enough, as well as indicating that he had not extended his defensive line far enough to the west. At Charleroi, the army that didn't pass through Brussels, Gen. Karl von Bülow's Second, occupied the north bank of the Sambre and began to force the bridges that spanned the dark, sludge-fouled river. Meanwhile the siege train that had reduced the forts of Liège had reassembled and was methodically taking out Namur's forts and the sprawling fortress that dominated the town.

The Battle of Charleroi (August 21–23), undeservedly overlooked amid the tumultuous events of those months, was played out against a cindery backdrop of pitheads, perpetually smoking slag heaps—not all the fire was aboveground—and the drab, soot-stained walls of one of the mingiest cities in Western Europe, the center of the coal-mining region of southern Belgium known locally as *Le Borinage*. Charleroi and, to a lesser extent, the nearby Mons were the first battles in history fought in an urbanized, industrial setting. (The attackers of Liège had largely bypassed its numerous factories: most of the fighting had taken place around the city in an almost rural setting.)

The Germans stormed through Charleroi and forced their way across the river bridges, establishing a small foothold on the south bank of the Sambre and then gradually expanding it. The mean, close-packed faubourgs—narrow, unpaved streets, factories, backyard privies, and mine workings—became a battlefield, like a nightmare out of Hieronymus Bosch. The vainglory that still suffused French military aspirations erupted in full late-summer bloom as regiments descending from the low hills and slag heaps made bayonet charges with bugles braying and battle flags unfurled. The Germans cut their attackers down by the hundreds. Red-pantalooned bodies littered the slopes, adding another 6,000–7,000 dead to the French toll of August 22. The fighting continued for another day. Lanrezac threw in fresh corps and made repeated counterattacks, but before long his army was in full retreat. Not far off, the forts of Namur lay in ruins and had to be abandoned.

August 22 had not only witnessed hideous French losses up and down the long line but also something as potentially threatening: a nine-mile gap, half a day's march, had opened between the Fifth Army and the BEF—which had arrived at a town just to the west, Mons, ahead of schedule. The Empire professionals hunkered down in makeshift trenches behind a wide canal. The landscape along that canal, called the Condé, was *Borinage* normal: an endless, mingy line of black-stained miners' cottages, interrupted by pitheads, massive ridges of hundred-foot-high slag heaps, and, across the water, scatterings of more cottages and industrial buildings that seemed to be settling into a sodden fretwork of drainage ditches. A "dirty-looking factory town" was one soldier's dismissive impression.

The British troops, in what would prove their first named action, occupied a shallow salient, one that practically shouted to be outflanked, especially from the west. But there were no Germans lurking in those anonymous Belgian woodlands. The BEF was supposed to move forward the next morning. The Germans suffered from an even greater myopia. A heavy mist obscured sightings from the air. About noon on August 22, their cavalry reported that the closest Allied troops were still fifty miles away.

At Mons, in the hours leading up to an unsought collision, blindness continued to affect both sides. Divisions blundered over an unfamiliar landscape, in a haze of misdirection. The same blindness possessed the townspeople who flocked to church that Sunday morning, unaware of what was about to happen. It was responsible for the overconfident behavior of the all-conquering German First Army, as it plunged down toward a dingy *Borinage* town and the welcome prospect of the obstacle-free open country that lay beyond. It should have frightened the British, whose left flank flapped dangerously in the empty air—as did their right. Should Kluck's army locate and overwhelm those excavations to nowhere, two matchless opportunities to outflank and roll up the enemy presented themselves. For Kluck's army, that excavation to nowhere represented a matchless opportunity to destroy the enemy. What was becoming a pattern of faulty intelligence let him down. Those missed chances went right to the top, to Moltke and the gerontological army commanders. Let that fine military historian Cyril Falls explain:

> Kluck could have outflanked the British, and with his superior numbers it might have been disastrous for them if he had. Unluckily for him, he had been placed [by Moltke] under the Second Army commander, General von Bülow, and that nervous old man ordered him to keep close touch and absolutely forbade him to swing wide. So Kluck came at the British like a bull with head down.

Kluck may have been the same age as Bülow, but he possessed the energy of the two combined—and the cantankerousness. He was a risk-taker, but, perhaps unfortunately for his side in these critical days, he would heel to Bülow's wishes and ignore his, and his side's, best alternatives.

The importance of Mons is not just what did happen there, but what did not. As Dennis E. Showalter and his collaborators, the Robinsons, have pointed out, going beyond Cyril Falls, if units of Kluck's First Army had swung around either of the dangling and exposed flanks of the BEF and compromised its rear areas, the Great War "might very well have taken a completely different course. Indeed, that result might have been certain."

Too often, the road not taken is the right one.

KLUCK'S FIRST ARMY HAD MADE its turn south and had begun to advance toward the French border; Mons was in the way. This early in the war, individual enterprise still mattered: that would soon become a lost characteristic. Edward Spears discovered that Lanrezac had failed to alert Sir John French that the nine-mile gap remained unclosed. Spears hurried off by car to warn him. He caught the Field Marshal at his temporary headquarters in the midst of a late meal. French immediately ordered a halt to the advance of the BEF.

For Great Britain, the unexpected encounter of August 23 became the stuff of legend, complete with supposed angelic vision in the sky. There had been some cavalry clashes the afternoon before, but the emergence from the woods of a growing number of gray-clad figures came without warning. Four, and eventually six, German divisions would face two British, both belonging to Sir Horace Smith–Dorrien's II Corps. Within moments, BEF riflemen, waiting in three-foot-deep "kneeling" trenches at the water's edge, behind the Condé canal, would begin to shoot down line after line of Kluck's tightly packed infantry, his bull with head down, as it advanced shoulder to shoulder. "Wherever I looked, left or right," remembered the German novelist turned Brandenburg Grenadier captain Walter Bloem, "were dead or wounded, quivering in convulsions, groaning terribly, blood oozing from fresh wounds." The well-trained British regulars fired .303 Short Muzzle Lee Enfield bolt-action rifles accurately and without letup—their opponents famously thought that they were coming up against massed machine-gun fire, and before long, gray heaps were scattered thickly over waterlogged meadows.

"Soon all that remained was the long line of the dead heaped before us," an Irish corporal remembered, "motionless except for the limb movements of some of the wounded."

For a change, Allied infantry exacted a disproportionate toll. Whether Mons was as much of a shooting gallery as British writers like to portray it is questionable. The losses cited in German regimental histories published after the war add up to around 2,000, which seems low; Belgian civilians hired to bury the dead, reported a higher figure, but not the improbable 10,000 casualties that some writers have claimed. A total of half that, comparable to French losses at Charleroi, is more reasonable. (The fighting retreat proved more costly to the BEF: the grand total of British casualties for the days of Mons is 4,150.) The Germans had suffered an unseemly early battering; as it had done at Liège with its calamitous coup de main attacks, OHL (Oberste Heeresleitung), the Supreme Command, deliberately spared the home front. The British chose to withdraw that night, leaving the Germans in possession of the battlefield and allowing Kluck to claim a victory—which he of course did. But the BEF was the tactical winner. For England, there was now no turning back.

IT WAS NOT, HOWEVER, THE weight of an entire German army that brought about the withdrawal from Mons. Once again, Spears had taken the initiative. At about 9 P.M. that same Sunday, Lanrezac summoned his staff to his office at a temporary headquarters and declared his intention to retreat. Spears, waiting outside the door, recognized that there was a new crisis in the making. Lanrezac had mentioned nothing about warning the British. "To retire without consulting them was to abandon them to certain destruction. Yet that was what he was proposing to do." The entire British 70,000-man force would be left, isolated and alone. Worse, French had not given up his intention to go on the offensive. The bad feelings and mutual contempt of Rethel could now have been set in concrete, that most characteristic symbol and substance of the Great War—and their hardening effects were not over.

Spears ordered his driver to head cross-country at high speed. He reached Le Cateau about 11 P.M. He made his report to French (who had also received a warning wire from Joffre). Offensive action of any kind was forgotten. Just in time, the entire British force made an early morning escape from Mons. Sir John, the grudge bearer, never forgave the French, nor ceased to suspect their motives, as long as he commanded the British Army on the Western Front.

Mons may have cost Kluck's First Army an irreplaceable day in the timetable of conquest, an unexpected whistle-stop on the track to Paris, but nothing that couldn't be made up. What mattered more were the irreplaceable opportunities that the Germans had missed. They couldn't get away fast enough from what seemed then the last big stop in Belgium. There was every reason to be impatient: France, and its pleasant countryside of fields and small copses beckoned, less than ten miles away, and with it, the end of the dismal *Borinage*. Now, it was the chase to the border, and only the intoxicating chase, that mattered. The BEF, which had abruptly pulled out of Mons early that morning, was crossing the border by the end of the day, its rampaging pursuers practically on its heels.

The breathtaking advance of German armies, not only beyond Mons, but almost everywhere along the line ending in the curious bulge of the Swiss border known as the *Bec de Canard*, the Duck's Bill, continued. The Western Front as a substantial and unbroken physical presence was far from being a completely formed one. It was on the verge of becoming an identifiable geographic feature but lacked certain essentials. Large stretches of it remained free of martial traces. Trenches, its surest sign, had not started their connected progress. The sleeve brushing the sea remained a deathbed fancy. The sea was in fact nowhere close. Hundreds of thousands of invaders ranged over the landscape of a largely rural Belgium—and now France. Open warfare still prevailed.

Was the Western Front ever, like the Great Wall of China, a creation of man-made geography, detectable from the moon? We'll never know. In 1914, we had barely learned how to get off the earth.

On August 24, German Patrols showed up at Maubeuge, the vast, decrepit French defensive complex on the Sambre River built around a star-shaped 1679 Vauban fortress, which was a wonder of miliary architecture in its time but offered scant protection from modern artillery.

More important, Maubeuge, just thirteen miles south of Mons, was a major rail junction, and a fortified one. Bülow's Second Army detached a 40,000-man siege force commanded by lieutenant general Hans von Zwehl; investiture began. Namur surrendered on the twenty-fifth, and in the Ardennes, Longwy hoisted the white flag the same day. Bülow's legions were already stalking Lanrezac's Fifth Army, fleeing from the slag heaps of Charleroi and into the woodsy countryside beyond. Hausen's Third Army had reached the Meuse and was beginning to cross. In Lorraine, trains were waiting to transport troops westward to bolster the two right wing armies.

They were never put to that use, yet another What If? of those waning days of summer. What if Moltke had followed Schlieffen's prescription for a strengthened right wing? As German victories accumulated, so did the missed opportunities that the forward surge of glory too often concealed.

"On the whole, the deployment ran like clockwork, systematically and without friction," the German official history, *Der Weltkrieg,* concluded. "It was a remarkable accomplishment." So far, the Schlieffen/Moltke Plan was living up to expectations.

SIR JOHN HAD LEFT HIS Le Cateau headquarters and hurried south, taking uneasy possession of an airless furniture-choked bourgeois townhouse near St. Quentin. Bad taste was hardly a concern at this point. He had briefly toyed with the notion of moving the BEF to Maubeuge, just below the Belgian border, for a needed rest. But he suspected that his army might have become trapped there, as indeed would have happened. This was a perilous time for his little army, an army that was, after one battle, already on the run.

The summer heat smoldered. Violent thunderstorms swept the paths of retreat. Uhlans, joined by Jaeger skirmishers and scouts, as well as detachments of regular infantry in open cars and lorries, scoured the countryside. Streams of refugees everywhere impeded troop movement. The dense beech forest of Morval intervened to separate the columns of the British I and II Corps, and they ended the day eight miles apart.

August 25 had been a dreadful day for Sir Douglas Haig. He had suffered a rampaging attack of diarrhea and was too weak to mount a horse; the GOC of I Corps had to direct the retreat from a staff car. That night he set up his headquarters at a sizeable village astride the Sambre. Landrecies was dangerously close to the advancing Germans—how close, he wasn't sure. His men blocked its streets with crude barricades and knocked out rifle-sized holes in the walls of cottages.

The events at Landrecies mirrored the confusion and discomfort of the retreat. During the night of August 25–26, I Corps did hold off the German advance in clashes that were mostly fought in the dark with bayonets: there was too much danger of shooting your own men. A howitzer dragged up to the front line fired point blank at the flash of enemy guns. At one point, Coldstream Guardsmen in an outpost heard the approach of men singing in French. The officer in command, a Captain C. H. Monck, called out a challenge: a voice "replied in French that they were friends. A light was flashed on Captain Monck's face. Simultaneously one of the sentry posts flashed a light up the road and revealed a group of German soldiers just in front. Captain Monck at once gave the order to fire. The Germans rushed in. Captain Monck was fired at with a revolver, but succeeded in getting back unhurt. . . . Private Robeson at the machine gun was able to send a hail of bullets down the road before the Germans reached and bayoneted him." But Private Robeson's last, desperate bursts into the mass of men and horses, unseen in the darkness, left a number of dead and wounded men on the road; horses collapsed, burying their riders under them, or broke free of their harness and, panic-stricken, galloped for the rear, overturning guns and ammunition-limbers.

A few hundred yards back in the village, Haig, usually so unflappable, was losing his cool. He stood on a doorstep, waving a revolver and exclaiming, "We must sell our lives dearly." He was apparently convinced that Landrecies was nearly surrounded. Around 11:30 P.M. he piled into a car with members of his staff and careened eastward for the next village. Convinced that Germans were lurking everywhere, they drove without lights. Others followed on horseback, leading Haig's horse. The frantic drive must have done little to calm unsettled nerves. Haig ordered I Corps to dump baggage and packs, and to hit the road south as soon as possible. It had not been, as one of his biographers writes, "Haig's finest hour."

He had too little imagination to stay panicked long. He knew what it was like to be under fire: he had taken part in that wild, dust-choked Boer War gallop to rescue Cecil Rhodes, after all. He soon returned to his familiar self, steady, taciturn, even a bit stolid. It was his duty to set an example, and duty was a word that he would practically trademark. He may not have possessed French's considerable gift for inspiring his men, but he had an instinct, just as valuable, for keeping disparate parts of his corps-sized war machine oiled and its gears meshing. Haig was obviously suited to his time, with its veneration of order and efficiency, and destined for greater things. A successful offense required vision; defense can get away with determination. Haig was rather better at defense.

If he spoke of it at all, he no doubt blamed his recent loss of composure on his brief and unseemly affliction, now cured. Real men don't get the trots.

JOFFRE, IN THE MEANTIME, HAD started to prepare for a vast counteroffensive, the germ of the plan that would develop into the Battle of the Marne. The Allied retreat would stop at a line that ran roughly from Amiens through the Aisne highlands to Rheims and Verdun: then his rebound would commence. He was also in the process of forming a new army, the Sixth, from divisions now serving on the borders of Lorraine and Alsace and from those protecting Paris. It would strike the German right wing, Kluck's First Army, from the outer flank of the German advance.

As if the German threat weren't serious enough, Joffre faced another from his rear. On August 25, the government, in the person of the minister of war, Adolphe Messimy, demanded that Joffre allocate three "active corps," the equivalent in size to an army, for the defense of Paris: they would occupy the entrenched camp that Messimy was digging around the capital. Joffre sensed that panic might bring on "the menace of governmental interference in the conduct of operations." This would "hamper my liberty of action at the very moment when it was most essential that it should be entire and complete." The essential Joffre took charge. He begged Messimy to be patient, and went on with his plans. It was Messimy and not Joffre who would be blamed for a month of French reverses. He would be fired the following day.

Joffre alerted Sir John that he would arrive at St. Quentin on the morning of August 26 and summoned Lanrezac to join the meeting. He dispatched an order designated as *Instruction Général No. 2,* detailing the outlines of his developing plan. It arrived after midnight, just as French's chief of staff, Sir Archibald Murray, who could no longer take the strain, had collapsed: only after injections of a primitive tranquilizer could he continue to function. That perennial schemer, Sir Henry Wilson, took over many of his duties. He had little chance to sleep that night. Whether distracted by constant interruptions and urgent demands, car dashes at dawn to give advice over the only nearby phone, or simply by his irresistable hanker to make mischief, Wilson neglected to pass on to his boss Joffre's *Instruction Général,* the principal reason for the meeting. It was not unlike the man to forget on purpose.

Joffre arrived at 10:30 A.M., and Lanrezac soon after, accompanied by Hély d'Oissel and Spears. "The windows and shutters were closed in the dimly lit chamber where the conference was held," Spears wrote, "and everyone spoke in an undertone as if there were a corpse in the next room." In the August heat, the house must have been stifling, and the smell of perspiring men shut up in a sealed room unbearable. Few could speak the other's language. Lanrezac was launching into a tirade about British lack of cooperation when Sir John appeared. Sir John asked Wilson to translate. The change in French's manner shocked Joffre. "I expected to find the same calm officer whose acquaintance I had made a few days before," he remembered, "but to my surprise, the British Commander-in-Chief started out immediately in a rather excited tone to explain that his army had been violently attacked. . . . He explained to me that since hostilities had begun, his troops had been submitted to such hardships that he could not for the moment contemplate resuming the offensive."

French, plainly agitated, went on to complain about Lanrezac, accusing the Fifth Army commander of having left him "completely isolated."

Lanrezac, French said, had given "no reason for the very unexpected moves he had made." Though Wilson attempted to soften the Field Marshal's harsh words, his intervention only made matters worse. As Victor Huguet, the French liaison officer to the BEF, observed, a "coolness" and "lack of cordiality" enveloped the gathering.

The generals adjourned to the billiard room of the pied-à-terre French had commandeered. There was no delaying the inevitable moment. Joffre began to discuss his proposal for a renewed offensive. The British field marshal, who was standing, leaned forward, with both hands resting on the green felt of the billiard table, and asked, "My general, what is your plan?"

"What?" replied Joffre, visibly disconcerted. "My plan?"

"Yes," Sir John broke in. "It isn't the first one?"

"Surely not," Joffre answered. Hadn't Sir John seen his latest version? Joffre added that he had sent the *Instruction Général No. 2* several hours earlier. "I saw by his surprise that he was not acquainted with Joffre's intentions, and I asked him if he had received a copy." French replied that he had not. He turned to Sir Henry Wilson, who admitted that he had indeed read the document in question but had delayed forwarding it. Can we even believe that much of his explanation? Joffre went over the essentials of his revised plan. He had the distinct impression that Sir John was not convinced. Had he become fixated on continuing the British retreat?

"The scene," Lanrezac later commented, *"needs no commentary."* By way of emphasizing the annoyance of Joffre and his delegation, he italicized the entire sentence in his memoirs.

Sir John invited the two French generals to lunch. Joffre, who never met a meal he didn't like, was more than willing to take a pause for sustenance. Lanrezac begged off, pleading that he had to get back to his own headquarters. "Marshal French was plainly in a bad mood," he explained in his memoirs. He left, never to see Sir John again. Joffre and French sat down to eat. "I gathered," the Field Marshal wrote in 1914, "that he was by no means satisfied with the action and conduct of his subordinate General. No very definite plans were then decided upon. . . . The Commander-in-Chief urged me to maintain my position in line, which I told him I hoped, in spite of heavy losses which we had suffered, to be able to do." French did little to hide his gloom, which only deepened as news of an engagement to the north began to arrive. Those first reports of the apparent plight of II Corps were hardly promising. Upset, Joffre drove back to his Vitry headquarters early in the afternoon.

"I carried away with me a serious impression as to the fragility of our extreme left"—in a word, the BEF—"and I anxiously asked myself if it could hold out long enough to enable me to effect the new grouping of our forces." When he returned to his Vitry headquarters that evening, "the reports which I found waiting for me from along the whole front were far from comforting. . . . From everywhere there arrived news of weaknesses which made me fear that the morale of the troops was broken; discouragement began to make itself felt in every grade of the army, and even in my own headquarters."

The feeling is inescapable: Joffre was touching bottom.

At that moment, General Horace Smith-Dorrien's II Corps was attempting to break off a battle with Kluck's First Army.

For its size, few battles in British history have aroused more controversy than the second one the BEF fought in 1914, Le Cateau, three days after Mons. It basically involved the three divisions that comprised the British II Corps, helped by a French cavalry corps and a Territorial infantry division. They confronted seven German divisions, which had a roughly two-to-one numerical advantage, 100,000 to 50,000. Le Cateau, short as Great War battles went, lasted only one day. It was more disorganized than complex. Neither was there anything complex about the issue that came to dominate, the deep-seated rancor of two generals.

When he decided to stand and fight at Le Cateau, did the commander of II Corps, Sir Horace Smith-Dorrien, deliberately defy French's order to retire as quickly as possible? Or did he, in fact, believe that Sir John had approved his decision, which, as close to the action as he was—twenty-odd miles closer than French—the man on the spot saw as his one remaining option? The best generals tend to write the most lucid orders, and clarity of command language was not always Sir John's special strength. Careless wording may have been the cause of the dispute.

After more than a century has passed, excellent historians are still arguing whether Le Cateau was a British disaster, a "foolhardy adventure" distinguished by poor leadership. Or was it "one of the most splendid feats of the British Army during the whole of the War." Curiously, Le Cateau rates scant mention, a few pages only, in the German *Der Weltkrieg*. Could the explanation be that Kluck's failure to outflank Smith-Dorrien represented one of their great missed opportunities of the war, and the less said the better? The British *Official History* toys with that explanation of the curious silence of its German opposite. Can a "What If?" question be more tantalizing—or less preordained for an answer?

Too, we have the matter of two of the main actors, the British generals Sir John French and Sir Horace Smith-Dorrien, he of the preternaturally long jaw who commanded II Corps. We are by now well acquainted with French and his failings. Sir Horace, too, had made his reputation in Africa. He was famed as one of the few officers to escape with his life from the Zulu siege of Isandwhana in 1879. He rose to military prominence in the late Victorian era for his role as an army chieftain in Egypt, Sudan, and the Boer War. But he was also renowned, in the tight circle of officer intimates, for his eruptions of violent temper and an unfortunate tendency to demean subordinates. His fits of wrath approached the legendary. He and French had been on bad terms for years. Other than the fact of rank, French was his master in only one respect: a gift for political infighting. You might add his ability to stay afloat. How many times in his career had he come perilously close to going under?

When the admirable James Grierson, the man who had made a fool of Douglas Haig in the 1912 maneuvers, dropped dead of a heart attack on his way to the Western Front earlier in the month, French had made no secret of his preference for Hubert Plumer to head II Corps. Plumer did indeed prove himself to be one of England's best generals, but that is another story. Kitchener chose Smith-Dorrien instead. Perception of character or a sense of who would fit in best with whom was never one of his strengths. Sir John (who was himself no stranger to bouts of rage and resentment) made light of Smith-Dorrien's leadership abilities, which were in fact considerable. Bad temper or no, he had a talent for making correct assessments under stress. Le Cateau would prove a test beyond the competence of all but a lucky few. That day Horace Smith-Dorrien had luck on his side.

AUGUST 24 HAD PASSED AND then August 25. The BEF, unable to shake Kluck's pursuing army, had kept up a running rear-guard action. Military men agree that there are few actions more difficult to pull off than a successful fighting retreat. Hard marching might outdistance riflemen, but the Uhlan cavalry clusters, forever snapping at heels, refused to be beaten off or outrun. When the two British Corps, led by Smith-Dorrien and Haig, had come up against the dense beech forest of Mormal, they had been forced to split. A summer deluge in the middle of the night slowed down the fleeing British marchers of the II Corps, the same unit that had endured the worst of Mons. The downpours ended but were now replaced by a humid and murky fog; the marchers stumbled on. No one slept that night. By dawn on August 26, the fog had begun to lift. Above depressions still obscured by haze, the British could see figures in spiked helmets taking their places along the open crests of nearby groundswells. In some places the opposing forces were already in fighting contact.

Smith-Dorrien had by now reached Le Cateau, an unexceptional market town, distinguished only by the crossing, west of town of two Roman roads, both timeless and straight as the flight of an arrow, and by the fact—not that this would have mattered in 1914—that Henri Matisse had been born there, the son of a wealthy grain merchant, who had tried law and had once served as an administrator in a local court before he turned full-time to painting. A bad heart had kept him out of the war. Matisse was in Paris, within the sound of approaching gunfire, as Smith-Dorrien, the man on the spot, made the only decision he believed he could make.

To begin with, his intention had been different. Smith-Dorrien had complied with Sir John's wishes, sending out orders at 10:15 the previous evening for a general retreat to start at daybreak on August 26. But overnight his situation rapidly deteriorated. Uhlans were now making threatening gallops into the northern suburbs of Le Cateau; leading detachments of Kluck's infantry followed, too close for comfort. Smith-Dorrien decided that he had no choice but to pull back and make a stand in the low hills south of town, bare except for random splotches of woodland. It was too much at that point to ask his men to keep going. He worried that the Germans would reach his weary few before they had a chance to break away. What is the old military saying? Never show the enemy your back. Fighting would mean facing him.

At 3:30 A.M. he sent off a message by car from Le Cateau to St. Quentin, which arrived at GHQ at 5 A.M. His intention, he said, was to delay the Germans with a "stopping action" that would last only long enough to allow the II Corps to get away with a minimum challenge. About an hour and a half later another message for Sir John arrived. Smith-Dorrien wanted to speak to him or to his chief of staff on the phone. The only line available was at the railroad station. Since Sir Archibald Murray was hors de combat, it was Sir Henry Wilson and aides who went to the station in Wilson's limousine. He had apparently woken from a brief nap—which might explain why he had not yet read Joffre's *Instruction Général No. 2*. The *Instruction* had only arrived at some point after midnight: more urgent matters were at hand.

"H.W.," an aide wrote, "had no time to put on his leggings and drove off with about six inches of bare leg showing above the top of his ankle boots. He was quite calm, although he thought that 'Smith-Doreen' was in the devil of a hole." When he spoke to Sir Horace, who had asked for help from the I Corps, he turned down his request with a dismissive "troops fighting Douglas Haig cannot fight you." Wilson said—and this was a legitimate concern—that he was more worried about the Germans outflanking II Corps from the west and possibly cutting it off. Smith-Dorrien answered that he was "fully confident and hopeful of giving the enemy a smashing blow and slipping away before he could recover. He replied, 'Good luck to you. Yours is the first cheerful voice I have heard these three days.'" But Henry Wilson could not resist having it both ways. A moment later he was cautioning Smith-Dorrien that "if you stand and fight there will be another Sédan." Sir Horace had already made up his mind. As they spoke, Wilson could hear the rumble of gunfire on the other end of the line.

At 9:10 A.M., Sir John wired back, giving Smith-Dorrien "a free hand" but reminding him that "this telegram is not intended to convey the impression that I am not anxious for you to carry out the retirement and you must make every endeavor to do so." That seemed to be the permission Smith-Dorrien sought—or so he interpreted it. The commander of II Corps would make his stand. The best generals tend to write the most lucid orders, but the clear rhetoric of command was not always Sir John's signal gift. Careless wording, distorted by fatigue, could produce later hard feelings and recriminations; this was not the last time it happened. Sir John could share the same difficulty with his own language as he did with foreign tongues. In the diary entry he made that night, he omitted to mention his mid-morning wire. Perhaps he should be forgiven: the previous hours had been more than packed with event. But forgetting on purpose was not beyond the man. Even this early the field marshal may have been beginning to build his case against his unwanted subordinate.

THE DEFENDERS HAD NO TIME to initiate more than cursory spadework: Many British riflemen on that eleven-mile-long front took on the advancing Germans lying prone in low grass. James Lochhead Jack, then a captain in the Cameronians, observed frenzied efforts of his men to defend themselves. "They were entrenching as well as they could with their wretched little tools, augmented with some village picks and spades; the field batteries were trotting to their stations, many of these only 200 to 400 yards behind the foremost infantry and practically in the open as there had not been time to 'dig in.'" The Germans charged repeatedly, sometimes running over their stubborn adversaries and knocking them to the ground: bayonets were still much in evidence. More often the British line held. Battlefield communications were as always a problem. There were no radios, no telephones. Horseback riders or runners scurrying on foot had to carry messages. The British relied on bugle calls to summon reserves. Senior officers rode behind the lines, shouting encouragement. Men fled. A staff officer rounded up one group of fugitives, yelling at them, "For God's sake, men, be British soldiers." They had fought two battles in three days, this one more desperate and at a greater disadvantage than the first. No wonder men cracked.

The old century still reigned in those spreading cornfields—or wheatfields, as North Americans would call the principal crop of the region. Fences hardly existed here. The long, straight main highways dated back to Roman times. The encounter could have been Borodino or Antietam—the only difference being that in the past antagonists stood up in extended lines, side by side with cannon, as they banged away at one another with muskets that were as hard to fire as they were inaccurate.

Was this the last battle of the nineteenth century? Perhaps that is what set Le Cateau apart from the copious bloodlettings that were already becoming routine.

Certainly, the fighting formations, with men and guns gathered in lines, belonged to another era. These may have been nineteenth-century tactics—but they were, as Max Hastings has pointed out, executed with twentieth-century weapons. Napoleon or George McClellan didn't have machine guns, and they still fired cannonballs. Le Cateau was the largest single battle a British army had fought since Waterloo.

Should we think of it as the last battle of the nineteenth century? Perhaps that is what set it apart from the copiously simplistic bloodlettings that, less than a month into hostilities, were becoming routine. Already the nature of war was changing. More than Mons, it was an artillery battle, and the size, concentration, technical sophistication, and intensity of the new ordnance was like nothing soldiers had ever before experienced. They had to endure what the British Official History called a "hurricane of shrapnel." A direct hit by a high explosive shell could practically dissolve a human form. There were few places where one could hide on that battlefield. "We stayed there all day under very awful shell fire," reported a British company captain. I saw one officer with his arm blown off, still riding his horse giving instructions. Of course he soon fainted from loss of blood, but just imagine doing your duty with your arm blown off, in awful agony, knowing that you had only a few minutes more to live. . . . I saw an artillery major blown high in the air and falling down in pieces. . . ." Officers and the horses they rode were simply 'blotted out" by direct hits.

———

BY MIDAFTERNOON, THE GERMANS WERE working their way around the far right of the II Corps line, down the valley of the little river Selle. They pushed forward a menacing three and a half miles, almost, but not quite, reaching a place where no flank remained to be refused.

By that time, Smith-Dorrien had given the order to retire. That most difficult of battlefield operations, the retreat under fire, began again. "Our artillery with superb courage," Jack wrote, "attempted to save their pieces, the teams galloping straight forward through corn sheaves under annihilating rifle fire. Many teams were shot down but others succeeded in getting guns away, some of them no further than two or three hundred yards from the enemy. . . ." Le Cateau cost the BEF thirty-eight guns, a significant number. Without the superhuman efforts of some anonymous individuals, that figure might have been worse.

Even the Germans admired the courage of the same men they were busy slaughtering. It was still that kind of war. A Leutnant Schacht, who commanded a machine-gun company just west of Le Cateau, ordered his twelve guns to turn their fire on batteries, less than a mile away, that were preparing to move off. The killing commenced. "There could not be greater activity around an upturned ant heap. Everywhere men and horses were milling around, falling down. . . . Soon many had disappeared." Suddenly Schacht saw more rescue teams approaching at a gallop. "We could not help but think, 'Are they mad?' No, with extraordinary bravery they were attempting to pull out their batteries at the last minute." The first vehicle "was ready and drove off, with three horses in front and one man on top and managed to get away. . . ." In the midst of all the confusion, a second team apparently did escape, but the rest were not so fortunate. "Men lashed out at the poor creatures, but soon could do no more as they were hit and fell."

Gunfire ceased. Only one living creature seemed, to the onlooking Leutnant, to have survived in that part of the battlefield. A horse "remained standing in amongst this wild hail of fire." Then it did what came naturally. It "started to graze, whinnied for water and shook its head tiredly."

THE WEIGHT OF GERMAN NUMBERS and the burgeoning casualty count had begun to tip the scales. "The trickle of wounded," Jack later wrote in his journal, "who, carried on stretchers or sustained by damaged comrades, had since early morning hobbled southwest along the Roman way now amounted to a stream." By midafternoon Smith-Dorrien recognized that the time had come to break off the battle. If the II Corps waited longer, it risked being outflanked—from opposite sides—and trapped. "I was told," said Jack, "that orders to withdraw had been received, and that our leading troops had all been obliterated leaving none between this battalion and the Germans."

It was just after three P.M. The critical moment had arrived. Le Cateau was, Nick Lloyd has written in his lively, learned, and thoughtful history, *The Western Front*, "the closest the BEF would ever come to being engulfed." Somehow things began to go right for the British—briefly, but just long enough to save them. War can be a matter of doors blowing open, and, just as abruptly, slamming shut. Prevailing wind could be as good an explanation as any. Can you get through before its direction changes? The brazenness of his pullback caught the Germans off guard. They had been doing better in this battle than they had done at Mons. This was more of an artillerymen's battle, and the German guns were murderously effective, as the increased Allied casualty figures would demonstrate. But the men of the First Army were equally fought out and marched out as their enemies. Perhaps, too, something intangible made the difference: call it the strength of desperation.

It has been remarked that the British are at their most superb in retreat. There is probably as much truth as malice in that observation.

All the while a remarkable pattern was taking shape, one that only open warfare, with its relative freedom of movement, could produce. Three adjacent lines, one German and two British, were making their parallel ways south, racing in view of one another. If the Germans could manage to pull ahead, they might be able to swing westward, cross the southbound Roman road to St. Quentin, and block the British retreat. By 7:00 that evening they had pushed as far as they could go. They followed the narrow valley of the Selle River, which ran through Le Cateau. Germans contested the ridges to the west of the stream with British riflemen and machine gunners. Their frustration mounted. In the late August dusk, they could see the unbroken lines of the retreating BEF, little more than a mile away, but could do little to slow its progress. That retreat was not a pretty sight. To quote the historian of the British 5th Division:

> Transport, guns, and Infantry were hopelessly mixed up. . . . This road presented a truly alarming spectacle; it was packed with vehicles, double-banked and moving at a snail's pace with frequent blocks—guns, ambulances, and small bodies of tired Infantry without Officers were crawling along past derelict motor-lorries and wagons. . . . every carriage was crowded with wounded. . . . To make matters worse a steady rain set in and continued throughout the Pitch-dark night.

One brigade diary commented, "It looked to be the break-up of an army." So near and yet so far to that ragged line, the Germans could at least comfort themselves that they had probably destroyed the British contemptibles, reducing them to a fugitive rabble that they could round up at a later day. Had Sir John French's worst fears come true?

SMITH–DORRIEN DID MANAGE TO EXTRICATE a surprisingly large portion of his II Corps. On the far left, elements of the French General Jean-François Sordet's I Cavalry Corps and a French Territorial division of men in their early middle age held off the three divisions of a German corps long enough for the threatened BEF 4th Division to pull out of the line and escape. In the fading misty light of a damp late summer afternoon, a British sapper, on the Roman road plunging south, recalled a landscape of men fleeing for safety. "One could barely see the infantry . . . streaming back across fields under a hot shell fire . . . and every moment we expected to see the Bosche cavalry appear over the crest." British artillery stationed along that straight Roman road hastened to discourage any enemy infantry or horsemen who probed too close. None did. At five P.M. rain started and kept up throughout the night. Men made their blind way through woods or in the dark. Lt. Bernard Montgomery was one of those fugitives who followed irregular cross-country routes to evade German cavalry patrols. Some did not receive the order to retire in time and kept fighting, resistance that continued only as long as their ammunition lasted. They had no choice but to surrender. A column of Gordon Highlanders fleeing south blundered into a substantial German detachment, and found itself trapped: the Germans captured 500 of the Highlanders—though a few did slip away and actually made it all the way north to the safety of Antwerp.

Smith-Dorrien's losses in the line had been heavy, but were nowhere near the "at least 14,000 officers and men" that Sir John cited in his memoir. His bitter memories had simply doubled what would become the official figures. Even the careful estimation of the British *Official History*, 7,812, seems on the high side. More recent recalculations have reduced the figure to 5,000; perhaps 2,500 of that number ended as prisoners. Estimates of German casualties range from 2,000—the figure derived from regimental histories, which seems low—to 9,000. The needless destruction of archival records in an air raid in the last days of the Third Reich makes it difficult to establish a true figure.*

Though French lauded Smith-Dorrien and his stand in his official dispatches, he privately never forgave him for disobeying his orders. In a conversation on April 30, 1915, Sir John told Haig that Smith-Dorrien had deserved court martial. This was another time of high stress. The Germans had attacked again, this time with a new weapon, poison gas. The battle known as the Second Ypres, another of those interminable Great War struggles, had another month to go. Smith-Dorrien, by then commanding the just-formed British Second Army, floundered at first,

---

* According to that capable British historian Spencer Jones, "a detailed study produced by the British War Department in 1933, when the original documents were still available, listed German losses as 8,970 killed and wounded." Should that figure be reasonably accurate, it would give Le Cateau a different complexion. There is a big difference between 2,000 and 9,000. Not only would the revised estimate explain why Kluck's pursuit began so tentatively but also that the difference in relative strength between the two sides may have been shrinking more rapidly than historians generally acknowledge. An Allied advantage in the war was no longer unimaginable.

but then recovered handsomely. He also recommended abandoning Ypres itself and straightening the line behind it, an operation that had the potential for saving thousands of lives. A week later French, whose hatred of his subordinate knew no bounds, fired Smith-Dorrien, by telegram and without explanation. There would be no sacrificing Ypres. Symbol had triumphed over strategy.

Again and again that August of 1914 the Germans seemed on the edge of triumph. Le Cateau could have been a giant step in that direction. That it was not may well be the result of Smith-Dorrien's determination to stand and fight. Had he followed Sir John French's order to continue to retreat, it is likely that Kluck's prowling columns would have taken advantage of the separation of the two British corps, destroying each in detail. Or they might have outraced them to squeeze the life out of the British in a double envelopment—creating what would be known in a later world war as a "cauldron." As it was, a week would pass before I and II Corps rejoined. If we think of Mons as a tactical British victory but an operational loss, Le Cateau was the opposite: a tactical defeat but an operational deliverance.

Not surprisingly, the Germans viewed Le Cateau as one step further in the march toward victory, widespread and, for the moment, unstoppable. "Without question, the battle at Le Cateau was a success for the First Army," the German official history maintained, though with one major reservation. "The British had narrowly escaped destruction with considerable losses. Covered by strong cavalry, they retired southwest in darkness, pouring rain, and disorder. . . . However, the double-sided envelopment that First Army Headquarters had devised . . . had not materialized, and the chance for a decisive blow on the right wing had disappeared. . . . The lack of quick and reliable communications exacerbated the problem." Such failures to clinch the deal would surely be taken care of soon. They hardly seemed to matter in these heady days. Many members of the OHL staff were by now convinced that the major battles had been fought. Even "Gloomy Julius" showed signs of coming down with what Dennis Showalter calls the "Victory disease." The fall of Namur on August 25 freed up two corps, some 70,000 men, from the center of the German line. You would have thought them bound for one of the two armies on the right, surely Schlieffen's solution. Moltke dispatched them to Prussia instead. Those trains waiting in Lorraine to carry troops westward could now be released for other purposes.

No one has adequately explained Moltke's decision. Had his newfound optimism convinced him that the war in the West was all but over, and that now it was time to deal with Russia? It may be that he ordered the transfer of corps in the opposite direction as the quickest way to deal with the panicked grumbling in Berlin, brought on by the menace of an unexpectedly early Russian invasion, and the pleas of refugees, some of them influential aristocrats, who were flooding the German capital. Or was it just Moltke being Moltke, the eternal tinkerer, who could never leave well enough alone, the man who could not stop adjusting or giving a screw an unnecessary last turn. It was a choice that Moltke would soon come to regret: in the next three weeks, those departed corps could have made a big difference—though probably not enough to have changed the eventual outcome of the Marne battle. In the event, by the time they arrived, the victory at Tannenberg had made them extraneous.

When members of his staff questioned his decision, Moltke replied that he felt that reversing orders would undermine confidence in his command. And then he delivered a summation in three-words: "Order—counter-order—disorder."

Kluck waited until the next day, August 27, to resume his pursuit. Faulty intelligence, ever the bane of both sides in 1914, would prove his undoing. As an information gatherer, his cavalry underperformed and misled him. Reconnaissance aircraft added little valuable information. He ended by veering away from the British, chasing phantom divisions headed southwest in the direction of the Channel. The two BEF corps fled straight south. Two days after Le Cateau, thirty-five miles separated the Germans from the British. The gap only widened. Le Cateau, that golden opportunity, ended with Kluck's First Army, in the words of Jack Sheldon, "off-balance and ill-placed to carry out the great encircling movement which might have seen at least the whole of II Corps defeated and captured." As he notes in *Le Cateau*, the excellent account he coauthored with Nigel Cave, "German errors had let their chance of dealing a truly crushing blow slip through their fingers. The opportunity never arose again."*

In that sense, Le Cateau is far more important than it has long been made out to be, an overlooked key moment in the history of the opening of the Great War—like Mons, another blown chance for the great German gamble.

The arguments about August 26, 1914, will probably never be settled. There is one fact, though, that too many seem to overlook: the II Corps got away.

THE BRITISH RETREAT CONTINUED, SOMETIMES interrupted by brief, inconclusive, but always deadly rearguard clashes. The Germans would catch up, only to be left behind again. In the meantime Joffre ordered Lanrezac's Fifth Army to counterattack, in a surprise delaying action. On the morning of August 28, Joffre, driven precipitously over jammed, shell-cratered roads by his racecar chauffeur, showed up at Lanrezac's headquarters to demand that he push an attack against Saint-Quentin, now in German hands. Lanrezac, beginning to sound like Sir John French, pleaded that his men needed rest. "Do you want me to remove you from command of your army?" Joffre burst out. "You must follow my orders without argument." His voice rose. "The fate of the campaign is in your hands."

After a moment's pause, Lanrezac replied that he would obey his commander in chief.

The French commander had already started to prepare for a vast counteroffensive, the germ of the plan that would soon flower into the Battle of the Marne. The Allied retreat would stop at a line that ran roughly from Amiens through the Aisne Highlands to Rheims and Ver-

---

* The British *Official History* agrees. "There is no doubt," it notes, that the German First Army "not only suffered heavy casualties and wasted a whole day in time, but owing to misconception of the situation and indifferent staff work, lost a great opportunity of enveloping three British divisions." This may be another reason why German official accounts of the time said so little about Le Cateau.

dun: then he would launch his rebound. He was also in the process of forming a new army, the Sixth, from divisions now serving in Alsace and Lorraine and in the entrenchments around Paris. It would strike the German right wing, Kluck's First Army, from the flank.

But an attack aimed to distract and stall the German advance would come first. Lanrezac was to strike across the Oise River toward Saint-Quentin. He needed to draw Kluck's legions eastward, away from the area where Joffre's new Sixth Army was even then beginning to detrain. That evening, the twenty-eighth, Lanrezac moved his headquarters south, to a schoolhouse in Laon, a little city built on a butte.

Lanrezac asked Haig to support his attack. Haig at first agreed—but said that he would first have to inform GHQ. In an angry phone call, French refused his request. Retreat and recuperation had become an obsession. When Haig telephoned Lanrezac in the early hours of August 29 to inform him of Sir John's decision, the French general was, as a Haig biographer has written, "understandably livid."

The attack began. Lanrezac's left wing crossed the Oise and disappeared into the dawn mist. At first it made ample gains, close to three miles. Promptly at nine, Joffre turned up at the school building. What followed has to be one of the strangest episodes in the history of command. With hardly a word, except for an occasional grunt of affirmation, Joffre sat all morning in Lanrezac's office, looking on while the general managed a struggle that grew more complicated by the hour. When Lanrezac submitted an opinion or asked Joffre a question, he did not say a word but contented himself with a nod of the head. Spears sized up Lanrezac's performance at the Battle of Guise, as the widening brawl around a town on the Oise River came to be known. "Far-sighted he was, and clever, too, too clever perhaps, and too critical. At Guise he manipulated his units with the consummate skill of an expert at the great game of war, but he played his hand without zest or faith." Had Lanrezac made what Joffre considered a wrong move, he probably would have fired him then and there. He didn't. At noon, apparently satisfied, Joffre left.

Combat raged over a front of thirty miles and essentially broke into two parts. The French attack to the west, which the Germans called the Battle of Saint-Quentin, saw Kluck's army slow, stop, and push the

French back to the Oise. Then, Bülow's Second Army crossed the river and hit the French from the north. Lanrezac responded by turning to face Bülow. As the military historian John Terraine has noted, "This swinging of units about on the battlefield was what pre-1914 generals had been trained to do; it was an exercise in the Napoleonic style which they understood; it was something that the conditions of the rest of the war would make improbable. But at Guise it worked."

The second part of the battle belonged to the French; it can be counted as their first important victory of the war. They disrupted the hitherto relentless German advance, causing it to veer eastward. And Joffre did discover another general who would rather fight than flinch, Louis Franchet d'Esperey, a leader in the mold of Foch. A stocky, bullet-headed man who had been a corps commander, d'Esperey rallied troops on either side of a shattered corps, mounted his horse, and, accompanied by his staff, led an assault. Long lines of infantry, sweating in their trademark red trousers and dark-blue wool overcoats, dashed forward, bayonets raised, with regimental flags billowing and drums and trumpets signaling the advance. "For perhaps the last time in the war—in history," Terraine wrote, a Napoleonic demonstration was successful. Franchet d'Esperey caught the Germans off balance and hurled them back to Guise, the first big Allied victory in the war.

The French made no attempt at a follow-up. Lanrezac refused to withdraw unless ordered to do so, declining to move without written instructions. An error in the postal department of Grand Quartier général (GQG), Supreme Headquarters, delayed the orders: he waited, while his army courted encirclement and destruction. The Fifth did escape, but too close to the point where retreat would have been impossible. Joffre could no longer risk uncertainty. On September 3, he once again showed up at Lanrezac's headquarters. This time he fired him. "You are used up, undecided," he told Lanrezac. He expected an argument. The face of the man who had just won a battle he had not wanted to fight lit up, and he was soon on his willing way to retirement.

That night Franchet d'Esperey took command of the Fifth Army.

The next day found Joffre's armies pulling back all along the line. Meanwhile, the BEF did not come to a full stop until it reached a point southeast of Paris, having marched two hundred miles in thirteen days. On the afternoon of August 29, while the lines of Guise still swayed bloodily back and forth, Joffre met with his British opposite, then pausing at Compiègne. He pleaded with him to hold fast. Sir John refused. He talked of withdrawing, not to the Paris region but to the British base at Saint-Nazaire, at the mouth of the Loire. There was even talk at his temporary headquarters of reembarking the army for England, with the idea of landing on the Continent for a second time and resuming the war later in the fall—if, that is, there was still a war to return to.

Sir John's apparent failure of nerve had come close to handing Germany the upper hand on the Western Front, and a permanent one. London was aware of French's panicky behavior, and it would have been within its rights to dismiss him on the spot. But there was a problem. Who might have replaced him? Grierson was dead. Haig and Hubert Plumer were unknown quantities. Sir John's machinations, his openly expressed dislike of the two men, and his misgivings about their abilities may have done Rawlinson and Smith-Dorrien lasting damage. The urbane Ian Hamilton, who had his supporters, was a disaster waiting to happen—as he would soon prove at Gallipoli. Except for the Secretary of

This German photograph, taken during the Battle of the Marne, captures a Western Front scene that would become iconographic: in one direction, a long column of infantry riflemen march toward the front line; in the other, horse-drawn ambulances (soon to be replaced by motorized vehicles), with their freight of wounded and dying, head for aid posts in the rear. (Ullstein Bild/Granger Collection)

State for War, Field Marshal Lord Horatio Kitchener of Khartoum himself, enigmatic and unapproachable, no one of the stature necessary to fill even those diminutive boots seemed available. *Faute de mieux,* Sir John French would remain.

It took the intervention of Field Marshal Lord Kitchener of Khartoum, the recently appointed secretary of state for war, to stiffen French's resolve. On September 1, a day in which Kluck's army occupied Soissons, just sixty-two miles northwest of Paris, Kitchener boarded a fast destroyer, and then a special train, showing up at the British embassy wearing his blue field marshal's uniform. Was Kitchener, who did not outrank Sir John, trying to pull rank? His special position in the cabinet did give him a small, if unspoken, edge. Behind closed doors, a testy exchange took place; in the end Sir John gave in. The Little Field Marshal's troops would return to the firing line, where they would remain, said a telegram from Kitchener to the government, "conforming to the movements of the French army." Sir John left the meeting in a huff. But that day Kitchener may have saved the war for the Allies.

4

The Antwerp Diversion

SEPTEMBER 6—OCTOBER 13

WE NOW RETURN TO THE STORY OF ALBERT AND HIS OVERMATCHED BELGIAN Army.

After lunch on August 5, the king left his Brussels palace and drove to his new headquarters in Louvain. He would not see his capital again for more than four years.

The field army, about 90,000 rifles, that Albert found gathering behind that pleasant but innocuous stream called the Gette seemed hardly prepared for war. The king immediately noted a dearth of officers and experienced noncoms. Men, just called to the colors, wandered aimlessly in the concentration areas. They did not salute the few officers they encountered and lacked the stamina to march any significant distance. "The troops could not bivouac, for they had neither tents nor waterproof sheets," wrote Albert's military advisor, Capt. Émile Galet. "Moreover, there were no field-kitchens, and cooking utensils had to be collected from farm to farm." There was an almost holiday feel to this unreal convocation. "The soldiers strolled about with their relations and friends who had come to see what war meant. Parents joined their sons as a matter of course, even when on outpost duty." Galet, in evident disbelief, tried to put a good face on what he saw: "Marvelous enthusiasm on all sides, but what an army!"

Though modernization of the Belgian military had started, it had far to go. Change, for example, had not affected uniforms, which still had a decidedly nineteenth-century look. The most distinctive dress feature was the cylindrical, flat-topped billed shako, with a red pom-pom attached to the front rim and a black oilskin cover, headgear held in place by a strap under the chin. The Belgian Army's failure to prepare for a new kind of warfare was also reflected in the preponderance of infantry and cavalry: it had no mobile artillery, and all its big guns were immured under the concrete of the fortress rings of Liège, Namur, and Antwerp. The entire army possessed only 102 machine guns. These were typically Maxims mounted on bicycle-wheeled carts hitched to pairs of 110-pound mastiffs bred to pull heavy loads. (The British had rejected the use of dogs out of qualms about cruelty to animals.) Could there be a more perfect definition of obsolescence than those big dogs?

Both sides were equally blind to the whereabouts, intentions, and true size of the forces opposing them. It's strange to think of armies blundering in a landscape that, apart from the forests of the Ardennes, is so open, so benevolently rolling, so domesticated. Cavalry was effective as a screen but inept at discerning significant movement changes. Albert's cavalry troopers, in their characteristic fur shakos or square-topped Polish lancer caps, *czapkas*, which looked like upended griddles, were no better or worse than their German counterparts. Albert's cavalry scouts failed to warn him of the massing of two German armies, almost 600,000 strong, which were about to march through his country, threatening to envelop and trap his little army.

Belgian intelligence completely misread the omens, perhaps out of wishful thinking. It is as good an explanation as any. The first nighttime slaughters of German troops storming the Liège forts on August 5 and 6 were followed by several days of quiet. To an extent, the Germans had learned a quick lesson about tactical profligacy. They sensibly elected to wait for the siege train to come up. The Belgians, meanwhile, began to think that they actually had stopped the invaders. Then the huge mortars of the German siege train arrived and briskly took out, one by one, the twelve forts that ringed the city. Intelligence failures also led to a near mutiny of Albert's officers, the result of an underestimate of German strength and a near-fatal embrace of the French spirit of the offensive. The latter was abetted, indeed shamelessly provoked, by a Colonel Adelbert, the head of the French mission to the Belgian Army,

Amid the pastures and apple orchards of a village called Haelen, on August 12, overconfident German cavalrymen neglected to reconnoiter, and, after wasteful gallops against massed rifles and machine guns, retreated. By the time this photo was taken, the human bodies had been removed and buried, but a heavier detritus of battle was harder to dispose of—some 400 dead horses. (*L'Illustration*)

a man whose determined assurance greatly influenced all who listened to him.

On August 12, the day the siege train began its reduction of the Liège forts, German cavalry was already roaming the rural landscape to the west of the city. One patrol of more than a thousand horsemen, a reconnaissance in force, reached a village called Haelen, and crossed the Petite Gette over a partially demolished stone bridge. In the fields and orchards beyond, uhlans in silver casques ran up against dismounted Belgian cavalry and cyclists. The fight went on all day: sabers and lances were no match for machine guns and massed rifles. In photographs of the aftermath, you can see bloated horse corpses littering the road out of the town—the Germans lost some 400 mounts. As Western Front engagements went, Haelen was decidedly minor—the two sides combined suffered upward of 1,500 casualties—but the so-called Battle of the Silver

Helmets briefly gave the Belgians something to crow about, their one victory of the summer.

Confidence soared. Colonel Adelbert told Albert's generals that they should accept the "retreat of the German cavalry as final and the projected attack through central Belgium as postponed or even abandoned." He "encouraged the painful suspicion amongst our own officers," Captain Galet wrote, "that the Belgian Army was, to put it mildly, playing a pusillanimous part." The operations section of the general staff even began drawing up plans for the restoration of the bridges across the Gette, after chasing off the Germans.

While the French mission pushed ardently for a shift to the offensive, it was silent about when Albert could expect help from Joffre's French armies or the British, who, by August 14, were beginning to land at Boulogne. Joffre wanted the Belgian king to remain in his Gette position until French help arrived—a prospect that seemed to grow more indefinite by the day. For Albert, that was one option. The other was to retreat north twenty or thirty miles, heading for the protection of the forts of Antwerp. Three concentric rings of fortresses surrounded the major port of the nation: a few were built of concrete, with gun-emplacement cupolas of solid cast iron. But after the experience of Liège, it was doubtful whether the majority of Antwerp's defenses could stand up to modern heavy artillery. Still, Belgians thought of those defenses, reputed to be among the strongest in Europe, as their "national redoubt."

How long could Albert afford to wait for the promised reinforcements? As Bülow's Second Army swung southward toward Namur and Charleroi, Kluck's First Army began to cross the Meuse and fan out over country highways. By August 18, reports of both German massing and forward progress were alarming and could no longer be denied. The messages that flooded into Belgian headquarters were full of impending disaster, and from all over:

> "10:30 a.m. Have been able to arrive by skirting Lummen at 300 metres from enemy. A peasant reports that since 3 a.m. a column of all arms has passed through Lummen. . . . I have seen three infantry regiments, three batteries, a long column of vehicles,

then an infantry regiment. The regimental bands played through Lummen." (From a cavalry scout.)

"11.35 a.m. (telephone message). The line of the Gette is attacked along all its length by infantry and guns. The defense has given way at Geet–Betz. The Cavalry Division is abandoning the defense of the Gette . . ."

"11:50 a.m. The Germans have attacked Haelen. Our forces there have been driven back."

"At 1.50 p.m.: German troops have been passing since 11.0 a.m. . . . . About 60 guns counted. The number of Germans who have passed Landen estimated at 8,000." (A cavalry report.)

As the attacks along the Gette built up, the Belgians were beginning to take unacceptable losses. In one clash their casualties amounted to 1,600 men and 30 officers, about what the British would suffer a few days later at Mons. Then word came from Joffre that the French and British were too far away to help. Albert, still at his Louvain headquarters, made up his mind to begin a withdrawal to Antwerp before daybreak the next morning, the nineteenth. His order came none too soon. Even so, some units found themselves having to fight their way back. By the end of the day, most of Albert's army had reached the presumed safety of the outer ring of the Antwerp forts.

But the crossfire of messages, and the sniping at Albert from below, grew increasingly intense. On the morning of August 19, when he learned of the exodus from the Gette line, Colonel Adelbert was quick to lodge a complaint with the Belgian chief of the general staff: "The military consequences of this abandonment," he said, "may be grave." He did everything but charge that the Belgian king had lost his nerve. Albert had one of his generals point out to Adelbert that his frontline troops "no longer had the resisting power to fight a fresh battle which endangered our communications with Antwerp." That closed the case. The moment the French minister of war, Adolphe Messimy, learned of Adelbert's indiscretion, he recalled him and gave him what amounted to a reprimand: a combat command. By the time the mischief-making colonel had begun his circuitous route back to Paris and the shadows of history, Brussels fell, as did Namur, and French and British forces were in retreat from Charleroi and Mons. Only Albert had been wise enough to avoid an armed confrontation that might have proved Belgium's ultimate and complete undoing.

But Albert's command problems persisted. Once in Antwerp, he continued to be the target not only of some staff members but also of their political allies. As his faithful aide, Emile Galet, wrote, "The retreat of the Army from the Gette upon Antwerp excited bitter comment, and gave rise to hostile criticism from those officers who considered that the national honor had been compromised by the surrender of territory before insignificant forces." There was talk of giving the command of the army to someone more endowed with the offensive spirit. Without consulting its king and commander in chief, one division launched an exploratory probe by two infantry regiments, a regiment of cavalry, and six four-gun batteries. This patent act of insubordination was hardly a minor undertaking, but it accomplished nothing except the loss of 300 men. This near disaster came as a complete surprise to Albert, who decided that its lack of success was demonstration enough of its recklessness. The retreat to the Antwerp forts continued. As the true size of the German invasion became apparent, the general staff began to have second thoughts about freelance adventures.

ANTWERP, THE COMMERCIAL HUB ON the Scheldt, is one of the great ports of Europe (and of the world, for that matter), the unofficial capital of Flanders, site of a royal palace, and a painter's refuge for Rubens, van Dyck, and Pieter Bruegel the Elder. It may have represented a temporary deliverance for Albert's beleaguered little army, but it was at best an uneasy one. The experience of Liège and Namur cast doubt on the ability of the Antwerp forts, especially those in the older inner rings, to stand up to the battering of the inevitable German siege train. But there was a problem that seemed more immediately pressing: The port's only access to the sea, at the mouth of the Scheldt River, passed through the territory of the neutral Netherlands. If the Dutch government chose to become prickly about that neutrality, or worse—and this did not seem out of the question in the summer and early fall of 1914—if it allied with Germany, Antwerp could no longer expect help from the water. Some in the British cabinet, like Sir Edward Grey, the foreign minister, felt that violation of Dutch neutrality was a risk not worth taking. Others, like Kitchener and Winston Churchill, the First Lord of the Admiralty, maintained that Antwerp must be defended at all costs and by every means. The strategic consequences were too great. The loss of the city, they warned, would irrevocably influence the outcome of the war. Having once taken Antwerp, the Germans could advance to the North Sea coast, scooping up every port from Zeebrugge south. Should they reach Calais, they would be able to invade England with ease.

But Antwerp was a concern for the Germans too. The menace of the Belgians in their "national redoubt" seemed real enough to merit detaching troops from the campaign in France. Though the Dutch had effectively blocked the Scheldt passage, there was nothing to stop the British and French from landing reinforcements on the North Sea. Ostend and Zeebrugge were still open—not to mention the Channel ports. As an outstanding historian of the war, C.R.M.F. Cruttwell, pointed out, the Germans "could not move forward without being continually reminded of an actual and potential threat to their rear." Communications with the south and the supply and reinforcement of the legions invading France were clearly vulnerable to attacks from Antwerp. There was even the possibility of the Allies extending the general front north of the French border all the way to Antwerp, thus denying the Germans access to the North Sea.

None of this was lost on Albert. On August 25, just six days after the escape of his army from the Gette, he mounted a sortie in the direction of Louvain, his recent headquarters. He hoped to relieve pressure on the French and British, who were then retreating to the south from Mons and Charleroi; he even entertained fugitive thoughts of retaking Brussels. A hasty "scratch force" (as John Keegan called it) of Germans managed to contain the Belgian attackers, not a few of whom were by nightfall streaming back to the protection of the Antwerp fortress rings. At least Albert had shown "die hard" doubters that he was neither afraid to attack nor lacking in personal courage, spending the entire time with his artillery on the firing line. But his army had also proved, rather too conclusively, that it was as yet "incapable of offensive warfare." The king's military advisor painted a picture redolent of fiasco, and one that, by the time the two-day sortie was done with, had cost three to four thousand casualties:

> The infantry did not deploy fully, the greater part of the divisions remaining strung out along the road, while the heads of columns alone came to grips with the enemy. They fell into disorder at the first severe check and, with their officers decimated, the men speedily went back. The artillery, impeded by the enclosed country and hampered by inadequate telephone equipment, gave the infantry scarcely any support. The engineers were not employed in co-operation with the infantry. The generals and the staffs, full of enthusiasm at the start, quickly lost heart. The rank and file did not lack courage, but were handicapped by their poor training and the want of officers.

Albert did accomplish one aim, which was to draw German divisions away from the south, where they would be needed in the battles shaping up across the French border. By the late afternoon of the twenty-fifth, rising to his bait, enemy reinforcements were beginning to detrain at the Louvain railroad station.

But there was a price, and a high one. The German reaction to Albert's sortie produced one of the ugliest moments of the Great War. It began when the German defenders of the outer villages, many third-line reservists, themselves gave in to panic and began to turn back in the direction of Louvain. We will never know exactly what happened next. Warned that the city might be on the verge of an uprising, the considerable force still guarding it began to fire on retreating troops who were mistaken for an advancing enemy. Adding to the confusion, riderless horses dashed through the streets. A curfew required that doors be kept open and unlocked: soldiers fired into hallways, killing occupants. In front of their families, men were dragged into the streets, beaten, and shot. More men were rounded up and marched to the railroad station, to be executed. Priests, thought to be the ringleaders of an uprising, were special targets.

Then the torching began. About 11:30 P.M. German soldiers broke into the library of the university, dashed gasoline through the interior, and set the building on fire. Some 300,000 volumes burned, including irreplaceable medieval manuscripts and incunabula, the first printed books. The Germans fired at those who tried to fight the blaze. In the next days, fire destroyed one-sixth of the city, and 248 of Louvain's citizens died violent deaths. The flaming houses incinerated whole families.

From the first day of their invasion, the Germans had made it abundantly clear that they would not tolerate resistance by irregulars, which they viewed as illegal, punishable by death. The Germans regarded the supposedly rabid civilian response to their invasion as an illegitimate "People's War," which justified a harsh response. They recalled the Franco-Prussian War of 1870–71, when French guerrilla bands referred to themselves as "franc-tireurs" (free-shooters). There were many veterans still alive who remembered that irregular resistance, and it exerted a deep and continuing hold on the German popular imagination. When war broke out in 1914, the term revived immediately. On August 12, 1914, Moltke himself released an order that from now on

> Every non-uniformed person, if he is not designated as being justified in participating in fighting by clearly recognizable insignia, is to be treated as someone standing outside international law, if he takes part in the fighting, interferes with German communications with the rear, cuts telegraph lines, causes explosions, in short participates in any way in the act of war without permission. He will be treated as a franc-tireur and immediately shot according to martial law.

The phrasing might be tortuous, the words of a man with a wheeze and a hundred distractions, but the meaning was clear. Could there be a stronger endorsement of the franc-tireur threat than one that came from the chief of the general staff himself?

August 25 in the university town of Louvain turned into a night of flames and death. The German version of what happened, depicted in this 1915 painting, had Belgian franc-tireurs, imaginary terrorists, sniping from rooftops. But panicked Germans firing at other panicked Germans, all trying to put down a rebellion of apparitions, turned into a frenzy of killing and a deliberate burning of cultural treasures. (INTER-PHOTO/Friedrich/Mary Evans)

The franc-tireur could be anybody, or everybody. He was all but invisible. In France, because most men below the age of forty-five had been called up, he was likely to be middle-aged. In Belgium, possible franc-tireurs could be younger, if only because conscription had existed for barely a year. To the Germans, Belgium was a breeding ground for guerrillas in waiting. You couldn't trust the man on the street, no matter how friendly or obliging he seemed. A franc-tireur might be a café proprietor, a worker in clogs, a peasant wearing a Red Cross armband, a village mayor or parish priest (men in positions of influence were thought to be particularly dangerous), even an occasional woman or a child old enough, and bold enough, to raise and aim a rifle. There was an undeniable strain of anti-Catholicism in the German view, especially in armies like their First, which had been conscripted from largely Protestant areas and which would all but burn its way through Romish Belgium on its way to make its wheel into France. A popular German explanation for the burning of

Louvain, for example, was that Belgian soldiers in civilian garb had remained concealed in the town and had from the rear attacked Germans trying to repel Albert's sortie from Antwerp. Franc-tireurs violated the notion of how a proper war should be fought. "Treacherous" was the adjective most commonly used to describe them. They were criminals and deserved to be treated as such.

Certain motifs in German accounts of the franc-tireur recurred: the church bell ringing a summons not to prayer but to revolt, priests inciting their parishioners to violence, machine gunners firing from church towers, and always, the sudden, unexpected ambush, usually in the dark, by shadowy figures who inevitably mutilated their victims. There was a suspicious sameness in the alleged episodes of freelance violence, and with good reason. The franc-tireur was a mirage, a mythically malign creature of the imagination. But how did German soldiers—and, more important, their commanders—come to believe in such phantoms?

To point to recurring "myths" such as the machine gun in the church tower or ambushes at night followed by deliberate mutilations was just a start. What sort of person was most affected by such bogeymen? For starters, many of the German soldiers had rarely, if ever, strayed far from the places where they had been brought up. Paranoia was part of their preparation for war. Their instructors had apparently warned them of the dangers of civilian resistance even before they left Germany. Not only did they find themselves in the midst of a hostile and unfamiliar world, but they also faced, almost immediately, another trauma, the trauma of combat. Massive armies were ready-made for massive delusions, and there had never been one so big, or so widespread. Also, the sheer speed the Schlieffen Plan required made soldiers particularly susceptible:

> The slightest unfamiliar noise or inexplicable occurrence produced acute nervousness and called for explanation which, in view of the warning about enemy civilians, easily took the form of mythic francs-tireurs. Punishing daily marches . . . often in oppressive heat, led to exhaustion which heightened the general nervousness.

Insecurity provided fertile ground for the spread of rumors. The specter of the franc-tireur was a case of guilt by association, an association many times magnified and distorted, the rules of war glimpsed in a circus mirror. It was also an essence of total war. Civilians had now become the enemy.

The franc-tireur may have been a figment of the collective German imagination, but there was nothing unreal about the trail of death and destruction left in his spectral wake. From the beginning of August until mid-October, the German invaders dispatched 6,500 civilians in France and Belgium, and destroyed 20,000 buildings, supposedly franc-tireur havens.

Thus Louvain was a premeditated action, fueled by unpremeditated panic, but its purpose never changed: to spread terror and awe of the conquerors. The rest of the world did not see it in the same lurid light. Germany never recovered from the stigma of Louvain, or from that of similar propaganda missteps. The then-renowned American war correspondent and popular novelist Richard Harding Davis saw the city in flames from a railway carriage where he and other neutrals, potential eyewitnesses all, had been locked in by German troops. He also saw men at the station marched away to be shot. Days later he was able to send a dispatch back to the United States. It was published on the front page of the *New York Tribune* on August 31. "At Louvain," he wrote, "it was war upon the defenseless, war upon churches, colleges, shops of milliners and lacemakers; war brought to the bedside and fireside; against women harvesting in the fields, against children in wooden shoes at play in the streets."

But the franc-tireur was not the only propaganda gift that the Allies seized upon. There was, for example, the naturally villainous made-for-poster countenance of the kaiser, with his pointed, upturned mustache, as well as the supremely mythical creature of evil he had created: the Hun. It is a story that, in this context, is worth repeating.

On July 27, 1900, the kaiser spoke at Bremerhaven before an advanced contingent of the German expeditionary force leaving for Asia: it was to join six other Western nations in putting down the Boxer Rebellion in China and lifting the siege of foreign legations in Peking. Members of the press boarded his steam-powered yacht *Hohenzollern;* they were handed copies of a prepared speech. That was the version designed for public consumption. While members of the press rushed off to catch trains home and file their stories, one reporter remained: what he heard were words, designed to inspire the departing troops, that not only weren't canned but rang a high note for bellicosity: "When you come before the enemy, let him be struck down; there will be no mercy, prisoners will not be taken. Just as the Huns one thousand years ago . . . made a name for themselves in which their greatness still resounds, so let the name Germany be known in China in such a way that a Chinese will never again dare even to look askance at a German."

The Huns. An ill-considered epithet in 1900, which an enterprising stray journalist noted would put the Germans at a propaganda disadvantage in 1914. They could never shake the brutish simian image of a thousand posters, rapaciously scowling and ember-eyed under its pickelhaube, emblazoned with the word "militarism." HALT THE HUN.

Germany's leaders felt that they had to set a stern example. That may have been effective for home consumption, useful for stamping out potential rebellion behind the lines, but not for winning the worldwide competition for allies and supporters, or the campaign to make certain that abstainers like the United States remained on the sidelines. The Allies took immediate advantage of German blunders, and they exploited them with a shameless will. "Remember Belgium" proclaimed an American war-loan poster of 1917 in which a silhouetted soldier in a spiked pickelhaube drags away a young girl as a town burns in the background. There can be no doubt about his intent. What seemed to make military sense turned into a public-relations disaster that no amount of persuasive savvy could paper over. Germany had lost the propaganda war almost before the real one had begun.

On September 9, Albert dispatched a second sortie, again a sally by besieged forces upon their besiegers. This one was more extensive than the first. "Its object," he told Joffre, "is not merely to disturb, but to dislocate the enemy's communications." At a key moment, when the German armies were reeling on the Marne, their forces in Belgium froze. Galet claims that the second "Great Sortie" deprived the Germans of

Attila in *feldgrau:* Without Louvain, posters like this would have been a stretch, its German soldier smirking amid an expanse of slaughtered innocents, most of them comely and female, as a city burns in the background. Even the kaiser's head of propaganda admitted that Louvain "aroused almost the whole world against Germany." (*L'Illustration*)

upward of twelve sorely needed divisions. Inasmuch as at least seven divisions were needed in Belgium just to guard supply lines southward, that seems an exaggeration. But the divisions held back, perhaps as many as five, would amount to around 90,000 men, a number that could surely have shifted balances.

The second sortie did show that the fighting potential of Albert's little army had vastly improved. But the Belgians suffered from a signal weakness, a lack of commissioned officers, company commanders in particular. Officer losses in the first month had been ruinous. The army did promote several hundred noncommissioned officers that autumn. They suffered from a lack of tactical education, the knowledge of what to do when under fire that sufficient training can make instinctive. At one point on September 10, the second day of the sortie, Albert's cavalry had actually entered Louvain and seemed on the verge of recapturing the city. But then orders came to retreat. The inexperienced officers in the division to the right had lost control of their men, who retired in disorder, leaving the cavalry attack in dangerous isolation.

In other places Albert's troops performed with unexpected bravery, in spite of fearful losses. An American correspondent named E. Alexander Powell recorded how men ran into a German trap at the edge of a village:

> Every now and then a soldier would stumble, as though he had stubbed his toe, and throw out his arms, and fall headlong. A bullet had hit him. The road was sprinkled with silent forms in blue and green. The fields were sprinkled with them too. One man was hit as he was struggling to get through a hedge and died standing, held upright by the thorny branches. . . . A man plunged into a half-filled ditch and lay there, with his head under water. I could see the water slowly redden.

They rallied. By nightfall the Belgians had gained a purchase in the village. But overall the sortie had cost them men they couldn't replace—8,000 of them. Even before the day began, Albert's regulars were down to 65,000 men, plus the 80,000 second-line troops garrisoning Antwerp.

Albert's sorties—there was a third at the end of September, by bicyclists who tore up rail lines on which the enemy so depended—genuinely threatened the Germans. As long as there were Belgian troops in Antwerp, German lifelines to the south remained vulnerable. At any moment Albert's raiders might choke off necessary and never-ending quantities of military supplies, munitions, and men bound for the still-expanding Western Front. The possibility that Albert's field army in Antwerp might be reinforced by British and French troops also disturbed them, with reason. Now there was a new peril that could not be overlooked: bombing attacks on Germany by planes using Antwerp as a base. Aircraft of the

Under fire during a late September sortie by Antwerp-based Belgian troops, a gutsy photographer snapped this incident at a hastily erected barricade in the eastern Flanders town of Aalst. Men scurry for safety from German fire coming from down the street; three are already down. In retaliation, the Germans would execute twenty civilians as *Francs-Tireurs.*(Simpson Charles Walter Collection, Imperial War Museum)

British Naval Air Service carried out two raids on airship sheds of the Rhine cities of Düsseldorf and Cologne, one of them destroying a shed at Düsseldorf and the Zeppelin inside it.

The Germans decided to eradicate the Antwerp menace once and for all. On September 27, a Sunday, the heavy artillery of Gen. Hans von Beseler's III Reserve Corps, belonging to the German Fourth Army, a newly constituted unit, began a methodical pounding of the outer ring of Antwerp forts. Beseler, a sixty-four-year-old engineer, who had won an Iron Cross in the Franco-Prussian War, was a siege specialist, and had been one of the generals proposed for the position Moltke would hold. He commanded the equivalent of five divisions, 60,000 reservists with limited or no combat experience. But it was his artillery that mattered, 173 heavy guns, including fifteen giants that ranged in width from 30.5 centimeters to 42 centimeters—12 to 16.5 inches—with ranges of between five to seven miles. No Belgian gun could reach that far. His plan was to smash a hole in the outer perimeter with artillery, and then, after a devastating three-day bombardment, let the infantry pour through. It worked. Within the first days, the Belgian garrisons had begun to abandon some of the forts in the outer ring; the Germans had stormed, and overrun, others, though suffering substantial losses.

The earth rarely ceased to tremble, but after a time soldiers became accustomed to the unnerving vibration. "What a spectacular evening," wrote a Belgian diarist named Arsène Bernard (who happened to command a regiment in the outer Antwerp perimeter). "Ominous silence, then interrupted by the boom of heavy enemy artillery, which continued shelling to the north. Fires lit by the projectiles are reflected in the sky; towards the west, Saint-Armand is in flames. Towards the east, in the direction of Malines, the sky is completely red." He noted, with the practiced eye of an artillerist, German "sausage" balloons regulating gunfire, and doing so with an efficiency that he could not help but admire. Early in the siege he looked up to see a *Taube* scout monoplane moving slowly (sixty miles per hour, maximum) across the sky. Suddenly, the pilot hand-dropped a bomb, which crashed through the roof of a building. It was the headquarters of one of his battalion commanders. Bernard was five hun-

Walking wounded: Bandaged Belgian soldiers (left), and a pair of British Marines (right), make their escape from the collapsing outer ring of forts, toward the uncertain safety of the port of Antwerp. Early experiments with inundation failed to slow the advancing enemy; too few Allied reinforcements arrived too late; and obsolescent siegeworks were once again no match for German heavy artillery. (*L'Illustration*)

dred meters away, and there was nothing he could do. The house burned "like a torch." He learned later that everybody had escaped.

On occasion, though, the Belgians gave as good as they got, especially at short ranges. Bernard watched as, across a canal, shells demolished houses that German reservists had just occupied. They "scampered off like rabbits." It was, he said, "pleasing to see."

The Belgian field army was preparing to evacuate Antwerp when the irrepressible Winston Churchill, with his pugnacious signature slouch and oversized cigar, arrived on the afternoon of October 3. The First Lord of the Admiralty asked Comte de Broqueville, the Belgian prime minister, to delay the departure. He agreed—on the condition that the Allies promptly send reinforcements. Churchill said that would be done and volunteered one brigade of marines, now in Dunkirk, and two of the Royal Naval Division. He promised that 2,000 marines would arrive in Antwerp within a day. He came without being asked, a man who refused to stay deskbound. He had an almost prurient hanker for action that his fellow ministers were fond of deriding. Churchill viewed Antwerp as one of the strategic prizes of the war in the west: what if the Western Front ended here and not miles to the south? It was still possible to deny the Belgian coast, and its most important port, to the Germans. If necessary, this former army lieutenant was ready to take charge of the defense of the city. He worried that he was already too late.

The following morning, October 4, a Sunday, Churchill (driven in a Rolls-Royce) led a procession of cars to inspect the outer ring of fortifications—those that were still intact and had not been captured. He wore a dark overcoat and what was then known as a box hat, a kind of truncated top hat "generally worn by elderly gentlemen on semi-formal occasions." The words were those of the British seaman who had organized Churchill's convoy. As the man recalled, "Mr. Churchill was energetic and imperative. He discussed the situation with his own staff and some of the Belgian officers, emphasizing his points with his walking stick. . . . He put forward his ideas forcefully, waving his stick and thumping the ground with it. After obviously pungent remarks, he would walk away a few steps and stare towards the enemy's direction. On other occasions he would stride away without another word, get in the car and wait impatiently to go off to the next area."

Churchill did not like what he saw. Sections of the perimeter had been inundated, but not to a depth that would impede a German attack. Moreover, the soggy earth did not permit the digging of deep trenches that might have shielded men from artillery fire. At one stop, Churchill "found the line very thinly held and asked where 'the bloody men were?' He certainly was not mollified when he was told that was all that were available at that point." During a subsequent inspection tour, an Italian correspondent observed Churchill's behavior under fire. "He was . . . enveloped in a cloak, and on his head wore a yachtsman's cap. He was tranquilly smoking a large cigar and looking at the progress of the battle under a rain of shrapnel, which I can only call fearful. . . . He smiled and looked quite satisfied." It was men like Churchill who led Bernard to observe, "The war, for the English, is a sort of sport. Their calm is admirable."

On the morning of Monday, October 5, Churchill telegraphed London to suggest that he resign his cabinet post and take command of the British forces there. Read aloud by Prime Minister Herbert Asquith, before the assembled group, his message met with a "Homeric laugh." (Churchill's detractors, and they were legion, felt that, for a navy person, he devoted far too much time to the terra firma of the Continent.) Gen. Henry Rawlinson, a dependable military man, was given the command instead; Asquith ordered Churchill to return to London as soon as possible.

During the next two days, 8,000 men of the Royal Marines and the Royal Naval Division, parts of three brigades, followed Churchill into Antwerp and took positions outside the city. Many of them were overage reservists. Some barely knew how to fire a rifle and arrived, commented Oxford historian C.R.M.F. Cruttwell, "without water bottles, haversacks, or bandoliers, and had to carry their ammunition in their pockets and their bayonets in their garters." They still wore blue uniforms and sailor's caps. Among the Royal Naval Division personnel were Arthur Asquith, the prime minister's son, and the poet Rupert Brooke. The young officers of the division were as elite as they were inexperienced. They came, not by sea but overland, by rail and by London omnibuses with advertisements still on them.

Brooke wrote that when the naval brigades paraded down its streets and prepared to take their place in the line, "Everyone cheered, and flung themselves on us, and gave us apples and chocolate and kisses." Belgian spectators passed around jugs of beer. They treated these raw British battalions like seasoned troops. Once settled in what passed for trenches, the new soldiers in their sailor uniforms adapted to unfamiliar circumstances with surprising dispatch, even enthusiasm. The *Official History* recorded that "the men of the 1st and 2nd Naval Brigades showed most creditable firmness under heavy artillery fire; without any training in field fortification, they entrenched themselves; without training in musketry, they used their rifles with effect; without any supply service or regimental transport, they lived on such food as could be procured locally from time to time, and one day it was turnips from the fields." They did manage to slow the progress of the Germans.

All the pieces seemed ready to fall into place, but the hour was late. The British 7th Division and the 3rd Cavalry Division—the British IV Corps that Rawlinson commanded—were already on transports bound for Ostend, on the North Sea coast. The French pledged to send the 87th Territorial Division—overage men all—and a brigade of Marine Fusiliers, to bolster Albert's effort to hold out. Including those already in Antwerp, that would make 53,700 men and 9,960 horses. In the event, none of these last reinforcements would make it to the besieged port before time ran out. On October 6 and 7, the 7th Infantry and the 3rd Cavalry, whose mission was now to cover the corridor of retreat for the Belgian field army, landed at Zeebrugge and Ostend, while 1,450 French Marines—almost five times that number had been promised—disembarked from trains at Ghent and prepared to take up blocking positions.

Beseler's approach, meanwhile, was methodically brilliant, not something that could be said of most Western Front commanders that fall. No amount of enemy determination could stand up to his siege train. The defenders resorted to a venerable military expedient, inundation, which left ponds of standing water not more than a foot deep, not enough to hold up Beseler's attackers, who sloshed through widening gaps and past pulverized ruins that had been, only a day earlier, intact defensive works. On the night of October 1, a staff officer told Colonel Bernard that the Germans had fired 297 shells into one fort; only 3 had failed to cause serious damage. He ordered him to begin preparing bridges for demolition. The Germans now brought up 420mm mortars that could hurl shells weighing more than a ton. Having breached the outer ring, Beseler waited for tractors and horse teams to drag his artillery forward, and then started on the second, garroting the life out of the city.

By the sixth of October, Bernard noted, "all hope had disappeared." That night large units began to pull out of the line and head for the coast. In less than a week, "the most powerful fortified position in the world," as he had once thought of Antwerp, "had ceased to exist."

LT. GEN. HENRY RAWLINSON, WHOSE IV Corps was then landing on the coast, appeared in Antwerp late in the afternoon of October 6—"by motor," as the British *Official History* quaintly put it—and toured the line with Churchill. The son of a noted Assyriologist, whose aristocratic connections helped his ascent up the military ladder, "Rawly" was dependable and intelligent but lacked the imagination that would have marked him as truly special; his greatest talent may have been, as he himself admitted, "falling on my feet." An inveterate intriguer, it was hardly surprising that Henry Wilson was a close friend. The French referred to him as "Le Nickelé," the man who wouldn't budge, an allusion to the difficulty inevitably experienced in dealing with him. He was given to grand, obtuse pronouncements: "The moment when a battle seems to be lost is the moment to refuse to accept defeat and to attack with every available man and gun." It was Foch warmed over, but without the dapper precision, the mystical edge, of the little Frenchman. Sir John had deliberately excluded Rawlinson and his IV Corps from the original BEF contingent that traveled to the Continent; Churchill found a different use for them.

Rawlinson and Churchill concluded that there was no choice but to retreat to the inner fortress ring, which would shorten the defensive perimeter from thirty to eleven miles—but which would also leave the city open to shelling once the Germans could bring their heavy guns forward. At a meeting of the Belgian Council of National Defense, held later that afternoon, Albert agreed with the decision. But the king and his council also concluded that Antwerp's days were numbered, and that they should begin withdrawing their field army across its main waterway, the Scheldt. They did not want to risk leaving thousands of men trapped in the city.

That night Churchill and Rawlinson left Antwerp together. The Belgian evacuation began a few hours later. Albert and his wife, Queen Elisabeth, waited until early the next afternoon to head west. The bridge their car took across the Scheldt was barely passable. "The road," recorded the faithful Galet, "was swarming with refugees . . . all mixed up with civil vehicles and military transport pressing on pell-mell in a panic and disorder which beggar description." The king pushed on and established a temporary headquarters in an Antwerp faubourg.

By the evening of October 7, one Belgian division and three British brigades still remained in Antwerp, literally holding the forts. As the German forces closed in, OHL, the Supreme Command, telegraphed Beseler to be quick: his men and his guns were urgently needed to the south, to cover the approach of four new German corps in the Ypres area.

By the next day, October 8, Beseler's artillery was in place and had started to shell both the inner ring of forts and the city itself. Some forts fell; others, disabled, had to be abandoned. Fires broke out, which could not be extinguished because the bombardment of the forts had also damaged the municipal waterworks. The commander of the British forces announced to Lt. Gen. Victor Deguise, the military governor of Antwerp, that he would withdraw his three brigades that evening. "Then it's over," Deguise said. "My men are used up." Under cover of darkness, the remaining Belgian division, accompanied by many of the fortress troops, made their way to safety across one of the Scheldt bridges. Most of the British force escaped across the other. The marines had been there four days; the Royal Naval Division just thirty-six hours. "It was a still starlit night," the *Official History* records:

> Many houses and barges in Antwerp were burning: the streets of the deserted town were littered with the broken glass of windows, and the debris of fallen buildings. Several huge reservoirs of petroleum near the upper bridge having been set on fire by the Belgian Engineers, thousands of tons of oil were flaming and heavy masses of black smoke hung like a pall over the river.

German shells stoked the inferno. Flames reached high in the air and withering blasts blew across the narrow road that was the British escape route. Men ran, praying not to be incinerated—and then had to hurry through shell bursts until they reached the bridge that would lead them to safety on the other bank. "Beyond the river"—to pick up the *Official History*—"not only troops, but refugees, with every kind and size of ve-

As the Germans closed in on Antwerp, their guns began to pound the inner city. The only hope of escape was to make it to the other side of the Scheldt River. But bridges were out or under fire. The passage for boats and barges across its shell-churned waters was equally treacherous. Even so, by the next morning Antwerp was a ghost town. (*L'Illustration*)

hicle three abreast on the roads, and cattle and other animals, formed an inextricable mass of confusion, moving westwards."

Confusion also reigned in Antwerp, where a major mix-up was playing out. Three battalions of the Royal Naval Division and a rear-guard Marine battalion stood around waiting for orders. When they finally arrived, they proved the wrong orders and were delivered to the wrong people.

Hours passed before the units were at last able to set out. Shellfire blocked their retreat. Then they discovered that Belgian gunboats were destroying the bridge they had planned to cross. The battalions started their search for rail connections. They found a train but were told that the Germans were storming a station just down the line. The report was not true, but the commander of the 1st Naval Brigade could tell that his men were done for. His only choice was to end their war. He marched three battalions, almost 1,500 men, three miles north to the Dutch frontier, where they were disarmed and interned for the duration.

The rear guard of the Royal Marines crossed the Scheldt without incident, reached one station but found there were no more trains, and marched on. Along the way, the battalion picked up 600 stragglers from the 1st Naval Brigade. The marines finally did find a train, but as it neared a village called Moerbeke, a German shell derailed the engine. Firing broke out on both sides of the stopped train. "Approaching darkness," notes the *Official History*, "added to the confusion of the scene. With difficulty, the Marine battalion extricated itself and attacked towards the village." There is some dispute about what happened next. Near the village, the marines collided with Germans and were surrounded: 5 officers and 931 men were taken prisoner. Most of the marines got off on the right side of the train, where the Germans were most densely concentrated. If they had disembarked on the other side, the majority would have gotten away. As it was, perhaps as many as 500 of the British pushed forward along the tracks and made good their escape in the dark. Later, a Belgian officer took charge of the train and guided it to safety. Not only were refugees and Belgian soldiers still on board but also a number of

Naval Division men. Totally exhausted, they had slept through the whole fracas.

On October 10, Lt. Gen. Victor Deguise formally handed his sword to a German colonel. A sergeant and a private accompanied him, the only members of his garrison whom he could find.

BACK IN ENGLAND, CHURCHILL WOULD endure a veritable firestorm of condemnation for what critics called "the Antwerp Blunder." They blamed him for the capture and internment of 2,500 men, losses that were out of his control. Even David Lloyd George, the minister of munitions, who had at first supported Churchill's enterprise, joined the jeering chorus. He was, his private secretary noted in her diary, "rather disgusted with Winston . . . and think the PM is too. Having taken untrained men over there, he left them in the lurch. He behaved in rather a swaggering way when over there, standing for photographers with shells bursting near him . . ." Sir David Beatty, who served under the First Lord of the Admiralty as commander in chief (C-in-C) of the Battle Cruiser Fleet, wrote his wife that "the man must have been mad to have thought he could relieve" Antwerp. The attacks so wounded Churchill that he seriously contemplated leaving public life. Friends like Sir John French talked him out of doing so. But, in fact, the five days he had been able to buy for the Antwerp operation would, before the month was over, make all the difference. That Churchill's initiative, ridiculous as it seemed to many at the time, may have saved the Channel ports is not out of the question. And it left open escape routes to the coast and to Flanders.

Albert, for one, did not view the brief British intervention as a "forlorn hope." He later told Gen. Archibald Paris, who commanded the Royal Naval Division at Antwerp, "Only one man had the prevision of what the loss of Antwerp would entail and that man was Mr. Churchill. . . . Delaying the enemy is often of far greater service than the defeat of the enemy."

5

Testimony of the Spade

SEPTEMBER 14—OCTOBER 4

ON SEPTEMBER 14, THE KAISER RELIEVED THE CHIEF OF THE GERMAN GENERAL staff, Generaloberst Helmuth von Moltke, of command. The reason was fairly straightforward: Moltke had suffered a nervous breakdown, one that was too overt to disguise. He had also presided over, and lost control of, what had become the largest battle in history, several adjoining battles, really, the two-hundred-mile-long collision centered on the Marne River east of Paris. The Battle of the Marne, as we now call it, had begun as a triumphal march of German arms but was clearly ending in disaster. Until later in the fall, the authorities hid from the German public both the outcome of the battle and the dismissal of its chief living architect. No German leader had been more responsible for going to war than Moltke, who had stubbornly refused to delay total mobilization or stop the trains jammed with troops from rolling west. Military considerations, he had told the kaiser at the beginning of August, had to take precedence over political concerns. Peace was out of the question. Now, six weeks later, Moltke had been overwhelmed by his own creation.

DURING THAT TIME, THE GERMAN supreme headquarters, OHL, had moved from Berlin to Coblenz to Luxembourg City. Moltke's biographer Annika Mombauer has described these nerve centers as "a blend of military headquarters and royal court." Billeted in a succession of grand hotels were the kaiser and his sizeable personal entourage; the chancellor, Theobald von Bethmann Hollweg; the minister of war, Generalleutnant (major general) Erich von Falkenhayn; and Moltke. "The Nephew" established his actual Luxembourg center of operations in an unused former girls' schoolhouse. "We have neither gas nor electric lights," he wrote his wife, "only dim petroleum lamps." The empty building had no facilities for telephones and wiring for only a single radio transmitter. It seemed an unlikely place in which to conduct the most highly industrialized war in history. He found himself out of touch with the armies bearing down on Paris. That forced him to make decisions based less on facts than on suspicions and indications that often turned out to be mistaken. Instinct replaced information. As the historian Holger H. Herwig has written, "Communications remained the Achilles' heel of the German armies in the West."

On September 3, German cavalry patrols rode into Écouen, eight miles north of the French capital, no more than a long rifle shot away from the present De Gaulle Airport. Falkenhayn, however, was uneasy. "Impressed on Moltke," the war minister noted in his journal that night, "the necessity of occupying the north coast and also of halting for rest on Marne." Moltke did neither. One of the enduring mysteries of that summer is why the Germans made no attempt to take the Channel ports, which were at that point totally undefended. And Moltke seemed not to heed Schlieffen's warning in his famous 1905 memorandum, not to permit the French—he had discounted British participation—to withdraw behind the Marne River: "If one allows them to proceed in this direction, it will lead to endless war."

The overarching German scheme for a quick victory began to fall apart, exposing its basic madness. Moltke's legions had pushed too far, too deep, too quickly. They had been too successful too soon. Armies lost contact with adjoining armies, generals with generals. They had failed to take the Channel ports or to destroy both the French Army and the nation's will to fight. A disregard for logistics proved the signal flaw in the Schlieffen/Moltke Plan. The farther the invaders advanced, the more basics like food and ammunition diminished. Living off the land had its limits. Artillery, the greatest German asset, could not keep up with the progress of the infantry; Moltke's seven armies paid for its absence, and for the mounting shell shortage. In his more energetic years, he had actually done much, if not nearly enough, to improve the logistical shortcomings that Schlieffen had ignored. "But in the final account," the often inspired Israeli military historian Martin van Creveld has written of the Marne campaign, "it was furious improvisation, not reliance on carefully-made preparations, that enabled the Army to reach as far as it did."

And it had been directed by a sick man.

On September 6, the French counterattacked. A newly created and largely scratched-together Sixth Army, aided by reserves brought up from Paris by the legendary taxis of the Marne, struck the German First Army along an exposed and overextended flank. In the process of cleverly extricating himself—too clever by half, perhaps—the German commander Kluck allowed a space forty miles wide to open behind him, between his army and Bülow's not-so-neighboring Second.

The BEF and the French plunged into the breach, causing panic on the German right wing. Suddenly the initiative passed from one side to the other. Hundreds of thousands fought, perhaps as many as a million on each side: casualties must have reached close to 200,000. The battle at times took on a life of its own. Moltke didn't just lose control; he failed to exert any control at all. For several crucial days no orders went out from Luxembourg City.

Even if that had not been the case, even if a breakdown of nerves had not assailed him, faulty communications would have done so in the end. Lacking accurate information about the armies he was supposed to control and direct, especially two on the far right of his complex maneuver, Moltke belatedly sought to correct the situation. He dispatched a trusted staff officer, Lt. Col. Richard Hentsch, who departed at 10 A.M. on September 8, with instructions to order a retreat, if necessary. In the next ten hours, he visited the headquarters of four armies: he diagnosed their condition as "serious but not hopeless." It was the nervous commander of the Second Army, Karl von Bülow, and not Hentsch who gave the order to retreat. Moltke's emissary left Bülow's headquarters early the next morning. His motorcade needed five hours to reach the headquarters of Kluck's First Army. What Hentsch saw dismayed him. Men and vehicles fleeing north clogged the roads. Landwehr troops fired at his cavalcade, and in places he had to force his way west. He used his authority to order a retreat by the First Army. The Second was already pulling back across the Marne. Soon the retreat became general.

Nerve failed Moltke; it failed his commanders. The will to move forward also deserted them. There is no other way to put it. They pulled back when they were still winning. As the influential British military historian B. H. Liddell Hart wrote, "The retreat was ordered rather than compelled, due to the panic fears of leaders so saturated with military convention that a slight indentation of their front and a partial bending of their flanks led them to conclude that, by the rules of the game, they were beaten." As the Killing Season lengthened, a failure of nerve would become a pattern with much of German military leadership.

You can regard the Marne as a realignment rather than as a terminal reverse for Germany. That would come later. The Germans were stopped, the Allies had denied them Paris, but they were by no means beaten. Even now the war was still theirs to win.

THE STRESS OF MANAGING A war on two fronts seemed to crush Moltke. His health broke again. Various diarists recorded that his face twitched and turned an unhealthy putty color. On September 8, Crown Prince Rupprecht of Bavaria, the most reliable of the German royal commanders, described Moltke as "a sick, broken man. His tall frame was stooped and he looked incredibly debilitated." On September 10, a staff officer wrote that he was "the image of a man whose nerves have completely crumbled. His excitement is such that he is unable to point on the map to the position that the army is now to hold. His trembling finger oscillates wildly on the map. . . . I am glad to know that there were only a few witnesses to this spectacle, which was far from uplifting."

Moltke's afflictions seemed to have affected the entire staff. "The OHL has lost its nerves," Rupprecht concluded.

The battle of the Marne was almost over when Moltke finally showed up in person at various army headquarters. There is a hint that he refused to leave Luxembourg City because he sensed intrigues festering around him, ones that might come to a head in his absence. It was not until the eleventh of September, a day of wet and misty gloom, that his caravan set out. He surveyed the situation, which seemed more dire than it actually was. The French, especially the tough new army commanders, Foch and Franchet d'Esperey, were rebounding. But Moltke's splendid armies were holding their own—though their own commander was in no mood to recognize it. By that night, Sewell Tyng wrote in his classic history of the Marne campaign, "All the German armies from the Oise to the Swiss border were in retreat. In the darkness, under an icy rain, the field-grey columns trudged northward, weary in body and depressed in spirit."

Moltke returned to Luxembourg City at 2 A.M. on September 12, in a rain that was still unrelenting. Though it was the middle of the night, he immediately reported to the kaiser on the results of his tour. According to an eyewitness, an angry kaiser "slammed his fist on the table and forbade any further retreat." It was too late: his generals were already turning north. Moltke took to his bed, where his wife and advisors hovered, attempting to comfort their distraught charge into sleep.

Moltke would issue his final order on September 14. An admission, hardly tacit, of defeat, it spoke of retiring "in good time" back across the Marne and establishing defensive lines. The Germans would come to regret the considerable territory they had won and then surrendered. Their commander in chief had denied his own aggressive scheme of attack. By the time Moltke returned to Luxembourg, the Schlieffen Plan, with its ever-moving, scythelike sweep through Belgium and northern France, was dead. "It was the hardest decision of my life," Moltke later wrote, "one that made my heart bleed." Falkenhayn had his own acerbic interpretation, jotted down about this time. "Our general staff has totally lost their heads. Schlieffen's notes have come to an end, and with this, Moltke's wits."

All along the line German soldiers received the order, incredulous. *They* did not feel defeated. A regimental commander wrote, "I saw many men cry . . . others simply expressed amazement." Another high-ranking officer stated what clearly seemed obvious to him: "This could not be. . . . Victory was ours." A captain of the 12th Grenadiers looked at his men "and scarcely recognized them. Covered in dirt and mud . . . their whole attitude showed utter exhaustion, and, worst of all, writ large on every bent head, was the word 'Retreat;' Undefeated and yet going back." Some simply broke into wine cellars and got drunk. They were passing through territory that they had fought for, and conquered, just days before.

The final unraveling took shape not long after, on the fourteenth. "Big crisis in the evening," a high-placed diarist at the Luxembourg City headquarters recorded, "immediately before dinner." Moriz Freiherr von Lyncker, chief of the military cabinet, told the kaiser that the time had come to dismiss Moltke of command and replace him with Falken-hayn. "H.M. agreed straight away." An ugly scene followed. The kaiser told Moltke that he must resign because of his "fragile state." It was an order, and one that took the Generaloberst by surprise. "I refuse to do this! I am not sick. If HM is unhappy with the conduct of operations, then I will go!" But he had no choice. To save face, Moltke agreed to re-main at OHL, but from this moment on he had surrendered all power.

Only in November was Moltke allowed to leave Mézières and return to Germany. The kaiser lent him his hunting lodge. Later he would com-plain to a friend, half-anguished, half-boasting: "It is dreadful to be con-demned to inactivity in the war which I prepared and initiated." He would die in June 1916, the victim of a stroke, predictably.

ERICH VON FALKENHAYN, THE MINISTER of war, was the man the kaiser chose to succeed Moltke as chief of the general staff. It was only the beginning of November, a month and a half later and after Moltke had vacated the OHL premises, that the German government made the change public. Until then, no word of it had leaked out. Not even the military leaders of Germany's closest ally, Austria, knew that Falkenhayn had displaced Moltke. Making the cover-up easier to pull off was the fact that almost everyone who was important in the German leadership had gathered in Luxembourg City, or then in Mézières, where Falkenhayn moved OHL almost immediately, to be closer to the front.

Falkenhayn was, if nothing else, a convenient choice. He was the man most available. "It did not seem fitting," he explained somewhat ingenu-ously in his 1919 memoirs, "to disquiet any further the population at

Erich von Falkenhayn, another favorite of the kaiser, replaced the broken Moltke as chief of the general staff on September 14. His most immediate task was to reverse the disaster of the Marne. He almost succeeded. He was young for his position, just fifty-three, secretive and prone to making snap decisions, profligate with lives, a commander who combined, one historian wrote, "strategic caution and operational ruthlessness." (© SZ Photo/Scherl/Bridgeman Images)

home, which was already sufficiently agitated by the events of the war, and . . . to give enemy propaganda further ostensible proof of the completeness of the victory obtained on the Marne."

The Austrian representative to OHL presented a telling portrait of Falkenhayn: "tall, slim, with a particularly youthful face, in which were a pair of very sharp and clever but sarcastic eyes, with the striking contrast of a very gray but very thick head of hair." Falkenhayn was fifty-three in 1914, underaged for his position, a young leader among old men—"By German reckoning," military historian Cyril Falls wrote, "almost an infant prodigy."

His career had not followed the traditional course upward. In 1896, Falkenhayn left the army to go to China, where he remained for six years, first as a military instructor, then as an infantry and staff officer in the German expeditionary force sent to help put down the Boxer Rebellion. His years in Asia gave him a cosmopolitan veneer that most German officers lacked. Back in Germany, Falkenhayn rose rapidly in the kaiser's army. He commanded an elite Guards regiment, a sure way to the sovereign's favor. By 1913 he had been promoted to lieutenant general and appointed minister of war. His Majesty liked him for his vigorous defense of army traditions, dueling included. He could never be mistaken for an intellectual or a progressive. "If cultural progress signifies that we can no longer count upon our army in case of war," he proclaimed before the Reichstag in the spring of 1914, "culture may go to the deuce for all I care." That was Falkenhayn to a tee.

Falkenhayn's memoirs, written in a chilly third person, are as tedious as they are mercifully brief: there aren't that many lines to read between. The sarcastic vigor of his journals is nowhere in evidence. He may be the most important German military figure of the first two years of the Great War, but he remains an elusive one. He was a superb organizer but rarely an inspired warlord at a time when a little inspiration might have gone a long way. Falkenhayn was forever unable to summon the common touch. "Aloof, reserved, notoriously ambitious," Liddell Hart writes in a notably incisive portrait, "Falkenhayn was not the man to inspire affection in his subordinates or trust in his peers." He could be tactless, and during the time that Moltke was forced to hang around OHL, forbade the deposed commander in chief from eating dinner with the rest of the staff officers.

That Falkenhayn was clever, a quick learner, and a tireless worker did not gain him friends—or the support—he would eventually need. Neither did his inclination to secretiveness. Count Harry Kessler, art patron, publisher, and, for the duration, a staff officer, recorded in his remarkable diary that "the mood in the general staff is shaped by the fact that Falkenhayn lets no one know of his plans. At most he speaks to [his operations chief] Tappen about them. All other staff officers are left completely in the dark until suddenly some order is given. So most of them are in a bad mood, offended, so to speak." Falkenhayn remained an outsider, but he rarely surrendered his remoteness.

Yet Falkenhayn seemed forever to lack an overriding strategic plan. Call it a vision, that special habit of sight (and foresight) that the greatest generals possess. Perhaps it is nothing more than a sure and never-erring instinct for the opponent's jugular. Falkenhayn, moreover, consistently failed to surround himself with brainy and imaginative subordinates, another sure indication of insecure leadership ability. Also, Falkenhayn's sarcastic mouth, and his barbed tongue, could get him into trouble. The men who served him did not love him, and he frequently reciprocated the feeling. As an old acquaintance, Fritz von Lossberg, delicately put it, "the unconditional trust that the troops and their leaders at the fighting front should have had in their supreme headquarters and its leader was reserved at best." There was another, less pleasant, aspect of Falkenhayn's leadership style, and one that did not go down well with his men: he was notoriously indifferent to the expenditure of human life.

Falkenhayn had one final characteristic worth noting. He was an incurable pessimist, a saturnine presence who consistently saw the worst in human striving. It is hard to escape the feeling that he was never convinced of ultimate victory. "If we don't lose the war," he once said, "we have won it." A draw seemed to be his scenario for success.

Falkenhayn's most pressing mission was to restore the morale of an army defeated through no fault of its own, by circumstances still a mystery to the common soldier. He called a halt to the retreat. He filled the last gaps in the line. His moves were quick and relatively sure-handed. For all his faults, Falkenhayn was a superior organizer, especially when it came to logistics. He set to work preparing Germany for the long haul. Again, to quote Liddell Hart:

> The technique of field entrenchment was carried to a higher pitch than with any other country, the military railways were expanded for the lateral movement of reserves, the supply of munitions and of raw material for their manufacture was tackled so energetically and comprehensively that an ample flow was ensured from the spring of 1915 onward—a time when the British were only awakening to the problem. Here were laid the foundations of that economic organization and utilization of resources which were to be the secret of Germany's resisting power to the pressure of the British blockade.

By the end of September, Falkenhayn had moved OHL from Luxembourg City to Charleville-Mézières, twin small French cities near Sedan and the Belgian border. They may have lacked grand hotels, but they were just fifty miles from the front, in this case, Champagne.

Falkenhayn was opposed to the one feature that has come to stand for the Western Front: the trench. As long as he could, he resisted a calculated descent into the earth and a surrender to a reliance on the spade. He wanted to avoid the warfare of the stabilized line at all costs, and any amount of human life was worth the price. The next two months would be consumed by his efforts to do so.

TRENCHES WERE HARDLY A NEW phenomenon in 1914. They were as old as city sieges, practically as old as recorded history itself. Some years ago, archaeologists found evidence of one outside the walls of ancient Troy; it dates back to the thirteenth century BCE, when the Trojan War is supposed to have taken place. Its function may have been more to impede attackers and their siege engines than to protect defenders, but it was a trench nonetheless. Caesar's legions dug trenches, and they were incorporated into Hadrian's Wall, running across northern England. Approach trenches, which sheltered besieging troops from cannon fire, were common in the 1500s, if not earlier. The first notable continuous defensive line in which trenches were a significant feature was the so-called Great Wall of the Dutch Republic. A combination of wooden redoubts and earthen ramparts, it was built in 1605 in an effort to hold off an expected Spanish invasion; the Spanish broke through it anyway. When Swedish armies invaded Poland in the 1620s, Polish propagandists scoffed at their siege techniques as "mole's work" and manifestations of a "grave-digger's courage"—while Polish military engineers hastened to copy them.

As the violent seventeenth century progressed, continuous trench lines became something of a military fashion, spreading over large stretches of France and the Low Countries. They were mainly single-line affairs—facing trenches with no-man's-lands between were a later phenomenon. Often their purpose was less to repel invading armies than to protect valuable territory from raiders, rogue bands that swept through a countryside, pillaging and raping. Trenches also became an offensive tool.

Artists of siege craft like Sébastien Le Prestre de Vauban would time and again tighten a noose of excavations around a strategically important citadel or town. It was one of those coincidences of history that so many of his earthworks crossed the Flanders plain south of Ypres. Vauban built the walls of Ypres and the citadel of Verdun. His handiwork even figured in the Great War. The military engineering of Vauban would have done the Western Front proud.

Not until the Great War would the pick and shovel earn more prominence than they did in the War of the Spanish Succession (1701–14). The French proved particularly industrious at digging. The most famous of their extended lines was known as Ne Plus Ultra—literally, "Go No Farther." More than a hundred miles long, it started at Namur on the edge of the Ardennes, passed close to Vimy Ridge, Arras, and Cambrai—household names two centuries later—and reached the English Channel. These great works featured linked entrenchments, fortifications, and deliberate inundations, all backed by a system of lateral roads. (There was one big difference between the extended diggings of that time and those emerging in 1914: since opposing trenches rarely existed, neither did a no-man's-land.) Call Ne Plus Ultra the Maginot Line of the eighteenth century. France put just as much faith in it. The system was notable less for its length than for its undoing. French engineers had designed this most elaborate of continuous lines to block the duke of Marlborough's invading army. He breached those supposedly impenetrable defenses. English politics saved France that time. Political rivalries forced Marlborough's recall, and his innovative campaign sputtered out.

Increasingly, maneuver became the rule and digging the exception. Though we do not think of the shovel as a primary implement of the Napoleonic Wars, it did figure in one notable episode: the defense of the Torres Vedras lines. In 1810 in Portugal, the future duke of Wellington's outnumbered army constructed a triple line of 114 redoubts connected by trenches. The strongpoints were about a mile apart and allowed for crossing fire by artillery—what might be called one of the earliest experiments with defense in depth. Torres Vedras worked: the French retreated, without even an attempt at Marlborovian dazzle.

At the beginning of the American Civil War, the defenses around

Washington, D.C., were a copy of Torres Vedras, as were those that Robert E. Lee, not yet a Southern saint, dug around Richmond, the Confederate capital, in 1861. For his efforts he earned the nickname "King of Spades." Digging was considered unmanly.

That attitude did not long survive the unprecedented range and intensity of Civil War battlefield fire. During the 1862 Peninsula campaign, one-third of Gen. George McClellan's Union Army was engaged in digging. By the final year of the war there could be no doubt about it: as the saying went, "Spades were trumps."

Trenches were everywhere in the Civil War, in all theaters of operations, and they should have been an omen. They were an omen disregarded. So were the futile Russian charges against the Turks dug in along the ridges of Plevna (1877) and the suicidal, if ultimately successful, Japanese attacks at Port Arthur in the Russo-Japanese War. Positional warfare had returned with a vengeance. But the message most Western observers brought home from Manchuria was that the Japanese had won by a fanatic reliance on the offensive. It seemed beside the point that the losers, badly generaled as they were, had exacted an enormous price with weapons that would become basic to the Western Front: hand grenades, machine guns, mines and countermines, barbed wire, and even some primitive experiments with poison gas.

While some of those observers went around counting bayonet wounds in corpses to prove the efficacy of the attacker's stabbing or cutting weapons—their armes blanches—at least one group, the combat engineers of the German Pioneer Corps, recognized the Russo-Japanese War for the dress rehearsal it was. In a 1907 article called "The Campaign of the Future," published in a British military journal, the author predicted war on the Continent. It was, he said, shaping up to be "siege warfare in the field." By 1913, as military historian Bruce I. Gudmundsson has pointed out, German military contractors were developing improved grenades, trench mortars, and flamethrowers.

It is true that none of the belligerents, including the Germans, were prepared for trench warfare. Both sides at the beginning of August expected that a decision would be reached in a month or so—"before the leaves fell," as the kaiser famously put it. But it was also true that before many days of the war had passed, men had begun to dig, mainly rifle pits of varying lengths to begin with, for temporary protection. They had even started to connect them.

YOU CAN MAKE A GOOD argument that trench warfare, the phenomenon for which the Great War is most remembered, originated on the same day that the kaiser ordered the dismissal of Moltke as chief of the general staff, on September 14.

September 14, 1914. Remember that date.

What if, in the week that led up to it, the BEF and the French, who marched into the gap between the German First and Second Armies, had moved faster and with more confidence? The BEF did manage several miles a day, but, with little German resistance, it was a rate that British military historian Cyril Falls characterized as a "crawl." Lt. Gen. Sir Douglas Haig, commander of the I Corps, remarked on September 7, "I thought our movements very slow today, in view of the fact that the enemy was on the run. . . . I thought [the cavalry] were not doing much, in fact our infantry was in front of their front flank!" But like a benign affliction, languor spread. As the BEF and the French units next to it headed for the Aisne River highlands, a cornerstone of northern France, Haig himself dallied and hesitated. Ever after, says his biographer J. P. Harris, he harbored "a sense of lost opportunity."

Sir John French's immediate goal that second week of September was the summit of the Aisne highlands, along which ran a highway known as the Chemin des Dames—the Ladies' Road. Originally a Roman road (which accounted for its straightness), the Chemin des Dames had been resurfaced so that Louis XV's two daughters could enjoy a smooth coach ride when they made one of their frequent visits to see their close friend (and the king's former mistress), the countess of Narbonne-Lara, who lived nearby. As if that wasn't history enough, Napoleon in 1814 had narrowly won the Battle of Craonne, near the eastern exit of the road. It had done him little good. He was sent to exile in Elba soon after, his first.

The Chemin des Dames is eighteen miles long and the ridge across which it runs is treeless, flat, and windswept, a bit on the arid side. Spurs extend knuckle-like into the narrow valley of the Aisne. That river is deep, sluggish, and an opaque brown, a natural moat. Between the spurs are ravines, steep and forested; in places, farms and small fields cling to their sides. The limestone spurs are wormholed with stone quarries and caverns, whose labyrinthian galleries could (and would) hold several thousand men each. As highlands, the Chemin des Dames are not especially notable—they generally range from three to five hundred feet high—but the drop-offs are sharp and the valley prospect as spectacular as it must have been inviting to artillery dug along the top. Joffre compared the Chemin des Dames to "an immense fortress prepared by Nature."

The British I corps of Sir Douglas Haig (left), was one of the Allied units trying to gain the strategically important heights above the Aisne River. Their chief rival was Johann ("Hans" to his men) von Zwehl (right) and his German VII Reserve Corps. Pushing his men in forced marches, ignoring orders to divert his two divisions, he attained his goal first—costing the Allies a chance to force the Germans into a continued retreat, and altering the nature of the war on the Western Front. (INTERPHOTO/Alamy Stock Photo)

AS IF THOSE DAYS OF late summer weren't already filled with drama, the two sides now competed to reach, and hold, the summit of the Chemin des Dames. The winner would have command of a key sector of the Western Front, the one closest to Paris. For the Allies that was just a starter.

They had visions of pouring through a gap that still was, on the night of September 12–13, an estimated twenty-five miles wide, held only by a scattering of infantry and cavalry. There seemed a real chance for a penetration attack, with the British and French bursting through on a narrow front and then fanning out, to shatter the Germans from the rear.

In the hours before dawn on the thirteenth, the British arrived at the Aisne River. It was pouring, and the temperature was more appropriate to November than mid-September. By prodigies of daring and ingenuity, crossing single-file on blasted bridges or commandeering rowboats, they managed to get a sizeable number of men across the narrow but swift-flowing river. The rain barely let up, but neither did the unceasing storm of steel, which took a small but steady toll. Even so, the Germans were apparently still in full retreat. Haig's I Corps settled down for the night, a mile below the summit of the ridge, confident that the rest of the way would be easy. Sir John told Maj. Gen. Edmund Allenby to prepare his cavalry division for a gallop to Laon. "The prospects of a break-through," said the *Official History*, "never were brighter."

MENTIONS OF GERMAN EXPLOITS ARE notoriously scanty in accounts of the Great War. There is a certain truth to the maxim that history is written by the victors. That may explain why the story of the German drive for the Chemin des Dames has been so long overlooked.

Lower-level commanders, unlike the panicked old generals at the top, did understand the seriousness of the German predicament. They moved troops with an urgency that was lacking on the other side. They scrounged reserves from all over to create a new, gap-filling Seventh Army. At a time when their Western Front armies were everywhere in retreat, good fortune did favor the Germans in one place as it had not done for many days: On September 8, the sprawling but antiquated fortress system of Maubeuge, just south of the Belgian border, surrounded and isolated for two weeks and pounded by the siege train, surrendered. That meant the release of the VII Reserve Corps, which on September 10 began a furious progress south to join the cobbled-together Seventh. If Maubeuge had held out even a day or so longer, which it might well have done, the

VII Reserve Corps would have had little chance to make a difference. But luck, too, the indefinable, and the determination of one remarkable man, intervened.

That man, undoubtedly one of the best commanders on the Western Front in 1914, was Johann von Zwehl. "Hans," as he was popularly known, never hesitated to drive his men hard or to take calculated risks when he thought the ends justified them. If he felt the immediate situation warranted it, he would disobey orders. And yet he was never reckless. Zwehl was a handsome man, with hair parted down the middle, heavy-lidded eyes, and a florid mustache, which came close to having a handlebar droop. His was not the look of a crew-cut Prussian. Besides his independence, the one serious count against him was his age, sixty-three in 1914. To him, it made no difference.

Zwehl had played a leading role in the taking of Maubeuge, for which he would be awarded Germany's highest decoration, the Pour le Mérite—the "Blue Max." It had been well earned. Maubeuge was one of the major German triumphs on the Western Front that summer. Then, after the briefest of intermissions, he prepared for his next assignment. At first his Army commander, Bülow, ordered him to march his VII Reserve Corps northeast to the Flanders coast after the British landed at Ostend and had commenced digging entrenchments around the port. But the British soon reembarked, and Zwehl was free to lead his men in a different direction. What if the British had remained? They didn't—and now Bülow needed Zwehl's corps, two divisions strong, to deal with the emergency developing to the south. These were tough men, Westphalians from the industrial cities of the Rhine, with a hardy strain of agricultural workers thrown in, and they responded to the challenge. Their destination was Laon, a large town perched on a solitary butte and built around a medieval cathedral with a commanding view—the same place where, two weeks before, Joffre had silently supervised Landrezac's handling of the Battles of Saint-Quentin and Guise. Early on the evening of September 12, Zwehl learned about the unfilled gap on the Aisne highlands and the approach of the British and, on either side of them, the French. He allowed his men a two-hour rest, then continued marching through the night. At 5 A.M. on the morning of the thirteenth—when the BEF was beginning to cross the Aisne—he ordered another stop. By now he was five miles south of Laon. His Westphalians had covered forty miles in twenty-four hours: as many as a quarter of his force had fallen out along the way. He could not afford to wait for the stragglers to catch up.

At 8 A.M. a dispatch arrived from Generaloberst Karl von Bülow. Bülow commanded the Second Army; as part of an army group, the First and Seventh were also under his orders. Zwehl was to begin filling the gap to the left of the First Army, the task he had been sent to accomplish. He gave his troops another hour and a half to rest and then roused them to finish their dash to the Chemin des Dames. But at 11 A.M. he received another order from Bülow. The French were attacking near Berry au Bac, the chalk mounds where the highlands subsided, and were threatening the right wing of the Second Army: Bülow ordered Zwehl's corps to come to his aid. Zwehl replied that his men were too far committed to change direction—and kept going. He had an absolute belief that he was doing the right thing. Had he not ignored Bülow's cry for help, the *Official History* writes, "he would have left the way clear for the British I Corps to establish itself on the Chemin des Dames ridge, and the flank of all the German forces west of it might have been turned."

By 2 P.M. the first of Zwehl's two divisions, the 13th Reserve, reached the summit. Its men immediately set to fashioning trenches, lines of them. They had won the race and would be ready when Haig's I Corps approached. Thus, by the afternoon of September 13, the *Official History* notes, "the crisis . . . was, for the Germans, practically past." The British, though they were as yet unaware of the fact, now confronted a continuous and ever-deepening line. The first genuine trench battle of the war was about to begin.

AT 3 A.M. ON SEPTEMBER 14, the two divisions of Haig's I Corps resumed their progress uphill. It is not easy to make sense out of the mounting derangement of the hours that followed, which the *Official History* called "remarkable even for a modern battlefield." Few other clashes of arms on the Western Front can have been quite like that day, a nightmare beyond nightmare, an anomaly of war more than an essence. It began in darkness and rain; it ended the same way. The men climbing the wooded ravines had to pull themselves up by grabbing branches. Fog was their only protection. No one could tell where the front was. As the unexpected din of gunfire swelled into a roar, orders, shouted, could barely be heard. Men blundered ghostlike out of that fog, clashed with, and killed, other specters, and disappeared again behind its gauzy curtain. "Everywhere on the ridge," said the regimental history of the Scots Guards, "there was the confusion of companies and battalions, which could not be avoided in the mist in an unknown country."

At midmorning the fog lifted, allowing the British artillery to unlimber and actually see where to fire: it immediately disrupted a German attack. Gunners on both sides fired over open sights. Losses mounted. "I was with a party under my Company officer, Capt. Brody, who was aside me most of the time," Pvt. Sam Owen of the Loyal North Lancashire Regiment recalled. "We attacked up the slope and things were rather hot as the Germans were firing their field guns down the slope. I looked back but could not see the Capt. I think a shell must have hit him and blew him to pieces as we never found a trace of him."

Despite its relatively low elevation, the summit of the Chemin des Dames is not just windswept but windcrushed: the few trees that grow along it tend to be little more than head-high. Much of the fighting swirled around one of the few buildings on that long ridge, the Troyon sugar-beet factory. It stood at a crossroads, an ugly, soot-stained brick industrial structure from the late nineteenth century, its two wings giving it the look of a large rusting staple, there to keep the building from blowing away. Its most prominent feature was a high, widemouthed chimney that was a ready-made observation post. Artillery soon knocked much of it down: that would not stop the spotters. The Germans occupied the factory first. The British attack commenced before daylight, and all through the next hours the fighting surged back and forth across three hundred yards of bare ground, now considerably cratered with shell holes that were converted into rifle pits. They were connected and gradually turned into lengths of trench.

The British took the building and the Germans seemed ready to give way. Then a battalion worth of German reinforcements, as many as a thousand men, rose from a trench and thronged over the crest. Numbers made the difference. The counterattack regained the factory. The Germans came on an exposed flank of the Cameron Highlanders and raked it with machine-gun fire. With half their number down and with ammunition running low, survivors "gradually dribbled back" to their predawn starting point. Fifty men did hold out until a mass of attackers, five or six deep, swarmed over and overwhelmed them. The attack soon lost its forward momentum but not its downward one; entrenching began.

British officers gathered at a farm to discuss what should be done. "We came to the conclusion," wrote a Grenadier Guards major named "Ma" Jeffreys, "that with the battalions so scattered and mixed up, no further advance should be attempted." But in the hard rain of that early evening, Haig, beginning to reveal a tendency to obsess on objectives unattained, ordered Brig. Edward Bulfin's 2nd Brigade (or what was left of it) to make a final attempt to regain the sugar factory. Advancing amid a dense litter of bodies, the British reached the top of the ridge, occupied by the now-battered building, but could not hold it. Their back-and-forth struggle continued in the rain. During that single day, Haig's I Corps had lost 160 officers and 3,500 other ranks, the equivalent of three and a half battalions. They were never able to secure the mill.

All this must have happened at the very time when the kaiser was bloodlessly dismissing Helmuth von Moltke.

Under the cover of the streaming darkness, those on both sides still standing unfastened short spades from their packs. Everywhere men began to dig.*

WHAT BEGAN AS A BATTLE in the open that morning of September 14 would, by nightfall, become a battle of fixed positions, ones that would hardly change for the next three years. The freeze in the opposing lines that took hold around the Troyon mill quickly spread, a going-to-ground that also signaled the end of the Battle of the Marne. "The fighting on

---

* In each German infantry company (ideally 259 men and 5 officers, but far smaller by now) half the troops carried entrenching tools.

14 September was a watershed," writes J. P. Harris. "The Allied counter-offensive was finally checked. The German ability to stand on the Chemin des Dames helped preserve their army from disintegration."

On the following night, at 8:30 P.M., Sir John French issued his Operation Order No. 26. "The Commander-in-Chief," it read, "wishes the line now held by the Army to be strongly entrenched." As if loath to admit the possibility of stalemate, French added, "it is his intention to assume a general offensive at the first opportunity." As the *Official History* noted, this "proved to be the official notification of the commencement of trench warfare," a ratification of the stable lines that the fighting of the previous day had established. "Siege warfare in the field" had arrived.

That matchless interpreter of the Great War, Hew Strachan, has written that those first trenches "were not yet ends in themselves, but means to an end." Their tactical function was to provide shelter from shellfire. Their operational one was to give tired soldiers a rest after the marchings and countermarchings and the fierce grapplings of the Marne and the Chemin des Dames. Now ground could be defended with fewer men, freeing up others for a war of maneuver elsewhere, presumably in the plentiful open country that still existed to the north. "Bitterest of ironies, trench warfare was adopted to enable mobile warfare to take place."

The Aisne excavations were the first manifestations of *organized* trench combat. The word "organized" underlines an important distinction in the way the war was beginning to be fought, as compared to the way it had been. It was no less than a switching of historical gears. What you might call ad-hoc digging had been going on since the war began. Before many days of September had passed, just over three hundred miles of the emerging Western Front, from the Swiss border to the Marne, could be counted as more or less stabilized. Numberless excavations, both Allied and German, of all shapes, sizes, and depths, from connected shell holes to fully dug trenches, some reasonably continuous, others widely separated, some facing similar enemy works, others not, already scarred the landscapes of the eastern frontier regions of France and Belgium. Many had been created for purposes of hasty defense or as protection for multitudes in flight—dug, say, perpendicular to a road or overlooking a tactically important river crossing or road junction. Even the French, who normally disdained the spade and the pickaxe—the Ne Plus Ultra urge did not yet grip this generation—resorted to these tools if they offered a chance to throw up a defense that would slow the advancing Germans.

But there was a difference between that random digging and what was happening on the heights above the Aisne. Before, trenches had been hit-or-miss affairs, with few or no opposing enemy lines, no observation posts, no communication trenches, no latrines or reserve trenches, no aid posts, and, most of all, barely a hint of a trench *system*.*

Those first burrowings above the Aisne on September 14 were a succession of narrow pits holding three or four men each, and separated from the ones adjoining by stretches of undug earth that functioned as natural traverses. Rifle pits were dug behind rifle pits, and connected. So were shell holes. As the nights passed—most of the work was done then—men on both sides began to extend the pits and make them deeper. "There was plenty of work on the Aisne during those days," remembered a Pvt. Frederick Bolwell of the Loyal North Lancashire Regiment, "the men in the front line connecting each single trench up with another, so as to form one continual line; also the making of bunny holes." (By way of explanation, a major in the Royal Irish Regiment put it more elegantly: "Every man had to dig a hole in the bank, and completely disappear like a rabbit.") In his history of the Irish Guards, Rudyard Kipling wrote that these

---

* A recent biography, *Haig's Enemy: Crown Prince Rupprecht and Germany's War on the Western Front*, by Jonathan Boff, sets the date of the commencement of trench warfare at least two weeks before the clash on the Aisne heights, at the end of August. That was when, after the Battle of Morhange, Rupprecht saw an opening of promise and dashed into the bare landscape south of Nancy in French Lorraine. Moltke did nothing to restrain him. The Crown Prince met with a minor disaster of his own. Meanwhile, his troops began to dig. That trenches appeared, I have no doubt; they belonged to the same stabilized lines I have mentioned above. But they did not initiate an extended, and rapidly expanding, system on both sides. I do take Boff's claim seriously, but without more direct evidence, I have chosen to go with the *Official History* and the date of the first major trench battle on the Western Front. Beginnings, their exact time and their location, matter, nowhere more so than in the narrative of the early days of the Great War.

first trenches were "little more than shallow furrows, for we did not know that the day of open battle was ended."

The very nature of combat on the Western Front was changing. The vertical marching lines on the dusty roads of August, miles long, driving southward or retreating in the same direction, would become the horizontal defenses of September and beyond.

What Kipling called "the casual ditch which they called a trench" was likely to be narrow and rarely deep enough to provide thorough protection, and in the cold, hard rain that saw out the summer of 1914, they tended to fill with waist-high water. Shellfire and snipers took a constant toll on both sides. "I got six," a Scots rifleman reported, summing up a day's work; "They put their heids too high above the heather." To avoid an unnecessary, and perhaps fatal, exposure of reinforcements, supply details, ration and ammunition parties, and stretcher bearers carrying back the wounded, troops on both sides began digging communication trenches to the rear, which, before long, linked with second-line excavations. More often, though, troops made the trek to the front line—the French called it *le feu*—in the perilous open. A system, no matter how haphazardly organized, was taking shape, a feature new to the emerging, and still evolving, Western Front.

Trenches might be an ancient phenomenon, but for these men, everything about them was uncharted territory. Improvisation became the new normal. Both sides introduced sandbags (which rarely contained sand but loose dirt or clay). They fashioned primitive periscopes by fastening mirrors to the ends of sticks. Foragers brought back wire and digging tools from now-deserted farms. Infantrymen set out anything that might impede an attack. "Our front is now well covered," said the war diary of the 1st Rifle Brigade, "with spiked sticks, barbed wire, entanglements, concealed holes, etc." When food didn't arrive, which happened too frequently, soldiers braved sniper fire to rummage for potatoes and carrots in fields that otherwise would have gone unharvested.

Once the two sides began to dig their opposing systems, they automatically created another inescapable feature of organized trench warfare, no-man's-land. The no-man's-land here—the phrase did not

German riflemen in *feldmützen,* or field caps, crowd a freshly dug frontline trench on the Aisne highlands. Trenches had existed before, but not trench systems opposing other systems, separated by a new phenomenon of siege warfare, no-man's-land (though it was not yet called that). Here, too, the first system-against-system trench battles took place. (Ullsteinbild/TopFoto)

become common currency for another three or four months—was unusually wide, as much as a thousand yards, but more often a few hundred. In one instance, only twelve yards separated the British and Germans. It was, as one historian has characterized it in a flash of poetic insight, "a new place on earth." A lot can go on in half a mile of open space. Observers from both sides, with telephone wires trailing, took to climbing trees or hiding in hollowed-out haystacks. British patrols came on other observers dressed as farm laborers: once they spotted the telltale wires, they dispatched them without mercy. Snipers and machine-gun teams also hid in no-man's-land.

The area between the trenches, the regimental historian of the Grenadier Guards noted, "was covered with unburied bodies, but for either side to venture out merely meant adding to their number." A captain of the Bedfordshire regiment recalled how "the weather became hot and the smell of dead bodies in the woods was dreadful, both German and our own which had fallen in odd places and not been discovered. Carcasses of horses and cattle were even worse. . . . It takes some doing to bury a cow which has swollen to three times its normal size."

This war, to use Samuel Hynes's phrase, was already promising to be rich in "battlefield gothic."

Almost by accident, the Germans were better prepared to fight a drawn-out battle of position, at least on the Aisne front. They made the most of it. On September 14—that day again—a trainload of engineer stores, which included heavy artillery, mortars, rifle grenades, hand grenades, searchlights, illuminating pistols, and periscopes, arrived at the railyards of Laon. It was a cache originally destined for the siege of Paris—which, for the moment, appeared to have been merely postponed. (What other use would searchlights have had but for the investment of a city?) All was not lost. Those same tools of urban siege warfare were ideally suited to a defensive stand in open country.

The myriad manifestations of a new (and sometimes old) technology would make all the difference in the next four years. For so much energy to converge on one place, the Western Front was, as military historian Paddy Griffith observes, "an unmistakably modern phenomenon." It represented "a mobilization of hundreds of active brains around a single theoretical problem—the problem of trench warfare—in a way that had no true parallel in the nineteenth century, but which would be seen again several times over the long subsequent history of warfare." With the arrival of that train, September 14—seize the day a final time— also inaugurated another sophisticated, and very human, creation: the transformation of the Western Front into an industrial battlefield.

As the British *Official History* noted: "At the beginning . . . the enemy was at a great advantage in his knowledge of trench warfare; and he had the material required for its practice, even if his men had not been generally trained in its use." The British, on the other hand, were ill prepared. The only engineer supplies that reached the British on the Aisne were small quantities of empty sandbags and barbed wire, along with some old-model 6-inch howitzers. They were quick learners. They had to be. The lessons of siege warfare observed in the Boer and Russo-Japanese Wars at the beginning of the century had not been lost on many up-and-

The German 5.9 howitzer, shown in a November 1914 photo, may have been the outstanding gun of the war. Its high-explosive shells could make a crater fifteen to twenty feet wide and ten feet deep—shells that had a tendency to bury men alive (which may explain why that happens so often to Allied soldiers in these pages). German artillerymen, unless they were Bavarians, wore helmets topped not with a spike but with a ball. (Imperial War Museum)

coming officers, including Haig, who spent a couple of years as the War Office's director of military training. But when Haig requested items such as hand grenades, night-camouflage suits, and increased numbers of machine guns, all in evidence at the German maneuvers he had attended before the war, the War Office turned him down: they cost too much.

WHERE THE GERMANS HELD A genuine advantage, and one they would not surrender until 1917, was in artillery, their 5.9 howitzer, in particular. The 5.9, British military historian John Terraine writes, "would seem to have been the most outstanding gun of the War, exceeding in effect even the famous French '75.' . . . The French had pinned their faith to the 75s, which were light and easy to handle, and had a prodigious rate of fire, but which were hopelessly outranged and out-calibred by the 5.9s." Those German howitzers, high-angle guns, could fire a variety of shells: "The high-explosive shell on bursting," explains the *Official History*,

> caused a tremendous concussion, and made craters 15–20 feet across and 10 feet deep. The high-explosive shrapnel, however, though it made a terrific noise, and produced much green and white smoke, was comparatively harmless. Ordinary shrapnel was generally burst too high to be dangerous. A small high-velocity shell ("whizz-bang") was very accurate, the burst and report of discharge being practically simultaneous.

The high-explosive shells, as the regimental history of the Grenadier Guards put it, "made holes big enough to bury three or four horses in." When they hit a trench, they might not register a direct hit but had a nasty side effect: they buried men alive.

Haig, in his September 16 diary entry, made no bones about the dominance of the enemy artillery: "Our own high explosive is of little use compared with the German, so the enemy's big guns possess a real moral superiority"—strange concept—"for some of our gunners. In fact, our gunners cannot 'take on' the enemy's heavy batteries."

Like endless trench battles to come, the Aisne lapsed into a duel of big guns. The British did their best to compete; their efforts that fall never did come close to measuring up. One officer figured that fifty German shells fell per minute. Artillery spotting became something of an art, though as yet a primitive one. Both sides stationed observers in trees, haystacks, and deserted farmhouses between the lines; the Germans used the by-now much-battered chimney at Troyon to peer at nearby British trenches. Though they now had the advantage of holding the high ground almost everywhere on the Chemin des Dames ridge, and the commanding views that came with it, they did not shun the air. Observation craft like the Taube or the Albatross biplane provided valuable tactical information. Stationary warfare also gave them the opportunity to experiment with captive kite, or sausage (as they were known more familiarly), balloons. With spotters dangling from wicker baskets, balloons made their first appearance on the Western Front, peeking discreetly above the ridgelines. But the models tested in that first autumn of the war were too heavy to rise higher than 1,600 feet, leaving them vulnerable to ground fire. By discarding the baskets and equipment in them, and by substituting a stiff saddle arrangement, observers managed to coax more altitude. It was not an assignment for the faint of heart, connected to Earth as you were only by steel cables and a telephone wire: the craft tended to buck in the wind and ground crews needed as much as an hour to haul them down by hand. Parachutes for balloonists weren't introduced for another year, nor were gasoline-powered motor winches. By then the balloons themselves were bigger, more stable, and could rise as high as five-thousand feet. The saddles had long since been discarded.

Because the Allies were lower down on the Chemin des Dames, artillery spotting from the ground was mostly impossible. Though French artillery commanders were initially dubious about the value of air reconnaissance, the British, like the Germans, increasingly relied on observation from above. Pilots took up artillery officers, whose job it was to locate enemy batteries and note their position on squared maps that would be sent to divisional artillery commanders. A few aircraft were equipped with wireless transmitters, an innovation. One pioneering observation aviator, Donald Swain Lewis, was adept enough to fly his plane and operate the wireless at the same time. A fellow airman noted in his journal that Lewis "came in from spotting with his machine shot full of holes; 'I believe he likes it!' "*

A wireless message, one of the first, was sent down from a British plane to an artillery battery on September 24, 1914:

4.2 p.m. A very little short. Fire. Fire.
4.4 p.m. Fire again. Fire again.
4.12 p.m. A little short; line O.K.

---

* On April 10, 1916, Lewis was flying over Wytschaete, a German-held village bordering the Ypres salient, when an antiaircraft gun scored a direct hit on his plane. The flight should have been just another day's work: a man who had done so much to perfect the art of observation died as he was showing an artillery officer the effects of trench mortar fire.

4.15 p.m. Short. Over, over and a little left.

4.20 p.m. You were just between two batteries. Search two hundred yards each side of your last shot. Range O.K.

4.22 p.m. You have them.

4.26 p.m. Hit. Hit. Hit.

4.32 p.m. About 50 yards short and to the right.

4.37 p.m. Your last shot in the middle of 3 batteries in action; search all round within 300 yards of your last shot and you have them.

4.42 p.m. I am coming home now.

On September 15, a lieutenant named Pretyman took five photographs from the air of enemy positions; they were the first of millions over the next four years. What aerial reconnaissance would accomplish represented a major change in the nature of making war: the near abolition of surprise.

There were offensive experiments perhaps left unremembered, such as the dropping of steel darts, "fléchettes," in the direction of massed men or horses. Pilots occasionally took potshots at each other with pistols or rifles. It is recorded that on September 22 an observer in a German Albatross two-seater fired on a Lt. G. W. Mapplebeck, hitting him in the leg and making him the first British aviator wounded in aerial combat. Soldiers on both sides learned to duck and hide when they heard the grinding buzz of a motor overhead.

But given the German command of the high ground, Allied daily wastage from shellfire remained constant, considerable, and predictable. On September 15, the Highland Light Infantry suffered 60 casualties; on the sixteenth, the 2nd Grenadier Guards, 70; and the King's Royal Rifle Corps (KRRC), 68. On the seventeenth, the artillery lost 40 horses. So it went. Snipers firing down from the spurs also made daytime movement on the river flats perilous and added to the daily loss. The Aisne became a model for the wasted, and all but forgotten, sacrifice of the fall of 1914.

Who didn't suffer? Consider some of the distressing events along the Aisne line on a single day, September 20. The hours of early morning had begun with stinging showers of hail, the eighth day of cold, foul weather in a row. "I had an awful night in the trenches last night," twenty-six-year-old lieutenant Bernard Law Montgomery of the Warwickshires, the future field marshal, wrote to his mother later in the day. "It poured rain all night and the trenches became full of water. I had to go forward visiting sentries. . . . I crawled about on my stomach in mud and slush and nearly lost myself." The bishop's son thanked her for a gift. "I eat the peppermints with a dead man beside me in the trench."

After an interval of relative inaction, the Germans attempted to seize the initiative that morning. Lines of men in spiked helmets and soaked gray uniforms emerged from trenches and advanced over the open ridge. September 20 began with a near disaster for the British. A battalion of the West Yorkshire Regiment was holding the far right of the line, where it merged with the French Fifth Army. Soon after dawn, Moroccans, badly cut up by artillery fire, gave way, leaving a gap that the Germans were quick to exploit. They enfiladed the British line and worked methodically from one long pit that passed for a trench to the next. The haze of battle descended. Some sources, including the West Yorkshire regimental history, say that a large number of German troops advanced, waving a white flag. Thinking that a mass surrender was in the works, the Yorkshires left their trenches and went out to meet them. Meanwhile, the Germans who had turned the flank got behind the men now in the open. They fired, and so did those who had "surrendered." Surrounded, the Yorkshires who weren't killed or wounded had no choice but to give up. But the killing in this sector kept on until nightfall. "The lost trenches," wrote the *Official History,* "were finally regained by a dashing counter-attack of the Sherwood Foresters, but at a cost of two hundred casualties, mostly from machine-gun fire." We know only that events in this sector did leave the British with 400 killed or wounded and 500 missing. The latter figure was certainly on the excessive side, even for those life-defying highlands; the white flag ruse might account for it.

"The whole affair was a mystery," said the regimental historian of the West Yorkshires, "but it was evident the lost companies had been first tricked and then shot down or taken prisoners."

The *Official History* gives a memorable picture of the confused fighting that day. British counterattackers, trying to keep the line next to the unfortunate Yorkshires from further dissolving, were met with machine-gun fire and "overwhelming shrapnel." Dismounted cavalry fought. Costly prodigies of sacrifice helped to stabilize the line. Other British troops made their way through a thicket "under heavy fire" and carried a German trench beyond it, only to fall into a machine-gun ambush. Troops broke; troops rallied, British fire proving too much for the enemy. Some German attacks were outright failures. They "tried to entrench themselves upon two bare knolls but were driven off them by shrapnel; and about 4 p.m. about two hundred men of the Wiltshire, Worcestershire and South Lancashire advanced, and after sharp fighting drove the enemy back to his own lines, leaving the ground behind littered with his killed and wounded."

In the afternoon, the skies cleared, and autumn in all its by-now tattered glory settled in. "Altogether the 20th September was a successful day for the British, though it cost the BEF nearly twenty-two hundred killed, wounded, and missing. The Germans had delivered four serious attacks at four different points and had, after first gaining some little advantage, been everywhere repulsed. The French immediately to the right and left of the British were subjected to similar onslaughts with much the same result."

The German VII Reserve Corps, which had participated in the general attack, reported that it was so exhausted and depleted that it was barely able to hold the line. One brigade, normally 6,000 strong, was reduced to 200 men, with 9 or 10 officers. That was the essence of General Zwehl's protest to General Herringen, the commander of the Seventh Army, who had ordered the attack to continue. The time had come to stop, to turn attention elsewhere. The attacks sputtered out. The Germans began to string stands of barbed wire, a purely defensive barrier, along the Aisne heights. It was an indication of the need to conserve manpower and to divert troop strength to the "race" developing as the line turned northward.

In the burgeoning annals of trench warfare, two further innovations are worth recording. On September 27, German troops hurled the first hand grenades, of the stick variety, into British trenches on the Chemin des Dames. The BEF had no grenades, and a request went out to the Royal Engineers to improvise some sort of handheld explosive device.

They came up with a missile that used gun cotton—which was soon re-placed by other experimental expedients, most of which posed a greater threat to the hurler than to the hurlee on the receiving end.

The other notable innovation was the first trench raid in force. At 8 A.M. on October 4, a subaltern named Merton Beckwith-Smith led a platoon of the Coldstream Guards across a hundred yards of no-man's-land, rushed a first trench with bayonets, finding it occupied only by fif-teen dead Germans, and then a second, where they shot or bayoneted twenty. Fire from a third—sure evidence of a developing system—forced the raiders to retreat. Beckwith-Smith was wounded and received a DSO. Three of the raiders died.

The Aisne, the first trench battle of the war, had ended in a stalemate, a costly one for both sides. Between September 12 and October 3, when the transfer of British troops to Flanders began, the British lost 561 offi-cers and 12,980 men—13,541. That many trained officers would prove difficult to replace. We shall never know the true extent of German losses (or those of the French, for that matter): they were probably as heavy or heavier. The Aisne, however inconclusive, was for both sides a dress re-hearsal for a more important confrontation.

At the beginning of October, Sir John French sent a report on the recent weeks of the war to King Edward VII. "I think the battle of the Aisne is very typical of what battles in the future are most likely to re-semble," French wrote, with considerable prescience. "Siege operations will enter largely into the tactical problems—the *spade* will be as great a necessity as the rifle, and the heaviest calibers and types of artillery will be brought up in support on either side."

6

Race to the Sea

THE AISNE FRONT MAY HAVE HARDENED INTO STALEMATE, BUT HOPES FOR A resumption of open warfare in the plains of northern France still glimmered in the imaginations of generals. In the last days of September and into October, few thought of Flanders, though day by day the war drew closer to it. Surely a decision would be reached on the plains of northern France, which were still open, still inviting.

This was the interval of the Great War that has come to be known as the "Race to the Sea." It lasted just a month—from September 17 to October 17, when the Belgian Army anchored itself along the Yser River and prepared to make a last stand. Those thirty-one days have practically dropped from the calendar of 1914 history. Not enough has been written, at least not in English, about the considerable events of this all-but-forgotten interval, which involved notable encounters, nonstop action, and the fall of one of France's largest cities. It left a swath of blood and disrupted earth more than a hundred miles long. At a very rough estimate—no exact figures exist—the combined casualty total for the two sides may have been as high as 200,000 to 300,000. It was an extended tactical brawl with no set strategic objective, except finding that sweet spot, that ever-evasive flank to turn while flanks still existed. Strategy, and a resumption of a war of maneuver, could begin then. The sea became an objective only as an afterthought, and a flankless one at that.

It was a month that started on the Aisne and ended across the Belgian frontier, near Ypres. Add a final lurch to the North Sea. Did that justify the familiar title? In the words of John Keegan, "A race it was; not for the sea, however, but to find a gap between the sea and the Aisne position before it was exploited by the other side." Both Joffre and Falkenhayn believed that they would reach a decision somewhere in northern France. They didn't—and found themselves in Flanders. Like cross-country runners, the two sides elbowed their way on a parallel rush northward, trying to get far enough ahead of the other to find an opening from which they might launch and achieve the ultimate outflanking move. Trenches followed them. The opponents recognized early that the relentlessly spreading defensive system was a measure of economy: fewer men were needed to hold it. Their hope was to free up more men for the initiative in the open, that ever-elusive great leap sideways. That was the real race.

Until the parallel lines began to probe French Flanders, nearing the coast, the sea remained an afterthought—as did the involvement of the BEF. Once the Channel ports—Boulogne, Calais, and Dunkirk—came in reach of the Germans, attitudes changed. "It still seemed possible, if the present German front held," Falkenhayn wrote in his memoirs, "to bring the northern coast of France, and therefore the control of the English Channel, into German hands." That may have been a thought that occurred only when a watery conclusion became inescapable. But the Allies perceived the same threatening possibility and began to garrison the ports and build up the defenses surrounding them.

Transport, explains Australian historian Trevor Wilson, was at the heart of the race. The side that had the better north–south railway system had the advantage:

> For against a force being transported by rail, troops having to move on foot would be too slow, and adequate motorized transport did not exist. But in the event each side had a railway system at its disposal . . . the Race to the Sea was in effect a series of parallel entrainments northwards, punctuated by sharp exchanges at places where the two sets of north–south railway lines were intersected by others running east-west.

That accounts for the focus of action around large towns like Noyon, Albert, Arras, Lens, Lille, Armentières—junctions all—and, in due course, Ypres. Rail connections in German-held territory still suffered from the ravages of the retreating French. Falkenhayn acknowledged the deficit in his memoirs. The sought-after enveloping movement, he said, "had been prevented by the superiority of the French network of railways." As Robert A. Doughty has observed in his justly respected study of French strategy in the Great War, "If Joffre had a secret weapon, it was the highly efficient French railway system." The industrial battlefield moved on rails.

A street in the Somme department town of Albert lies in ruin after the Race to the Sea had passed through. There was a reason why certain places like Albert, Arras, Lille, Armentières, and Roulers were so prized, and so fought over. They were rail junctions, and transport—who could get ahead of the other first—was at the heart of the race, as troops leapfrogged north in an unceasing effort to prevent potential envelopment from the other side. (*L'Illustration*)

Yet the "race" accomplished none of the things it was meant to do. As map games, its concepts were tantalizingly daring; execution was another matter. For the moment, neither the French—the British weren't involved until its final stages—nor the Germans could summon the number of fresh troops that might have made conclusive maneuvering possible. The profligacy of the first two months of the war, along with the exhaustion of near-continuous battle, had caught up with the men who fought, and perhaps with their leaders as well. One side could do no better than to maintain the pace of the other. The French, one of their own generals commented, were forever "twenty-four hours and an army corps behind the Germans." The same could have been said about the Germans. An American might invoke the words of the Confederate cavalry leader Nathan Bedford Forrest, whose prescription for victory is often rendered as: "Git thar fustest with the mostest." Neither side did.

SEPTEMBER 17 MARKED THE START of those parallel moves north. That was the day when Gen. Michel-Joseph Maunoury's French Sixth Army struck Gen. Alexander von Kluck's First Army, just as it had two weeks before on the Marne. This time Maunoury's objective was not an exposed flank but the tactically important town of Noyon, on the forearm of the newly created elbow of the Western Front. The country was hilly and wooded, not a promising place for an attack, and the French offensive soon stalled. (For the next two and a half years, until the Germans retreated from the town, Georges Clemenceau's newspaper *L'Homme enchaîné* would print in thick type at the top of the front page, LES ALLEMANDS SONT À NOYON—which was a mere fifty-six miles from Paris.) Blocked in one direction in this first attempt to outflank the Germans, Maunoury kept heading north. And both sides began to dig.

Joffre produced a new French Army, the Second, which took its place in the line above Maunoury's Sixth. He brought two army corps, as well as their commander, Castelnau, from Lorraine, and then took two corps from Maunoury. Maunoury's maneuvering days were over; his surplus legions were needed elsewhere. Joffre then added two more corps—four divisions—to the Second Army.

Joffre's choice for the new command was Gen. Édouard de Curières de Castelnau. A devout Catholic, he was a lay member of the Capuchin order, and was nicknamed the "Capuchin in Boots" or the "Fighting Friar." In a professional army dominated by anticlericalism, Castelnau's extreme faith did little to win him popularity, though his closeness to Joffre made him influential beyond his abilities. Before the war, he had been Joffre's right-hand man. The commander in chief had promoted him to head an army, the Second. That army had sustained a dreadful beating in August, at Morhange, from Crown Prince Rupprecht's Sixth German Army. But Castelnau had rallied his forces and administered one in turn when he stopped Rupprecht's pursuing Germans.

Gloomy by nature, Castelnau had been unhinged by the news of a son's death in battle—he would lose two more before the war was over. Under mounting pressure from the Germans, Castelnau had been preparing to evacuate the Grand-Couronne, the heights that sheltered Nancy, and to surrender the city; Joffre forbade retreat. It was a key moment in the war. The Germans, blinking first, relinquished their foothold on the heights and withdrew, leaving the field to Castelnau. Nominally, he had presided over the victory that buttoned up the Allied right flank all the way from the city of Nancy south to the Swiss border, not just in 1914 but also for the rest of the war. Castelnau had in fact done everything possible to deny himself that triumph. He had won in spite of himself.

During one of his incessant tours of the front—his chauffeur was a former race car driver—Joffre stops for an al fresco picnic lunch in a farmyard. Never one to miss a meal, he is the portly figure at left, quaffing, presumably, a glass of wine. Joffre had a habit of showing up at a general's headquarters, uninvited and unannounced. (*L'Illustration*)

The real victor was Joffre, who had made the right gesture at the right moment. It is all too easy to make sport of Joffre, with his girth, his great white walrus mustache, his silent but epic triumphs at the dinner table, his insistence on regular naps, his paperless desk and mapless office, his wild drives chauffeured by a former racecar driver, and his sudden, frightening descents on unsuspecting generals. But Joffre was also a commander who could make excellent decisions when it counted. The Grand-Couronne was one of them; the decision to turn and fight at the Marne was merely the most famous. Joffre was a man who changed history by keeping it unchanged. He denied the Germans the victory that at times had seemed so close. That was accomplishment enough.

Joffre retained his confidence in Castelnau: he eventually became his chief of staff. Of their relationship, Castelnau once said, "Except for sleeping together, we could not be closer." But he was not a fighting general, like Foch or Franchet d'Espèrey, better on the whole at defense than offense. Now Castelnau found himself in an offensive struggle, and events did not start off well for him. By September 24, Castelnau's Second Army had reached the Somme, when his outflanking move ran into the German XVIII Corps, which had just marched more than fifty miles from Rheims. The Germans pushed hard: now they were the ones attempting a flanking maneuver. They threw the Second Army back at Péronne. This time, though, it was the French who bent but did not break.

The "race" was still largely open warfare, and it possessed a distinct character, unlike any other interval on the Western Front. Regimental commanders, the Germans especially, could still be observed leading their men into battle on horseback. The Germans, given to harmonic uplift, brought regimental bands forward, to inspire the troops as they prepared to dash across stubble fields recently harvested to their rendez-vous with death. Farmyards became the scenes of desperate, obscure struggles as men crouched for illusory protection behind stone barns or haystacks.

Piles of unburied dead, French mingling with German, lay every-where. The weather was, in general, good, although the famously impen-etrable fogs of northern Europe rose up to consume the morning hours.

Officers blithely reconnoitered in front of forward lines, knowing that they had little more to fear than an occasional stray bullet. Troops suddenly materialized from the dense mist to swarm over surprised villages. In the murk, haloes ringed the fires of burning buildings. Sometimes the fog would lift without warning, revealing lines of men as they crossed fields, beyond cover; the killing resumed.

Falkenhayn countered with a major reinforcement of his own, the imposing Sixth Army, which he brought from Lorraine. The commander of the Sixth was the son of King Ludwig III of Bavaria—though a part of greater Germany, Bavaria still had its own monarch. Crown Prince Rupprecht was a quiet and thoughtful man, a forty-five-year-old widower with sad eyes and a university education, a passionate traveler and hunter, a lover of music (though he couldn't stand Wagner), solid, independent, and immensely popular with his men. Like them, he went through a learning process, and it was a costly one. He had won a notable victory at Morhange, his first big battle, a little more than a month earlier, and had come close to achieving another at the Grand-Couronne. But in the end, his attempts at pursuit had proved sanguinary fizzles. The French held; a great prize, the city of Nancy, remained out of reach. In the middle of almost ceaseless action, a telegram arrived from Munich, informing him that the older of his two sons had died of polio; he could not break away for the funeral. His relations with Falkenhayn were civil but increasingly chilly. It is almost a cliché to say that Rupprecht, who had spent a lifetime in the military, was the best and most professional of the German royal commanders. But beyond question he was as good a general as Germany had.

The arrival of Rupprecht and his Bavarians seemed precisely the tonic that the common soldier needed after the disappointment of the Marne. The Germans began to recover the gameness they had surrendered there. In the open downlands, where fixed lines did not yet exist, horsemen rode side by side with the infantry or made exploratory dashes in all directions. Cavalry still mattered. An account, ripe with enthusiasm for battle, records the charge of the 3rd Guards Uhlan Regiment on September 26. The uhlans fell on two companies of French Territorials, escorted by cavalry troopers:

With lances couched, the squadrons wheeled into line and charged with loud hurrahs! Half of the 5th Squadron plunged upon a retreating skirmish line, cutting down many of the Frenchmen in the hand-to-hand combat that ensued and sending others to the rear as prisoners. . . . The other half of the squadron . . . overtook a retreating column, and cut down a large number of the enemy, while shooting many of the remainder out of their saddles.

The account boasted, "The regiment had victoriously carried through a genuine cavalry charge and thereby added new laurels to its standard." The exploit had not been without cost: "At sunset we buried our dead as the cannonading and cheers of the attacking Bavarians resounded in the distance."

In the same area, two fresh corps, the II Bavarian and the XIV Reserve, attacked a weak French Territorial division holding the crossroads town of Bapaume, drove it back, and surged forward over the Picardy downland, almost reaching the key rail hub of Albert. A Lieutenant Koehler of the 17th Infantry Regiment made no effort to hide his elation. "Despite enemy attempts to halt us, we had advanced more than forty-five kilometers this day." Koehler was convinced that "just a few more days like today and we shall have taken Amiens and be marching on Paris."

Still, intelligence in an unfamiliar landscape was poor; rail-connections, unlike Joffre's, were uncertain; and Falkenhayn's instructions to Rupprecht were ill defined. Confusion prevailed. German units found themselves spread all over the map of Picardy, and out of touch with one another. A captain (who was also a count, a Graf) named Armansperg searched for his unit. "Where on earth the 1st Division was, nobody knew. I discovered very clearly during those days how very little even the higher staffs knew about the situation; how everything was shrouded in uncertainty. . . . All I could do was to go from one place to another and gradually build up a picture."

But faulty intelligence and still-unrepaired rail connections were not the only reasons for the failure of Germany to make the great outflanking movement that would regain the advantage it had lost. A colonel commanding a Bavarian regiment assessed the enemy. The men the Germans now confronted on the Somme, he said, were not the same troops they had beaten so easily in the first month of the war. "The battles in Lorraine had given our troops a feeling of superiority. They received an extremely rude shock when they had to accept" that the French "had changed. They were tough, daring and self-confident." He wondered where that new spirit would have been without the Marne and the order to withdraw that had turned a battle almost won into a defeat. That change, and the failure of nerve that had produced it, was something that neither Schlieffen nor Moltke had taken into account. The panic on high, the colonel said, "must be regarded as a crime against all things German."

Thoughts of Amiens, no less Paris, began to evaporate. In their search for an elusive open flank, both sides attacked without cease. Each successive village reached seemed to become a battleground. At Fricourt, Lt. Col. Henri Colin of the French 26th Infantry Regiment wrote in his journal, "We are nose to nose with the Germans . . . separated by no more than the width of a street." Both sides brought in searchlights. Troops of Rupprecht's II Bavarian Corps, its two divisions outnumbering the defenders, gradually forced them out. Colin had just been promoted to command after his three predecessors were killed. In his journal entry for September 28, he described how, after nightfall, he crossed a plateau that shellfire had already shorn of vegetation: "The spectacle is impressive. . . . All the horizon is ablaze, Albert, Fricourt, Mametz are in flames and the glow of burning villages lights up the night."

Rupprecht watched the fighting from a deserted mill on a ridge nearby. He could see the famous gold-plated Madonna that topped the basilica in the center of Albert. There was a prediction popular during those years: when the Madonna fell, so would Albert. It didn't; not then, at least.

Throwing in reserves made no difference: the casualty lists only lengthened. Artillery became the primary killing tool for both sides. One battalion commander, an Oberstleutnant (Lieutenant Colonel) Randebock, described how, once it was dark, "I went forward across the battlefield, right up to the furthest point where the men had fallen. They were lying so close that they almost touched. In one place I counted thirty in a row. Almost all had been killed by head wounds." Coordinated bursts of shrapnel fire from French 75s had obviously caught them in the open. Their patent-leather pickelhauben, with the characteristic spikes protruding through the canvas covering that concealed the shiny black surface of their headgear, had offered scant protection from the darting pellets released by shell bursts above.

Trenches were only the most notable feature of the advancing siegeworks. On both sides of the line, the new tenants went about turning villages into fortresses. Pioneers—field engineers—made loopholes in house walls wide enough for rifle barrels to poke through, filled in windows but left apertures big enough for machine guns, and converted cellars into shellproof dugouts. They dug trenches that connected buildings and ringed the villages with wire entanglements, tree barriers, and "wolf pits"—holes with sharpened stakes sunk into their centers. These defenses would hardly budge until the Allies launched the Somme offensive in July 1916.

The facing lines of trenches and dug-in strongpoints continued to move north. Brig. Gen. Marie-Émile Fayolle, commander of the French 70th Division, kept a secret journal. (It wasn't published until 1964, thirty-six years after his death.) In his entry for October 2, he wrote, "We are in a continuous line from Donon"—a pass near the Swiss border—"to Arras, and this line extends without cease toward the north. It will end by breaking open at some point. It's inevitable! . . . When that happens, perhaps the stalemate will end. I only hope it doesn't happen to us!"

Fayolle lamented the difficulties that an attacker now faced. He described the emerging vista of trench warfare, which in a matter of days had taken on an aura of permanence. He described an "entire land torn up," with barbed-wire networks already in place, reverse slope works perfectly concealed and difficult for artillery to locate, interlocking machine-gun emplacements, deep trench lines indented with tooth-shaped traverses, and underground shelters and command posts where men found safety during bombardments, only emerging to fire on attacking infantry. And then, the man who would one day become Maréchal of France, added an exclamation: "What a battlefield! One sees nothing out there. Yesterday I returned morning and evening. I didn't spot a single living person."

He was not likely to do so in daylight. Many thousands might inhabit the virtual cities they were creating and connecting, but these were cities of night. "All movements are made at night," a young French captain wrote home from the Somme, "and it is then we eat and orders are sent." Parties carried off the dead of the day and brought in food that was already cold. The empty battlefield continued its relentless spread.

Had there ever been a human-generated phenomenon quite like this? Every sunrise revealed piles of fresh earth that seemed as if by magic to have leapt forward during the night.

THE BATTLE LINES EDGED TOWARD Arras. Now the German Sixth Army had to contend with a new French force, the hastily scraped-together Tenth Army, commanded by Louis de Maud'huy, an aristocrat with a white mustache and still-thick hair. Haig, in his diary, described de Maud'huy as "a small active man, about 58. Sandy coloured hair, probably dye! Quite an old type of Frenchman whom one has seen on the stage of the Louis 14th period." The Tenth detrained near Arras during the last days of September, perhaps the most tumultuous month in military history, and immediately found itself in action. German cavalry was already ranging over the heights to the east of town, and de Maud'huy was convinced that the horsemen alone blocked his advance. So his army, still widely dispersed, wheeled to the southeast, in an attempt to outflank and envelop the Germans. He was not prepared to find Rupprecht's Sixth Army shadowing its cavalry. Maud'huy's own cavalry scouts underestimated the numbers and the closeness of the advancing German infantry, which had contrived a wheel of its own. Before long, it was the French who risked being outflanked and enveloped.

For the first week of October, and a few days beyond, the struggle for Arras unfolded along the ridges of Artois, with their cornfields (as Europeans call wheat) just harvested, their wide-spreading, shelterless pastures, and tight network of farming villages. The ridges dominated the town that the Spanish had once occupied: many of its buildings and its wide central square still had a Spanish flavor. Men fought aboveground and dragged artillery into the front lines, where guns could fire over open sights. By the end of the battle, trenches had appeared. They seemed to bring the startling casualty roll of the first days under control, replacing that essential trait of the Killing Season, open warfare, with stationary defenses.

Arras did have the good fortune to be defended by one of the best divisions in the French Army, the 77th Alpine, a unit made up largely of mountaineers, men accustomed to a rigorous life. It had just come from sharp fighting in the Vosges Mountains, its home territory. The commander of the 77th Alpine was a remarkable man, already something of a legend, named Ernest Barbot. He was a tall, lean, quietly thoughtful individual whose long face narrowed into a graying goatee. He wore a common soldier's blue greatcoat and a black beret. He refused to carry a weapon. Hands in his pockets, he habitually placed himself in the thick of any action; Arras was no exception. Being deliberately conspicuous would get him killed the following spring, when a shell burst ripped his chest open. The 77th Alpine came to be known as La Division Barbot.

The 77th Alpine marched into war almost as soon as it disembarked from the trains that had carried it. Outflankers were about to collide with outflankers, and the slugfest known as the Battle of Arras began sooner than anyone had planned. Neither side believed that the other was so close. On the evening of October 1, advanced units of La Division Barbot found themselves unexpectedly struggling with Rupprecht's Bavarians for possession of the ridge villages east of town. The house-to-house fighting continued through the night. At daybreak the bulk of La Division Barbot advanced in a thick fog that obscured all but the most immediate features of the landscape. Men ran into high fences and lost time and cohesion clambering over them. Units strayed and became separated. As the fog lifted, the French collided with dense lines of Bavarians. They tried to withdraw up a long slope: massed rifle fire cut them down and howitzer shells burst in their midst. But Barbot's disciplined men, after sustaining the initial shock of unexpected encounter, did manage to retreat in good order, killing more of the enemy than they lost themselves. All day the fighting swayed back and forth over open pastures and freshly harvested wheat fields, now swept by thresherlike shrapnel. Early in the afternoon Barbot, worried that his lines would give way, dispatched a messenger to headquarters, asking for reinforcements. They were promised. Meanwhile a breach did open. Though diminished in numbers, Barbot's riflemen plugged the gap.

It was dark and 7 P.M. by the time the fresh units arrived. The Bavarians had pushed the French back to the eastern suburbs. The next day headquarters ordered Barbot to retreat. That would have meant giving up the town. Barbot refused. In any event, Rupprecht had decided by then that Arras was not worth the human cost. For both sides, it was already unreasonably high. Of the 12,000 men of La Division Barbot who had reached the town on September 30, just 3,000 remained standing five days later. But Arras had held.

MEANWHILE, THE BY–NOW INEVITABLE TRENCHES made their semi–circuit around the town and headed in the direction of the nine–mile–long Vimy Ridge. Here medieval miners had hacked chalk from what became a labyrinth of tunnels, Huguenots had hidden underground in the sixteenth and seventeenth centuries, and the duke of Marlborough had launched his dazzling campaign of 1711 nearby, feinting and maneuvering through the trenches of Ne Plus Ultra.

No such operational adroitness manifested itself at Vimy in 1914, just the power of German numbers. Round-the-clock assaults did dislodge the French, as the Germans managed to gain outflanking positions at both ends of the heights, forcing Fayolle's 70th Division to evacuate them. The stream of contradictory orders he received didn't help: to attack one moment, to maintain a stance of "aggressive defense" (whatever that meant) the next. "This wavering is deplorable," Fayolle complained in his secret journal.

Where armies had, days before, raced across the landscape, they now seemed to disappear into it. The commander of the I Bavarian Reserve Corps, Gen. Karl Ritter von Fasbender, made a depressed entry in his diary: "Thus we sink deeper and deeper into the earth, eyeball to eyeball with the enemy. We lie for weeks, even months, largely passively across from one another. Few of us have the nerve to demand that the troops advance." But, pushed by Falkenhayn, Rupprecht made the demand, and the casualties on the German side climbed ever higher. Fasbender reckoned that his Bavarians lost an average of 7 officers and 240 men each day. On October 4, the kaiser showed up in the Arras sector. An inveterate war gamer, he suggested that German cavalry make a sweeping maneuver into the enemy rear. Knowing what that could mean in terms of lives lost, Fasbender stood by, speechless. Falkenhayn sensed his upset. "Just hold your position," he whispered. "That suffices." Two days later Falkenhayn decided to give up on the Somme and Arras and to continue heading north, in the direction of Lille, Flanders, and the Channel ports.

This German Army was no longer a well-oiled machine: Schlieffen would have been horrified. Confusion behind the lines was the rule rather than the exception. Infantry commanders operated without maps or neglected to reconnoiter terrain. Units strayed off course. Ammunition supplies were exhausted. Field kitchens didn't show up. Casualties soared. The shortage of experienced officers became a crisis; morale deteriorated. Men, ordered to attack, refused to budge from their trenches. They also refused to shoot when the other side ventured into the space between trenches to collect dead or wounded—and the French held their fire in return. "An ad hoc live-and-let-live system was beginning to take shape," historian Holger H. Herwig has noted. Most worrying of all, "hysteria or perverse sensitivity" (the general's words) became epidemic. The Allies would call it shell shock.

In the meantime the "race" had already moved north. The Germans had reached the great industrial plain of French Flanders, a stretch of surpassing ugliness in its original contours that the Industrial Revolution had reduced to a wasteland of smoking slag heaps and soot-blackened brick and mortar. Now the Industrial Revolution was being supplanted by a newer form of wasteland, the Industrial Battlefield.

ONE GENERAL IN PARTICULAR EMERGED as an inspirational figure in this interval, and in the battle for Ypres that would soon follow: Ferdinand Foch. A bandy-legged little man from the Pyrenees with a handlebar

When the war began, Ferdinand Foch was a corps commander who had never been under fire, best known for his writings on military theory. An apostle of the offense, he proved equally adept as a defender. By mid–October, Foch was Joffre's deputy and number two man in the French Army. (*L'Illustration*)

mustache and a bourgeois background, Foch had been a corps commander at the start of the war, an artilleryman who, in his forty-four years as a soldier (he was then just short of sixty-three), had never been under fire. He had gained peacetime fame for massing 100,000 men at a review in a rectangle of 120 by 100 meters—in his words "a mere pocket handkerchief." The former head of L'École Supérieure de Guerre, Foch was best known as a teacher and theoretician of military science, and had there been no war, he would have been remembered, if faintly, for those talents. His pronouncements would influence a generation of French officers, not always for the better, as well as France's opening moves of 1914.

His lectures had become "enshrined" (Liddell Hart's word) in two once-influential paeans to the offensive, *The Principles of War* (1903) and *The Conduct of War* (1905). He preached the gospel of the power of numbers in battle: "To charge, but charge in numbers as one mass, therein lies safety. . . . Numbers mean surprise for the enemy, the assurance that he cannot resist caused by . . . the rapidity and proportions of the attack which he has neither the time nor the means to parry." Foch wrote that in 1903, at a time when such massed attacks were deemed a prescription for success. Weren't the Japanese proving that at Port Arthur? By 1914, a revolution in armaments had changed everything. In the words of Liddell Hart, otherwise one of Foch's admirers, "numbers could be nullified by the mechanical progress which made one man sitting behind a machine gun the superior of a hundred or more who were advancing on him with a bayonet." The harsh experience of real war, as opposed to that of the lecture hall, put paid to such beliefs, too glibly dispensed, perhaps.

Foch had a gift for aphorism. "The art of war, like every other art," he wrote, "has its theory, its principles, or it would not be an art." He took that a step further: "The goal of the military art is action. Action alone is our concern. The rest is just literature." He was fond of quoting a favorite thinker, the Catholic reactionary and proto-fascist Joseph de Maistre: "A lost battle is a battle which one believes lost"—which he turned on its head. "If defeat comes from moral causes, victory may come from moral causes also, and one may say, 'A battle won is a battle we will not acknowledge to be lost.'" He had an unshakeable, all but mystical, confidence in himself. "One goes forward without knowing the future, without knowing if success will come. But it is necessary to go forward all the same, for in certain cases anything is better than retreat." When in doubt, attack.

Foch's military mysticism only grew more pronounced with age. He developed a tendency to speak in parables that his listeners might not fathom for days, if at all. E. L. Spears wrote that Foch "provided an endless source of fun, with his wooden movements, his cap on one side and his cigar that would never draw and that he was for ever re-lighting." At mess, a young officer imitating Foch's lecture style would pull out a chair and sit astride it, as Foch would do, and strike match after match while he tried to light an imaginary cigar, and then exclaim:

"Le perroquet, animal subtil. . . ." which was actually what Foch had said when he had tried years before to give a lecture on advanced guards. The general had stood for a quarter of an hour trying to get a word out, then the astonishing sentence had burst forth in time to prevent his dying of apoplexy. That had been the end of the lecture, and his audience had thought Foch had this time really gone off his head, but one cleverer than the others guessed the riddle. A parrot climbing up its cage seizes the bar with its beak, then another with its claw and only when these two points are firmly held does the second claw move up—and so should an advanced guard progress.

He rarely bothered to explain. "*De quoi s'agit-il?*"—What is the problem?—was his constant refrain. Some really did think him insane.

In argument, throughout his career, Foch tended to win by intimidation, deliberate arrogance, and a loud voice—irresistible, perhaps, because he never admitted to doubts. He could be rude, insufferable—and he could also inspire. He didn't care whom he was talking to. He told Albert in October 1914 that if he did not hold on to what was left of Belgium, he could forget being king after the war. In the same conversation, Foch, ever blunt, told the king that he would need forty-eight hours to get reinforcements to him. Albert waffled. To accept help from a foreign power, the constitution required him to consult his ministers first. "*Je me f——— de la Constitution, Sire,*" said Foch. Fuck the constitution.

But the man could fight as well as talk. The beginning of the war found him leading the XX Corps of the Second Army, an elite unit based in Nancy, where it watched over the frontier with Germany. Foch was a hands-on commander, forever an optimist and an opportunist, a believer in making the most of the moment. His energy astounded. At Morhange on August 20—it's hard to think that he had never before tasted combat—Foch's cool handling of the rearguard operation of his XX Corps helped to avert a complete catastrophe. Curiously, France's preeminent apostle of the offensive made his first great impression in a retreat.

The battle had begun with XX Corps, in the true Fochian fashion, advancing on the Germans, in violation of the orders of Castelnau, the commander of the Second Army, to stay put. Foch later claimed that Castelnau's order had never reached him, an explanation that Castelnau would forever deride as "puerile." It didn't matter. The Germans attacked first, storming down from the tableland around Morhange under cover of heavy artillery and a dense fog. They caught the French by surprise. An unexpected reverse quickly turned into a rout, with roads jammed with horse-drawn artillery, ambulances, staff cars, and troops fleeing for the elusive safety of the rear. Foch's two divisions held, shielding the retreat of Castelnau's army. As his exemplary biographer Elizabeth Greenhalgh concludes, "The question of the (non-)arrival of the order would not have mattered if the day had been a French success. It was not."

Joffre, meanwhile, had found much to admire in the former professor's sangfroid under fire. On August 28, he telegraphed Castelnau, asking him to dispatch Foch to his new headquarters at Romilly-sur-Seine. Joffre needed him, he said, "for an important command." That command was the new, and hastily cobbled-together, Ninth Army, which was forming up in Champagne, to the northeast of Rheims. Castelnau, to say the least, was not unhappy to see Foch go.

Though the Ninth would exist for barely more than a month, Foch responded to his new role as if destiny depended on his performance, speedily pulling together a ragtag force, mounting a defense, and then turning a perilous situation around at the last possible moment.

The Ninth Army found itself in a long, wide, water-soaked trough, a place of swamps crossed by narrow causeways, the marshes of Saint-Gond, named after a hermit monk who had lived here in the seventh century. To the west, the marshes rose into thick woods; to the east, into downlands, arid, chalky, and bare. A long, low ridge occupied the south, a final barrier before a flat and featureless expanse, the steppes of France, the vast plain of the Aube, where the southern horizon disappears into the haze of distance. Had the Germans been able to spill over that ridge line and reach those plains, muscling past Foch's improvised army, they would have been able (in Elizabeth Greenhalgh's words) "to break through and split the Allied deployment, rolling up the British and French against the coast, or continuing east to crush the French against the Vosges." You can make an argument that the miles that Foch's improvised army held were the same ones where the Germans still had their best chance for a breakthrough. Hence, the word "decisive" really could have meaning.

The stand of the Ninth Army happened just at the moment when France most needed a show of backbone. There may have been less to it than met the eye, but why quibble with results? Foch's accomplishment could easily have gone otherwise: Schlieffen and Moltke might have been vindicated after all. "It was evident that the only way we could hope to frustrate the plan which . . . the enemy had been methodically executing," Foch wrote in his memoirs, "was to take the offensive ourselves." Even he was at a loss for words to explain his victory in the marshes. He did not know at the time that the collective nerve of the German high commanders had failed them: they had ordered their incredulous legions to retreat and dig in.

The reverse in Allied fortunes came so suddenly that it seemed almost a gift of Providence. "The first days I was beaten," Foch told an acquaintance a year later. "The last day it was a question of holding on. Yet I advanced four miles. Why? I don't know. A good deal because of my men. A little because I had the will—and then, God was there." That was the devout Catholic speaking. But he had another explanation: "I was filled with a wild obstinacy." He talked of seeing "with the utmost distinctness the mission of sacrifice on which my troops were embarked. It was an almost physical vision startling in its clearness, blindingly bright." That was Foch the mystic speaking.

The day of crisis was September 8, 1914. That was the day when elements of Franchet d'Espèrey's Fifth Army and the BEF began to probe the empty space between the German First and Second Armies. It was the day, too, when Generaloberst Max von Hausen—who hadn't lost his nerve—ordered a surprise bayonet attack in the dark, scheduled for 3:45 A.M., German time (2:45—for the French, the depths of the night). All along the left side of Hausen's Third Army line, men fixed bayonets, first removing bullets from their rifles (and, in cases, stowing the bolts in bread pouches), so that they would not be tempted to fire random shots and give themselves away: they were to move forward in total silence until they struck. Foch had his own attack planned for 5 A.M.: Hausen's theatrical rite of mass impalement preempted it. The German divisions advanced under a pale moon, and then, as they collided with the enemy, bugles sounded, drums beat, and cheers rose. The blade-wielding procession overran the sleeping French; the entire right wing of the Ninth Army collapsed in the darkness. Some panicked units didn't stop until they were eight miles back, up on the narrow ridge that guarded the marshes; Foch's own headquarters, which had been far in the rear, was now virtually in the front lines. Not until the German spring offensives of 1918 would comparable gains be made on the Western Front in a single day. The rising sun would reveal, a German account noted, "Green hillsides dotted as if with red and blue flowers"—dead Frenchmen.

Foch always kept the big picture in mind, and he detected German weakness, especially on the right wing of their great sweep through northern France, where a forty-mile-wide gap now yawned. He sent a message to Joffre, calling his situation "excellent." He added that "the attack directed against the Ninth Army appears to be a means to assure the retreat of the German right wing," a correct diagnosis. Though the taking of that final ridge presented such promise to the Germans—fighting centered on a château continued all that day and into the next—perhaps Foch was right: this attack was less danger than diversion. The German First and Second Armies were indeed beginning to pull back, with the French and British following. Foch's words, magnified, became the statement forever associated with him in the public imagination: "My right is driven in, my center is giving way, it's impossible for me to move: the situation is excellent, I attack." He probably never uttered those legendary words, so Fochlike in its cadence as to be almost a parody of the master. But he might well have done so had he thought of them.

Everyone pushed limits that day and the next, Foch especially. "You say you cannot hold on," he said to a despairing corps commander, "and you cannot withdraw, so the only thing left is to attack." His generals thought him mad, that he had gone off his head. But Foch always had a plan. *"Audace réfléchie,"* his right-hand man, Maxime Weygand, called it, "premeditated audacity." Desperate situations can demand desperate solutions.

In the struggle for the marshes of Saint Goud, we encounter the essential Foch, the man who would become one of the best fighting generals of the war, if not the best. He was a man who never let crisis overwhelm his imagination. Here, the teaching of peaceful decades at last took shape. As beaten troops continued to stream back, a gap opened in the right wing of his line. Foch, as Greenhalgh writes, "had a better appreciation of the danger than Hausen of the opportunity." He ordered the imperiled corps commander not just to make a stand but to counterattack. With reservations about the sanity of his leader, the man followed orders. He made the counterattack. The gap closed.

Can there be a better example of *Audace réfléchie* than the *rocade,* or bypass, of the 42nd Division—a term used both in chess and, more mundanely, in European road construction. It was the ninth of September now. Foch was running out of men. He had lost 6,500 in the bayonet disaster. He ordered the man who commanded his best division, General Paul-François Grossetti, to lead his men from their position on the far left of the Ninth Army ten miles to the east—and then mount an afternoon attack. Grossetti—who will show up again in these pages—was a portly Corsican with a pointed white beard, boundless self-assurance, a short temper, but an otherwise unflappable demeanor. His division would march behind the ridge chain that rose out of the trough of swamps, and then pivot north in the direction of Fère-Champenoise, a central village that had fallen in the bayonet attack.

The afternoon-long passage of the 42nd was a magnificent spectacle. First came the ample figure of Grossetti on horseback, a pennon at his side, followed by a long procession of cavalry, artillery, and infantry, all deployed as if on a maneuver march. The scene was one calculated to raise the morale of spectators who had known little but retreat and defeat in recent weeks, and that, as much as anything, was its purpose. By the time Grossetti arrived at his jumping-off position, night was falling, and he judged that an unfamiliar landscape was no place to fight in the dark. His counterattack would have to wait. He reconnoitered himself, asking that a haystack be set on fire to guide him back. Grossetti's little group came on no Germans that night: the enemy had mysteriously vanished.

For the French a miracle had happened. The miracle was something that the Schlieffen Plan had never bargained for: a failure of nerve. When his division and other units of the Ninth Army entered Fère-Champenoise the next morning, it found streets littered with broken bottles up to ten inches deep. "It was difficult," Foch remembered, "to pass on foot, on horseback, or even in a car"—at the time tires were still mainly solid rubber, unpuncturable. The French came on hundreds of Germans passed out in the wine cellars, rudely awoke them, and led their staggering charges off to prisoner's cages. Riflemen picked off others, who tried to escape across the roofs. There was little serious fighting that day. Foch's army was too exhausted to mount much of a pursuit.

JOFFRE WAS CONVINCED THAT HE had at last found a commander with *cran*—"guts." On October 4, he summoned Foch, who drove cross-country from his headquarters in Chalons to Romilly-sur-Seine. He told Foch that he was making the former professor of military science his "*adjoint*," or deputy—his number two man. Foch's immediate task would be to oversee the two northernmost French armies—Castelnau's Second and de Maud'huy's Tenth Army, plus a group of territorial divisions made up of reservists aged thirty-four to forty. Foch would coordinate their movements with those of the British and Albert's Belgians. Joffre asked him to make his way north as soon as possible.

In the next fifty-seven hours, Foch would travel five hundred thirty miles, over cratered dirt roads and hastily repaired bridges, and (he remembered) "through villages disfigured by battle." At 4:30 A.M. on October 5, he arrived at the Picardy schoolhouse that served as Castelnau's headquarters, and, while the general dressed, caught a few moments of sleep on a bench. A haggard Castelnau entered the room and announced to his recent corps commander, now his superior, that after two weeks of continuous and unforgiving combat on the Somme front his army was "almost done for." He insisted that he had to retreat and regroup. Foch refused to listen. "You are speaking to a wall," he said. Soon they were shouting at each other. Not two months had passed since Morhange, but to Castelnau, Foch's failure to obey his orders still festered. Unintentionally rubbing salt in the wound, Foch left behind a written order that commanded Castelnau to hold on, no matter what the cost. Joffre, he said, would send reinforcements as soon as he could. Castelnau had no choice but to obey. But he would never forgive Foch for whatever had happened in the Lorraine debacle.*

By sunrise, Foch was on his way again. His next stop was the village of Aubigny, on the river Scarpe, the same little stream that passes through the northern outskirts of Arras. Here de Maud'huy had just established the headquarters of the Tenth Army. Foch encountered more downcast looks and gloom from the commander of the just-created army and his staff. The Germans were still cascading over the ridges around Arras and were securely entrenched in its eastern suburbs; the situation was going downhill—literally. Once again, Foch administered a jolt of verbal electricity.

"Maud'huy, I embrace you for all you've done," he began, "and for all you will do. You hear what I say, for all you will do!"

He ordered the staff to leave the room. Standing outside the closed door, they could hear Foch's voice, its theatrical anger mounting. "I won't hear anything! You understand! I won't hear anything! I'm deaf! I only know three ways of fighting—Attack—Hold on—Clear out. I forbid the last. Choose between the first two."

The brutal pep talk had the desired effect. De Maud'huy gave his word that he would not budge and would even try to envelop the enemy's flank in Lens, just to the north.

Foch visited de Maud'huy one more time, on October 6. When the general complained that he was still having difficulty containing the German thrust, Foch exclaimed, "Fight to the last man, but hang on like lice. No retirement. Every man to the attack."

The Tenth Army held, but the enveloping maneuver proved to be impossible to carry out. Meanwhile, new trenches began to snake amid the slag heaps and mine tipples of Lens, always pointing northward.

---

* Both men had already lost sons. Two of Castelnau's had been killed, one of them serving in Foch's XX Corps at Morhange. That can't have helped. Foch's only son was missing: his father would soon learn that he had died in the Battle of the Frontiers—along with his son-in-law, the groom at the wedding Sir Henry Wilson had attended in 1910.

We will leave Foch with a last word (he was never short of them): "We had to win the Battle of the Marne so as not to lose the war. Soon it will be necessary to win the Battle of the North Sea."

IN THE RACE TO THE Sea, the Germans could boast of one truly notable prize that autumn: the taking of Lille. The capital city of Flanders, French and Belgian, with a population of more than 200,000 in 1914, it was a center of the coal, iron, and textile industries, where canals and five main rail lines met. Its textile factories supplied four-fifths of France's needs. On a once-central island, Vauban built a star-shaped citadel in the late seventeenth century; it was still in use in 1914. Lille was the most populous French city—the fifth-largest metropolitan area in the nation—that the Germans took in the Great War.

The loss, a ludicrous foul-up, needn't have happened. Lille became the urban anchor for German forces in the northern part of the Western Front, and its conquerors made sure to keep its industries running. Most important, Lille was the terminus of the strategic lateral railway that ran across France to Metz. The severing of that route—which didn't happen until November 1918—was, for the Allies, an objective only a little less glittering than the taking of the Channel ports was for the Germans.

Outliers of Kluck's First Army had briefly occupied Lille in late August. At that point the northwest corner of France was basically empty of arms. After the Germans left, the garrison had somewhat expanded; the need for reinforcements did not seem pressing. Later, the Marne consumed the few men who might otherwise have been available. Not even the approach of the battle line, the ranging of German cavalry in the area, or the flood of refugees that swamped the city seemed cause for alarm.

The morning of October 3 found a division of German infantry probing the approaches to the city; a few shells struck Lille's eastern suburbs, without causing much damage. That afternoon fighting became intense. "A terrible street battle began," a twenty-year-old artilleryman named Herbert Sulzbach wrote in the diary he kept throughout the war. "We were right up at the front; the first barricades had been put up in front of a railway embankment, and the infantry swarmed over them all

Le commencement de la rue de Tournai, place de la Gare.

Les maisons incendiées de la rue du Dragon.

DANS LES RUINES DE LILLE

M. Pierre-Plessis, un jeune poète qui se trouvait à Lille le 13 octobre, date à laquelle les Allemands y firent leur entrée pour la seconde fois, a réussi à s'échapper. Tous ses efforts pour gagner les lignes alliées par Seclin ou Armentières ayant échoué, il se résigna à prendre le chemin le plus long. Déguisé en paysan, il parvint à gagner par la Belgique la frontière hollandaise. Il était sauvé. Il

vient de rentrer en France après un séjour de plus de trois mois dans les lignes allemandes. Il a dit aux lecteurs de notre confrère l'Intransigeant avec quelle superbe résignation la vaillante population lilloise souffre, en attendant la délivrance. Il précise ici les dégâts provoqués par les soldats du kaiser dans le chef-lieu du Nord.

Ces ruines ne sont à présent familières. Je sais leur grandeur tragique.

J'ai erré de la Grand'Place à la rue Faidherbe, et de l'Alhambra à la Préfecture, alors qu'elles étaient rouges encore des lueurs d'incendie. Les jours ont passé; elles me sont apparues plus tard ruisselantes de pluie ou fantômales dans des éclaircies de brouillard. Un soir, le vent furieux les a secouées, et les pans de murs trop audacieux se sont écroulés, mêlant le fracas de leur chute à la voix grondante du canon.

Pauvres choses mortes! Elles disent la rage de destruction dont se glorifient les soldats du kaiser. Bombarder est leur passe-temps, incendier est leur système, car, à Lille, comme en beaucoup d'autres endroits, les barbares continuèrent d'incendier... après le bombardement. Douze cent soixante maisons furent détruites!

Suivez-moi:

Voici l'église Saint-Maurice, trouée en deux endroits; autour d'elle des décombres, à perte de vue.

Voici la rue du Sec-Arembault intacte, mais les rues de Béthune et de l'Hôpital-Militaire n'existent plus.

Voici la Grand'Place et le Corps de garde : les Allemands y pointent sur le perron deux mitrailleuses. Voici la rue Faidherbe, amas de briques et de fer tordu. Le café Jean et l'Alhambra dressent vers le ciel leurs pierres noircies. Le quartier central a souffert davantage, mais de droite et de gauche, dans les autres rues, on voit des maisons éventrées. La Préfecture fut saluée par quatre-vingts obus. Elle a résisté. Le Musée qui lui fait vis-à-vis n'a pas trop souffert, mais un grand nombre des trésors qu'il contenait furent détériorés. Fort heureusement la fameuse « figure de cire » avait été mise à l'abri et les conquérants de passage sont fort mécontents de n'avoir pu la faire fondre... ou la voler!

Dernièrement ils se fâchèrent : « Nous voulons voir la belle fille de Lille » Le général ajouta même : « J'exige! » Les menaces furent sans effet. On lui répondit : « Elle est au Louvre! »...

L'hôpital militaire fut gratifié de tant de grenades incendiaires qu'on dut évacuer les blessés et qu'on ne parvint à maîtriser les flammes qu'au prix de rudes efforts. Les envahisseurs, en entrant dans la ville, coupèrent les conduites d'eau; porter secours aux sinistrés était impossible; il fallut être les muets témoins de l'inutile destruction!

Depuis un mois, les officiers allemands font des ruines de Lille le centre de leurs excursions. Ils viennent de Bruxelles, Tournai, Roubaix en auto. Munis de petits stéréos, ils prennent des vues pittoresques. Ils sont fats, gantés, grossiers et sentent la saucisse. Je me suis heurté à plusieurs sur le trottoir. Les hair sans les connaître est de l'enfantillage, car on ne peut les hair vraiment qu'après les avoir connus! Je les connais et je les hais!

PIERRE-PLESSIS.

Ce qu'il reste d'un immeuble bombardé de la rue des Arts.

Un obus a traversé le fronton du Corps de garde, sur la Grand'Place.

L'Alhambra et le café Jean, rue Faidherbe : cette vue a été prise du Marché aux poulets.

Deux Allemands, un infirmier militaire (à gauche) et un soldat du landsturm, déambulent rue Faidherbe.

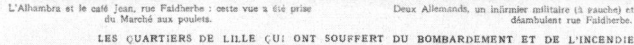

LES QUARTIERS DE LILLE QUI ONT SOUFFERT DU BOMBARDEMENT ET DE L'INCENDIE

The capture of Lille, one of France's great cities, marked Germany's signal triumph in the Race to the Sea. Though the city surrendered after a brief siege, which spared its center, the eastern outskirts were badly roughed up. The photos above were taken by a young man named Pierre-Plessis, who found himself trapped in Lille when the Germans entered. It was winter before he escaped. Disguising himself as a peasant, he made his way across Belgium and managed to cross the Dutch border. He somehow avoided internment and reached Paris. There, in February 1915, *L'Illustration* published this series of secret photos of an occupied city. (*L'Illustration*) with bayonets fixed, and now a dreadful fire was directed at us, and a hail of shots from every window, cellar-opening, and skylight." The German gunners unlimbered their artillery pieces and began firing down the narrow faubourg streets; the façade of a house collapsed, and the building burst into flame. Sulzbach, a limber driver who came from a family of wealthy Jewish bankers, tried to control "wildly rearing animals." He saw the first dead and wounded lying in the street. Orders arrived to pull back the guns. The Germans tried to enter the city by another route but machine-gun fire stopped them. The artillerymen "bivouacked in a meadow and lay in the straw recuperating from our generous baptism of fire."

The next day, October 4, the Germans renewed their attacks. Still, a last train of mobilized French troops was able to leave the Madeleine station and head south. Why were they not held back to defend the city? What misplaced priorities were at work? There are no good answers. Castelnau, apparently, balked at mounting a full defense of Lille: his Second Army, he told Joffre, was already stretched too thin. As he had done at Nancy, he was prepared to give up a major French city and retreat to safety.

Desultory fighting continued. Several times, under fire, Sulzbach and his companions had to throw themselves to the ground. They foraged—"and found some marvelous wine in a deserted château." He made notes in his journal, "lying among the horses." He began to grow a beard. His unit buried its first dead. He found something unfair and ungentlemanly in those early confrontations. "The enemy had fixed it up in such a cowardly way—he didn't let us fight properly, man to man, he just fired on us out of a snug hiding-place!"

In 1914, innocence did not shy from announcing itself. That was its voice.

The more the German siege pressed in on Lille, the clearer it became that they owned a monopoly on urgency. Instead of trying to secure reinforcements, the military commanders of the city (and their political counterparts) continued to send men away. On October 9, the prefect of the Department of the North, the state-appointed administrator for the region, ordered the evacuation of all fit men between the ages of eighteen to forty-eight. But he neglected to check whether the Germans controlled the flight routes. They did. By nightfall the greater number of those designated to escape had returned to the city after hours of dodging through enemy-infested country. The same day, part of the military garrison left Lille, some to participate in the defense of Arras, which had already been saved, others to protect the detraining of British troops to the west. Everyone seemed to believe that the British would come to the rescue. They were too far away to make a difference. A high-ranking staff officer declared complacently that the reduction of the garrison was "without doubt the result of a misunderstanding." No one bothered to rectify it. During the early evening of October 10—the day that Antwerp surrendered—Sulzbach waited to go into action in the eastern suburbs, the faubourgs. He could not believe what he saw: "Strangely, the trams are running, as though there weren't any war!"

Even today we can't be completely sure what really happened at Lille, or how high responsibility for its collapse reached. The deliberate official smokescreen baffled even commanders like Foch, who could have helped. By the time he recognized the peril to the city, and gave the order to send reinforcements, Lille was beyond saving.

After a forced march from the Rheims area of 147 miles in seven days, the German XIX Corps arrived on October 11 to take part in the final siege, along with cavalry and the 26th Division of the XIII Corps. With the troops already in place, the Germans had four divisions— against two French regiments and change. The new formations showed up as Foch was still trying to round up motor transport to speed the move eastward of the British II Corps. The added German corps made the difference. That morning the French defenders in the citadel received German officers, who advanced under a flag of truce. They wanted to discuss terms of a possible surrender: the French did nothing to discourage their approach. The Germans noticed immediately how scant and shabby the garrison appeared. That was all they needed to see. They would clearly be back before long.

The Germans waited until the early morning hours of the twelfth to begin what they hoped would be the final pounding of the city. "You could see a huge fiery glow: Lille was burning," Sulzbach wrote. The bombardment went on through the day. The Germans poured some 15,000 shells on Lille, destroying an estimated 980 buildings and damaging several thousand more. Entire streets were reduced to smoking ruins. The wounds, though, were more psychological than physical. Lille was ready to give up. It remained only for the prefect of the Department of the North to make an official decision. At 6 P.M. someone thrust a white flag from the tower of a landmark in the center of the city, the Church of the Sacré-Coeur. A carrier pigeon flew off to de Maud'huy's headquarters, carrying a message that announced the surrender.

The surrender of Lille merited a special celebration, which took place in the central square, above, on October 13. Troops of the German Sixth Army marched into the town, with bands playing, and soldiers' voices raised in patriotic song. Its commander, Crown Prince Rupprecht of Bavaria, accepted cheers from its open staff car. The war seemed to be turning again in Germany's favor. (*Michelin Illustrated Guides to the Battlefields (1914–1918): Ypres*)

The Germans marched into the city the next day, October 13, singing "Die Wacht am Rhein." They halted in front of the island citadel—it was "in unbelievably scruffy condition," Sulzbach said—where men of the XIX Corps brought out hundreds of prisoners. Bands played. Rupprecht drove through the streets in an open staff car. The German High Command directed the city government to pay an immediate levy of

1,300,000 francs, with another 5,000,000 due at the beginning of November. Days later, parts of the central city were still smoldering.

ONE MISSING ELEMENT IN THE tumultuous tapestry remained: the British.

Once it became clear that Sir John French's divisions could not advance beyond the Chemin des Dames, the strategists in London began to consider departure from that front. For the British, the Aisne highlands had become not just a dead end but also an isolated one. On September 15, Winston Churchill crossed to France, carrying a message from Kitchener for French. Kitchener had asked him to broach the possibility—indeed, the advisability—of moving the BEF to its "natural station" on the Channel coast. Both men worried about the German threat to the almost undefended ports now that Paris was no longer in jeopardy. The Aisne front was hardly the best place to protect them, or England itself. Besides, the British Army belonged on the left of the line, where the home island and the Royal Navy were closest.

Churchill drove from Calais to French's headquarters at Fère-en-Tardenois south of the Aisne. It is a measure of that uneasy autumn that he felt it necessary to take a wide detour: there was always the risk of blundering into German cavalry, and a captured Churchill would be a genuine prize. He presented Kitchener's case to Sir John; French raised no objection. Acting as a friend and intermediary, Churchill had (in the words of his biographer Martin Gilbert) "succeeded in averting serious friction over the major question of future strategy."

On the twenty-seventh, Churchill again visited French. No persuading was necessary. By now the field marshal could scarcely wait to begin shifting his troops northward. He wrote to Joffre, making a formal request "to disengage us from our present position as soon as possible and put us on the left flank of the Allied forces." The British Army, he said, would be better utilized in the north—where, also, its cavalry, immobilized on the Aisne front, could be released to operate against the German flank. Nothing, though, was more important than the shortened lines of communication with England, which could only be maintained as long as the Allies were able to deny Germany the Channel ports. "There remains the question of *when* the move should take place." And then French pressed his plea home:

"I submit that *now* is the time."

Joffre's lengthy reply was elaborately polite and prompt, reaching the British marshal the following day. He agreed that French's ultimate goal was a sensible one—in his memoirs he called it "irrefutable"—but there was one problem: Now was not the time. "The movement contemplated . . . would inevitably entail certain complications, not only in the position of the troops but also in those of supply trains, etc. It might possibly create confusion in the general disposition of our armies, the extent of which it would be difficult to foresee." In other words, it would interfere with the "race" northward. Joffre (who always referred to himself in the third person) asked the British commander to delay as long as the northern flank remained open. The name Ypres went unmentioned.

But Sir John did persist. Joffre gave in, with grave reservations. Whether or not it was an afterthought confirmed by the way events worked out, he came to believe that he had made a mistake, something that he did not often admit, and in public. In his memoirs, published posthumously in 1932, the year after his death, he spoke of the problem Sir John had created. One result, he said, was "the almost complete interruption during ten days of the transport of the French troops towards the northern theatre of operations." Worse—and this was a charge that still seems dubious: "the definite loss of the rich region centering in Lille was due, in my opinion, to this operation, my consent to which was accorded only with the greatest regret."

You have to wonder. What if Lille had been saved, but Ypres lost, opening the way to the Channel ports?

French's demands may have seemed rash to Joffre, but the actual British withdrawal from the Aisne highlands and the river valley below was managed with deliberation and care. It began on the night of October 1–2. All movements, including the replacement of units in the line by French troops, were carried out after dark, to hide the large-scale transfer from suspicious aerial eyes. "The French filed in," noted a divisional account, "as our men filed out. There was no interruption from the enemy."

A photo, taken somewhere in northern France, captures a moment in the clandestine transfer of the BEF from the Aisne highlands to Flanders. Cavalry units—in this case, the Eleventh Hussar Regiment (Prince Albert's own)—made the entire journey on horseback. For almost two weeks, the Germans believed that the British were still dug in below the Chemin des Dames. (Pitman Thomas Tait (Major-General) Collection, Imperial War Museum)

During the day, men remained in their billets. They marched in the dark and took roundabout routes, sometimes as much as an added fifty miles, to reach railheads at staggered intervals. Thus the British avoided sudden, and noticeable, increases in train traffic. The cavalry, too, moved at night, traveling by road and taking the same billeting precautions during the day. It worked.

A German wireless message intercepted on October 3 stated that all six British divisions were still dug in. Not until October 8, when two of three British corps had moved out of line and troops were already detraining at Abbeville, at the mouth of the Somme, did German air reconnaissance take note of unusually heavy rail traffic and the movement of lorries and marching columns. The Germans guessed that their destination was the lower Somme valley, perhaps to reinforce a drive eastward into the great plain of northern France.

The two divisions of Sir Horace Smith-Dorrien's II Corps moved first, stopping long enough on the south bank of the Aisne to pick up new greatcoats and blankets. It was clear now that the war would last beyond autumn. By the night of October 3–4, the entire corps was heading for the Compiègne railyards and would soon be boarding freight cars (regular passenger cars for the officers). On the far left of the Aisne line, III Corps handed over its trenches to the French on October 6, and by the next night, its two divisions were on their way to Abbeville. GHQ also moved, first to Abbeville, then to more permanent quarters at Saint-Omer, close to the border with Belgium. Not until the night of October 14–15 did Haig's I Corps completely vacate its Aisne trenches; the men boarded trains between 4 and 6 A.M., while it was still dark. Their destination was the rail center of Hazebrouck in French Flanders, and by the time the first contingents arrived, they could already hear "the sound of heavy gunfire coming from the south-east."

The surreptitious transfer of the BEF to Flanders, Sir John French's most lasting contribution to the war, was complete.

1

Accidental Tourists

IN THE EARLY DAYS OF OCTOBER, THE GERMAN SUPREME COMMAND LOOKED to success in three separate operations. First, as they moved steadily northward, Falkenhayn's armies continued to probe for a breakout point. A new determination to restore their former advantage had replaced the defeatism that had marred the last days of the Marne. Think of the events of the next days as the Schlieffen Plan in reverse. If his armies could out-flank the French, Falkenhayn believed, Paris was still attainable. Oppor-tunities beckoned—and promptly disappeared. Who, now, stops to recall the battles of Noyon, Albert, or Arras? More such local struggles were bound to present themselves. Surely one link in the flimsy Allied chain had to snap. So far the only winners were the trench diggers.

The second key to German success was the taking of Antwerp and Lille: those two major European cities would fall within two days of each other. They were auspicious triumphs, though the cost in time lost was yet to be reckoned. There was a third possibility that had a certain swash-buckling attraction: Eight cavalry divisions, three corps' worth, were to sweep across Flanders, and, it was to be hoped, gather in the Channel ports. As far as the Germans knew, they remained practically undefended.

One more operation, as yet unannounced, was taking shape, and it was the most promising of all. The German Fourth Army, commanded by the Grand Duke Albrecht, was forming up south of Brussels and would be, by the middle of the month, ready to head for an area north of the Lys River, roughly close to a once-famous textile center, Ypres. This was not the same Fourth Army that had been the principal victor at the

Battle of the Frontiers. The emergence of Falkenhayn and the rapidly changing character of the war in the west had brought about reorganizations, reshufflings, and repositionings, not just of regiments, divisions, and corps, but of entire armies. The Fourth was no exception, and was almost entirely a new force. It would be comprised of the divisions commanded by Hans von Beseler, which had just swallowed Antwerp and were now tasked with striking down the Belgian coast and into France, as well as four reserve corps, eight divisions strong, just arrived from Germany. On paper, the Fourth was formidable, as many as 160,000 troops, the majority fresh. The British, whom Falkenhayn still believed to be dug in on the Aisne highlands, were not, in his reckoning, a factor.

He calculated on the disruptive strength of surprise: a lightning breakout to the sea, a joining with Beseler and then the two combining to make a turn south, taking the Channel ports, and, at the right place and moment, another wheeling, this time away from the coast, perhaps down the valley of the Seine. Falkenhayn's aim was, in his own words, nothing less than "to obstruct England's Channel traffic, effectively attack the Island itself, and turn the French flank." Though he never mentioned its name, Paris had to be his ultimate goal. That surprise thrust, followed by the turn at the coast, had the potential to become Falkenhayn's strategic ace in the hole, Schlieffen resurrected. Would the last man on the right finally brush the Channel with his sleeve?*

The plan was daring; it was also risky. The risk lay in the character of the reinforcements he proposed to draw on. Beseler's augmented three-division corps was not the problem. Though it had lost men in the siege

---

* Much about Falkenhayn's intentions has to be informed surmise. The greatest enigma of this period has to be Falkenhayn himself. The German commander in chief was not a person who felt comfortable confiding in others. His secret ruminations remained secret. His memoirs, published at the end of 1919, offer only limited help about his immediate intentions, and speculative diversions none. Records that might have shed light on his intentions that first autumn, both operational and strategic, would be destroyed in the next war. Falkenhayn's one biographer so far, Holger Afflerbach, shuns the counterfactual. I don't mean that as a knock; many fine historians, and Afflerbach is one, refuse to venture into the speculative. Robert Foley's *German Strategy and the Path to Verdun,* a truly exemplary study, is mostly concerned with the subsequent military politics of a stalemated conflict. Unfortunately for history, Falkenhayn died a relatively young sixty-one in 1922. Except for his bare-bones memoir, he remained silent to the end.

of Antwerp and had left behind several thousand more to garrison the captured port city, those who had reached the coast and now were advancing down it at least had some battle experience. The other eight reserve divisions were composed mainly of men who had, in a flush of enthusiasm, volunteered upon the declaration of war. Most of them had escaped the obligatory three-year term of military service, or were older men for whom lessons once learned were far enough behind them to be all but forgotten. Their training had been meager; many of the officers who drilled them had been brought out of retirement and were unversed in the latest innovations in tactics and weaponry. Falkenhayn felt that he had no choice but to use these fresh but practically uninitiated legions. "There was no longer time," he wrote, "to exchange the young troops for tried formations."

THE I AND II CAVALRY Corps, led by Gen. Georg von der Marwitz, set out on October 2; the IV Cavalry Corps (Lt. Gen. Gustav Freiherr von Hollen), two days later. Not only did they aim to outflank the French line, but they also aimed to mask the movements of the Sixth and Fourth Armies, as the one continued to push northward and the other prepared to advance through Belgium from Brussels to the sea.

For a few days more, cavalry still mattered. There was something of the Wild West, wilder even in those swarms of opposing horsemen, wielding their swords and lances, firing their short repeating carbines, the French in their nickel-plated breastplates and prowlike helmets, the German Hussars wearing round, black caps with silvery death's-head facings. The troopers would dash up roads unused to war, clatter across bridges to envelop towns still unscathed, dismount to fight on foot in narrow Old World streets—and then gallop on. The artilleryman Herbert Sulzbach observed the passing of a seemingly endless line of cavalry with appropriate awe:

> One cavalry regiment after another rides past us. The 23rd and 24th Dragoons from Darmstadt, mounted chasseurs from Trier, regiments from Metz, Karlsruhe, Bruchsal, Mulhouse and Cas-

sel; they trot past us for hours and hours; they look terrific with their lances, and you feel that something very big is going to happen. . . . You feel that a great battle is in preparation and you are suffused with hope and excitement.

German uhlans—whose chief weapon was the lance—lead a calvary foray, like the one that swept into Ypres early in October. Cavalry turned up everywhere in the early months of the war. The speed and mobility made these horse soldiers, with their distinctive square-topped helmets, ubiquitous as long as open warfare lasted. "Uhlan" became a general word for cavalry, the result of so many mounted men, who didn't belong to uhlan regiments but did carry lances, being lumped with them. (World of Triss/Alamy Stock Photo)

Swarms of horsemen were now ranging all over the area on both sides of the Franco-Belgian border. Much of their energy was spent disrupting communications: tearing up rails, bringing down telegraph and telephone wires, and blowing up railroad bridges. It is hard to follow their wanderings. They did meet with scattered harassment from Belgian cyclists, gendarmes, and armed inhabitants, men who didn't seem to worry about being caught and executed as franc-tireurs. The uhlans, as the German cavalrymen were known—the word actually refers to mounted lancers, which not all of them were—occasionally faced more demanding resistance. In a village south of Ghent, factory whistles signaled their approach and Belgian armored cars attacked. Machine gunners hidden in hedges fired on them, as did riflemen from windows and roof openings. The German troopers had to dismount and fight on foot. They routed the ambushers with bayonets. But disengagement was hardly easier beyond the village confines. "It was impossible to see over the flat country on account of those damned hedges and gardens!" read an after-action report. "The artillery could do nothing." The uhlans were fortunate to escape with a minimum of casualties. Meanwhile, to the west, the 6th Cavalry Division, scouting forward from the rail center of Roulers, had reported that the next large town beyond, Ypres, was free of enemy troops.

The Old World put on a notable show at Ypres, whose central square, the Grande Place (or Grote Markt), appears in a prewar photograph of market day. Looming in the rear are the two truly impressive buildings of Ypres, both with architectural features dating from the Middle Ages: the Cloth Hall (center) and St. Martin's Cathedral (right), both relics of the vanished age of Flemish opulence based on the wool trade. (*Michelin Illustrated Guides to the Battlefields (1914–1918): Ypres*)

YPRES MUST HAVE BEEN A magical place in the early fall of 1914, if magic can be attributed to the down-to-earth Flemish. As a center for crafts and culture in the Middle Ages, it had equaled the more famous Bruges and Ghent. But by the beginning of the twentieth century, it had become a self-consciously quaint refuge from the modern world, an involuntary time machine. Its old streets were a definition of the picturesque. That some were unusually wide has an easy explanation: they had originally been canals. One extraordinary structure, the thirteenth-century Cloth Hall, dominated, a Northern European wedding cake. Trading center, warehouse, market, exposition hall, office building, meeting place for local guild representatives as well as for merchants from all over Europe and the Levant—this bulky, sprawling medieval megabuilding still evoked the wealth and power that the Golden Age of Flanders once boasted. Oceangoing ships towed up the stream called the Yperlee—later widened into the Yser Canal—could edge up to the Cloth Hall and unload their goods in return for woven cloth. Ypres linens were mentioned in Chaucer's *Canterbury Tales;* its cloth reached Russia. Ypres, at its prosperous height in the thirteenth century, was said to possess four thousand looms and its population to approach 40,000, a figure never again matched, not even in the fall of 1914, when the Great War turned it for a brief time into what was, in every sense, a boomtown. In November of that year, its population would sink from 18,000 to next to no one in a matter of days.

There was something inescapable about the Cloth Hall, something comfortably bizarre and unexpectedly cosmopolitan—if you could think in such terms that early. The same might be said of its narrow, many-windowed late-Renaissance addition, the Nieuwerck, heaving up like the bow of a galleon becalmed in cobblestones. On market days, the center of town would come to life. The Grande Place, the three-acre main square that the two buildings overlooked, would be crowded with stalls and covered farmers' wagons. A small orchestra would play light music from a central bandstand. Tourists strolling these antique streets would become aware of the high, square belfry tower of the Cloth Hall, with its minaret-like campanile and studded Gothic foolscaps at facing corners. Or, bicycling in the surrounding countryside, they would hear the deep clanging echoes of its carillon intricately chiming the hours. It's not hard to understand why the Germans lobbed shells into the Cloth Hall so methodically for four years, as if going for a cultural jugular of what remained of Belgium.

History has rarely left Ypres alone. The town was deep in the "cockpit of Europe," as Flanders has rightly been called, a political, economic, and military intersection that, like the triumphantly sagging figure at a significant crossroad, of Christ on a crucifix, has long dominated. (If He didn't take sides, sides were taken for Him.) Over the centuries, Rome, France, Spain, Holland, Austria, Great Britain, and Germany have contested it, as well as tribes, dutchies, and principalities dimly, if at all, remembered. It has been said that "when God had made this good Flanders, He put it between all in order that it might be devoured by one after another."

Caesar's legions pursued Belgae tribes in this area—though the Romans wisely confined their incursions to the dry summer months. Even in the first century BCE mud was a campaigner's occupational hazard. The town of Ypres itself began to take shape a thousand years later, in the tenth century, growing up around a ruined castle, a relic of Norman invasions. The thirteenth century would witness the flowering of Ypres and the woolen trade. (Baudoin IX, Count of Flanders, laid the foundation stone of the belfry of the Cloth Hall, its oldest part, in 1201.) The political and social unrest of the fourteenth century saw the beginning of the decline of Ypres. In 1386, an English army, supported by the rival town of Ghent, overran it and drove out many of its artisans and wool traders. There were repeated invasions by the French; Flanders later fell under the sway of the Hapsburgs and the Spanish—who besieged Ypres for eight months in the sixteenth century, plundering and massacring when it finally fell. The Bubonic plague added to the death toll. The French took over again. That supreme fortress builder of the late seventeenth century, Sebastian le Prestre de Vauban, made plans to fortify the town, his characteristic star-shaped brick battlements rising out of the still, dark waters of an outer moat. He devised an intricate system of canals, dikes, and water-carrying ditches to improve communications and to drain the countryside. But his principal intention—Louis XIV's chief military engineer died before his plans were implemented—was to create in Ypres an outlying bastion to shield the larger and more important port stronghold of Dunkirk.

In 1830, Ypres became part of the new kingdom of Belgium. Townspeople, in a rebuilding mood, always, partially tore down Vauban's walls for their brick and stone. The Cloth Hall, though, was never at risk to deconstructors. By one of those curiosities of history, its belfry was encased in scaffolding when the first German shell struck on November 22, 1914. Restoration work was under way. The town was fixing up its chief ornament in anticipation of the tourists who had begun to discover it in increasing numbers and who would surely throng its winding streets in the summer of 1915.

LATE IN THE AFTERNOON OF October 7, the German 3rd Cavalry Division, plus cyclists and infantry, 8,000 men in all, entered Ypres. The curé of St. James Church, Fr. Camille Delaere, recorded in his diary that their appearance was announced with a show of cannonading: the curé described "the whistle of shells, the explosions, the humming of bullets, the appalling sight of my poor people flying in terror. Fathers and mothers all weighed down with children and bundles, with pale faces and frightened eyes, running like madmen to the Grande Place to hide from the enemy approaching so rapidly and to escape the bullets." Shrapnel balls pierced the centuries-old stained glass of his church and a shell exploded against the bell tower.

The long column of German cavalry galloped down the road from Gheluvelt—a name to remember—followed by horse artillery and lorries heaped with ammunition and provisions. It took six hours for the procession to pass through the Menin Gate to the center of town. Two stone lions flanked the passageway through the Vauban ramparts: the inhabitants (so one story goes) had placed straw in their mouths, hoping that the Germans would not show up until the animals had made a meal of it.

Horses and their riders filled the Grande Place, where troopers stacked their rifles. Officers entered the Nieuwerck, which served as the hôtel de ville, the city hall. They demanded a levy of 70,000 francs. There were only 65,000 francs in the municipal treasury; the Germans took them. They also demanded that the post office till be opened, found only 127 francs, and took them too. The Germans also did some late-afternoon pillaging, scooping up food and men's clothing, underwear especially. From Madame Heursel's jewelry store on the rue au Beurre, they lifted 35,000 francs' worth of watches. "The railway station had also to suffer,"

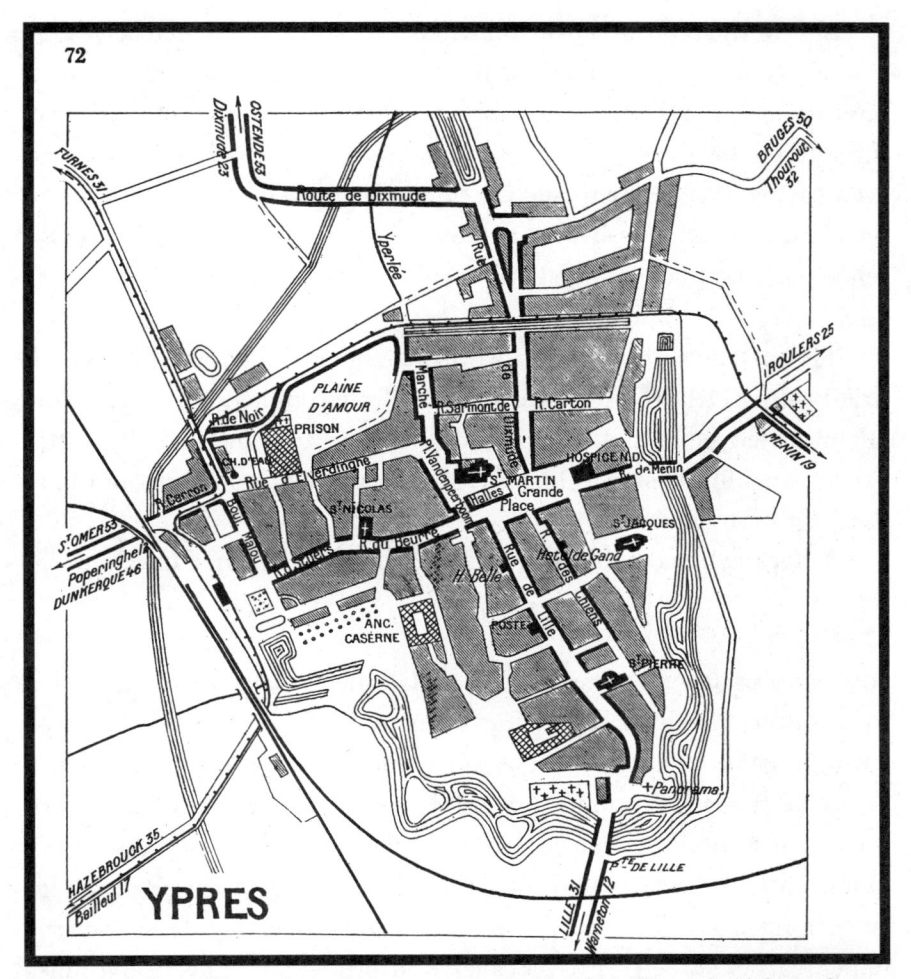

This street plan of Ypres shows the town as it looked in 1914. The main highway from the east, the Menin Road, entered (right center), passing twin lions of the gateless Menin Gate, and leading to the Grande Place. The Cloth Hall (center) presided over that busy square, and had for seven centuries, since the laying of the first stones of the main tower in the 1200s. (*Michelin Guide to Ypres and Its Battlefields*, 1919)

an eyewitness recorded, "the telegraph and telephone lines being all cut. . . . A great number of horses were put in the waiting-rooms at the station, destroying all the cushions and furniture. The soldiers demanded shelter in whatever house they pleased, and no one dared refuse them anything. . . . The most anxious of all were those who were actually housing wounded Belgian soldiers." In one case, Germans spent the night in a room underneath recovering men.

But for the most part, the uninvited tourists behaved themselves. "A marvelous evening mood spread through the ranks," a Bavarian captain remembered. Many used this respite from war as an opportunity to stroll through the town, admiring "a scene right out of the Middle Ages" and even paying cash for items such as pricey Belgian cigars. "The shops on the main street were as elegant as those of a large city," one uhlan captain remarked. And then he added, "We could almost feel the proximity of the sea."

"Twenty or so cavalrymen with their horses took over my church hall," Father Delaere wrote. He refrained from commenting on the odorous mess left behind. The curé did note that someone had chalked in French on a blackboard: "The Germans fear God, but apart from Him they fear nothing in the world."

As for the lions of the Menin Gate, the straw remained uneaten.

FOR MUCH OF THE NEXT week the three German cavalry corps continued to roam the Flanders area. A Lieutenant Count Stolberg-Rossla of the 23rd Dragoon Regiment—the cavalry, among all the combatants, was a favored refuge for the military-minded aristocracy—rode with a party of horsemen in the direction of Dunkirk. Did his superiors really expect him to enter and occupy one of the Channel ports, or was he off on a freelance burst of glory? Stolberg-Rossla and his band arrived at a spot on the upper reaches of the Yser River called Rousbrügge Crossing, twelve miles from Dunkirk. His squadron ran up against a barricaded bridge and, after a brief skirmish, retired. Twelve miles. Remember that distance.

Now British troops were beginning to take their place in the line, beside French units and, north of Ypres, the much-diminished Belgian Army. By October 11, noted the *Official History*, "a complete though thin line of alternate infantry and cavalry corps was established to the sea." A few gaps remained to be filled. By the next day the new arrivals were involved in fierce firefights, the first between British and Germans in Flanders. North of La Bassée Canal, a major waterway, Sir Horace Smith-Dorrien's II Corps found itself in a landscape like none other the BEF had yet disputed, a stretch of almost sublime ugliness. Here was ground that was, the *Official History* said, "little better than a morass. . . . It was dismal country to work over and depressing to dwell in. And it was to become worse." What a dreadful place this must have been to see or breathe your last in. Death had become a major industry in these featureless hectares. Over the next week, from October 12th to 18th, the II Corps lost close to 3,000 men. One of them was a major general, Hubert Hamilton, Lord Kitchener's former military secretary, killed by a shrapnel pellet as he surveyed that naked landscape.

But this was a landscape that could abruptly change around the next hedge-obscured corner or with a sudden rise of elevation. Even as the soggy plain was being contested, so were the low but attractive heights just to the west. On October 12, Lt. Gen. Edmund Allenby's cavalry corps collided with elements of the German IV Cavalry Corps. The Germans were holed up in a monastery at the crest of a hill called Mont des Cats. There was no stirring Lady Butleresque gallop to glory. Instead, dismounted cavalrymen of the 4th Hussars and 5th Lancers sneaked and dodged their way through hop fields on the lower slopes and after a hard, but brief, fight at dusk, drove the enemy from the hill. The Germans had to leave behind a badly wounded royal, the kaiser's nephew, Prince Max of Hesse; he later died. (He gave his gold pocket watch to the Irish doctor who tried to save his life.) On October 13 the British rode on, heading for the ridges that cupped Ypres.

Such furtive sorties on the part of both sides may not have amounted to much, but in one respect the German cavalry had proved its usefulness. The French and British were totally unprepared for the arrival of the German Fourth Army—or any new force, whatever its size—and in the coming days their ignorance nearly led them into a mistake that could have proved fatal. At risk of belaboring the already obvious, the deficient state of military intelligence in 1914 was once again notable. How else could whole armies advance through long-domesticated landscapes of a small nation and not be detected? Faulty information, or the total lack thereof, was surely one of the principal causes of an ever-lengthening war, one that had begun to spin out of control, taking on a life of its own.

Cavalry's days on the Western Front were dwindling to a precious few. The closing of the line, by now inevitable, would doom it, as would the machine-gun and massed-artillery fire. On October 15, a Lt. Carl Friedrich Erich Holck of the 9th Dragoon Regiment, a well-known jockey in Germany, went on a patrol mission to find out the position of the British 4th Division astride the river Lys. Holck, who would later die in air combat, "accurately located" the whereabouts of the division—the official German fails to say how, exactly—and returned to confirm his sighting. His may have been one of the last scouting exploits by horsemen on the Western Front. Until Holck made his discovery, the Germans believed that the 4th Division was still dug in on the Aisne heights. This was one further bit of evidence that the Allies were making a major troop shift.

In the next days and weeks, thousands of men, with their mounts, gear, and fodder supplies, would be loaded on trains and shipped east. On that other front, a far more open one, horse soldiers still had the ability to alter the tilt of a battle. Those who remained found themselves employed as dismounted infantry. For counts, barons, and former jockeys mired in freshly dug trenches, it was an unsought comedown. No wonder so many of them switched to the cavalry of the skies.

ON OCTOBER 10, ABOUT THE time that Antwerp surrendered, a meeting that included Albert, his defense minister, Lt. Gen. Rawlinson, and Gen. Paul Marie Pau, Joffre's representative, took place in Ostend. Pau, who had lost his right hand in the Franco-Prussian War, had retired in 1913, after a distinguished, if unspectacular, military career. He had returned to duty when hostilities broke out. Joffre put him in command of the Army of Alsace on the French far right, but his force was so disastrously roughed up that Joffre relieved him of command and dissolved his army. But the commander in chief saw other uses for him. Thereafter the grandfatherly looking Pau served frequently as Joffre's emissary at meetings like the one at Ostend. He had, in fact, accompanied Albert on horseback in the retreat from Antwerp.

The meeting lasted barely half an hour, but those thirty minutes were evidently unpleasant ones. The subject was nothing less than the fate of Belgium—and, to a lesser extent, of Albert himself. Joffre had insisted that Pau persuade the Belgians to take part in a major offensive that would sweep the Germans back from French Flanders, retake Lille, and keep the entire coast in Allied hands. Albert would have none of the French plan. He had to regroup his men, most of whom were still marching or on trains headed south, and allow them needed rest. Pau backed down. For the moment, as he admitted, "The Belgian Army is not in a condition to fight." But he infuriated the king by suggesting that Albert give up personal command.

Since notes of the meeting are lacking, the decisions made can only be guessed at. Albert's faithful shadow, his chief of staff Émile Galet, was the main witness. The official story, and one that seems reasonable, is that Albert insisted on keeping whatever small portion of his nation that still remained. He would make his stand on "the last strip of national territory." Once the Germans controlled all of Belgium, he pointed out, they would be free to set up a figurehead government, which much of the world would be forced to recognize. This was not the moment "to resign to others the duty of leading" Belgium "in the desperate struggle that was approaching."

There are, however, indications that Albert toyed with the notion of sending his army to France. The next morning, October 11, Pau telegraphed Joffre that the Belgian Army would be crossing the border into France—and that, in fact, one division would arrive by train in Calais that day. (The French had started to prepare barracks there for the entire Belgian Army.) Had that happened, there might well have been no stand at Ypres. But the transfer of the division never did take place. Joffre complained that any movement by the Belgian Army might hinder French transport moving north. Then Albert changed his mind. He recognized that he needed every man available close by. The idea of making a stand on the Yser River, where his divisions were gathering, had begun to take shape.

Albert wanted no part of French offensive schemes. "It might suit the Allies, who had at their disposal a military machine of almost unlimited resources, to undertake hazardous adventures," wrote Galet (who spoke for Albert), "but for us, reduced to the remnant of an army standing with its back to the frontier, such adventures were out of the question." That for Albert's Belgians the next battle "would assume a defensive form was a foregone conclusion."

There was no better stretch of ground for that defense than the Yser River, which emptied into the North Sea at Nieuport; its canal extension bent southward at Dixmude and headed for Ypres. The river itself, which rose in the sandstone hills just across the border with France, was forty-eight miles long. The position along its left bank "formed a veritable natural entrenched camp," and the built-up banks were ready-made parapets. The river may have been narrow, but it was much too deep to wade across. The bridge crossings were few; the Belgians soon dynamited them. Once the brigade of French Marines reached Dixmude from the east on October 15, it linked up with the Belgian Army. The river rampart took shape. As the British military historian C.R.M.F. Cruttwell wrote, "The Yser, merely the largest of the numerous intersecting dikes, is surely

Six days after the Germans made their first (and last) visit to Ypres, it was the turn of the Allies. Here, a long line of infantrymen of the British Seventh Division parades through town. By evening, some of these men would be digging trenches. (Imperial War Museum)

the most insignificant stream that is assured of an immortality in history."

EARLY IN THE AFTERNOON OF October 14, a day of cold, hard autumn rain, the 7th Division, led by a long line of horsemen, entered Ypres, the first British troops to arrive in the town. A military marching band followed the cavalry across the Grande Place, playing "Tipperary" *and* "La Marseillaise." The division, part of Rawlinson's IV Corps, had landed on the Belgian coast a week earlier, but Antwerp, its destination, had fallen before the 7th could reach the port. It had retreated west, stopping in Roulers the previous night. The French 87th Territorial Division, middle-aged reservists, had already arrived in Ypres. Though destined for Antwerp, they, too, had never come close.

Braving the rain, an animated crowd deluged the troops with pears, apples, pipe tobacco, cigarettes and matches, cups of coffee, and glasses of beer. One of the spectators was an Irish nun from an abbey that had existed in Ypres for two hundred and fifty years. "What excited the most curiosity," she wrote, "were the 'petticoats,' as they were styled, of the Highlanders." The burgomaster emerged from the Nieuwerck with a delegation of prominent locals to welcome the newcomers formally. He suggested quartering the horses in one of the vast ground-floor rooms. As they were led in, the horses began slipping on the marble floors. They ended up being tethered in the wide street that ran between the Cloth Hall and another splendid medieval edifice, St. Martin's Cathedral. The rain stopped. The crowd could hear the occasional crack and rumble of distant rifle and cannon fire that came from the south.

While a British billeting team "engaged in chalking the doors of houses with the number of men to be accommodated," the British *Official History* noted, "a party of Uhlans appeared." They had apparently slipped into some back streets at the east end of town. The billeting parties fired on them, a Yorkshire quartermaster "bagging" one German trooper; the rest fled to the refuge of a wood, where a cavalry detachment rounded up the remaining twenty.

A car passed through town, carrying a captured uhlan and, seated in back next to him, a British officer who exhibited to eager onlookers his lance and distinctive square-topped helmet. A pair of new-model antiaircraft guns, one on the back of a lorry, the other horse-drawn, set up shop on the Grande Place and promptly began pumping away at, but not hitting, a passing Taube observation craft—also pursued, but not caught, by five or six British planes. The bakers of Ypres had to work an extra shift to provide enough bread for the arriving troops.

Later that afternoon, as if to signal the new reality of that war, men of the 7th Division went out to dig the first trenches on what would soon become the battlefield of Ypres. Before long, the division would be on the march again, probing for enemy forces—wherever they might be. "The country people," the divisional historian later reported, "were full of rumours of the advance of large bodies of Germans and the 3rd Cavalry Division [which belonged to Rawlinson's IV Corps] reported several encounters with hostile patrols and the presence of the enemy in force a little to the Eastward. Accordingly the troops started to entrench."

THE CHIEF PLAYERS WERE RAPIDLY taking their places in the Flanders landscape. Four battalions and a machine-gun company belonging to the French Marine Fusiliers advance guard marched into Dixmude on October 15, the day after the 7th Division reached Ypres. With a population of 4,000, less than one-third that of Ypres, Dixmude was little more than an oversized village, though the concentration of buildings in an otherwise empty rural landscape gave an impression of greater size. Dixmude was another of those Old World places favored by genre painters, a town of ancient houses with crow-stepped gables painted bright green or yellow, a sixteenth-century church, and a narrow residencia where Spanish governors of the district had once resided. The Yser ran through Dixmude, so narrow in stretches that the houses on either bank seemed to touch. Outside of town, pastures, sugar-beet fields, and, shading the roads, endless lines of poplars stretched off into the sealike horizon. In the weeks to come, the town would prove to be one of the anchors of this part of the Western Front.

The marines immediately set to work digging trenches on the eastern outskirts. The Germans were close behind: shrapnel began to burst over the roofs, and most locals, except those who took shelter in their cellars, joined the swelling refugee ranks. The marines repelled a raid by cyclists and an armored car. German attacks intensified as more of their men came up, but the makeshift trenches held. As yet, the marines had no barbed wire. That Sunday, October 18, a tall Belgian officer wearing a closely buttoned cape and eyeglasses visited the front line with the marine commander, the stubby, bearded Rear Admiral Pierre Ronarc'h.

By the Yser, the officer shook hands with the admiral and then paused for a moment, wrote a French journalist, "gazing at the triangle of marshes, all that remained to him of his kingdom." It was Albert.

IN QUICK SUCCESSION, THE GERMAN Fourth Army, with Beseler's III Reserve Corps on its right, had swallowed Ghent, Bruges, and, on October 15, the North Sea port of Ostend. The conquerors then headed south for Nieuport, at the mouth of the Yser. You might say that the Fourth had won the Race to the Sea, but not from the direction intended, nor with the places desired.

It is hard to associate the parochial order and unnerving stillness of the Flemish countryside with the sights and sensations of those wild days: the singing columns of German soldiers (they lifted their voices partly out of enthusiasm, partly to bolster morale and esprit de corps), the leaden skies and constant rain, the dust of summer churning into the mud of autumn, the unseasonable thunder of distant cannon fire, the villages burning on the night horizon, and, permeating everything, the rancid odor of thousands of marching men in their sweat-steeped woolen uniforms, an odor that lingered in the air, mingling with the pungently familiar barnyard smells long after the columns had disappeared into the mist.

Screens of cavalry swept in front, uhlans searching for the enemy rear guard. Somewhere ahead were the Belgians. The greater number were refugees, packed into the last trains or fleeing by car, by cart, or on foot, heading for the French border and already crowding into the Channel ports. (A quarter of a million made their way to the U.K., most of whom returned when the war was over.) The exodus of populations on such a grand scale was a new phenomenon—but then, so was the "front" that caused it. Mixed in with the refugees were units of Albert's army. It is hard to imagine less martial-looking groups of men. They wore a mélange of uniforms and headgear. All manner of containers from bottles, cans, and flasks hung from their belts. Instead of knapsacks, the one item they all seemed to carry was a bag of rough gray cloth called a *balachon*. Many would turn up at the Yser wearing *sabots*, wooden clogs.

In the first two and a half months of the war, the Belgian field army had shrunk to an estimated 53,000 effectives, less than half its original size; by October 15, nearly 90,000 were casualties. It was a demoralized force that reached, and crossed, the Yser, men who had only known defeat. "We had reached our limit," Galet admitted. Even the king himself was losing hope. "Situation very bad," his wife, Elisabeth, wrote in her journal on October 15. "Everything seems black to Albert."

Though his original preference had been to continue the retreat and reorganize his shattered forces behind the French border, he changed his mind. He was too intent on retaining that tiny piece of his country. The following day, October 16, the king met with Foch. Their conference over lunch took place at the town hall of Furnes, where the king had established his headquarters. Foch, who had driven from Dunkirk on roads packed with refugees, was late and in a bad mood. Galet described an introduction decidedly on the frosty side.

> The General's reputation as a military writer was, of course, well known, and on greeting him, the king graciously complimented him on his knowledge of strategy. He responded with that brusqueness which has become legendary: "There is no such thing as the art of war!" This remark rather chilled the atmosphere.

Foch then insisted that Albert make a stand along the Yser, half a dozen miles to the north. The general-king said that he had already resolved to do so, if with some reluctance. Though he was determined to hold on to a small portion of his nation, he also pointed out to Foch the disadvantages of the front outlined by the river. It would be impossible to dig trenches more than a couple of feet deep in the low-lying, water-logged soil of the Yser line: to resist the enormous German siege guns, trenches were necessary, and the deeper the better. He warned that his men could not hold out for long. Once again he refused to agree to the voluble Foch's demand that his men join in the offensive he and Joffre were planning along the whole Flanders front. Always a clever negotiator, the king apparently used his reservations about the offensive, as well as his conviction that a big German attack was coming on the Yser, to extract from Foch a grudging promise of reinforcements.

Whatever his private misgivings, Albert kept them to himself. Once he had given his word, he held to it. Even as his wife was scribbling that gloomy entry, he issued a general order: "The line of the Yser constitutes our last line of defense in Belgium. . . . This line will be held at all costs."

The progress of the Germans had been just slow enough to allow Albert's men an interval of rest. It was at ten minutes after six on the morning of October 17 when they woke to the first sound of cannon fire along the Yser.

8

October Surprise

THE LEAVES MAY NOT YET HAVE FALLEN FROM THE TREES OF 1914, BUT WITH each passing day, hopes of a quick ending receded. Both the Allies and the Germans had gambled on a short war in the west; both were losing their bets.

There was another reason, obvious but rarely discussed, for a war that soon escaped the control of the men directing it. Those first months lacked great captains. Schlieffen, the one military genius of his time, if a somewhat mad one, was dead. The new war with its mass armies was a conflict on a scale and of a complexity that no one was prepared to deal with. It daunted the very men who had been preparing for continental combat their whole lives. Too many may have been adept at confronting grand strategic concepts but not operational or tactical realities.

There is no better example than Moltke. Chronic health problems alone should have disqualified him for command. But even if he had been in the pink he would have faced unexpected difficulties. Poor communications and not a lack of innate ability doomed him. He had too many variables, too many unforeseen contingencies, on too broad a front— fronts—to deal with in too little time, much of it spent in the information-starved dark. He sent the man who was potentially his best general, Ludendorff, to the Eastern Front, where, at the end of August, he master-minded Germany's biggest victory of 1914, Tannenberg. It went for nothing: the German war plan was predicated on a quick win in the west. What if Ludendorff had been involved in the Marne and had been avail-able to buck up his former boss, Moltke? The German military managers on the Western Front that fall were mostly overaged and unwilling to take risks. The three generals on the right of the great scythe—Kluck, Bülow, and Hausen—were all sixty-eight. Falkenhayn may have been younger and a veteran of colonial wars in China, but he had a talent for throwing away his best chances, a pessimist's gift for too much caution when caution was not called for, too little when it was.

Few military managers on the Allied side, the French especially, had ever been under fire. Joffre may have done so once, in a skirmish with Black tribesmen on the way to Timbuktu. A few of his generals, like Lanrezac, Castelnau, or Pau, had fought in the Franco-Prussian War; if anything, the memory of their ancient brushes with death had made them overly wary in venturing into the unfamiliar, and ever-changing, territory of this new conflict. Foch, the former professor of military science, had not experienced combat until Morhange. He quickly took to it. Lower-level commanders like Louis Franchet d'Espèrey and Charles Mangin, who had cut their martial teeth in colonial disturbances—Mangin had been wounded three times—rose fast after war broke out.

Many British officers—and their men—had served in the Boer War, a nasty and prolonged struggle that was not just another colonial slugfest. Men like French, Haig, and Allenby had all learned their trade in South Africa. Close encounters of a violent kind were all very well, but they did not make up for imagination, or the lack thereof. (Foch did have it, sometimes too much, French too little.) Once these early commanders ran out of flanks—and they were doing so rapidly—most of them ran out of ideas. That could be said of both Joffre and Falkenhayn. In Joffre's defense, his refusal to panic, his preternatural calm, at the Marne and the Grand-Couronne, probably saved France. In those two weeks he flirted with greatness. But in the end, tranquility or a sense of order should never be confused with genius. There was more than a little truth in Liddell Hart's perception: "Joffre was not a general, but a national nerve sedative."

Donkeys there were: both sides had their share of them, at no time more than in 1914.

Peace had been no preparation. As one French general wrote of the sour atmosphere at headquarters on the eve of the war, "Did not an un-

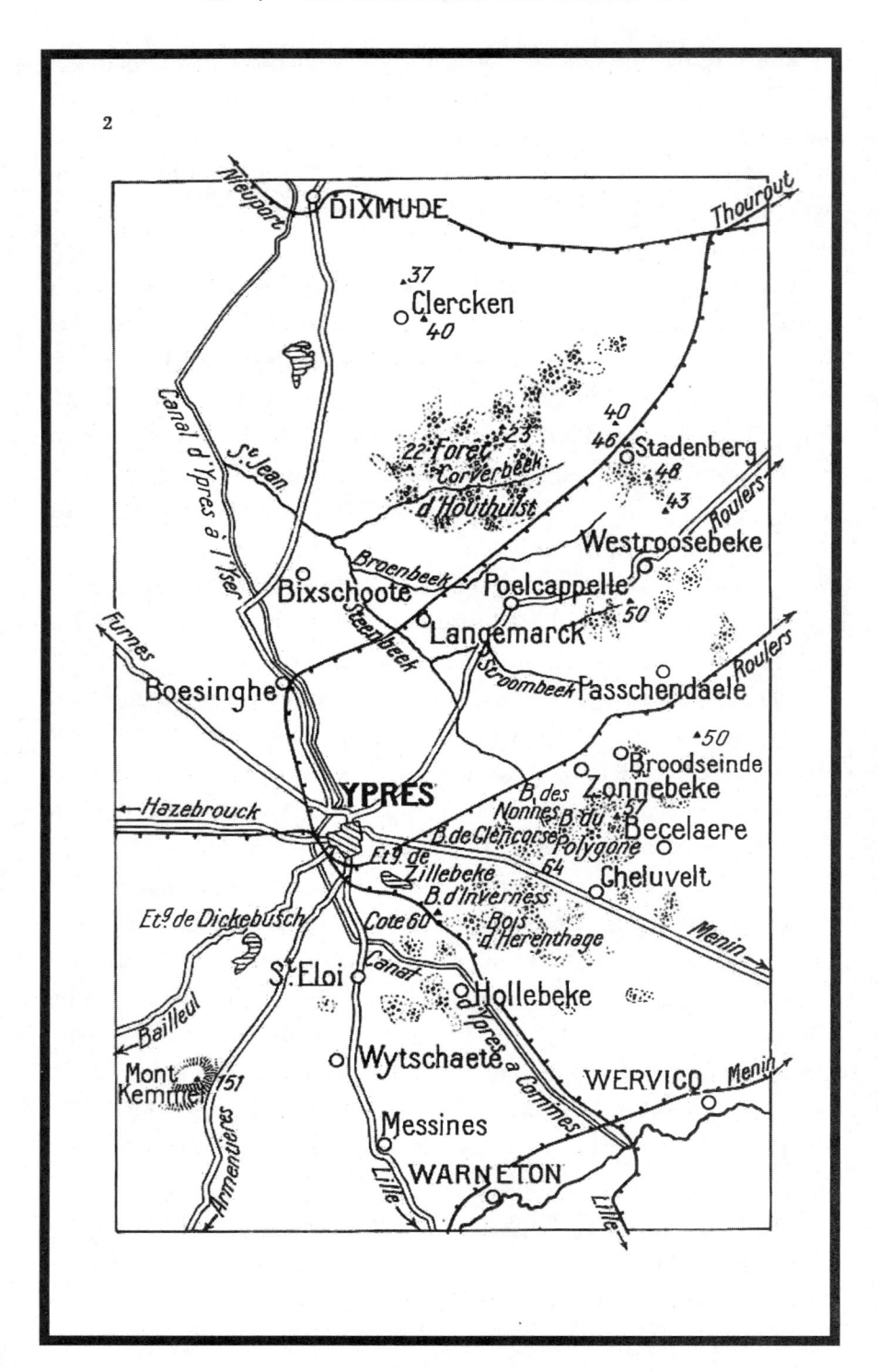

fortunate spirit exist within the army's staff—the deadly result of a peace that had dragged on too long, and of the frustrated ambitions of all these officers cluttering up the departments?" Officers who had never been able to prove their worth on the battlefield made better use of their political and social connections. When, with little warning, war did burst on the world, great numbers who had distinguished themselves as desk warriors were not ready for the challenges of the open field. As Joffre concluded of one general fired after August was not half over, "It did not lie in his power to change his peace-time mentality to that required in war."

A measure of that unpreparedness was the number of generals and colonels who were dismissed in the first five months of the war. Uncertainty can defeat the stoutest of intentions; and stress is no respecter of rank. The example of the French is worth citing, if only because they kept such graphic records. Most of their officers who cracked, or otherwise failed to measure up, were sent back to the 12th Military Region in the interior, whose administrative center was the city of Limoges—which led to the terms *limogés* or *limogeages*, slang for high officers who had been sacked. The reasons varied, as reasons will: an onset of nerves that interfered with giving orders or produced other forms of indecision; exhaustion that paralyzed the will; a teary breakdown; overt fear; a lack of *cran*, guts. In writing a brief but perceptive biography of Joffre, André Bourachot, a retired French general, examined the records of the *limogés*. As he observed, "In 1914 generals received no training in how to with-

Facing page: In the fall of 1914, the area in Belgian Flanders surrounding Ypres and its neighbor thirteen miles to the north, Dixmude, presented a peaceful rural vista, flattening as it swept toward the sea and the Dutch border. Most of its busy multitude of villages were destined to become casualties of war in the next four years. Water was the inescapable element of this landscape, something that this 1920 Michelin Guide to the battlefields doesn't show. The water table lurked just beneath the surface, and humans had struggled for centuries to control the surfeit of moisture and the mud it produced, building an intricate network of drainage ditches that poured into the bekes—brooks—canals, and rivers such as the Lys (at lower right, unmarked). The canal that extended from Dixmude to Ypres had once been the route inland for seagoing vessels that docked at the Cloth Hall, that great medieval omnibuilding, where they were loaded with the woolen goods the region was famous for. When two units of the BEF met below Mount Kemmel (lower left), the Allied line from the North Sea to the Swiss border closed for the duration. The Germans needed a few more days, their final line sealing shut in the Houthulst Forest (center, top).

stand the pressure for a long period. They were not even aware what lay in store for them, since they had no previous experience of modern warfare." Lack of endurance proved a frequent undoing. "Any general who failed to organize his command for the long haul ceased to be of much use after 48 hours spent without sleep while receiving an avalanche of bad news." Battles that were expected to last no more than a few hours went on for days, even weeks and months.

Telling notations, Bourachot discovered, appear in the dossiers of the *limogés:* "Professional inadequacy," "Slow on the uptake," "Commanded feebly," "No operational competence," or, simply, "exhausted." The bigger the command mistake, the greater the cost in lives. The ratios of that Killing Season were elementary.

A general named Louis Bonneau was the first *limogé,* a man whose "slowness and indecision" irritated Joffre. On August 8 his VII Corps had made a publicity-grabbing dash into Mulhouse to an emotional welcome by the French population of the Alsatian city, which had been part of Germany since its formal annexation in 1871 at the end of the Franco-Prussian War. Military bands played "La Marseillaise" and young women decked gun barrels with blue, white, and red flowers. German reinforcements counterattacked, nearly enveloping Bonneau's defenders and forcing them into a hasty and unseemly retreat. Those who had so recently celebrated the coming of the French now faced harsh reprisals. There were executions. Joffre sacked Bonneau on the thirteenth. The war was just ten days old.

Most prominent of the dismissed were two army chiefs, one of them Lanrezac, the Fifth Army commander, who would rather fuss than fight. Joffre visited him about 8:30 A.M. on August 28, and "as soon as I saw him, I was struck by his physical condition. Marks of fatigue lined his face; his color was sallow, his eyes bloodshot. He immediately began, with gesticulations which betrayed his nervous condition, to raise objections to the orders he had received the day before, alleging the tired condition of his troops . . . The tone of the conversation became heated . . ." Joffre fired Lanrezac a week later.

The other notable general Joffre fired that first month of war was Pierre Ruffey, commander of the Third Army; Ruffey had an unfortunate tendency to badmouth everyone in sight, including Joffre. Some of those derogatory remarks got back to his boss. The Third Army also had an excessively high casualty rate and had been battered at the Battle of the Frontiers. On August 30, the generalissimo visited Ruffey. "His excited way of talking made me feel that it was impossible to take what he said seriously. . . . I judged it imprudent to leave General Ruffey in command of his army." He accepted his dismissal "without any apparent regret. He dined that same evening at my table."

Between August 12 and September 30, 1914, Joffre dispatched 96 officers, most of them generals, to an early retirement. By the end of the year the number had reached 162. For most of the dismissals, there were ample reasons. At the Battle of Charleroi, a general named Sauret, a corps commander, not only lost track of his men and failed to issue orders but also disappeared for most of the battle. "Professional inadequacy" was the charge that earned him a one-way trip to the 12th Military District. Generals who openly expressed defeatism, especially in the rough going of the early weeks, were soon out of a job. Some thumbed their nose at the system, like the general who housed a "woman of loose morals," and lived with her, in the town where his headquarters was located.

Adolphe Messimy, the minister of war when hostilities broke out, wrote Joffre on August 24 to urge him "to send officers relieved of their command to G.H.Q. by motor-car and there have them court-martialed. I consider that . . . there are only two punishments, dismissal and death." After all, he reasoned, that's how it was done in the French Revolution. Joffre, who considered dismissal punishment enough, found Messimy's demand a little extreme. Yet some dismissed officers shared Messimy's opinion: they committed suicide. A General B—, unnamed, was found hanging in the bathroom of his apartment on December 1, 1914. He left a note: "I have decided by my own free will to kill myself, as I am unable to live with being forcibly retired during the war." Others blew their brains out, and at least one unfortunate had to be forcibly restrained from doing so.

The Limoges factor had one positive side. Joffre did request that officers, generals in particular, who displayed notable courage or leadership qualities be reported to him, putting them in line for promotion as

Joffre may have been quick to sack high-ranking officers who could not stand the strain of combat command, but he also replaced them with men who showed what he called '*cran*'—guts. One was Charles Mangin, seen peering over a trench parapet, right, who would eventually lead armies. Mangin was famously profligate with lives but believed that in this war there was no way around big losses. (*L'Illustration*)

positions became (ominous word) "vacant." Some outstanding commanders emerged that way in the fall of 1914. Franchet d'Espèrey, who replaced Lanrezac after Guise as head of the Fifth Army, was one. Charles Mangin, who eventually commanded two armies, was another. At a time when French arms were reeling, Mangin gained fame for an exploit near Namur at the end of August. Holding a Lebel rifle with a bayonet fixed to it and looking like an ordinary soldier, the general led his brigade into a burning Meuse village, which he recaptured from the Saxons who held it. He ended the day sitting with an NCO named Lefin on a pile of rocks, sharing half a baguette, a tin of corned beef, and a water bottle. A week later Mangin, a tough-looking, sharp-faced man with dark-brown hair in a crew cut, a dark mustache, and a hooked nose, found himself leading a division, replacing a major general who had taken the Limoges route. Some called him "the butcher" and an "eater of men," but he had a common feel that his troops appreciated, and a frankness of attitude. He acknowledged his reputation. "Whatever you do," he said, "you lose a lot of men." Could there be a better summation of leadership in the Great War?

Then there was Fayolle, the consummate gunner and secret diary keeper. On August 3, as he left Paris on the slow train carrying the 6,000 men of his brigade to Nancy, close to the border with Germany, he made a notation: "I am afraid of being afraid, of not being up to my task." Soon after his arrival, he visited the headquarters of Maj.-Gen. Charles Bizard, the commander of his division, the 70th Reserve, part of Gen. Fernand de Langle de Cary's Fourth Army. Fayolle found him "merry and full of good cheer." During breakfast the next morning, Fayolle heard the first distant thunder of cannon fire. As time passed, the rumble came closer and grew louder. The menacing sound clearly unnerved Bizard. He began to suffer, his dossier said, from "a symptomatic trembling and was hesitant in the way he spoke, slow on the uptake." Word got back to Langle de Cary. On August 13, the day after the sacking of Bonneau, Joffre fired Bizard. Fayolle was the natural leader who replaced him, stepping on the first rung of the ladder that would lead to the exalted perch of Maréchal of France. In a matter of hours he had gone from commanding a brigade of 6,000 to a division of 15,000. He would head groups of armies before the war was done.

Fayolle, the brigadier, allowed himself a rare moment of immodesty: "I am going into the campaign as a Major General!!! . . ."

HAD THEY NOT SURRENDERED AND been sent to Germany when the city fell, the commanders of the Lille garrison surely would have joined the tarnished ranks of the *limogés*. Instead, the French leadership, and not just Joffre, publicly blamed the British for the loss of Lille. They focused their wrath on Sir John French and what they viewed as his lack of goodwill. The feeling was, as the French president Raymond Poincaré noted in his diary, that the BEF should have been able to "retake Lille without striking a blow." Foch wanted to fire Sir John and replace him with his friend Henry Wilson. Joffre agreed but felt that he should formally ask the advice of Poincaré before approaching London.

A genuine crisis in the Anglo-French coalition was brewing, but one the British newcomers seemed not to be aware of. They were too busy getting settled. Advanced units of the II Corps of the BEF, the first to leave the Aisne, were just beginning to take up positions to the north of the French, along La Bassée Canal, when Lille surrendered. The BEF divisions were twenty impossible miles from the city: there is no way they could have reached it in time. Meanwhile, Germans were taking over the intervening countryside in ever-increasing numbers, and digging in. Cavalry, mostly dismounted now, light infantry, and cyclist battalions concealed themselves behind hedges and knocked loopholes in house walls. The two British divisions of the II Corps, the 5th on the right by the canal and, above it, the 3rd, would find themselves becoming rapidly outnumbered. By the time October was half over, the Germans in this sector would have built up a 2-to-1 superiority. Stalemating defensive systems were beginning to replace a freewheeling warfare of maneuver on the Western Front. Before long open space would have totally disappeared—except for that dangerous stagnant swathe between the facing lines.

FEW, IF ANY OF THE combatants, could grasp the size—you are tempted to say "immensity"—of the battle taking shape. From the mouth of the Yser River and the North Sea, through the polders of Dixmude and south to Ypres, then arching across English-like downlands to Armentières and the low, almost ridgeless ridges overlooking Lille, and finally, the mean, windswept slag heaps around La Bassée Canal, was a daunting mix of mini environments. Both geographically and emotionally, two Flanderses exist, a French and a Belgian, divided by the narrow, polluted, marsh-fringed trough of the Lys, which here forms the watery border with France. It was an unfordable stream, five feet deep and from fifteen to twenty yards wide, its floodplain crosshatched by narrow, boggy brooks and drainage ditches that hindered movement of cavalry and infantry alike. Half a dozen floods in a single year are not unusual. "The floods of the Lys are the most dangerous of all in the Flemish plain," observed the geographer Johnson, "and the river has not inaptly been called 'the scourge of Flanders.'" A king of France once asked his advisors, "This river of the Lis, is it so evil to pass that one cannot find passage save at well-known crossings?" One of them replied, "Sire, yes; there is no ford, and the stream flows upon marshes which one cannot traverse." Bridges mattered.

What happened on the opposite banks that fall was interrelated: this was essentially a single battle. The characteristics of the landscapes and of the villages and towns north and south of the river may have been different—Western Europe, as noted before, is a checkerboard of small environments existing side by side—but otherwise, everything was the same. Even the casualties of the two battlefields matched. The objectives of the combatants also complemented each other. The Allies sought envelopment to begin with and, when that ceased to be possible, containment—though they never surrendered the breakthrough notion. The Germans, for their part, sought a breakthrough to the coast and the Channel ports, easier to accomplish through Ypres than from the marsh-impacted south battlefield. That would be followed by a rolling up of the Allied line and the resumption of the march on Paris, presumably in the spring. Maybe the taking of the ports was all that was needed for victory. Neither side took seriously the possibility of stalemate.

The area around Ypres offered an ideal jumping-off place for any offensive, better for the Germans, since flat, unobstructed country spread out immediately to the west of town. The ground south of the Lys did not lend itself to movement unfettered by geography. Cavalry was useless here. Artillery may have been an effective killer; but it already created as many problems as it solved, destroying or blocking the arteries of natural or man-made drainage channels. The water table, which was only a couple of feet below the surface, tended to rise in the fall: trenches here could not be dug down but had to be built up with extensive breastworks that had the unfortunate effect of further blocking drainage systems.

But in the first days of war in this area, trenches did not yet exist, and troops of both sides struggled forward through a tight complex of woods and orchards, hedges and haystacks, small enclosed fields, streams and deep ditches lined with pollarded willows, muddy lanes, and farming villages where wealth was often measured by the size of the manure pile in the barnyard. Below La Bassée Canal, coal country took over, with its multiple rail lines, blackened brick factories, girdered pitheads, and towering slag heaps. Both sides immediately converted those man-made hills into observation stations. Otherwise the miles south of the Lys were (and still are) a flat, charmless landscape—as the *Official History* put it, "dismal country to work over and depressing to dwell in. And it was to become worse." The BEF had reached France's Rust Belt, which, even as early as 1914, had become, as Ezra Pound put it, "an old bitch gone in the teeth."

THAT BLEAK LANDSCAPE WITNESSED A series of British misadventures, inaugurating a four-year plunge into the mud of Flanders. Their introduction to a new phase of the war was every bit as frenzied and shocking as Mons or the September 14 duel for the Aisne highlands. October 12 was a day of thick, dark, freezing fog, with visibility down to twenty yards until midmorning. The BEF's first objective was Givenchy, a village on a faint rise that straggled along a muddy road. German snipers were concealed in its church steeple, behind top-floor cottage windows, haylofts, and hedges that still retained their leafy summer thickness. As the fog lifted and the advancing figures took shape, German riflemen began to make gaps in the long, thin, extended lines of infantry, occasionally interspersed with squadrons of cavalry. At one point, an advance of 250 yards cost 43 casualties, 11 dead among them. By nightfall, the British had an uneasy purchase on Givenchy.

The following day the Germans of Rupprecht's Sixth Army counterattacked; the British gave way. Stubble and beet roots hardly provided shelter: rescuers had to grab wounded men by the ankles and drag them to the relative safety of drainage ditches. One group retreated to a farmhouse, which the Germans set on fire. The men trapped inside, the brigadier commanding the British defenders of Givenchy later wrote, "put it out with wine from the cellars, for they were cut off from the water supply." Eventually, though, they had to surrender. "That day," wrote the same brigadier, Edward Gleichen, "was a terrible day: Givenchy was bombarded heavily by the Germans for hours, and rendered absolutely untenable. The Bedfords . . . stuck to one end of the village whilst the enemy was in possession of the other; but the heavy artillery was too much for them, and after losing about sixty casualties, many of them killed by falling houses, they gradually fell back to trenches in rear of the village." That "terrible" day cost the British close to a thousand men.

Three days later the British retook Givenchy and, said the historian of the 5th Division, "found some of their buried and wounded men there." They were able to force their way almost to the limits of a bigger town, La Bassée. Enfilade fire from brick stacks across the canal swept the attackers, and the Germans unleashed, said the divisional historian, "a tornado of shells." The British lost another thousand men. Then it was the turn of the Germans to attack. "They attacked all day, and again at 7 pm, 11 pm and 2 am," a British subaltern wrote. "We drove them all back and they must have lost heavily . . . But we were able to hold on . . ." The Germans were introducing a new feature to the Western Front: the night attack. And, in the predictable course of things, the BEF counterattacked, several times over but never at night. It was able to reach the outskirts of La Bassée, and there the battle died down. In its first nine days in Flanders, October 9–18, the British had lost 4,500 men; the German casualties were roughly similar. La Bassée was as far as the British could manage in this sector for another four years—what their *Official History* described as the "high-water mark" of their first Flanders offensive.

FOR A FEW DAYS MORE, both French and British commanders regarded a confrontation like the one at La Bassée as little more than another step in the relentless movement north, and not for what it was: a consolidation and strengthening of the German line that was a necessary prelude to a truly vast offensive. Until it was almost too late, the Allies remained indifferent to the possibility. Staffs were too busy working up their scheme for a breakout north of the Franco–Belgian border. They still glimpsed space available for their grand maneuver, at least as far as Bruges and maybe farther. They were aware of a certain German buildup in Flanders, but not alarmed by it. "We must push, push, push," Sir Henry Wilson wrote in his diary on the thirteenth, "as we have nothing in front of us . . ."

The French and British considered themselves ready to go on the offensive, but one on the scale that Falkenhayn now contemplated, one calculated to seize back the initiative in the war, was unthinkable. The blindness of their leadership astounds. Push, push, push: no buzzword obscured the basic deficiencies of the newly arrived Allies more. At that moment, thousands of fresh German troops were detraining at rural stations south of Brussels, preparing to march westward toward Flanders and the Channel ports. Because cross-country rails in Belgium were still under repair and lorry transportation for moving men was unavailable, they had to make the last part of their journey on foot.

As always, Falkenhayn arrived at plans and decisions in a hurry. In the past month he had created a new army, the Fourth. (He had dissolved the old Fourth and parceled out its units to the armies on either side of it.) Now he rushed to prepare what he hoped would prove a decisive blow. Instead of relying on battle-tested but exhausted veteran units, he had stocked the new force with four reserve corps, eight divisions. They were made up largely of recent volunteers, predominantly young, as well as men recalled from civilian life, who had long ago gone through training and seen active service. There were considerably more of the latter than legend would have it: too many years of peace may have dulled the necessary belligerent edge.

Time was not on Falkenhayn's side. Time made up his mind. It would take too long, and might involve too great a risk, to bring veteran units into the Flanders position, filling the empty, and relatively quiet, spaces they left with green troops. Not that many weeks were left before winter shut down operations. Here, waiting in Germany, just a train ride and some hard marches away, was an entire fresh army, more than a hundred thousand men, that he could throw into battle immediately. What it lacked in experience it made up in enthusiasm and patriotic fervor. Just the march to the front, optimists among the commanders hoped, would give the reserve troops the necessary cohesion to fight as frontline units. There was one more factor that might tip the balance: Allied planners, most notably Joffre, did not calculate on Falkenhayn's using reserve formations as attackers. They would not dream of doing so. Why would he?

Once again, intelligence had failed.

THREE DIVISIONS OF BESELER'S III Reserve Corps, released from the siege of Antwerp, were now in close pursuit of the fleeing Belgians and were menacing the frail barrier of the Yser River. They, at least, were veterans by now, victorious ones. Their mission was to sweep southward along the coast, as far as they could go. Dunkirk was already in their reach. The size of the entire new army was just short of 200,000 men. The greater part of the Fourth would enter the line north of the Lys, extending the front to the Channel. The newly formed force would link with Rupprecht's Sixth Army, which had handled the defense of La Bassée so capably, and, presumably, with Beseler on the coast.

In committing untried men to the climax in Flanders, Falkenhayn recognized that he was making an enormous gamble. He risked losing everything—or winning much more.

As the French and British headed north toward the Yser (and beyond, they hoped), the danger that they would cut the Germans off from the Belgian coast mounted, as well as (in Falkenhayn's words) "the danger of an effective encirclement of the right wing." At the very least he had to prevent both. "If this was not done, then drastic action against England and her sea traffic with submarines, aeroplanes and airships, which was being prepared as a reply to England's war of starvation, was impossible. . . . It was also questionable . . . whether the occupied territory in Northern France and Western Belgium was to be held; the loss of it would necessarily have led to evil results."

Balanced against those threats were the Channel ports. Paris might be a wild dream; the ports were not.

He summoned Grand Duke Albrecht of Württemberg, the royal commander of the old Fourth Army as well as the new one, and Maj. Gen. Émil Ilse, its chief of staff, to his new headquarters at Mézières. Albrecht was a bland, humorless individual, efficient to a fault but not a hands-on leader; he had established his headquarters in Brussels, seventy-odd miles from the jump-off point of the contemplated offensive. He kept his distance; you seldom feel his presence. Albrecht was fifty, on the young side for such a command—but then, he was high nobility—a man with a measuring eye and a handsome countenance that verged on hardness. As commander of the old Fourth, he had helped to orchestrate the slaughter of the French at the Frontiers and the swallowing of the iron mines. He had overrun Sedan. That fall he was, along with Rupprecht, the most capable of the German Army commanders on the Western Front.

Nevertheless some in the High Command had their doubts about Falkenhayn's decision. A General Loewenfeld, who had inspected the new divisions before their departure, was blunt in his negative assessment. The inferior quality of their junior officers worried him; he warned that their rudimentary and abbreviated training left them unprepared for concentrated shellfire or for what would happen when they advanced "in thick masses at relatively short distances from the enemy." His qualms went for nothing. The Supreme Commander had already made up his mind.

On October 10, Falkenhayn briefed his listeners on his plan to resume the invasion of France. Albrecht recalled his instructions. "The new Fourth Army is to advance, without regard for casualties, with its right wing on the coast. The fortified ports of Dunkirk and Calais are to be isolated—they were to be captured later—and then, leaving St. Omer off to the left, to swing down towards the south." Falkenhayn's objective (he later wrote) was "to obstruct England's Channel traffic, effectively attack the Island itself, and turn the French flank." A bold concept, a war-winning maneuver, even.

Falkenhayn set the jump-off date: October 20. "The prize to be won," he later reasoned, "was worth the stake."

THOUGH FEW RECOGNIZED ITS SIGNIFICANCE at the time, October 14 was a notable day in the chronicle of the Western Front. The first British troops, the IV Corps, comprising the 7th Division and the 3rd Cavalry Division, reached Ypres and threw out outpost lines connecting them with the

French and Belgians to their north and their own troops coming up from the south. That should have been remarkable enough. But at some point—the exact time was not recorded—riders of the Royal Scots Greys and a party from the 3rd Cavalry Division met below Mount Kemmel, a hill 512 feet high, a few miles below Ypres. There, in the curious phrase of the *Official History,* they "joined hands." Did they remain on horseback? Did they offer cigarettes to one another? Were they aware of the sound of gunfire approaching from both north and south? Before they turned and disappeared into the rainy mist, did they complain about the weather, which had been beastly for days? We shall never know. These were not men with a writer's sense for detail. But they had shared an important moment. Though none of them probably suspected it, they had closed the barrier, "frail indeed in the north, but still a continuous one," that now stretched from the Swiss border to the North Sea, a distance of 470 miles—of which the British then held just thirty-five. Within hours, one supposes, trench diggers would have rushed in to cement the handshakes. (The Germans, unaccustomedly laggard, would not complete their line until October 21, in the Houthulst Forest, twenty miles to the north.) In retrospect, it seems no accident that the Gordian knot that was trench warfare was finally tied near Ypres.*

By closing the Western Front, cavalry had nearly written an end to its long history, at least as the art of military horsemanship (if we can dignify it with that charged word) was practiced in Western Europe. It had helped to provide its own undoing. At Ypres the mounted warrior ceased to matter. No longer would he be the shaper of decisions, the creator of destinies. He had become just another casualty of this war. In a few days, a week or two at most, trenches—and all they represented—would supplant and solidify the thin connective membrane forged below Mount Kemmel, their webs growing in depth and complexity as they spread inexorably over the landscape of France and Belgium. That October day, cavalry, as a major tool of war, became as obsolete and discredited as an alchemist's beaker.

---

* The regimental history of the Royal Scots Greys gives the date as October 15, but I must go along with the citation in the *Official History,* a day earlier.

———

THE OPEN FLANK THAT JOFFRE, Foch, and French sought—the dreams of generals died hard in those months—may have disappeared, but Sir John continued to probe for it in the area around Armentières. The chimera of that open flank, as Richard Holmes has called the lure of the exploitable gap, was one of the things that had drawn French to Flanders.

Problems abounded, and not just the ones of self-delusion or the unfamiliarity and, increasingly, the sodden inhospitality of the new territory. Faulty intelligence about the size and strength of German forces and their exact whereabouts also misled Sir John. (The same might be said, to a lesser extent, for the disregard of the Germans for their opponents.) Another problem—though French didn't see it that way—was the man who led the III Corps (4th and 6th Divisions), Maj. Gen. William Pulteney. A stocky, shortish man with a big, cheerful mustached countenance, he was an Etonian and a Scots Guardsman from an old family: he had spent the bulk of his career in Africa and had distinguished himself in the Boer War (and as a big-game hunter). French regarded Pulteney as imperturbable and willing to do anything asked of him, which may have accounted for his steady rise. He was widely known by his nickname, "Putty," a reference to his malleability but more likely a comment on what existed between his ears. A subordinate called Pulteney "the most completely ignorant general I served during the war and that is saying a lot." A donkey's donkey he may have been, but Pulteney was also a survivor, ever willing to shift blame for disasters to subordinates. In the British Army, thanks to the traditions of regiment and class, dimness was not a disqualifier.

The Battle of Meteren was a fair example of Pulteney's penchant for indecision. On October 13, he dispatched his two divisions in five parallel columns to march toward the front, wherever that might be. Meteren, four miles south of the Belgian frontier and twelve from Ypres, blocked their way: though just arrived, the Germans were already entrenched there. This was dead-level country where cottages lined the roads for miles and the staked frameworks of hop fields filled the land behind. There was too much rainy mist that morning for artillery to be of much use, though once it lifted, according to a German eyewitness account, shellfire set much of the town on fire.

By about one in the afternoon, two companies of the Royal Warwickshire Regiment were working their way along both sides of the road leading into the western limits of the village, while the Germans prepared to pull out. It was at that moment that the GOC (general officer commanding) of their division, the 4th, arrived at a forward command post. He reported that Pulteney was upset by a report from a reconnaissance aircraft that 500 Germans were occupying Meteren. One captured German claimed that the British outnumbered "our forces six-fold." In addition, stubborn German resistance was holding up the nearby 6th Division. Both circumstances convinced Pulteney that his men must wait for the entire corps to attack. The Germans, who had been preparing to pull back, suddenly recognized that the British attack had halted, returned, and opened fire. It was midafternoon before another British brigade could resume the attack, and evening before the village fell. By the time the Germans disappeared into the rainy darkness, they had inflicted 708 casualties.

One of the wounded was a twenty-seven-year-old lieutenant in the Warwicks named Bernard Law Montgomery. We met the bishop's son earlier, chewing peppermints next to a dead man on the Aisne highlands. That morning he had led a successful bayonet charge and had himself captured a German. (The memoirs of the man who would become the most heralded British general of the next world war indicate that he had done so after a well-aimed kick in the groin.) He was reorganizing his platoon when a rifle bullet tore through his back. As he fell in the mud, one of his men rushed forward to bandage him and carry him to safety. But a bullet smashed into his head, and he fell across Montgomery's body. The two, one dead, the other barely alive, lay there while the Germans continued to pump bullets into them; another bullet caught Montgomery in the knee. He shouted to the survivors of his platoon to stay where they were.

For three hours, until darkness fell and he was at last rescued, Montgomery lay under the dead man: perhaps it was for the best that he passed out. Finally, two men, who must have detected sound or movement in the inert form—it was not like Montgomery to admit that he might have been groaning—dashed forward, slung the shattered subaltern in a greatcoat that passed for a stretcher, and lifted him through a hedge. At a dressing station, he somehow attracted the attention of a doctor, who decided to send him back in an ambulance; a grave was already being dug for him. Montgomery woke up in a hospital in England, to find that he had been awarded a DSO and been promoted to captain. The Great War fighting days of the future victor of El Alamein were over.

The next day, October 14, the III Corps continued its deliberate slog eastward. Once again, it rained. The British ran into pockets of stubborn opposition, but nevertheless managed to occupy a sizeable town near the border, Bailleul. Hollen's German IV Cavalry Corps retreated, taking with it more than 500 wounded in carts. The Germans had to leave behind 85 men who were too badly hurt to be moved. Air reconnaissance reported a division-sized column, with cavalry protection, pulling out of Armentières, the biggest town in the area after Lille.

In spite of ample evidence that he faced only token immediate resistance, Pulteney refused to be hurried. But token was too dangerous for his taste. Not before midafternoon on October 15 did orders go out to seize four bridges over the Lys in the vicinity of Armentières; battalion commanders weren't briefed until six, after dark. At the Pont-de-Nieppe at Armentières, a small party of Germans with four machine guns held up an entire company. As men of a Hampshire battalion were preparing to deal with the rear-guard annoyance, word arrived that they were to wait until light. Though there was plenty of illumination from burning buildings, Pulteney, several miles away, had decided that rain and fog made conditions unfavorable for a night advance.

Pulteney's III Corps did finally take the bridge called the Pont de Nieppe, but failed to advance into Armentières. Not until the following day did Putty's 4th Division occupy the town. A delegation of citizens approached the British to say that the Germans had left. The 4th Division proceeded through the dingy streets of the unlovely textile center in triumph. "We were loaded up with gifts of eats and smokes by the excited populace."

Reports began to reach Pulteney that two corps of Crown Prince Rupprecht's Sixth Army were beginning to entrench along the ridge that separated Armentières and Lille, its northern swell known as the Pérenchies Ridge and the southern, Aubers Ridge. Pulteney did recognize that he risked exposing his right flank to enfilade fire from a numerous enemy concealed on higher ground. As Anthony Farrar-Hockley put it in *Death of an Army,* the Germans "would have a grand view and a grand shoot." The best solution seemed for the 6th Division to make a direct assault on the Pérenchies Ridge—though a less costly one would have been simply to stop and dig in where its advance had taken it—which is where the line ended anyway. So, on the morning of October 18, two days before Falkenhayn's offensive was to begin, all three brigades of the 6th Division surged up the long, gentle rise of Pérenchies Ridge—which might be described more accurately as a plateau slanted upward. The 2nd Leinsters, Irishmen, fighting along the paved main road from Armentières, reached Prémesques at 10 A.M. From that inconspicuous village they could see Lille spreading across the plain just three miles away. Not until the fall of 1918 would any Allied soldier who wasn't a POW again enjoy that view.

BY SCREENING THE ADVANCE OF troops across Belgium, the German cavalry had performed one task superbly. The Allied High Command's knowledge of the approach of the Fourth Army was decidedly limited. According to Belgian and French intelligence sources, the *Official History* reported, "certain large new formations, composed of a mixture of young men and old, had been detrained south-west of Brussels, and were moving forward." Air observation backed up these reports to an extent, though it downplayed the size of the German concentrations. The good luck of bad weather that persisted through those mid-October days had kept aircraft largely grounded, and as the British official history of the air war admitted, "the formidable enemy movement against the Ypres line developed undetected." Sightings on the ground had also been sparse. The Belgian Army, which might normally have spotted new enemy initia-

Weary German Fourth Army marchers from one of Duke Albrecht's reserve divisions take a roadside break. An anonymous photographer took this shot during their four-day trek across Belgium toward the coast, a surprise attack designed to outnumber, outflank, and overwhelm Allied defenders, including the badly beaten Belgian Army. (*L'Illustration*)

tives, was in disorganized retreat along the coast, far from the principal lanes of German march. It was concerned only with its pursuers, and with staying intact.

On October 14—that day again—the Fourth Army had begun its progress westward from the rail stations where it had detrained, marching along four parallel paved roads in seemingly endless columns. The men arrived in greenish gray woolen uniforms and canvas-covered patent leather helmets with the characteristic spikes poking through the cloth—pickelhauben. They wore calf-high leather boots and carried heavy, full packs, along with six ammunition pouches, bayonets, canteens, mess kits, entrenching shovels, and their rifles slung over their shoulder, the ensemble weighing as much as seventy pounds. The packs were nicknamed "monkeys"—the probable source of the expression "monkey on your back." Each morning cooks provided them with a quarter of a loaf of bread and a piece of cheese or sausage, their midday meal, hardly adding to the weight of the things they carried or making for a full belly. At night, field kitchens on wheels, able to boil coffee and cook stew while moving—

popularly known as *Gulaschkanonen,* "goulash cannons"—were supposed to show up. Their unreliability was a common source of complaint throughout the war.

Behind the leading brigades, horses pulled divisional artillery. Cavalry ranged over open ground, reconnoitering and screening. Jaeger companies—light infantry—fanned out. They carried no packs and were ready for immediate action. Those advance probers scoured woods and farming hamlets. Any suspicious person or persons unfortunate enough to be swept up in their dragnet were likely to be executed on the spot as franc-tireurs.

With the coming of darkness, the columns broke, with thousands searching for shelter. Barns, cottages, and the undersides of wagons were not always available; officers appropriated châteaux and the more substantial houses along the way west. Often the marchers had no choice but to stretch out in damp, stubbly fields, bundled in groundsheets. It rained on and off those four days. That many men must have left behind an odorous trail of refuse and human waste, calling cards of an unwanted invasion.

For many, carried away by the enthusiasm of the moment, those first days must have seemed like a glorified outing in the country—for the younger among them, a kind of martial *Wandervogel,* that typically German urban middle-class youth movement, a highly organized return to Nature. They sang, of course, all the time. In those first days, there was no enemy to hear them, and prepare. At night they might glimpse the lightning-like flashes and hear the thunder of distant artillery. Or the columns might be abruptly halted while they took on fleeting enemy cavalry skirmishers or fired in the direction of a retreating armored car. All still seemed part of the romance of war.

Not until the end of their march did advance units encounter resistance worth the name. They had crossed the north–south highway that ran from Bruges through Roulers and down to Menin on the Lys. By the night of October 18–19, six German divisions, three corps, or 100,000 or more men, were west of the road. The Fourth Army had progressed that far without being detected. Though skirmishes were growing more intense, the various Allied headquarters refused to take their implication seriously. Foch and French were still contemplating their grand right hook. They were convinced that Rawlinson's IV Corps was facing only cavalry.

BUT FOR THE ACCIDENT OF an imprecise word, Rawlinson's 7th Division might have blundered into the oncoming Fourth Army. Rawlinson and the staff of the IV Corps, now headquartered in Ypres, incorrectly interpreted the meaning of Sir John French's Army Operation Order of 7:10 P.M. on October 17. It directed the 7th to "move"—a leisurely term—on the Lys town of Menin; French meant "attack." The division advanced 4,000 yards early the next morning and dug in. Men of the 7th could spot freshly dug trenches a little more than a mile away. Advance units of an as-yet-unestimated German force had obviously dug them. Rumors spreading among the local peasants hinted that it was sizeable. By the time, meanwhile, that Rawlinson and his staff discovered their misreading, it was already early in the afternoon of the eighteenth. In a dark cloud

The first BEF troops to arrive from the Aisne highlands fought along the Franco-Belgian border. Sir John threw them into battle immediately, disputing obscure villages at great cost. Here, British riflemen position themselves in a roadside ditch that passed for a trench and wait for the enemy to emerge from the mist. (Imperial War Museum)

of agitation, a liaison officer from GHQ arrived at Rawlinson's headquarters to spell out the precise meaning of Sir John's order. Even so, Rawlinson had to postpone the attack until the next morning. It never, in fact, took place. Sir Henry Wilson, who had come down with a near-terminal case of the Fochian bug, was livid. "Owing to nothing but absolute incompetence and want of regimental officers," he confided to his diary on the nineteenth, "we have lost the finest opportunity of the war and are now being thrown on the defensive. Maddening and perhaps disastrous."

But the delay may quite possibly have saved an entire division from being cut off and overwhelmed by the German forces gathering in front of it—"a piece of good fortune," the *Official History* later said.

October 19, the eve of the battle that we now call the First Ypres, was another wet and windy day. The British and French, as well as the Belgians still settling behind the Yser, remained no more than dimly aware of how many Germans were closing in on them. It was the Marne in reverse. At dawn, ten to seventeen miles in fact separated the opposing armies; as the hours passed, that distance rapidly narrowed. One British regimental history took note of how "tenacious peasants continued their autumn work, cattle grazed in the fields, women and children appeared at the cottage doorway with the wondering air of possessors disturbed in their peaceful rights, but otherwise unmoved by the marching of troops as by the flight of civilians refugees along the Route Nationale"—the official name of the Menin road. In the sky, puffs of black smoke, "thick and wooly," burst silently, "followed by a hollow explosion." The volume of skirmish fire mounted.

On the German side, officers ordered the reservists to spread out in lines and then move forward. They advanced, shoulder to shoulder. Ditches, hedges, barnyard wire fences, and their own enthusiasm undid the precision of their closely packed formations. Some moved forward along the highway to Dixmude, others approached the Houthulst Forest, the largest tract of woodland in the Ypres area, or probed the faubourgs of the junction town called Roulers. Less than two hundred yards ahead of the Germans, French dragoons of Gen. Antoine de Mitry's II Cavalry Corps banged away with their short carbines, which may have looked like toy guns but could be deadly at short range. The French unlimbered 75s and commenced to fire. Men dropped, not romantic phantoms but real men who had been swallowing the last of their luncheon sausage, smoking a final cigarette, or making a crude joke about their foreign opposition just minutes before. The lines closed and surged forward. By nightfall the French had pulled back, leaving battered villages and their surviving inhabitants cowering in cellars.

The rail center of Roulers—it was on the Lille–Ostend line, with connections to the interior and beyond—was the main bag of the Germans on the nineteenth. That morning de Mitry's cavalry still held the town itself, though not the empty flanks on either side of it. Rather than bypassing Roulers and cutting it off, the troops of the German 51st Reserve Division marched directly into the town and immediately found themselves hemmed in amid its narrow Old World streets. House-to-house fighting had not been part of their meager training. Farrar-Hockley has described the scene:

> For a little while, de Mitry's cavalrymen were at an advantage . . . and the local householders were ready to help with directions, point out sniping posts, aid the wounded. Lacking assistance amongst the maze of buildings, alleys and backyards, and as yet untrained to react quickly under fire, the Germans were unable to make use of their greater numbers and heavier weapons. . . . Sections and platoons dashed off prematurely or in the wrong direction. Orders were given and countermanded in the same breath. The middle-aged commanders, themselves inexperienced in this type of fighting, were hard put to collect and keep their platoons let alone to launch them in a concerted assault.

Gradually numbers and the zeal for self-sacrifice prevailed over confusion. Outside of town, fresh troops took advantage of the open flanks and swarmed ahead. French cavalrymen in their breastplates and Roman-like helmets hastened to dash through narrow alleys or clamber across red-tile rooftops. The survivors found their horses and galloped back five miles, to the safety of the Passchendaele Ridge. The Germans followed them into the night.

In the weeks and years to come, the fall of Roulers would prove critical; like Lille, it was another prized railhead lost, and would remain equally—and tantalizingly—out of reach for the next four years.

The French 87th Territorial Division, which held the village of Passchendaele on the ridge to the west commanding Roulers, waited apprehensively that night of the nineteenth. Raoul Nel, a doctor serving with this unit of men in their thirties and forties—in peacetime he was a urologist, but war was no respecter of medical specialties—detected signs of the enemy's approach: flares illuminating the dark sky, a steady beat of gunshots, and, ever closer to the French lines, the shouts that were the German version of the Rebel Yell. Nel could see a stream of refugees "fleeing in throngs" along the railroad tracks that passed over the ridge near the village. During rare empty minutes, the fledgling battlefield surgeon kept a journal. "In front of us the fires become more sinister as the night darkens; through a distant, confused noise come screams, piercing human cries, gunshots . . . silence . . ."

On the following night, German attackers reached Passchendaele and, charging with bayonets, overwhelmed the French defenders. The French "withdrew in haste." The guns on both sides picked up the tempo of the night action. "The English batteries behind us fire without interruption. You would think the sky was going to burst open. . . . Whistlings crisscross the air, near and far, cracklings—fantastic, rapid, unexpected—seem to split our skulls. . . . In the distance, through the glow of fires, we see the horizon burning; the clouds have become red; the sky is colored purple in places, black in others." In the confusion of sound and the staccato clash of shadow and violent light, German numbers pushed the defenders out of Passchendaele and off the ridge. For the moment the bayonet had triumphed, an event increasingly uncommon on the Western Front. Nel and his medical team did manage to pile many of the French casualties into horse-drawn "ambulance cars" and race down the long slope to safety. Allied troops did save a gun battery, but "the seriously wounded and the dead had to be left in the hands of the enemy."

"It's our baptism of fire," he wrote later. Nel, the recent urologist, would have to learn his new skill quickly. He did.

MEANWHILE THE BRITISH 7TH DIVISION had resumed its progress toward Menin, a town on the Lys a little bigger than Ypres. The division commander, Sir Thompson Capper, a man notorious for being a hard driver, was surprised when GHQ complained that he was "backward in advancing." More annoyed than chastened, he ordered an attack the next morning, beginning at 6:30 A.M. on the nineteenth; one brigade made an advance of two miles. Then, just before noon, an order came to abandon the attack. GHQ had received disquieting, and frighteningly believable, reports of a substantial German buildup. The impending loss of the Passchendaele Ridge may have contributed to its nervousness. The 7th Division abruptly retreated. By the end of the day, it would find itself three and a half miles behind its morning jump-off line, but—what it did not know at the time—had narrowly avoided walking into a trap. The Germans were waiting for an attack, which by now they had come to think inevitable. It was not difficult to read the operational habits of the Allies. In the event, the British did what was beginning to come naturally. They dug trenches.

But Sir John French was not ready to give up his hopes of a decisive attack. That night, in written instructions to the commander of the I Corps, Sir Douglas Haig, French revealed the magnitude of his self-deception. "He estimated," Haig wrote in his diary soon after, " 'the enemy's strength on the front Ostend to Menin, at about one corps, not more.' I was to march via Thurout and capture Bruges. Defeat Enemy and drive him on Ghent [which was another 25 miles southeast of Bruges]." Wilson, no fan of Sir John, had his doubts. He could not resist a private journal barb the next day: "Bruges for all practical purposes is as far as Berlin, and to-morrow's fighting will settle that." The man who had so brilliantly planned the movement of the BEF to the Continent now found himself a kind of sub chief of staff, something of a hanger-on at headquarters whose only real function was to be responsible for maintaining a presentable relationship with the French. Hardly a day passed when Wilson and Foch did not visit each other.

Up front, movement for both sides was beginning to slow down. In the developing Ypres sector, trench diggers kept busy. It sometimes seemed that the spade had replaced the rifle in importance. Entrenching continued from the eastern fringes of Ploegsteert Wood down to the Lys, or as close as diggers could manage before the ground turned too water-logged to excavate. On the far side of the river, beyond the floodplain, trenches started again and worked their way up the ridge, where the two southernmost British corps maintained an uncertain hold. The Leinsters burrowed in at Prémesques, as did the Sherwood Foresters at Ennetières, a nearby village that was just as close to Lille but lacked the view. "We can apparently get no further for the Germans have brought up strong reinforcements," Lt. William La Touche Congreve reported from the 3rd Division's temporary headquarters at Neuve Chapelle, "and also have a strongly prepared position which we are now up against. So it looks like another siege unless we are strongly reinforced here."

On October 19, the day before the official beginning of Falkenhayn's great Flanders offensive, troops of the First Battalion of the Cameronians—the Scottish Rifles—ride in London double-decker buses, still adorned with advertisements for luxuries few of the common soldiers had ever known or would ever have a chance to savor. They were headed for Laventie, a village in French Flanders just below the Lys. (Imperial War Museum)

The Cameronians, Scottish troops, were sent forward in forty urban motor buses, "bearing their homely London labels and advertisements," Cap. James Lochhead Jack wrote, "including 'Pears' Soap' and (I think rather callously under the circumstances) 'Dewar's Whiskey'"—a treat denied to the ordinary soldier. Men of the Royal Welch, who were on foot, looked on enviously. The buses and their cargo "were in our thoughts a good deal in the later stages of the march." That was one of the weary Royal Welch marchers speaking. Many of them, riders and hikers alike, would soon be beyond caring.

German aggressiveness was manifest everywhere. One episode during the night of October 18–19 confirmed the relative change in strength and fortune. Earlier that day the 2nd Royal Irish Battalion, already under strength, had stormed a hamlet called Le Pilly, a gathering of peasant cottages south of the Lys so insignificant that it doesn't appear on most maps. They took the place, little more than a narrowing of a dirt road, but lost 200 men in the process. Dismounted French cavalrymen were supposed to occupy the next village but never reached it. Night fell. In the dark, the Royal Irish didn't recognize how isolated they were; the Germans did. They decided to strike before dawn. Guides led two battalions of Westphalians, close to 2,000 men, along a muddy track. They split up, each battalion getting ready to go in from opposite sides of Le Pilly, squeezing it in a pincer. A barrage opened, and a neighboring British battalion reported "a thunder of gun-fire to the northward." The German shells crushed roofs and walls—though most of the defenders had dispersed to gardens and to the edges of fields. It was now the morning of October 20, and massed British rifles held off the attackers, but at a high cost. In the midafternoon the Germans made a fresh assault. The British fire slackened: ammunition was running low. The commanding officer of the Royal Irish, Maj. E.H.E. Daniell, ordered the remains of his force, many of them walking wounded, to fix bayonets. They charged, and the Westphalians massacred them; Daniell was among those cut down. In two days of fighting, the Royal Irish had lost 257 killed and 290 captured, of whom 240 were wounded. Only thirty escaped to their own lines.

The disaster at Le Pilly marked a turning point for the British in French Flanders, but it was not the only one that day, October 20. From

La Bassée to the mouth of the Yser, fifty-six irregular miles, the Germans had gone over to the attack. The laboratory of war that was Ypres was about to witness a three-week experiment in mass warfare, a budding operational masterwork that would, its clever but cynical scientist-in-chief calculated, restore the fortunes of Germany. Falkenhayn's sweep toward the Channel ports and the sea, his October surprise, was in sight of its goal.

ARC OF FIRE

Riflemen of the Second Battalion of the Scots Guards pause in the digging of the first Salient trenches at the edge of a field near Zandevoorde. Those trenches in the south face of the developing Ypres Salient were about shoulder-high and as yet offered little protection. Though already harshly "blooded," these men in their billed caps can still muster an apprehensive smile for the official photographer. (Imperial War Museum)

9

The Salient

OCTOBER 20–21

ON OCTOBER 20, 1914, A TUESDAY, FALKENHAYN LIT HIS GREAT ARC OF FLAME. It was 9 A.M. German time, 8 A.M. Paris. He had the advantage of surprise: the Allied leaders were blind to the true size and extent of his gathering divisions. The Germans outnumbered their opponents by as much as 2 to 1. He had no unity-of-command problem to distract him. His opponents had to coordinate the defensive movements, as well as the idiosyncrasies and national requirements, of three armies.

Falkenhayn could rely on mainly fresh (if untried) troops. The British and French were forced to feed tired divisions piecemeal into extended and increasingly thin lines; the Belgians had no more divisions left to feed. The Allies, once the Race to the Sea had ended in its unfortunate draw, had no settled plan to fall back on. Outflanking the enemy was now out of the question. They may have dreamed of movement and maneuver; static, stubborn defense was, for the moment, their only option.

Ypres began not so much by accident, as so many conclusive battles have done, as by the process of elimination. It almost goes without saying that the closer the opponents were to the sea, the fewer openings for a flanking movement presented themselves. Two that remained tempted Falkenhayn. One was the Yser, where Albert's little army appeared to be on the verge of collapse and Ronarc'h's French Marines probably were not a serious obstruction. The other was the Ypres corridor to Dunkirk, just under thirty miles distant. (A third, possible but less likely, was the straight ahead slog of Rupprecht's Sixth Army: once it could get beyond the shaft and slag-heap wasteland around Armentières, relatively open rural country beckoned.) He elected to go with the first two. That late October day, as the leaves were turning yellow and beginning to fall, Falkenhayn seemed to have every prospect of success.

But a look at a map—a succession of maps, rather—of the developing battle reveals a signal defect of Falkenhayn's plan: the pressure was equal everywhere, too equal. The cartographic images of the First Ypres—as we now call that initial battle—resemble those late-Renaissance paintings of the ordeal of Saint Sebastian, his entire body, torso, legs, neck, and head, pierced by a score of arrows. Let each arrow indicate the thrust of a German corps or division, opposed by the flat, smooth lines of the Allied defense. Yet no single sector takes precedence over another. This was the principal weakness of Falkenhayn's offensive. Ordinarily, concentrated breakthrough attacks would allow the offense to spread out and conquer from behind, once the enemy line had been breached. This was all but impossible with Falkenhayn's broad-front approach. The arrows might penetrate the flesh of the Allied Saint Sebastian, but the wounds were not deep enough to disable or kill.*

INDEED, WHEN REGARDED FROM THE vantage of a reconnaissance aircraft— and many were in the sky that day—the launching of Falkenhayn's great Flanders offensive did seem impressively continuous. It wasn't. Combat centered on a handful of hot spots. The smoke and flame of exploding shells began to merge, hiding the gaps. The Fourth Army was still settling in as individual units found their places in line. Some would not see action for another day or two, or even several more.

But in those first hours, the Flanders offensive did assume an almost unbroken fury south of the Lys. The Fourth Army may not yet have been fully in place, but Rupprecht's Sixth was, and he was determined to push the Allies away from his new prize, Lille, and off the ridges that threatened it. His first objectives were Prémesques and Ennetières, villages that were the potential anchors of an Allied upland

---

* Legend has it that Sebastian did not succumb to arrows but, healed back to life, suffered the martyrdom of assassination. His non-Christian assailants clubbed him to death.

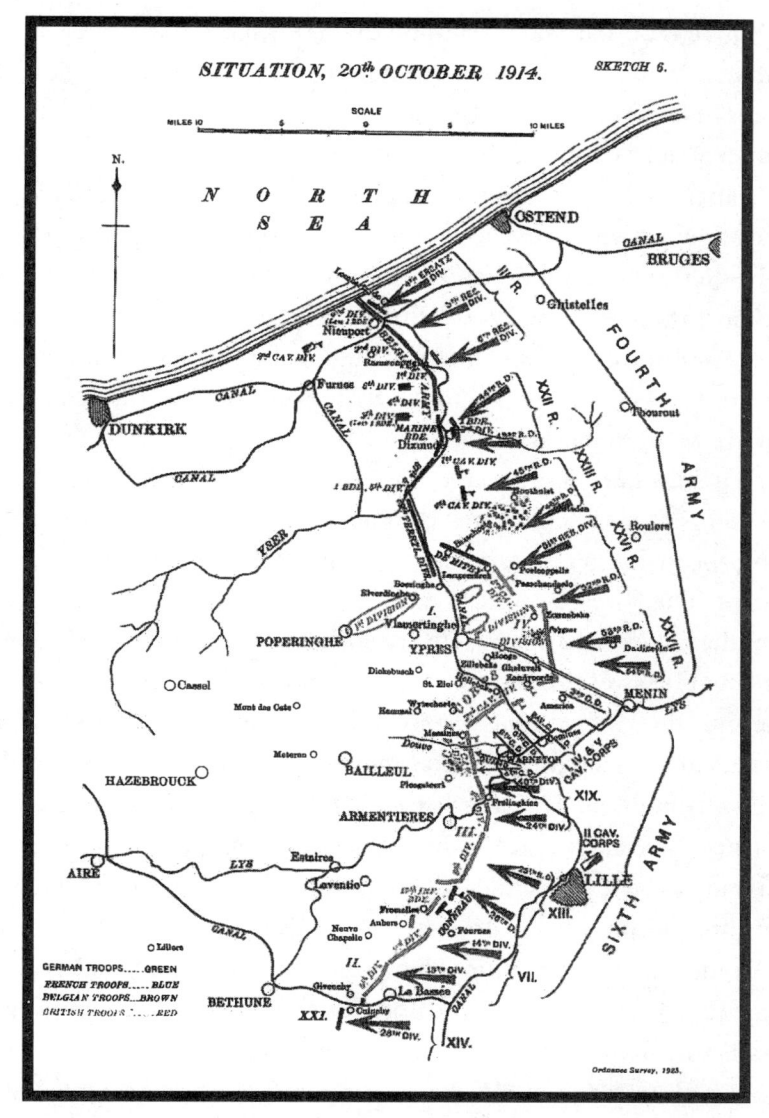

Erich von Falkenhayn's great drive in Flanders, which he officially inaugurated on October 20, extended from La Bassée (bottom center), fifty-odd miles to the North Sea. Each black arrow indicates a German division, a total of about 300,000 men, of whom as many as a third ended up as casualties. It was truly a broad-front offensive, an impressive sight on a map such as this, but not always the soundest expedient for the deep penetration he sought and counted on. You can detect a salient in formation, but it is only an impromptu bump caused by the abrupt retreat of British and French units escaping Roulers (center, far right): Call it as yet a small *s* salient. (The ovals behind the Allied line represent advancing British reinforcements.) Langemarck, where, later that week, the British would slaughter waves of German reservists, appears near the point (center) at which the BEF and the French Army met.

line. Three BEF battalions, supposedly 3,000 men, but by now a number much diminished by days of uninterrupted combat, defended Ennetières. They belonged to the Sherwood Foresters, Midlanders. The German attacks continued on and off all day on the nineteenth, mostly falling apart as British rifle fire cut down the long, close-packed lines of men as they patiently advanced across the fields. In this part of the battle, the Germans could depend on Rupprecht's veterans, men who had for almost three months known little else but combat, from Morhange and the Grand-Couronné to Arras and Lille. As fighters, these impromptu veterans were equal to the BEF professionals, though perhaps not up to them in marksmanship.

That advantage disappeared once night fell: it is not so easy to pick off shadows. Now shellfire was coming in from three sides of a narrow salient; the major in command asked permission to retire. Twice Brigade denied it. The Foresters were "on no account to withdraw." They continued to dig. They held out into the twentieth, the official start date of the German offensive. Three German battalions, dispatched from Lille, broke into the eastern houses and connected barns of Ennetières and, working along its single street, began methodically to overrun the village building by building. It was early evening now. In the dim light, survivors re-formed on a slight rise on which a windmill stood, its outer walls cratered and riddled, its paddles askew and shattered by gunfire. They saw troops approaching from a neighboring village, and assumed that they were coming to relieve them. They were not. The Sherwood Foresters recognized their error too late. But, in fact, masses were converging across fields, shoulder to shoulder, from all directions. This was the way Falkenhayn's scenario of attack was supposed to work, as his battalions pressed defenders into an ever-tightening circle. By its count, the German 122nd Regiment netted 576 prisoners. Another British group, 2 officers and 60 men, held out in cottages until the early hours of the next morning, when they, too, out of ammunition, surrendered. In the end, 2 officers and 253 other ranks did escape the disaster of Ennetières.

At nearby Prémesques, the village with the view of Lille—on a clear day, that is, which October 20 was not—fighting started at dawn and continued all day. The Germans annihilated two companies of the Leinsters, Irishmen, and recaptured the village, though a sizeable part of its temporary garrison escaped. The following day, the twenty-first, Sulzbach and his horse-drawn guns arrived in Prémesques.

"We all pull forward, get our first glimpse of this battlefield, and have to get used to the terrible scenes and impressions: corpses and more corpses, rubble, and the remains of villages. The bodies of friend and foe lie tumbled together. Heavy infantry fire drives us out of the position which we had taken up, and this is added to by increasingly heavy British artillery fire."

SULZBACH'S UNIT, THE 2ND BATTALION of the 77th Field Artillery Regiment, found a safer, if not necessarily more pleasant, spot to set up camp: "We are now in an area of meadowland, covered with dead cattle and a few surviving, ownerless cows. . . . Trenches hastily dug by the British are full of bodies. . . . A dreadful night comes down on us."

Sulzbach saw British prisoners being led back to improvised pens by the hundreds. The British III Corps, trying to hold on to a twelve-mile front on both sides of the Lys and attacked by two German corps, risked being squeezed in a vise if the enemy penetrated too deeply on either side of the river. That would be the worst-case scenario, not to mention one that might lead to a German breakout to the sea, trapping Allied troops by the thousands. Another German objective was the capture of the coalfields around Béthune, just to the west of La Bassée. That would mean the loss of the major remaining concentration of French coal reserves, one that a nation at war could now ill afford.

Gradually, though not without severe losses, the German Sixth Army pushed the Allies off the ridges. It took less than a week for the line to reach the sodden lowlands. Whenever possible, the British recruited local civilians to dig trenches or, where the water table was especially high, to erect breastworks, so-called command trenches: better village folk than the uncertain labor of exhausted infantrymen who could hardly stay awake. Parallel German diggings appeared. The first rolls of barbed wire arrived on wooden reels, and pioneer detachments, field engineers, strung it after dark. The Germans, too, were hard at work doing the same thing. Between pioneers, a live-and-let-live relationship developed.

The lines at the foot of the ridges took shape and before long assumed the look of permanence. "Little did we think when we were digging those trenches," Pvt. Frank Richards of the Royal Welch Fusiliers said, "that we were digging our future homes."

WE NOW TURN TO THE considerable action above the Lys.

At 10:50 on the morning of October 20, without quite knowing what to expect, Maj. Gen. Thompson Capper's 7th Division dispatched a reconnaissance in force, eastward along the road to Menin. It was his second attempt to force his way in that direction. Was there any truth in the continued reports that large numbers of enemy troops were approaching—although no commander on the Allied side yet believed that they could be the vanguard of an entire army? It was an uncomfortable repeat of what had happened the previous day. A line of skirmishers advanced but soon ran into heavy shellfire. Brimming with purpose, armored cars made cavalry-like dashes in the direction of the Lys, and returned. Sir John French remained as eager as ever to begin swinging his Fochian scythe, and he had been pressuring Rawlinson, Capper's immediate superior, to get on with the final preparations for his big show. But it became increasingly clear to those closer to the action that the 7th Division was heading for trouble. Rawlinson once again ordered it to pull back: Germans were massing up ahead, in numbers too numerous for British skirmishers to handle. But French refused to forgive Rawlinson for what he viewed as an excess of caution, an opportunity missed.

German attacks on the 7th Division began in the afternoon, "preceded by scouts and snipers, and covered by artillery and machine-gun fire," noted the history of the Grenadier Guards:

> Almost for the first time the Germans were now distinctly seen, and there was something almost reassuring in the fact that they

looked like ordinary beings. Hitherto they had seemed a sort of mysterious bogey, something far away on the black horizon, an evil force associated with burning houses and fleeing inhabitants. Though their attack was all according to the book, they never succeeded in reaching our trenches.

The results were the same all along the 7th Division's eight-mile front, which was still little more than an outpost line. The divisional history rendered the pointillism of combat, with barely connected dibs and dabs of units spread out across the landscape. "Effective assistance was given by the 104th Battery . . . which caught German infantry advancing in mass. . . . The Yorkshires' machine-guns took full advantage of some admirable targets. The Wiltshires were quite hard pressed but the enemy were beaten off every time with heavy losses, the XXXVth Brigade R.F.A. [Royal Field Artillery] co-operating effectively and catching the Germans as they came over the ridge; the Scots Fusiliers . . . caught a company working forward along the edge of a wood and drove it into the trees in disorder."

For the green and barely trained German regiments, the first experience of combat was hellish. They attacked shoulder to shoulder, in the prescribed manner they had learned on parade grounds. Men of the XXVII Reserve Corps hurried up the ridge toward a large village, Becelaere, and were met with concentrated rifle fire from the thin forward lines of the 7th Division regulars. Late in the afternoon of October 20, they took the village, mainly by weight of numbers: in the fading light, the new soldiers had their first glimpse of the distant towers of the Cathedral and the Cloth Hall of Ypres. That enticing view hardly made up for their losses. Accounts spoke of meadows "carpeted" with corpses. Wounded lay untreated where they had fallen, and many died before aid could reach them. Men retreated toward the relative safety of the burning village. Chaos ruled the night. Ammunition columns, machine-gun sections, horse-drawn vehicles, and reinforcements jammed roads and open ground. A stream of walking wounded headed for the rear, hoping to find treatment. The men in the front lines went without food and drink. It rained. Shivering soldiers in soaked greatcoats got little sleep. Orders went out for the attack to resume once light returned.

To the left of the 7th Division, the British 3rd Cavalry Division still held the two miles of ridge from Passchendaele to Westroosebeke on the morning of the twentieth. There it was in touch with de Mitry's French Cavalry Corps. But, under pressure from the German XXIII Corps, the French gave way, retreating through the dark, spongy recesses of the Houthulst Forest. In a single afternoon, the French surrendered as much as four miles, although the Germans didn't follow them until the next morning. Rawlinson's 3rd Cavalry found its left flank suddenly exposed, and it, too, retreated. In turn, the French Territorials in Passchendaele pulled back. At 12:30 that afternoon, after a brief but fierce fight, the Allies abandoned the village, which the Germans promptly occupied.

The painter Paul Maze, a Frenchman who worked for the British staff as an interpreter and scout, always carried a camera. He took this shot of a stream of refugees, seemingly without end, that clogged roads and blocked progress of troops and supplies. (Imperial War Museum, Paul Maze Collection)

The Territorial Division's retreat must have been difficult; available escape routes were clogged with refugees, who streamed through the Allied lines and made desperate haste to get down the long, low ridge, out of the path of war. Some led heavy Flemish three-wheeled wagons, drawn by horses and piled high with furniture and the precious accumulations of a lifetime; cattle, tethered to the wagons, trailed behind. Others accompanied carts drawn by ponies or dogs, or pushed wheelbarrows, carrying both possessions and children too small to walk. Older children trotted by their mothers' sides. Gasping for breath, old people practically ran. "All had a look of terror in their eyes," remembered a regimental historian, "and all hurried madly to safety, spurred on by the thought of the burning villages that lay behind them." Writing home, a British officer noted, "There is not a soul left in the country. All the farms are deserted, and the cows and pigs wander about aimlessly. The men milk them in the intervals of shelling! The crops are splendid, but wasted, it is as if a plague has passed over the land." The Germans did nothing to stem the human flood in this sector: they must have welcomed the chaos they were creating.

It is recorded that in the neighboring village of Zonnebeke, a mile down the road from Passchendaele, a baker named Van den Bulcke made bread deliveries that morning, and noted in a heavy ledger what was owed him. Then he loaded up a cart—perhaps the same one he had used to make his deliveries—and joined the retreating throng. Van den Bulcke carried his ledger all the way to Quimper in Brittany. Not until 1922 did the baker return to Zonnebeke—and of course did not neglect to bill his surviving 1914 customers for their final distribution of bread.

That same day, October 20, the two divisions of I Corps finally arrived and prepared to take up positions outside of Ypres, next to those of the 7th Division. Maj. George Darrell "Ma" Jeffreys of the Grenadier Guards described, in the classic language of an English country squire and proper Church of England man, his passage through the town: "Crowds of people in the streets, to see us march through, and there seemed to be a tremendous lot of priests and nuns. Rather a nice old town with narrow, cobble-stoned streets, and some fine buildings." In the countryside to the east, he could hear "a lot of firing . . . in the afternoon and all night, but we saw no enemy. A pouring wet night."*

Many of those who stood by watching Jeffreys's detachment pass were refugees just arrived, people with no place to go, nothing better to do. The more fortunate among them found space on friendly floors; British and French soldiers and Belgian wounded had already filled most houses. Day and night the streets swarmed with the new homeless. Religious orders did their best to feed them. Ypres was a town caught in a sudden uproar. A nun, Dame M. Columban, who belonged to an abbey of Irish Benedictine sisters who had originally fled to Belgium in Cromwell's time, chronicled the never-ceasing hurly-burly that had overtaken them:

> Outside, the noise grew ever louder. The roar of cannon, the rolling of the carriages, Paris omnibuses, provision and ambulance cars, the continual passage of cavalry and foot soldiers, and the motor-cars passing with lightning-like speed, made the quiet, sleepy little town of Ypres as animated as London's busiest streets. At night even the Allied regiments poured in, profiting by the obscurity to hide their movements from the Germans; while, contrasting with the darkness, the fire from the battle-field showed up clearly against the midnight sky.

THE NEXT MORNING, OCTOBER 21, the advance of the I Corps toward Bruges, twenty-five miles distant, was supposed to begin. Still, the Allied generals refused to surrender to reality. Foch was inevitably the fountainhead of new enterprises. His enthusiasm for the offensive—which at all times the stolid Joffre backed—swept Sir John French along, almost until

---

* A legendary soldier, whose name will turn up again in these pages, Jeffreys served in the Grenadier Guards and as a colonel commanded Maj. Winston Churchill in 1915–16. He had acquired the nickname "Ma" because in Aldershot, where the Guards were based, a Mrs. Jeffreys, known as Ma, kept a well-known house of prostitution. The subalterns were, as a fellow Guardsman recorded, "quick to transfer the sobriquet to their brother officer."

it was too late. Foch never met an offensive he didn't like: offense, in his view, was always the best defense.

But all through that Tuesday the evidence of an unforeseen German effort grew, from intercepted wireless messages—the enemy often didn't bother to use code but spoke in the clear—from loquacious prisoners belonging to corps and divisions hitherto unidentified, from increasingly accurate aerial reconnaissance that reported marching swarms of infantry, and from the rising number of German offensive actions. On the night of the twentieth, French issued his Army Operation Order No. 39. This was no longer the man who, a day, even hours, earlier, had been talking about vigorous attacks. Now his tone had changed: "The Commander-in-Chief intends to contain the enemy . . ." Though the Allies had not abandoned the offensive, you can already sense a hedging of bets: "As ground is gained," read another order from Haig's I Corps a few hours later, "it must be entrenched." Those words marked a decided change in the nature of the campaign—and, indeed, the war on the Western Front—a first hint of the big freeze to come.

By the following morning, the British field marshal must have known the worst. French seemed to lose his nerve—as he had done once before, in early September, when days of retreat had left him ready to evacuate the BEF from France—until Lord Kitchener intervened. Now it was Joffre who came to see him at his new headquarters in Saint-Omer, just over the border from Belgium. Joffre, who was on one of his lightning journeys, announced that he was transferring the French IX Corps from the Champagne front to Ypres; Grossetti's 42nd Division, which had made that memorable march at Saint-Gond, would reinforce the Belgians at Nieuport. He also advised French that sea dikes had been opened to flood the approaches to Dunkirk, the Channel port most immediately threatened. Sir Henry Wilson was present, in his capacity both as deputy chief of staff and as translator. "Doubleh-Vay" (as his friend Foch called Wilson) was one of the only generals at GHQ who could speak adequate French. Wilson described the scene in his diary:

All went satisfactorily until Sir John asked for facilities to make a great entrenched camp at Boulogne to take the whole E.F. [Expeditionary Force]. Joffre's face instantly became quite square and he replied that such a thing could not be allowed for a moment. He would make some works to safeguard against a coup-de-main [surprise attack], but an entrenched camp he would not allow. Sir John was checkmated straight away. . . . So that nightmare is over.

Or, at Ypres, was it just beginning?

THAT WEDNESDAY, OCTOBER 21, THE Western Front reached another milestone. At the foot of the Passchendaele Ridge, the land spreads out in a wide plain that barely rises above sea level. There, the day before, two fresh divisions of the German XXIII Corps, just arrived, had forced de Mitry's French cavalry corps to retreat into the Houthulst Forest, the most extensive piece of woodland in the area. Its dark, spongy depths are so humid that the trunks of trees are green and crusted with moss to a great height. The German 46th Reserve Division did enter, and occupy, the forest the next morning. The division, noted a semiofficial German monograph, "had to cross a stretch of country which put these partially trained troops and their inexperienced officers to a very severe test. The great forest of Houthulst with its dense undergrowth made it difficult to keep direction in the attack and to maintain communication between units fighting an invisible opponent." But, it must be added, an imaginary one. The phantom French cavalrymen had already fled.

One week after the Allies had sealed their side of the Western Front, the retreat of de Mitry's cavalry had allowed the Germans to close theirs for good. Between the North Sea and the Swiss border, other than marshland, rivers, or impossible mountain drops, no more gaps of any significance remained.

GERMANS SUDDENLY SEEMED TO BE everywhere. As the endless lines of the Fourth Army fanned out, their troops swarmed over Roulers, up the Passchendaele Ridge, and into Houthulst Forest. They occupied the outskirts of Dixmude and, closer to the sea, threw their first rude bridges across the Yser. Battalions of the Sixth Army's XIX Corps had already established themselves on the north bank of the Lys, passing over on pontoon or footbridges or in assault boats, always under fire. They occupied a railroad embankment and dug machine-gun emplacements. The troops were mainly Saxon regulars, men from the nation's southeast who had a reputation for being the most ardently German of the Germans. By the time darkness fell on the twentieth, they had, by cutting through fences and hedges strengthened with barbed wire, fought forward to within three hundred yards of a developing strongpoint, the British-held Ploegsteert Wood. At 6:30 A.M. (5:30 French time) the next morning, an extended line advanced in silence through the thick predawn fog. There was no advance artillery barrage. The Saxon regulars swept over the unsuspecting British, killing some still asleep.

But this time surprise failed to clear the field. In the fog, the Saxons were as blind as their adversaries. The British rallied. At a place called Le Gheer, where houses were loosely strung out along a north–south dirt track, the two sides brawled with bayonets, clubbed with rifle butts, and fired rifles at close range. But the British held on to the flanks, and the Saxons barely penetrated the dense wood with its soggy floor deep in slippery leaves. The struggle for those mean Le Gheer cottages lasted most of the day, until orders arrived for the Germans to withdraw. "Sniping prevented the counting of the dead," the *Official History* noted with a certain grim satisfaction, "but wherever the enemy had penetrated the front line, the ground was littered with German corpses." Two days of combat, according to German sources, cost Infantry Regiment 104 alone (two other regiments were involved) 12 officers and 720 other ranks killed, wounded, and missing, irreplaceable regulars all. The British did not get off unscathed. The 12th Brigade lost 468 officers and men, also regulars and also irreplaceable.

The Saxons refused to give up. They clung to trenches at the edge of Ploegsteert Wood, but accurate British small-arms fire frustrated their continued efforts to break through. They found themselves huddling in muddy trenches, unable even to evacuate their wounded or bury their dead. Food couldn't reach them, and they could only relieve thirst by scooping up puddles of water in shell holes. The surviving Saxons eventually made it back to reserve trenches fifty yards to their rear. Already enemies were learning to exist that close to one another. Such short but increasingly permanent distances were becoming the established order of trench warfare, as the sides developed their defenses, trench systems that, in places, would almost touch.

Elsewhere, just to the north of Ploegsteert Wood, confusion overtook the British on October 21. Fatigue was largely to blame. Regiments that had been in action, or just advancing and withdrawing, settling in and then being moved for no apparent reason, their men getting no more than a couple of hours of sleep a night, were beginning to make errors that might have been avoidable otherwise. A brigade of Maj. Gen. Hubert Gough's 2nd Cavalry Division, mostly dismounted now, held the village of Hollebeke, which had become the southern hinge of the bulge developing east of Ypres. Its lines and gunpits were too thin and hastily dug, too irregular to be called a salient quite yet. (Gough had been a prominent troublemaker in the Curragh incident, but that was forgotten now.) About midmorning a dispatch rider brought to brigade headquarters instructions from Gough, indicating a possible line of retreat—but only if necessary. A strung-out brigadier and his staff misinterpreted Gough's "anticipatory" plan as a command to withdraw immediately. Yet another misunderstood word had dire potential. The brigade abandoned the village and the Hollebeke château, as did two other brigades on either side of it. A gap of more than a mile opened. German cavalry, also turned infantry, followed at a careful distance, clouds of smoke from exploding shells, "like giant puff balls" (one observer remembered) bursting in the blue autumn sky. The entire 2nd Cavalry Division was now in retreat. Gough rode forward, found staff officers of the brigade that had first broken, and commanded them to turn their men around.

"I shall expect to learn that you are in your original trenches within the next 30 minutes," he said. "Are you quite clear?"

Less than an hour later all three brigades were back in line. By the end of October 21 they had recovered (at the cost of 4 officers and 11 men, already a minimal reckoning on the Western Front) everything but the château, which for the moment remained in German hands. Apparently the Germans never realized they could have ended the day at least two or three miles closer to Ypres, with the southern flank of the Allied line in peril of dissolving.*

That night the opposing cavalries, German and British, settled down, facing each other across an empty interval of 1,000 to 2,500 yards. It wasn't called no-man's-land yet. A regimental historian described the horse soldier's new role. The cavalry, he wrote, had "gradually congealed" from "a fluid line of mounted men occasionally dismounting to use their rifles" to "a rigid line of dismounted men occasionally using their horses to move from one part of the battlefield to another."

FOR THE 7TH DIVISION, HOLDING a disconnected series of trenches that made a right-angle bend at a hamlet called Kruiseecke and then continued northward for four miles through Zonnebeke, nothing changed, except that its losses mounted. It could ill afford them. The main task of the division was to keep the line steady while the I Corps took its place to the north—and presumably prepared to start its advance. All day German artillery firing from its newly gained positions around Passchendaele made life hot and miserable for the 7th. In the judgment of General Farrar-Hockley: "The corps staff had drawn a line on the map for the 7th Division to hold without regard to contours and, unhappily, General Capper, the divisional commander, had accepted it. His infantry were therefore dug in on forward slopes in full view" of German batteries on high ground. Throughout the day and into the night of October 21, the German gunners kept up a harassing fire on well-registered targets. The 7th lacked the trench-fighting experience that the other divisions had

* The failure to exploit that gap, as well as the lackluster performance of the German cavalry in this sector, may have contributed, according to the *Official History*, to the firing of Generalleutnant Gustav Freiherr (Baron) von Hollen and his replacement by Gen. Georg von der Marwitz. Matters such as demotions had always to be handled delicately, especially when nobility was involved. Marwitz, in a letter written the following evening, acted as though nothing special had happened in the first hours of his new job. "I passed a dull day beyond the long, over-extended front." But it is significant that Hollen went from commanding eight cavalry divisions in France and Belgium to one infantry division on the Eastern Front, the 37th, though it was a first-rate one (but in a region of less importance).

picked up on the Aisne. And, to make matters worse, the ground it held was sandy. Trenches crumbled, rifles jammed, and the troops discovered that they didn't have enough picks and shovels to dig new, better-sited protective excavations. Searches of nearby farms turned up few useful tools. Barbed wire, moreover, had not arrived. In places the German infantry ended the day just a hundred yards distant, but they did not attack. That night the 22nd Brigade of the 7th Division evacuated Zonnebeke, which the Germans immediately occupied. Darkness allowed the British to withdraw to less exposed positions. For both sides, once again, exhaustion was the only winner.

Besides Zonnebeke, the Germans could boast of a couple of small successes along the eight miles of overextended front held by the 7th Division, though those were no match for the savage rebuff they encountered almost everywhere else. About four in the afternoon of the twenty-first, near the nearby ridge crossroads at Broodseinde, troops of the 52nd Reserve Division discovered that the left flank of the trenches held by the 1st Royal Welch Fusiliers was in the air and vulnerable. The Germans punched through the opening and hooked behind the British defenders. After a firefight lasting three hours, the Welch, surrounded, ran out of ammunition. Improvised white flags waved. More than a hundred men surrendered. Later, in the waning hours of the night, near the same Broodseinde crossroads, a heavily laden British supply column blundered into the lines held by Reserve Infantry Regiment 238 (which had also helped to capture the Welch). This time it bagged 3 officers and 115 other ranks. But the battalion of the South Staffords, which the Germans had been trying to reach and overrun, did get away by striking out across fields and pastures and melting into the darkness.

October 21 may have been short on accomplishment for both sides but was long on an indifference to death that is hard to understand more than a century later. At Zonnebeke, a west-facing village on the Passchendaele Ridge, a British soldier remembered how German volunteers would sing and wave their rifles in the air while attacking: "As fast as we shot them down, others took their place. Even when their own artillery barrage caught them by mistake, they kept on advancing. They were incredibly, ridiculously brave." Or take the attack of German reservists on the Wiltshire Battalion regulars entrenched at Polygon Wood, the north-extended forearm, the worker's salute, as it were, beyond the elbow at Kruiseecke:

> The enemy came on with great resolution and in close formation, line upon line, not once but several times, and the battalion took full advantage of its chances. . . . Evening found the Wiltshires exhausted but triumphant; the ground in front of them was heaped with German dead and wounded, a testimony at once to the battalion's musketry and to its opponents' determination and devotion.

Devotion. It is a quasireligious word that has deserted our lexicon.

This war did, of course, also partake of the theatre of the absurd—as, for instance, what happened to a battalion of the Irish Guards on the evening of the twenty-first, also near Zonnebeke. Rudyard Kipling (whose son served with the Guards, and would be killed in 1915) records the story. The battalion, Kipling wrote, came under a heavy burst of artillery fire and was forced to lie down in a plowed field: then, "a hare started up which was captured by a man of No. 2 Company to the scandal of discipline and the delight of all, and later sold for five shillings."

Only two days into the battle, mass killing had begun to seem commonplace. As darkness fell on the front where the German XXVII Reserve Corps faced the 7th Division, British observers noted helmeted men wearing white armbands gathering before Becelaere. It was obvious that one of the patented German night attacks was about to take place: the armbands would make the men visible to one another in the dark. The British dragged guns to within 200 yards of their forward trench line. The *Official History* tells the rest. "The guns were run up to the crest and were just in time to catch the Germans on the sky-line shoulder to shoulder at 1,200 yards' range. There was much shouting, but nothing more was seen until next morning, when many bodies were visible on the forward slope."

———

WITH FOCH'S BACKING, FRENCH HAD ordered the newly arrived I Corps to drive toward Bruges on the twenty-first. Among other benefits, he hoped the attack would relieve pressure on the beleaguered 7th Division. The designated jump-off time was 7 A.M.; the 2nd Division, joining with the 7th at Zonnebeke, was in position half an hour earlier. But the 1st Division, headed for the sizeable village of Langemarck (population 7,438 but emptying fast), was held up by French troops streaming across the Yser Canal and by more pitifully interminable lines of refugees. It was 8:30 by the time the 1st Division got into place. The better part of another hour passed before it was ready to start north to the Forest of Houthulst, still presumed to be empty of Germans. The I Corps' objectives for the first stage of its advance were the ridge villages of Westroosebeke and Passchendaele, which the Allies had abandoned the previous day.

Below those villages, the few ridges like Pilckem, wide, gentle land swells, are hardly worth the designation. Fields are enclosed by thick, impassable hedges and are seamed by brooks—"*beek*" or "*beke*" is the familiar Flemish suffix—and by ever-present drainage ditches. Farmyards, cottages, and scattered clumps of woodland further obscure long views, as do the mists (or in summer, heat hazes) that frequently envelop the landscape. Artillery fires blindly here, and attackers are hard-pressed to discern what or who lurks beyond the next obstruction. "Owing to the enclosed nature of the country," Operations orders warned, "it is important that guns should be pushed close up behind the firing line . . . at every opportunity."

Take what happened the morning of the twenty-first to a battalion of the 2nd Division, the Oxford and Bucks, south of Poelcappelle, yet another of those view-blocking congeries of mean brick houses and barns that lend no particular distinction to the area. Troops came up against a hedge interwoven with barbed wire—an obstacle favored by both sides at the time. But when the British tried to pass through a gate, a machine gun opened on them and (says a divisional account) "officers and men tumbled over one another—killed or wounded." The Oxfords did get through, but with a loss of some 30 men; they took even worse casualties, 190 men, in the flatlands beyond, when they encountered German trenches and the kind of aggregated rifle fire that the British had hitherto been masters of.

But the 2nd Division did make it across the Zonnebeke–Langemarck road, pushing forward by as much as two thousand yards, more than a mile. Two companies of Coldstream Guards reached the ridge just south of Passchendaele, but found themselves isolated and were eventually ordered back. The artillery of Haig's I Corps may have enjoyed the best day of all: one battery had what the *Official History* called "the target of a lifetime—thick waves of advancing infantry in the open at short range." For both sides, the 2nd Division historian said, October 21 was "a busy day for doctors."

That morning attack of the I Corps "progressed slowly but steadily"— the clichéd words are those of a regimental historian—and then ground to a halt as the two British divisions collided with three advancing German ones, the 46th Reserve, the 51st Reserve, and the 52nd Reserve. Now it was the turn of the Germans to go on the attack. The din swelled into what a British participant described as "one unending roar." Several thousand men of the 51st and 52nd Reserve Divisions, hardly tested in battle, battered the British line from Zonnebeke north to Langemarck, held for the most part by the 2nd Division. At Langemarck, that line took a right-angle bend in the direction of the Yser Canal. The trenches that the 1st Division began to dig there faced the Houthulst Forest. Already the German 46th Reserve Division was heading south through it.

As men in their spiked helmets and smelly *feldgrau* woolens emerged into open meadows and started splashing through a succession of swampy streams, some of them waist deep, the sun made a rare appearance. Was it a relief? Perhaps not. "To die by daylight," the poet R. G. Vliet wrote, "is the worst terror."

For the British 1st Division, which faced the 46th Reserve, October 21 was a day when insubstantial landmarks cast long shadows, as if to prove that military history has the power to defy the elementary laws of physics. Koekuit, a group of farm buildings on a slight rise two thousand yards north of Langemarck, changed hands repeatedly, and became the tip of a salient within a forming larger salient. Another bulge, Kortekeer Cabaret, a mingy crossroads tavern a mile or so to the west, found itself the anchor of what passed as the Allied front, one of the places where the onrush of the Germans was brought to a halt. Even ditches, which became ready-made trenches, assumed a preternatural importance as lines of defense—and, in cases, as deathtraps. A quote from the regimental history of the Gloucester gives a feeling of the confused, ditch-bound give-and-take of those hours:

> On the left of D Company heavy machine-gun fire opened. Shortly afterwards Lieutenant Caunter through his field-glasses saw columns of the enemy about to debouch from a road near the railway about 700 yards on the right front. In three intense bursts of rapid fire the Gloucesters broke up the threatened attack. The enemy, however, shelled the position and several wounded men lying in the ditch were killed.

October 21 was a day, too, in which divided command nearly undid the Allies. For the Germans, it was again a day of missed opportunity.

Early in the afternoon the situation had seemed promising for the I Corps. The German attacks had let up, and the 46th Reserve Division appeared to be pulling back toward the Houthulst Forest. The British even had reinforcements close at hand, a rarity for them. Then, at 2 P.M., the commander of the French front, Gen. Victor d'Urbal, ordered his cavalry corps to retire and take up positions west of the Yser Canal. Joffre had promised to send the IX Corps, with its two infantry divisions, veterans of the marshes of Saint Gond; but they wouldn't, and didn't, arrive for another two or three days. For the moment d'Urbal could only depend on two Territorial infantry, and four cavalry, divisions: he worried that a German breakthrough might unhinge the line and open the way to the Channel ports. He later explained that "it was indispensable to remain in possession of the line of the Yser and its crossings." He probably believed what he said, but this master of the hot-air directive could have cost his side the battle.

His order to retreat came about the time that, not far to the south, the British 2nd Cavalry Division was making its mistaken withdrawal from Hollebeke and the left wing of the 7th Division seemed to be dissolving at Zonnebeke. For an hour or so the Germans had a luck-sent opportunity to pinch off much of the tiny British Army.

But the GOC of the French 7th Cavalry Division, the dapper Major General Hély d'Oissel, immediately grasped the threat the British now faced. He was on the left of the I Corps, and saw that if he withdrew, the Germans could practically march through the open gap. Hély d'Oissel refused to obey d'Urbal's order immediately, insisting that it be repeated. The time he bought made all the difference. The left flank of Haig's I Corps was briefly uncovered. But the 1st (Guards) Brigade, commanded by a brigadier named Charles FitzClarence, was able to extend its line a thin and precarious three miles. This would not be the only instance in which the quick thinking of FitzClarence saved the Allies from disaster that month. By the middle of the afternoon the 2nd Cavalry Division, thanks to Gough, had closed the Hollebeke gap: the 22nd Brigade may have lost Zonnebeke but, despite heavy losses, it never came close to breaking.* In the event, Falkenhayn's two German armies, saddled with their broad-front operational plan, probably lacked the troops to exploit temporary advantages in particular sectors. Even so, the disintegration of the Allied line had been a near thing.

IT WAS LONG AFTER DARK when Ma Jeffreys wrote in his diary: "The whole sky to the east was lit up by the glare of fires, presumably started by the Germans, who made a counter-attack on our positions about 10 p.m. As they approached, someone called out, 'Don't fire, we are Coldstream.'" (Another writer elaborated on Jeffreys's account. "It was characteristic of German thoroughness of method to master this regimental idiosyncrasy, and say Coldstream and not Coldstreams.") As the German "spiked helmets could be clearly seen against the light of the fire," Jeffreys contin-

---

* The commander of the 22nd Brigade, Sydney Lawford, established a justified reputation as a fighting general at Ypres, leading attacks (sometimes on horseback) armed only with a walking stick. He rose to become a lieutenant general, was knighted in the field, and led the 41st (London) Division. Lawford ended as the longest-serving British divisional head in the war. Nicknamed "Swanky Syd," he had a fondness for natty outfits; Lawford was as famous for his amatory exploits as his military ones. They would later lead to his forced retirement. Today he is remembered, if at all, as the father of the Hollywood actor Peter Lawford. Indeed, he played aristocratic bit parts in a handful of movies—all, alas, uncredited.

ued, "our men were not taken in, and they were repulsed with heavy loss." The engagement was over in a couple of minutes; the Germans left behind a hundred dead and wounded.

Jeffreys's night was not over. The major, a man with intense eyes and a huge inverted fantail of a mustache, traveled back to 2nd Division headquarters in nearby Saint-Julian, to report the situation. He passed along a road "crowded with transport moving up," as well as walking wounded, ambulances, both motorized and horse-drawn, messengers, men separated from their units, and refugees moving rearward. "I was tired and wet." After the burst of afternoon sunshine, it had started to rain. At headquarters, the division GOC, Maj. Gen. Charles Monro, greeted Jeffreys pleasantly. "He was full of confidence: said the German troops in front of us were a raw lot—'mostly cooks and waiters.'" Jeffreys, who had just spent a vexed interval confronting those cooks and waiters, recorded a two-word exclamation: "I wonder!"

HISTORIANS THRIVE ON CATEGORIES; HISTORY couldn't care less. In July 1920, just short of six years after the events described here, a British military group, grandiloquently christened the Battles Nomenclature Committee, issued a report. Among other findings, it designated the events of October 21 and the three days following as the Battle of Langemarck—a subdivision of what came to be known as the First Battle of Ypres. (The Committee named October 19 as the start of Falkenhayn's offensive; the *Official History* goes with the twentieth, the date I prefer.) As the time of armed encounters lengthened, it is true, they became increasingly hard to comprehend, an unending bloody blur. Langemarck was indeed briefly a center of action, as well as the reputed locus of spontaneous vocal outbursts that would soon take wing in legend.

But we need first to turn to that part of the story of the first two days not yet told: events as they affected the Germans. So far, most of the present chapter has been seen from the Allied side. That, obviously, gives us less than a full account. For the Germans, the attack began to stray from Falkenhayn's plan almost from the moment his troops began their advance on the morning of October 20. We recognize just how much when we read the accounts of ordinary soldiers exposed for the first time to violent death. We have to dig a little deeper, and read between the lines of the numerous regimental histories that appeared in Germany all through the twenties and into the early thirties, when they became tools of Nazi myth-making and of dubious value. As a general rule, the closer the publication date of a memoir or a regimental history was to the the war itself, the more accurate it was likely to be. Letters and journals, written in the heat of an event, can be the most valuable testimonies of all—if, of course, they have not been too heavily censored. (The best French accounts, curiously, were written during the war. Later, the public did its best to avoid confronting the trauma—though they were reminded of it almost every day by the sight of women in black—widows, mothers, sisters, or fiancées of the dead.) Most of the narratives in German were never translated into English. That is changing now, mainly through the efforts of British historian Jack Sheldon, who has compiled (and, as of this writing, is still doing so) a series of books on the German Great War experience on the Western Front. Sheldon's extraordinary and important work—as well as his collaborations with another authority, Nigel Cave—offer an entirely different, and altogether fresh, view of the events I have recorded here. Many, though by no means all, of the translations from the German about the experiences of 1914 quoted in these pages come from Sheldon's books. For the military historian, the study of the Great War will never be the same.

THE NIGHT OF OCTOBER 20–21 found two reserve corps of the Fourth Army in possession of the ridge five miles to the east of Ypres, and beginning to move down its lower slopes; a division of another was about to enter the Houthulst Forest. The Germans expected, and hoped for, the kind of largely unobstructed progress that had to this point distinguished their progress through Flanders. Army orders, which arrived during the night, called for an advance to the Yser Canal, and the establishment of bridge-heads on its far banks. The 46th Reserve Division was to occupy the Houthulst Forest. The 51st and 52nd Reserve Divisions were to take Langemarck, smashing through it on their way to the canal; they were to sweep across Pilckem Ridge, which overlooked the waterway and the towers of Ypres three miles away.

Three long columns of the 51st Reserve Division marched from Westroosebeke, at the end of the ridge, to Poelcappelle, which the Germans had occupied on the twentieth. The stop-and-start trek, just two and a half miles long, required five hours. The 15,000 men, who had been up all night, jammed the single street of Poelcappelle. As dawn broke in the foggy fields beyond the village, men could finally lie down and catch a brief nap, either sitting on their packs, heads in their hands, or stretching out in the wet grass. Some found barnyard pumps and washed up. Field kitchens appeared. Many of the reservists had gone without a hot meal for several days and had resorted to eating scraps left in discarded knapsacks by retreating Belgian troops. Beyond hunger and the desire to sleep, one newly minted soldier remembered, "there was a feeling of anxiety—really sharp anxiety that bit and gnawed away at us."

Now as the German troops waited to go forward toward the village of Langemarck, shrapnel began to burst over their heads. The first wounded went down. Platoons and companies spread out into skirmish lines, and those lines of men, thousands of them, moved forward, shoulder to shoulder, in the prescribed attack formation. They pushed through gardens and hedges. Already rifle and machine-gun fire from an invisible enemy began to take a toll in the mist. "The Feldgrauen lay piled in heaps along the road and in the ditches," said a *Vizefeldwebel* (staff sergeant). As he led his men across a stream bed, a shell exploded nearby, driving a splinter into his stomach. Stretcher bearers carried him back through the barrage to Poelcappelle; he was lucky to have escaped this second shell storm. "I was delivered, semi-conscious, to the regimental aid post . . . and there the injections of our battalion medical officer, Dr Mirbel, delivered me into a marvelous dreamland."

The attacks everywhere broke down, and junior officers tried with little success to get them started again. The long lines split into platoon- or company-sized groups, already reduced. They became lost. They got turned around and attacked in the wrong direction. They cowered behind hedges. A corporal of Reserve Infantry Regiment 235 wrote, "There was no order. I have no clue where our platoon commander was. . . . Men were falling all around me; we were in a witches' cauldron of artillery fire." Lines turned and ran, British gunfire following them. Shrapnel pellets whipped down on them. Survivors of Reserve Infantry Regiment 235, crashing through a field of chest-high fronds, came on their colonel, sprawled lifeless amid the sugar beets.

A few men from Reserve Infantry Regiment 236 actually made it into the outskirts of Langemarck, with its burning houses, collapsing roofs, and ammunition exploding in flame-consumed buildings. As they waited in vain for support, they dug lengths of trench with whatever came to hand: bayonets, helmets, a few spades. Lost men wandered aimlessly in the inky black night, now streaming rain. They were, perhaps fortunately, unaware of the cheerful orders that emanated that night from General der Infanterie Freiherr (Baron) von Hügel, commander of the XXVI Reserve Corps, headquartered at Westroosebeke:

1. I am delighted that today the Corps, during its first serious battle, has beaten off and driven back the enemy all along the line.
2. Tonight the Corps is digging in in the captured positions, organizing, and replenishing with food and ammunition. Strong forces . . . are preparing to resume the offensive in the morning . . .

How many casualties did the Germans sustain in that day of rout and panic? We shall probably never know.

OCTOBER 21, A WEDNESDAY, BEGAN for Sir John French with his unpleasant meeting with Joffre, and the dismissal of his armed camp notion: the day went downhill from there. Not long after the departure of the generalissimo, Intelligence informed French of the German buildup. Why the new information had taken so long to reach him is puzzling: perhaps it was his tendency to ignore what he didn't want to hear. Now, though, he was properly dismayed. Intercepted messages indicated that no fewer than four new corps had arrived to reinforce the German Fourth Army. As he later reflected, "all my worst forebodings as to the enemy's increasing strength were realized. . . . This, taken with the speed in which they appeared on the field, came like a veritable bolt from the blue."

That afternoon he met with Rawlinson and Haig, the commanders of IV and I Corps. Rawlinson's failure to reach Menin still rankled—as, perhaps, did the distinct chance that the IV Corps commander may have acted appropriately. French told his two generals "that in view of the unexpected reinforcements coming up of the enemy, it would probably be impossible to carry out the original role assigned to them." That put paid to his cherished offensive. At 8:30 P.M. on the twenty-first, Sir John issued an order to start entrenching all along the line. Not only were there no more openings in the Western Front but also, as the Allies began to dig in, the shape of a wedge had begun to impose itself on battle maps of the area. This was the moment when the Ypres Salient was created.

LET US PAUSE TO CONSIDER the possibilities still very much open to the Germans. On the Yser front, the Belgian membrane of defense was perilously frail. There seemed little to prevent Beseler's III Corps from continuing its sweep down the dune route toward Dunkirk, threatening Ypres from behind. Other corps might strike down from the ridges, breaking into the open of the maritime plain and joining with those advancing from the coast, to squeeze Entente divisions in a vise, narrowing and, finally, eliminating potential escape routes. Could they have fought their way out? Or would they have been encircled, trapped in what would come to be known in the next war as a "cauldron"? Would the Germans have at last pulled off the dream of their operational thinkers, the double envelopment, a Cannae in the Low Countries? After that, nothing could stop a breakthrough to the Channel ports. "Had they done so," writes historian Ian F. W. Beckett, one of the chief chroniclers of the Great War, "it would have had the same result as in 1940, spelling the imminent defeat of Belgium and France, forcing the evacuation of the British Expeditionary Force (BEF), leaving Britain isolated, and heralding the possibility of a German invasion of Britain."

For the Allies, that was their greatest fear.

One outcome was now certain: Ypres had to happen. In a matter of days, it had become the keystone of western Flanders. Remove it, and the whole edifice of resistance would crumble. For both sides, nothing could be more clear.

ON WEDNESDAY, OCTOBER 21, WORD of the German approach to Ypres, ever closer, spread through the town, as did speculation that heavy shelling would commence by evening. People took to their cellars. The Irish nuns lay down to sleep on sacks filled with straw; no one undressed. The bombardment failed to materialize, though the next day a Taube flew over town, its observer dropping bombs by hand. "The Germans nearer meant greater danger," wrote Sister Columban. Finding food was a problem more pressing than an occasional Taube. "What were we to eat? For weeks, no one had seen an egg. Now, no milk could be got. Fish was out of the question—there was no one left to fish. To complete the misery, no bread arrived, for our baker had left the town." They sent out the Abbey's handyman to scour the streets. He returned with four packets of Quaker Oats and a promise of a hundred salted herrings. Curiously, restaurants were still open.

"Our life, by this time," the sister added, "had become still more like that of the Christians of the first era of the Church, our cellars taking the place of the catacombs, to which they bore some resemblance."

AT 12:12 P.M. ON OCTOBER 22, French dispatched a telegram to his boss, Earl Kitchener. The Weathercock's good spirits had inexplicably revived since the gloomy encounters of the previous day. "Here and there we were driven back," the British commander said, "but our successes predominated, and everywhere the enemy suffered severe losses. . . . In my opinion the enemy are vigorously playing their last card, and I am confident they will fail." French would come to regret his optimism. As the military historian John Terraine wrote, "It was not their last card that the Germans were playing, but their first."

10

Shoulder to Shoulder

FOR THE GERMANS, THE STRUGGLE TAKING PLACE AROUND YPRES WOULD BE-come more than a battle. Over the years its story would go down as "Der Kindermord bei Ypern," the so-called Massacre of the Innocents at Ypres. The "Innocents" were the student volunteers in the reserve corps who were slaughtered in droves but who went to their deaths singing— a phenomenon we shall presently examine in greater detail. In German Bibles, the word "*Kindermord*" was applied to the children King Herod killed after the visit of the Magi to the baby Jesus, and it had, in both cases, the connotation of "holy innocents." One thing is incontrovertible about the unending attacks in which they participated. A massacre had taken place, a massacre of innocents in the military sense, and one that deprived Germany of the human potential that a nation wastes at its peril.

It is possible to forge a rough statistical portrait of the volunteers of 1914. In Germany, as many as 250,000 to 300,000 joined up that August, the first month of the war. (The entire German Army at this time mobi-lized about 5 million, typically reservists who had already done their ac-tive duty.) Most of the volunteers were young.

According to British military historian Alex Watson, over 55 percent were under twenty, the age at which men became eligible for peacetime military service; 88 percent were younger than twenty-five and 95 per-cent were single. The majority, contrary to myth, were not educated, upper-class youths, university students, or recent graduates. (That Au-gust, no more than 11 to 12 percent of the *Kriegsfreiwilligen*, war volun-teers, were in university.) The greatest number belonged to the urban middle class, which Watson describes as a "broad group of people ranging from the Reich's economic and intellectual elite to office workers and skilled artisans." They "made up the bulk"—just over 66 percent—of the volunteers of August. You can argue that the Great War was the first middle-class war.

When the war began, the army found itself unprepared to handle the numbers of men available to it. Uniforms and equipment were in short supply and often weren't issued until the new and unanticipated soldiers were sent to the front. They barely had time to exchange their dark-blue training tunics and trousers for new field uniforms, gray with a greenish tint, calf-high boots, and shiny patent leather spiked helmets, the famous pickelhauben, covered with canvas on the battlefield. Some showed up for combat wearing visored hard leather police or fire-brigade helmets, or were given packs confiscated from Belgian troops, some still stained with the blood of their previous owners.

No one contemplated that the volunteers would be needed so soon. Their instructors—and their line officers and NCOs, too—were likely to be men who had come out of retirement when the war began or civil servants with temporary commissions. Most had never experienced combat. They had little comprehension of the demands of modern warfare and were unfamiliar with machine guns or the latest model Mauser (M1898) rifle, the standard weapon of German infantry. They had probably forgotten the tactics prescribed in the *Drill Regulations of 1888*, except for the reliance on close-order attacks. Even fewer would have been acquainted with the more recent *Drill Regulations of 1906*, which regarded both close- and open-order tactics with equal favor. Though the 1906 regulations may have offered more leeway for methods of attack, they were hardly paragons of military realism—or of the new varieties of weapon-based warfare that were already being fought. Take this description of "The Charge":

At the proper distance from the enemy the command **March, March** is given.

The drums beat to the charge continuously, while the buglers blow the signal "advance quickly."

Immediately before the assault the command **Charge____ Bayonet! Hurra!** Is given. The leading rank charges bayonet, everyone continually hazzaing, rushes on the enemy for the hand-to-hand encounter, until the command **Company ____ Halt** is given. The two front ranks bring their pieces to the "ready." If the enemy is beaten, a pursuing fire is, by command, opened as soon as possible . . .

German recruits in training camp practice skewering head-shaped dummies with the bayonet. The weapon was a favorite of drill instructors and journalists, but in the confines of trench warfare, it was an impediment. The recent civilians would be taught useless details of discipline and maneuver by men who had never known combat, on placid drill fields that had no resemblance to the battlegrounds they would soon encounter. (Chronicle/Alamy)

The volunteers filled their days with close-order drill and bayonet practice—not knowing that the bayonet—the arme blanche—was becoming an increasingly irrelevant weapon, which would inflict no more than one-third to a quarter of 1 percent of all Great War wounds. They carried out their exercises on flat drill fields, not on irregular ground that might have given them a hint of the real war terrain they were about to face. (Many officers believed that training men to rely on cover promoted cowardice.) Their instructors tried, in the limited time given them, to make obedience a habit that depended on the discipline of repetition, which must be "absolute and unthinking." William Balck, at that time a well-regarded German writer on tactics, put it another way. "Love of life and fear of death," he said, "are overcome in a soldier by discipline." This may have worked for the conscripts who spent their two mandatory years (three for a cavalryman) being kneaded into soldiers. The volunteers had two months and sometimes as little as five weeks.*

Not even the dreary hours of parade-ground drilling could completely dampen the enthusiasm of the volunteers. It was the greatest asset they possessed, their only asset, really. By the lights of some tactical commentators, they had too much. Balck again: "For enthusiasm, we would substitute faithful, unselfish performance of duty and unquestioning subordination of the will of the individual to that of the leader." Discipline would help the volunteers to bear inevitable losses.

What the superannuated instructors taught—or didn't teach—would make all the difference in actual combat, as would the leadership of line officers. Both proved deficient, irrelevant to the plain and unpleasant battlefield realities that the volunteers would soon confront. The tactics of "review," those offensive and defensive formations created and rehearsed for show on the drill field, prevailed. They recalled a past, too recent for comfort, when class was the arbiter of human potential and aristocratic officers manipulated peasant soldiers, most of whom were unlettered, through discipline pounded in by rote. Instructors who belonged to an earlier generation made the mistake of treating the new volunteers as if they were scum from the lower depths, not the representatives of an ambitious middle class. Indeed, by early September, German military authorities were receiving complaints that "the treatment of the mostly educated war volunteers by the NCOs is in places degrading and inconsistent with the regulations." Far from acting as models of behavior under

---

* Apparently some did not even have that long. Can we believe the claim of a regimental history of the Gloucestershires that at Koekuit on October 21 a company "captured two young *Einjahrige* (volunteers) from a Jaeger regiment. These proved to be quite youngsters, with only two weeks' training."

fire, officers were more often distrusted and despised. They failed to act as the necessary magnets drawing disparate individuals together into smoothly functioning units. They were as afraid as the men they commanded, and that fear was catching.

Class distinctions had another consequence, and a calamitous one: Members of the middle class had long been discouraged from applying for commissions. The German Army went to war with a shortage of junior officers. As the perceptive military historian Bruce I. Gudmundsson has pointed out, "The unwillingness of the German Army as an institution to put anyone but members of the traditional officer caste in command of units on the battlefield had a profound effect on the tactics that the German infantry would use in the opening months of World War I."

Tactics and class were intertwined. Waves of men, anonymous and inferior, advancing shoulder to shoulder, with officers commanding from the ends of long lines, were the favored formation of attack. The waves might be separated by as much as five hundred yards. There was also the smaller company column attack, a Prussian innovation that went back to the Napoleonic wars. The three platoons, each one ideally eighty men strong, that made up a company would bear down on the enemy. This close and deep formation "permitted the company commander," Gudmundsson writes, "to keep his entire company in sight and within the sound of his voice." The three platoons could easily spread out "into a dense firing line in which every rifle in the company could be employed against the enemy." In the last weeks of September and the first two weeks of October, the volunteers practiced such formations endlessly. Rote accomplished little but to make them aware that they were in the army now.

As far as line officers of the old school were concerned, rigid control was the essence of success in battle. To lose that control was a commander's worst fear. An independent soldier was an ineffective one. The aggregated firepower of a unit trumped individual initiative, that unfortunate trait of the middle class. The many supporters of the "old Prussian drill" maintained that (in the words of military historian Steven D. Jackman) "a dispersed attack, carried out by men lacking strict discipline, would degrade into a mob of shirkers and lost men, who became impossible to move forward." Once soldiers stopped to take cover, officers were not sure that they could force them to budge. Momentum would dissipate, as would the Furor Teutonicus that inspired and sustained the attack.

That was all very well—in theory. But what would happen if the officers were killed or badly wounded, precisely the circumstance, and a fairly frequent, if not inevitable, one, in which the initiative of a trained NCO was most needed. If an officer died, would the attack he led die with him?

Attacks by infantry advancing in close order resulted in a higher rate of casualties than open-order ones. Studies conducted in Germany during the 1870s put the casualty rate of close-order attacks as high as 60 percent. (Between 50 and 60 percent was the rate for the German Army at the First Ypres.) Columns took somewhat heavier losses because shots that passed over the front ranks hit men in the rear. Experimenters at the Spandau Marksmanship School also found that if they narrowed the interval between man-sized targets from four or five meters to two meters, they doubled the percentage of shots that struck home; if they decreased the interval to a single meter, they quadrupled it. Even proponents of close-order attacks conceded that the price might be high but was worth the shock value of a remorseless thrust by a dense line: ends justified the costly means. None of these calculations, however, anticipated the new math of trench warfare.

Early in the 1900s, it is true, some German infantry commanders tried out so-called Boer tactics, which South African irregulars had used to harass and frustrate the British expeditionary force sent to put down their rebellion. These open-order tactics featured dispersed small units and loose, elastic formations armed with repeating Mauser rifles that made the most of the irregularities of vegetation and terrain. "Riflemen, trained to fire as individual marksmen," Gudmundsson writes, "would destroy the enemy's will to resist by accurate fire rather than the weight of their own bodies." There was one huge problem. It was difficult for platoon, company, or battalion commanders to control units spread over distances ranging from several hundred to several thousand yards. Boer tactics enjoyed a brief vogue and were then forgotten. It would take the experience of close-order massacres in the Great War to merit a second look.

At Ypres, though, the men who might have led an open-order revolution were wanting, relegated to the anonymous ranks. Tactical experiments could wait. Shoulder to shoulder it would have to be.

IT WAS OCTOBER 22 NOW, the third day of Falkenhayn's vast offensive. As the intensity of the struggle diminished in one sector, the rhythm of confrontation swelled in another. The tectonic plates of slaughter constantly shifted. The battle never really let up.

During the day, the noise level remained "a shrieking hell," as one young Scots officer described it. Exploding shells blew in trenches, everyone's; both sides lacked enough picks and shovels to redig them. The trenches were shallow scrapings anyway, rarely more than three feet deep, some separated by gaps of "two, three or even four hundred yards." Those open spaces were easy enough to cover with artillery or rifle fire during the day, but once darkness fell the Germans made probing attacks with some success. British commanders tended to feel that night actions of their own were perilous, risking fatal confusion, an aversion that persisted through the entire war. Their German adversaries had no such qualms.

There were no dugouts or communication trenches, and the Royal Engineers' stock of barbed wire was limited to a two-mile length for the entire British Army—which then held some thirty-five miles of front, from just north of Ypres to La Bassée and the canal named after it, a distance that, over the next days, continually expanded and contracted. Reserves concealed themselves in the numerous, and still intact, patches of woodland; artillery began to establish itself on reverse slopes, out of sight. Trench systems, with long connecting avenues of communication trenches, second and third defensive lines, deep dugouts with bunks, field kitchens, advanced aid posts, and latrines, mortar pits, machine-gun nests, and listening saps to detect suspicious enemy sounds, did not yet exist. The makeshift lines made life difficult in other respects. "It was only at night," the British *Official History* noted, "that supplies could be got up to the troops and the wounded removed, and as soon as it was dusk the streets of Ypres and the roads radiating from Ypres were crowded with vehicles passing backwards and forwards."

The British suffered their worst losses from the steady bombardment by high-explosive and shrapnel shells. "The enemy's fire had now become more accurate," wrote the historian of the 7th Division, "and the trenches were terribly knocked about, men being buried and rifles put out of action . . . Parties bringing ammunition up by hand lost heavily in crossing the open." The British dug deeper.

ABOUT THREE IN THE AFTERNOON on the twenty-second, British troops guarding the approaches to Polygon Wood watched as Würtembergers, south Germans, members of the 54th Reserve Division, spilled over the low ridge that ran from Becelaere to Zonnebeke. The British unleashed a torrent of shrapnel and machine-gun fire. "The German masses staggered," said the *Official History*, "and as one battalion diary states, their dead and wounded were literally piled up in heaps almost before a rifle shot was fired." *In heaps.* It was a phrase that, with variations, often recurs during the next days. What the Germans lost at the First Ypres, and could never recover, was that potential cadre of young men who might have developed into capable junior officers—and, indeed, into the civilian leaders of the future, men who might have erected a bullwark against radical outliers like the Nazis.

The Allies suffered similar irreplaceable losses, if hardly in such daunting quantities. Their junior officers, professionals all at this point, were easily recognizable targets. Decent diets proved their undoing: most were at least a head taller than the men they commanded, a fact that did not escape German snipers. Neither did the telltale mustache that all British officers affected. Captains and lieutenants, along with the occasional major or colonel, deliberately placed themselves in harm's way. It was expected of them. Officers were conspicuous also because of the weapons they carried. A captain named Jeffrey of the Green Howards led a bayonet charge that afternoon, waving a pistol—not a private's weapon—in one hand and a sword in the other. (Swords would soon disappear from the front lines, though not from ceremonial parades; officers took to carrying unnotable rifles.) There was no mistaking Jeffrey's rank. A rifle bullet cut him down. "I am wounded somewhere," he is supposed to have called out as he expired. "Carry on, men, carry on!" This was the language of 1914, the upper-class idiom of sacrifice that would soon become as extinct as Captain Jeffrey.

FIVE MILES TO THE NORTH, at Langemarck, where the line took another sharp bend and headed toward the Yser Canal, the Germans dispatched more close-packed swarms. But the XXVI Reserve Corps command began to display less confidence than it had just hours before. It requested a pause to rest and regroup. Had the extent of its losses of the previous day, the twenty-first, begun to sink in? Albrecht's headquarters in Brussels insisted that the Fourth Army attacks go on. Brussels reasoned that once the division took Langemarck, it could power itself through the gap and take Ypres from the north. Two reserve regiments would pour down the faint incline from Poelcappelle toward Langemarck; more would emerge from the Houthulst Forest and, advancing from the other side, help to lop off the bothersome Langemarck protuberance.

As the troops of the German 46th Reserve Division streamed out of the trees in columns and started across the spongy meadows, British artillery caught them in the open. Eventually the Germans did overrun British-held Koekuit; but farther along, the Kortebeek, a stream narrow but deep, presented a major obstacle. Men hesitated to cross—relatively few Europeans could swim in those days. They were more afraid of the water than of the shrapnel that swept down on them. Some waded across, the water rising to their belts and higher; others improvised flotation devices from heavy pieces of wood or anything they could inflate. Hundreds eventually huddled on the south bank. The officers who survived urged their men forward, and a scattered few of the attackers crossed over a railroad embankment and even secured a brief foothold in the forward British trenches. That was as far as they got.

They were the successful ones. The experience of another volunteer of Reserve Infantry Regiment 215, belonging to the 46th Reserve Division, was more typical of that day. Striding fearfully through a field of shoulder-high sugar-beet plants, he saw the friend next to him collapse, riddled by machine-gun bullets. He and his fellows crawled forward. An officer ordered them to their feet. "We made some progress, but the majority were hit." Those who were still alive threw themselves to the ground again and "pressed their faces against the cold earth. There was an eerie rustling in our ears. It was the sound of bullets cutting through the leafy tops of the beets." Nearby, "an old officer"—this was the sort of person who led the reservists—"groaned and pressed his hand against his body, as though he could reduce the intense pain of a stomach wound by so doing." The narrator could hear the approach of a second assault wave crashing through the beet fronds. "It did not even get level with my position. All I could hear were screams and groans."

The Germans refused to surrender their Langemarck obsession. As the afternoon of the twenty-second waned, long, packed lines of fresh attackers of the XXVI Reserve Corps swept across from Poelcappelle. The predictably concentrated rifle fire held off the German swarms, though some of the attackers did get as close as twenty-five yards from the shallow trenches the British 2nd Division held. These were moments that called for stiff upper lips, as when the regimental history of the Worcesters described the unending concussion of bursting shells and the proximity of the charging Germans as "most trying."

THE BRITISH 1ST DIVISION HELD the next four miles of line, from Langemarck west to a hamlet called Steenstraat on the Yser Canal. The closer the Germans came to the canal, the more October 22 improved for them. At the canal, where the line assumed an elbow shape and headed north toward Dixmude, the two sides facing each other across the water, the problem of divided command became acute, one that would plague the Allies until the final spring of the war. It was not entirely clear at what point the French took over from the British. The place was somewhere just below the German-held village of Bixschoote, where the British were beginning to entrench. The commander of the grandiloquently named Détachment d'Armée de Belgique, Gen. Victor d'Urbal, not an individual renowned for his good manners, ordered an attack on Bix-schoote by a brigade of the 87th Territorial Division, but neglected to inform his British counterparts. His intention was to outflank the German XXIII Corps, preventing it from reaching the canal—it had already done so—or, in the worst case, from crossing it. That flanks had just disappeared from the Western Front escaped this recent cavalry leader, still accustomed to the unfettered swoops of mounted maneuver.

The Territorials marched out of Ypres at five in the morning, mostly men in their late thirties to early forties, whose active service was suppos-edly long past. They were needed now. In their long blue greatcoats, red trousers, and overladen backpacks, they were a force of six battalions, about 6,000 men. Late in the morning, after a six-mile march, they ar-rived at half-dug and disconnected trenches, held by the Scots Guards. Unwarned, the Scots were surprised to see them. The Territorials paused to fix bayonets before moving across fields and a scattering of woods toward Bixschoote a mile away; dismounted cavalrymen, brandishing sa-bers, brought up the rear. "This time, captain, we'll get them," an NCO named Vaudoir assured his company commander. A Scots Guard lieuten-ant, W. B. Lawson, climbed out of a trench to point out the best route of attack and to warn of possible hazards. Suddenly he crumpled, struck in the head by a sniper's bullet. The French lieutenant to whom he had been talking took a few steps forward; another bullet cut him down.

The Territorials made their halting way across fields recently har-vested toward Bixschoote, a village that the German 45th Reserve Divi-sion had occupied just a day earlier. The Germans, Dr. Nel wrote, were already "well-hidden, dug in, lying in wait." The Territorials began to encounter fire that was, a witness said, "terrifyingly accurate." The in-souciant Sergeant Vaudoir was pushing a front door open when a shot from within the house smashed into his temple. Another shell shattered the head of the company adjutant, his brains gushing down what re-mained of his face. Shattered glass from exploding greenhouses flew down the contended streets, mixing with the lethal passage of bullets. The French managed to maintain a foothold in the village for much of the afternoon, but the Germans pushed them back, house by house. The Territorials finally broke and began to stream toward the Allied lines. British guns laid down a protective barrage.

At a forward dressing station in the front line, meanwhile, Nel and his fellow doctors and medics hastily bandaged the most seriously injured. His diary doesn't say if they were under shelter of any kind, but the medical team did wonder whether it was too exposed. "Bullets and shrapnel are now whistling all around us . . . a shell fragment buries itself in the ground right at our feet, spattering us with dirt." They kept working, cramming the wounded into horse-drawn ambulances and then returning for more. A colonel tried to rally the fleeing troops for another attempt to take Bixschoote; they were beyond obeying orders. Panic was now general. "At the Boesinghe railway bridge, a log-jam. A dragoon captain energetically directs traffic . . . in the crush of retreating troops crossing the bridge." The concealment of nightfall could not come quickly enough.

Next to the bridge crossing the doctors turned an inn called the Parrot into an impromptu aid station, filling the main downstairs tap room with wounded men. Nel continues his story: "The room is packed, and offers a tragic spectacle. There are dying men, with shattered limbs held on with scraps of flesh or fabric. . . . Doctor Vallais uses scissors to cut the tissue holding an arm to a shoulder.

"The red blood spurting from wounds soaks the bandages, splatters the walls . . . the pale faces of the wounded, their mingled cries of pain and calls for help . . . the shouts of the waiters pouring beer and, when that ran out, water, into the parched throats of famished combatants."

For the failed attackers of Bixschoote, most of whom had never seen action before, unless in colonial scuffles, it had been a first experience of war, and an unsavory one. As Louis-Ferdinand Céline (soon to enter the line nearby) remarks in his novel *Journey to the End of the Night*, "You could be a virgin in horror the same as in sex."

BIXSCHOOTE ENCOURAGED THE GERMANS. THEY kept up the pressure in this part of the line. Along the northern face of the developing Salient—the word deserves to be uppercased from now on—they could point to another small success on the twenty-second. That was at Kortekeer Cabaret, the crossroads pub that the British 1st Division now held. Men of the Cameron Highlanders and the Gloucestershire Regiment, exposed and undermanned, were strung out in detached parties from Langemarck to Steenstraat on the canal. The German nibbling commenced. *Einjähriger,* volunteers, of the 46th Reserve Division attacked troops of the Gloucestershire Regiment. According to the *War Narratives* of the Gloucesters, it was "a particularly fine feat of arms . . . These lads . . . advanced with the utmost determination, singing patriotic songs, and though suffering appalling casualties, actually succeeded in driving back their seasoned opponents." The singing is what stands out: a legend was gathering momentum.

The gaps—one of which was four hundred yards wide—presented a considerable peril to the defenders. Haig, who commanded the I Corps, sent up troops of the Black Watch, in reserve on Pilckem Ridge, to stabilize a dicey situation. At this early point in the war, the British Army allotted each battalion two machine guns; the Black Watch established one of theirs in a ruined windmill. Gunners set it up behind a high window and steadied its tripod with bags of meal. From time to time the crew would move the gun to another window; it helped to hold off the Germans through much of the afternoon. Eventually the Germans brought up a field gun, and its shells began to strike the windmill. Three or four machine guns joined it. "The windows of the mill," said the regimental history of the Coldstream, also involved in the fight, "became quite untenable." As the gunners struggled to carry the weapon to safety—one man was wounded—the building went up in flames. They escaped. Darkness came on. The Germans breached the line and seized the pub. They worked their way behind the Cameron Highlanders and began to take them prisoner, a few at a time. They captured fifty-four.

Later that night Haig assembled five battalions led by Brig. Gen. Edwin S. Bulfin, a dapper, thin-faced Irish Protestant who would become one of the heroes of the First Ypres. He never seemed to have a cigarette out of his hand. Haig ordered Bulfin to take back Kortekeer Cabaret at dawn.

FOCH REFUSED TO GIVE UP plans for an Allied offensive. He ordered a major counterattack, to begin on October 23. But its objectives were wildly out of reach. The Belgians and Grossetti's 42nd Division were to drive eastward toward a large village called Ghistelles, nine miles away. Naval gunfire from British monitors anchored offshore would clear their way. Ronarc'h's Dixmude garrison was to attack across the soaked polders toward Thourout. The IX Corps, just arrived, would head cross-country for Roulers, which, even at that early date, was beginning to take on for the Allies the character of a mirage.

There was little evidence of advance planning. To reach Roulers, the Allies would have needed to retake the Passchendaele–Westroosebeke Ridge, which they had relinquished too easily. Foch appealed to Sir John French to support his attack "by acting offensively" along his whole front. As for the Belgians, Foch asked them "to associate yourselves in these offensive movements to the limits of your resources." General d'Urbal met with Albert, mainly to introduce himself. The fighting qualities of the Germans were, he said, so lackluster that he had no qualms about the success of the offensive. "The interview ended rather abruptly," the king's biographer Émile Cammaerts wrote, moments after Albert "had expressed his astonishment that, in the circumstances, the Allies had not yet reached the Rhine."

It is easy to disparage Foch's intentions, too easy. Allied reinforcements were arriving in considerable numbers. The Indian Lahore Division was ready to take its place in the southern Flanders line. The French IX Corps, with two divisions of infantry and two of cavalry, was approaching the Yser Canal. The Germans may have originally held a numerical advantage, as much as 2 or 3 to 1, but three days of hideous losses, especially among junior officers, had brutally hacked away at that edge.

The time was actually right to push back against the Germans. "A major counter-attack by the Allies," Farrar-Hockley writes, "might have unbalanced them, sufficiently at least to force them to withdraw some distance." But it was not to be. Even with the reassuring presence of Grossetti's division, the Belgian front was in precarious disorder; the

Germans had just managed to establish a bridgehead across the Yser. Ronarc'h's marines were having a hard time holding on to Dixmude. Foch's orders called for the general attack to begin at 9 A.M. on the twenty-third. The infantry divisions and the dismounted cavalry of the French IX Corps would not begin to be in position until later in the day. The message from d'Urbal announcing the big push did not reach the British GHQ at Saint-Omer or Haig's I Corps headquarters at Ypres until shortly before 2 A.M. That hardly gave the British time to organize any sort of offensive action and was an invitation to confusion, which is more or less what resulted.

The indefatigable and ever-competent Maj. Ma Jeffreys of the Grenadier Guards recorded in his journal, "A message came to say that French troops were to attack through us in the afternoon with the object of taking Passchendaele and that 'an officer who could speak French' was to be sent as Liaison Officer to General Moussy"—who commanded a brigade of the French 17th Division. The French-speaker chosen was Ma Jeffreys; the attack was part of Foch's scheme. What Jeffreys witnessed in the next hours would present a diverting contrast in national styles of command. Jeffreys found Gen. Jean Baptiste Albert Moussy standing in the middle of a road near Saint-Julien, not far behind the front line, in the company of two smartly dressed staff officers. "He seemed to have no Headquarters, as we understand them," Jeffreys observed, "to which reports could go, but he walked among his troops with the two staff officers, and seemed more like an umpire at a Field Day than a commander of attacking troops." His men began to come under shellfire. Though it did little damage, it repeatedly brought them up short. Moussy walked among his troops, and whenever he saw a group halted, he coaxed it into moving again. *"Allons, Allons, mes enfants. En Avant! En Avant!"* Always they would reply, *"Bien, mon Général,"* and resume their advance. Sometimes he would joke with them, saying, *"Il faut absolument arriver à Passchendaele ce soir, ou pas de souper, pas de souper."* You absolutely have to get to Passchendaele this evening, or no dinner, no dinner.

The attack, which had to pass through British-held trenches, soon ran into a wall of German fire, and stopped. "General Moussy went for-

George Darrell "Ma" Jeffreys of the Second Grenadier Guards was a legendary soldier, a man who began the war as a major and ended it as a major general. At one point, in 1915, he was Winston Churchill's commander. He took the former cabinet minister to task for bringing too much baggage, leaving him a spare pair of socks and his shaving gear. (© National Portrait Gallery, London/Art Resource, NY)

ward and stood at the cross-roads on the Zonnebeke-Langemarck road, a most unhealthy spot." Moussy "showed not the slightest sign of fear, and nor did his two Staff Officers, who laughed and joked at the bursting shells." The normally unflappable Jeffreys stood with them, "though inwardly hating it."

The advance never did reach Passchendaele, or even come close. The Allies would need another three years to get that far.

From this moment on, the First Ypres became as much a French as a British battle. That pointed to an essential problem, and one we have already touched on: there was no unity of command, no single warlord who could impose order on a potentially chaotic situation, no authority (in Farrar-Hockley's words) "to make a plan and insist upon it." Foch may have fairly exuded dynamism as no other general in Flanders did, but the former professor was not yet the leader or coordinator of international armies he would one day become.

BULFIN'S ATTEMPT TO REGAIN KORTEKEER Cabaret went off in the mist of early morning on October 23. Two battalions advanced on either side of the road to the tavern, a distance of more than a thousand yards. Thirty guns shelled the roads that the Germans would have to use to send up reinforcements. The country on the west side of the road was somewhat rolling—as rolling as you could find a few feet above sea level—and was broken up by numerous hedges marking the limits of pastures and plowed fields. The Loyal North Lancashires moved forward unseen, though at one point wire that the Germans had strung during the night briefly held them up. The 1st Queen's Battalion, on the unobstructed east side of the road, began to take rifle fire from long range: the command went out to widen the distance between the skirmishers. This was no shoulder-to-shoulder attack. A Lt. J.G.W. Hyndson, a company commander in the Loyals, described their progress:

> We are now close to the "Bosche" [sic] trenches, and must pause to wear down his nerves until he dare not show a hair, before we can complete the attack. We commence to fire for all we are worth . . . I noticed the Germans dodging past a gap in the hedge some 250 yards to my front, and order a section to fire at them as they slip past.

It was like peacetime on the rifle range. His men entered into the task "with zest"; Hyndson saw "many of the flitting figures" fall. "We afterwards found 20 or 30 dead Germans in this area."

The Germans were paying most of their attention to the Queen's; the final dash of the Loyals took them by surprise. The Queen's charged at the same time. The British stormed houses firing from their hips. German resistance crumbled.

> Suddenly the glorious sight of masses of grey-coated men standing up to surrender meets our gaze . . . Isolated bodies of Germans still continue to resist and must be rounded up; one

particularly brave man established on the top of a windmill continues to fire, and refuses to surrender, so we have to set fire to the building; but in spite of this he goes on firing until the building collapses and its brave defender perishes in the flames.

Bulfin's attackers had gone so far forward that they came under fire from their own artillery. Hyndson continues:

I shout to the men to get back to a house flying the Red flag . . . On reaching the house, what a sight meets my gaze! The whole place is crammed with German dead, dying and wounded, all lying together on the floor, packed as tightly as sardines.

When the British entered the tavern itself (and presumably disarmed the men holding the building), they discovered as many as sixty prisoners crowded inside, waiting to be escorted to a long detention. "They came skipping out of the Inn in great delight," remembered an officer of the Queen's. Hands were pumped, backs were slapped, and laughter and shouting erupted. A momentary party interrupted the killing. Men stripped badges from their former captors who had themselves become prisoners. They collected souvenirs and broke out German cigars. It was with difficulty that their officers ordered them into trenches to prepare for inevitable counterattacks. Meanwhile the British herded, or had carried back on stretchers, 791 prisoners, 352 of whom were unwounded. They had killed 490 Germans, at a cost of 47 killed and 184 wounded.

The Germans did make ineffectual attempts to regain what was now the Kortekeer salient. That it was a salient, potentially hard to defend, worried Bulfin, and after dark he withdrew his battalions to freshly dug trenches south of the cabaret: the tactical value of the place wasn't worth the price of holding it. Around midnight the Germans made a determined effort to crack the 1st Division line, advancing in close order and (no doubt to identify their positions in the dark) singing.

———

ALL THROUGH THE TWENTY-THIRD AND into the night, the Germans continued to target Langemarck. Its fetid smoking ruins remained for them a fatal lodestone. In assault after assault, the undertrained legions of the 51st and 46th Reserve Divisions suffered hideous losses. "Doing tremendous execution" became a phrase favored in British regimental histories.

But the terror could be equal on both sides of the line. In a letter to his sister written a couple of days after the event, Capt. Harry Dillon, nicknamed "Rabbit," the commander of A Company of the 2nd Battalion of the Oxford and Buckinghamshire Light Infantry, described what it was like to be on the receiving end of a mass attack. Dillon's men faced the XXVI Reserve Corps, which his battalion had mauled the day before. ("The leading Germans got within 25 yards of our trenches," another officer had written of that earlier encounter, "but then could stand it no longer and ran back.") This time the Germans came on singing and shouting. Listen to Captain Dillon, a Boer War veteran who had spent

BEF troops repel a German mass attack. Though this contemporary representation is imagined, similar events did happen, notably around the village of Langemarck. A British officer described how "One saw the great mass of Germans quiver. . . . I have never shot so much in a such a short time: it could not have been more than a few seconds and they were down. . . . [O]ut of the darkness a great moaning came." (*Illustrated London News* Picture Library)

most of his military career in Africa. His letter to his sister, describing events that began about 5:30 P.M. that evening, is one of the unforgettable documents of the Great War on the Western Front.

When it appeared in a local newspaper, Dillon's account must have had the effect—though through words—that Alexander Gardner's photographs of Union and Confederate corpses at Antietam had for Civil War–era Americans. In a few flicks of the eye, the nobility of war vanished. Eternity could not have been more empty of life and redemption than those corpses. God was dying on our watch:

> The night came on rather misty and dark, and I thought several times of asking for reinforcements, but I collected a lot of rifles off the dead, loaded them and put them along the parapet instead. All of a sudden about a dozen shells came down—and almost simultaneously two machine guns and a tremendous rifle fire opened on us. It was a most unholy din. The shells ripped open the parapet, and trees came crashing down. . . . Presently the guns stopped, and I knew we were in for it. I had to look over the top for about ten minutes . . . before I saw what I was looking for. It came with a suddenness that was the most startling thing I have ever known. The firing stopped and I had been straining my eyes so that for a moment I could not believe them, but, fortunately, I did not hesitate long. A great grey mass of humanity was charging, running for all God would let them, straight on to us not fifty yards off—about as far as the summer-house from the coach-house. . . . As I fired my rifle the rest went off almost simultaneously.
>
> One saw the great mass of Germans quiver. In reality some fell, some fell over them, and others came on. I have never shot so much in such a short time: it could not have been more than a few seconds and they were down. Suddenly one man—I expect an officer— jumped up and came on. I fired and missed, seized the next rifle and dropped him a few yards off. Then the whole lot came on again and it was the most critical moment of my life. Twenty yards more and they would have been over us in thousands but our fire

must have been fearful, and at the very last moment they did the most foolish thing they possibly could have done. Some of the leading people turned to the left for some reason, and they all followed like a great flock of sheep. We did not lose much time, I can give you my oath. My right hand is one huge bruise from banging the bolt up and down. I don't think one could have missed at the distance and just for one short minute or two we poured the ammunition into them in boxfuls. My rifles were red hot at the finish, I know, and that was the end of the battle for me.

The firing died down and out of the darkness a great moaning came. Men with their arms and legs off trying to crawl away; others who could not move gasping out their last moments with the cold night wind biting into their broken bodies and the lurid red glare of a farm house showing up clumps of grey devils killed by the men on my left shoulder further down. A weird awful scene; some of them would raise themselves on one arm or crawl a little distance, silhouetted as black as ink against the red glow of the fire.

Screams pierced the night. The British could hear the Germans collecting their wounded and dead; they held their fire. Dillon felt himself being sucked into a void where death was sovereign, one that filled him "with a great rage." Here was an officer and a gentleman for whom thoughts of summer houses and coach houses came as naturally as the sense of duty that led him to pick up a rifle and obliterate human beings who shared his same outlooks and sentiments. The senselessness of the Langemarck slaughter appalled, even if it was his mission to continue. Unreason had become the motivating essence of this Great War, and his. Langemarck made that clear. "The whole thing is an outrage on civilization," Dillon told his sister. "The whole of this beautiful country is devastated—broken houses, broken bodies, blood, filth and ruin everywhere!"

At about 11 P.M. troops of the French 17th Division showed up to relieve the 2nd Division and to take over the Langemarck sector. The next morning they found (and counted) 740 corpses in front of the trenches the Oxfordshires had held. The number had obviously been greater before the Germans cleared the battlefield. That their wave had broken so close to the British trenches made the scant casualties suffered by Dillon's battalion hard to believe: 2 officers wounded, 2 other ranks killed, and 5 wounded. Curiously, too, the Oxfords sustained most of those casualties in parts of the line where they were shelled, and not where they were directly attacked.

11

Singers in the Mist

OCTOBER 23–24

THE BRAVERY AND TENACITY OF THEIR GERMAN ADVERSARIES IMPRESSED THE defenders—but did not prevent the killing from continuing. German volunteers crawled along drainage ditches, sprang up to dash across a broad planting of turnips or sugar beets, and then withered away under suddenly awakened fire. Here, leaf fronds outlasted flesh. Young officers carrying regimental colors would dash ahead of their men, plant the flag as a point to make for, and be shot dead. A general named Rohden, a brigade commander, attempted to rally his troops by riding among them on his horse. Did it inspire his men to greater wonders of offensive effort? The general (and, apparently, his horse) survived; his troops may not have been so fortunate.

For Germany, a human tragedy was taking shape.

Even German courage had its limits. Only night and fog, the dense darkness of Flanders fields, could hide the ground strewn with bodies like animal droppings. Attacks began to falter, troops drifted to the rear, individuals first, then sections, and finally entire lines, shoulder to shoulder in reverse. Company officers did their best to stop a general stampede. "Mentally and spiritually we were totally spent," a rifleman remembered. "The men are all burnt out," another said.

There is no satisfactory way to estimate German casualties for the days of Langemarck. Many of the *Feldwebel,* sergeant majors who were supposed to keep records, had been themselves swept away. The German High Command, moreover, deliberately covered up the enormity of its losses, afraid that home-front morale would crack. But even the generals had only an inkling of how high the casualty rate really was. Far removed from the action, they had lost control of it. Three battalions of the 46th Reserve Division's Reserve Infantry Regiment 215, for example, with an original strength of around 2,200 officers and men, had shrunk to four companies, weak ones at that, perhaps 600 to 700 men, or less than one-third of their number when they made their first battlefield appearance on October 20. Some small units had taken 90 percent casualties. After a day of nonstop fighting, October 23, which included a German mass attack, men of the Welch and Gloucestershire Battalions counted 1,500 corpses in front of their trench north of Langemarck. A single machine gun dispatched as many as 400 to 500 of those. One British regimental historian put the three-day German casualty total in this sector at not much less than 10,000 men—a rough estimate but not an unreasonable one. Given the number of regiments involved, and a loss rate of as much as 50 to 60 percent, it might have been on the low side.

THE TOWNSPEOPLE OF YPRES, AND few had left as yet, probably had only a dim awareness of the massacres going on so close to them. How could they truly grasp what they did not see? By this time the sounds of battle rarely died down. They were as constant as the unending roar of a cataract around a bend in a river: unseen and mostly out of mind—gray noise we might call it now, louder and more ominous than white. You became conscious of it at fugitive moments. You went on about your business. Sound marked an invisible boundary. Nothing beyond that constant rumble seemed to matter any longer. "For the future," Sister Columban mused, "we only knew what was happening in and around Ypres. And was it not enough? The windows already shook with the heavy firing. The roar of the guns in the distance scarcely stopped a moment. From the garret windows we could . . . see the smoke of battle on the horizon." She grew reflective. "To think that, at every moment, hundreds of souls were appearing before the judgment seat of God! Were they prepared? Terrifying problem."

IT IS NOTEWORTHY, AND NO doubt intentional, that Alexander Watson, in his essay on the German volunteers of 1914, segues immediately from Harry Dillon's description of the massacre at Langemarck to a discussion of combat-induced mental breakdowns among the same group at the same time. Watson, one of the most original of a new breed of Great War scholars, cites the official figure for Fourth Army psychiatric casualties at the First Ypres. That figure was only 387 men: it is, he writes, "almost certainly unreliable." It was also probably a vast underestimate. But to suggest new numbers, new percentages, at this remove of time is pointless, not to say impossible. One observation does seem appropriate: though these reserve regiments may have seen hard fighting later in the battle, mainly defending against the offensive-minded French, after the first few days the majority were pulled out of the line at Ypres and were mostly not used again as attack troops.

You don't have to look far to find reasons why psychiatric casualty estimates were lower than they should have been. Not the least of them was the widespread distrust of psychiatry as a medical discipline. There was a tendency to dismiss the wounds of the mind not just as evidence of underlying moral infirmity but of downright insanity that had afflicted the individual long before he had reached the front. The most widespread explanation was that shell concussions had damaged the brains of sufferers—hence the phrase "shell shock" (which first appeared in print in the January 1915 issue of the influential British medical journal *The Lancet*). How better to explain the wildly varying hysterical symptoms than to blame them on the shock of a shell burst—blindness, inability to move a limb or to speak, deafness, violent tremors, morbidly extreme insomnia, uncontrollable fits of weeping, to name just a few. In general, they left no exterior physical marks, only the havoc inside.*

---

* The first British troops to show extreme symptoms of war neurosis began arriving back in England early that fall. Examining doctors came to the conclusion that the brains of these sufferers had been damaged by the concussion of shells exploding nearby—hence the expression "shell shock." Though the original explanation for hysterical symptoms fell out of favor, the phrase stuck. Eventually, in later wars, it evolved into "combat fa-

But the uncomfortable truth was that the *Kriegsfreiwilligen* never should have fought so soon or in such a crucial operation. The briefness of their training meant that they had no opportunity to develop that greatest of soldierly strengths, unit cohesion, the reluctance to let down the man next to you that can pass for courage.

There might have been one further reason for the low reported rate of breakdowns. So many of the volunteers were dead before they had a chance to fall apart.

Langemarck brought about a change in the character of the war the combatants hardly noticed at first. It was more than just the diminishing number of mass attacks in the open of the sort that had distinguished the early days of Falkenhayn's offensive. In an inconspicuous footnote, the chronicler of the Welch regiment touched on the nature of that change: "After 1914 one seldom saw Germans except as prisoners in a battle raid." It became increasingly rare to see—no less to encounter—an actual living enemy. And yet the combined population of the Western Front in mid-October 1914 was 4 million men, an instant metropolis. The over-populated but apparently untenanted sweep of the trenches, almost five hundred miles long and growing more intricate and connected by the day, had become an empty battlefield.

THE STORY OF OCTOBER 23 was not over. Though the French had come to grief at Bixschoote, Allied troops were still holed up there. Firefights broke out far into the night. The flames that now consumed the windmill at Bixschoote lit up the battered village and the corpse-littered meadows that surrounded it. In the gathering darkness, men groped in search of human shapes that would welcome, and not kill, them. It was said that a

---

tigue" and "post traumatic stress disorder" (P.T.S.D.), both increasingly psychological in nature.

More than a century later, explanations continue to change. Recent research, led by Dr. Daniel Perl of the Uniformed Services University of the Health Sciences in Bethesda, MD, examined the brain tissue of men who had served in the Middle East and had later died. All had been exposed to violent explosions on the battlefield. Perl and his team discovered a pattern of scarring in all the brains examined. Had the original diagnosis of "shell shock" been the correct one after all? Had we indeed come full circle?

This drawing of a singing student volunteer comes from a Nazi-era book, by which time the legend of young men who went to their deaths with the lyrics of patriotism on their lips had long since become generally accepted as real. (From Reinhard Dithmar, *Der Langemarck: Mythos in Dichtung und Unterricht*, Neuwied Luchterhand, 1992)

Hauptmann Arthur Dehrmann, commanding the 2nd Battalion of Reserve Infantry Regiment 211, was the first officer to direct his men to sing "Deutschland, Deutschland, Über Alles!" as a way of identifying themselves. A few moments later, a random bullet struck him in the neck, and he fell, mortally wounded.

It is possible that the phenomenon of the singing attacks originated at Bixschoote with the unfortunate Captain Dehrmann, though we do have evidence that they first manifested themselves earlier. Certainly by the night of the twenty-third they were real enough, and had a necessary purpose. Singing a familiar German song such as "Deutschland, Deutschland Über Alles!" or "Heil Dir im Siegerkrantz" (Hail to the Victor's Crown) was a recognizable signal, much more believable than a cry of "Don't shoot—We are Germans," which was too easy to imitate. Troops in nearby rifle pits or trenches might respond with the words of "Die Wacht am Rhein," reassuring their invisible neighbors that they were friendly.

It was only later that the glorified version of the story, inspirational but wildly impractical, took hold—and would soon be embellished into legend. That version even acquired its special locus, Langemarck, and as a PR creation was carefully nourished by both the kaiser's Germany and Hitler's. The basic account has student volunteers, called the Children's Corps by scornful veterans, advancing silently in the autumn fog of Flanders, "a wide sea of white air," as one chronicler put it. There is no preliminary artillery barrage that might tip off the enemy. The volunteers are discovered anyway, and bullets from a source hidden in the mist chop down their close-packed rows. They continue to throw themselves "into this hell with childlike trust." But nothing avails. They lie in the open, unable to advance or retreat. "In this hour, they have become men."

Then the miracle happens. A voice rises in song, another joins in, and another, all taking up "the holy words." The young soldiers arise as one and storm forward: they sing as they run, some with their heads wrapped in bloody bandages. Their "burning eyes" give them the look of "unreal figures from an old saga." In some versions, the volunteers sweep over the enemy trenches; in others, the song dies as they die, and silent gray heaps litter the damp fields of Langemarck.

Unfortunately for the myth, Langemarck, for all the death it witnessed, may never have experienced a singing attack, though villages nearby, like Bixschoote, did. But Beck-skota (as it is pronounced), that rough, turnip-eating name, does not lend itself to martial fantasy in the same way that the vaguely Teutonic vibrations of Langemarck do. As one former student volunteer put it in 1933, the first year of Hitler's reign, "the name sounds like a heroic legend."

According to the official army bulletin of November 11, 1914, which appeared on the front pages of many German newspapers, "West of Langemarck youthful regiments stormed first lines of the enemy trenches and took them, singing *'Deutschland, Deutschland über alles.'*" But that single dispatch is only the beginning of the confusion and misinformation that propagandists produced. Singing volunteers took no Allied trenches at Langemarck on November 10. But in the aftermath of Ypres, Germany needed a myth such as the self-willed sacrifice of the young volunteers to believe in. The self-willed sacrifice of the young volunteers, based ever-so-loosely on fact, was the ideal PR invention.

We are now entering fantasyland, and no one escorted us into its skewed premises better than Adolf Hitler himself. In *Mein Kampf* (My Struggle), the former private in Bavarian Reserve Regiment 16 describes his baptism by fire—or, as he puts it, the "iron salute" he received near Gheluvelt on October 29:

> Then a crackling and a roaring, a singing and a howling began, and with feverish eyes each one of us was drawn forward, faster and faster, until suddenly past turnip fields and hedges the fight began, the fight of man against man. And from the distance the strains of a song reached our ears, coming closer and closer, leaping from company to company and just as Death plunged a busy hand into our ranks, the song reached us too and we passed it along: *Deutschland, Deutschland über alles, über alles in der Welt!*

The landscape of oblivion: This panorama of Passchendaele Ridge was taken from British lines in April 1915, but the prospect late that previous October can't have been much different. Many of the trenches—seen here as upheavals of white clay—had been dug and the wide, grassy interval between the trenches, soon to be called no-man's-land, had already

By the time Hitler wrote (or dictated) those lines in 1924, while incarcerated for his part in a failed Munich putsch, the invention of myth and not the establishment of fact were uppermost in his mind. In this instance, Hitler was busy pushing what would become one of the most persistent semifictions of the interwar period and a cornerstone of the Nazi experience, the image, seemingly translated into hard reality, of young patriots sacrificing their lives for the greater good of the Fatherland. Whether or not he took part in an actual singing attack is open to debate: Truth was always the least of his concerns.

The singing attacks happened. In a signal twist of the story, recent German historians deny that they did, though there is plenty of evidence for them. But their reality is far less exalted and ennobling than the legend would have it.

Why would men sing going into an attack? Except as the stuff of Nazi-era PR, mystical miracles played no part. Among poorly trained soldiers, singing must have helped sustain morale and create unit cohesion in the face of unexpected and disconcertingly heavy casualties, including

been established. Both sides produced such panoramas, which have provided us with an extraordinary historical legacy. We now know what the Western Front looked like. (Imperial War Museum First World War Panorama Collection)

the loss of most of their officers. There is a more mundane explanation. Singing preformed the function of the mostly defunct battlefield drum, allowing units to keep in touch amid the confusion of noise, autumn fogs, unexpected ditches, hedgerows, bekes, contradictory orders, unseen enemies, and the dark. Singing familiar patriotic songs may also have lessened the danger of friendly fire. Still, that soldiers sang all that much seems unlikely. It is just that when they did, everyone noticed.

WHEN WE CONSIDER THE DAILY (and sometimes hourly) German assaults and the ceaseless pounding by their superior artillery, the surprise is that the Allies did not experience more genuine crises in the early days of the struggle for Ypres. There were only two, really, between October 21 and 24. The first came on the twenty-first, when the gaps opened on either side of the developing salient. Command misunderstandings, unfamiliarity with the terrain, and fatigue, the great leveler, had all brought that first crisis about, and the Allies were fortunate that their opponents were themselves too dispersed, too inexperienced, and momentarily too blind to take advantage. All were sleepwalkers; all stumbled. The Germans, apparently, never recognized their opportunities. Their broad-front operational plan made it difficult for them to exploit the unexpected.

Just three days later the Allies presented them with a second opening, and one that could have made all the difference. Once again, the way to Ypres opened.

It happened at a place called Polygon Wood, which was then just behind the elbow held by the British 7th Division. Polygon Wood was a square mile or more of close-growing Scotch firs, with undergrowth of oak, beech, chestnuts, and heather, crosshatched with horse paths, or rides. On a map, the whole woodsy tangle looked like a hatchet, the long, sharp edge pointed toward the town of Ypres. Polygon Wood spilled over the long ridge surrounding Ypres: it occupied vital high ground. If, with a quick strike, the Germans could seize it, there was little to stop them from pouring into open, downward-sloping country, all the way to Ypres, less than four miles away.

Polygon Wood was the site of a Belgian Army cavalry school, though the cadets who had trained there had by then ridden off to war. The wood took its name from an elliptical-shaped training ground fenced in by white-painted railings, the eternal badge of horse country; a straightaway ran down its middle. The first British troops who arrived here, many of them cavalrymen, found the jumping fences, triple bars, stiles, and railway gates still in place, and irresistible. In the midst of German shellfire, young officers raced and put their mounts through horseshow paces until an irate brigadier reminded them what they were there for. To the ordinary British soldier, the place became known simply as Racecourse Wood.

Dawn on October 24, a Saturday, began with the usual unrelenting German bombardment—they had a rough advantage over the British of five heavy guns to one. Many of the British trenches in the area had been dug in sandy soil, with the predictable results. Shells cut telephone communications between the firing line and headquarters.* The Germans began their attacks as early as 5:30 A.M., while it was still dark, though the main onslaught would not come for another half hour. It was cold and pouring rain, and the thick Flanders fog limited visibility. The rain kept up all day. We know that a Hauptmann Dehgen, sword in hand, rallied reluctant troops, who followed him forward. About 8 A.M., a report reached Divisional Headquarters of the British 7th Division, a couple of miles down the Menin Road at Hooge, that the Scots Fusiliers and the 2nd Wiltshires were in trouble in Polygon Wood. The next thing headquarters heard was that the Germans were in Polygon Wood and pushing forward. Stragglers from the Scots Fusiliers reported that entire units of their battalion had been buried alive in the shelling or had been

---

* The first military experiments with the field telephone go back to the late 1870s, when the British Army tried out the new invention on the Northwest Frontier of India and in Africa. But it was not until 1914 that the device began hesitantly to come into its own on the battlefield. Those original frontline telephones, besides depending on Morse code—officers had to dictate to telegraphers—were difficult to transport and broke down; their wires to the rear, hastily buried, were too frequently chewed by artillery fire or by the hooves of cavalry horses. Signals carried only short distances and were easy to intercept. That moving target, the runner, was still the principal, and most reliable, carrier of messages between frontline trenches and command posts in the rear. Hitler was a runner. Their losses were daunting but considered necessary.

overwhelmed and captured. Nobody knew what had happened to the 2nd Wiltshire Battalion, but it was obviously nothing good.

A scattering of the Wiltshires did reach safety, and they were able to tell bits and pieces of the story. At roll call the next morning, only the quartermaster, the sergeant major, and 172 other ranks remained of 1,000 men. No officers were left. Not until 1918, after the Armistice had been signed and POWs repatriated, did the story of the stand of the Wiltshires emerge.

It started with the Germans seizing the village of Reutel, just behind the front line. While the remaining Wiltshires were trying to hold off a frontal attack, other Germans belonging to the Reserve Infantry Regiment 244 got behind them. They began to work down the British trenches from right to left. Before long the whole firing line had been overpowered. Four hundred and fifty men, many of them wounded, threw down their rifles and raised their hands in surrender, along with the colonel, senior major, and other officers. German accounts admit to bayoneting those who resisted to the end and waited too long to surrender: such was the unofficial code of soldiers in that war. "The survivors on their way through their captors' lines had the satisfaction of seeing that the enemy's trenches were full of dead and the corpses were stacked in heaps in the copses . . . They were also warmly congratulated on their resistance by the commander of the 54th Reserve Division which had taken them."

The Germans were now able to pour into Polygon Wood and out the other side. For a few moments nothing seemed to stand between them and a complete breakthrough into open country, with only token resistance in their way.

Without quite knowing how ominous their situation was, the British threw in every reserve available. Their orders were to fight the Germans to a standstill and not allow them to get beyond the wood. Maj. Gen. Thompson "Tommy" Capper, the unpredictable but inspirational commander of the 7th Division, sent cavalrymen, the Northumberland Hussars, from Hooge. They rode up the Menin Road past streams of walking wounded, dismounted, left their horses behind, and entered the wood on foot. They would be the first Territorials to be involved in more than a skirmish. The Territorials were Great Britain's volunteer reserve force, some of it already trained, which could serve as a Home Guard and, in an emergency, as reinforcements overseas. The Hussars would lose 300 men that day, including the colonel who commanded them.

The Warwickshires, just relieved from the line, where they had already suffered big losses, also joined the fight. Capper rushed in other units, including a regiment of French cavalry. His Hooge headquarters in a country gentleman's château prepared to make a last stand with as many cooks, clerks, cyclists, and batmen—the personal servants of officers—as it could muster.

The 5th Brigade of the 2nd Division had handed over its part of the line to the French the night before, and, after a march of several miles across country, was preparing to bivouac in pastures just to the east of Ypres.* Before its men even had a chance to prepare and eat breakfast, the brigade was on the march again, bound for Polygon Wood. The 2nd Worcestershire Battalion and the 2nd Highland Light Infantry took the lead, reached the southeast corner of the wood around eleven, and plunged in. They had two other battalions in support, but they had only the vaguest idea of where they were going and of what and whom they might encounter on the way. "To avoid shooting our own men," the Worcestershire regimental history notes, "instructions were given not to fire in the wood but to use only the bayonet." This would be one of the few instances in the war in which it was the dominant weapon.

In the dense underbrush, the two battalions lost contact. Maj. E. B. Hankey, who led the Worcesters, ordered his by-now disorganized troops to halt and fall back out of the wood. He re-formed the line and started off again, with himself in the lead: he ordered his men to keep him in sight and follow his direction. Hankey was a natural leader, one of several on both sides who would emerge in the battle for Ypres, a man who would survive four years of war to command, first, this battalion, and, later, a brigade of a weapon not even dreamed of at this point, the Tank Corps.

Ahead of the Worcesters and the Highland Light Infantry, hard,

---

* The field that was the brigade's destination, close to the junction where the Potijze–Zillebeke road, a dirt tract, and the Ypres–Roulers rail line cross the paved highway to Menin, would soon become famous as the behind-the-lines shell-storm deathtrap called Hellfire Corner.

blind fighting raged amid the trees and undergrowth. The resistance of the Northumberland Hussars and the Warwickshire did slow the progress of the Germans and prevent them from widening the breach. The British caught one battalion of Reserve Infantry Regiment 246 in a crossfire, cutting down half its men. German artillery fired on its own units. The bravery of individuals, too, held up the Germans, like that of a Lt. H.W.V. Steward of the Scots Fusiliers, who stationed himself with his platoon along a ride and grabbed a rifle, shooting at least eleven Germans and forcing others to abandon two machine guns.

Then something unforeseen happened. The Germans stopped. Had they become lost in the forest? Or, more likely, had most of their officers been wounded or killed, leaving ordinary soldiers without direction? These were not men who had been trained to take charge; nor were they prepared to take initiative in emergencies. By teaching men never to act without the guidance of an officer or an NCO, the German Army made it inevitable that attacks died with their officers. As the not-unprejudiced British *Official History* wrote, reserve troops "sat or stood about helplessly and without precaution. Either they were content to rest after reaching the objective they had been given, or they did not know what to do next." And it was now, around noon, that the Worcester and the Highland Light Infantry collided with the German Reserve Infantry Regiment 244.

Men on each side "forced their way through bushes and brambles into the fight," the Worcestershire historian writes:

At one point a party of the Worcestershire charged cheering . . . Everywhere the men of the Regiment plunged forward with bayonet and the Germans gave way. Back through the wood they were driven, and after them in a long ragged line came the Worcestershire, shooting and stabbing, hunting out the broken enemy from behind trees and bushes and cheering fiercely as they charged forward.

The pursuit continued until the Worcesters reached the edge of the woods, where they ran into "a storm of shrapnel and machine-gun bursts" and were themselves stopped. The Worcesters' adventure cost them 6 officers and 200 men. Meanwhile, a confusion of small-unit struggles was taking place. One part of the British advance ran into one of those unexpected local obstacles: tobacco-drying grounds that became "ready-made wire entanglements on which the men's packs and accoutrements caught." Close by, the Highland Light Infantry met substantially less resistance and lost only 5 men. Nothing could better illustrate the lottery of war.

A young German cavalryman from Freiburg, Hans Schroeder, who had ridden forward, described the chaos that had engulfed his side:

> We have advanced barely two hundred paces into the wood, which is bare of foliage, when rifle bullets begin to strike ever nearer and nearer to us. Then isolated men approach us from the right, and we see more and more retreating field-greys . . . Now the first shells are sweeping in . . . A deafening roar, echoed a hundredfold—trees break, splinters fly, earth, dirt and stones whirl through the air . . . A heavy bough comes down on me, crashing on to my helmet and stunning me for a moment. I try to mount; my saddle slips. The last of our stragglers runs past me. "Quick, quick, the English are close upon us!"

Schroeder escaped the wood and galloped across fields to the Becelaere–Broodseinde road. It was late afternoon now, damp and misty, and the British had recaptured Polygon Wood. He watched a Jäger battalion pass, "composed almost entirely of Marburg students." They reached the road and moved forward in a shoulder-to-shoulder attack:

> The next few moments are terrible; I shall never forget their ghastly, inhuman tragedy. As soon as a Jäger raises his head, to attempt the jump over the ditch at the roadside, one or two shots whip across, and the man leaps up into the air and falls on his back. Eight or ten Jägers are shot down in this fashion, until it at last becomes clear to them that they are being fired on by snipers posted behind the trees at the edge of Polygon Wood, and that their only chance to go forward lies in a mass attack. . . . Shout-

ing hurrahs, the battalion storms the wood . . . And disappears amid its lethal thickets.

A British corporal named A. G. Chambers described Polygon Wood at the end of the day. He had been sent with other troops to consolidate positions. "All the paths," Chambers wrote, "are strewn with dead and wounded. There are a few of ours among them. It has been mostly bayonet work and the ditches literally run with blood." From all sides he could hear "groans and moans" in German. "The stretcher bearers are working like mad—I gave one poor chap some water, he had been bayoneted through the chest, he could speak a little English." German shelling started, and Chambers was forced "to lie down among this horror of corpses. I lie alongside a little German officer, quite dead, I am sure he is no more than 19. They all appear to be either old men or young boys." It was, someone said, "a nightmare of a wood."

That morning Reserve Infantry Regiment 244 had 57 officers and 2,629 other ranks. By evening, only 6 officers, 77 NCOs, and 671 other ranks remained. Reserve Infantry Regiment 246 lost in that single day 16 officers, 18 NCOs, and 1,800 other ranks—70 percent of its strength. In the dark, it withdrew from its exposed positions at the edge of the wood. Its men were too tired and demoralized to bury their dead, many of whom they left to rot amid the shattered oaks and heather.

Another door to Ypres had failed to open.

CLOSE BY POLYGON WOOD, AT Zonnebeke, the French 17th Division attacked. Fighting went on all day, house by house, block by block. Machine guns concealed in a police barracks swept the main street, holding up the French advance. Finally the colonel commanding the attacking regiment ordered a 75 dragged up to a bend in the street. It opened fire, and within moments the German defenders in the building were scattering for safety. By nightfall the French had taken the village. Between Zonnebeke and Langemarck, they pushed their line forward between five hundred to a thousand yards. In the Zonnebeke area, a new phenomenon was observed: opposing trenches that were uncomfortably close to one another. There was a place where Germans entrenched on one side of a hedge and the British on the other. Just six yards separated them. This was not the record for proximity, but close to it.

At one point that night, German troops caught the notes of a trumpet playing "Strömt herbei, ihr Völkerscharen," a song in praise of the Rhineland, its wine, and its women. Then silence engulfed the battlefield.

12

The River Redoubt

THE WALL OF FLAME AND SMOKE WAS NOW SPREADING TO THE NORTH—AND taking an abrupt turn west—at last running into the sea. The Western Front had reached its watery limits. On the twenty-first an observer of the Royal Flying Corps, flying above the Houthulst Forest, scrawled a report: "Dixmude can hardly be seen for a mass of shells. French sailors having hellish time—much smoke rising from area of Nieuport . . ."

Dixmude and Nieuport were the two strongpoints that anchored the line held by the brigade of French Marine Fusiliers and the shredded remnants of the Belgian Army. Between them, the Yser is really just a large creek, slinking through pastureland and fields of wheat, turnip, and sugar beets; it is about sixty feet wide and no more than ten feet deep. Both banks are built up in dikes, the left one (behind which the Belgian troops and French marines crouched) commanding the right by a few feet. Infrequent bridges span the river. Farms built on barely perceptible hillocks as protection from flooding can be seen here and there. The few trees and the isolated villages—hamlets, really—stand stark and conspicuous. A couple of miles behind the left bank, across polders divided and subdivided into an intricate fretwork of canals, creeks, and drainage ditches, was the Nieuport–Dixmude Railway. In 1914, it ran absolutely straight along an embankment nowhere more than five feet high (and sometimes as little as three), the dominant elevation in the area. A glance at a map made an uncomfortable fact plain: this embankment was the Belgian Army's last line of defense, the closest thing to a natural barrier in the area. Meanwhile the Germans and their artillery massed behind the opposite bank and prepared to cross the river.

Flush from its success at Antwerp just days earlier, the right wing of the newly created German Fourth Army descended on the last Belgian strongholds. Beseler's III Reserve Corps (5th and 6th Reserve Divisions, augmented by the 4th Ersatz Division) had reached the North Sea, pivoted, and was making its relentless way south. His troops were the only part of the Fourth Army that could be described as experienced, the ones who could boast of the taking of Antwerp. Thanks to them, the church bells of Germany had rung for days.

Once Albert had made the decision to fight on the Yser, as the naval historian and strategist Sir Julian S. Corbett wrote, "the race for the sea may be said to have resulted in a draw. The Germans would reach the coast, but not at the point that was vital to their plans." If the Allies could not hold them at the Yser, and the Germans were able to break through, they would, as Corbett put it, "have Dunkirk and Calais at their mercy. . . . No part of the Allied line gave so much cause for anxiety."

On October 15, the Germans entered the port of Ostend. Three days later, in villages on the right bank of the Yser, the pursuing III Reserve Corps caught up with the retreating Belgians, and their first serious clashes since Antwerp occurred. They all went in favor of the Germans. Several outpost settlements fell to them. The next day they took, lost, and retook a village called Keyem, three miles north of Dixmude. Belgian troops attempted to escape, sprinting across mushy fields, where German machine guns and artillery caught them in the open, and "reaped a dreadful harvest."

The giant siege train that had crushed the forts of Antwerp began to arrive and systematically pulverized the brick walls and tile roofs of the farming clusters where the Belgians sought sanctuary, as well as the more substantial and august buildings of the nearby market town of Dixmude. By nightfall on the nineteenth, at least half of the bank of the Yser was in German hands; the III Reserve Corps began to probe for places to cross—as did the 44th Reserve Division, which was taking up stations to its left, facing the French Brigade of Marines. Then came the as-yet-intractable bulge around Dixmude. Sheltered behind embankments on either side and separated by a width usually less than a hundred feet, the enemies kept up a duel of small-arms fire over the murky waters.

It seemed only a matter of time before the German surge would continue. In their oceanside villa at La Panne, ten miles south of the Yser, Albert and Elisabeth organized their few remaining belongings so that, if necessary, they could make a quick exit. People everywhere in that last unoccupied corner of Belgium were preparing to flee. At Nieuport, only a small bridgehead protected what was locally known as the Goose Foot, the complex of locks and gates where canals, vaarts—creeks—and the Yser itself converged.

A mile or so to the east of Nieuport, a scattering of Germans did make it across the little river on the twenty-first, but it wasn't until the next day, in the hours just before dawn, that significant numbers succeeded in following. Pioneers constructed the first bridges from barrels, and nailed planks or doors ripped from nearby houses and barns to them. "The nearer we approached the river, the more frequently bullets cracked overhead," an anonymous NCO of Reserve Infantry Regiment 35 wrote home. "Only the occasional groan showed that not all of them passed by harmlessly." His unit had to move in the dark through ditches where the mud was a foot deep. The Germans fashioned another jury-rigged bridge. "This comprised a barge wedged across the river, to which a few planks had been attached at either end. The planks had become so slippery that it was necessary to crawl across them on all fours." Shells aimed at the new bridgeheads threw up geysers of muddy water. Sometimes they hit men huddled along the embankment they had just gained. Not even the night protected. "Every three paces we came across corpses or wounded men groaning. . . . Somebody shouted that the enemy was trying to filter past us. We . . . saw, not thirty paces to our front, dark forms which were getting closer and closer . . ." Gun flashes punctured the dark. "We hardly dared expose the tips of our noses," the NCO said. The Belgians pressed to the embankment. "There were flashes next to me and the shadowy figures collapsed. 'Fix bayonets!' They threw themselves at our muzzles. Our lads were both in front of and behind the wall. The black shadows scattered . . ."

Daylight hardly relieved the lethal confusion of fighting at close quarters. The Germans made it across in other places. They clung to their hard-won gains on the left bank, and as the days progressed managed to widen their bridgeheads. The cost was steep. Rows of the dead lay just above the water's edge; more corpses floated down the sluggish river. The Belgian trenches nearby, shallow, water-filled excavations, were themselves little more than drainage ditches choked with floating bodies.

There is little that is inviting about this part of the world. The terrain, even under normal circumstances, is fertile but bare, and given just a few days of artillery battering, even more denuded than ever, can often be featureless as a damp pool table. The soggy meadows of autumn extended to the horizon in all directions, that unblemished vista being interrupted by the blue swirls of exploding shells. Maurice Dewez, the literary Brussels doctor turned battlefield surgeon, who published under the name Max Deauville, described the scene at night. Some buildings, he noted, burned "like ardent furnaces; others, half-consumed already, exhibited the fluttering light of a lamp going out." The fires, he wrote in his journal (he was a frontline surgeon with the Belgian Army), "are scattered across the plain . . ." The Yser, with its deep and sticky mud that smelled of pigsties and crushed and burned barnyards, as well as newer deposits of mortality, had to be one of the war's most unpleasant battlegrounds, a premature Passchendaele.

On October 23, the Germans managed to wrest the most prominent loop of the Yser from the Belgians. That gave them their first foothold of real consequence on the left bank. The slaughter caused by German 210mm giants dug in along the far edge of the loop had already forced the Belgians back to its base, and units of the German 5th Reserve Division soon occupied the empty space left behind. Meanwhile, to the east, closer to Dixmude, pioneers of the 6th Reserve Division spanned the little river with a prefabricated bridge, the first of several. By the early morning of October 24, a Saturday—the same day that the Germans broke into Polygon Wood—the division had succeeded in sending across the majority of its riflemen and its artillery, as many as 20,000 that day. Another drenching gale had blown in from the Atlantic. To the Belgians, withdrawn to the railroad embankment, and now huddled behind it, a final calamity seemed only a sodden mile or so away.

IN ONLY ONE PLACE, THE coast, did the Allies have any real prospect of slowing the German advance. It was the sea, the traditional source of Great Britain's power, which might yet come to the rescue.

Word had reached London that 6,000 Germans of Beseler's 4th Ersatz Division were advancing on Nieuport.* A more alarming prospect was that the Germans would land troops at La Panne, the last town in Belgium, where Albert and Elisabeth had relocated. Churchill, wasting no time, ordered a flotilla to head across the Channel, and to begin shelling the moment it arrived. As he wrote to his friend Sir John French some days later: "I do trust you realize how damnable it will be if the enemy settles down for the winter along lines which comprise Calais, Dunkirk or Ostend. There will be continual alarms and greatly added difficulties. We must have him off the Belgian Coast, even if we cannot recover Antwerp." He put his naval secretary, Rear Adm. Horace L. A. Hood, in charge of a flotilla that came to be known as the "Dover Patrol," two light cruisers, some destroyers, several French warships, and two to three monitors—which were essentially gun turrets on floating platforms.†

A storm was disrupting Channel crossings, but—Corbett again—

---

* Ersatz divisions originated as reserve or replacement formations. To quote Bruce I. Gudmundsson: "They were the product of the 'layered' mobilization system of the German Army, one which satisfied administrative convenience in order to get as many relatively young men to the front as quickly as possible" (email to author, March 5, 2013). Some army depots found that they had more young men than the reserve divisions could handle when they were formed in August 1914. These extra men ended by joining mobile—that is, designed to move with armies in the field—Ersatz units. By the time it reached the Belgian coast, the 4th Ersatz Division had already seen action at the Grand Couronné and the siege of Antwerp. Normally a Corps comprised two divisions, 34,000 men at peacetime strength. Beseler's III Corps, perhaps because of the importance of its assignment, added a third. If anyone could reach, and carry, the Channel ports, it was the conqueror of Antwerp.

† The shallow-water monitors, which could come as close inshore as a few hundred yards, had originally been built in England as gunboats for the Brazilian Navy on the Amazon. When war broke out, the Royal Navy appropriated the almost-completed *Javary*, *Madeira*, and *Solimoes*, renamed them *Humber*, *Mersey*, and *Severn*, and sent them to join the Dover Patrol.

"To wait for the weather might mean to lose all: it was a question of hours, and the Admiralty without hesitation resolved to take the risk." The admiralty also risked leaving the northern entrance to the Channel unprotected. Churchill decided that he had no choice. By 1 P.M. the first ships were steaming out of Dover; the monitors set out a couple of hours later, weather or no. Hood's flotilla did arrive off the Belgian coast by midnight on October 17, but shelling did not begin until the next morning. Belgian soldiers gathered on the beach to watch the spectacle. Albert's queen joined them, recording the scene in her journal:

> The bombardment becomes so powerful that we leave the house and walk up the dune to watch the ships. We can see the flash each time a gun is fired. Between 14:00 and 15:30 it becomes almost unbearable, windows vibrate, we can feel the shaking.

The principal targets of the Dover Patrol were the villages nestled in the dunes north of Nieuport that the Germans had recently occupied, as well as newly fortified farms where they had cached bridge-building equipment. The British *Official History* noted, "The material effect of naval heavy shells, according to German accounts, was small, as they broke up into a few large fragments, but"—the words are those of a 5th Division staff officer—"the moral effect on the troops was great." Formations of the 4th Ersatz were so distressed by the shelling from the sea that their cohesion totally broke down. The remnants of eight battalions retreated to Middelkerke, leaving only one battalion in the forward trenches. In a letter to his wife, a German prisoner of war said that he and his comrades had been obliged "to lead the life of cave dwellers owing to the terrible artillery fire from the fleet." Beseler apparently decided to hold off on assaulting Nieuport.

After something of a romp down the nine miles of dunes from Ostend, casually swallowing shore villages like Middelkerke and Westende as it advanced, the 4th Ersatz Division stalled just above Nieuport and the mouth of the Yser. The unrelenting bombardment by Hood's Dover Patrol largely neutralized its progress. Beseler ended by moving the division to the left, out of range of the naval bombardment, to join the forces

Belgian onlookers on a North Sea beach observe a British monitor, headed south for the safety of Dunkirk after bombarding the German forces that threatened Nieuport. Naval gunfire stopped their advance; it may have saved the Channel ports as well.

attacking the railway embankment: Nieuport could wait. That would explain why, days later, German troops were absent when they were most needed. The Germans eventually did pack the dunes north of Nieuport with batteries of coastal artillery. The fire from these new guns was so dense and accurate that it compelled the Allied ships to retreat more than two miles out to sea. The counter-shelling damaged several of Hood's ships. They had found the remedy, too late.

Hood's Dover Patrol may well have saved the Channel ports. It had shown the Germans, in Corbett's neat summation, that "there was one flank they could not turn." This had to be an unobserved turning point of the Great War. As Oxford historian C.R.M.F. Cruttwell remarked in a series of lectures he delivered in 1936, the Yser line (and, indeed, the defense of Ypres itself) "could hardly have stayed, had not the British warships continually galled the open flank of the enemy advancing over the sand-dunes. This was the first and only time that the fleet had the opportunity of directly influencing the course of operations in the West."

Churchill's almost instinctive reaction to the German threat was a measure of the best side of the man. He could be right, at the right time; he wasn't always. His activities along the Belgian coast went almost unnoticed, except by his critics, who were as always legion. They included the prime minister, and they put down Churchill's efforts to stop the enemy at the mouth of the Yser as his "Dunkirk circus." His resolve has to be one of the key moments of that fall, if not of the entire war.

THE 44TH RESERVE DIVISION, COMPOSED mainly of *Kriegsfreiwilligen*, volunteers, and reservists recalled to the colors, began to occupy the right bank of the Yser sometime in the evening of October 22. Its four regiments took their place along the embankment closest to Dixmude, just the left of Beseler's III Reserve Corps. They faced Belgian infantry and, closer to the market town, French Marines, mainly riflemen and a few machine gunners. A noisy firefight, embankment to embankment, had already broken out when the new division arrived.

One of those volunteers was an eighteen-year-old named Peter Kollwitz. Though he did not come from a typical background, he was in other ways representative of the kind of person whom Falkenhayn had thrown into battle. Peter had been raised on the periphery of greatness. His mother, Kaethe Kollwitz, was the most important female artist in Germany. She had established herself as the graphics bard of the German working class, a major figure whose work is too little known outside her own country. She was a bellwether of the Left, which caused her difficulties throughout her life. Her subjects, many of them executed in series of narrative etchings, could be brutal: peasant uprisings cruelly put down, the hunger-ravaged faces of strikers, the sufferings of working–class women, the hardships and hopelessness of the proletariat. But her work was as delicately limned as the depiction of a society garden party or a croquet tournament. Almost as an act of political defiance, she had eschewed color and oils for the starkness of black and white. She was often too poor to afford models. Not infrequently, she used her sons instead. Kollwitz had a sure sense, so appropriate for a time of unrest and confrontation, of the collision between the promises of the future, too long unkept, and the mounting social grievances of the present. I think of the lines of John Dos Passos about social divisions in the United States: "all right we are two nations." That was Germany as well in the early years of the twentieth century.

Peter Kollwitz's father, Karl, was a doctor. who by choice practiced and lived with his family in a working-class district of Berlin. Peter was, like many young Germans, a prodigious hiker. He staged amateur theatricals. He showed talent as an artist. How far, or where, he would have taken his talents will forever be a question without an answer. In Peter Kollwitz we have a glimpse of the potential that Germany—all the combatants, for that matter—so thoughtlessly sacrificed on the battlefields of 1914.

The Kollwitzes were people for whom radical politics were practically a blood right—and yet, they supported this war in its early months. As Peter's mother wrote, "Back of the individual life . . . stood the Fatherland." At first they and people like them welcomed the war as a means of bringing about the social change that had eluded them for so long. "Deep in our hearts," the novelist Thomas Mann wrote at the time, "we felt that the world, our world, could no longer go on . . . War! It felt like a purification, a liberation, and a tremendous hope."

The first days of August, when the Continent was exploding, found Peter and his family vacationing in Königsberg, the Baltic town in East Prussia where his mother had been born. "I remember hearing the departing soldiers singing as they marched past our hotel," Kaethe Kollwitz later wrote. Her husband, Karl, ran out to watch them. "I sat on my bed and cried and cried and cried."

Her son hastened to enlist when he returned to Berlin. His outpouring of enthusiasm for the war briefly convinced his mother. Germany seemed fixated on the notion of sacrifice and the death of the hero, *Heldentod*. "Heroism" was the enchanted word that united an unstable nation, one in which the rigid distinctions and divisions of class ran deep and bitter. Rivers of heroes' blood would flow homeward and revitalize Germany. "Rushing off to war," the historian Robert Wheldon Whalen points out, "was an act of love." What seemed the highest and most noble form of idealism had captured the fancy of a nation. Peter Kollwitz was no exception.

The *Kriegsfreiwilliger* had just two months of training, if that. There is a final snapshot taken of Kollwitz by a family member. In his tunic and field cap, Peter slouches against a barracks wall; he holds a cigarette with studied nonchalance. Underneath the youthful bravado, though, you sense a certain edgy vulnerability. His mother gave him a flower before she left, a pink.

His division entrained for the Western Front in mid-October, unloaded at Termonde, south of Brussels, and then marched for four days cross-country, almost to the sea. There had been showers throughout the day when the 44th Reserve Division arrived on the Yser, October 22, and dense fog. A gale from the sea was gathering force, a four-day blow. It was the same storm that would wash over the massacre at Langemarck the next evening, and would go on to drench Polygon Wood. Orders came for Peter's regiment, the 207th Reserve, to fight its way in the dark across to the left bank and make for Dixmude. Improvised bridges would be waiting.

Night fighting was full of unpleasant surprises and concealed terrors, even for veteran troops. The German High Command was more enamored of the practice than the common soldier. On the other side of the river, Belgian troops and French Marines had set fire to haystacks, to illuminate the soggy prospect of drainage ditches, sudden vaarts, and water meadows. Nearby, and under nonstop bombardment, flames consumed Dixmude; not even the rain could put them out. Flares sputtered downward and exploding shrapnel rounds bounced their brief, bright flashes off the low clouds. Bullets snapped branches, thudded into tree trunks, ricocheted off stones. Peter's column would have to step aside on the muddy track to allow medics carrying stretchers to pass, or walking wounded. The whip cracks of small-arms fire intensified as the line of marchers approached the river in the thick and oily darkness, almost a texture by itself, of a Flanders night. Peter Kollwitz was about to enter his *Heldenzon*, the zone of heroes. We can only imagine his terror.

Peter's regiment nowhere made it across the Yser, advancing only as close as a high embankment, where the new soldiers joined a long firing line, near a bend in the river a mile or so above the burning town. Already the humid air reeked of powder smoke; the concentrated noise of thousands of rifles deafened. The *Kriegsfreiwilligen* climbed the lips of the berm, lay down, and commenced firing. The promised bridges were not waiting. Perhaps seventy feet across the water, no more than a stone's throw away, was a parallel embankment, behind which enemy troops crouched, the dull flash of their rifles punctuating miles of darkness. They had no difficulty picking off the pioneers who had rolled barrels down to the water's edge and brought planks to nail on top of the makeshift pontoons. Morning would reveal the bodies of the bridging crews, bobbing in the still river.

Dawn arrived, gray and foggy—"this great friend of humanity," a French Marine officer called it. "When you begin to see your neighbors, you don't fear the enemy as much." Men slid down the embankment, stood up, and stretched their legs, speculating with their fellows on the possibility of a hot meal. Food did not always make it to the front lines, on time or anytime. It was hard to avoid looking at the dead. They lay in long rows, like lines of prone puppets, their strings severed. Most of them had wounds to the head or upper body. The corpse of Peter Kollwitz lay in one of those rows. The first of his regiment to die, he had survived less than a night of combat, perhaps only minutes. "At dawn the regiment buried him," Kaethe Kollwitz wrote a friend that November, "his friends laid him in the grave. Then they went on with their terrible tasks."

Grief such as his mother experienced when she learned of his death was another, less reported, part of the Western Front narrative, and it was woven like a black band into the fabric of subsequent European history. People were unprepared for such loss, loss that left few untouched. Men boarded a train or waved goodbye at a barracks gate, and disappeared forever. No wonder survivors could remember the day, the hour, the weather, the last words exchanged, with such clarity.

That unreality was underscored by the way that you found out that your husband or son or fiancé had died—"gone west," "snuffed it," or "become a landowner" were some of the soldiers' euphemisms. If you were lucky, an official letter brought the bad news. (In Great Britain, only the next-of-kin of deceased officers received telegrams.) But sometimes— this was especially the case in Germany—you simply glimpsed the name of a loved one on a huge casualty list posted on a municipal wall, or your last letter to the front came back to you stamped "Dead—Return to Sender." Kaethe Kollwitz and her husband were almost more fortunate. A Berlin friend told them. His son had enlisted with Peter, and had seen him hit before he was himself wounded. The Kollwitzes went to visit him in the local military hospital where he was recovering, and to get details of how their own son's life ended.

There was nothing remote about the aftereffects of loss. Statistics do not indicate what happened to those left behind by the men slaughtered at Langemarck, Kortekeer Cabaret, Polygon Wood, or on the Yser. More than 80 percent of them were not volunteers like Peter Kollwitz but reservists who already had families or were becoming established in trades, farming, white-collar jobs, or professions. Soldiers, as

Near Dixmude, on the night of October 22–23, an eighteen-year-old German volunteer named Peter Kollwitz died on the banks of the Yser, minutes after coming under fire for the first time. His mother, Kaethe, was already renowned for her graphic depictions of the working class in turmoil and for her sculptures. Her memorial to her son, "The Mourning Parents," recognizably the figures of the artist and her doctor husband, Karl, keep watch over Peter's grave in the German Military Cemetery at Vladslo, Belgium. (Photograph by Hugo Maertens)

has been often pointed out, were not the only war victims. Others included the women reduced to poverty by the death of a husband and wage earner; the children left to roam wild while their mothers worked; the families broken apart; the parents deprived not just of the consolation of heirs but of support in their old age; the intellectual and political movers and shakers stripped by sorrow of their imaginative energy, their power to persuade. Considered in this light, the phrase "home front" takes on new meaning. "First he fell in battle," Kaethe Kollwitz wrote, "and then I did."

So much of nineteenth-century optimism had been founded on a belief in the future, and for thousands already, and thousands more to come, that was gone now. Grief, spread wide enough, and the anger that inevitably follows, can be an unspoken ingredient of social breakdown, a negative force; and the paralysis it brings a very real affliction. "I walk in half-darkness," she wrote, "there is seldom a star, the sun has set, long ago and forever."

IT IS HARD TO GIVE coherence to the events of those last days of October on the Yser. Attacks and counterattacks were broken as much by the depth and weight of mud and by exhaustion as by artillery and machine guns or massed rifle fire. Men skidded forward or backward in small, uncoordinated groups, taking advantage of whatever cover they could find, flopping in the sodden fields, hunkering in frigid, water-filled ditches. Corpses of every kind turned into sheltering promontories. In the midst of whistling bullets, untended herds of cattle still grazed in the meadows, unconcerned by the dead animals and humans among them. Occasionally a cow would suddenly collapse on its knees and roll over, lifeless. The animal next to it would sidestep and resume grazing.

The Yser may be one of the dampest rural spaces in Western Europe, but potable water has always been in short supply. The water near the surface of the polders is likely to be contaminated by animal, human, and fertilizer wastes; deeper down, below an impervious layer of clay, the water is brackish, still flavored by the sea. "The water is very bad, quite green, but it is drunk, as no other is available," a German officer recorded in a diary found on his body. At forward aid posts, surgeons, chaplains, and ambulance drivers pitched in to quench the thirst of delirious men, boiling stagnant water from bekes and drainage ditches.

For medical personnel, too much water, and not enough, was but one problem. Sanitation was another: barns and stables were hardly ideal places to prevent or contain potentially lethal infections such as tetanus. Doctors had to deal with a multitude of injuries they had never confronted before. In his diary memoir, *Jusqu'à l'Yser* (Passage to the Yser), a small and undeservedly forgotten gem, Max Deauville described one of those improvised barnyard aid posts near the river:

> The wounded come one by one, at times supported by a comrade, or carried on a torn up door. . . . Reddened bandages and muddy equipment are already scattered around on the ground. In places, the straw is stained with blood. In the back of the barn, one of our riflemen is close to death. He was shot clear through the stomach. He is stretched out, his head resting on a sack. His torso appears almost naked under his torn shirt. His hand is clenched on his chest. His mouth is open, his lips white, his eyes stare fixedly at a point in infinity.
>
> A Frenchman who has had the tissue of his forearm torn off by a shell, cries and screams; with regular pulsations, his artery pumps strong, warm jets of red around him. The procession goes on like this, always the same. Now the French are mixed with our men; it's the only difference. All of them are black with gunpowder.

THE RAIN CONTINUED. SO DID the fires. At one place, where shells had ignited fuel tanks on the left bank, even the Yser went up in flames. The circumstances of that conflagration on the river, a mile or so above Dixmude and close to where Peter Kollwitz had died, evidenced a savagery that was notable, even in this increasingly brutal and chaotic battle. The two petrol tanks and the houseboat that was ordinarily the home of their caretaker were the setting for a firefight that went on for much of October 24. Germans of the 6th Reserve Division had positioned machine guns in the houseboat and turned it into a floating fort, which commanded a nearby trench that the French Marine Fusiliers had recently held. Again and again, when they tried to retake the houseboat, the machine guns swept the ground and brought down the attackers. The marines finally did regain their objective, but had trouble fitting in with the dead and wounded who already choked it.

Suddenly, in the midst of a tempest of rain, wind, and gunfire, the tanks exploded. Plumes of thick black smoke billowed upward, to be lost in the low, unbroken cloud ceiling, and torrents of flaming petrol poured out in every direction, burning men alive. One French battalion commander, wounded, refused aid: he didn't want to slow the attack. A moment later, flames engulfed him. That night marine patrols crept forward, looking for survivors. They found only bodies, carbonized and unrecognizable. As for the tanks, blackened, crumpled, and empty, they remained in German hands for the rest of the war, occasionally useful for observation and sniping.

No one—least of all the idealistic German student soldiers like Peter Kollwitz, thrown into battle for the first time—was prepared for this sort of war. "In what bitter disappointment I now sit here, with horror in my heart," twenty-three-year-old Albert Buchalski wrote during a break in the fighting at Dixmude. "It was ghastly! Not the actual shedding of blood, nor was it shed in vain, nor the fact that in the darkness our own comrades were firing at us—no, but the whole way in which a battle is fought is so revolting. . . . The attack, which I thought was going to be so magnificent, meant nothing but being forced to get forward from one bit of cover to another in the face of a hail of bullets, and not to see the enemy who was firing them!"

Then, in a sort of logically illogical flourish that might occur to a philosophy student like himself, Buchalski added what may be the saddest afterthought of the next four years: "If one could only accomplish something, then, no doubt, the bullets wouldn't hurt so much!"

ON THE TWENTY-FOURTH, BELGIAN DEMOLITIONS teams blew the remaining Yser bridges, but it was too late to do more than slow the by-now relentless crossing of enemy troops. The German bridgeheads on the left bank of the river were widening and deepening. Beseler ordered his III Reserve Corps to bring heavy artillery across, and its demoralizing effect was immediate. Increasing numbers of Belgian troops drifted to the rear; those who remained to fight began to dig in along what all acknowledged was their last line of defense, the Nieuport–Dixmude railway embankment.

German shells were now landing close to the Belgian Army headquarters at Furnes. The army prepared to shift its headquarters to a safer spot near the border with France. Though roofs were crashing around his command post, the king elected to remain with his military operations staff. It was the sort of gesture, hardly empty, that was Albert's special knack. The Belgian General Staff made frantic pleas for the French reinforcements to hurry. Should the center not hold, their Operations Division warned Col. Charles Brécard, the head of the French mission to the Belgian Army, "it will be necessary to consider a retreat." The danger was plain, as Brécard hastened to inform Foch: the entire Yser front was on the verge of collapse, one that would open the way to Dunkirk.

Under pressure, d'Urbal agreed to send reinforcements. Just in time, four fresh battalions of the French 42nd Division, some 4,000 men, showed up in Pervyse, a large village close to the front, and in the center of the line. Another large contingent from the same division had already taken up positions in Nieuport. Leading them was Foch's favorite goateed showboat, the generous-bellied Corsican, Paul-François Grossetti.

Grossetti's day had already been unusually busy. At three in the morning of the twenty-fourth, a Saturday, his chauffeured car had bounced him up a muddy lane near Pervyse to a place called the Vogelsteen Farm, the temporary headquarters of the 1st Belgian Army Division. A Belgian staff officer, Cap. Commandant Prudent Nuyten, accompanied him. Grossetti discussed with the division commander how best to distribute his infantry battalions and six batteries of artillery. Later that morning, again accompanied by Nuyten and, this time, a British liaison officer, Col. Tom Bridges, Grossetti hiked through watery fields to the railroad embankment. While the two men scanned the battlefield with binoculars, Grossetti took a seat in the folding camp chair that would become his trademark. Nuyten pointed out that the embankment offered the Allies an ideal line of defense, one that would replace the winding riverbank with a straight line from Nieuport to Dixmude, a critical saving of three miles of front. Grossetti agreed. By way of insurance, the Belgians had also started digging fortifications along the Loo Canal, some five miles back.

FOCH ARRIVED AT FURNES JUST after lunch, to check the situation. Bridges, a deft memoirist, left an acute portrait of this "horsy-looking little man chewing a cigar which he constantly tried to light, and with a little stick that he always carried. He was a model of simplicity, directness and apt criticism, helped out by expressive and frequent gesture." Bridges admired Foch, whom he found "quite unhampered by considerations of vanity or personal ambition." But Bridges did feel that Foch failed to "give due consideration to local conditions on the Yser" or the dismal state of the defenders. "The weather was abominable and the infantry were in very poor shape. Muddy, unshaven, often too tired to march or even shoot, they crowded the wet trenches (water was found only two feet down) in a condition bordering on apathy." It did little good to preach the offensive to such beaten men. But that was never Foch's way. With some impatience, he listened as the Belgian commanders described their plight. His response was vintage Foch. "You held out for eight days; you will still hold for another eight days." And then he added, all but punctuating his phrases with his never-motionless hands, "You do not talk about retreat when it comes to the very existence of your country."

Bridges himself may have been less conspicuous—showboating was not a part of his repertoire. He had ridden with John French at the relief of Ladysmith and was a friend of Churchill. Bridges was himself an inspiring leader who ended by commanding a division. When it came to feats of practical ingenuity, one exploit during the retreat from Mons stood as the measure of the man. On August 27, he arrived in the town of Saint Quentin to find several hundred British troops whose commanders were about to surrender them. Bridges would have none of it. "If one only had a band, I thought! Why not? There was a toy-shop handy, which

A single exploit made the rotund Corsican Paul-François Grossetti famous. The commander of the French 42nd Division brought a folding camp chair to the main street of a threatened village, Pervyse, and sat there for hours under shellfire, directing its defense. (*Guides Illustrés Michelin Des Champs De Bataille (1914–1918): Le Yser*)

provided my trumpeter and myself with a tin whistle and a drum and we marched round and round the fountain where the men were lying like the dead playing the British Grenadiers and Tipperary and beating the drum like mad. They sat up and began to laugh and even cheer." Soldiers joined in with mouth organs. They marched out of town, and eventually back to their regiments, to the sound of his impromptu band.

Meanwhile Belgians taken prisoner on October 24 told German interrogators of the appearance of the 42nd Division, adding, erroneously, that the French in Nieuport were preparing to take advantage of the absence of the 4th Ersatz Division, which had moved over to buttress the attack on the center of the line. The French reinforcements, said the prisoners, intended to work their way up the coast and then strike the III Reserve Corps from the flank. Their story, which sounded plausible, caused a certain amount of panic at Beseler's headquarters. The unflappable general dismissed the threat. He refused to weaken the attack he was developing. His instinct proved correct. Reinforcements or no, the Belgians were hardly in shape to switch to the offensive. A sortie along the dunes was out of the question.

Beseler may have distinguished himself for his excess of calm, but ordinarily sangfroid, unless taken to its outer limits, does not make for legends. Grossetti's performance on the afternoon of the twenty-fourth did. He ordered an aide to bring his signature folding camp chair to the center of Pervyse's principal intersection, the most intentionally conspicuous place he could find. There, with shells exploding around him, the general plunked down his considerable bulk and sat throughout the ebb of the day, leaning on a cane, a sedentary policeman directing traffic in a maelstrom. As buildings dissolved in flame and smoke and masonry crashed to the street, men would dash up to him, receive orders, and dash away. He sent counterattackers forward, "in the face," Farrar-Hockley estimated, "of an enemy three times his strength." Even the pretense of a riposte was enough to check the Germans. He also bought time to reorganize his defense. When night fell, and the shelling eased, he walked away, unharmed, his aide following, the folding chair in his arms. "I don't know how much will be left tomorrow of the 42nd Division," Grossetti told d'Urbal, his commander, "but so long as one man remains the Germans will not cross the railroad."

ON OCTOBER 25, THERE WAS a lull in the fighting, but not in the hard rain that had blown in from the sea. After a week without relief, the attackers were as worn out as the defenders; their losses, too, had been heavy, and they no longer enjoyed the excessive numerical advantage that they had begun with. The landscape itself was proving an equalizer. A diary found on a dead German officer, quoted earlier, hinted of a general breakdown on his side:

> I have no idea where the enemy is, nor what strength he has. . . .
> In the other lines they are also suffering heavy losses, which are
> certainly out of proportion to the results we obtain. . . . The help
> given the wounded leaves much to be desired. . . . The sanitary

companies are kept useless on the other side of the Yser. It is equally impossible to get regular supplies of food and water. For several days we have had no hot food. The bread, etc., is hardly sufficient. The emergency rations are exhausted. . . . Man is reduced to the state of a beast.

A crisis even more serious was taking place behind the Allied lines. The previous night, upon his return to his new headquarters at Cassel, just across the frontier, Foch had given the order to inundate the polders north of Dunkirk. Water would act as a wall. At dawn on the twenty-fifth, Brécard informed the Belgian operations staff at Furnes of Foch's intention. Consternation took hold. A sheet of water spreading behind the Belgians would have cut off their main route of retreat. "So, under those conditions," Nuyten said, "we will have the enemy in front of us and water in our rear!" The indications, long buried by subsequent official hagiography, are strong that retreat had been all but decided on. It was that or be trapped. Only a direct appeal to Foch from Albert's prime minister, Baron Charles de Broqueville, prevented the release of the water. He protested to Foch that the Dunkirk inundations would force the Belgian Army to evacuate the last fragment of the nation it clung to. Foch gave in. That same morning he wired Joffre that he had decided to postpone the operation.

The focus now shifted to Nieuport. The town at the mouth of the Yser and its hydraulic system were "the key to the door," wrote that genius of French military engineering, Vauban, in 1706. He had built much of the Flanders canal network with defensive inundation in mind. "Once Nieuport and Furnes slip from our grasp, we will soon have the enemy at the gates of Dunkirk." Two years later, France's Marshal Vendôme inundated the area between Nieuport and Bruges, to check the advance of the Duke of Marlborough. The Nieuport area had been inundated once more in 1793, during the wars of the French Revolution, and again in 1813 and 1814, when Napoleon was in retreat and this corner of the Continent still belonged to France, part of the Département of the Lys. But there had been no fighting here for a century, time enough for the new states of Belgium and Germany to forget a potent military expedient.

GIVEN THE RIGHT TOOLS, STRONG backs, favorable soil and water conditions, and the will to sacrifice great stretches of arable land, carrying out a successful inundation is not difficult—except, perhaps, for the intervention of enemy guns. The topography of the Lowlands, with water close to the surface, hectares of polder land that within the memory of human records were under the sea, and an intricate network of drainage ditches, creeks, or vaarts (a Flemish word meaning "channels"), canals, and tidal rivers, is the ideal environment for this maneuver of desperation. In a hydraulic system such as that of the Yser, you encounter a main river channel, into which just that sort of watery network flows; the struggle to regulate tides, to keep large stretches of rich land from being submerged under the sea, has been going on for centuries.*

That war with the sea has long been focused on waterway junctions—centers of operation, to use a military phrase—like the Goose Foot at Nieuport. Here canals and vaarts join the main channel of the Yser. The place where a canal empties into the stream is closed by sluice gates, great doors that open outward to allow barges to pass. In a hydraulic system, the flow of water in the vaarts—which are only navigable by shallow-draft local boat traffic—is regulated by weir gates, which are raised or lowered when the tide goes out or comes in. Normally at low tide you raise the

---

* I originally derived much of my information on the hydraulic system of Nieuport and the subsequent inundation of the Yser while researching an article, "Albert and the Yser," later published in *MHQ: The Quarterly Journal of Military History*, Vol. 1, No. 4, Summer 1989, 106–116. Two Belgian historians were especially helpful, and I shall forever be in their debt: the late Professor Henri Bernard and Professor Emeritus Luc De Vos of L'École Royale Militaire in Brussels. I have tried to summarize De Vos's careful descriptions of the workings of the Yser hydraulic system—and how it can be manipulated to cause an inundation. Professor Bernard sent me a copy of his book, *L'An 14 et La Campagne des Illusions,* which contains the Great War diary of his father, Maj. Arsène Bernard, one of the truly useful documents I quote in this book. Almost two decades after my article appeared, a remarkably useful book, Paul van Pul's *In Flanders Flooded Fields,* was published in the U.K. It is the story of 1914 on the Yser front. Van Pul is a talented amateur historian who has made military inundations his specialty. He is a professional land surveyor, a retired officer in the Belgian Army who now lives in Canada. If there are errors here, they are my own.

weir gates so that the vaart can drain. At high tide you lower them, sealing the vaart from onrushing water.

But suppose that, in time of war, the need arises to stop the advance of an enemy army, and you lack the strength of arms and men to do so. In this part of the world, inundation can be, and has been, an equalizer, a last resort, creating a barrier of water separating you from your enemy, an amphibious no-man's-land. To initiate an inundation, you reverse the normal process. You crank gearboxes to raise the weir gates at high tide, allowing vast amounts of water to rush in, and close them at low tide, trapping the seawater and causing it to spread across a polder as it searches for a nonexistent opening. By the same token, you can inundate by opening sluice gates at high tide and closing them at low. In both cases the process may have to be repeated a number of times. One creek, the Noordvaart (or North Vaart), was the key to the operation. It began at the railway embankment, flowing north until it emptied into the Yser at the Goose Foot. The Noordvaart had no built-up banks: thus an inrush of seawater could easily cause the creek to overflow, flooding the polder plain in front of the railroad embankment.

It is not clear who initiated the inundation option. Even a local farmer named Pieter Ghewy made an early pitch. After Mass on Sunday morning, October 18, he barged unannounced into a schoolhouse near the village of Ramscappelle, just behind the railroad embankment, where a divisional staff had made its temporary headquarters. He said that he wanted to see the commanding general. The innocent bravado of the old man must have impressed: he got his interview. Maybe it was just a slow morning, with a group of strung-out officers trying to catch their breath before the next blows fell.

Ghewy, who owned a tract of land on a low rise nearby, actually spoke to a commanding officer in the schoolroom that served as his office. He said that from an attic window of his house he could see German positions across the river: they were no more than a thirty-minute walk from his house. Inundation, he added, was the only solution, and the sooner the better. It had been successful a hundred years ago, and it could be now. "My grandparents," he said, "had had to move their cattle into the sand dunes and the land had been barren for a few years after the flooding in 1814 with seawater." But his grandparents had reclaimed the farm and had worked it ever since.

The general ended the interview by saying that he would consider Pieter Ghewy's plea—which is, in any negotiation, tantamount to saying no. He may have recognized the environmental hazards of long-term saltwater damage, as well as the high cost of paying for the prolonged, and perhaps permanent, loss of arable land: they seemed more daunting than the immediate German threat. In a matter of this import, a farmer might suggest; only the king could decide.

A week passed; the inundation scheme languished. One man who did bring it up was Prudent Nuyten. An officer risen from the ranks, who ended in the early 1930s as the Belgian chief of staff, Nuyten was a Fleming at a time when most officers were French-speaking Walloons; only common soldiers, cannon fodder, were Flemish. At the time the war began, he had just been appointed a full professor at the Royal Military

Charles Cogge, a fifty-nine-year-old water supervisor, was one of the few men who understood the Yser hydraulic system who had not fled to France. He braved shellfire to advise Belgian military authorities how to flood a landscape they could no longer defend. The initials on his cap stand for "Northern Waterworks or Veurne"—or, to use the French spelling, Furnes. Cogge wears the medals promised him for his help. (Arterra Picture Library/Alamy)

Academy in Brussels, teaching military and international law. Since August, he had worked out of General Headquarters. He could do a little of everything well, and did not hesitate to take the initiative. Though not an engineer, Nuyten had already made himself knowledgeable about the intricacies of water management: nothing hereabouts was more important.

After Baron de Broqueville had made his protest to Foch about the Dunkirk inundation on the morning of the twenty-fifth, a Sunday, all manner of practical problems remained. How could the Belgians best produce an inundation of their own, and where? Nuyten's first task was to collect available information, from tides to available tools, on the drainage system in the area.

But he soon discovered that the hydraulic engineers he might depend on had all fled to France. Nuyten could not even lay hands on tidal charts. Someone finally volunteered a possible name. There was a water supervisor, Charles Cogge, who, despite the German shelling, had refused to budge from his Furnes home. But it was a Sunday, and Cogge, as was his habit after attending Mass, had stopped at a local tavern called Le Petit-Paris. A messenger found him there.

By the time Cogge arrived at the Furnes hôtel de ville, where General Headquarters was located, it was 11:30. While the autumn storm rampaged outside, Cogge and Nuyten huddled over a map of the local water system. Cogge, who would become an improbable hero, was fifty-nine, with a short, scraggly beard and a drooping mustache, narrow, appraising eyes, and a wheeze. He took an immediate liking to his fellow Fleming. Cogge confirmed that it was possible to strengthen the Belgian line of defense by submerging the stretch of land between the Yser and the railroad embankment. He pointed on the map to an old and long disused work called the Spanish Lock on the left bank of the Yser Channel, to the west of town, close to where the river reached the sea. Its huge wooden doors, sluice gates, were presumably still in working order. Cogge estimated that they could flood the polder between the river and the embankment in eight tides, or four days. The big advantage of the Spanish Lock was that it was free of Germans. But there was a quicker way, which would require only three tides, and a day and a half. This was the wider and deeper North Vaart Gate on the Goose Foot.

Once again problems immediately presented themselves. The faster inundation might risk stranding the troops of the 42nd Division, who held a bridgehead on the right bank of the Yser, just above the Goose Foot. But a greater difficulty with the North Vaart option was the complexity of its execution, which required the raising and lowering of heavy weir gates at four precise moments during the day. It was an operation likely to be spotted by German forward observers, who would surely call in artillery fire. Nuyten, who did not want to risk tipping off the enemy, decided to recommend the opening of the Spanish Lock. He could not have been aware of Foch's estimate that the Belgians could hold out for only three more days. That would be October 28. Even with Grossetti's reinforcements, could the Belgians resist that long? They seemed ready to give way at any moment, and in any number of places. Time now seemed to be on the side of the Germans.

Nuyten took Cogge to the offices of General Headquarters, where he met Galet, Albert's right-hand man. He told Galet that he had found a way to set a flood between the Yser and the railway.

Officers gathered around the old water supervisor and agreed with his recommendation. Belgian engineers would carry out the inundation in two stages. They would begin by flooding the area between the river and the embankment. That would stop the German infantry. Then they would inundate an even wider stretch from the embankment to the Loo Canal. That would mostly put Allied troops out of range of enemy artillery. But they needed Albert's approval first. Galet went in search of the king, who was in the building. Albert immediately ordered the necessary work to begin. But he hesitated to order the second stage of the plan. Did this early environmentalist have reservations about what seawater could do to such rich land? Did it seem to him a flood too far? Did he think he could hold the Germans at the embankment? We can only ask the questions."*

---

* Albert was not alone in his doubts about the need for an extended inundation. Another man of influence locally, Emeric Feys, also expressed strong reservations. Feys, whom some writers (including myself in an earlier account) have given credit for suggesting the possibility of inundation, was a Furnes judge and a dabbler in antiquarian research. A high-ranking staff member had billeted at his home. Feys, the story goes, pointed out to

By nightfall, soldiers of the Engineer Corps, sappers, had started to close the culverts along the railway embankment. Small creeks ran through these culverts. Once the inundation began to take effect, the blocked creeks would back up and overflow. But the closed culverts would prevent the flood from spreading behind the embankment, Albert's fear. The sappers worked without letup in the gale, often under fire. In places the enemy was only a few hundred yards away now. The Germans apparently did not suspect that anything out of the ordinary was happening. Perhaps they were too tired to care. But all the effort and risk of the sappers would go for nothing if the Spanish Lock scheme failed.

ON OCTOBER 26, THE GERMANS renewed their attack. South of Nieuport, near the embankment, troops swarmed over a large group of retreating Belgians and captured a hundred. Elsewhere they made some gains until furious small-arms fire and shrapnel stopped them. Once again, the intervention of Grossetti's French battalions prevented a breakthrough at the embankment. Once again, too, the attack bogged down in the mud as the storm swept over the battlefield and the shivering, soaked men lying in the open.

The Germans did not know how close the Belgians were to disintegrating. Between Pervyse and Ramscappelle, a four-mile stretch, Belgian troops had run away: some turned up in Furnes, five miles behind the

---

the colonel that deliberate inundation of the Yser had saved Nieuport from invading armies in the past: why couldn't it be tried again?

It is more likely that Feys, a lawyer to the core, threw a certain amount of cold water, as it were, on the inundation proposal; he may even have contributed to the decision to reduce the amount of flooded land. Feys pointed out that everyone in an area of almost ninety square miles, which included hundreds of farms and more than ten villages and hamlets, would have to be compensated for the long-term damage by the seawater that would have to be let in. He even produced an official document that showed that his wife's grandfather had been compensated for damages suffered in the 1793 inundation.

I should note that Paul van Pul's study has led—indeed, forced—me to correct my original narrative, "Albert and the Yser," written over thirty years ago. The misjudgments that I made were based on the researches then available. They mainly concerned Charles Cogge, whom I portrayed as a figure of slight derision, a foxy local. Think of him instead as someone who enjoyed moments of glory in late middle age. Three decades too late, I celebrate him. We should all be so lucky.

Albert, in braided *képi* (center), visits troops in their dugouts hollowed into the eleven-mile-long railway embankment that ran between Nieuport and Dixmude. For four years it would be the Belgian front line. The king, who doubled as commander-in-chief of his little army, was rarely out of touch with it. (*L'Illustration*)

embankment. Their artillery was breaking down as gun barrels and carriages wore out from too-constant use; shells were running low. General d'Urbal told Foch that he could no longer count on the Belgians. That night Brécard wired d'Urbal a message in code that said the Belgian Army was falling apart. He added that its General Headquarters was preparing plans for a withdrawal to the Loo Canal. Foch passed the information on to Joffre: he said he would deal with it in the morning.

When Albert learned of the intention of his generals, he had one of his rare fits of anger. The embankment must hold, and would—"*à outrance*" (at all costs)—he said in a general order, issued that evening. But as the king regarded German progress that day, one perception did seem hopeful. He came to the conclusion that concentrated breakthrough was all but impossible with Falkenhayn's broad-front approach. Galet later wrote "that German tactics—which were no longer a mystery to us— might be successful along a more or less extended front, owing to the enemy superiority in material, but by reason of the breadth of front involved were not likely to lead to a deep or sustained penetration." The

Germans might force a retreat, but as long as they failed to make a significant break through the line, they could never spread out and conquer from behind. Albert had put his finger on the principal weakness of the entire German offensive from La Bassée through Ypres to the North Sea.

AT SIX IN THE MORNING of October 26, Captain-Commandant Victor Jamotte picked up Cogge, and the men drove off in the continuing downpour to check for the most likely places on the embankment to plug culverts. Jamotte had become head of the Directorate of the Inundation Service, a post and an operation that the army had created on the spot the previous evening. Heading for Dixmude over rain-slicked cobble roads, crowded with supply wagons and sullen, drenched marchers, they had to take numerous detours because of traffic jams, German bombardment, and sometimes both at once. They stopped to squish through shell-swept meadows to the embankment. Vaarts twenty to thirty feet wide were natural candidates, and they saw men already at work damming them, sometimes standing up to their waists in numbingly cold brown water to fill the openings with whatever was available—wheat sheaves from nearby fields, for example. Cogge scouted for, and identified, smaller, and less obvious, culverts. Intense fighting was going on ahead of them. Cogge, who left a memoir in Flemish of his 1914 adventures, described his flirtation with enemy shellfire:*

> Shortly afterward the Germans started to bombard ferociously and like that we were in the middle of a hail of steel and lead. The officers retreated quickly but I was short of breath and could not move that quickly . . .
>
> Out there stood six guns apparently without ammo because they were not firing.
>
> "You are retreating slowly, old man," the gunners said. "You're lucky they didn't mow you down."

---

* This translated quote comes from Paul van Pul's *In Flanders Flooded Fields*, Pen & Sword, Barnsley, South Yorkshire, U.K., 2006.

"Bah, bah!" I replied. "There's more room around me than on me so it would be pure luck if one of those hummers struck my head."

But then all of a sudden I heard one of those loud whistling sounds so I quickly ducked behind a small stable. There were all these manure heaps around us and see . . . zut, boum, bang, all those heaps flew up in the air and the manure was spread out around the field in a flash, quicker than the farmer could have done it.

"What do you say, old man?" shouted the gunners. "Be happy you got here, eh?"

Jamotte and the old water supervisor returned to Furnes by 11:30 A.M., their tour of inspection completed. There, Jamotte introduced Cogge to Capt. Robert Thys, the officer who would be in charge of the Spanish Lock operation, scheduled for that night.

Thys would become another leading actor in the inundation drama. Jamotte's deputy, he was a hydroelectric authority who would now be in charge of the hoped-for flood in front of the embankment. He was thirty years old, a narrow-faced man of middle height, with lank straight dark hair parted down the middle and glasses, a smoker.

Thys motored toward the French border with Nuyten, to inspect Foch's inundation there. They discovered that French sappers had temporarily dammed the canal from Furnes at the border and that the inundations covered only one polder east of Dunkirk, a safe distance away from their own territory. There would be no sheet of water blocking a Belgian retreat. The two returned to Furnes, much relieved. By this time it was a little after six in the evening of the twenty-sixth, dark already and made darker by the storm. Thys reported his findings to headquarters—which immediately ordered him to open the Spanish Lock.

He encountered an immediate dilemma. Thys didn't know, exactly, how to find the Spanish Lock. He drove to Cogge's house to ask whether the old man would join his party as a guide. He found that Cogge had gone out; only his wife was at home. He was at a friend's house, she said. Thys invited her to take a seat in his car. She refused, saying that she wanted nothing to do with modern inventions. Instead she walked in front of his car to the house her husband was visiting. Cogge agreed to accompany Thys; his wife objected. Her husband, she argued, had just made two dangerous trips for the Belgian military. He was an old man and suffered from bronchitis. If he visited the Spanish Lock, he risked being killed by German snipers concealed on the other side of the river. Cogge's daughter appeared and agreed with her mother. Thys had an inspiration. He said that he would be back. He drove off to locate the deputy chief of staff of the Belgian Army. The two men came up with a solution. Thys returned with a promise to pay Cogge 2,000 francs—about $700 now—and award him a medal. Cogge's wife gave in, and the water supervisor climbed into Thys's car.

AS THYS'S CREW HEADED FOR the Spanish Lock, the Germans were beginning to menace the bridgehead north of the Goose Foot. Lucien François, the twenty-one-year-old second lieutenant who was in charge of the pioneer units guarding the fan-shaped complex of converging waterways, received orders to destroy the swing bridge at its southern end. That might slow any German advance. By this time the Goose Foot was under constant fire from German artillery. François began to oversee the wiring of the bridge with explosives. Shells burst without letup around the demolitions party. At one point, as he was unrolling wire, a nervous soldier pulled a detonator from the charge. A sergeant volunteered to crawl under the bridge to retrieve the fallen detonator and reattach it. Then, just as François was preparing to push the plunger that would set off the explosion, he received a message: a French lieutenant colonel asked him to delay until midnight, time enough for three battalions of the 42nd Division to make it back across the Goose Foot. François and his crew had by now been working for eight hours, under constant fire. The French battalions appeared, and scurried to safety. At 11 P.M., François blew the bridge.

ALBERT HAD ONE FINAL HOPE: help from the British. Early in the evening of the twenty-sixth, the king, Galet, and Col. Tom Bridges set out for Sir

John French's headquarters at Saint-Omer. Bridges had called ahead to ask if they could dine with the British commander. It would be one of the few times during the war when Albert left Belgium. He thought that Bridges, who was certainly familiar with the plight of the Belgians, might back him up. "A few reliable battalions in the line would make all the difference," Bridges wrote. Their car was passing through a village called Berques when French sentries at a roadblock stopped and challenged them. "As we had not got the countersign," Galet remembered, "I was compelled to disclose the identity of His Majesty." Security had been breached, but the French Territorials, no doubt impressed by the large car and its august passengers, allowed the travelers to continue.

The party arrived at Saint-Omer around 8 P.M., an hour late. French and his large entourage, Galet noted, had already sat down to dinner, "as unconcerned as if no such thing as a battle were going on." Considering the dire circumstances that had prompted the meeting, Bridges could not resist a dash (or was it a splash?) of sarcasm in his observations. "The sight of a galaxy (or was it a jealousy?) of generals and staff officers with swords and medals, spotlessly turned out waiting to receive him, reassured the king. These did not look like people who were going to be driven out of their positions. They were far too comfortable." Sir John welcomed the newcomers, and the meal continued, followed by cigars. Albert complained that he could not afford good tobacco.

After dinner, when the two commanders were alone, Albert put forward his request for British reinforcements. French was sympathetic but admitted that his little army was too hard-pressed itself to spare a man. Albert apparently asked French to provide the queen with an armed escort, if necessary, and to help her reach England. The most promising information the field marshal could report was that the French IX Corps was due in Ypres, with more reinforcements to follow. "Notwithstanding our lack of success," Galet wrote, "the atmosphere of phlegmatic imperturbability which we had found at British headquarters had raised our drooping spirits.

"We left about midnight. It had stopped raining and the night was calm and clear, the sky studded with stars."

ABOUT THE TIME ALBERT WAS leaving Saint-Omer, Robert Thys parked his car about half a mile from the Spanish Lock. He discovered that someone, whether Belgian pioneers or German gunfire, had blown a bridge, and he could drive no farther. Thys sent Cogge ahead, accompanied by an escort, while he went in search of a few soldiers to help open the lock gates. The Germans were now shelling both the Goose Foot and Nieuport itself. Cogge and the policemen who were escorting him took shelter in the lee of a building. Thys, also held up, was unable to join them for a couple of hours. It was 2:30 A.M. when the entire party arrived at the Spanish Lock.

The little group had to work in the dark, keeping as quiet as possible. Thys presumed that with the French evacuation of the bridgehead, the Germans would have begun to spread along the dunes on the opposite bank, a little over a hundred feet away. Nothing proved easy. The men couldn't find the necessary tools, which had apparently been stolen, along with the key to the padlock that secured the chained flood doors. They needed a crowbar to bend open a link. The Spanish Lock hadn't been used since the late 1860s, and the men had to open the gates on their rusty hinges by hand, using ropes. Then they had to wait for the moment when the rising tide in the river channel made the water level higher than that of the vaart, the pressure forcing the doors open. The doors slowly swung back. But retaining rings had long ago been removed, and the doors could not be anchored with gate hooks. As the drag on the doors that now came from the vaart side increased, the soldiers could no longer hold them open. They risked being catapulted into the dangerously turbulent lock chamber. Abruptly, at 3:45 A.M., the doors snapped shut. No amount of exertion could open them again. The men straggled the half mile back to the parked automobile. The inundation attempt had failed.

ALBERT WAS RUNNING OUT OF options. His manpower reserves were rapidly diminishing, and Sir John French had denied him reinforcements.

The Germans were inching closer to the embankment. Once they crossed it, and the tenuous Belgian and French line disintegrated, the battle was as good as lost: the coastal route to Dunkirk would be open. The Germans might even be able to take Ypres from behind—if, once they had Dunkirk, they needed to take it at all. At this rate, before many days were out, Albert would be a king without a country.

LATE IN THE AFTERNOON OF the twenty-sixth—light was fast failing—what was left of the regiment Dr. Max Deauville served left the farm where he had set up his temporary *poste de secours*. "The line isn't long. It moves gloomily on its way." His use of the present tense gave immediacy to his memory. "The cannon fire continues without interruption." Reaching a small field, the line paused to wait for the entire battalion to reassemble. Presently they formed a square on the brown earth. "Among the dark uniforms of the soldiers, the lighter uniforms of the officers are rare. . . . Sergeants, in front of the companies, call the roll. And in this desolate field, surrounded by trees in which the shadows thicken, few of the names they call speak up."

The doctor looked around, and noted trenches underwater. They were filled with corpses.

13

The Great Fear

"DRAMA" IS NOT A WORD TO BE BANDIED ABOUT WITHOUT CAUSE. BUT THE saga of the Yser, so intimately related to events happening just a few miles away in the Salient, still had tumultuous acts to play out.

The next centered on the siege of Dixmude, the town at the eastern end of the long, straight railroad embankment from Nieuport. Dixmude in 1914 may have been little more than an outgrown village, with a population of scarcely 4,000, but it was not an unimportant one. It was a market hub, with an imposing flour mill that was the tallest building in that part of Flanders. Rail lines ran through on their way to Brussels. Barges, too, stopped to load up with sacks of flour and the dairy produce of the surrounding area. The river narrowed and took a bend here, a canalized branch heading for Ypres, fourteen water miles from Dixmude.

A millennium ago, before the polderizing of the landscape, the village had been a full-fledged port at the head of a bay—a bay that no longer exists. Dixmude itself was a paradigm of the Old World, its step-gabled houses cheek by jowl and a small cathedral dating back to the early 1500s, a bit of a magnet for second-rate artists looking for the inspiration of the picturesque. They can't have been tempted to stray far from the village: the drab but damply prosperous countryside could never supply much in the way of visual stimulation. Out there, boredom competed with barnyard odors. Dixmude did have a military attraction, however, and one that now threatened to overwhelm its insistent quaintness.

The Siege of Dixmude began on October 15 when the French Marine Fusilier Brigade from Brittany arrived. Here, closely pursued by elements of the German Fourth Army, released by the fall of Antwerp, it turned and fought to deny the Germans another potential opening to the Channel ports. Because there was so much else going on in the prodigious Flanders struggle (and no doubt because there were no British troops involved), the stand of the French Marines at Dixmude has long been overlooked. It shouldn't be. This had the stuff of an epic, a market-town Thermopylae. Had the Germans managed to open a breach, they could have, at a single stroke, forced their way behind Albert's Belgians and Grossetti's French reinforcements, racing cross-country for Dunkirk and rendering the defense of the Yser, with a potential inundation, irrelevant. For the invaders, the overwhelming of the Dixmude choke point became an obsession.

Any measure of Dixmude's savage month is inseparable from the role played by the marine brigade commander Rear Adm. Pierre Ronarc'h. He has to be one of the attractive figures of the early years of the Great

Rear-Admiral Pierre Ronarc'h, the stubby, broad-shouldered, bearded man wearing a Sam Browne belt (center), poses with his officers—those, that is, who survived. It was Ronarc'h who led his mostly Breton French Marine Brigade in the month-long defense of Dixmude. Forgotten now, Dixmude was another of those loci of peril that would make the difference in the Salient battles. (The Print Collector/Alamy)

War, and one of its outstanding mid-sized unit leaders: sometimes the actions and decisions of men like him counted for more than those of the highest generals. Ronarc'h was a short, compact, broad-shouldered man in a billed officer's cap, with a graying mustache and a pointed beard known as an "imperial" sprouting underneath his lower lip, after the fashion of the era of Napoleon III. (In times of stress, though, and they would be numerous that fall, he reverted to a full beard.) A Breton, not surprisingly, Ronarc'h was, at forty-nine, the youngest admiral in the French Navy, a torpedo-and-mine expert who had distinguished himself in various wars of empire. But he had also fought on land. In the Boxer Rebellion of 1900, he had commanded French Marines in the so-called Chinese Relief Expedition, at one point directing a well-conducted retreat that saved valuable artillery.

His men respected his steady leadership and his refusal to give in to panic. He seemed unflappable. Once, at Caeskerke, a village just to the west of Dixmude, where Ronarc'h maintained his command post in the tiny railroad station, a heavy, high-explosive shell from a 210mm mortar scored a direct hit on the building while the admiral was inside. The blast lifted him off the ground and knocked him unconscious. He soon revived, rose to his feet, and, brushing the dust from his uniform, resumed giving orders. Ronarc'h could constantly be found in the front lines, advising, encouraging, assessing, and occasionally berating. He went to lengths to avoid wasting lives, a trait that set him apart from so many commanders in the Great War. Though a professional soldier, he privately believed that war was madness, a scourge that must disappear from the planet.

There was no denying his democratic streak. As Jean Norton Cru, that gifted listener and evaluator of French Great War accounts, observed, Ronarc'h was a flag officer who had, almost by a gift of nature, the soul of a *poilu*.* He often marched with his troops, notably during the dispiriting retreat from Ghent. Nights on the way west he would sleep in his car. At Caeskerke, he slept on straw in a dugout and could feel the earth tremble

---

* *Poilu* was the popular word for the French common soldier. It meant, literally, "the hairy one," after *poil*, body hair from the upper lip down—the mustaches or beards that French infantrymen almost universally affected.

as shells struck all around. Sometimes cows would wander in and munch on his bedding. A château was not for him.

THE ORIGINAL STRENGTH OF RONARC'H'S Marine Fusilier Brigade was 151 officers and 6,434 other ranks, a total of 6,585. By the time it reached Dixmude, it was already short of that number, and getting shorter by the day. His sailors were really soldiers, infantrymen. A battered regiment of Belgian troops fought with them. The brigade soon found itself opposing an entire German corps, the XXII Reserve, with two fresh divisions, the 43rd Reserve and the 44th Reserve, Peter Kollwitz's unit. In terms of rifle strength, the Germans outnumbered Ronarc'h's little force by 4 brigades to 1. But his marines had an advantage in training and experience, as well as being commanded by men who were career officers. His force was, in fact, composed almost entirely of professionals, much like the BEF. That would make a vast, and equalizing, difference in the days to come.

In his orders to Ronarc'h on October 16, Foch did not mention going on the offensive. As he said, "Under the present circumstances . . . your tactics must be confined purely and simply to resisting on your actual position. . . . Your mission is to stop the enemy in his tracks." Foch, the guru of the offensive, was (in Anthony Farrar-Hockley's words) beginning to learn "the wisdom of laying off."

The German XXII Reserve Corps began to show up in villages just to the north and east of Dixmude on October 18. Since it had detrained south of Brussels, it had been marching for four days. The only signs of war the new soldiers had observed were dead, wounded, and derelict cattle, empty farmhouses, and a trail of discarded enemy equipment. "Up until then we had not heard a single bullet fired," said a *Kriegsfreiwilliger,* a volunteer fresh from training barracks. "This had already become tedious. To march day after day without ever catching sight of the enemy was boring." For the moment he had to content himself with watching flashes from artillery to the west "flaring up into the sky like lightning bolts."

Maj. Gen. Emil Ilse, the Fourth Army's chief of staff, was convinced that no place was better suited for tearing open a hole in the Allied line, and securing an operational coup, than Dixmude. He had learned that Grossetti's division was about to arrive and hoped to force a breakthrough before it took its place with the Belgians.

On October 19, Germans of the 43rd Reserve Division showed up at a village called Beerst, across the river and two miles north of Dixmude. The Belgian GHQ requested that the marines attack and drive them out. They had to move across almost totally flat polder land that offered no cover except for a few irrigation ditches and the predictable hedges. Cows grazed unconcernedly as the soldiers in their red pom-pom hats passed. An occasional farm or an isolated cottage, deserted now, interrupted the monotony of this tranquil landscape. Under a thick shroud of autumn clouds, German observation craft circled—"ugly birds," the men moored to the earth called them—watching for suspicious movement below. Every so often they would fire flares of various colors, and, moments later, shell bursts would erupt across the landscape. The marines mostly kept away from the road, which shellfire swept unceasingly. Jean Pinguet, a captain leading a company of 250—in the naval parlance used by the Marine Fusiliers, he was a *lieutenant de vaisseau*, ship's lieutenant—described the approach of a high-explosive shell: you first heard a whistle "in a particularly disagreeable manner." Then came the explosion, which resembled the sound "of a glass clock breaking, only much louder."

German rifle and machine-gun fire from Beerst was brisk. "Every moment one of our men rolled over among the beetroots," a junior officer reported: he was himself wounded in the action. In order to move more freely, men threw off their greatcoats. Perhaps too casually, a captain with the aristocratic name of de Maussion de Condé stood up amid the sugar beets to scan the scene with his binoculars: a bullet, no respecter of birth, struck him in the forehead. By way of example, officers still felt that they had to act with such deliberate insouciance—and, indeed, they were required to do so.

Flames had begun to consume Beerst. The Germans and their machine guns were mainly sheltered in outlying houses at the southern limits of the village. The marines entered at the back and began a methodical sweep; the Germans retreated. By 5 P.M. the French were in total command. Three hours later Ronarc'h received an order from Belgian headquarters to evacuate. They had discovered, they said, that powerful German columns were approaching from the east: they needed to pull back and bolster the line on the left bank of the Yser. There were fears, too, that the marines would be isolated, and trapped.

Ronarc'h was not pleased. The aborted capture of Beerst had cost too many men. His Marine Fusilier Brigade had lost 13 killed, including 2 officers, and 85 wounded, of whom 4 were officers, and 11 missing, most of whom were probably dead. Now he was being told to retreat. He kept his frustration to himself—but not to his memoirs, when they appeared in 1921. He would have much preferred to have spared precious lives and spent the nineteenth perfecting the trench defenses of Dixmude and clearing fields of fire in anticipation of the German attack that was sure to come within days, if not hours. Now he might not have that opportunity. On the body of a German officer killed at Beerst, marines found a general directive, to take Dixmude "at any price" that same evening. To the German Fourth Army, advancing with apparent relentlessness, such thinking did not seem overly wishful.

Indeed, promptly at 11 A.M. the next morning, the first heavy shells— marmites, the French called them, stewpots, or saucepans—dropped on Dixmude. A marine wrote home that you could see the shells coming, "and they are heralded by a creaking sound, as if of ungreased pulleys." In a place that so evoked the past, houses, their roofs high and steep in the Flemish manner, caught fire, holes appeared in the elaborate façade of the hôtel de ville, the town hall, and in the early sixteenth-century Church of St. Nicholas; shells shattered the stained glass of its rose window. Much of the town, and whole centuries with it, went up in flames.

THE GERMAN OFFENSIVE TIMETABLE HAD clearly been interrupted before the first troops arrived. Paranoia had caused the delay. Regiments advancing on Dixmude had already run into fire, not from the deadly apparitions the Germans called franc-tireurs, but from retreating Belgian regulars, cavalry and foot soldiers, who had killed a couple of their pursuers. Volunteers, *Kriegsfreiwilligen,* fresh from their training barracks, had passed through dim constellations of rural villages, some of them mere hamlets. War was still a lighthearted, if footsore, experience for the new soldiers, and yet they couldn't help but feel edgy when they thought about the civilian assassins who might lurk with their hunting rifles behind curtains and half-drawn shades along the streets their tramping numbers poured down. As a German soldier marching into Belgium reasoned, "An honest bullet in honest battle—yes, then one has shed one's blood for the Fatherland. But to be shot from ambush, from the window of a house, the gun barrel hidden behind flower pots, no, that is not a nice soldierly death."

Eessen, two miles east of Dixmude, was one of those villages, part of the outer perimeter of the defenses of the larger town. Units of the 43rd Reserve Division arrived there on October 20, just before nightfall. Shooting started. Marching men and equipment in transit jammed the roads that funneled into Eessen, adding to the confusion. Men fired at random. Rumor and panic swept the packed files of infantry and transport. Locals, the word spread, were signaling the French defending Dixmude; ambushed German stragglers had been mutilated, some castrated, others decapitated. Convinced that franc-tireurs were on the loose, the commander of the 201st Reserve Regiment ordered the torching of the village, even though his men had suffered no known casualties.* (It seems possible, even probable, that the panicked German volunteers did all the shooting, mainly at one another.) At least one villager was pulled from his home and shot on the spot. The soldiers dragged others from cellars where they had sought refuge and pulled three men out of a brasserie. They shot them all. German soldiers claimed to see muzzle flashes coming from the church. It, too, was set on fire, and if there were indeed men inside, the flames and the collapsing roof immolated them. In all, forty-seven villagers died, but not one German; 245 Belgian civilians were deported to Germany. (Some 13,000 to 14,000 Belgians were deported in

---

* The *Franktireurkrieg*—war on irregulars—is a facet of the Flanders struggle that has gone largely unreported. We owe the uncovering of German military violence against civilians in France and Belgium, which was more widespread than originally believed, to the patient, and at times inspired, digging of two Irish researchers, John Horne and Alan Kramer. It's hard to think of a more convincing (or damning) work of historical detection than their *German Atrocities, 1914: A History of Denial*.

the first months of the war.) Chaos had trumped the timetable: there would be no storming of Dixmude that night.

The record of unprovoked killings in the rest of Belgium and occupied France is reasonably well known; that in the Ypres area is not. As Horne and Kramer note, Eessen was not the only place in western Flanders that suffered an orgy of reprisal for imaginary crimes against the invading armies. On the road to Dixmude, units of the 43rd Reserve Division shot townspeople and set suspect buildings on fire in several villages, including Beerst.

Some of the most notable excesses occurred just to the south, where other reserve divisions were pushing toward Ypres. At Roulers, which German cavalry had briefly occupied on October 15, the uhlans collected all civilian firearms and destroyed them. Four days later, the Germans of the 51st Reserve Division attacked Roulers again, and (as we have related earlier) fought French cavalrymen from house to house, rooftop to rooftop. As they pushed through the town, they herded locals and used them as human shields. Though the townspeople had been relieved of their guns, German officers alleged that civilian irregulars had fired on them. They retaliated by burning some 250 buildings and either shot or incinerated 31 people.

Horne and Kramer write that one witness described how 40 to 50 villagers were rounded up in a field and "told by a German officer 'who was fuming with rage' that they were enemies who deserved to suffer, before four men were selected and executed." The Germans then gathered a group of 150 inhabitants, whom they forced ahead of them as they advanced up the road to the village of Staden. They occupied the place and shot more villagers, including the curate. At Ledeghem, a village to the south of Roulers, soldiers of the 242nd Reserve Regiment took a group of town notables hostage. An officer boasted that his troops had torched thirty-four buildings and executed eighteen civilians in revenge for two small girls firing on Germans outside the village. (Two eight-year-old girls and a woman were in fact executed, along with the other supposed franc-tireurs.)

———

A SIGNAL MODEL FOR THE sort of irrational frenzy that produced the franc-tireur atrocities was the so-called Great Fear of 1789. In the summer of that year, within days of the storming of the Bastille, towns and villages all over France prepared to meet an onslaught of "brigands," supposedly backed by the aristocracy and foreign monarchs in a nationwide counter-revolution. In a pioneering 1932 study of mass hysteria, *The Great Fear of 1789*, French historian Georges Lefebvre described the contagion of panic that swept France as the Revolution began. Between July 20 and August 6, 1789, a period of two and a half weeks (the worst of the 1914 excesses on the Western Front were concentrated in the similar brief interval), strange things happened from one end of the nation to the other, from the Lys River to the Mediterranean. Phantoms ruled; panic took wing. "Fear bred fear," Lefebvre wrote.

As the Great Fear spread from rural village to rural village, and laid siege to larger towns, tocsins sounded, and the cry went up, "The brigands are coming!" Harvesters put down their tools and fled their fields. Local militias marched out in search of roving marauders or to aid neighboring villages—and were fired on for their good intentions. Flocks of sheep raising clouds of dust caused alarm, and sentinels fired at shadowy figures approaching town walls. In the village called Ennetières in French Flanders—the same place where the Germans would surround hundreds of Sherwood Foresters 125 years later—a priest gave absolution to his wailing congregation.

The events that Lefebvre's book records would resonate in the Great Fear of 1914. When "an assembly, an army or an entire population sits waiting for the arrival of some enemy," Lefebvre says,

> it would be very unusual if this enemy were not actually sighted at some time or other. It is the excitable individuals who respond to this sort of atmosphere, especially when placed in isolation or on guard duty, or when they feel particularly exposed or else when some responsibility suddenly lies heavy on their shoulders. A suspicious character, a cloud of dust, less than this even: a sound, a light, a shadow is enough to start an alarm. Auto-suggestion plays an even greater part and they imagine that they

see or hear something. This is how whole armies fly into panics, usually at night, and this too lies at the origin of the panics which started the Great Fear.

Lefebvre could have been talking about Louvain or Eessen or Roulers.

How did German soldiers—and, more important, their commanders—come to believe in a phantom, the franc-tireur? A young Belgian sociologist, Fernand van Langenhove, in his book *The Growth of a Legend: A Study Based Upon the German Accounts of Franc-Tireurs and "Atrocities" in Belgium,* set out to understand the reasons for what he saw as a collective delusion. Even though he carried out his research in the middle of the war—he worked for the Belgian government in exile in Le Havre—he came up with answers that still make sense. "Deliberately confining himself to German sources in order to avoid the charge of contamination by Allied propaganda," Horne and Kramer write, "he exploited internal contradictions in the German evidence." Nothing damned the Germans more than their own explanations. The result was a major study in the dynamics of mass hysteria.

To point to recurring "myths" such as the machine gun in the church tower or ambushes at night followed by deliberate mutilations was just a start. What sort of person was most affected by such myths? In the words of the two Irish writers, van Langenhove described "the trauma of German soldiers snatched from civilian life and invading unknown territory with its attendant terrors." Many of these men had rarely, if ever, strayed far from the places where they had been brought up. "The sheer speed necessitated by the Schlieffen Plan made the troops vulnerable to disorientation." Not only did they find themselves in the midst of a hostile and unfamiliar world, but they also faced, almost immediately, another trauma, the trauma of combat. Massive armies were ready-made for massive delusions, and there had never been one so big.

Rumors traveled as rapidly across the landscape as the newly articulated trench systems. In Flanders, clashes between the advancing German Fourth Army and Allied rear guards and patrols provoked retaliation against franc-tireurs—who generally proved to be locals who had the misfortune to get in the way. A new phenomenon of this war, the Irish writers point out, was the blurring of the distinction between soldiers and civilians. As time went on, and other wars followed, it practically ceased to exist.

Wars and revolutions favor such fears, and the Great Fear of 1914 on the Western Front has to be among the most notable. The franc-tireur may have been a figment of the collective German imagination, but there was nothing unreal about the trail of death and destruction left in its phantom wake. In West Flanders, there were eight incidents between October 19 and 21, in which 161 civilians died. What happened in West Flanders was not publicized as widely as, say, Louvain and Dinant, but it still added to a growing toll that could not be ignored. From the beginning of August until mid-October, the German invaders executed 6,500 civilians in France and Belgium, and destroyed 20,000 buildings, supposedly franc-tireur havens.

No matter what the rationale, these executions were atrocities. There is no getting around the word. Germany's leaders felt that they had to set

Ronarc'h's Marine Brigade, caps topped with its trademark red pom-poms, parades through an unidentified French city. Some 9,000 Frenchmen fought in the month-long Dixmude battle, just under half of whom became casualties. (BMH Photographic/Alamy)

a stern example. That may have been effective for home consumption, useful for stamping out potential rebellion behind the lines, but not for winning the worldwide competition for allies and supporters, or the campaign to make certain that abstainers like the United States remained on the sidelines. What seemed to make military sense turned into a public-relations disaster that no amount of persuasive savvy could paper over.

THE DEFENSE OF DIXMUDE BY Rear Admiral Ronarc'h's Marine Fusiliers has been lost in the general accounting of the First Ypres, undeservedly so. The Germans plainly understood the importance of an early capture, and its operational potential. The Germans planned to converge on their target from three directions, north, east, and south—advancing along the roads from Beerst, Eessen, and Woumen—and to cross the river and consolidate on its west side, behind the embankment of the Dixmude–Ypres rail line.

Memories were short those days; they had to be. New challenges were constant, and thrust old ones to the background. Commanders could only hope that they had retained some useful wisdom in the process.

Beerst was a case in point. Ronarc'h put its unsatisfactory abandonment behind him and returned to Dixmude to supervise the preparation of defensive works in whatever time he had left. He ordered trenches dug and the stringing of whatever barbed wire had reached the Marines. It was dicey work. Enemy artillery far outranged his. The first German shells from those untouchable guns struck at 6 A.M. on the twentieth. Throughout the day the bombardment was ceaseless, and reduced much of the town to ruins. There were sometimes twenty to thirty explosions per minute. The entire quarter around the church was in flames. Shellfire practically cut Dixmude off from the rest of the world. Ronarc'h sent men to scrounge telephones from deserted houses, but even when they came upon the apparatus they were looking for, they couldn't always make them work. What transmission wire they were able to stretch was too often promptly severed by exploding shells, human clumsiness, or hungry cattle. The deep mud of the roads delayed dispatch riders on motorcycles. Ronarc'h had set up headquarters in the railway station at a nearby hamlet, Caeskerke, where he could communicate by one means, the telegraph.

DIXMUDE GRADUALLY DISINTEGRATED. AROUND 8 A.M. on October 21, a 150mm shell exploded in the midst of a section of marines, normally 60 men: it killed 9 and wounded 25. If anything, the intensity of the bombardment picked up after lunch. The church, already battered, caught fire. At 2 P.M. a marmite plunged through a stained glass window of the hôtel de ville and exploded in a room next to the one where Belgian staff officers were meeting. When the smoke had cleared, an eyewitness wrote, "the most horrible scene you can imagine was revealed. Amid the debris of shattered furniture, fallen bricks, broken plasterwork, rubbish, and dust . . . you could not take a step without knocking into someone who was dying, or who belonged to a shapeless tangle of corpses. Brains were stuck to the walls and blood dripped down, severed arms and legs littered the floor . . . a veritable abattoir. There were exactly 43 victims: 19 killed and 24 wounded."

This must have been about when the British observation plane flew above Dixmude and its pilot noted, "French sailors having a hellish time."

Though the townspeople who remained in Dixmude sought shelter in the relative safety of catacomb-like connected cellars, a few did venture outside. In a letter, a young woman described how house walls trembled, were enveloped in fire, and came crashing down. "There was a stench of burning flesh so strong that, surely, bodies must be roasting in the flames nearby." Her letter continued, "A soldier near me was hit by a shell and knocked over. We cut open his greatcoat and improvised a bandage, and the poor lad, lying in the middle of the street, waited for stretcher-bearers to show up. Another shell cleanly killed a horse. . . . Again and again, I encountered our blood-soaked wounded. One of them could no longer remain standing. He fell, picked himself up, and fell again, as he tried to flee from the flames that licked his face." A corpse she spotted lacked both arms and head.

This was just the second day of the bombardment.

Ronarc'h and the Belgian commanders did their best to persuade the holdouts to leave; the burgomaster requested the civilian population to evacuate, and an exodus began. Most, but not all, were gone by the end of the day. They took advantage of a lull in the shelling, and he could report "a continuous marching past of pitiable refugees carrying bundles or pushing carts full of a thousand familiar objects that they didn't want to leave behind. There pass the sick, the invalids, also some wounded, small children, and nuns. Women in their best clothes floundered ahead through the mud, with admirable resignation."

One building did resist the torrent of gunfire, the hulking, dark monolith on the east bank of the Yser where flour was milled. From a platform of reinforced concrete that roofed its five floors, observers had an almost aerial view of the battlefield—as did the field pieces the marines manhandled to the top. The mill was about the height of a New York City tenement, but this was the Low Country, and the prospect was matchless. In the daytime, it gave the defenders a preview of any attack forming up in front of them.

THOSE ATTACKS, UTTERLY PREDICTABLE, BEGAN on October 20, but they were sporadic and uncoordinated, launched when men, and undertrained ones at that, had barely had time to establish themselves. Their eagerness to take Dixmude proved their undoing, as did the unexpectedly troublesome terrain. Companies blundered into hedges, fences, and water-filled ditches, up to fifty feet wide, and virtually uncrossable. Some attacks continued into the night, to no avail. Ronarc'h's brigade, by contrast, was dug in and ready with machine guns and massed rifles. The virgin attackers were no match for professional soldiers like his marines.

The Germans decided to wait for more troops to reach the line and held off major attacks by the 43rd Reserve Division until the next day, October 21. Even then, delay followed delay: they weren't able to mount a significant effort until early in the afternoon. The same obstacles that had hindered the original attacks had not disappeared overnight. Now a new one presented itself. Friendly fire took an unexpected toll, especially of Reserve Infantry Regiment 202, advancing up the road and through the woods from the "castle" of Woumen on the east bank of the river. To make themselves identifiable to their own side, the attackers wore white armbands and sent one of their men up a windmill to wave a yellow flag. Their artillery paid no attention and continued to fire on them. Worse, the yellow flag attracted enemy machine guns and a hailstorm of shrapnel.

The situation was even more unpromising for those attacking from Eessen, a mile or so to the east of Dixmude. The marines who had, with such effort, brought the guns to the roof of the flour mill proceeded to open fire. They were improvising—though I prefer to think of them as being among the first experimenters in the laboratory of war that Ypres and the plains of Flanders would become. They witnessed a spectacle that would, before many more days were passed, never happen again, because of them and improvisers like them.

What they saw was a succession of long, dense waves rising from trenches a half mile or more distant and methodically approaching across the muck and spikes of newly harvested fields or pushing through the hip-high fronds of sugar beets. This was a mass attack in its full flower, the apotheosis of shoulder-to-shoulder shock as proclaimed in tactical handbooks, on drill fields, in military colleges, or at central headquarters far removed from the scenes of real carnage and real persons suddenly and unwillingly launched into eternity. Ronarc'h's artillerymen fired over the burning town without letup, as did the Bretons entrenched in front of it: the human waves slowed and stopped, some breaking into tiny individual figures who began to run back while the lines diminished in size and closed up, the more obedient gathering themselves and continuing to move forward. Time and again they would come on, in ever diminishing numbers, never quite reaching their goal. It took just an afternoon to disprove the offensive teachings of a century, lessons and habits that would take much longer to unlearn.

Near Eessen, a Berlin *Kriegsfreiwilliger* of Reserve Infantry Regiment 201 (the 43rd Division), named Karl Classow, found cover from "lacerating fire" in the scant protection of a furrow. When he heard a trumpet and drum signaling a charge, he got to his feet, only to see comrades "twisting, tumbling over and collapsing, but we charged on with bayonets fixed." As bullets from an unseen enemy took out their platoon and section leaders, cohesion vanished. In the confusion of the stalled attack, German machine guns brought down their own men. Once again Classow looked for whatever cover he could find. He dove behind a dung heap, a common feature of this rural landscape. "When can I, an inhabitant of a great city," he later wrote, "have ever imagined that my life would be saved by a miserable little dung heap in Flanders?"

Classow then dashed for a nearby ditch. It was full of dead and wounded. From a company that had started the day 250 strong, only 70 were left. "The battlefield itself seemed to have died," he said.

Elsewhere, on that lethal road from Eessen, men plowed through fields of beet that offered no protection. They could see the outlying houses of Dixmude. The defenders were firing from every window. The survivors looked in vain for officers to take charge. "This was not to be wondered at," a *Kriegsfreiwilliger* said. "After all we had only been soldiers for two and a half months and we simply could not operate independently." Survivors of the first attacking waves of Reserve Infantry Regiment 203 found themselves in a slight dip between two beet fields. Nobody dared to stir. Those who did rise for a quick view were shot through the head. Only the coming of night saved them. A largely leaderless mob fled back toward Eessen. They frantically tried to dig in, but found they lacked the tools to do so. Others sought illusory shelter behind haystacks. A volunteer named Friedrich Meese remembered,

> Our wounded lay out to our front . . . under fire from both sides. Weeks later, when on patrol—in the meantime we had never actually got back to this point—I saw them there and had to crawl over them: row after row of dead. They were the ones who up until then had been numbered among the missing.

The missing. "The word" was, wrote Meese, "a miserable and tough one for everyone who knows what it means."

The following day there were no further attacks, but the shelling remained undiminished. German kite balloons showed up, with observers in baskets suspended from the sausage-shaped craft, peering down with powerful binoculars on the battered town. No suspicious object, no potentially dangerous movement, seemed to escape their snooping, or the shellfire that it produced. French observation aircraft spotted numerous German batteries, though most of them were out of range of Allied guns. Ronarc'h reported a relatively calm afternoon: "We profit from it to repair badly battered trenches, to evacuate the wounded, and even to bury whatever German corpses we can safely recover in front of our lines." Elements of Grossetti's 42nd Division had begun to take their place with the Belgians. The shelling continued throughout the twenty-third. Forward posts beat off attacks that were launched with suicidal regularity at one-hour intervals. "These attacks, which are ineffectual," said Ronarc'h, "appear to be made by very young troops."

The Fourth Army planned another big push on Dixmude for the twenty-fourth, but when a train carrying artillery shells derailed, headquarters in Brussels postponed the attack. That General von Beseler's III Reserve Corps had crossed the Yser and established a bridgehead seemed a promising sign. But morale was sagging: at one point, soldiers in the front lines went without food for thirty hours, sleep on the soggy earth was all but impossible, trenches filled with water, wounded remained unevacuated, and in gun battles in the dark, Germans once again killed Germans. Unburied dead rotted in the incessant rain.

Brussels decreed that the Dixmude offensive would go on.

ON SUNDAY, OCTOBER 25, AFTER a daylong break in the weather, the skies opened again. Between 1:30 A.M. and 6:30 A.M., and into the morning of the twenty-sixth, the XXII Reserve Corps made fifteen attempts to break through: trenches were taken and retaken; the dead piled up in the drenched dark and were trampled underfoot. Dixmude held.

The midmorning found Ronarc'h in his command post, the tiny railroad station at Caeskerke, a mile or so up the line from Dixmude. He learned that a battalion of Grossetti's 42nd Division had just relieved a marine battalion commanded by his longtime friend Capitaine de

Frégate—Lieutenant Colonel—Jeanniot, which went into reserve, "very diminished in strength and very tired."* If it was possible, the bombardment grew in intensity. That was the day that the howitzer shell crashed through the depot roof, knocking the admiral unconscious.

Meanwhile, along the road heading south to the château at Woumen, the shelling had become "very lively." The writer was the leader of a section, a lieutenant named Charles Poisson, who, when his journal appeared in print, used the pseudonym "Claude Prieur." Three months before, when the onetime marine fusilier officer had been mobilized, he had been a Jesuit in training: a "Fish" about to take holy orders became a "Prior." The shelling caught his men in the midst of an unpleasant job: throwing gray-clad cadavers from the October 21 attack into an enormous shell hole, a ready-made grave. The novice priest took the bombardment as a blessing: "They only wanted to relieve us of the sight and the smell of their dead." The men hurried back to the protection of their trench, dug behind the south wall of a cemetery. To distract them, one of Poisson's officers began to count in a deliberately high-pitched voice the number of shells that fell close to their line. In fifty-five minutes he counted a total of sixty-nine shell bursts. The men survived without a scratch.

Then, Poisson and his marines could see German troops of Reserve Infantry Regiment 203 forming up in the middle of the Woumen woods. They estimated that there were 200 of them. Though the Germans were at least half a mile away, Poisson ordered his men to start firing at will. Machine guns joined massed rifle fire. "The range was good," he said, "and the result satisfying." The attackers twirled, spun like trapped animals, turned sideways, plunged into ditches, but were unable to conceal themselves completely. The machine guns blocked their advance; the rifle fire, their retreat. The sight of the enemy in the open, falling in droves, seemed to egg on Poisson's men, as if they took sudden pleasure in kill-

---

* The designation of rank for the officers and men of the Marine Fusiliers Brigade was nautical, even though this infantry of the sea fought mainly on land. Ronarc'h himself, the brigade commander, was a *contre-amiral*, rear admiral, the equivalent of an army brigadier. His friend Jeanniot, who led a battalion, was a *capitaine de frégate*, a lieutenant colonel. Poisson, a lieutenant who headed a 60-man section, was called an *enseign de vaisseau*. A private, a rifleman, was a *matelot sans spécialité*—that is, an ordinary seaman.

ing. "I sense how much the sight of the enemy, so long awaited, is a violent stimulus, one that intoxicates." To quote a French journalist at Dixmude, "A frenzy of extermination possessed our people." It was all Poisson, the aspiring man of God, could do to convince his men to stop firing.

CONFUSION, MORTAL CONFUSION, PREVAILED. AS the night settled in, the storm only made it worse. Early in the evening of the twenty-fifth, the Germans gathered themselves for a new attack, this time from the direction of Eessen, in the dark, of course. Men stood up, and in greatcoats stiff with mud and soggy from the unremitting downpour, in boots full of cold water, and on empty stomachs, moved forward. Machine-gun and small-arms fire from the flank immediately cut them down. The survivors of yet another broken attack returned to their starting points. Once again, there were no rations, hot or cold, waiting for them. Before long word came from division headquarters: the commanders would not tolerate failure. The attack would resume.

It was not just the resistance of the marines and the Belgian troops holed up in Dixmude that worried the *Kriegsfreiwilligen* but the apparent threat, equally potent, of franc-tireurs "shooting from every bush, tree or ruined building." The comment, by one of the few who did survive, makes the German frame of mind and its effect on the dubious adventure of the next hours more understandable. Paranoia, once again, was in the driver's seat.

Two companies of Reserve Infantry Regiment 201 stumbled into the darkness and disappeared. All but a handful of these attackers were never seen again. Unbelievably, though, they did manage to sneak into Dixmude, where almost everyone was trying to stay out of the rain. Later that night, at about 1 A.M., a battalion (or what was left of it) of Reserve Infantry Regiment 202, including its commander, a Major von Oidtmann, followed that first group. He led them at a run. Oidtmann's men arrived at a half-inundated trench held by a few Belgian troops. Lookouts spotted them coming and ducked. The Germans seemed so numerous that they didn't try to stop them. The Germans crossed the trench in a single bound and also vanished into the night. The Belgians neglected to warn anyone that the Germans had broken through.

Led by the major, the detachment surged over the barricade the marines had erected on the eastern edge of Dixmude. Somewhere along the way stragglers from RIR 201 spotted the advancing shadows of Oidtmann's unit and joined them. Without firing a shot, men from the two regiments passed the railroad station and gained the Grande Place, the center of town. There, as the French and Belgians suddenly recognized what was happening, fighting broke out. Belgian troops fired down from windows. They seriously wounded two of the German company commanders, one of whom they were able to drag away. There were silent clashes with bayonets and rifle butts on narrow side streets, where many of the houses were on fire. The rubble of collapsed buildings and of dead humans and animals littered the ground. Mausers in hand, the main German force headed for the bridge over the Yser. Drums and trumpets sounded, and hurrahs! and shouts of "Long Live Germany" battled with the thrashing wind and rain of the storm. As if directing traffic with his sword, Oidtmann tried to encourage his men to cross. A car driven by marines stopped at the head of the bridge and turned its headlights on the Germans swarming forward. Machine guns opened up; men dropped. Others hid in buildings that hadn't been destroyed. A few approached the flour mill, where they captured a Belgian officer, bound his hands and feet with wire, and shot him.

For the Germans, desperation now held the whip hand, and a middle-of-the-night decision at the 43rd Reserve Division headquarters only worsened an already bad situation. In an attempt to relieve pressure on the beleaguered Dixmude attackers, division command cobbled together a force and sent it up the road from Woumen and the south. Shuddering light from shell bursts illuminated the oncoming Germans, and Ronarc'h's marines swept them with fire. It was another fiasco in the rain-soaked darkness. In the words of Jack Sheldon, the division "had done everything humanly possible to carry out the orders of their superior headquarters. Now it made no difference what orders were given; there was nobody left to obey them."

About sixty men, including Major von Oidtmann, did succeed in pushing past the guns at the bridge and escaping to the open country beyond. They struck out across the polders and headed in the vague direction of Caeskerke, hoping to reach the safety of their own forces on the right bank while it was still dark. Now it was the Germans who seemed overcome by a frenzy of extermination. They began to fire at any light they saw burning and at anyone who happened to get in their way. They apparently killed two cooks and wounded a driver. A doctor named Duguet and the chaplain of the 2nd Marine Fusilier Regiment, Abbé Le Helloco, stepped out of a casualty-clearing station to investigate the noise. But they failed to extinguish the hurricane lamps inside. The Germans fired at their silhouettes in the doorway. The doctor, hit in the spine, collapsed, mortally wounded; the priest, though gravely wounded, managed to administer last rites: he lived.

In a nearby house, Varney, the commander of the 2nd Regiment of Marine Fusiliers, doused the hurricane lamps on his table and left by the back door: he escaped. Another commander, Ronarc'h's friend Capitaine de Frégate Jeanniot—a battalion commander—was not so lucky. "This little stout, grizzled officer, rough and simple in manner, was adored by the sailors," wrote journalist Charles Le Goffic. He spotted marching men, whom he ordered to stop. They did, but they were Germans, who took him prisoner. They also captured a Belgian doctor named van der Ghinst. Meanwhile, Ronarc'h, who had been up most of the night at Caeskerke, learned that Germans were somewhere in the area. He decided to wait for daylight, which was now only a couple of hours away. He had a hunch that the enemy would be coming in his direction.

Oidtmann's party was in fact approaching, herding some twenty prisoners in front of it as a shield. As it pushed through the icy water of a wide ditch, the major recognized that his men and their prisoners were lost in a confusion of ditches, water-filled shell holes, and soggy meadows. The rain had not let up, and now the sky was turning gray with the menacing promise of dawn. The Germans would have to hurry, but in what direction? A shot rang out, almost lost in the turmoil of the storm, wounding one of the party. Marines had spotted the Germans in their unmistakable uniforms. The Belgian doctor rushed to help the fallen man, but the major ordered van der Ghinst to leave him behind. For the first time they caught sight of the tantalizing banks of the Yser, the water so close and the banks so close together.

But now a battery of Belgian artillery blocked their way. Then the fugitives saw marines approaching. While the attention of their captors was momentarily diverted, the doctor and two other prisoners made a dash for safety. No one tried to stop them. They plunged into a ditch, where they crouched, wet to the skin. They could see the Germans heading toward the river and took note of what happened next. They watched as Oidtmann called a halt for a quick conference.

As long as the Germans were herding prisoners, their escape was all but impossible. If they didn't want to become prisoners themselves, there was one option. Some raised Mausers and began to kill their captives. They shot Jeanniot in the head, blowing away the front half of his skull, then stabbed his body with bayonets. The man standing next to him raised his hands just as his executioner pulled the trigger: though shot in the shoulder, he took advantage of the general confusion to get away. Bullets to the head dispatched many of the others. Then the Germans started to scatter across the polders. Marines surrounded them. Other Germans, found hiding in town, were marched out—109 of them. One of the freed prisoners, a Belgian named Deliens, grabbed a rifle from a marine and bayoneted Major von Oidtmann. He was soon dead.*

Ronarc'h came up. Someone noted that a young *Feldwebel*, a sergeant major, was still carrying a revolver. First making certain that he had been relieved of his weapon, Ronarc'h interrogated him. But, he said, "he was so arrogant and insolent that I ordered him to turn his back to me, so that I would not give way to the temptation to slap him in the face." Suddenly

---

* There is a certain lack of agreement on the fate of Major von Oidtmann. Every source concedes that he was killed—but under what circumstances? German accounts, obviously wanting to highlight his bravery and not his involvement in the murder of Jeanniot and the other prisoners, imply that he died somewhere along the way, perhaps at the bridge. French and Belgian sources will have none of that evasiveness. The major was there until the end. It was he who ordered the shootings, and his former prisoners did not forgive his fanaticism.

the NCO took off, plunged through a vaart, and began to sprint across a polder. Marines followed him, guns drawn, and brought him down.

Ronarc'h turned to face the other prisoners. "I had a great desire," he later admitted, "to shoot all of them for having murdered Commandant Jeanniot, my old friend of more than thirty years, whose body at that same moment marines brought up, laid low by bullets and bayonets." However, his questioning convinced him that many of the German soldiers had refused when ordered to kill prisoners. They included recent students from Berlin: this was not the kind of war that they had volunteered to fight. A drama within a drama had plainly taken place.

Dr. van der Ghinst emerged from his hiding place and told Ronarc'h what he had seen. The admiral's diary entry could not have been more matter-of-fact, emotionless words that betrayed the anger and sorrow he felt. "I asked him to point out the soldiers who had carried out the murders. The doctor indicated three of them in a way that admitted to no doubt. I had them shot on the spot."

EVERYONE SUFFERED IN THE WATERLOGGED landscape that Ronarc'h described as "this accursed polder." In *Souvenirs de la Guerre,* the arresting memoir based on his diary, the admiral quotes at length from a field notebook that Belgian troops found on a dead German officer. His life had ended near a hamlet called Oud-Stuivekenskerke that possibly had fewer inhabitants than letters in its name. But then, that was what men on both sides had been reduced to dying for. The repetition of certain words and phrases is a measure of the stress and terror that the writer must have experienced in his sojourn on the front, as he scribbled in pencil during rare moments of respite:

24 October.—The fighting continues. . . . Terrible situation. We know nothing of the general situation. I have no idea where the enemy is, nor how big a force he has, and there is no place to obtain information. . . . Our heavy losses have little relationship to the results we obtain. The enemy artillery is too powerful and too well

hidden, and since our weaker artillery can't silence it, an advance by our infantry has no effect, and only achieves heavy and useless losses.

Help for the wounded equally leaves much to be desired. . . . The medics are kept uselessly behind the Yser. It is equally impossible to come by a regular supply of water and rations. We haven't tasted a hot meal for days. Bread and scraps are scarcely sufficient, the reserve rations are exhausted. . . . Man is reduced to the state of beast.

Bad leadership from above, and in cases no leadership, as well as an inability of officers to deal with the basic needs of the men they commanded, comes through in every page of these brief, desperate remarks. At a time when the best German general on the Ypres front, Beseler, was on the verge of a breakthrough at the railway embankment at Pervyse, the Fourth Army chief of staff, Ilse, remained obsessed with Dixmude. He and his boss, Duke Albrecht, were eighty or more miles away from the Yser front. As General Farrar-Hockley reasoned about the struggle for the embankment, in a counterfactual scenario that is as elementary as it is telling: "If the shells of the 350 and 420 [mm] guns had been fired at this line, it must have broken beyond repair." A simple redirection of the siege train might have changed everything.

But let us pick up the diary again:

26 October.—The night was frightful. A terrible storm and rain. I felt as though I had been turned to ice, and I had to remain standing, with my feet in the water.

The situation is the same as all the other days so far. No forward movement, in spite of the unending battle, in spite of the roar of cannon and the cries of alarm of the human lives needlessly sacrificed . . .

Our company has suffered a great deal. Our colonel, our battalion head, and many other officers have been wounded and several are already dead . . .

The situation is terrible. To be machine-gunned without letup, and to know nothing of the enemy, nor of his approximate strength. It is to be hoped that the situation will clear up soon.

On the twenty-sixth and the twenty-seventh, there were some welcome changes. The commander of the 43rd Reserve Division, as well as those of its two brigades (each comprising two three-battalion regiments, 6,000 men at full strength), were fired: "relieved of command" is the military expression that allows no ambiguity. The officers who replaced them had all experienced combat. They made a point of moving their headquarters just behind the front. The new bosses quickly recognized that the volunteers had been trained in ways that had little relevance to the necessary skills of the present war. They brought in engineers to teach the *Kriegsfreiwilligen* how to construct, and position, proper trenches—which they also moved closer to the enemy, to shorten attack distances. And they encouraged more active nighttime patrolling in the still-nameless empty space between the lines.

Most of all, they discontinued for the time being the large-scale assaults that had witnessed so much unnecessary dying. Men had to learn how to be soldiers first. For the Germans, too, the laboratory of war was beginning to show results.

As for the anonymous diarist, these changes came too late.

27 October—At dawn, I profit from a moment of respite to read the good wishes that have come to me from home. What a joy! But soon the illusion vanishes. The situation remains muddled. One mustn't think about tomorrow.

It was at this moment that a bullet, or a bursting shell, cut short his diary, and his life.

14

"Hanging on by Our Eyelids"

OCTOBER 25–26

IN THE BOOK CALLED *1914*, HIS SELF–SERVING, SCORE–SETTLING, BUT RARELY edifying memoir, Sir John French regarded the battle of Ypres with a certain amount of satisfaction. To him, the date October 26—the same evening that Albert made his visit to plead for reinforcements—represented the successful conclusion to its first phase.* By his reckoning, Allied operations up to that point had established "a line to the sea which, if it could be held, brought the Germans face to face with the challenge: 'Thus far shalt thou go and no farther.'" There was no better proof, he reasoned in the book, than "the desperate but abortive attempts they made to break through in the second phase of the battle." That second phase was the one about to begin, lasting (by his later reckoning) from October 27 through October 31. In his nightly telegram to Lord Kitchener, sent after Albert's departure, French had assured the secretary of state for war that the Germans were "quite incapable of making any strong and sustained attack." Those words came close to matching the unreality of his memoir. Sir John often seemed to inhabit a private dream world.

Even when his ghostwritten book appeared in the spring of 1919, it was sometimes hard to tell which way the wind was blowing for the weathercock. One moment all was hopeless for the Germans; a page later, a contradictory breeze had taken over and it was his own men who were

---

* Perhaps uneasy in retrospect about having given royalty a brush-off that night, French made no mention of his Saint-Omer interview with Albert.

hanging by a gallant thread. One side's desperation was not necessarily the other's deliverance. He rarely manifested the long view. "In my inmost heart," French said, "I did not expect I should have to fight a great defensive battle." He would soon be forced to do just that.

At GHQ, he surrounded himself with mediocrities, lightly educated second sons from horsey backgrounds. They mostly towered over this man who, except for his middling height and constant lack of funds, belonged to their class. Their dim influence was telling. His closest confidants were men like Sir Henry Wilson (French's "evil genius" one non-admirer called him), forever undone by his own machinations—he also held his boss in low estimation—or Archibald Murray, his chief of staff, a man buffeted by nerves and indecision: he once fainted on hearing bad news. French, though, was not really intimate with anyone male; a vindicative streak continually tripped him up. He owed whatever distinction he took credit for to the good sense, initiative, and courage of his lesser commanders, to the professionalism of his small, and ever-shrinking, army, and to a preternatural gift for his own survival.

In June 1922, he would accept the hereditary title of 1st Earl of Ypres, a place where his good fortune had been beyond his control. "Although Ypres as a city has ceased to exist," French wrote, "I am thankful to know that no German soldier has ever set foot within its walls"—as always, his sense of recent history failed him—"save as a prisoner. Here, as at Verdun, they did not pass . . ." His main contribution that autumn may have been the burgeoning hold that Ypres—"Wipers," as so many of his countrymen called it—would gain on the British imagination.*

FOR THE NEXT FOUR DAYS, October 25 through 28, no action could be considered crucial; none had the potential of a turning point. Fresh French divisions arrived. The Yser front seemed ever more in danger of buck-

---

* French accepted the title, but with misgivings: his finances were in their usual tattered state, and the prerogatives of an earldom came at considerable cost. After his death in 1925 the title passed to his painter son, Dick, from whom he had long been estranged. French did make up with his second son, Gerald, who had won a DSO in the war. In years to come, Gerald would become his chief defender, not an easy task.

ling, the first inundation attempt had failed, but somehow the Belgian and French defenders continued to cling to the railway embankment and to Dixmude. A relative lull settled over much of Flanders. In another of his ritual telegrams to Kitchener, Sir John attributed the apparent gaining of the initiative to a battle that the Allies had "practically won."

The Germans, meanwhile, were deliberately biding their time as they prepared to launch a new onslaught. Within a few days they would have an advantage of 2 to 1 in numbers of available infantry, and 10 to 1 in artillery. They did not completely lie low. The Germans did try human wave attacks one more time, south of the Lys. Rupprecht's Sixth Army sent its 14th Division, veteran infantrymen and not untrained reservists, storming down the faint groundswells that passed as ridges, in an attempt to swamp the British II and III Corps in the spongy strip of impoverished soil between Armentières and the canal of La Bassée. This is open country, sullen in aspect, and even though the predictable darkness of late afternoon had fallen—the date was October 24—the British riflemen made sport of the German masses, so easily recognizable in their spiked helmets as they pressed on the village of Neuve Chapelle. "It was a wild evening of volleys fired at the flashes of the enemy's fire," wrote military historian Cyril Falls in his Great War chronicle of the Royal Irish rifles, "or at dim figures distinguished in the darkness." The Germans made momentary breakthroughs, "men meeting with shouts and oaths on the wet, slippery ground, thrusting at one another with bayonets. For an hour the affair was doubtful. Then gradually the enemy was shaken off, and by 6 p.m. the attack was definitely repulsed. . . . Heavy losses had been inflicted on the enemy, to judge by the noise of the wounded in front of our lines . . . Those who have heard that sound remember it."

Two nights later, in house-to-house fighting, "a wild fury of rush and counter-rush"—"wild" is again the operative word—the Germans did take the village of Neuve Chapelle, a battered cluster that would gain incarnadined prominence in the following months. Here, the two lines were only a hundred yards apart. The capture of the village was a bellwether. A similar struggle for another village in the Salient itself, Kruiseecke, had equally promising results for the Germans. Apparently there are no records to indicate that Sir John viewed either operation as a trial run.

Kruiseecke wasn't much of a village, a single street about three hundred yards long, running in a north–south direction. But, occupying a knoll some fifty feet higher than the general level, the place was a tactically important local feature. As views went in that area, Kruiseecke's could be considered commanding, all-important for artillery support and observation in this basin-like landscape, with Ypres itself at the shallow bottom.

The struggle for Kruiseecke, largely overlooked today, was an early epitome of war on the Western Front, and a near-disaster for the British. An entire division, the 7th, and the corps it was part of, came close to destruction. One of the best brigades in the BEF, the 20th, was nearly annihilated by the shells that dropped at a rate of 150 an hour, or between 2 and 3 per minute, from dawn to dusk—what seemed for the time an unprecedented weight of steel. Kruiseecke came close to ruining the career of a general, who would, for better or worse, rise to a position of influence in the British Western Front hierarchy, Henry Rawlinson. It severely depleted the cadre of trained officers and took the lives of hundreds of the core of riflemen on whom the BEF depended. The Germans, perhaps, suffered equally: with their casualty-counting system in disrepair, it's hard to tell.

Kruiseecke never should have happened, and only did so because of Sir John French's fixation with the offensive. Did a too-heavy dose of the Fochian serum lead him to deny the warnings of his own competent chief of intelligence, Gen. George Macdonogh, that the German buildup was huge and potentially unmanageable? "Although I looked for a great addition to the enemy's numbers . . . the strength they actually reached astounded me," French wrote in his memoir. "This, taken with the speed in which they appeared on the field, came like a veritable bolt from the blue." It's a sentence that defies comprehension. To quote a perceptive biographer, George H. Cassar, French "had closed his eyes to some very obvious probabilities. The one remaining hope of a strategic victory for the Germans lay in seizing the Channel ports and rolling up the Allied line. For this purpose it followed that they would need to concentrate every available man. If the Allies had thinned their line on the Aisne and elsewhere in order to bring troops northwards, what was to prevent the

Germans from doing the same thing at the same time?" That was precisely their intention.

THE STORY OF KRUISEECKE BECAME tangled in British headquarters politics as old wounds and bitterness unexpectedly reasserted themselves. Too often self-control, carefully nurtured, surrendered to the relentless stress of those days. The antagonism between French and Rawlinson had been simmering for years. A decade earlier, French had accused Rawlinson and Henry Wilson—a man who played all sides—of masterminding a blocked appointment of his aide-de-camp. Antagonisms could also go back to arcane feuds of officer cliques, resentments involving class, money, gambling, and women as much as doctrine, disputed promotions, orders obeyed or disregarded, insults feigned or real, and even something as seemingly minor as seating at mess.

Dealing with those buried feuds grew more urgent for certain high officers than events on the battlefield, especially when private quarrels long hidden threatened to become public. Perhaps they accounted, too, for French's failure to respond sooner to the German buildup. Did a pout take precedence over the enemy threat? It does not seem out of character.

Sir John, as we remember, had originally dispatched Sir Henry Rawlinson's IV Corps, then comprised of the 7th Division and the 3rd Cavalry Division, in the direction of Menin, on the Lys. That was on October 18. Though French pressured him to move swiftly, Rawlinson elected to proceed with caution. He was beginning to hear reports that German forces had already reached the Menin area; they were even now advancing in his direction. Rawlinson's rush to hesitation would prove wise. On the nineteenth, a Monday, two fresh German corps, four divisions, turned up to block the progress of his single division. He managed to pull back his advance guard but lost 150 men in the process.

Four battalions of the 20th Brigade of the 7th Division withdrew and dug in on Kruiseecke Hill, holding a line that formed a blunt salient of forward trenches. For the German artillery concentrated opposite, the sight of plainly visible trenches on a hillside was an invitation to turn them into a shooting gallery. But French demanded that the 20th hold on until relieved: he still intended to restart offensive action. Despite mounting losses, the brigade would not move from that ugly little bulge for a week. "It was impossible to leave the trenches by day," noted a regimental historian, "and rations and supplies had to be brought up by night; there was no telephonic communication and messages between the headquarters of the Battalion and the companies to the rear had to be sent by runners."

The 7th division was everywhere stretched dangerously thin, responsible for more line than any other unit in the BEF, eight miles of front at one point. That meant that the average dispersal of riflemen was one every seven yards, considered a dangerously wide spacing. There was as yet no second line or troops to hold it, no communication trenches protecting passage to the rear, and few dugouts. French ignored Rawlinson's requests for help or for making changes before they were forced on the British. One of the latter might have been as simple as agreeing to a withdrawal to a less-exposed position. He could not forgive Rawlinson for what he viewed as a priceless opportunity missed. Sir Henry Wilson, that steadfast switcher of allegiance, egged him on.

Major General Henry Rawlinson—"Rawly"—commanded the IV Corps, the first British unit to reach Ypres. Directed by Sir John French to locate and engage the German vanguard, Rawlinson hesitated. He suspected that he risked being enveloped by a vastly larger force, and he was right. French felt otherwise, that Rawlinson had disobeyed orders. He nearly fired a man who would become one of the most important British commanders. (Imperial War Museum/Robert Hunt Library/Mary Evans)

At a meeting of the corps commanders the next day, the twentieth, Rawlinson found Sir John "very cold to me and evidently still angry about Menin." The Little Field Marshal should have thanked him instead: Rawlinson's caution had saved his division from disaster. French could never bring himself to do so. He remarked in a diary entry that the IV Corps commander had "disappointed" him. For Sir John, grudges, like old soldiers, never died. Neither did they just fade away.

NO BRITISH DIVISION ENTERED BATTLE that fall with more severe handicaps than the 7th; no division was more pressured or held on more stubbornly; no division would be more in danger of disintegrating and yet survive; no division in Flanders suffered more casualties, 9,865 (the next claimant to that unfortunate distinction, the 3rd Division, numbered some 1,500 fewer); and no division saw its performance more disparaged or more disregarded by the commander of the BEF.

The division, which could boast battalions belonging to some of the most illustrious regiments in the British Army, such as the Grenadier Guards, the Scots Guards, or the Green Howards, had been hastily assembled at the end of August. It gathered in virtually the last remaining trained regulars in the empire. Good as its individual parts were, the division didn't yet mesh as a unified fighting force. That was a cause of much of the difficulty it experienced in its first days in the line. The 7th lacked the combat tempering of the first six divisions, and its rawness had already cost it dearly. Many of its men arrived in Flanders woefully out of shape. The army had rushed them from wide-flung colonial bases in Egypt, Malta, Gibraltar, and South Africa. They had spent long periods of inaction cooped up on crowded, sweltering troop ships. The GOC of the division, Maj. Gen. Thompson Capper, had attempted to restore vigor to his enervated formations by sending them on long marches through the New Forest of southern England, and to some extent he had succeeded.

The 7th Division was one part of Henry Rawlinson's IV Corps, the 3rd Cavalry Division being the other. It was never a complete two-division corps, which was another problem, given its overstretched situation. But as the trench lines solidified, horsemen were suddenly superfluous: during the whole of October, the cavalry division could never depend on more than 1,200 dismounted riflemen out of its entire 4,000 men for combat duty. That added up to little more than a battalion of infantry. And a quarter of those riflemen were required to serve behind the lines as "horse holders."

The 7th faced other problems. Its staff, so hastily assembled at the end of August, was inexperienced in the conduct of the new form of earthbound war, a siege almost five hundred miles long, one that had no precedent in history. Capable staffs were a key, not just to success but survival. In addition, there were mutterings of discontent that focused on the personality, opinions, and peculiarities of its commanding officer. One captain who served with Capper described him: "His steely blue eyes, beneath a thick crop of dark, wiry hair, stared at one with the look of a religious fanatic." Capper was a man who thought nothing of exposing himself to fire. "He wasn't brave; he simply did not know what fear meant." Once, the same officer remarked to Capper on his seeming recklessness and the chances he took. "Capper turned on me almost fiercely: 'I consider it to be the duty of an officer in this war to be killed,' he said." Some of his staff claimed that he was mad.

A story, perhaps apocryphal but accurate in its way, went the rounds. Capper is supposed to have come into the staff mess one time during the battle, announcing, "What! Nobody on the Staff wounded today; that won't do!" He ordered everyone in the room to go up to the front line. That attitude didn't always sit well with those he sent out to risk their lives in encouraging his troops. Haig found him "too full of nerves and too much of a crank to get the best out of his officers." As far as his staff was concerned, that evaluation was a gross understatement. And yet, behind those deep-set eyes, the high forehead, and the obligatory officer's mustache lurked a steadiness and determination, a penchant for inspiring, that held together a division too often on the verge of cracking. In spite of their terrible losses, his men gave him unswerving support. As one close associate said, "No one but Capper himself could, night after night, by sheer force of his personality have reconstituted from the shattered fragments of his battalions a fighting line that could last through tomorrow."

THE FRICTION BETWEEN CAPPER AND his staff reflected, but hardly exceeded, the tension in the topmost reaches of command. At this point, relations between Rawlinson and French were turning frostier by the day. In matters of headquarters politics, French revealed more genius for maneuver than he did on the battlefield, operating with a deftness that he ordinarily reserved for the bedrooms of London. The near-destruction of Rawlinson was one of his signal triumphs, and it came close to doing away with a potential rival, a general who would rise to lead an army. (The BEF was not yet large enough to split into armies.) Few people in the emerging world of command on the Western Front watched their own backs quite so assiduously as the forever-insecure Sir John. In the end, it would do him no good. But that is another story.

Almost a year later, at the Battle of Loos, Capper's luck ran out. He was, of course, in the thick of things. Legend still attended him. One story had him running forward with his men as he led an assault. Another had him riding a white horse between lines while brandishing a sword to encourage them. He was actually shot in the back by a sniper's bullet. The same battle and his mishandling of it cost French his job. In December 1915, London relieved him of command. Gen. Sir Douglas Haig replaced him.

The cause of the present discord between the general and the field marshal was simple. Rawlinson had originally reported to Kitchener, not to French. Messages between French and Rawlinson had to travel through the War Office, where Kitchener insisted on monitoring all telegraphic communications even if it added hours to their turnaround time. French once remarked to Rawlinson, "I do not understand whether you consider yourself under my orders or not." By the time French's GHQ and the IV Corps did establish a direct link, the damage had been done, leading to a clash of command that could not have taken place at a worse time.

Rawlinson's IV Corps was edging toward disaster. Time and again, the only way to patch the line was to "putty up." That was the expression that described the emergency shift of hastily appropriated units, not always infantry, to bolster threatened units and plug dangerous widening gaps. It was not unusual to find artillerymen, pioneers or dismounted cavalry, even the proverbial clerks and cooks caulking leaks. Haig, to his credit, was especially adept at impromptu rescue operations. He became the Allies' fireman of Ypres. On the afternoon of October 22, responding to a request by Rawlinson, he had sent up reinforcements from his I Corps to relieve the 22nd Brigade of the IV Corps, which was barely holding on. But for Capper's energetic leadership, and the troops that Haig had made available, the entire 7th Division might have buckled under the German weight; it didn't. As Rawlinson could write in his journal the next night, October 23, it is "just as well that the I Corps have come up here for the Germans have massed large forces in these parts and had I to meet them alone I should have been overwhelmed and had to give up Ypres."

French displayed little sympathy for a fellow officer's predicament. The British commander blamed the perils of the 7th Division on what he perceived as Rawlinson's faintheartedness. He seemed to pay little heed to the shattering losses the 7th had suffered. Between October 22 and 24, just three days, it had lost 120 officers and 2,700 other ranks, or 45 percent of its officers and 37 percent of its men. Rawlinson especially worried about the growing officer deficit, adding in a telegram to French sent on the twenty-fifth that "most of our troubles and losses have come from being on such a wide front. We have to take up these wide fronts in order to get our flanks far enough out to avoid envelopment by the Germans. We want more men, and always more men."

A new division, the 8th, was forming in England, and would become part of Rawlinson's IV Corps. But it was not scheduled to arrive in Flanders for another two weeks. That might be too late. "We are only hanging on by our eyelids," Rawlinson told Sir John on October 25. Rawlinson's telegram concluded with the comment that "when the 8th division arrives, it will be easier to hold a front of eight miles." Did Sir John sense a nagging tone in Rawlinson's words? Or find them freighted with an implied reproach? Given the unpredictable whirligig of moods that could seize him, those words, too blunt to be diplomatic, might have been more measured, if not wholly anodyne. Rawlinson would have been better off if he had sent no message at all, especially since d'Urbal's French IX Corps and Haig's 2nd Division were in the process of taking over a sizeable portion of the Salient: the front held by the 7th Division would shrink from eight miles to four.

Sir John exploded. When Rawlinson showed up at Saint-Omer on the night of the twenty-fifth, French refused to see him. He raged to his staff about Rawlinson's "cheeky" words and said that he was ready to fire him. Sir Archibald Murray, French's chief of staff, emerged from closed doors to give Rawlinson "a long talking to." At the same time, French's military secretary, Sir William Lambton, sent Rawlinson a note that advised him to apologize "and eat humble pie if you want to remain in command." Lambton's note ended with words that were less advice than an order: "Don't be a fool, and climb down." Rawlinson proceeded to deliver a letter of apology by hand. French now took a magnanimous tack—if, given past disagreements, he did stretch the truth. "We have always been great friends; let us remain so!"

But French's tantrum had not run its course. His Army Operations Order No. 40 of October 24 not only ordered a broad front attack—nothing came of this unbelievable plan—but also transferred Byng's 3rd Cavalry Division to Allenby's Cavalry Corps. Rawlinson was rapidly becoming a commander without a command. Once again Henry Wilson was in the thick of the intrigue. Wilson and Rawlinson were longtime friends, having tramped the battlefields of the Franco–Prussian War together as young officers. At his suggestion, Rawlinson would leave for England on the morning of the twenty-seventh, both to instruct the new 8th Division in what to expect from war as it was now being fought, and to get out of the way. Once the 8th Division arrived on the Continent, it would become part of a reconstituted IV Corps. That same day, French put the 7th Division under Haig's command; he wrote Haig, "He [Rawlinson] is not really wanted here." Still, he didn't fire him, and in not doing so, may have saved Rawlinson's military career.

EVEN AS RAWLINSON WAS REMOVING himself from harm's way, a relative lull in the hitherto nonstop action settled on the Flanders battlefield. The operative word here is "relative." By no means did death take a holiday. The two sides were merely catching their breath.

Tot up some of the other events of October 25 and 26. They would have considerable bearing on the outcome of the long battle. French units took over five miles that the British had formally held. From now on, Ypres would no longer be a mainly British battle. The twenty-fifth was the day, too, when attackers of the British 2nd Division made it up the Passchendaele Ridge, and almost reached the village of Passchendaele itself before the Germans turned them back. Had the British succeeded, the capture of this otherwise nondescript agricultural settlement might have deprived us of one of the signature names of the Great War. October 25 was the day when some burying parties of the 2nd Royal Scots Fusiliers came under fire from a house a few hundred yards from Gheluvelt and attacked it, with only shovels in hand. Swinging their improvised weapons, they captured twenty Germans, including an officer. Then they completed the mission they had set out to perform, burying a captain and other dead, whose bodies had been lying in the open for days. That was the afternoon when General Grossetti plunked his considerable bulk in a camp chair at the Pervyse crossroads, and directing newly arrived troops, brought the German advance across the Yser to a temporary halt. That stormy night saw Major von Oidtmann's nightmare trek through Dixmude and its murderous conclusion at dawn on the polders beyond.

And then there was Kruiseecke.

The same night of October 25–26, in the same downpour, British control of Kruiseecke at the tip of a salient a couple of miles south of Gheluvelt, a kind of pimple on the point of a nose, began to falter. A blindly lethal slugfest erupted. Men on both sides, as if intoxicated by a heady brew of high ideals and low rhetoric, contested a place that had no significance and only marginal tactical importance. The events at Kruiseecke were a symptom of what was emerging as a European civil war, one that disputed, and exalted, not ideology—that would come later in the century—but national power, identity, and prestige. Another symptom of the obsessively bitter enthusiasm that this European civil war ignited was the ceaseless rifle fire that characterized the first year of combat on the Western Front. One British officer in the Kruiseecke salient spoke of "sheets of lead going over our heads all night."* Only genuine anger motivated by true feeling could produce such concentrated and continuous shooting. Could there be a better contribution to the national mission of honor than an overheated rifle barrel? At last, the ordinary mortal could, to use a German word, participate in the rites of *Heldenzon*—the hero's zone—which had become, of course, the Western Front. (Too many, of course, shed *Heldenblut,* hero's blood, died a hero's death, *Heldentod,* and were hastily covered with dirt in a hero's grave, *Heldengrab.*) That sacred language was the nineteenth century speaking to the twentieth, and for the moment most still believed in what Hemingway deprecated as "The Big Words" and were inspired by them. How else to explain the desperate but willing convulsion that was Kruiseecke, as opposing nationalisms groped forward and collided in the pitch-black downpour swamping that single Flanders street?

OCTOBER 25: A DAYLONG TORRENT of shells replicated the torrents of nature. "Never have I been through such a day as it was," remembered an officer of the 2nd Scots Guards. "It was a veritable hell on earth." The Scots Guards belonged to the 20th Brigade of the 7th Division, an elite unit, and held the elbow of the Kruiseecke salient, which bent upward at that mingy cluster of cottages and barns. Here the Germans, obviously looking for a trophy village capture, concentrated their shellfire: attacks

---

* Just consider the amount of rifle ammunition expended each day by a single unit in late October 1914. The 2nd Battalion of the Green Howards, which held a few hundred yards along the northern base of the Kruiseecke salient, just above the Menin Road, was not even close to the center of the action. Their regimental history notes that "every night, under cover of darkness, ninety-six thousand rounds of ammunition were brought up; and on one occasion when, in the middle of the day, more ammunition was urgently required, the six ammunition carts came up, 'delivered the goods' and returned without casualty among men or horses."

were sure to follow. A Captain George Paynter reported that some of his company's trenches were "blown in," and two of his subalterns buried alive and "had to be dug out." According to the regimental history of the Grenadier Guards—their 1st Battalion was next to the Scots—shell bursts "buried half a dozen men at a time, all of whom had to be dug out with shovels. Some of them had as much as three feet of earth on top of them and many were suffocated before they could be rescued." Searchers pulled out the lucky ones, blue in the face, most of whom promptly returned to the line. The unnatural avalanches of sandy soil not only leveled trenches and entombed their occupants but also clogged gun barrels. There was as yet little or no wire available, and the digging of communication trenches to the rear or even the linking of neighboring excavations was too hazardous to attempt. Tempting gaps beckoned everywhere along the line.

The German attacks started at sunset and intensified under cover of darkness. Paynter—who would eventually command his battalion—picked up the story: "Then we noticed masses of troops advancing on our trenches. It was extremely dark and raining in torrents." The cold rain soaked the opponents to the skin; they fought on. Some of the Germans "got as far as our trenches and were shot down, others lay down in front calling out 'we surrender,' and 'don't shoot; we are Allies,' 'Where is Captain Paynter "G" Company?'" How had they learned his name? Were they trying to trick the Scots Guardsmen? The Germans did take advantage of the gaps. "Parties got through the line on my right and left and commenced firing on us from behind, others got into houses. We shot at and silenced all these. Fresh lots kept coming on. . . . After about a couple of hours all was quiet."

The German assault troops formed up behind farm buildings, dismounted cavalrymen mixed in with the infantry. In the last light, they watched the shells of their heavy artillery throw up fountains of sandy earth. Then, with the fall of night, the guns went silent. Trumpets and drums sounded and the attack commenced as successive lines picked their way ahead. British artillery tore holes in the advance but could not stop it. Closer to the village, the attackers were able to improvise, slipping through hedges and fences, making crouched runs along drainage ditches or behind blasted walls, guided by the glow of the burning village. They did their best to avoid British machine-gun fire. The Germans began to fight their way along the single street, clashing hand to hand. The British retreated, then pushed back through the village.

The official history of the 7th Division is frank about the confusion of the next hours. "The exact sequences of events on the night of October 25th / 26th is even more than usually difficult to ascertain." Advantages continued to seesaw. Early on, some four to five hundred Germans overwhelmed the northernmost trenches, held by the 2nd Scots Guards. A Lt. William Holbech led his men in an attempt to retake the trenches with the bayonet; only Holbech and a few of his men returned. It was a moment of peril: the loss of the trenches had opened a gap of a quarter of a mile, and the Scots Guards battalion was in danger of disintegrating. The Honorable H. Fraser, a major second in command of the battalion, hastened to Kruiseecke with three hundred men, all that remained of two companies. They filed silently through the single street, keeping close to the houses on either side. The only sound was the drumming of the rain. Fraser met Holbech, who whispered to him about the loss of the trenches. In the middle of the village, a cinder track led to one of the trenches that the Germans had captured; Fraser headed down it with forty men. On their way, they came on two cottages full of wounded British, who told him that the Germans were gone. They had left behind a single sentry, who had himself fled.

Fraser left with Holbech to investigate some freshly dug trenches nearby. Suddenly someone switched on a flashlight. A command in German broke the silence, as did a rifle volley. Fraser ordered his men to charge, and they dashed forward with fixed bayonets. None of them reached the trench. A bullet killed Fraser instantly; another wounded Holbech. Only a sergeant named Mitchell and four men returned to tell what had happened.

Now it was the turn of the British. A report came in to the new commander of the relief force, Maj. John Viscount Dalrymple, that Germans occupied a large house by the road, the same one the man he replaced, the late Major Fraser, had taken. Dalrymple ordered his men to surround the house. German soldiers appeared at the front door and began to fire at the Scots. Dalrymple's men killed the Germans in the front yard and called on whomever was inside to surrender. Men poured out of the building with their hands up. But other Germans, who were concealed behind bushes nearby, began to fire on the Scots Guardsmen. They killed Sergeant Mitchell, who was standing next to his commander. Dalrymple grabbed two German soldiers and, pushing them in front of him, made them shout to the men in the bushes not to shoot. They emerged from the bushes and surrendered. In all, the Guardsmen herded 187 men and 5 officers to brigade headquarters.

In spite of all the British heroics—which, unfortunately for the defenders, were matched by those of the Germans—the end of Kruiseecke was plainly at hand. The Scots Guards dispatched patrols to root out possible snipers. A lieutenant with yet another aristocratic name, the Hon. James St. Vincent Broke de Saumarez, led one group. In his search he came on what can only be described as a house of horrors—"an estaminet in the village which was full of wounded men. It was a terrible sight; every other man had expired. They had been there for days with nobody to look after them . . . Some of the wounded men were clean off their heads." One was Lieutenant Holbech—Saumarez spelled it "Holbeach"—who, after Major Fraser's disaster in the dark, had been dragged inside and left in what must have been originally an advance dressing station.

Soon the village would be exposed to dawn light, both stormy and dangerous. The Germans were about to lay down their inevitable barrage. Saumarez's Guardsmen didn't have much time. They had to perform a hasty triage, evacuating those who, like Holbech, seemed still to have a chance.

The coming of daylight made further searching of the village too chancy. In any event, "that difficulty," the Scots Guards regimental history commented dryly, "was solved by the German artillery, which destroyed every house in it, and must have buried any Germans left behind there." Some of the attackers from the previous day had remained huddled in water-filled outlying trenches, close to the British. They fed back to their artillery, via runners, target information and range corrections, which increased its rate of fire. Lord Dalrymple and his company sergeant major "counted over 120 shell bursts within 100 yards round them in two minutes." Saumarez had returned to the front line. A single shell buried his entire platoon. He and his sergeant dug furiously trying to free the men caught under that avalanche of sand. They got to most, but not all, of them in time.

Saumarez's adventures were not over. The young lieutenant left the uncertain cover of his trench and attempted to determine whether there were still Scots Guardsmen on his right. He heard the approach of a shell and ducked into a wrecked cottage to take shelter from the blast. It knocked him unconscious. "When I came to my senses," Saumarez later wrote, "there was a badly wounded man lying on me and above this wounded man lay a dead one. In this position I was unable to move as a great many bricks had fallen in the ditch all around us and we could only just breathe through the debris." He lay in that position the entire day. When darkness fell, he heard German voices. Then a Guardsman who had been lying in the ditch discovered the lieutenant and pulled him out. They crept into Kruiseecke, where they found more British soldiers, who told them that the village had fallen. Making their careful way in the dark, the men eventually reached their own lines.

A week of combat had taken its toll. By October 26, the line held by the 7th Division's 20th Brigade was perilously stretched; the widening gaps invited attacks. Before the morning was far advanced, the previous day's brash German probes began again, once more squeezing the apex of the Kruiseecke salient from the south and the east. The Germans outnumbered the defenders 15 battalions to 4. At 9 A.M. the siege train returned to action, and the bombardment soon grew in intensity. German troops, who had hidden in the woods all night, crept forward, taking advantage of the cover that hedges provided. At least one party made it through a gap between the Scots Guards and the South Staffordshire battalions, or what remained of them. This proved the opening wedge. The Germans then resorted to a ruse, and one that worked. A shout, "Retire!" went up, and some of the South Staffordshires, believing that the order was legitimate, pulled back. The commanding officer of the battalion was able to halt the retreat, but the damage had been done. Confusion ruled.

The South Staffordshires found themselves fired on by both the Germans and their own men. This was the moment of indecision the Germans, many of them dismounted cavalry dragoons, had waited for. According to one report that is unusually candid about the brutality of close combat, "the Englishmen began to leave their front trenches. When our troops saw this, they tumbled pell-mell from their insufficient dugouts . . . without further orders, determined to wreak revenge upon a foe who had inflicted such heavy losses on their forces." They went at it with a pent-up abandon. Covered by machine guns, they swept over the east-facing trenches held by the Scots Guardsmen and the Grenadiers and found their way into the ruins of the village. For the British, it was by this point a fight as unequal as it was hopeless. "As some of them displayed an inclination to use their weapons," the report continued, "it was necessary to demonstrate the uselessness of further resistance on their part with lead and rifle butts." The dragoons were invoking a timeless rule of war: *If you want to live, don't resist.* Swarming into the narrow trenches, they did take a hundred prisoners. Meanwhile, German infantry began to overpower the south face of the elbow, swallowing two companies of the Border Regiment in the process; only 70 men escaped—the equivalent of about 15 percent of a normal two-company complement.

The German sweep continued. Having broken through the south face, they penetrated the village in ever greater numbers. Now the two Guards battalions, the Scots and the Grenadiers, were their main opposition. Early in the afternoon the Germans began to fire on the front trenches held by the Guardsmen. The defenders might have escaped by an opening that still remained, but their orders said to hold out to the end; they held. "At last," said the Scots Guards regimental history, "the Germans were on them on all sides in overwhelming numbers, and surrender could not be avoided. Bushes and houses in the rear screened the assailants until they were actually in the trenches." The commander of the surrounded Guardsmen, Major Viscount Dalrymple, suddenly noticed Germans and British mixed up, and brawling, in the next trench. Escape was no longer an option. He ordered the last five men who were with him to smash their rifles; then they surrendered. When Dalrymple's father died in December, making his son the 12th Earl of Stair, he was a prisoner of war in Germany.

By the best estimates, Kruiseecke fell at 2:30 that Monday afternoon. Capper, at 3:20 P.M., did try to inform Maj. Gen. Julian Byng, the commander of the 3rd Cavalry Division, that a calamity was in the making: "part of 20th Inf[antry] Bde is retiring but we do not know how much." Men of the 7th Division began to stream back in disorder, telling all who would listen of their rout at Kruiseecke.

In his diary entry for October 26, Haig described hearing that the 7th Division "is giving way." The commander of I Corps sent a staff officer to ascertain what was happening. "He reports several battalions in great disorder passing back through our first brigade." Haig "rode out about 3 P.M. to see what was going on, and was astounded at the terror stricken men coming back. Still there were some units in the division that stuck to their trenches. I arranged for the necessary number of units from the 1st Division to support the latter . . ."*

Rawlinson, about to leave for England, reported "some confusion and much shelling" when he visited the 7th Division for a last time at dusk. At this point he was largely irrelevant, and he knew it. He noted with approval that Capper seemed to be everywhere, and would spend the entire night shoring up the line. The 7th Division had temporarily disintegrated but would recover. Haig was already taking charge. He was at his puttying-up best. He sent elements of I Corps to take over parts of Capper's line. He helped to pull shattered units together. There was no chance now for a withdrawal turning into a rout.

What we might call smoke and mirrors slowed the progress of the Germans, as did the coming of darkness. After its debacle in the morning, the Border Regiment assembled from its headquarters the usual collection of noncombatants: clerks, cooks, drivers, and scouts. Joined by fugitives from the frontline trenches and by strays from other regiments, this

* Haig refused to let go of his obsession with the dire consequences of badly sited trenches. "It was sad to see fine troops like the 7th Division reduced to inefficiency through ignorance of their leaders in having placed them in trenches on the *forward* slopes where Enemy could see and so effectively shell them."

scratch group helped to establish a new line and turn around the rout of the 20th Brigade. Resistance by isolated groups of Scots and Grenadier Guards, who fought on until forced to surrender, also slowed the German advance, as did the machine guns of the neighboring 21st Brigade, which became a killing cornerstone of the restored British line.

The Germans themselves contributed to delays. Overwhelming as their numbers were, their lack of training and discipline became evident. Third–line troops like the 11th Landwehr Brigade behaved like third–line troops. Artillery shells may have been plentiful, but resupply of food and emergency rations was chaotic, if nonexistent. Famished soldiers stopped to scavenge rations from the dead; they even attempted to "still our hunger" with unripe apples discovered in empty farmhouses or potatoes dug up from fields. What would become a Western Front paradigm manifested itself. After the capture of their trophy village, the Germans advanced several hundred yards, and then, as it grew dark, paused to dig trenches.

For both sides in that small episode of the continental civil war enacted on the frail heights of Kruiseecke, the losses seemed vastly out of proportion to the worth of the prize. As they were led off to captivity, captured Scots Guards experienced at least one gratifying moment: the sight of the broken ground in front of their trenches "paved with German dead." The German losses may have been severe, but they (and the French) could still depend on reserves without limit—for the moment. But for the little army of the British, the casualties were shattering. During just the 25th and 26th of October, the Border Regiment lost 250 men and 9 officers. It was worse for the South Staffordshires, who lost 13 officers and 440 other ranks. Out of a battalion that normally would have numbered just under 1,000 men and 30 officers, only 460 men and 12 officers of the 2nd Scots Guards reported for roll call that evening. The casualties in the 20th Brigade (some 4,000 at full strength) for the two days of Kruiseecke exceeded 1,000. The toll mounts. "The losses of the 7th Division in its nine days continuous fighting," notes the *Official History,* "amounted by the evening of the 26th October to 43.6% of the officers and 37.2 of the men." For three brigades, the total for the holding of the Kruiseecke salient was 162 officers, and 4,320 other ranks—a loss equivalent to the size of an entire brigade—all this blood shed over a single rural village. The loss among officers grew more appalling by the day. Officers and riflemen alike were irreplaceable.

Despite Sir John French's nightly drumbeat of optimism, with its inevitable dismissal of German offensive potential, the decision makers in London became increasingly uneasy. The loss of Kruiseecke and Neuve Chapelle on successive days was cause enough for concern. That was not all. Before thick cloud cover made aerial reconnaissance impossible, reports had come in of sizeable train movements and of long columns of troops marching west to reinforce the Fourth Army. What if the Allies experienced a war-changing reverse at Ypres? What if the Germans poured through a sudden gap and a forced re-embarkation was necessary? Consequences had to be anticipated. Kitchener that day dispatched officers to reconnoiter defensive positions around Calais and Boulogne.

KRUISEECKE IS NOT A NAME that we readily associate with the First Ypres. It was soon forgotten, a place and event that did little to embellish the BEF legend. The French, meanwhile, were just beginning to show up in the Salient; their role would expand soon enough. Though the British have managed to appropriate the lion's share of credit, as it were, for the outcome of the First Ypres, the part the French played cannot, and should not, be underestimated. By the time the battle ended, they had more divisions engaged and controlled a greater length of the Flanders front— including, in point of fact, the entire Salient. Foch and Joffre called more shots than Sir John French. As inexact as casualty figures were for those weeks, the French losses were probably greater than the British. Ypres in the fall and winter of 1914 was as much a French as a British battle.

Even as the British were making their last stand at Kruiseecke, the 17th and 18th Divisions of the French IX Corps, both blooded at the marshes of Saint Gond, were taking their place in freshly dug Salient trenches, lines of men wearing red kepis, dark blue-gray double-breasted greatcoats, the skirts buttoned back to make movement easier, and baggy red trousers, notorious targets that the wearers often discarded in favor of brown or black corduroys. They carried heavy and uncomfortable

1893-model knapsacks, wooden frames covered with canvas or dark leather. Inside, they kept everything from clean linen (long and short underpants, an extra pair of socks—new ones were issued once a month—flannel shirts, suspenders, puttees, reserve laces, and, for the middle-aged men of the territorial units, nightcaps. To this assemblage add cleaning and maintenance equipment (shoe brushes, polish, tins of grease for their Lebel rifles, a sewing kit, a pair of round-tipped scissors), toiletry articles (bandages, towel, mirror, soap, razor and strop, toothbrush, comb) as well as personal items (tobacco and rolling papers, first-aid kits, matches, tinderbox, flashlight, nickel silver and aluminum bracelet with identification disk, individual service record booklet, and a *Prayer Book for Soldiers*). An entrenching tool hung from the left of the pack, a second pair of shoes was strapped on the right, and on top were strapped blankets, tent canvas and poles, and a mess kit. The weight of the pack was anywhere from sixty-four to seventy-seven pounds in dry weather, more when it rained. "I don't think that the warriors of the middle ages, clad in iron, were more weighted down than we were," one *poilu* wrote.

For many, a German bullet or shell blast would soon ease that uncomfortable burden.

From his headquarters in the Belgian border town of Rousbrugge, Gen. Victor d'Urbal issued an order on the evening of October 23 to the head of the IX Corps, Pierre Dubois: "At the stage we have arrived at now, the smallest upset of equilibrium at one point can tip the balance in our favor for good." The omens, d'Urbal said, were promising. "The troops you face . . . appear mostly to belong to recently raised corps without great value." He suggested that Dubois take advantage of this deficiency in combat experience and push immediately for Roulers.

Joffre's deputy in the north approved. "There must be decision and activity," he said, Foch to the core.

Hardly had the French reinforcements taken position than d'Urbal's order arrived. Hély-d'Oissel, whose composure may have saved the British a few days earlier, was now commanding the French 7th Cavalry Division opposite Poelcappelle. A large village at the flattening base of the Passchendaele Ridge, it would prove for years to come a proverbial bone in the offensive throat of the Allies. October 24 was no exception. Hély-d'Oissel's dismounted cavalrymen pushed forward perhaps a half mile before riflemen and machine gunners concealed in fortified farmhouses or behind hedgerows stopped them. But a couple of miles to the south, at Zonnebeke, Dubois's 17th Division did clear the town, with the aid of a field piece that flushed Germans holed up in the central police station.

The twenty-fifth was that rarity for late October in Flanders, an interval that was warm and clear. As always, the gains were small, the casualties high. Attackers fixed bayonets that would never be used, enjoyed a final cigarette as they prepared to clamber up crude ladders into the open, whistles blew, and, even as they emerged from their trenches, bullets riddled them, making drill-like holes in suddenly smoking cloth. Shell bursts scattered and obliterated obedient advancing clusters of red-pantalooned men. Shards of steel tore faces away, and you could no longer recognize a man who had been your neighbor for ten years. The impact of bullets lifted others from their feet; they turned somersaults and were dead before they touched the ground. The wounded crawled back to what they thought of as safety, leaving a trail of blood behind them.

At the end of the twenty-fifth, the British still clung to Kruiseecke, barely. North of them, the French IX Corps made methodical, determined, if slow, progress: a mile here, a few hundred yards there, nothing elsewhere. Roulers remained over the ridge and untouched. The sky began to cloud up, and by nightfall a hard rain was falling.

ARTILLERY AND, INCREASINGLY, MACHINE GUNS remained the chief German strengths; the grenade was yet to become the infantryman's weapon of choice. There, too, the Germans had the lead. It seemed no problem for a military that was long trained in siege craft to convert that offensive skill to the defensive. The British and French, meanwhile, were just beginning to improvise; they only began to do so as trench warfare took hold. Ypres was the ideal laboratory.

As for the bayonet, most men who had actually seen combat agreed that the weapon was wildly overrated, except by drill instructors and journalists. In the Great War, British armament experts calculated, out of one sample of 200,000 wounds, bayonets caused only 0.32 percent. (A later American Surgeon General's report gave an even lower figure: 0.24 percent.) One British corps commander was quoted as saying, "No man in this war has ever been killed with the bayonet unless he had his hands up first." Most bayonet wounds, to be sure, were immediately fatal, and did not make it to the casualty returns.

Bayonets mainly won their plaudits from people who didn't have to use them. If the arme blanche, as a bladed thrusting weapon was known, did not live up to its reputation as a killing instrument, another, the once-disparaged machine gun, was beginning to earn lethal notoriety on the Western Front. Those most frequently used were variations of the gun invented by a semiliterate mechanical genius named Hiram Maxim, who rose from humble beginnings in the rural backwoods of Maine to wealth, prominence, British citizenship, and a knighthood. Hiram Maxim's automatic gun was pure devilish inspiration: the harnessing of the energy, hitherto wasted, that the recoil of a gun released. You just squeezed the trigger, and the recoil action created by the explosion of the first round provided the energy that ignited the next round and the next. In July 1883, Maxim registered a British patent for what he called a "Machine" gun "in which the feeding, firing, extracting and ejecting devices are operated by the force developed by the recoil of the breech block." Someone else probably wrote the words, but no matter.

By the beginning of the twentieth century, Maxim's guns, or adaptations of them, were turning up throughout the world. The Japanese made deadly use of them in their war against the Russians. Vickers, which had bought out Maxim, now produced the British version; it became the standard automatic weapon for the army. The German adaptation was called the Maschinengewehr 08, or MG08, after the year, 1908, when it was adopted. In 1914, the German Army used MG08s exclusively.*

Most versions of the Maxim—and the MG08 was no different—were fed by a fabric belt holding 250 cartridges: with a quick exchange of belts,

---

* The French preferred their own Hotchkiss Model 1914, with its barrel wrapped in its distinctive doughnut-shaped steel rings that provided radiating surface for air cooling. Its rate of fire and range were roughly equal to the water-cooled British and German guns.

a gun could fire 500 to 600 rounds a minute. Gunners, though, found that short, well-aimed bursts were more effective killers. The most distinctive feature of Maxim's invention was a cylindrical jacket filled with about a gallon of water that cooled its central barrel—though in cases of emergency, gun-crew urine served the purpose.

That the opposing armies hesitated to rely on the machine gun until the fall was far advanced should not come as a surprise. It was not suited to the war of movement that the opening battle plans called for. "The machine guns in use," one Western Front veteran wrote of those early days, "were clumsy, too large to be manhandled for more than short distances, and were water-cooled with delicate mechanisms that too often jammed under the rough conditions of the battlefield, and when water failed they soon seized up. . . . Rapid fire by trained riflemen was more reliable." Machine guns, said one senior German commander, "serve only to clutter up the marching columns." Another German officer was even more dismissive. "The heavy machine gun with its protective shield will be the death of the offensive."

As the days passed, and Falkenhayn's offensive grew more intense, trench lines were connected, deepened, and became increasingly sophisticated in construction, like these near La Bassée, their sides shored up with woven branches. These French troops had taken over from the overextended British: the Salient itself eventually became entirely French-held. (Imperial War Museum)

When we regard the Great War today, we find it hard to escape the feeling that the Germans owned the machine gun. That was not necessarily true in 1914. Of the Western Front contenders, Germany had in fact been the last fully to endorse the machine gun. Boer War pressure had forced Great Britain to act first: in 1898, it adopted the gun, allotting two guns to every thousand men, or a battalion. The French did not attain that ratio until 1909; the Germans only matched it, with reluctance, in 1913. If, just a year later, the Germans ended with more machine guns in Flanders, it was mainly because they had more divisions there.*

Only now, halfway into the autumn of 1914, as the lines became increasingly immobile, did machine guns begin to be accepted as the murder engines they were. It little mattered whether or not machine guns were difficult to manhandle into position: once in place, they no longer had to be moved again. With a secure view of the prospect before them, they were ready to start killing. They were only less efficient than artillery—the casualty ratio of artillery and mortars to that of machine guns and rifles being roughly 5 to 4. The Germans hastened to establish a genuine advantage in machine guns. In the early months of the war, the German gun works at Spandau produced 200 per month, a figure that would, by 1915, reach the thousands. For the moment, though, machine guns were ideal for defending the close rural environment of the Salient, clearing it for the offensive that would sweep the enemy from the field once and for all.

THE FRENCH NOW HELD THREE miles of the Salient itself, the British five. On the night of October 25, Foch floated a coded proposal to Joffre for an extensive push out of the Salient, marking the French takeover of its top half. Foch's plan was, to say the least, ambitious. Divisions would advance

---

* British military writers had an unfortunate tendency to confuse the size of German regiments with that of battalions. So, it was not uncommon to find them asserting that in 1914 the Germans had six machine guns per 1,000 men—a "regiment." That would have meant that an actual regiment, normally 3,000 men, had eighteen machine guns, an impossibility. But then, the Germans thought that the concentrated fire of the BEF could only come from machine guns and not rifles.

to the north and envelop the Houthulst Forest. The IX Corps would re-establish its hold on the Passchendaele Ridge and threaten Roulers. If the French could accomplish this, they might divert the German forces attempting to breach the Yser line. The French would maintain close contact with Haig's I Corps, which would swing south toward the Lys. Foch did not seem daunted by the fact that the BEF had already failed once in this enterprise a week earlier, with near disastrous results. Nor did he pay much heed to the imminent fall of Kruiseecke, which, curiously, had little apparent effect on the gathering French attack. Foch was more concerned by the telephone call that came from Colonel Brécard, the liaison man at Belgian headquarters, reporting that the Belgians were preparing to retreat along the entire Yser front. As we know, that didn't happen, but it didn't stop Foch from erecting another of the offensive dream castles in which Sir John French too readily sought refuge. At Ypres, the Allies persisted until a dangerously late hour in clinging to the illusion that offensives here remained possible. This one, Foch assured Joffre, could have "the greatest consequences."

The next afternoon Joffre telephoned his approval.

Foch's scheme did not so much involve new attacks as a redirection of efforts already ongoing. Poelcappelle and not the ridge village of Passchendaele became the main objective, if only because it was closer to the Yser and the beleaguered Belgians. Grossetti, Foch's old favorite, now would command French troops defending the Yser line, including Ronarc'h's marine brigade. But unless the inundation of the polders along the river could be made to work in the next days, no marvel of defense that Grossetti, Ronarc'h, or the fading Belgian Army could perform in that northern sector of the Flanders front would matter. The Germans were already hammering on the door that opened on the dune route to Dunkirk and Calais, one that armies had favored for centuries.

In a special order to General Dubois dispatched at 18 hours—6 P.M.—on October 25, d'Urbal spoke of enlarging and deepening the narrow hole already punched in the German line between Poelcappelle and Zonnebeke: it was narrower than it was deep. A little before midnight, he sent another message to the commander of the IX Corps: "Poelcappelle must be carried before noon," he said, and added that they had to win the ground at any price, "*and win it quickly.*" By way of emphasis, he underlined the words. The village of Poelcappelle had little importance except for offering a lesson on how an obsession can develop. The Allies would spend the better part of four years trying to retake it. Few places in the Ypres area were more fought over or less deserving of the blood shed there.

D'Urbal, too, was consumed by Fochian offensive flights of fancy. They had developed into what amounted to a communicable military disease. But even before Foch received Joffre's go-ahead, his drive out of the Salient sputtered. From the beginning it was clear that it would fall short of its stated aims. For one thing, the switch of emphasis from Passchendaele to Poelcappelle meant switching the direction of artillery fire, delaying the attack and giving the Germans an added opportunity to deepen their trench defenses and make them more complex. They were beginning to string barbed wire. For another, the uncertainties of autumn weather were forever conspiring against firm intentions. That morning a thick fog, no doubt the dividend of the previous day's mildness, cut down visibility and rendered counter battery fire inaccurate, if not impossible. The attack was scheduled just after dawn on the twenty-sixth, and a newly arrived French division, the 31st, was supposed to join the battle that day. The French, four battalions strong (a putative 4,000 men, but by this time many fewer), didn't leave their trenches until three in the afternoon. The attack unfolded slowly, as men dodged from hedge to hedge, garden to garden, house to fortified house, swept by, and withering under, intense fire. In their red pantaloons, the French might as well have been wearing targets. In this domestic setting, death was at all times their neighbor. Still, the IX Corps moved the line forward as much as three thousand feet. For all the distractions and delays of those long hours, its performance was not without distinction.

From his headquarters in Ypres, Dubois ordered the attack on Poelcappelle to continue. It was now six o'clock and night was settling in. Almost immediately, the French ran into a barrier of barbed wire, just strung up. It was, as yet, an unfamiliar obstacle; the attack stalled. Hély d'Oissel's dismounted 7th Cavalry Division, the main force driving on Poelcappelle, paused to wait for the 31st Division to join it in the line. The

31st never arrived. There had been delays in transporting battalions forward, delays in assembling reserves, delays that had no logical explanation. Unfamiliar terrain hindered progress; units lost their way in the dark. The three regiments of the 31st bivouacked without ever coming under fire.

Now fatigue entered into the offensive equation. Even the IX Corps commander had to admit that troops who had been fighting day and night for four consecutive days had begun to wear down. Fatigue certainly explained why, at one point during the afternoon of the twenty-sixth, units of the 18th Division had strayed in front of the British on their right. By the time the French had recognized their mistake and pulled back, their advance had lost whatever momentum the attack had started with. It was the same all along the line. The French tried to put the best face possible on the situation: they maintained that, between the opposing sides, a state of equilibrium now prevailed. They were as tired as they were probably right.

15

One Day

IT WAS NO DOUBT A RELIEF TO ALL THAT TUESDAY, OCTOBER 27 WAS A DAY IN which the actions and reactions of the combatants were, for the first time in a week, free of desperation. For the moment, no backs were against the wall—except, perhaps, those of the Belgians, who were barely clinging to their last line of defense, the railway embankment between Dixmude and Nieuport. For once killing was not the main objective of those hours.

The undetected advance of the Fourth Army across Belgium had been a potentially masterful move. But that thrust to the sea, so initially promising, had run up against surprisingly stout resistance by patched-together Allied forces. Early gaps had opened, which more experienced, better-trained troops might have exploited. What if the Fourth Army had, as planned, kept right on going? Though the Germans had a decided edge in manpower and available artillery, the inferior quality of the green troops of Falkenhayn's reserve divisions had nullified that advantage, as well as the even greater one of surprise. In war, surprise generally makes the difference. Falkenhayn later argued that he'd had no choice but to gamble on using untried troops. By the time the Race to the Sea had reached Flanders, he wrote in his anorexic memoirs, "there was no longer time to change the young troops for tried formations."

Now he proposed to do just that, to make a swap for inexperience. If, with a bracing of veteran troops, the German Army could still throw back the enemy in Flanders and reach the sea, "it could expect to force a favorable change in the whole situation" on the Western Front. "The prize to be won was worth the stake."

ON THE MORNING OF OCTOBER 27, Erich von Falkenhayn boarded a special train at Charleville-Mézières and took the lateral railway line, only just reopened, across northern France to Douai, the coal-mining and industrial center where Crown Prince Rupprecht had recently established the headquarters of his Sixth Army. It was a journey of just over a hundred miles and three hours. Falkenhayn arrived around noon. Rupprecht and his chief of staff, Generalmajor Konrad Krafft von Dellmensingen, met his train, and escorted him to their headquarters in town.

Falkenhayn wasted no time spelling out the reason for his journey— "dictating" might be a more apt word. After just a week, the supreme commander felt the time had come to make a major adjustment in his stagnating Flanders offensive.

TWO BATTALIONS OF THE BRITISH 2nd Division, the 2nd South Staffordshires and the 1/King's Royal Rifle Corps (KRRC), operating to the right of the French, briefly came as close as anyone to breaking into the open. Had more units of Haig's I Corps been involved, they might have done so, then making the wheel south that Foch had called for. The fight here on the twenty-seventh started as a scramble up the ridge beyond the village of Broodseinde. It was a small preview of 1917. True, the landscape was still recognizable as such, and there was less mud, though mud was a Flanders constant three out of four seasons. There had already been much rain that October, and uniforms tended to become coated with grayish-white clay, transforming combatants on both sides into apparitions in motion (who had an unfortunate penchant for turning abruptly inert).

The KRRC did have a minor celebrity in its midst, a denizen of the London social pages, a twenty-three-year-old subaltern who was, by virtue of birth, a semi-public figure, the foremost popular fixture involved in the Ypres struggle. He was Prince Maurice of Battenberg, the fortieth, and youngest, of the late Queen Victoria's grandchildren. His mother, Princess Beatrice, had been Victoria's closest confidante, almost an assis-

Prince Maurice of Battenberg, the youngest grandson of the late Queen Victoria, served as a subaltern in the swanky King's Royal Rifle Corps (KRRC). On October 27, as he was leading his platoon across an open field, a burst of shrapnel killed him; he was the most celebrated British casualty of the war thus far. (Maidun Collection/Alamy Stock Photo)

tant queen. His father, Henry of Battenberg, was a German prince, who had little to do but hunt, fish, ride, serve as honorary colonel of a fashionable regiment, and fend off accusations that he had introduced hemophilia into the royal line; a malady of European royalty, it was already there, in the young person of the Tsarevich Alexis, for one. Maurice had spent the first nine years of his life, until Victoria's death, in whatever palace or castle where she happened to be: he was baptized in one of the most important, Balmoral Castle in Scotland, on October 31, 1891. The little prince, whose soldier father died from malaria in Africa when he was four, thought nothing of roaming grand halls and bedrooms, and bursting into his grandmother's private chambers at any time of the day, unadmonished. He grew up keen on polo and aviation, was a marksman, and a reputed fine fellow. He joined the army and found his way into the KRRC, a regiment laden with prestige and tradition and a safe haven for the highborn.

Maurice was a haughty-looking young man, with a standard officer's mustache, still somewhat wispy, a cleft chin that matched the tight part down the middle of his lank, dark hair, and eyes that stared out with empty vigor. We can be reasonably certain that he was not afflicted with hemophilia, though uncontrolled bleeding, its chief symptom, did kill his brother Leopold after a hip operation. (Had army doctors detected the condition in Maurice, they would have discreetly turned him down or shuffled him off to non-combat duties, as the KRRC did with his brother.) He became a model soldier. No doubt, as was then the habit of officers in elite regiments, he wore, even in battle, uniforms tailored on Savile Row, with the KRRC's distinctive black buttons, conspicuous for their bugle-and-crown motif, and blackened Maltese cross cap badge. In the first weeks of the war, when military publicists paraded acts of audacity, however slight, before the multitudes, Maurice had crossed an Aisne River Bridge under fire and (said a dispatch) "daringly searched a house on the other side alone."

On October 27, Lieutenant Prince Maurice was leading his platoon over the Broodseinde ridge, near a village the French had captured the day before, Zonnebeke. He had spent the previous night in a scratch of trench on the hillside, drenched by the unforgiving remains of the coastal storm. His uniform was damp, if not soaked. The two British battalions had tired of waiting for the French to move on their left. Their opportunity for a significant advance, perhaps as far as Passchendaele, was diminishing by the minute. It was already midafternoon.

Maurice led his men across an open field and a little stream, the Heulebeek, but here (says the official historian of the 2nd Division) "a terrific shell and rifle fire played havoc with the riflemen." The two battalions suffered 273 casualties, many in those first minutes. One was Maurice, hit in the head by a burst of shrapnel pellets. His platoon sergeant—a man named O'Leary—draped the prince's bespoke form across his shoulders and, under fire, tried to carry him to the safety of a forward aid post. Long before the two arrived, the prince had expired. For the British public, there was a crude symbolism in that scene of the commoner supporting the dying royal. Despite rumors, hemophilia had played no part; headgear had. Cloth-billed caps, such as the one Maurice wore, offered the head no protection. That would be true until the opposing armies introduced steel helmets in 1915 and 1916.

The two battalions continued over the ridge, down what passed for a slope, and moved into a shallow U-shaped valley of open cultivated land. They had almost reached a string of houses and barns, Keiberg, the hamlet that gave its name to the spur they were attempting to ascend. They manhandled an 18-pounder into the front line. German fire grew in intensity, forcing them to dig in where they lay. They had gained more than a thousand yards that day—an achievement, given the new and unfamiliar conditions of trench warfare. At 3 P.M., a message arrived from the GOC of the 2nd Division: "The hour is late. A thorough reconnaissance will be needed tomorrow prior to an attack." That was as far as the British would go. Several days later German attacks pushed them back. It was late September 1918 before Allied troops again set foot on this same ground.

By that date, the name Battenberg had been changed to one that George V, the present king, found less offensively Germanic. A literal translation of Battenberg was "Battenhill," a fair description of the uplands in Hesse where the family had originated. That wasn't grand enough. The family elected to raise the nomenclatural elevation to Mountbatten. The name stuck.

Maurice was not buried on the spot, as usually happened. During the night of October 27–28, an ambulance picked up his body and transported it back to Ypres. Great Britain could not risk having the Germans overrun the grave of one of its princes. Maurice was the most prominent British casualty in the war so far, and in fact the only member of the royal family to be killed in the war. A fellow officer described Maurice's burial service on the edge of the municipal cemetery. "The guns were making such a noise," he said, "that you could not hear the chaplain's voice." With each passing hour, the war seemed to move closer to the town. On the twenty-ninth in London, the *Daily Sketch* printed a page of photographs showing scenes from Maurice's life as a royal. Above them, a headline read, "THE JOLLY PRINCE WHO DIED FOR HIS COUNTRY."

Innocence was still having its age.

———

"IN THE MORNING, I SET out on horseback for Zonnebeke, accompanied by a mounted guide." So began the entry for October 27, 1914, in the diary of Sous-Lieutenant Pierre Petit. He had been dispatched to meet up with a patrol in the village, captured two days earlier by the French 17th Division, but not yet thoroughly pacified: German stragglers hidden in basements were still taking potshots at passing French columns. Petit, who belonged to the headquarters staff of the 34th Brigade, had been ordered to root out those strays and, should he take prisoners, bring them back for questioning.

Petit was twenty-three years old, the same age as Maurice, who was about to buy the farm, as it were, on a ridge a mile or so south of Zonnebeke. He came from a nondescript corner of southwestern France and would, in later life, become a banker. He was of middle height, with a dark mustache and the beginnings of a beard, in looks a bit like a young and upright Toulouse-Lautrec. This day he carried a camera. He also kept a journal.

Petit already had a story to tell about Zonnebeke, not the sort that normally finds its way into military histories, at least not official ones. Three evenings earlier, on October 24, about the time the French were ready to proclaim total occupation of the village, a shade prematurely perhaps, Petit had escorted the commander of his brigade, a Colonel Simon, to view the conclusion of the action. The party advanced on horseback up the main road that led through Zonnebeke to Passchendaele. Without warning the routine inspection spun out of control. What Petit described as "a mad desire to dash off on the attack" seized the colonel. He drew his saber and broke into a gallop. But the road was paved, wet and slippery from recent rain; the colonel had to slow down. The quick-thinking Petit had just enough time to catch up and direct the party to the shelter of a wall. Had they gone a few feet more, the horsemen would have found themselves in the no-man's-land that was the high street of Zonnebeke, irresistible moving targets.

A regimental command post was nearby; the officers dismounted only to find that they had arrived just as the Germans were mounting a counterattack, a final convulsion before they abandoned the village. Bullets were slamming into house fronts; Petit and his party must have caught glimpses of gray uniforms swarming across the single street. This was the moment, as darkness fell, when nameless demons overtook the colonel on horseback. Simon completely lost his head: the highest-ranking officer in the area was suffering a breakdown under fire. Even the most unsophisticated spectator could sense that something was wrong. Simon grabbed the arm of the regimental officer in command, also a colonel, and cried out, his meaningless words rising above the din: "You're

A young French sous-lieutenant, Pierre Petit, carried a camera when he investigated the just-captured village of Zonnebeke on October 27. A companion snapped a picture of him by a shell hole at the gates of the local château (above). Later, Petit and his men routed a group of Germans from a cellar and marched them (left) back to headquarters. (From Pierre Petit, *Souvenirs de Guerre*, Académie Européenne du Livre, Nanterre, France, 1989)

not leaving me to eat with those brutes. Tell your men to howl!" *Like the animals they are,* he seemed about to add—and then, out of the maelstrom of madness, shouted, "Howling like shipmates caught in a whirlpool."

Minutes later, the French had beaten off the counterattack; Simon calmed down. Night came, and with it, a lull. The French had finally taken Zonnebeke, more or less. The regimental commander assigned Petit to escort a by-now–subdued Colonel Simon down the ridge to division headquarters, the first stop on the road to Limoges. The man said nothing that the sous-lieutenant saw fit to record. He had already said more than enough.

Now it was the twenty-seventh, and Petit was entering Zonnebeke once more, again on horseback. He found the promised patrol, and their investigation began. Stray cattle wandered everywhere; otherwise the single cobblestone street was deserted. Where were the Germans hiding? Petit took photographs of the abandoned village, and then asked one of his men to snap a photo of himself, posing in front of a shell hole at the gates to the château. His collar is up and his hands are in his pockets: it was almost November, and turning cold.

The château, in the midst of a wooded park, dominated the village. The patrol entered, rifles at the ready. They checked the grand rooms on the ground floor. There were no Germans waiting to pour fire on any unfortunates who happened to probe the wrong corridor. But they did find, curled up on a normally forbidden sofa in the salon, "a poor little greyhound bitch." When an occasional shell would detonate on the grounds, or when volleys of machine-gun fire would pour through glassless window frames, she would tremble, terrified. Mirrors were cracked, bottles unstoppered, furniture turned upside down. The owners had obviously left in a hurry. They had even forgotten to take the pedigreed hunting dog with them.

Petit and his party returned to the village, leaving the dog behind. He had more serious matters on his mind. Toward noon, the sous-lieutenant boasted, "I routed thirteen Germans out of a basement." His diary gives no further details. How did the patrol come on them? Were there warning shots fired? Did the Germans resist? You suspect not. They were Landwehr troops, the dregs of the Fourth Army to begin with, and by now hungry, tired, isolated, and demoralized. Petit photographed them and sent them down under guard to division headquarters for interrogation. Later, the commander of the 17th Division, a general named Pierre Guignabaudet, clasped Petit's hand and thanked him.

The Walloon owner of the château, a man named Emmanuel Iweins, Petit learned later, had escaped to France and spent the duration in Normandy. There is, of course, no record of what became of the greyhound.

OCTOBER 27 WAS GRAY AND sunless, but the ceiling was not low enough to keep observation aircraft from the skies. Later in the day, that low ceiling would have consequences.

From the moment on August 6, 1914, when the German Z-6 Zeppelin dropped bombs on Liège, the sky had become an undeniable precinct of war. Just six years had passed since the Wright brothers had shown up in Paris to make their first demonstration flights, ones that caught the fancy of a continent. Would-be aviators rushed to emulate them. The following summer, on July 25, 1909, Louis Blériot crossed the Channel in just thirty and a half minutes.

Military men began to regard aircraft as possible war-changers, and soon the major European powers were experimenting with fledgling air arms. Military aviation made an astounding technological leap in those last years of peace. By the end of 1911, Italy was testing powered flight in actual combat, in an otherwise forgotten and forgettable colonial altercation in Libya called the Italo-Turkish War. Italian aviators performed the first tactical reconnaissance of enemy territory from the air, as well as artillery observation, the dropping of primitive aerial bombs, the directing of naval gunfire, aerial photography, and wireless air-to-ground and ground-to-air communications. Guglielmo Marconi, the foremost radio specialist of his time, arrived to give advice. The Italians instituted the tradition of the dawn patrol. They also suffered the first loss of a plane shot down by ground fire—in this case, massed rifles. The only element missing was aerial combat, presumably because Italy's Ottoman adversaries lacked aircraft of their own. A then-obscure officer named Giulio Douhet, later famed as a prophet of air power, proclaimed: "A new weapon

"Taube" was a generic name for a German monoplane with a variety of wing shapes, produced by several manufacturers. An unarmed observation aircraft, it had a top speed of 60 mph and a ceiling of only 4,000 feet. Though Taubes performed useful service in the first months of the war, they quickly became obsolete. (ART Collection/Alamy)

has come forth, the sky has become a new battlefield." Other nations looked on, and, as it were, took notes.

The Great Eruption came. Rumpler Taubes, monoplanes, buzzed Paris, arriving at the end of each day, always at the same hour, to drop a few bombs, by hand. People took to calling them "the six-o'clock Taubes." Life went on. By mid-October, aviators could see the opposing trench lines unfolding from horizon to horizon, a landscape split apart by fresh, continuous scars of upturned earth, already widening in places. And yet, on either side of that gulf, increasingly unbridgeable, were just-harvested fields and villages, as one observer wrote, "looking quite normal, as if no such thing as war existed." For these men in their flimsy machines, flight could make up for, and nullify, the violence and chaos below, the sights and smells of human waste and wastage.

Aviators could feel as though they were standing still in relation to the earth: as you climbed or dove, you had no sensation of speed, except for the stinging Arctic-like rush of air past your face. You flew in an open cockpit, and had, as one veteran pilot later noted, "no heater, no oxygen, no parachute, no radio link with other planes or with the ground, and no compass worth the name. These deficiencies were in keeping with the construction, wooden frames braced together by wires and covered with highly inflammable draped fabric." In some 1914 planes the wooden frames were not even covered with fabric, the wings only, with elongated cockpits mounted in front. These craft looked like flying box kites. A mixed bag of aircraft went to war. Each machine performed its tasks alone, and uniformity of design or performance was not important. As yet, there was no need for formation flying by craft of equal ability. Jasta, Escadrille, Squadron: these were words of the near future.

By the standards of the time, these 1914 aircraft were fast, and getting faster. The official world record, set in 1913, was 127 miles per hour. The top operating speed of the lumbering creatures that inhabited the Western Front skies that fall was from 60 to a little over 100 miles per hour: the former figure was more common. A Taube needed fifteen minutes to reach 2,500 feet, and an entire hour to gain an altitude of 6,500 feet. Allied pilots dreaded returning from a mission to encounter the prevailing westerly wind if it was blowing particularly hard. "The wind," said the 1914 volume of the *Official History of the Royal Air Force*, "was the heaviest trial for pilots . . . it made it easy to get at the enemy and difficult to get away from him." A strong headwind might cause those early craft to stand still, and there were instances in which they were actually blown backward.

In those first months of the Western Front, both sides emphasized reconnaissance. "Aerial observers," John H. Morrow Jr. wrote, "could detect with the naked eye individual men at 1,200–1,500 meters and troop columns at 2,500–3,000 meters altitude. Such observation sufficed in the war of movement . . ." That early emphasis on spying from above, as if airplanes were simply an extension of the cavalry, was largely responsible for aircraft that were slow, deliberate, hefty, and a bit stolid, like the commanders they serviced. Two-seaters, they were designed for pilots of average ability, stable craft that could practically fly by themselves while the men at the controls, or their observers, jotted down what they saw on the ground and drew rough maps. Aerial cameras and wireless transmitters did not come into general use until the following year, technological advances that turned these machines into flying laboratories of observation.*

But already the airplane was beginning to forge a revolution in the way war was waged. It was yet another harbinger of the industrial battlefield. The closing of the line made air reconnaissance increasingly necessary for the day-to-day conduct of the war. Machines in the sky became a constant presence in a soldier's life. That fall a French artilleryman pointed out to a British war correspondent a Taube hovering overhead. "There," he said, "is that wretched bird which haunts us."

At Ypres, the greatest gift to German offensive hopes was the weather. Autumn, as it advances, is rarely kind to Flanders. Low clouds, fog, hard rain, and finally snow, a general inclemency, persisted through much of the season, keeping reconnaissance craft grounded at key moments. But the Allies did observe enough to convince their intelligence services that a mammoth attack was coming, though the commanders at the top treated the reports their airmen brought in with skepticism. Foch, who was capable at this stage of the war of making as many inane as wise utterances, had once been heard commenting, "Aviation is fine as sport. I even wish officers would practice the sport, as it accustoms them to risk. But as an instrument of war, it is worthless." *C'est zéro* was his phrase. Was the true strength of the German Fourth Army really that menacing? Almost too late men like Foch and French discovered that it was. Though the generals on both sides insisted on emphasizing reconnaissance aircraft, they displayed over and again a reluctance to accept aerial evidence that went against their operational preconceptions.

* As *The War in the Air,* the official British history of the Royal Air Force, notes, "The deadly and effective method of directing artillery fire on hostile batteries by means of wireless telegraphy played a great part in winning the war, but for the First Battle of Ypres the wireless machines were not ready in quantity." In vain did division and corps commanders call for them. The Allies were experiencing a severe ammunition shortage, and means of ranging artillery that expended as few shells as possible had to be found. One method that did work imperfectly was to drop Very lights from a plane flying at a prearranged height over an enemy battery, while an observer on the ground took its angle of elevation and another with a range finder figured the distance to the target.

Almost no one, except science-fiction writers and a few prescient aviation authorities, thought the airplane would develop into the offensive weapon it did become. Technology ended by outstripping the imagination. That fall offensive actions in the air were mainly freelance affairs. Pilots, or their observers, would drop grenades, improvised gasoline bombs, live artillery shells, or weighted darts—fléchettes—preferably on troops marching in long lines in the open, as British aviators did to advancing German columns during the BEF's long retreat.

Combat "kills" remained rare. Though accidents, with their predictable fatalities, were the inescapable price of the aerial experiment, they were less the result of enemy action than of aircraft inadequacies, inaccurate navigation over unfamiliar territory, or misinterpretation of reconnaissance reports that were not always trustworthy to begin with. The sight of planes spiraling earthward in flames, their occupants choosing to leap to their deaths rather than being burned alive ten thousand feet above the earth, belonged to the near future.

It was not that pilots didn't try to eliminate their opponents. Clever maneuvering could lead to happy outcomes. By mid-September the British had downed five German observation planes by harassing them from above and forcing them to land behind Allied lines.

Airmen did begin to carry guns aloft, but rarely got to use them. A young British officer, Archibald Wavell, bored with life in the Intelligence Corps, yearned for more active soldiering. The future field marshal persuaded a pilot friend to take him along on a reconnaissance mission over the Ypres front. He told Wavell to bring his revolver in case they encountered a Boche. They did. Wavell's friend shouted to him to be ready with his gun, and went in pursuit of the German. What happened next was a little epitome of war in the air that fall:

> The observer's seat . . . was wretchedly cold and my fingers were frozen out of all feeling; I was very doubtful whether I could shoot off my revolver when I wanted to; I also had a suspicion that the Boche would probably be armed with a more effective weapon. So I was relieved when it became obvious that we should not catch him.

Not until October 5, 1914, did one aircraft actually shoot down another. A French Voisin III pusher, with engine and propeller in the back of the fuselage and armed with a machine gun in the front cockpit, fired by the observer, brought down a German Aviatik in flames west of Rheims. Both occupants died. (*L'Illustration*)

Frozen fingers or no, airmen still sought that elusive "kill."

Not until October 5 did one aircraft, a French Voisin III pusher, actually shoot down another, west of Rheims, the observer killing the German pilot with a burst of fire from the Hotchkiss machine gun he had mounted in the front cockpit as an experiment. It worked.*

Men may have been ready for combat in the sky; the aircraft of 1914 were not. Weather, as expected, rendered a fatal encounter of this sort all but impossible at Ypres. The role of the airplane in the battle was insignificant. As *The War in the Air* put it, those who flew above the troops on the ground "could only watch them and help them with eyes." Infantry and artillery continued to dominate. But as is often the case with military

---

* In a pusher aircraft, the engine and propeller were in the back of the fuselage, behind the pilot's head.

history, one lasting feature of British wars did emerge for reasons that were unexpected.

The infantry tended to regard anything that flew with suspicion and not a little envy, frequently firing on aircraft with little distinction between friends and enemies. The original British insignia added to its confusion. In mid-August, when the British had dispatched sixty-three planes, practically the entire Royal Flying Corps, across the Channel, commanders had ordered the painting of Union Jacks on the undersides of wings. This was done to discourage friendly-fire losses, the result of mistaken identities. But looking up from the ground, even just a thousand feet, and especially on a foggy day, an infantryman could make out only the red cross part of the Union Jack. It looked like the German Maltese cross marking.

This is precisely what happened two days running, October 26 and 27, both days of low clouds and rain. In the first episode, an observer reported, "The machine came down in flames and was completely demolished. Pilot and passenger had both been wounded by our own infantry fire when at a height of about a thousand feet with the large Union Jack visible." There was a similar unfortunate repetition not a mile distant the next day. Maj. "Ma" Jeffreys of the Grenadier Guards recorded it in his journal. A British aircraft was flying low and dropping Very lights at a prearranged height over German lines as a ranging signal for artillery. The "British aeroplane" was "mistaken for German and heavily fired on by Black Watch, who brought it down in flames, all the men cheering as it came down. A dreadful sight, as we . . . were watching and realized it was British."

The War in the Air mentions only the first incident. Were the two the same? It is hard to believe that they were. Jeffreys's diary, trustworthy to a fault, has too much immediacy to borrow from a previous day—or to rely on hearsay about the loss of aircraft and aviators, still an event of moment. Moreover, he had witnessed the downing himself. Whatever the day, there were consequences. The higher authorities of the RFC could no longer tolerate such misidentifications: lives and valuable machines were at stake. The unfortunate occurrence of the twenty-seventh seems to have made the difference. The RFC adopted the French circular marking—with a change. To preserve national distinctions, the corps alternated blue for red on the outer ring, then the same white, but red for blue on the inner roundel. The two air forces have not changed the insignia of their aircraft since.

THE MEETING THAT FALKENHAYN HAD convened in Douai was curious in one obvious respect: most of the principals who should have been there were absent. Neither the commander of the Fourth Army, Duke Albrecht of Württemberg, nor his chief of staff, Maj. Gen. Emil Ilse, were present, nor were the generals who would be leading the revised version of the Flanders offensive that Falkenhayn was about to propose. That puzzling omission is an indication of the haste with which Falkenhayn had conceived both the operation and the decision to announce it.

Crown Prince Rupprecht of Bavaria, who led the German Sixth Army in French Flanders, was the most solid and well-trained of the German royal commanders. Popular with his men, he tried not to be profligate with lives. His superior, Falkenhayn, was, and Rupprecht objected to his impulsive ways, but often had to go along with them. (Mccool/Alamy)

Even before the meeting began, Rupprecht was in a testy mood. OHL—obviously prodded by Falkenhayn—had ordered the rearrangement of divisions just as they were about to take a key destination, Neuve Chapelle. It gave no explanation. Rupprecht, never an unreasonable man, was ready to go to Mézières and appeal to the kaiser. "Either I will command the army or I will resign," he wrote in his journal. "It cannot keep on in this way. Falkenhayn lets himself be swayed by every silly rumor, making hasty arrangements, which in hindsight are disastrous, weaken the morale of the troops, and undermine faith in those who lead them." He wished for Falkenhayn's replacement, and underlined that wish in his journal entry. There was, and never would be, much love lost between the two.

Falkenhayn wasted no time spelling out the reason for his visit. The supreme commander announced that the time had come to make a major adjustment in his Flanders campaign, reinforcing and redirecting it. He may have been interfering in the way Rupprecht complained about, but given the costly stalemate of the first week, Falkenhayn's new scheme made a certain sense. It called for the installation of an army group between the Fourth and Sixth Armies. That group would concentrate along the largely inactive southern face of the Ypres Salient, a long sector that ran for about nine miles, from Saint-Yves, just above Ploegsteert Wood, to Gheluvelt, on the Menin Road. The new force would break through a neglected part of the British line and slash in a northwestward direction, taking Ypres from the rear and branching out in determined bids to reach the sea. Falkenhayn proposed that the army group be led by one of Rupprecht's best corps commanders, Max von Fabeck, who, Rupprecht noted, "on account of his tough nature, is known as an energetic and capable leader. Good!"

Falkenhayn went on to inform his listeners that he was already moving veteran divisions northward by rail and by motor transport. Why had the latter not been done earlier? He would stock Army Group Fabeck (as the new formation would be designated, after its commander) with the XV Corps (the 30th and 39th Infantry Divisions), which had been stationed on the Aisne front. That corps would join the II Bavarian Corps (3rd and 4th Bavarian Divisions) from the Péronne sector on the Somme. The 26th Division, already belonging to Fabeck's XIII Corps, would jump off from the north bank of the Lys and was poised to drive for the village of Messines and the key ridge that was named after it. These five divisions had all, in that sinister Western Front word, been "blooded." A sixth, the 6th Bavarian Reserve Division, now awaited its chance to share the experience of combat. Part of the Fourth Army, and just arrived from Germany, it was at that moment marching north from Lille toward the Belgian border.

German numbers in both men and artillery seemed sufficient to swamp the Allies. The margin was fast rising. Eleven and a half divisions, including cavalry, dismounted infantry for the time being, defended the Allied line from the Lys to the Yser Canal at Bixschoote. On October 27, seventeen and a half German divisions opposed them: two days later that number would swell to twenty-three and a half. The Germans were about to hold an advantage over the French and British defenders of the Ypres Salient of 2 to 1. Though we can only estimate combat-diminished divisional strengths, Fabeck's new Army Group probably amounted to a bit under 100,000 men, more than enough to turn the tide. One colonel prepared to attack with two battalions, each holding a frontage of only 350 meters, or approximately 1,100 feet. That was roughly one man for every foot of front. Falkenhayn also provided Fabeck with substantial quantities of artillery: 262 heavy howitzers and mortars, as well as 484 smaller guns.

"After lengthy negotiations," Rupprecht wrote, "the command of Fabeck's group was transferred to me." But Falkenhayn could not resist a barb, saying, "He cannot understand why forward progress is so slow with us." Rupprecht countered that the supreme commander failed to understand that his men had encountered a strong enemy fighting from fixed positions.

The renewed general offensive, mainly by the right wing of the Sixth Army, to which Army Group Fabeck was now attached and acted as an extension of, would begin on October 30. The Fourth Army would join in with attacks that would spread along the rest of the Salient. There was a good chance that units of the Fourth would soon penetrate beyond the railway embankment that ran along the Yser. Would the way to Dunkirk suddenly open? Oddly, no one spoke of the possibility of inundation, perhaps because they doubted that the Belgians could pull off an exploit of such magnitude.

Falkenhayn all but demanded a breakthrough on that first day.

The meeting wound down. There was some desultory small talk that Rupprecht recorded. He found particularly strange Falkenhayn's regret that relatively few of his generals had fallen in battle. Generals, he claimed, should make examples of themselves in attacks. Sounding like a German Tommy Capper, he remarked that if a few fell, it would create a good impression on the troops. These were the words of a man who had cut his military teeth killing masses of Chinese fanatics (read: patriots) in the Boxer Rebellion. Rupprecht replied that such sacrifice was counterproductive. Generals exposing themselves at the very front of an attack would be unable to control a battle.

The sarcasm, the belittling, the impatience of the supreme commander went unrecorded. Late in the afternoon he boarded his special train and steamed back across northern France.

YPRES ITSELF NOW BECAME A target. Early in the afternoon of October 27, six heavy shells, apparently fired from guns concealed in the Houthulst Forest six miles away, struck near the Church of Saint-Jean in the southern part of town, just behind the Vauban walls. The explosions killed several people. Were the Germans aiming for the headquarters of the French IX Corps, a few blocks from where the shells hit? "Nobody thought much about it," remembered Gen. Pierre Dubois, the corps commander.

ON THE THREE FRENCH MILES of the Salient, the encounter at Poelcappelle continued all that day without letup. The French 31st Division, newly arrived in the line, now led the main assault. Hély d'Oissel's 7th Cavalry Division covered its left flank. Both belonged to the IX Corps. D'Urbal called for "vigorous and incessant action, pushed home everywhere." He announced that the first company to enter Poelcappelle and the first to enter, and hold, Passchendaele would receive special citations of honor. The French attacked; the Germans counterattacked. The struggle here took on the nature of an encounter battle, a *bataille de rencontre*, with repeated unplanned-for collisions that tended to cancel one another out. The French won at most a few hundred yards of hedge, dirt road, shell-torn peasant cottages, and small fields, at a cost of over 2,000 casualties. Dubois, the decent and candid man who headed the IX Corps, tried to

A sergeant-at-arms in the French cavalry named Destouches, better known in later life as the novelist Louis-Ferdinand Céline, posed in uniform for a formal portrait, complete with breastplate armor and prow-shaped cuirassier helmet. His war, short and brutal, ended on October 27, when he suffered painful wounds, life-altering ones, after delivering a message under fire. He had endured that "vast furnace," in which "the least depleted will emerge the victor." For him, that was already too much. (adoc-photos/Getty Images)

put the best face possible on those meager results. "We did achieve partial progress," he wrote, "but without attaining our assigned goals." He called his losses "rather painful."

One of Hély d'Oissel's troopers was a twenty-year-old sergeant-at-arms who served in the 12th Cuirassiers, a former jewelry salesman named Louis-Ferdinand Destouches. Destouches, who would later become better known under his pseudonym, Louis-Ferdinand Céline, would survive to write one of the truly memorable novels of the twentieth century, *Journey to the End of the Night* (*Voyage au Bout de la Nuit*). There is every indication that his own journey to that destination of personal darkness began on the afternoon of October 27, 1914.

Céline endured less than three months of combat, though he was under fire practically nonstop from mid-August to the end of October. At that point he may have been done with war; but war was never done with him. In almost every one of his novels, war—*this* war—is a presence. Death would take hold of his imagination, a spent bullet setting off a creative sequence, nurtured by pain and isolation, that culminated in a masterwork of our time.

In Céline's novelistic version of the fall of 1914, time and place become garbled and unrecognizable. You cannot regard *Journey* as autobiography in any but the loosest sense. You must separate the real Destouches from the novelist's protagonist, Ferdinand Bardamu, in this detached and deliberately indifferent tourist guide to a death trip hurtling down "a long tunnel full of mists and terror" (as one Paris critic described the progress of the non-pilgrim). Céline captures the rapid and ever-changing transition from hallucination to horror, the wildness of history that was the illogical essence of those first months of war. You cannot fault *Journey* for exaggeration: the casual brutality of officers, the carrying out of senseless orders, the constant soul-destroying fatigue, the careless lottery of mortality could as well be the stuff of countless Great War memoirs. But it's the relentlessly demotic drumbeat of the absurd that makes his novel different. In avoiding conventional realism, Céline still manages to get at an undeniable essence of the war—or, perhaps, of war itself. "Soon we'd be at the heart of the storm, and the very thing we were trying not to see, our death, would be so close to our noses that we couldn't see anything else." Bardamu and his hapless companions had reached an outermost darkness, the end of their night.

Had Céline been aware of Grossetti and his folding camp chair, ostentatiously braving shellfire? You wouldn't be surprised if he was: the story, still fresh, must have spread along the French and Belgian line. There is an episode in *Journey* that comes close to it, though with an ending more sour and grisly, but Céline to the core. In this case we find Bardamu, the author's mouthpiece, standing with his colonel at the end of a raised Flanders highway. Bardamu holds out the open orderly book while the officer writes out a stream of man-killing commands. "Down the road, way in the distance, as far as we could see, there were two black dots, plunk in the middle like us, but they were two Germans and they'd been busy shooting for the last fifteen or twenty minutes." The colonel roams around the open road, paying no heed to the bullets whizzing by. "Now I knew it for sure," Bardamu muses, "he was worse than a dog, he couldn't conceive of his own death."

Couriers arrive, all pale with fear as they bob into the open, all delivering messages for the colonel from his commander, a General des Entrayes—as in *entrailles*, entrails. In this pre-Patton era, the novelist's creation might also be translated as "Old Blood and Guts." The general was, apparently, modeled after d'Urbal. Message after message demanded that his willing accomplice, the colonel, shovel ever more lives into the furnace.

As a dismounted cavalryman delivers yet another exhortation from the general, a shell explodes, knocking Bardamu to the surface of the road. Once he is able to get back to his feet and the smoke has cleared, he finds the colonel dead, his stomach split open and spilling guts, and the messenger decapitated.

"I had had enough, I was glad to have such a good pretext for making myself scarce." Make himself scarce from that "vast furnace," in which "the least depleted will emerge the victor." That may be as good a summation as any of the new kind of warfare that seemed about to dominate: attrition, the static combats of wearing down.

In a Céline novel, heroism doesn't exist, only vainglory, and the good get going.

This could well have happened. It didn't, at least not to Louis-Ferdinand Destouches. His real experiences had little in common with the events portrayed in his novel. They were, if anything, more dramatic.

What had begun as a life of bourgeois aspirations would be shattered and unrecognizably rearranged by war. Destouches was born in 1894, in a suburb just west of Paris. His father was an insurance clerk; his mother made, and sold, lace. Later he would take his pseudonym from his grandmother's first name: Céline. When she died, she left rent-paying property and a shop in a Paris arcade, which his mother took over. Her ambition for her son was for him to become a department-store buyer. But for that, he would need other languages: his parents sent him first to Germany for a year and a half, and then to England. Young Destouches ended up an apprentice salesman for a fancy jewelry store.

It was a time when every young Frenchman in his late teens was expected to do military service: the term had just been upped from two years to a controversial three. Destouches decided to get his service out of the way and then return to the jewelry business. He was eighteen when he enlisted, joining an elite cavalry regiment, the 12th Cuirassiers, so named because of their breastplate armor. They also wore silver-plated leather helmets with prow-shaped domes and metallic visors. (In the field, they slipped brown or beige covers over the helmets to prevent flashes of the sun that might give away their presence.) Destouches mastered his fear of horses and became an accomplished rider. By 1914 he had risen in rank to sergeant-at-arms; he affected the wispy beginning of a mustache. He participated in strikebreaking, running down protesters. On Bastille Day, 1914, he was one of several thousand horsemen who galloped in procession before President Raymond Poincaré. Destouches was always something of a political conservative: his bourgeois roots showed.

So, when the unexpected expected war came, there was no springing from a café seat to join an enlistment parade—as Bardamu impulsively does. Destouches was mounted and ready. Even a twenty-four-hour train ride into Lorraine did little to dim the enthusiasm of his regiment. "Morale is pretty much like that of a troop on maneuvers," he wrote his parents—and then admitted, "It is true that we have not yet been under fire . . . I haven't taken my boots off for 9 days and it will probably be this way until the end of the campaign."

By the third week of August, the 12th Cuirassiers found themselves not only under fire but swept up in the retreat from Morhange. The fighting during the next month was more or less continuous. On September 12, the Cuirassiers joined the bloody but successful effort to keep the Germans from crossing the Meuse at Fort Troyon, nineteen miles south of Verdun. Again, to his parents, this single long and barely punctuated sentence: "I never have seen nor ever will see such horror, we stroll up and down the length of the spectacle almost unaware of the danger from habit and especially from the crushing exhaustion we have experienced for the past month a sort of veil falls over your consciousness barely three hours a night and walking rather like an automaton moved by the instinctive will to win or to die Nothing new on the battlefield almost in the same line of fire for 3 days the dead are continually replaced by the living to the point where they form little hillocks that are burned and at a certain point you can cross the Meuse without getting your feet wet over the bodies of Germans . . ."

On October 4, the regiment (or what was left of it) detrained at Armentières. Four days later, Destouches found himself in a file of dismounted cavalrymen leading their horses along a path in Ploegsteert Wood, just north of the Franco–Belgian border. As they searched for the enemy, they blundered into a German infantry post hidden in the trees. A bullet in the head brought down the bugler next to Destouches. Another hit a lieutenant in the thigh; blood gushed from under his breastplate. "We got back on our nags. We lit out every man for himself. . . . We had lost our map and compass. . . . We guessed our direction, we felt our way, by the wind of the bullets, so to speak." Though trench lines were rapidly taking shape, cavalry could still range over the landscape for a few days more. German horsemen swept through Ypres. North of Béthune on October 10, French and German cavalry collided in a cemetery and fought, hand to hand with sabers. Destouches was one of them.

We now come to October 27. The 12th Cuirassiers found themselves at that forever unredeemable village, Poelcappelle, mostly unhorsed, as it were, reluctant infantry. At a time when communication by field telephone was uncertain, and at *le feu* nonexistent, runners carrying messages or (in the case of the Cuirassiers) mounted couriers were indispensable. Late in the afternoon of October 27, Destouches volunteered to carry a dispatch from his regiment to a colonel at brigade headquarters: the shellfire that afternoon was so unrelenting that other couriers were reluctant to take the risk of a dash on horseback across open fields. Destouches galloped to the rear, reached his destination, delivered the message, and headed back. It was about six in the evening; darkness was already settling. He was passing through a small wood when a ricocheting bullet smashed into his right arm. Somehow he made it to a *poste de secours*. Destouches's father, who saw his son in a hospital bed a little over a week later, wrote, "the bullet that hit him by ricochet was twisted and flattened by its first impact; it presented barbs and irregular edges that occasioned a rather large wound; the bone of the right arm was fractured."

At first, though, the medics who examined Sergeant-at-Arms Destouches didn't think the wound was particularly consequential. The next day an officer wrote the young NCO's father a letter that was somewhat offhanded: "Your son was wounded . . . That's the nature of war, where, less than ever before, one can never assume what the next hour will bring. It seems that his wound is not serious, but he has been evacuated, I know not where . . . I wanted to alert you immediately in describing the exemplary conduct that he has never ceased to display." He could hardly have been talking about the Bardamu character, who wondered whether he was "the last coward on earth." Destouches himself was mentioned in dispatches and won the military medal; the magazine *L'Illustré National* portrayed the speeding sergeant (complete with Germans firing in the background) on its front cover.

It is a measure of the fierceness of the struggle for Poelcappelle that so many wounded and dying crammed the tents around the forward aid post that the first ambulances, all of them horse-drawn, were too full to accommodate Destouches. After that first, cursory examination, medics would have dressed his wound, administered a tetanus shot, attached a tag describing the nature of his injury and what kind of treatment he had received, given him food and a drink of wine, and dispatched him to a casualty clearing station farther behind the front. Medical officers decided that he was fit enough to make it on his own. Destouches had to walk more than four miles before he found another group of ambulances that could take him.

The wound was more serious than the first medics had assumed. This time the medical officer examining him wanted to amputate his right arm. Destouches refused. He was sent back to have the bullet removed. His journey, again probably in a jolting horse-drawn ambulance—motorized ones did not come into general use until 1915—ended at a hospital in Hazebrouck in French Flanders, twenty-five miles and a day's journey from where he had been wounded. A local doctor performed the operation and extracted the bullet. Destouches declined an anesthetic. He was apparently afraid that the doctor would remove the afflicted limb while he was unconscious. What pain he must have endured in the process, pain that surpassed understanding?

Destouches always claimed that he had suffered a second, invisible injury that afternoon. On his gallop back from delivering the message, a shell exploding nearby knocked him from his saddle. He remounted his horse, bleeding from his left ear—and then the ricocheting bullet hit. Examinations could uncover no evidence of a head injury. Céline/Destouches, in later years a doctor himself, had a plausible explanation. When he fell from his horse, he had fractured a bone in the back of his head. The bone had healed, but in the process had pinched a nerve. "He could always tell when the pain was coming," Céline's widow told his scrupulous French biographer Frédéric Vitoux. "At such times he wanted to be alone. Alone with the unbearable pain. He drove people away. . . . That would tend to remove him from the world."

How much did the experience of that single afternoon, and the continuing agony he suffered, affect his outlook, hurling him into what he called "a black voracious void"? His later life bore the marks, too, of post-traumatic stress disorder (PTSD), even of possible permanent trauma to the brain. Do we dare to suggest "shell shock," actual physical damage to the brain, which recent medical researchers have begun to reinvoke? The prospect of his own death increasingly occupied his imagination. Was it the trauma and anguish of October 27 that unlocked his genius, even as it caused his life to take other turns, not all of them pleasant? Was it that day that, in the words of an early biographer, Patrick McCarthy, made him "one of the loneliest figures in twentieth century literature"?

Céline/Destouches did have a second operation on January 19, three months later, this time under anesthetic. If we are to believe his recently resurrected novel, *Guerre* (2022), his return to relative good health was a rough passage, one that left him unfit for further service. The arm remained painful and stiff. On December 2, 1915, Destouches received a provisional discharge—that is, without pension.

He became a wanderer, drifting from London and Central Africa to New York and Detroit. Tropical fever nearly did him in. An autodidact of boundless ability, this man who cultivated solitude studied his way through major exams and into medical school. The compulsive wayfaring stranger settled down to become a doctor in a lower-class section of Paris. He began to write, and discovered that he had a positive talent, not only for innovation but also for literary disruption. His first novel, *Journey to the End of the Night*, was published in 1932. A darker side of his personality emerged. He wrote and published antisemitic pamphlets. To be sure, dislike of Jews could practically be a genetic disposition of the French bourgeoisie. Céline/Destouches was brought up with it. How could the turn-of-the-century Dreyfus affair, which saw the railroading of a Jewish officer to Devil's Island on a treason charge, have been quite as divisive without an attitude so prevalent in the class that had nurtured the future novelist? During the Second World War Céline collaborated with the Nazis. He fled France and settled in Denmark until the French authorities allowed him to return. The worth of his books would remain clouded by his personal history.

At one point his hero Bardamu notes, "When you have no imagination, dying is small beer." When it came to imagination, the author was cursed with too much.

You have to believe that the fall from the horse did happen. You have to believe, too, in the invisible injury that caused the unbearable pain and the clamorous ringing in his ears that recurred for the rest of his life. "I've never stopped sleeping with that atrocious noise . . ." Céline wrote in *Guerre.* "I caught the war in my head. It's trapped in my head."

THE FRENCH TROOPS UP FRONT shared none of the confidence of their generals in *offensive à outrance,* offensive to the limit. One of those skeptics of the battering ram was Dr. Raoul Nel, the assistant medical officer for the 2nd Battalion of the 79th Territorial Infantry Regiment. He had already spent too much time dealing with the shredded residue of those attacks. Nel belonged to the 87th Territorial Division, made up of what in 1914 constituted middle age, reservists thirty-four to forty years old. Nel himself was in that age group, probably close to its outer limits.

Nel and his division, nominally a Breton outfit, would spend close to two years around a single Flanders village, Boesinghe, on the Yser Canal. He kept a diary, which has to be one of the most sharply observed and evocative documents of the Great War.

On the twenty-seventh, Nel's battalion received orders for a new attack. At dawn, the Territorials were to proceed to a jumping-off position in front of the trenches. To the doctor, as he looked across what was not yet known as no-man's-land, it all seemed hopeless from the start:

> Once again, men are dispatched into the zone of death. This is how the ground of attack in front of the trenches could be described, for without preparation, without explanation, or any means of individual protection, in full daylight, with only the armor of thin cloth, companies, officers in the lead, are thrown out in front. Already warned by those who have gone before, they have no more illusion that they will conquer, but with resignation and discipline, they accept the sacrifice that is commanded . . . Countless bullets rain down on the units that advance in the midst of this hail of steel which fills the air, whistling above, beside, whipping the earth, perforating chests, exploding skulls, breaking arms and legs; and when enough officers and men are put out of action, the rest retreat to escape a total massacre.

The result was predictable, and soon apparent. The attack gained a hundred meters at most, four hundred feet, and then the companies— "decimated, disoriented, demoralized"—returned to their starting point. Before the twenty-seventh was over, the 2nd Battalion of the 79th RIT (Territorial Infantry Regiment) had taken 91 casualties: 12 killed, 75 wounded, and 4 missing.

Nel described the death of an outstanding officer, a captain Alexis Spire of the 7th Company. As Spire was about to lead his men forward, a fellow captain shouted, "So where are you going? We can't raise our heads and even in the trench we have to be careful."

"It's an order," Spire answered. "I execute it."

Wrapped in a long, dark-blue cavalry coat with silver buttons, a shepherd's staff in his hand, he advanced "to his death. His body, left where he had perished, could only be brought back later, and with the greatest risk to those who retrieved it."

Another company, the 8th, had only one officer left, a Captain Maricourt. Nel encountered him at the regimental aid post at the so-called

Ferme du Général (General's Farm): he had a gash in his hip that didn't seem serious: "He is visibly happy to have gotten off so lightly." In a trench next to three haystacks, Nel stumbled on the remnants of Maricourt's company, all looking disoriented. "We're back from the attack," they told him, "and we no longer have anybody to command us." And in a nearby beet field, he encountered an adjutant named Rayer, of the 5th Company; a bullet had cut through both of his cheeks. The wounds gaped, and speaking must have been a torture. "Do you think I am sufficiently injured to be evacuated? Must I return to the front?" Nel reassured him that his fighting days were over for the moment, and pointed in the direction of the regimental aid post.

Nel and his team set up a post of stretcher bearers at a group of buildings called the Ferme des Peupliers (Poplar Farm). But to transport a wounded man from the front line to this place was a long and arduous process: "The number of stretcher bearers is limited and the numbers of wounded to transport is great." The medics went to work with a will. For the rest of the day, they plugged away, dressing wounds, "without the slightest pause."

That evening, the colonel commanding Nel's regiment ordered a group of doctors, male nurses, and stretcher bearers to go up to the front line and clear it of "the wounded who are clogging up the trenches." There was an undeniable hazard in the operation, especially since it was a rare night of clear skies and a bright moon; as communication trenches had not yet been dug, the medics had to approach the forward trenches in the open:

We go silently, impressed by the very silence that surrounds us. We pass close to the cadavers stretched out on the ground; the moon's rays light their wax-like faces, a little frozen foam pearls at the corner of their discolored lips. We come to the trenches of the engineer corps, then the trenches of the front line, to the post of Commandant Turin.* But we look in vain for the wounded to

---

* In the French Army a commandant commanded a battalion and was comparable in rank to a major.

be evacuated; they were all taken away during the day, we are told. With the greatest good fortune, we return without even a single shot being fired at us.

In his journal, during those waning hours of October 27, Nel scribbled a question that seemed no longer to have an answer:

"How long will this nightmare last?"

THE FAILURE OF THE SPANISH Lock operation had plunged Belgian headquarters into gloom. On the twenty-seventh, that mood touched bottom when three German shells, fired from guns five miles away, hit the Furnes railroad station at two in the afternoon, killing a number of people. By now there were so many German batteries embedded along the dunes that Admiral Hood's flotilla dared venture no closer than two and a half miles from shore, much reducing the accuracy and field of its fire. The German guns began to zero in on the British ships; one of the destroyers sighted a submarine. Hood's flotilla retreated to Dunkirk.

The Germans were clearly gathering strength for a renewed push across the mouth of the Yser; time was running short. Victor Jamotte, head of a newly created Inundation Directorate, resolved to have another go at the Spanish Lock, but would have to wait until the return of high tide after dark. French engineers spoke up: the quickest and most efficient way to inundate the polders between the Yser and the railway embankment would be to lift the eight North Vaart gates at the Goose Foot. Jamotte replied that the execution would be too risky. German patrols might already be lurking in the wedges of land between the locks.

Belgian pontoneers—the military engineers who supervised the waterways—tried one more experiment. They set a 250-kilogram explosive charge in the earthen levee separating the Furnes Canal from the North Vaart. The creek was a foot lower than the canal, and their hope was that the water released would end by swamping the polder to the east. The charge went up sometime after 5 P.M. and opened a sizeable breach.

Water poured out, but not sufficient to cause an overflow great enough to swamp the polder. Another attempt at deliberate flooding had failed.

Only one possibility besides the dubious North Vaart one seemed to remain. Jamotte ordered that a fresh attempt be made to open the Spanish Lock. Late in the afternoon of the twenty-seventh, a new team of pontoneers assembled; Thys drove off to pick up Cogge from his Furnes home. At headquarters, panic could barely be restrained. Some army officers talked of retreating behind the prepared defenses of Dunkirk. But this would be tantamount to surrendering Belgium to the kaiser, with all the negative constitutional ramifications that might involve for Albert. Would there, in fact, be a nation for him to return to? Germany had not made the elimination of Belgium a specific war aim, but victory inevitably has a way of tampering with, and erasing, boundaries. No wonder Albert clung so stubbornly to his tiny remaining corner of Belgium.

The crew that would make the second attempt at opening the Spanish Lock took a roundabout journey—bridges had been blown—and found their way to an isolated inn on the south bank of the Yser channel: from there it was a trek of a mile to the lock. The building was deserted. The owners must have fled the establishment just minutes before. They had left potatoes still boiling on the stove. The men passed the pot around. Then they tried to catch some rest before they set out. The tide would not be in again until the hours of early morning.

The little party left the inn just before 1 A.M., a corporal and a soldier carrying ropes, machetes, pickaxes, shovels, and other tools. The sky was clear, the moon full. When they had almost reached their destination, they met a gunnery captain, with a crew dragging a 75mm cannon. Fearing a repetition of the previous night's misadventure, Jamotte had ordered the gunners to blast away at the floodgate. A lieutenant of the engineers accompanied them: he carried a demolitions charge in case the .75 failed to do the job. It was a panic-driven prescription for a fatal setback. Once the gates were destroyed, no one could stop the tidal flow. The inrushing waters might swamp more than just the targeted area along the Yser, too much more. Thys convinced them to leave.

It was about 2 A.M. when his crew reached the lock. The soldiers immediately set about digging rifle pits on either side of the opening to the Yser channel. They then attached ropes to the heads of the flood doors, the men in their holes keeping a firm hold.

Cogge, in his brief memoir, remembered the scene. "It was all fire," he wrote, "the sky was red and along the channel people were still fleeing. It was awful to hear all the noise, the crying, the lamenting and then the shooting and the explosions."

Thys, lying on a flat stone, kept measuring the water level. Would the tide never rise?

"Charles," he would whisper, "it's taking so long."

"Yes, yesterday the weather was rough, but today it's calm. That could make a difference of two hours. But don't worry, it will come."

Not until about 6:15 A.M. on the twenty-eighth did the doors begin to swing open. The soldiers in the facing rifle pits held fast to the ropes as the seawater surged through.

AT I A.M. ON OCTOBER 27, in the occupied city of Lille, an alarm bell woke the sleeping troops of the 16th Bavarian Reserve Infantry Regiment. The List Regiment, as it was called, after its organizer and commander, a professional army colonel named Julius List, wondered what was up: were they in for yet another annoying drill, called at a deliberately inconvenient hour? The night was dark, the starless dark of mid-autumn. The three-day blow had passed. A never-ending rumble of artillery came from the west and lurid flashes lit the sky. The 3,000 men of Bavarian RIR 16, most of them barely trained volunteers who had arrived from Munich three days earlier, filed out of the large, once all-glass public building where they were gathered. Shellfire during the recent siege had blown out most of the panes, and to sleep there was like camping in the open, in a field of broken glass.

An hour later the List Regiment finished assembling on a wide avenue that was a natural open space, Le Place de Concert. The Bavarian RIR learned that it would be setting out for the front before dawn, and, within a day or two, would cut its fighting teeth against the British. List's Bavarians would temporarily join the 54th Reserve Division near Gheluvelt, a Württemberg outfit from the other south German province. Then a staff officer read out an exhortation from Crown Prince Rupprecht pointing to the British as their true enemies, the British who had betrayed a nation it had never fought before by joining France and making war against the Central Powers. Rupprecht described the British as

> that people whose antagonism has been at work for so many years,
> in order to surround us with a ring of enemies and strangle us.
> We have to thank them above all for this bloody, terrible war. Here
> is the enemy who stands most in the way of restoration of peace.
> Onwards! Onwards!

The List Regiment began its march through Lille. The long line threaded its way through army transport, motorized and horse-drawn, which even at that early hour crowded the streets. The siege two weeks before may have been brief, but the city had taken a battering. Wounded, brought in from the battlefield, crammed the railroad station, which doubled now as a hospital. It was shell-scarred and, reported an eyewitness from the Bavarian RIR 16, "a shambles. . . . There were burnt out gables and smoking piles of rubble everywhere."

The regiment headed north, toward the Lys, which it would presently cross. As the day took shape, so did the appearance of the marchers. They were dressed in greenish-gray uniforms, with "RIR" 16 sewn in red onto their epaulettes and narrow red stripes down the side of their trousers, which were tucked into new leather boots. A thick leather belt was buckled around their jackets. Because spiked hard leather helmets, pickelhauben, were in short supply, they wore billed oilcloth hats—nineteenth-century shakos—with a gray cotton covering that was supposed to give their headgear the appearance of regulation helmets. The shakos, meant for home-guard troops, *Landsturm,* looked martial enough, if outmoded, but offered no protection. Worse, from a distance, they could be mistaken for the billed caps the now-hated British wore.

The march, twenty-five miles long, under full packs, began in darkness and ended in it. They sang. The thunder of big guns grew in volume, to be joined by the distant rising babble of small arms as they drew closer to the front. Ration carts didn't catch up to the Lists until 9 P.M., by which hour they had crossed the Lys into Belgium and were about to reach the village of Dadizeele, where they would spend the night. They had set out believing that their primary mission was only to act as reserves for the German line. The Lists arrived, to find that the regiment had been incorporated in the revised offensive scheme that Falkenhayn had submitted that afternoon to Rupprecht. In a little more than a day, they would be seeing action for the first time.

One of the *Kriegsfreiwilligen*, Adolf Hitler, a scrawny, sallow man in his midtwenties, with an inverted V of a mustache, was not enthralled by his accommodations. "I couldn't sleep, alas," he wrote to a Munich acquaintance. "There was a dead horse four paces in front of my pallaise"— his mattress was probably just a pile of straw. The carcass "looked as if it had been dead for two weeks at least. The beast was half decomposed.

In the early morning hours of October 27th, the 16th Bavarian Reserve Regiment marched out of Lille, bound for Belgium and the just-created Salient. One of the 3,000 *kriegsfreiwilligen*—volunteers—was Adolf Hitler, who would do hazardous service as a dispatch runner. He is the gaunt man here sporting an inverted V of a mustache (right), in a mid-1915 group portrait with two other runners and an adopted dog. (Getty Images/Ullstein bild Dtl.)

Just behind us a German howitzer battery fired two shells over our heads into the dark night every 15 minutes. They kept screaming and whistling through the air, followed by two dull thuds in the far distance. . . . We had never heard anything like it before."

The specter of the franc-tireur continued to hover, though the new roar of the howitzer went far to overawe it. The closer you came to the front, the less threatening that phantom freelance killer seemed. In Munich, before the departure of the regiment, officers took what they deemed a necessary precaution. One of them, Ludwig Waldbott Count Bassenheim, observed in his war diary that his "company provided the troops with ropes to hang franc-tireurs; every three men received a readily prepared noose. The ropes are heavily sought after by the men."

One final occurrence worth noting took place around midnight. A report reached the headquarters of the 6th Bavarian Reserve Division that a franc-tireur had shot and wounded a messenger on horseback. (It was probably friendly fire, but no matter.) Orders had gone out for a general roundup of locals. The Lists, who had been on their feet for twenty-four hours, kept their ropes in their packs.

IV

NE PLUS ULTRA

Can there be a better representation of the developing deadlock, and its frustrations, on the Western Front than this look backward at the commander of a Scottish battalion wading through a rain-inundated trench below the Lys? (Imperial War Museum/Robert Cotton Money (Major) Collection)

16

The Bargeman's Solution

DURING THE AFTERNOON OF OCTOBER 27, WHILE FALKENHAYN AND RUP-
precht were disagreeing on the proper role of a general in combat, and
Kriegsfreiwilliger Hitler was marching to his rendezvous with a putrefying
horse, Gen. Max von Fabeck and his chief of staff, Lt. Col. Friedrich von
Lossberg, received their orders to prepare a major attack. Both the offensive and their role in it leading an army group must have come as a
surprise. So did the haste of the operation. Falkenhayn gave them just
two and a half days to get ready—in cases a day less than that—or just
over sixty hours until jump-off.

For the moment the only thing definite was the timing. Specifics such
as objectives and location of the attacks, which divisions might be shifted
from what sectors on the Western Front, and how much artillery support
to expect were still to be decided. Forced to sacrifice deliberation for dispatch, Fabeck and Lossberg contemplated their sudden task with a certain trepidation, and with good reason.

The man chosen to head Army Group Fabeck was a tough, solid, and
dependable infantry leader of the old school, until now an ideal corps
commander. Lossberg described Fabeck as "a very good soldier overall,
but his innate roughness often got the better of him. . . . Even when the
troops had conducted a difficult attack he could not find the praise and
the fiery words." He was more likely to single out "an incorrect position
of the helmet or other uniform deficiencies. Whenever possible I tried to
keep him away from direct contact with troops."

Lossberg, the lieutenant colonel universally known as Fritz, had the

General Max von Fabeck (right) confers with the kaiser, as Falkenhayn looks on. This photo probably dates from early 1915, after Fabeck's promotion to command the German Eleventh Army on the Eastern Front. Though tough and dependable, Fabeck was a compulsive martinet whose greatest talent lay in failing upward. (Imperial War Museum/German First World War Official Exchange Collection)

imagination his superior lacked. He would soon establish himself as the supreme practitioner of puttying up, the inventor of the elastic defense, the impresario of impregnability, who gained a reputation as his side's chief fireman on the Western Front, a military savior many times over. He was one of the few German officers (or Allied, for that matter) genuinely touched with genius. You can make an argument that no single military leader was more responsible for keeping Germany in the war so long. For the time being, though, he had to apply his considerable talents to the coming offensive.*

---

* The Imperial German Army was notably stingy with promotions, even in wartime. In almost all cases, advancement in rank depended on time served, and whether or not a candidate had managed to get around the notorious "major's corner," the undoing of many careers. No doubt officers at the top feared that brilliant and innovative younger colleagues would threaten their hold on power and influence—even their jobs. There was no instance more glaring than that of Hermann Geyer, one of Ludendorff's most prized theorists, who ended the war holding the same rank as he did when it began: hauptmann (captain). Lossberg himself was eventually promoted to major general—generalmajor— and chief of staff of an army group, but his advancement came late in a war that he had mostly spent as a colonel.

Fabeck may have been the epitome of the conventional leader, but at Ypres he was blessed to have the gifted lt. colonel Fritz von Lossberg as his chief of staff. In the years to come, Lossberg would devise many of the defensive innovations on the Western Front that helped keep Germany fighting and formidable. He has to be ranked as one of the few military geniuses that the Great War produced. (Smith Archive/Alamy)

In the hours and too few days that followed, the mismatched couple set up their new headquarters in a village called Linselles, just south of the Lys. October 28 found them dashing around, visiting various other headquarters and establishing new ones, advising and explaining. They made no attempt to hide the difficulty of their assignment. "We were convinced that our attack would run into strong resistance," Lossberg wrote. Aerial observation reported "heavy activity on the rail lines between Dunkirk to Hazebrouck, and increased road march traffic toward Poperingne." They examined the situation of their partners on either side, the Fourth and Sixth Armies. They reconnoitered the long line now held only by dismounted cavalry, which their army group was about to take over. Were their chief opponents, the British, as close to breaking as Falkenhayn claimed? (Lossberg doubted that they were.) How prepared for offensive action was their artillery? How could they deal with their most serious deficiency, a shell shortage that was more pressing than Falkenhayn admitted?

They did not receive specific directions for the attack and its immediate objectives from OHL until seven-thirty in the evening of the twenty-eighth. They had to work nonstop. Falkenhayn had given Fabeck, Lossberg, their staff, and the divisional commanders little more than two days to prepare—and, in the case of a preliminary attack scheduled for the twenty-ninth, only hours.

For the next few days nothing less than the war on the Western Front hung in the balance. More than just a cliché, tipping points were actually ready to tip. Intangibles were beginning to work in favor of the Germans. Momentum was not the least of them—momentum backed by the reinforcements that were beginning to arrive. A change had taken place with the capture of Kruiseecke, and it was spreading. Now, all along the line, from the Yser to the Lys, it was the Germans who were forcing the Allies back on their heels. Now it was the Allies who were making small but critical mistakes. Fatigue accounted for most. Even their best soldiers were fought out.

The Germans had the advantage of numbers, both in respect to men, many of the new arrivals being rested veterans, and artillery, still the best of any army. And they had surprise working for them. Few on the other side thought that the renewal of the general offensive would come quite so soon. Time was the worst adversary of the Germans—though the truncated hours of preparation that Falkenhayn demanded could work in their favor. An attack without the lengthy warning artillery buildup that was already becoming standard on the Western Front might give them just the edge they needed.

Army Group Fabeck had two principal targets to start with. The first was Ypres itself, the proverbial bone in the throat, the sticking point, the stubborn roadblock preventing an advance into open country, the Allied dike with not just a finger but an entire annoying fist stuck in its venerable masonry. The obstacles to overcoming the bastion of Ypres may have

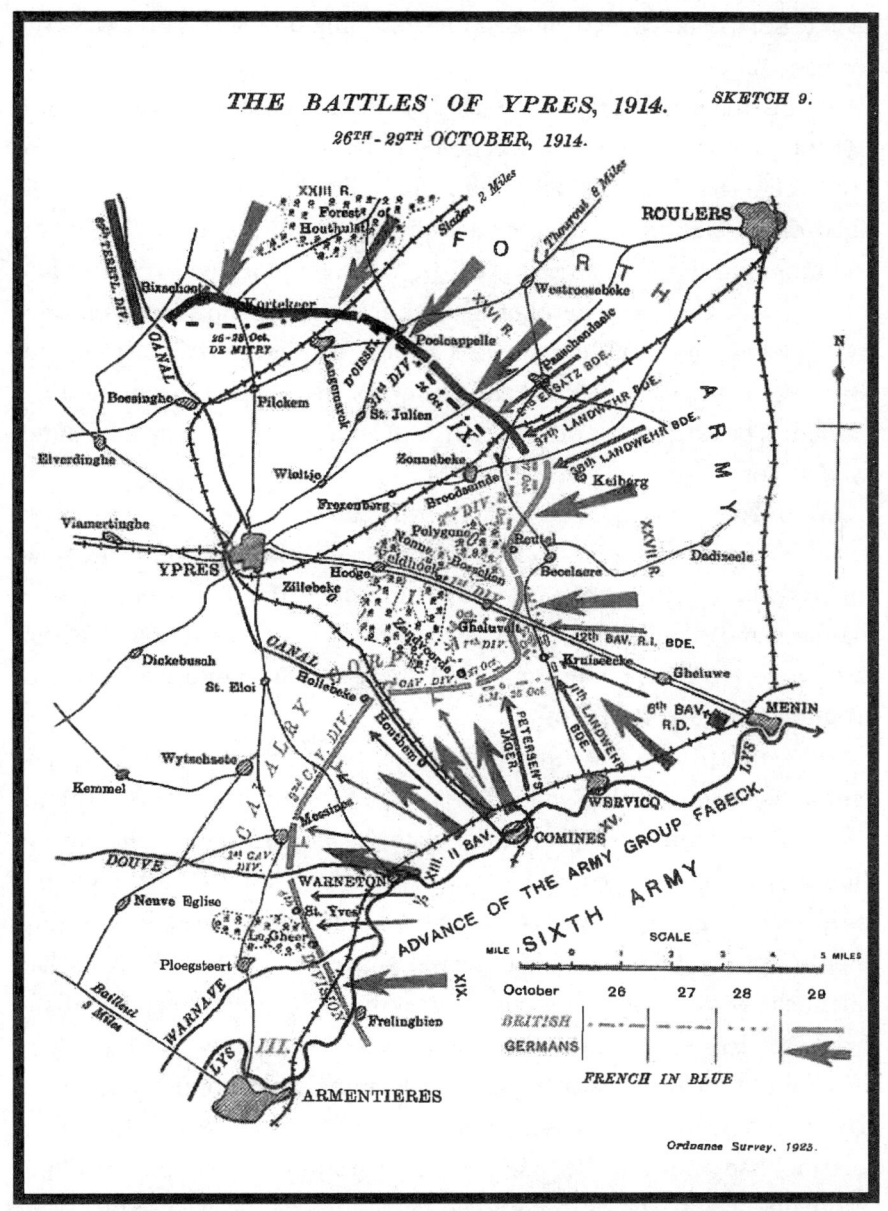

THE BATTLES OF YPRES, 1914. SKETCH 9.

26TH - 29TH OCTOBER, 1914.

By October 26, the Salient had taken definite shape, and by now was a feature rating a capital *S*—although that day the Germans had nipped off a triangular bit of territory around the village of Kruiseecke (broken line center). On the twenty-seventh and twenty-eighth, there was no perceptible budging of the line in either direction. But the twenty-ninth marked the opening of the offensive by Army Group Fabeck, which struck the soft southern underbelly of the BEF, mainly held by dismounted cavalry, and widespread units at that.

been legion. Balance them against one gleaming prospect: Ypres was "the key of Flanders."

Ypres, too, with its Cloth Hall and Cathedral, possessed the last major cultural monuments left in unoccupied Belgium, the only gifts worthy of a sovereign that German arms could still offer the kaiser. He clearly relished the thought of a ceremonial approach on horseback to that medieval omnibuilding that so reflected the vanished glory of Flanders. In a war like this, there was another bitter but practical consideration: once you attack the cultural heritage of a nation, you have gone far to neuter your opponent. Why else did the Germans single out Louvain and the Cathedral of Rheims for destruction, and later in the year, the Cloth Hall itself at Ypres?

With Ypres in hand, presumably, little could hold the Germans back. As military historian Gary Sheffield points out, the capture of the town "offered the enticing prospect of blasting open the Allied positions in Flanders and reopening mobile warfare, with the Channel ports within easy reach. In the late autumn 1914 there was no more vital piece of ground on the Western Front."

Messines Ridge was Group Fabeck's second major objective. The handle, as it were, of the sickle-shaped high ground that cupped Ypres, it offered a panoramic prospect of the plain that extended from the town to the sea. Messines Ridge may have been about two hundred feet high, but in this part of the world even that slight elevation could be a force multiplier. Height, as I have already observed, made might. Once the ridge had fallen, the possibilities for a major breakthrough would be substantially increased. Fabeck's left-hand divisions would then move on quickly to the chain of "Monts" that began with Kemmel and ran in a southwesterly direction toward the sea. Though barely five hundred feet high, Kemmel had an unexcelled view of the surrounding area. Possession of the chain, or any part of it, could go far to impede, or even to block entirely, an Allied retreat from Ypres toward Dunkirk and the sea.*

---

* The tallest of the Monts is Mont Cassel, all of 577 feet high. Foch had his headquarters here in 1914, and it is said, wrote the geographer Douglas W. Johnson, that he could "on a clear day see the flashes of the guns from the dunes at Nieuport to the chalk upland at Vimy Ridge."

Few on the German side, at least no one who was listened to, seemed to reckon on the hindering effect that a possible inundation might have on their operations. The Fourth Army command did not appear to recognize that inundations had happened in this area before, that history could repeat itself. No one envisaged how inundation of the Yser channel could prevent that most glorious prospect, a trap-shutting junction between Army Group Fabeck and Beseler's III Corps heading south from the Yser. That would have been a double envelopment straight out of the Cannae playbook that Schlieffen had so admired, one that might have trapped thousands of French and British troops. For a heady moment distance seemed to evaporate. Ypres was just twenty-six overland miles from Dunkirk, forty-six from Calais.

The likelihood is that Falkenhayn would not have attempted to take the Channel ports immediately. He didn't have to. Just isolating them would have served his purpose—and it would have saved lives needed for later campaigns. Let Sir John French build his great armed camp; let the English escape from Dunkirk the way they would a generation later. They would have been as good as out of the war. Let the right wing continue its Schlieffenesque swing south. This time many sleeves would have brushed the sea. Without the growing aid from Great Britain, how long could France have continued fighting? A second Marne-like "miracle" would have been at best doubtful.

Maybe there was still a chance to rescue 1914. Only the no-man's-land of the Goose Foot stood in the Germans' way

Perhaps, though, the Allies would not have gone down to defeat so easily. Campaigns of maneuver might have emerged again on the Western Front, shorter and, given the lethality of open warfare, even bloodier—too bloody to sustain. Peace might have come years earlier. As for more distant consequences, consider a couple—just for fancy's sake. If the war proved to be shorter, would the United States have become involved, except as a Wilsonian peacemaker? The American century might have been postponed indefinitely. European leadership in the world would have survived decades longer, with Germany as a likely leader. Adolf Hitler might have ended shouting antisemitic fantasies on Munich street corners. Could there have been a Second World War without him?

That brings us to the scenario that did happen. It is in some ways the most improbable of all.

THE ATTACK WAS CONSIDERED SO crucial that the kaiser himself had scheduled a special trip to Flanders, to be on hand for a possible triumphal entry into Ypres. "This breakthrough," announced one German order of the day, issued on October 29, "will be of decisive importance":

> We must and will conquer, settle for ever the centuries-long struggle, end the war, and strike the decisive blow against our most detested enemy. We will finish with the British, Indians, Canadians, Moroccans, and other trash, feeble adversaries, who surrender in great numbers if they are attacked with vigor.

The directive, found on the body of a dead officer, reflected the importance the Germans attached to the restart of their great Flanders offensive. Though it appeared under Fabeck's name, its careless fervor hardly seemed the sort of exhortation that would trip off the pen of that stolid, by-the-book but dependable commander—nor did it smack of Lossberg's rational way with words and inspired battlefield concepts. (Indians there were, along with some Senegalese at Dixmude, and by the beginning of November, some North African units would show up in the Salient. But Canadians would not take their place in the Flanders line until late in the coming winter, and there were no "Moroccan" units.) Could Falkenhayn himself have produced that message? It seems unlikely. The words do not sound like ones the chief of the general staff would use. His written style tended to be matter-of-fact to a fault, if not a little pedestrian.

A more likely candidate was the commander of the XV Corps, just transferred from the Aisne, General der Infanterie Berthold von Deimling. He was a notorious loose cannon, a perpetually intemperate man who had a tendency to talk too much and push men beyond achievable limits. He was an avowed racist, an attitude that the message in question fairly reeks of. The corpse with the message was found somewhere south of the Menin Road, and belonged to either the 30th or 39th Division, which Deimling commanded. That makes his authorship more likely.

There are few German generals whose careers were quite so bizarre as Deimling's, as much for his role during the war as before or after it. He was a rabid Anglophobe, an inclination no doubt picked up from his years in the German colony of Southwest Africa. In 1904, he had been responsible for driving Herero tribespeople into the desert, where hundreds, even thousands, died of thirst and starvation, or were killed by pursuing Germans. By the imperialist logic of the time, eradication made him a colonial expert; he became a favorite of the kaiser, who ennobled him. In 1913, the influence of the All Highest secured Deimling command of the XV Corps, headquartered in the Alsatian city of Strasbourg. He responded to protests over the behavior of his troops by staging daily parade marches through the streets. Provocative oratory threatening reprisals for local protests became a Deimling trademark.

With the coming of war, the two divisions of the XV Corps fought in Alsace and on the Aisne; then, at the end of October, they moved to Flanders. Deimling's testy disregard for human life would earn him the epithet "Butcher of Ypres"—but then, there were several generals who merited that accolade. When the use of poison gas was first considered for the Salient in the spring of 1915, Deimling's sector was Falkenhayn's natural choice. It turned out that the wind blew in the wrong direction, and the honor of releasing the gas went to another general. Deimling was equally profligate with lives at Verdun in 1916, where he directed the capture of Fort Vaux. His fellow generals waited until the following year to force his retirement. He was simply too dangerous to keep around.

With the end of the Great War, the life of that puzzling and curiously malign figure entered a new phase. A man who had never lacked for energy picked up the most unlikely of causes: pacifism. Was the collapse of the German monarchy the last straw for him? Was he overwhelmed by ghosts? Deimling even tried to push Hitler in a new direction, a classic case of backing not just the wrong horse but, as far as the cause of peace was concerned, soliciting the jockey from hell.

———

MASTERMINDING SUCH A WIDE-RANGING OFFENSIVE operation apparently didn't bother Fabeck and Lossberg; lack of time to prepare increasingly did. Being restrained, moreover, by a shell shortage was no way to run the sort of attack Falkenhayn envisaged, and he did arrange to have stocks of shells transported on the lateral railway from the Argonne and Champagne, both quiet sectors for the moment, as well as more explosives from Germany. The condition of the attacking troops was also cause for worry. Men who were supposed to go into action early on the thirtieth would spend much of the previous day moving into position. Some would have to make lengthy and fatiguing approaches in the dark on the night of October 29–30. They would have no chance to scout out the unfamiliar ground over which they had to advance at first light. Fabeck requested a breather of twenty-four hours; Falkenhayn, impatient as ever, turned him down. Any delay might risk betraying his latest surprise.

Fabeck and Lossberg's plan also called for a preliminary attack on October 29, aimed mainly at the Menin Road, the seam, as it were, between the British 1st Division, on the north side, and the 7th on the south. Fabeck/Lossberg wanted to distract British awareness of the buildup along the southern flank of the Salient. The sooner they could take Gheluvelt the better. They needed to capture the observation posts just beyond the village on the reverse slope of the Passchendaele Ridge, with their unobstructed views of Messines Ridge. This would cut down on harassing fire when the time came to storm the ridge. At this point, moreover, the Menin Road, the most convenient way to Ypres, four and a half miles away, would be all downhill.

For the attack of the twenty-ninth, which would mark the true opening of Army Group Fabeck's offensive, they would use dismounted cavalry and infantry units still in position, adding to that force two regiments of the 6th Bavarian Reserve Division. Except for the Bavarians, fresh troops who had not seen action, these were mostly veterans. The attack would sweep forward along both sides of the Menin Road. It would capture the key north–south crossroads, where the dirt track from Kruiseecke crossed the main paved highway, and then advance another mile west to overrun Gheluvelt and those potentially troublesome observation posts.

———

THE MORNING OF OCTOBER 28 was bright and clear, which could be a rare occurrence in a Flanders fall. Beyond the normal amount of sniper fire and some desultory shelling, there was little apparent activity on either side of the line. Observation aircraft reported an unusually large accumulation of transport—a line of vehicles fifteen miles long—on the roads leading up to the German lines; Allied aerial scouts attributed much of it to refugee traffic. They had come to recognize that the Germans preferred to make major reinforcements by night, when they could not be spotted from above. In this case they were probably mistaken.

Fourth Army headquarters sent out a radio message to the XXVII Reserve Corps, stationed just north of the Menin Road, requesting that the two divisions postpone any attacks scheduled for that day and wait for the general assault on both sides of the road, which would take place the next day, the twenty-ninth. It went on to state that the attack against the British would jump off at 5:30 A.M. Brussels had carelessly sent the Morse code message in the clear. Time pressure was almost certainly the reason for no coded safeguard. The senders would have needed extra minutes to translate the message into code, and the receivers more minutes to decode it. The shortcut must have seemed worth the risk. Instead it would cost Falkenhayn his surprise and perhaps much more.

The British GHQ at Saint-Omer happened to possess a wireless set specially modified by the Italian Marconi Company, the pioneer wireless manufacturers of the time. It was able to listen in on the enemy. All the British needed were telegraphers who understood German. They had them. GHQ phoned the intercepted message to Haig's I Corps headquarters, still at the Hooge Château. The three divisions Haig now commanded would be the ones directly affected. Though Hooge promptly sent out the warning at 3 P.M. and gave it priority, the communication took hours to reach the front lines, which were as little as three thousand yards away; some battalion commanders did not receive word until midnight.

Uncertain communications were to blame. "Telephone equipment of all kinds was very scarce and lines bad," a staff officer wrote of 1914. "My recollection is that messages forward of Divisional HQ were almost ex-clusively sent by runners." It was rare to find telephones in the front lines, or even in brigade headquarters. Wherever telephones did exist, cut wires were not the only impediment. Simply using a field telephone was difficult. As Col. R. M. Powell, who commanded the signal company of the 2nd Division in 1914, wrote:

> The hand telephone attachments were quite useless for any but short distance, and the only conversations between Division and Brigade consisted of "speaking over the key," i.e. the staff officer dictated his conversation to the telegraph operator, who sent it by vibration in Morse—the receiving operator "translating" it to the staff officer on the other end; a very slow and unsatisfactory process.

Improbable as it may seem, the role of the telephone actually re-gressed rather than improved as the war went on.

"Visual signaling," writes British military historian Brian N. Hall, "via electric lamps, flags, and heliograph was subject to interference from dust, smoke, and poor weather conditions, as well as dangerous to the life of the signaler; the message carriers, both human and non-human, were slow, vulnerable, and unreliable." Pigeons were used, and sometimes dogs carried messages. In the absence of communication trenches, usually the case at Ypres that fall, runners had to emerge from brigade or battalion headquarters dugouts, dashing and diving in the open to frontline posi-tions; they kept being gunned down. Adolf Hitler, never one to shy from risk, became a runner. To him, it must have seemed safer than being an ordinary infantryman.

For as long as the war lasted, neither side solved the problem of com-munications. As Hall writes (and it was also true of the Germans and the French), "The absence of suitable, mobile 'real-time' communications imposed profound restrictions on the successful conduct of British op-erations on the Western Front." An October 1932 "Report of the Com-mittee on the Lessons of the Great War" concluded that communications failures often led to "the general air of uncertainty and absence of command that characterized nearly all of the British Army." Messages never seemed to arrive on time. Unnecessary attacks were not called off; necessary ones were not ordered. Until now, generals had been able to direct battles in person, exercising "voice control." In this war, generals rarely inspired by their presence. The men who did the actual directing, deciding, and inspiring were the brigadiers, colonels, and majors, who were in the middle of the action. "After infantry had gone over the top," the British military historian Gary Sheffield writes, "the commanders who mattered were junior officers, NCOs or even privates, and the radius of their ability to command was limited to the distance they could shout." The noise of the battlefield limited even that frail cone of recognition. The generals just took the credit—or the blame. As Sheffield, one of the most perceptive chroniclers of the war, says: "The era of the Great War stands as the only period in history in which high commands were mute."

His is a notable verdict. It was also the subject of the disagreement between Falkenhayn and Rupprecht the previous afternoon. How close to the action should a general go? (The German supreme commander, it is true, may have been less concerned with the problems of communication than with the need of leaders to be visible examples.) The inability to communicate has to be considered one of the inhibiting essences of the way the Great War was fought and an explanation of why so much death resulted from command decisions made by men in the dark.

ON THE TWENTY-EIGHTH, THE GERMANS shelled Ypres again. "We heard," said Dame Columban, speaking for the Irish nuns, "that several houses in the Rue Notre-Dame had been struck, and all the windows in the street broken. The owners innocently sent out for a glazier to have the panes of glass repaired, little thinking that, in a few weeks, scarce one window would remain in the whole of Ypres." Others were not so sure, and deluged the Benedictine convent, pleading to be allowed to sleep in the cellars. But farmers still drove in wagons piled with provisions, and patrons in uniform crowded the restaurants that had stayed open.

Some of the German shells had, in fact, found a singularly accurate mark, smashing into the building where Dubois, his chief of staff, and other key officers lived and planned operations. They also hit an adjacent monastery that housed clerks, messengers, and chauffeurs. The explosions killed several, wounded at least ten, and wrecked cars. Dubois gave only the barest details in his memoir, and didn't bother to mention his own escape, which must have been a near thing. But then he was a general and not a journalist. There were widespread mutterings that spies must have been involved: Dubois dismissed the uncanny accuracy of the German barrage as "a happy accident."

As the mood of unease grew, people began to abandon town, packing wagons or carts or automobiles, and leaving quaint old buildings empty, a momentarily beautiful Potemkin village. The streets had not yet become dangerous. Casual batterings were all very well, but as long as the Germans believed that Ypres remained within their grasp, they would hold off leveling it. Better that the town stay reasonably fit for a king—or a kaiser.

BRITISH TROOPS PASSED THE LAST hours of October 28 making sure that their rifles were free of mud, dust, and sand, and were ready to fire—not always easy to accomplish, since oil for rifles had not been available for days. Men smoked. They tried to catch a couple of hours of sleep. Sleep presented, as much as anything, a brief opportunity to nullify the sour odors of dampness: the wet wool uniforms, the upturned manure-smelling earth, the myriad unwashed bodies, the ever-present reek of death, the fog itself. These were men exhausted after days in the firing line, with hardly a break. They were fought out, and now they would have to fight again.

The British had other worries besides fatigue and un-oiled rifles. The previous evening, ammunition that proved faulty had been issued to I Corps units like the Scots Guards, the Black Watch, and the Coldstream Guards. The brass cartridge cases were too big for their rifles. Anthony Farrar-Hockley, himself a decorated veteran of a later war, explained the imperfect ways they dealt with their predicament.

> A sharp movement of the bolt would force the round into the breech of the Lee Enfield but the empty case could not be ex-

tracted by the flick of the right wrist. After firing each shot, it was necessary to lower the butt to the thigh and tug the bolt back. When the breech became very hot or where fragments of sand or grit became lodged in the moving parts behind it, the riflemen were forced to place the butt on the ground and kick down on the bolt lever with his boot to free the weapon.

The expected German phalanx might present wall-to-wall targets, but would the British be able to shoot fast and often enough to stop the advance before it swept over them?

The defending troops could, moreover, depend on only a minimum of artillery support. Along the front held by the 1st (Guards) Brigade of the 1st Division, the most seriously threatened sector, a shell shortage (far worse than that of Group Fabeck) limited British guns to nine rounds per day. Here, even the trenches themselves, originally dug as a support line, were unsatisfactory for defense. They were too deep, too narrow, lacked traverses, and had the additional disadvantage of being covered with wooden planks, which presented more danger than protection. The sharp flying splinters spun off by a direct hit by a high-explosive shell could be deadly.

Small details—worse, an accumulation of them—had the power to change outcomes.

One officer, waiting in reserve behind the line, noted that the Germans spent the night "letting off myriads of different colored Very lights, unexpected salvos of shells, fired off haphazardly, and angry bursts of machine-gun and rifle firing at intervals." The purpose might have been to keep their opponents on edge, their own spirits up, or to disguise suspicious and persistent sounds. British soldiers reported hearing a heavy rumbling, which continued until about 3 A.M. It was the noise of wheels grinding along the pavement of the Menin Road as German guns moved up to the line, before being manhandled into position on both sides of the highway. A thick mist began to settle, making the darkness of an October night even more impenetrable.

———

IT WAS RARE, EVEN GIVEN the many-faceted drama of the Great War, to see a man of the people take center stage. Medal winners, Red Barons and Sergeant Yorks and privates awarded Victoria Crosses for wiping out machine-gun nests, may have performed legendary and laudatory deeds, saving countless lives in the process, but they didn't change the course of the war. Hendrik Geeraert did. He was not just bold; he knew where to go and what to do, at the right time. He helped to save what was left of his country, and perhaps the Allied cause that fall as well.

Hendrik Geeraert was an unlikely hero. He was a Belgian barge captain, a big, rough-hewn man with a thick, drooping mustache, graying hair, and the makings of a potbelly. He wore wooden clogs, a much-battered barge skipper's billed cap, and sometimes a kepi with a tassel: he was never without headgear of some kind. He is remembered as being blunt-mannered and uncommonly powerful. He had a habit of standing with his arms folded, except when he was holding a drink. Geeraert was

Hendrik Geeraert has to be the most unlikely hero of the Great War. A barge captain from Nieuport, he was a rough-hewn man, uncommonly powerful, barely literate, but with a way with machinery. He knew every peculiarity of the intricate local canal system—and where fleeing canal keepers had hidden the tools necessary for a widespread inundation. (public domain)

a bit of an alcoholic—or, as a lockmaster acquaintance put it, "He is a great enemy of full glasses."

He was fifty-one, the son of a fisherman, and a native of Nieuport. He had eight children, all born on French or Belgian barge canals. He was barely able to read or write, but had a way with machinery. He was also familiar with every hydraulic peculiarity of the local canal system.

On October 21, a second lieutenant of the engineers named Lucien François was about to conduct a first experiment with inundation, the opening of sluice gates to a navigable creek northeast of town. The object was to slow the advance of the rapidly approaching Germans, but François had only a vague idea of how to carry out his orders. One of his corporals remarked that he had acquired a new drinking companion, a civilian, who might be able to help. His name was Hendrik Geeraert. The corporal told François that the man knew both how to open and shut sluice and weir gates, and where the tools needed to operate them were probably hidden. He did retrieve the tools and, under his direction, the engineers successfully opened the gates at high tide and closed them at low. The limited inundation worked.*

The barge captain cemented his authority when he pointed out a hitherto unknown culvert that ran under the Yser and emptied into the flatlands beyond the railroad embankment. By inundating the creek, the engineers risked flooding their own lines. Geeraert recommended blocking the culvert. The engineers followed his directions, avoiding the disaster of an inundation in reverse.

THE FRONT LINE, LIKE THE weather, was mostly calm on Wednesday, October 28. For the Allies, though, the day was not a particularly good one. Admiral Hood and his ships kept up fire along the coast. But the Germans, who, in the words of Julian S. Corbett, "now seemed to regard the

---

* A distinction has to be made between sluices and weirs. The place where a canal empties into another stream is closed with *sluice* gates, which open outward to allow boats to pass. In a hydraulic system, creek flow is regulated by *weir* gates, which are raised and lowered.

squadron as the determining factor in this part of the great battle," had brought in heavy coastal artillery. Their powerful new batteries forced Hood to move his ships farther out to sea, and to take evasive action, making accurate bombardment difficult. A direct hit on the forward gun of the destroyer HMS *Falcon* killed the commander of the vessel and seven crewmen, and wounded another sixteen. An acting sub-lieutenant managed to bring the battered ship back to Dunkirk. Other ships took hits and casualties: in that single day, the flotilla lost 12 killed and 49 wounded. The squadron spotted a U-boat, gave chase, and then also retreated to Dunkirk. Hood's flagship, the HMS *Venerable,* which had been steering a zigzag course to make it a less inviting target for a submarine, ran aground on an uncharted sandbar, and had to wait for the high tide and the help of a destroyer to free it. Fortunately, it was out of range of German batteries.*

The mood of gloom seemed contagious. Colonel Brécard, the French liaison man at Belgian headquarters, visited Grossetti and found him uncharacteristically pessimistic. He was worried about the heavy losses his division had suffered and the mounting exhaustion of his troops. Ronarc'h, too, felt that his men could not hold out much longer. At the beginning of the day, Brécard admitted in a coded cable to d'Urbal, "The artillery alone has enabled the Belgian Army to hold out and endure." But the diminishing supply of shells and the deteriorating condition of the remaining guns were undeniable. The commanders on the spot were convinced that the Germans would launch a big attack north of Dixmude the next day, October 29. How much longer could they resist? Only the inundation could save them. But as Brécard remarked to Foch with dour hope, "The flood between the Yser and the railway is not yet complete."

Water may have been gushing through the Spanish Lock, but it was a flood that wasn't flooding. A second high tide on the afternoon of the twenty-eighth revealed unexpected problems. A watercourse called the West Vaart was supposed to carry the deluge in a sweep around Nieuport,

---

* A little more than a month had passed since September 22, when a single German submarine, the U-9, torpedoed, and sank, three British armored cruisers in the North Sea; 1,400 of their crews perished. The resulting fear of submarines goes far to explain the sometimes panicky behavior of Hood's flotilla off the Belgian coast.

at which point it would be diverted north, past the railway embankment, where it would begin to spread out and flood the landscape. Not a mile from the Spanish Lock, an old culvert under the Furnes canal became partially blocked with "a mishmash of nets, kegs, broken boards, jolly boats and whatever other floating debris a constant bombardment can produce." Then, a few hundred yards beyond, another blockage, a hidden weir, once more slowed the flood. Hardly a puddle had yet formed on the polders east of town, between the railroad embankment and the Yser River. How long could the battered remnants of the Belgian Army and its French allies afford to wait?

Geeraert felt that the Spanish Lock operation was futile. He had maintained all along that the quickest way to flood the polders would be to lift the eight weir gates of the North Vaart. Military engineers would need windless cranks to operate the gearboxes; he was the one person left in the empty town who knew where they had always been stored. Had the Germans already sent advance patrols to the Goose Foot? Geeraert dismissed the immediate risk. He persuaded the head of the engineer's battalion, Commandant Bourlon, that they had to act fast, before Germans actually did show up.

By now it was the night of the twenty-eighth. Geeraert led Bourlon and a party of engineers to the Goose Foot. Since the blowing up of the bridge, the single line had to balance its way across the narrow top of the lock gates. They stooped, trying to present targets as small as possible to potential ambushers. They paused to gather on the opposite side, on the wooded island next to the North Vaart weir gates. Then they moved forward again, fearing that at any moment a torrent of bullets might stream out from the bushes and trees. Nothing happened. Geeraert was about to look for the concealed windlass cranks when a messenger dashed up. He ordered them to call off their search.

It seemed that, just minutes before, Captain Thys, the man who had supervised the opening of the Spanish Lock, had returned to Nieuport from the Belgian High Command in Furnes. At the headquarters of the engineers he learned of Bourlon and Geeraert's mission. His rage can be implied from his actions. Thys reasoned, as Paul van Pul writes, that "if one man of the detachment was taken prisoner, or if the Germans made the right deductions, the whole enterprise could be ruined. Within a short time the road to Dunkirk would be open for the enemy." Thys phoned High Command. Whoever he reached agreed. Thys dispatched the messenger.

THE NEXT MORNING, OCTOBER 29, a thick fog settled on Flanders, from the North Sea to the Lys. A high tide pushed water through the Spanish Lock for a third time, but the results were again disappointing. Observers peering over the railroad embankment could now see some puddles of water, newly formed, in the polder near Nieuport, but the fields beyond remained free of pooling. Those observers had to take care: the Germans had brought fresh batteries across the Yser, and had begun to pound the embankment at close range. At 12:30 P.M., as if to warn Albert and his High Command that no place in that last corner of Belgium was safe, heavy shells once more hit the Furnes rail station. Not long after, at Ramscappelle, a village just two miles east of Nieuport, the Germans reached the embankment.

There could be no doubting it. The German Fourth Army was building toward its breakthrough effort on the Yser front. In the late afternoon, about 4 P.M., the Belgian High Command decided that it no longer had a choice. The Spanish Lock enterprise wasn't working. Once darkness took over and the tide was right, its pontoneers would venture again into the no-man's-land of the Goose Foot and attempt to open the North Vaart floodgates. That the Germans might already be there was a risk they now could not avoid.

FABECK AND LOSSBERG MAY HAVE intended October 29 to be a diversionary prelude to their big push, but the day soon got out of hand. If events are sometimes hard to follow, it is because they involved so many small and frequently disconnected struggles within the main one for the Menin Road: advantages swayed back and forth as the body count soared. Communications predictably broke down. Brigade and battalion commanders did not know what was happening a few yards in front of, or next to, them.

The leaders who should have imposed direction waited in vain at the ends of silent telephone lines. On the German side, lack of preparation showed. Captains and not generals or colonels ended up running the battle. Picture an open-air brawl spread out over four miles and involving perhaps 25,000 men, all bent on murder. The Germans could summon greater and fresher numbers; the British held the high ground. Disorder established an order of its own. October 29 became an early confirmation of a defining failure of the war for everyone concerned: the total inability of a guiding intellect to take charge.

The murky encounter along the Menin Road began, fittingly enough, in murk. Day broke; the fog did not. It was almost a physical presence, like thick silt stirred up on a river bottom. By mistake, the British artillery probing for the presumed lines of German infantry shelled its own front lines. The German attack jumped off punctually at the ordained time, 5:30 A.M. A British officer jotted in his diary: "Terrific shelling which begins at the first streak of dawn, and continues without ceasing throughout the day. It is certain death to leave one's trench." But in some parts of the line, the Germans did not bother with an opening barrage. They made the eerie choice of a silent advance, with booted feet shuffling cautiously forward. The men standing in the trenches, rifles at the ready, could see no farther than thirty to forty yards. They must have wondered at the continuous muffled tread approaching in the fog. It took the packed German lines several minutes to make it across the space between the diggings. Small obstacles impeded progress. So did unexpected large ones: hedges, cottages, gardens, orchards. The still-invisible shuffle drew closer. In places the Germans must have stumbled into man-made hindrances: "there was wire—or rather a wire—in front of the trenches," the British *Official History* reported, "a single plain strand, with tins containing pebbles slung on it, South African fashion, to serve as alarms." The rattle of many cans alerted the defenders, who fired into the mist. Opposite the Scots Guards, north of the Menin Road, a light wind caused the fog to lift momentarily, exposing troops as they stepped forward shoulder to shoulder. The Guardsmen began to fire, at less than their normal rate because of their defective ammunition; even so, they brought the advance to a standstill.

Other parts of the BEF line weren't so fortunate: two battalions of Bavarians appeared out of the fog and all but ran over the mixed companies of the Coldstream Guards, Black Watch, and Gloucesters protecting the crossroads between Kruiseecke and Becelaere. These may have been elite units of the BEF, but even their discipline and training could not withstand the crushing numbers and the undetected abruptness of the attack. The fresh German troops overwhelmed them in a matter of minutes and then started to work their way northward. Suddenly the Germans were able to pour fire on the British from three sides. By 6:30 A.M. they had captured three companies and occupied their trenches. They surrounded the right flank of the 1st Scots Guards and practically destroyed it. The Germans now aimed for a breakthrough. It was not to be. They got within one hundred yards of the Guards, who opened fire. The attack collapsed. "God knows how many we killed," said the commanding officer of the battalion, Lt. Col. Victor Mackenzie.

Commanders close behind the front line had no real idea what was happening and were slow to react. Poor communications came close to doing the British in that day. When the Scots Guards sent a runner to Brigadier General FitzClarence, commander of the 1st (Guards) Brigade, the messenger simply disappeared in the smoke of bursting shells, never to be seen again. It wasn't until about 6:30 A.M. that a wounded Gloucestershire officer, a Lieutenant Duncan, making his way to a dressing station, stopped at FitzClarence's headquarters to inform him of the loss of the crossroads and of the men defending it. FitzClarence set about locating reserves for a counterattack. FitzClarence, who seemed to be everywhere in the next days, did succeed in initiating one, which apparently slowed German progress.

Major General Capper, whose 7th Division held the sector south of the Menin Road, was even more in the dark. He did not learn of the German advance until 10:15 that morning, by which time there was a real possibility of a breakthrough. He immediately sent forward what reserves he could muster, two understrength battalions. As one, the 2nd Borders, crossed the crest line of the ridge, it ran into, writes the division history, "a tremendous storm of fire from guns, rifles, and machine guns." The colonel in command was wounded in the leg. Several other officers were hit, and casualties were heavy, but they managed to hold off the Germans, who attacked, as usual, shoulder to shoulder. An officer of the Border Regiment cited a perfect example of the lottery of war. In a sunken road he sat down between a subaltern of the Gordon Highlanders "and a lance-corporal of ours when a shell burst killing both instantaneously." The narrator was unscathed.

For the next hours, the fighting, always at close quarters, surged and ebbed. It's hard to form a true picture of the disconnected wildness of October 29, with its fog-obscured brawl along the ridgeline. Of the accounts of that day, none gives a better depiction of the prevailing chaos than the regimental history of the Grenadier Guards. The Grenadiers were holding the area just south of the Menin Road, a landscape broken up by cottages, orchards, gardens, and copses, a hard place for units to stay together and cooperate, especially since trenches were not continuous. And, at dawn, their own guns, misjudging distance in the fog, had heavily shelled the Grenadier forward positions.

> The problem was how, with three companies and no reserve, to stop a force ten times as numerous. The Germans had taken all the houses near the Menin Road, and the thin line of Grenadiers, with their left turned back to face the road, was all there was to stop the rush of the enemy.
>
> And indeed it was a formidable rush. They came on in such numbers that an officer afterwards said the attacking force reminded him of a crowd coming on the ground after a football match. Shoulder to shoulder they advanced . . .

These were not targets on a musketry range, but "full-length Germans not a hundred yards off, alarmingly visible, and in such numbers that even for the worst shot there was not the slightest difficultly in hitting them, especially as they were often three or four deep." The remaining Grenadiers retreated to a small wood, and from its shelter managed to hold off their attackers.

One event of those desperate hours seems almost emblematic of the day, a small epitome of the war. A company of the 1st Gloucestershire

Regiment found itself on the south side of the Menin Road, by the partially ruined windmill. A lieutenant named A. D. Harding was wounded. Two men from his platoon—a Private Ireland and another whose name has been lost—"volunteered to bring in their commander." They dressed his wound. The German attack resumed, along with heavy shellfire. Ireland was wounded in the leg; a piece of shrapnel killed his companion. The private hoisted Harding on his shoulders and limped back with his burden to safety. He set the officer down on the floor of a trench. It was only then that he discovered that he had been carrying a dead man.

THANKS TO THE FOG THAT had helped the Germans surprise British units in the early morning, they had been able to force a wedge between the 1st Guards Brigade of the 1st Division and the badly roughed-up 20th Brigade of the 7th. In the gap that opened, they moved up the Menin Road and began to shell Gheluvelt. One lieutenant colonel of the Guards wrote, "From our position we could see Gheluvelt and it did not seem as though anything could live in it in such fire." The closer you came to the front line, the more remote the prospect of victory became. That night, during a lull, the same officer, a man named Wilfrid Smith, wrote home. Dejection assailed him:

> I can't see how these battles are to end. It becomes a question of stalemate. . . . You can't get on because there are no flanks, and you cannot therefore get round them [the Germans]. As soon as you outflank, an airplane gives away the show, and the enemy meet it, and vice versa with us, so it is a never-ending business.

For the moment, the spirit of boldness and enterprise had clearly passed to the German side. One captain named Obermann, of Reserve Infantry Regiment 247 of the 54th Reserve Division, crawled out to scout the British positions. Later Obermann would lead his men along a concealed route to the British trenches that he had discovered. His reconnaissance saved many lives—but not, unfortunately, his own. A burst of machine-gun fire mortally wounded him. He died in the arms of his adjutant. A lance corporal named Rominger dashed across the Becelaere–Kruiseecke Road and took out the machine gun. That one gun had killed 15, including Captain Obermann, and wounded 74. The German attackers found scattered around the position they had just captured numerous dead Scots Guardsmen, recognizable by their kilts and bare legs.

The Bavarian Reserve Infantry Regiment 16, the unit to which Hitler belonged, arrived at their fogbound starting point at 5 A.M. on October 29, just north of the Menin Road. They had already marched four miles in the middle of the night. Their food wagons had failed to show up, and they would go into their first battle on empty stomachs. Hans Mend, a cavalry dispatcher for the List Regiment and, later, a memoirist, spoke of those hours as "a last awakening for many of my comrades." Skies, he remembered, "were flaming red from burning villages."

Faced with their first genuine test, they were full of enthusiasm, though not one of them had yet experienced war. They were even unfamiliar with their rifles, Gewehr 98s, the standard battle rifle of the German Army, a bolt-action Mauser. It was sturdy and accurate, but did have disadvantages, holding only five rounds and being four feet long (almost five with a bayonet attached), not the ideal weapon for the narrow confines of warfare that increasingly involved trenches. Their rifles and bayonets had been issued just days earlier.

As the Bavarians reached their first destination, the crest of a small hill, they noted new mounds of earth marked by simple wooden crosses topped with the pickelhauben of their late owners. The Lists would advance down the slope into a little valley and then fight their way up the next hill. Gheluvelt was at its summit, as well as its eighteenth-century château. The Bavarians pushed forward, with difficulty. "We can barely see anything of our own troops, or the enemy because of the fog," an officer wrote in the List regimental war diary. The men of the 1st Battalion of the List Regiment—Hitler's—had to squeeze through openings in thick hedges and step over corpses of the recent fallen, human and animal. Shellfire swept over the attackers. They had been ordered to make exclamations of triumph as they advanced, and raise shouts of "Hurra."; Now they were crossing British trenches: the British popped up and commenced shooting from behind. One soldier wrote his sister, "It was terrifying the way my comrades fell all around me with ghastly injuries."

This seems to be the point where, in *Mein Kampf*, Hitler interjected his now-famous description of List's doomed legions singing *"Deutschland, Deutschland über alles . . ."* All this was Hitler's imagination. Singing, as I have pointed out, probably did happen, but his version was pure mythologizing. By the time he wrote these lines in the early 1920s, there was nothing he did without purpose or design.

THE GERMAN ADVANTAGES DWINDLED. THE fog, their early accomplice in surprise, was burning off. British resistance hardened. August Haugg, an NCO who led a platoon in the 1st Battalion, at first took part in the attack, and then, shot through the foot and lying helpless, observed its ebbing fortunes through the pocket telescope he carried: "The 'List' men poured down into the valley and with loud shouts of *Hurra*, the charge went in against the gnarled old hedges"—hedges that concealed British marksmen. "I could not participate; I lay there on my own from 11:00 A.M. until it went dark."

Only then was he finally rescued. Through it all he had witnessed the battle raging in the valley below. "Men went down, shot like hares; one man threw up his arms then disappeared entirely." Like so many exploding axes, British shells knocked over one poplar tree after another, their severed branches raining down on the disabled Haugg. But when a nearby stack of straw caught fire, those branches protected him from the heat and flames. "Down below," he continued, "I could see the battle develop from bush to bush, from hedge to hedge, climbing up the slopes, ever closer to Gheluvelt. Ghostly figures, glowing blood red from the dying rays of the sun, flittered about behind the wooded outskirts of Gheluvelt as the 'List' men took cover on the bushy slopes . . ."

That was, for the List Regiment, its "Iron Greeting"—as Hitler would phrase it in *Mein Kampf.* But what actually happened on October 29, 1914, was in no sense an incarnation of the romance of war. The untested troops advancing as though on a Munich drill square found themselves trapped, and mowed down, mainly in a crossfire of rifle bullets. High explosives and shrapnel shattered the close-packed lines. Württemberg riflemen mistook the List Regiment's cloth-covered *Landsturm* shakos for billed British caps and began to fire into the backs of their own men. The Bavarians had to rip off the covers, revealing their shiny oilcloth headgear. That, too, made them enticing targets, this time for the enemy.

The List Regiment would lose 349 men killed and 750 wounded, one third of its entire strength, in a single day. A Prussian officer surveyed the prospect of sprawled bodies. "Why aren't the Bavarians getting forward?" he exclaimed. "Why are they lying down out there?"

The officer he questioned replied that there were indeed long lines of Bavarians lying on the ground, but that they were not resting: they were all dead or wounded.

Not long after, a hard rain began to sweep in from the North Sea.

GERMAN LOSSES HAD NOT BEEN totally in vain. Troops of the 54th Reserve Division had established a foothold on the ridge. That afternoon these south Germans from Württemberg had managed to occupy buildings on the eastern edge of the village of Gheluvelt, had set up machine guns in them, and had penetrated the woods bordering the grounds of the Gheluvelt Château. A captain C. R. Berkeley of the 2nd Welch Regiment described the clash that, for the time being, stabilized the confrontation. His men met Germans "advancing in rather a dense line. On the appearance of our men, the enemy hesitated, some stopped and opened fire, and some continued advancing slowly. We had great difficulty in getting into any position where we could use our rifles, as anyone showing himself clear of the houses and enclosures received a hail of bullets . . . We managed to establish a thin line, whence we were able to stop the enemy."

The Germans, in an October 29 prelude to Army Group Fabeck's main thrust, attacked the British dug in across the Menin Road, below Gheluvelt. Aided by a thick fog, they overran elite units and threatened to achieve the goals set for the next day's drive. But the fog lifted; British resistance stiffened. For once, machine guns like the Vickers Mark I (above) dominated the defense. (Bridgeman Images)

This may have been the German high-water mark that day. It didn't last, thanks to the enterprise of a lieutenant named G. D. Melville. He set up two machine guns on a mound and enfiladed the Germans advancing north of the village. Melville's initiative may have made the difference that afternoon. His guns, said Berkeley, "did such execution that the enemy fell back, taking with them those in front of the village."

At 4:15 P.M., the 1st Division's brigade commanders, Edward Bulfin, Charles FitzClarence, and Herman Landon, held a crisis meeting near the château with their battalion commanders. They agreed that the cross-roads had been lost for good but that they would set about digging a defensive line on the outskirts of the village: that night. Bulfin's 2nd Brigade occupied the new trenches. He was worried. "Do not like the situation at all," he wrote. "Went back to Landon who did not like the situation any-more [*sic*] than I did. Raining heavily. Got back to my headquarters after midnight. Road being heavily shelled." Clearly, something was up.

The BEF began to tot up its losses for the day. In twelve hours of combat, the 1st Gloucester Battalion lost 7 officers and 250 men . . . The

1st Black Watch, 5 officers and 250 men . . . The 1st Scots Guards, 8 officers and 336 men . . . The 1st Grenadier Guards, 20 officers and 450 men . . . And so it went. The attrition rate of trained, veteran officers was especially alarming. Units returned from combat with only a captain or two and a handful of subalterns who survived. "Without question October 29th had been a bad day," wrote the historian of the 7th Division. "The heavy casualties and the exhaustion of the surviving officers and men were really the most disquieting feature in the situation, more serious even than the loss of ground, though this meant that once again new trenches had to be dug and that the work of the previous days had to be begun all over again."

The "bad day" had stretched the British to the limit, but their continual counterattacks had deceived the Germans about their actual strength. As the regimental historian of the Grenadier Guards wrote:

> The enemy was apparently quite unaware how threadbare this part of the line was. . . . Had they only known that there were no reserves at all, and that all that lay between them and Ypres were just the remains of a battalion, with hardly an officer or non-commissioned officer still alive, the result of the battle . . . would undoubtedly have been very different.

Fabeck waited until night fell to begin preparing his main attack in earnest. October 29 had provided a mere foretaste. Now, when no aircraft could hover above to observe their forward movement, five regular army divisions began to march north from the Lys River to their jumping-off trenches. They would relieve the divisions of dismounted cavalry, pressed up against the south face of the Salient; only the two divisions of the German I Cavalry Corps would remain, to join Fabeck's push. The Allied commanders suspected nothing, with one exception. The German big guns had been registering all through the twenty-ninth, a fact that the I Corps artillery commander did report to Haig. He took the warning seriously. Putting Sir John's demanded offensive action on hold, the British master of puttying up ordered his men to improve trenches, string wire, and reorganize. Meanwhile, Fabeck's replacement divisions were still filing into unfamiliar lines, rushing to meet their early morning attack deadline and the surprise of a new landscape.

JUST AFTER 7 P.M. THAT same Thursday evening, October 29, dismounted cyclists and carabineers—cavalry soldiers armed with carbines—from the Belgian First Army Division crossed the narrow and slippery Furnes Lock; they had to move in single file. One of them slipped and plummeted into the water. Did the splash alert a hidden enemy? His companions quickly, and as silently as possible, dragged the soaked and shivering man from the water. The soldiers fanned out and hid amid the hedges on the side of the island bordering the gates of the North Vaart weir. Geeraert, Captain Umé, and three pontoneers followed. Once across the entrance to the Furnes Canal, they dashed in short bursts across the wooded island toward the North Vaart. As far as they knew, death lurked behind every tree, bush, and building on the little island; even shadows were unfriendly, especially if they moved. This night was, quite possibly, their final chance.

High tide arrived just after 9 P.M.; they would have to raise the eight double doors in the shortest time possible. Geeraert retrieved the hidden windlass handles, the cranks needed to lift the gates. They were stored where he had expected them to be. The five went to work. They moved from gearbox to gearbox in the streaming darkness—this was the same storm that had begun to hammer the plateau of Gheluvelt thirty miles away—"each time," writes Paul van Pul, "popping the square keyhole of the heavy handle over the corresponding, well-greased shaft protruding from the cast iron box, after which they started cranking frantically." To lift the heavy metal door, two men had to grasp and crank the single handle of each windlass. Slowly they raised one, then another, and finally, all eight.

Where were the Germans? They had to be somewhere close by. Perhaps they were trying to find shelter from the rain, or from the continuing British bombardment from the sea. Though the Belgians did not know it, Beseler's III Reserve Corps was too consumed with its preparations for the final attack on the embankment, which was scheduled to go off early the next morning, to pay attention to the Goose Foot.

The first stage of the operation took just twenty minutes, frantic ones that seemed endless. The dark seawater surged through the open gates, overflowing the banks of the North Vaart, which were not built up with dikes, and spreading over the plain. The little party managed to let out several hundred thousand cubic meters of water—no one knows the exact amount. Then the five men, followed by the platoon of guards, returned the way they came.

In another six hours, the entire procedure would have to be reversed once the tide started to ebb. The five men would have to return with the windlass cranks to lower the weir gates, trapping the water that was now rushing through them. They waited, alone, in the cellar of an abandoned tavern. They had allowed their military vanguard to retreat to the safety and shelter of their lines in Nieuport. Did the inundators search for something to drink? Did they have candles or an oil lamp to light the basement space? It is hard to think of them sitting for tense hours in total darkness. Frightening possibilities must have multiplied. Could they get the gear mechanisms to work properly—and promptly—the second time round? And most tormenting of all, would a German patrol be waiting for them to show up? Would the enemy notice the roar of escaping water and come to investigate? Would the Belgians walk into an ambush? As Captain Umé later admitted, "We were sitting there, pale with fear."

From Nieuport to Dixmude, the German bombardment of the embankment line kept up all night. The thunder of their guns seemed almost to merge with the blasts of the storm sweeping in from the North Sea, the explosions shaking the vaulted ceiling of the basement where the inundators waited. The Germans were paying special attention to the six miles that separated Ramscappelle and Pervyse—in normal times nothing more than short stops on the rail line. Out in the polders, eight German regiments, perhaps 20,000 men, waited to go forward, minutes before daylight. They would attack the front between the two villages—and, once they had broken through, drive for Dunkirk.

A little before four in the morning the little Belgian group returned to the North Vaart weirs to close the gates. The five inundators went about their business with dispatch. The tumult of the guns to the east concealed whatever suspicious sounds they might have made.

No movement came from the German side.

17

Dead Sea

OCTOBER 30-31

AS DAWN BROKE ON OCTOBER 30, ALLIED COMMANDERS SEEMED OBLIVIOUS to the massing of new German divisions along the southern flank of the Ypres Salient or the ominous nighttime rumble. Since the British misadventures of the opening days of Falkenhayn's great offensive—remember the chaotic struggle for Ploegsteert Wood or the inadvertent gap at Hollebeke—little urgent activity had taken place in this part of the Salient. Though little more than a week had passed, those events already seemed so remote that they could have belonged to another place, a different war. Time itself seemed bent out of shape, expanded here, compressed there, a telescope gone haywire.

The British, especially, had paid scant attention to the Ypres Salient's soft and yielding underbelly; they had little choice. They had garrisoned it with three divisions of dismounted cavalry, supported by two newly arrived Indian battalions. They held nearly nine miles of disconnected trenches running west to east from Messines Ridge to the village of Zandvoorde. This was the most vulnerable part of a British line already dangerously overextended; in places it amounted to little more than a string of outposts. The total effective force of Lt.Gen. Edmund Allenby's Cavalry Corps, including the Indian infantry, was about a thousand rifles per mile. The isolated British and Indian detachments had practically no artillery support. According to one reliable estimate, the Germans now outnumbered the Cavalry Corps 6 to 1.

Zandvoorde itself was a cluster of houses on a 130-foot rise, which qualified as a ridge in this flat country. It overlooked a woods-fringed corridor of flatland, spreading out across the Lys into a prospect of some of the dreariest country in this part of Europe, a soggy and featureless tableau of mingy peasant farms and isolated copses where, in the cold months, the water tables rose to form a network of pond-sized puddles that defied large-scale movement. Beyond were the massive slag heaps and coal mines around La Bassée. A defunct and largely dried-up canal that had once run between Ypres and Comines on the Lys bisected the corridor. This part of French Flanders is a near wasteland, and the coal-blackened hand of man has done it no favors.

The next seven and a half miles, from the eastern slope of Zandvoorde Hill to the junction with the French at Zonnebeke, were held by Sir Douglas Haig's I Corps, now (with the addition of the 7th Division) three divisions strong. Ten days of nonstop combat, including the sanguinary brawl the day before on the steep back slopes of the Gheluvelt Ridge, had brutally diminished I Corps. The first light revealed hillsides and woodland patches littered with the dead of both sides. The unofficial truce that allowed stretcher bearers to collect the wounded would end in a matter of minutes.

That night Maj. Gen. Hubert Gough, GOC of the 2nd Cavalry Division, decided, after hearing enough reports of unusual enemy movement, to go forward and judge for himself. A light wind carried the reluctant metallic scrape of wheels dragged through mud and "a queer long cry every now and then as if a crowd was shouting in the distance." No one ever came up with a decent explanation of the "queer, long cry," but there could be little doubt about the rumbling noise. The Germans were bringing heavy artillery into position.

Meanwhile French ordered Haig and his I Corps to mount a counterattack the next morning. A final sentence, potentially fatal to so many, went out for the fifth consecutive day: "Operations will continue tomorrow in accordance with previous orders, Acknowledge." Haig waffled on purpose. "Orders as to the resumption of the offensive will be issued in the morning when the situation is clearer . . ." The reservations he had privately voiced in August about French as a commander must have grown by the hour. Haig did request that his 2nd Division improve its trenches and string up the barbed wire that had just arrived. His determination to go his own way could well have saved the British on October 30.

LOSSBERG, THE MAN CHIEFLY RESPONSIBLE for formulating the offensive blueprint, worried that for all the operational soundness of the German plan, the offensive might run into unanticipated obstacles. One way to handle such contingencies was to keep his scheme as simple as possible. It was, for a change, a narrow-front attack rather than a broad-front one. Broad-front attacks, like Falkenhayn's original fifty-mile-long push, tend to be political solutions rather than strictly military ones. They are designed to keep every commander happy. Morale—especially morale among the leadership—was an important consideration in any rebound Germany might hope to achieve that fall. Loner he may have been, Falkenhayn must have sensed that he had spirits to raise, amends to make. So, in the beginning of his great Flanders offensive, he had given equal emphasis to the attacks of his Fourth and Sixth Armies. Lossberg regarded the Fourth Army's indifferent performance as a perfect example of the curse of the broad front. All its five corps had been deployed in line, and its onslaught "had lacked any depth from which as the attack progressed a main effort could be formed against the tactically correct point." This time, however, Army Group Fabeck intended to exploit and extend to the breaking point the presumed weakest Allied links, ones of limited width.*

The most serious restraint Fabeck and Lossberg had to deal with was a personal one, Falkenhayn's impatience, his refusal to give his new but hardly fresh divisions even an extra day or two of rest and preparation. Some of the troops Fabeck would have to depend on had been pulled out of ongoing fights. The 26th Division, for example, which was

---

* Dwight Eisenhower's broad-front strategy of 1944–45, calculated to appease the British in general and Bernard Montgomery and Winston Churchill in particular, was a model example. Military historians have never ceased to argue whether or not the widened drive prolonged the war on that later Western Front by many months. A broad-front strategy certainly held few benefits for the Germans in the fall of 1914.

supposed to strike the fortified village of Messines, had just been involved in a three-day action near Fromelles, in northern France. It then had to march for a long day and take up positions on the plain that extended to the east of the ridge named after the town that was its objective; there it relieved a division of dismounted cavalry. It was already the evening of October 29: the 26th prepared to attack the next morning at 6:00. The division had arrived in darkness—which at that time of year fell at 4:30 P.M.—and would advance into darkness the next morning, without having had an opportunity to assess the lay of the land it would be fighting over. The same rush to attack, moreover, gave the greater part of the arriving artillery little or no time to register targets—although as Lossberg discovered, his guns lacked the shells to waste on such ordinarily necessary preliminaries.

There may have been another reason for Falkenhayn's unseemly haste: the following day, October 31, the kaiser was arriving at Rupprecht's Sixth Army headquarters in Douai and would be staying for several days. He wanted to harvest the public-relations glory of a triumphal entry into Ypres.

Falkenhayn's haste did have one positive result for the Germans. Allied commanders were caught off guard. They regarded the attacks of October 29 not as a preliminary event, an overture, but as a discrete one aimed solely at the capture of Gheluvelt and its château and the gaining of a foothold on the summit of the ridge. Intelligence largely failed the Allies. It was not entirely their fault. This time there were no wireless leaks. Fabeck and Lossberg hid their intentions adroitly. All movement near the front was carried on at night, shutting off reconnaissance from the air. Corps commanders ordered men to stay out of sight during the day. Even the weather cooperated as fog blanketed the daytime landscape. Prisoner interrogation was the customary way to come by advance warnings, but since many of Fabeck's new divisions were still taking their place in line during the night of October 29–30, the Allies had not yet snared fearful unfortunates with compromising information to spill. By the time they learned of German intentions and the arrival of fresh formations, the crisis would have almost passed beyond control.

The Allies may not have been ready for Group Fabeck when its full force hit them. But were the Germans prepared to take advantage of their advantage?

IT IS NOT EASY TO comprehend how the civilized world of Europe had become so lethally divided so quickly. October 30 was far from the bloodiest day of those three months, but it was a wall-to-wall slaughter nonetheless. Both sides participated in what can only be described as mass murder. An entire continent was suddenly bent on homicide (or, some would argue, suicide and self-mutilation). Was this crumbling of humanistic values the inescapable outcome of the halcyon interval that was the nineteenth century? In that apparent paradise so abruptly and irrevocably lost, people were more likely to die of disease than of cannon or gunshot wounds. Bacteria and not battles were the levelers of their time. We know, of course, that this world was far from paradisiacal—except for a fortunate few, and even they were not immune from its health perils. Also, with that century of summer afternoons (Henry James called it the most beautiful phrase in the English language) came the stasis and stagnation of a great ennui, of positions in life that were frozen and would never change. It has been called the corrosive illness of the age, the malady of the bourgeoisie triumphant.

This might be the place to pause for a moment and ask some of the questions that George Steiner posed almost half a century ago in a memorable lecture series that appeared under the title *In Bluebeard's Castle:* "Is it reasonable to suppose that every high civilization will develop implosive stresses and impulses towards self-destruction? . . . towards a state of instability and, finally, of conflagration?" Did we succumb to what he called an "itch for chaos"? "What turned professional, essentially limited warfare into massacre?"

We can detect the outlines of a new era beginning in those last months of 1914, the era of deliberate mass extinction, of legitimized slaughter and state-sanctioned murder, of the elimination of the best, a terminal leveling. The world had never seen its like before, and humankind took to it with a righteous will. Rifle fire rarely let up in that early spree of violence. It was an easy step from the Great War to the purges of Stalin, the Second World War, the Holocaust, Hiroshima, and the Killing Fields of Cambodia. Where was God in all this? He was, perhaps, the chief casualty of the Killing Season.

OCTOBER 30, THE FORMAL BEGINNING of the Army Group Fabeck offensive, announced itself at 6 A.M. (Allied time), with the firing of more than 260 guns, concentrated along the Salient line from its Lys River crossing a couple of miles below Ploegsteert Wood to Gheluvelt on the Passchendaele Ridge. Fabeck felt that the British were by now susceptible to breaking; the French, in his view, presented more of a problem. His intuition was not entirely unfounded. By the standards of 1914, that assembly of heavy artillery was prodigious. Fabeck's *Schwerpunkt,* his point of main effort, was on either side of the Comines Canal, where he deemed the underbelly of the Salient to be the softest, defended by outpost strong points and the fewest troops. To his knowledge the French were not in the picture yet. Here, he located the majority of his guns.*

The German cannon fire started with a short, rolling barrage that signaled the onset of the main bombardment. Gunner's light had arrived, the time when targets could be made out at battle ranges by ground observers. In a few moments the German heavy artillery joined in, the shell bursts racing across the landscape. They reserved a special fury for the little hill of Zandvoorde. There, where German observers could easily see them, the trenches all faced forward, climbing the slopes like ladder rungs.

Maj. Gen. Julian Byng's 3rd Cavalry Division was responsible for Zandvoorde itself. Capper's beleaguered 7th Division, now part of Haig's I Corps, took over at the foot of the hill, its thin diggings running off to the east. Byng himself rode forward just before 6 A.M. to visit, as was his custom, his outpost line. He was about three quarters of a mile from

---

* By way of comparison, when Haig launched the Passchendaele campaign on July 31, 1917, he had 3,168 heavy guns at his disposal, locked almost wheel to wheel.

Zandvoorde when the ridge and the ground immediately in its rear erupted in tall geysers of earth; the soil under his horse began to tremble. It was useless to attempt to get through, and Byng turned back. For seventy-five minutes, fire poured on the trenches of the 1st and 2nd Life Guards (ironic name), dismounted cavalry.

At 8 A.M. the shelling stopped, and troops of the German 39th Division, along with Jägers—elite riflemen—and machine-gun platoons, rose from their trenches and moved forward. To add inspiration, drums crashed, bugles blared charging notes, and a regimental band played a rousing martial accompaniment, the last sound that many would ever hear. Two battalions, 2,000 men, stormed the little hill of Zandvoorde, each battalion advancing on a frontage of 1,150 feet, for the combined force of one man to every two feet. Those were just the men attacking Zandvoorde. That morning Fabeck's lines extended for twenty miles.

British observers could make out spiked helmets bobbing through the mist, indistinct forms hopping drainage ditches, crashing over mostly harvested gardens, pushing around farm buildings, shouldering through hedgerows and scattered copses—the predictable Flemish obstacle course. Terrified birds and animals fluttered and scattered out of their way. Even after the fierce bombardment, the British still had 300 to 400 hundred men left. When the commander of the 7th Cavalry Brigade saw the German lines approaching, he dispatched orders to retreat. It was too late. The moment artillery spotters saw men fleeing in the open, up the hill and out of the thickest of the fog; the closer the running figures got to safety, the easier they were to make out. Now it was the Germans' turn to do the massacring. Artillery fire cut off and annihilated the British cavalrymen. The first lines of Fabeck's attackers reached the bottommost trenches and began climbing the hill. One can imagine the messy business of rifle butts and spades shattering heads, bayonets and trench knives slashing and stabbing, rifles and automatic pistols firing at close range, and perhaps a few ball grenades filled with black powder hurled for good measure. The Germans had the clear advantage in numbers; their opponents gradually gave way. Only a few wounded men survived and were taken prisoner.

By 9 A.M. the German infantry had reached the top of the hill and had overrun the village of Zandvoorde itself. The intensive shelling by Fabeck's artillery had battered the Household Cavalry dug in there: trenches everywhere had been blown in and men buried alive. But survivors of Byng's 3rd Cavalry Division did escape and made it back a couple of miles, where they re-formed in the woods around the village of Klein Zillebeke. Given the inevitable breakdown in communications, the British commanders in the rear could only assume the worst. Another hour or two would pass before they knew for certain. Passing along messages to neighboring units when under fire was virtually impossible. Lengths of trench were likely to be separated by considerable and dangerous distances.

The victorious Germans in Zandvoorde manhandled a battery, six guns, up the slope and aimed them toward the trenches at the bottom of the hill, held by the Royal Welch. In the words of the 7th Division historian, the guns "did terrible execution among the Fusiliers." Two British field-gun batteries still on the ridge to the east saw what was happening and immediately set to firing. They swept the Germans in enfilade, forcing gun crews to bolt for shelter. But lethal damage had been done. A battery commander was heard to remark a laconic essence of the British predicament. "We had very little ammunition," he said, "but plenty of time to look for targets." They did. After an hour, though, their ammunition ran out. A quick-thinking officer set fire to a windmill, and the blaze created an impromptu smoke screen, which covered the escape of the batteries. They had bought an extra hour, delaying the German advance. But for the Royal Welch Fusiliers, it wasn't time enough.

The actual fighting for the positions held by the Welch began when units of the German 39th Division, recent veterans of the Chemin des Dames, approached the decorative moat that surrounded the Zandvoorde Château and the main British trenches just to the east of that many-windowed monument to Walloon new money. The Welch resisted the first attackers. Farm buildings became temporary strongpoints; rings of corpses surrounded them. But then German numbers began to make a difference. Artillery, dragged forward, fired over open sights. The fighting broke up into a series of hand-to-hand struggles, brutal forgotten actions. Forced back, the Welch relinquished the château. Now they were scattered amid short slits of trench. It was impossible to know what was happening to the right or the left. Hedge-enclosed fields limited vision.

The noose began to tighten. The pressure from the front did not let up, no matter how many Germans the Welshmen dispatched. The Germans seized a farm to the rear of the beleaguered battalion and began to block the British right flank. Jägers worked their way behind the Welshmen and, discovering a ditch concealed by a long hedge thirty yards away, set to firing. Snipers joined in. All the while, batteries were blasting away at the Welshmen from above, shrapnel "raking their trenches from end to end," said the *Official History*. British rifles began to jam, ammunition to run short. The Germans wiped out post after post. The lieutenant colonel in command, the regal-looking H.O.S. Cadogan, saw his adjutant, a Lieutenant Doones, hit and collapse. Leaving the safety of his trench, Cadogan ran to him, and himself went down, shot dead. Within twenty minutes, the battalion had ceased to exist.

A Lieutenant Wodehouse, wounded and taken prisoner, remembered the chaos of the end:

> About 8 a.m. the shelling increased and we saw large numbers of Germans advancing down a slope about 1,500 yards to our front. Also I believe large numbers were seen coming around our exposed right flank. The batteries on the ridge were now firing point-blank into our trenches, so that it was difficult to see what was happening, and the rifle fire also increased from our right rear. No orders were received, so it was thought best to stay where we were, and about midday the whole battalion was either killed, wounded, or taken prisoner. . . . I was taken to a dressing-station in Zandvoorde and patched up.

Of some 400 who had been upright when the sun rose, by noon, six hours later, the commanding officer and 275 of his men were dead. Four officers and 50 other ranks were taken prisoner, almost all wounded. Only 86 survivors, some of them shot up, escaped to make roll call that evening.

Now it was the turn of the 2nd Battalion of the Royal Scots Fusiliers, next in line, to deal with another German division, the 30th, also just transferred from the Aisne Heights. The Scotsmen weren't as close to, or as menaced by, the enfilading artillery on Zandvoorde Hill, though shellfire was soon turned on them. Communications had almost completely broken down. The frontline units were in tatters. They had been in the trenches since October 17, a day short of two weeks, and were exhausted. In that time they had lost 8 officers and 500 men. The battalion now numbered fewer than 500.

At 12:45 P.M. a runner, who had somehow made it through the curtain of fire, arrived with a message from brigade headquarters, advising the Fusiliers to withdraw. One company succeeded in doing so, but the next three could not escape. The ground across which they had to flee was rising and open, and bursting shrapnel pinned them down. They chose to remain and attempt holding off the German infantry. Not until after dark did the 130 Royal Scots Fusiliers who had survived the day reach safety.

The Green Howards just to the north, also menaced, also managed an escape. From first light they were harassed by "the deadly accuracy of a few snipers who never seemed to miss." They killed the colonel who commanded the battalion. A message from brigade headquarters ordering the Yorkshiremen to retire was dispatched around noon, but snipers once again claimed the first runner, and word did not make it to the firing line until 3:30 P.M. The battalion, fortunately, was able to follow an escape route shielded by trees and hedgerows: it reached safety with only— only—11 casualties.

Counterattacks may not have had a chance of reaching, no less regaining, Zandvoorde, but they did bring the German attack in the sector south of the Menin Road to a standstill. The German 39th Division had plans to advance to the Klein Zillebeke woods; the attack never took place. Trees obscured, and prevented, the Germans from seeing how thin the British line was. The *Official History* speculated that "possibly they could not conceive that so weak a line should dare to deny the way to the coast." German commanders believed that sizeable Allied reinforcements were about to be filtered into the line. They were "paralyzed by the thought that fresh British forces might appear at any moment from the shelter of the woods and surprise them." In the Great War on the Western Front, it was usually the Allied troops on the offensive; the accepted scenario saw the continuation of attacks long after any further benefit could be secured, a pattern that faulty communications and weak central control went far to explain. In this case, the Germans stopped too soon. Their commanders doubted their own success. The German generals were rarely as good as the men they led.

At 4 P.M. the order came to call it a day and dig in.

A similar want of enthusiasm gripped the II Bavarian Corps, pushing north on either side of the Comines Canal. They let their heavy guns do most of the work. It was, on the whole, a waste of precious shells. The thin and scattered line of the British cavalry, most of it dismounted, presented few targets to exploit. The remedy was to move the guns forward, which was done at midday, and which seemed to have a bracing effect on the Bavarians. They now began to menace the village of Hollebeke and its grand château. So many of the trenches in front of the village were blown in and flattened that holding them was out of the question. The 3rd Cavalry Brigade of Gough's 2nd Cavalry Division began to perform a wheel backward.

It was a moment of genuine danger. No trenches existed in this back area to which the British had retreated, and they had to utilize whatever natural cover they could find. They concealed themselves behind hedges and in ditches. A gap on the left of Gough's 2nd Cavalry Division opened. Only a handful of dismounted cavalrymen filled it. There were no reserves behind them. Had the 4th Bavarian Division pushed through between the village of Klein Zillebeke and the Comines Canal, nothing could have stopped it from marching to Ypres, just three miles distant. Once reinforced, the Germans might have gotten between the three divisions of Haig's I Corps and the town, cutting them off and surrounding them. The GOC of the 2nd Brigade of Haig's 1st Division, Edward Bulfin, expressed just that apprehension in the October 30 entry of his diary: "Found cavalry had retired early this morning leaving huge gaps which the Germans could have marched through. My men working like bees . . . Don't feel a bit happy, no sort of reserve."

Haig (whose I Corps was by then responsible for seven miles of front) felt concern enough to ask his neighbor on the left, the French General Dubois, for help. He agreed to lend units to Haig from his IX Corps. Maj.

John Charteris, the head of intelligence for I Corps, noted in his diary, "We had a splendid French general—Dubois—who never fails; a great soldier and most loyal ally. He sent help at once, the gap was filled." That was early in the afternoon. But the German commanders were too far back to act quickly, and were themselves in the dark. They failed to recognize their opportunity and take advantage of it.

To Haig's zeal to "putty up," in defiance of his commander's orders to attack, and his trust in the French, we must add a German breakdown in communications. Both had saved the British that day. But would the Allies be so fortunate on the morrow?

THE GERMANS MAY HAVE BEEN just three miles away from Ypres by the morning of October 30, but even that late in the siege, life there still made some pretense of normality. "Business went on as usual," said one British observer, "except that trade had never been so brisk. Long lines of troops, transport wagons and lorries streamed through the town unmolested." People hardly paid attention to the distant roar of battle, and the first artillery shells to hit came as a surprise.

That day Raoul Nel and a fellow doctor traveled to the venerable town to replenish supplies that had been destroyed when a shell hit their medical wagon some days earlier. Nel described the trip as "an escape" that "brought us a ray of sunlight in our sojourn of drama." They even found a restaurant and enjoyed a leisurely lunch: "To cap our day of celebration we drank, while we ate, some French champagne!" But already there was an unwonted element of menace. Aerial bombings happened every day now. The two doctors met a woman in tears: just that morning an explosive device, dropped by hand, had torn her flat apart. Even as they spoke, a Taube passed over the central market square: while people scampered for shelter, a machine gun sprayed the sky from a nearby roof. The plane buzzed on, unscathed. So far, damage to the town had been limited to hit-and-miss bombing from the air and the recent shellings, none of which had affected quotidian activities. But as the German lines closed in, Ypres could expect a measure of daily buffeting. So far, the Cloth Hall and the Cathedral seemed exempt.

Nel and his companion purchased what supplies they could find, loaded their horse-drawn wagon, and headed north for Pilckem, the village where their aid post was located. They arrived in time to witness the burial of two officers, acquaintances whose bodies were now neatly wrapped in tent canvas.

"I think about our fate," Nel wrote. "The Grim Reaper is among us; she walks through our ranks, her face a grimace. To the orchestra of gunfire, she moves about, busy night and day, without stop, in a macabre dance, from the trenches to all our little posts, her scythe already dripping with blood. Today she has chosen her victims . . ."

He, at least, was fortunate enough to sleep through another night.

"Pressed up again each other in the straw under our outspread greatcoats, we warm ourselves little by little and soon, given our fickle spirts, revive our stubborn hope for a better tomorrow."

AS HUBERT GOUGH'S 2ND CAVALRY Division wheeled backward and retreated into the woods, the II Bavarian Corps followed at a safe distance. By the middle of the afternoon the gap crisis had passed. Still, that brief opening was an indication of how fragile the British line in the underside of the Salient had become. A lack of initiative and not stiffening British resistance had slowed German progress. Had the divisions imported from more stable parts of the Western Front already become too inured to the relative security of trench warfare? Did combat in the open seem too fraught with the dangers of being exposed to fire? The siren song of safety had, this early in the game, become one of the delusive drawbacks of trench warfare.

There was, to be sure, more hard fighting that filled those waning hours of daylight. The struggle for the village of Hollebeke on the western side of the Comines Canal was brief but intense. One participant, a reserve second lieutenant from a Bavarian infantry regiment named Herman Kohl, described how "blow after blow was struck, but enemy machine guns"—more likely concentrated British rifles—"fired mercilessly and tore holes in the ranks. . . . The potential of every building, right up to the rafters, was cunningly exploited for its defensive possibilities. The

Major General Sir Hubert Gough (left) examines dispatches. It is the afternoon of October 30, and the vanguard of Fabeck's Germans is less than a mile away, and edging closer. The hulking marble pile in the background is Hollebeke Château. The photographer, a Frenchman named Paul Maze, was a post-Impressionist painter, who had put his brushes aside to become a scout and Gough's interpreter. (Imperial War Museum/ Paul Maze Collection)

dense woods served as one long endless barrier to progress. Fire blazed down from the treetops, serving its deadly veto on the Bavarians storming forward." Friendly fire nearly stopped the attack. "The commander gave the sign and the trumpeters blew 'halt.' The battle was paused as runners raced back to the battery position." Hollebeke, "that blood-soaked bulwark," held out until twilight.

Just to the east, across the canal, in the midst of wide lawns, probably cropped by recently developed rotary hand mowers and by sheep, and a network of ornamental moats and gravel drives, rose another elephantine temple to the plunder of the Industrial Revolution. The Hollebeke Château looked more like an American magnate's summer "cottage" from turn-of-the-century Newport than a Walloon nobleman's weekend estate in rural Belgium. The building and its sculptured, parklike grounds captured the aesthetic eye of Gough's interpreter, a Frenchman named Paul Maze, who had already made something of a reputation as a post-Impressionist painter:

"A lovely drive led to this lodge with a double alley of silver-stemmed poplar trees . . . [F]alling leaves were twisting and circling towards the ground like yellow butterflies. The sky was a very clear blue—the sun shone softly on all this lovely colour, impressing on my mind the last glory of summer.

"The situation on our front had become threatening. The enemy's big guns, having newly arrived, were now in action, and the black smoke of the shell bursts of 'Jack Johnsons' was multiplying everywhere." Maze mounted his motorcycle and drove down the wide drive to the neoclassic pile. The Germans were advancing from the south, and the firefight squall line mounted in volume as the storm front drew closer. But there was still time to slip indoors. Maze, the artist, discovered, and hastily examined, an extraordinary collection of miniatures. He wished that they could somehow be saved: time had long since run out, as he was forced to recognize in the next moments.

"While I was looking around, the whining of shells passing over the house had become continuous, and the reports of loud explosions were coming from the park. I looked out of the window and through a screen of smoke and splashing shells, I saw an ominous animation about the ground." Shells were plunging into the waters of the moats; while officers were rounding up Indian troops, some of the first to arrive on the Western Front, for defensive duty elsewhere, reserve squadrons of cavalry and regimental horse transport were cantering across the lawn; a general and his brigade staff were supervising last-minute packing before falling back to safer quarters; and orderlies were loading wounded into ambulances.

"The fire of musketry was coming alarmingly nearer, together with sudden outbursts of machine-gun fire. We were being heavily attacked . . ."

About 2:30 P.M., vanguards of the 4th Bavarian Division reached the southern edge of the château grounds, but were slowed down by enfilade fire from Hollebeke Village. The dismounted troopers of the 1st Royal Dragoons repulsed several attacks, firing into cleared fields. There was no panic. They evacuated all their wounded and made sure to carry off their most precious possessions, machine guns; only Maze thought about the miniatures. Then, on orders from Lt. Gen. Edmund Allenby, the commander of the Cavalry Corps, the Royals withdrew a mile to newly established defensive positions that extended eastward in the woodlands beyond Klein Zillebeke. Though the British had by now vanished from the scene, the Bavarians displayed an excess of caution as they moved by fits and starts across the exposed lawns and parkland. By this time they were fighting phantoms. It was not until after dark that men of Infantry Regiment 22 reached the château itself. They found it empty.

Maze, a rangy figure on a motorcycle, seemed to be everywhere in the Messines Ridge area. The following year he would meet Winston Churchill, then a major serving in Ploegsteert Wood, and the two would frequently paint together. (Imperial War Museum/Paul Maze Collection)

PAUL MAZE HAS TO BE one of the remarkable bit players of the war. He had largely given up painting for the duration—though he still carried sketchpads and a portable camera—to become an interpreter and unofficial liaison man for Hubert Gough and, later, Sir Henry Rawlinson. Fairly bursting with charm and good taste, Maze was a favorite of generals, a gangly figure forever riding his motorcycle on missions of importance. They trusted him. As the war continued, he took to crawling out into no-man's-land to sketch and listen. He was wounded four times.

At the end of 1915, he first encountered Winston Churchill on a muddy road near Ploegsteert; they talked about art. Churchill, whose political career had tanked after the Dardanelles fiasco, which he had promoted, was now a major, and leading a battalion on the Western Front; in his spare time he had taken to painting landscapes. A close friendship developed, and over the years Maze would frequently advise Churchill on technique; he became something of a mentor. At the end of August 1939, Maze and Churchill found themselves in a field in Normandy, painting side by side. It was close to the twenty-fifth anniversary of the Battle of Mons. Churchill turned to Maze and said, "This is the last picture we shall paint in peace for a very long time."

Maze's account of his Western Front experiences, *A Frenchman in Khaki*—colors were never far from his mind—is one of the notable memoirs of the war, a book as singular as its author. It appeared in 1934, by which time Hollebeke Château was nothing more than a mound of rubble rising from a watery swale in a Flanders beet field.

MOST OF THE ACTION THAT afternoon and into the evening took place west of the Comines Canal, in the flatland corridor below Messines Ridge. The British pullback from Hollebeke was gradual: The "strong hostile counter-attacks" and the hand-to-hand clashes that a German official account described never took place. Gough's 2nd Cavalry Division lacked the manpower necessary for even a minimal demonstration. All it wanted was to make a safe exit. But an order to retire did not reach one group of Indian troops, the Punjabi Musalman Company of the 57th Wilde's Rifles. This was one of the first colonial units to show up for the British in Flanders; more troops from the Indian Army were arriving there every day. In other parts of the Western Front, Moroccans and Algerians had been fighting for weeks. The French had no problem shipping established African units across the Mediterranean. Those colonial troops included the Foreign Legion, large numbers of whom were already stationed in France.

Between Hollebeke and a hamlet named Oosttaverne, close to where the ridge rises, troops of the 3rd Bavarian Division caught up to and showered the Indians with machine-gun fire from both flanks. The Indians, men who had fought on the Northwest Frontier, lost 80 of 140 before they managed to shoot their way out of the German trap. Second Lieutenant Kohl spoke of his first sight of Indian corpses: "Bronzed Indian troops lay there, cut down in rows."

The Indians took sizeable losses in those first encounters but also proved themselves tenacious fighters. They were particularly adept with that largely superfluous weapon, the bayonet. The remnants of the Punjabi Musalman Company eventually sought shelter in a trench on the ridge, northeast of the village of Wytschaete. That night they ran into a group of Bavarians. A man named Havildar Ganga Singh, who had been a bayonet fencing champion in his Indian home district, killed four of them before his bayonet broke. He picked up a sword, a weapon probably discarded by its former officer owner as useless for trench warfare, and fought on. He finally collapsed from loss of blood and no fewer than five wounds—but not before he had dispatched more of the enemy. He survived; the Bavarians retreated. In another night battle in a farmyard, Indian troops of the 129th Baluchis, wielding bayonets, chased Bavarians from the outbuildings, killing 10 and wounding 3; 14 surrendered.*

The Sepoys (as the Indian troops were known) even came away with a Victoria Cross that day. A unit that came up to cover the retreat of the beleaguered Punjabi Musalman survivors also belonged to the 129th Duke

---

* The detail about the discarded sword should not surprise. Consider the following words from a British cavalry officer, which Peter Hart quotes in his illuminating *Fire and Movement*. Swords, the cavalryman wrote to a friend in the infantry, "were an awful nuisance, because when they moved they made such a noise, tripped them up when they tried to run and caught in everything in the trenches—and were too big to be useful even in opening bully beef tins!" Once trench systems had begun to cover the landscape of the Western Front, it became obvious that the sword had to go. On January 22, 1915, the British Army abolished the carrying of swords by infantry officers—although the weapons still turned up in non-battle situations such as troop reviews or formal photographic portraits.

Maze pictured a column of freshly arrived Indian troops, the 129th Baluchis, marching across a field to take up positions near Hollebeke Château. The Baluchis, and units of the Lahore Division of the Indian Army, would be immediately thrown into battle. One of the Baluchis, Sepoy Khudadad Khan, won the Victoria Cross that day, the first Indian soldier to win the U.K.'s highest award. (Imperial War Museum/Paul Maze Collection)

of Connaught's Own Baluchis. The Baluchis' two machine guns fired at the advancing Bavarians, considerably slowing their progress. A shell burst destroyed one of the guns. Then the British captain who commanded the battalion took a debilitating wound in the head. All except one member of the crew of the other gun were killed. That left a Pathan named Khudadad Khan, who was himself wounded. He kept firing, holding off the Bavarians long enough to make certain that his companions had escaped. They had indeed made it to the safety of the ridge. No one can know how many Bavarians he killed. They charged, finally; Khudadad played dead as the Germans dashed by his prone form. His ruse worked. After dark he crawled and limped his way back to his own lines. That December he was still in the hospital when King George V presented the Victoria Cross in person. He was the first Indian soldier to receive Great Britain's highest award for bravery.*

The arrival of Indian troops, even in small numbers, stiffened sagging British resistance. Except for a scattering of men still in the British Isles, they were the only trained troops available; Canadian and Anzac reinforcements would not begin to show up until 1915. Allenby's Cavalry Corps had by now become so diminished in numbers that its defense consisted of little more than a scattering of strongpoints, which the Bavarians took without difficulty. These were the only sizeable gains the Germans made that day, up to two miles, and they left them bumping up against Messines Ridge. But in the process, the 3rd Bavarian Division outran its artillery, ammunition supplies, and its ordered destination. Gough's 2nd Cavalry Division made its way back to the crossroads village of St. Eloi, three miles south of Ypres, where it established new headquarters and, as it were, caught its breath.

Meanwhile, the Germans had been shelling Messines itself since daybreak. But light field guns could make only dents in the thick walls of that aged village. The heavy artillery that might have done an effective leveling job arrived too late to be of use. To move the big cannon close to the front lines, gun crews had to wade knee-deep in mud. The guns themselves sunk to their axles. The crews had to attach long tow ropes and haul them through boggy ground and over churned-up tracks. All the time they were under fire.

By 6 P.M. the heavy artillery had still not arrived. The 26th Division, South Germans from Württemberg, went forward with the attack anyway. From the beginning things started to go wrong. Orders arrived late. Preparation was haphazard, goals too exalted. A pair of regiments began their advance across flat, open terrain that offered scant protection besides a few drainage ditches and hedges. As patched-together units of

---

* Most sources, including his Victoria Cross citation, give the date of Sepoy Khudadad Khan's exploit as October 31. However, Gordon Corrigan's authoritative *Sepoys in the Trenches* convincingly argues for the October 30 date. Geography clinches the matter. The area between Hollebeke and Oosttaverne, an interval of two miles, where the Sepoy manned his gun, was by the thirty-first firmly in German hands. The exact site is unknown, but the general area was militarily irrelevant by the following day.

dismounted British cavalry and hastily assembled companies of Indian infantry poured fire down on them, the exposed Württembergers began climbing the steep slope to the village. They did not even reach the outer walls. There would be no Mount Kemmel that night.

October 30 had been a day that left no one happy. The British had lost two key villages, Zandvoorde and Hollebeke. Zandvoorde, with its low but dominating ridge jutting out into the flatlands, was the more important. The Germans had nearly wiped out one of the BEF's best battalions and seriously mauled two others. The way to Ypres had been briefly exposed.

But in the miles around Gheluvelt, Fabeck's legions, two corps' and four divisions' worth, had barely advanced. Even though the II Bavarian Corps had made substantial gains, they had not yet established a foothold on Messines Ridge. Army Group Fabeck had so far achieved none of its announced objectives for the day.

The sky cleared and the moon shone. A Bavarian corporal named Knauth, stationed near the Comines Canal, remembered the hours that followed: "That night there was strange, eerie silence. Hardly a single shot was heard and not a word was spoken aloud. A farmhouse to our front was burning . . . There was no crackling to be heard or fallen beams to be seen, it was all rather like a theatrical backcloth."

But the silence was not total. Allenby's cavalrymen, camped in the woods east of Klein Zillebeke, could hear, a mile or so away, a military band playing a late-night serenade of light opera in the Hollebeke Château.

IN HIS UNCOMPLETED MEMOIRS, PUBLISHED after his death in March 1929, Foch described the chaotic events of October 30 and paused to make an observation:

> Generally speaking, during a modern battle, where nothing is clearly seen, especially in an enclosed country, the results obtained are learned only through reports which show what localities are held by troops at the end of the day. But, when the line has been pierced or even merely thrown back, these reports come in

slowly and are not clear and definite, the liaison between organizations having been weakened. In fact, it is precisely when the situation is gravest that a commander gets the least information from the front and runs the greatest risk of having no time in which to make dispositions to repair the harm.

The "gap" that may have opened in the woods near Klein Zillebeke was a case in point. October 30 may be the moment when the idea of a gap became an all-consuming obsession for both sides: the sudden breach in the continuous trench line that troops could pour through, and in the process break the stalemate. Everybody eventually came round to the German way of handling the trench problem that fall; and it would dictate the way war on the Western Front was fought for years to come. An army corps would batter a line and then, so the scenario went, stream through the opening it had created. In a word, a gap. Once broken, would the entire line come apart as more big units penetrated it? "Let's hope," General Fayolle's diary entry for October 2 had concluded, "that doesn't happen to us."

The gap. Foch couldn't shake his apprehensions. From his headquarters across the frontier in Cassel, he sent out a staff officer, a Captain Requin, "to get information on the spot." Requin returned about 10 P.M. and informed Foch that a gap did indeed exist on the cavalry front, somewhere north of the Hollebeke Château, too close to Ypres for comfort. He added that the British did not have enough men to plug it. Foch telephoned GHQ in Saint-Omer, trying to come up with a more precise picture of the British situation. A staff translator on the other end informed the general that "nothing more definite was known." Foch's reaction to what he saw as deliberate British vagueness was etched in acid. "As is their custom, when the news is bad, they remain silent."

Foch's fear was not the capacity of his own troops to stand up to the German pressure but that of the BEF. Notes from his intimate daily diary, the unpublished *Journées,* talk about the crisis of October 30: "Ypres and all her communications are in jeopardy. The danger is great. So much more so as the English do not have any reserves." The risk was that the Germans, knowing that they faced overstretched and under-strength

British resistance, also suspected that a gap—if not gaps—existed, and would attempt to push through it (or them) at first light. The other danger, only less menacing than the actual capture of the town, was, as he put it in his memoirs, that the enemy would "establish himself firmly a short distance from Ypres. This would prevent any movement through the town and bring about a retreat under the fire of enemy guns of all our troops fighting east of the town; that is to say, of the greatest portion of the army. This would amount to almost a complete disaster." Foch had no idea that the Germans were themselves worried about the sudden arrival of British reinforcements, which might tip the balance back in favor of the Allies. Such reinforcements, however, territorial regiments and Rawlinson's new 8th Division, were still on their way. An exception was the London Scottish Regiment, even now taking positions on Messines Ridge. Neither side, let it be said again, excelled in the gathering of intelligence, nor, for that matter, in its implementation.

Foch soon placed another call to GHQ: far from the front lines, phones worked perfectly well. The reason for his second call was to announce that he was, in spite of the lateness of the hour, driving over to consult with Sir John French. This was an emergency.

Foch set off for St. Omer, fifteen miles from Cassel; he arrived about 12:30 A.M., in a downpour. Sir Henry Wilson, French's temporary chief of staff while Archibald Murray was in London, was waiting for him. The two old friends were on a first-name basis: Foch called Wilson Henri or "Doubleh-vay"—*W.** Foch took immediate note of the widespread mood of depression and indecision that enveloped the BEF headquarters. The inescapable message to Kitchener had been sent but not the customary daily operations order, reviewing the main actions of the past twenty-four

---

* "It is of historical note," Liddell Hart remarks, "that the British forces were usually referred to by the French staff as 'L'Armée W.'" In the French official history of the war, for example, Haig's I Corps is called the 1er [Premier] C.A.W.—the British First Army Corps. To the French, Wilson seemed to represent British arms, and the "Doubleh-Vay" first letter on his surname gained a notoriety that lasted in French military circles throughout the Great War. Wilson, after all, was their chief go-between with the British Army, an angular and elongated Colonel Blimp, a figure who might have been conceived by Vorticists. Wilson was actually Irish but that seemed to the French beside the point. In the context of late 1914, perhaps it was.

hours and spelling out the objectives of the next, something of a ritual, had never gone out. As French's able biographer, Richard Holmes, wrote:

> When Sir John retired to bed that night the situation was still unclear. GHQ was not sure of the details of the fighting, and had not yet realized the weight behind the German attack. French was not dissatisfied with the day's results, telling Kitchener that the enemy had thrown substantial forces against him, but adding that he hoped to regain the lost ground in a counter-attack.

That was standard French; this was not a standard moment.

Before long Sir John came down the stairs from his bedroom, buttoning his beribboned field marshal's blue evening-dress tunic, "from one sleeve of which," wrote Foch's chief of staff, Maxime Weygand, "indiscreetly peered the embroidered border of his night shirt." Foch left two versions of what happened in those minutes. In his memoirs, the two commanders "studied the situation together. The British had no forces available for stopping the gap. So far as I was concerned, I would have, on the morning of the 31st, eight battalions of the XVI Corps detrained at Elverdinghe . . . I suggested to the Field Marshal that I should send them without delay to close the breach in the British line. . . ."

Foch's description of the sleepy encounter in his *Journées*, presumably written just after the fact, is notably at variance with the memoirs. The urgency of his words is unmistakable.

> I see Wilson, explain the situation to him, ask him theirs, which is clear; they have nothing available. On the morning of the 31st I will have 8 battalions (of the 16th Army Corps). I can provide these to them as support, to occupy Wytschaete, to defend St Eloi . . . [N]aturally, he accepts. We go to find the Marshal to whom we communicate this . . . He is deeply moved, touched, troubled, grateful for my initiative . . . "You are rendering me a great help," he tells me. He thanks me . . . there is not a moment to lose.

Thus, in the *Journées*, it is Foch and Wilson who decide to send reinforcements to the south face of the Salient. Only at this point do they have Sir John woken up to inform him of a done deal: French can do little more than mumble platitudes of thanks. The difference in the two accounts makes it plain that, by now, Foch was calling the shots and had taken charge of the battle—as he would eventually take charge of the war.

"We are all in for it," French said, his voice full of gloom.*

"We shall see," Foch replied. Foch, as was his wont, seized the moment, and his words produced the desired tonic effect. "In the meantime, hammer away, keep on hammering, and you will get there. It's surprising the results you can attain in this way." What Foch said often mattered less than to whom he said it, and when. A sense of timing had to be one of his greatest talents.

Foch did not hesitate to toss in an incentive: eight battalions and three artillery batteries of his 32nd Division, which were then arriving from Compiègne at the railroad station at Elverdinge, just west of Ypres. There, a relay of packed lorries and open cars, their headlights off, shuttled back and forth throughout the night to reinforce the lines—stirring stuff, when you think about it, the taxis of the Marne in Flanders. To avoid being observed from the air, the transfer had to be completed before sunrise. By that time, 8,000 fresh troops had been deposited along the threatened front.

The Germans were unaware of their coming. This was precisely what they had feared. These reinforcements, in addition to the ones Dubois had already contributed to Haig, might not change anything on October 31, but they would go far to strengthen the line from Wytschaete to St. Eloi on November 1, All Saints Day—if, that is, the British could hold on long enough.

---

* The quote first showed up in B. H. Liddell Hart's *Foch—The Man of Orleans*. There can be no better reflection of Sir John's depressed state of mind than the words "We are all in for it." Several subsequent accounts of the exchange between the two generals leave out the "in," reading "We are all for it." That doesn't really make sense in the fraught context of their late-night meeting. I have obviously chosen to go with the Liddell Hart version.

———

EVEN AS FOCH CALMED AND encouraged Sir John French at Saint-Omer, Hendrik Geeraert and Capt. Fernand Umé, sheltered in the cellar of the abandoned tavern on the Goose Foot, tried to deal with their own malign specters—the probability (or so they saw it) that Germans would at the last moment show up at, and overrun, the hydraulic system, stopping the inundation at midflow. Would patrols still appear out of the shadows to undo their work and annihilate them? On the six-mile stretch of the Nieuport–Dixmude railway embankment between Ramscappelle and Pervyse, eight German regiments waited in the gale. It was just before 4 A.M. that the little group of pontoneers approached the floodgates at the North Vaart for the second time that night. As they worked, they could hear German mortars and artillery opening up all along the embankment, just to the east.

When Falkenhayn set Fabeck's push in motion, he surely downplayed the chance that thousands of acres of Belgian farmland, rich but curiously barren in aspect, might disappear underwater for the duration. The Germans were not aware of the open flood doors at the Spanish Lock, and only close-up inspection would have revealed what was going on there. No German troops had yet taken up stations along the opposite bank of the outer Yser channel, between the Goose Foot and the sea. Nothing, not even the noisy demolition of the Furnes Lock swing bridge on October 26, had aroused German suspicions that Belgian pontoneers were tinkering with the hydraulic system. Confined to their own cellar shelters north of the river, advance detachments of the 4th Ersatz Division hesitated to brave the tempest and investigate the Goose Foot.

That they did not take the risk was largely the doing of Adm. Horace Hood's Dover Patrol, which kept the 4th Ersatz, the coastal division of the III Reserve Corps, pinned down for crucial days. Naval gunfire scattered units advancing along the dunes to the north of Nieuport and saved the town; it shattered German morale; it forced the 4th Ersatz to keep out of sight. Remnants of eight battalions retreated up the coast to Middelkerke, leaving only one much-diminished battalion close to the river. Historians may argue how much actual damage Hood's guns did or didn't do. Keeping the Germans from the Goose Foot was, in the end, more important. The Belgians had difficulty believing their good fortune. No wonder Geeraert and Umé were convinced until the end that potential ambushers lurked behind every tree and bush. Their very absence seemed proof that they were lurking somewhere close. That the Germans so far hadn't discovered the intentions of the Belgians remained the best, the only, hope of the Allies on the Yser front.*

How long that slim advantage might last was problematic. By the final days of the month, the Germans were, perhaps too late for their own good, learning how to deal with the Dover Patrol. They had come to view it, in the words of Sir Julian S. Corbett, the British official naval historian, "as the determining factor in this part of the great battle. From now onward it became the chief target of their heavy batteries, and it began to suffer more than it had done since the beginning of the operations." By October 27, there were so many guns on the dunes that it was unsafe to come closer than four thousand yards from the shore. As Corbett said, "it was increasingly difficult for the vessels to get any result from their fire." As the days passed, the squadron faced a new danger, submarines, which sailed from the base newly acquired, at Ostend. Sub scares, real or imagined, were constant. Then, on the morning of October 31, the seaplane-carrier *Hermes*, which had just delivered its cargo to Dunkirk, was returning to Dover. Eight miles from Calais, it was torpedoed and sunk by a German submarine, the U-27. Nearly all the crew were picked up from the chill water. But "the incident," Corbett wrote, "raised the question whether the risk the ships were running was worth any further good they might do." Still, until that moment, the Channel had proved a flank that the Germans could not turn.

THERE HAD BEEN MASSED ATTACKS on the railway embankment day after day, with patient lines of infantrymen in their canvas-covered pickelhauben—

---

* Hood would go down with more than a thousand of his men at Jutland on May 31, 1916—only six survived—when an explosion split apart the HMS *Invincible*, the battle cruiser he commanded.

to be less conspicuous, soldiers sometimes unscrewed the spike—and water-logged uniforms slogging forward through swampy, clinging clay that sucked at their boots and slowed their forward motion to a dangerous and excruciating slowness. Under gray skies, they collapsed in gray heaps on the gray trampoline of clay. The dead littered the battlefield in front of the embankment, along with the wounded whose weakening calls persisted for long hours. The sky broke open in sullen downpours. The Belgians seemed on the verge of giving way, but somehow they held on, stiffened by the resistance of Grossetti's French regiments. Even they seemed close to breaking. For that matter, how long could the Germans continue before they, too, lost the will to go forward?

When Beseler ordered a new all-out attack on October 29, one of his corps commanders, Generalleutnant Erich von Schickfus und Neudorf, requested a formal review of the orders. He commanded the 6th Reserve Division, dug in opposite Pervyse. He argued that the ground was beyond saturation, his men exhausted, beyond endurance, and preparation had been inadequate, beyond rashness. Beseler agreed to reconsider. But he was under pressure from Duke Albrecht. Reluctantly, Beseler went ahead.

The unenthusiastic gray lines rose up yet again and trudged forward. The assault on the embankment continued into the afternoon, gaining little or nothing. Though major seawater release by Geeraert and Umé was still hours away, German infantrymen were already beginning to notice that water was rising. A Hauptmann Moeller of the 5th Reserve Division, pushing on Ramscappelle, observed: "The enemy has flooded the ground to our front. The trench encircling the farmstead in which the company is located is filling constantly. It sounds just like a waterfall." The Germans blamed the torrential rains of the past days, and to an extent they were right. But the Spanish Lock inundation efforts, unsuspected by them, were also taking effect at last.

So Beseler's orders for all-out attacks that afternoon, and even bigger ones at daybreak, were perhaps not unreasonable. If the Germans did not cross the embankment in the next hours, they might not have another chance. They were running low on shells, both shrapnel and high-explosive, and worse, on manpower. Too many Peter Kollwitzes had been wasted early on. Any dash for Dunkirk would require troops to sustain it. As for the shell shortage, it would have to be tomorrow's worry.

WHEN GEERAERT, UMÉ, AND THE other members of their crew emerged from their basement hideaway in the early hours of October 30, the all-night bombardment must have been the least of their worries: Ramscappelle was a couple of miles to the southeast, and no shells were striking anywhere near them. Nor was a German patrol waiting to ambush them. They must have gone about their work, relieved. The tempest muffled any loud sounds they may have made. Lowering the weir doors proved easier than raising them: gravity helped. The water, already risen substantially on the inland side, was trapped. The work of the inundators was not over. They would have to return on following nights to complete the operation.

IN A SHELTER BEHIND THE embankment, Lt. Col. Arsène Bernard, still commanding a battalion of Chasseurs, light infantry, in the Belgian 3rd Division, had stretched out on bales of straw to catch a couple of hours of sleep. He was stationed just north of the village of Pervyse, at the eastern end of Beseler's attack. His rest was soon broken. At 4:30 on the morning of the thirtieth, he noted in his diary that he was "woken by hell-like cannon fire." Before long, the German waves were emerging from the thick mist, to crash against the last obstacle holding them back.

The laboratory of war was back at its experiments. At Pervyse, the Germans relied on a weapon seldom used until now, the grenade, probably the serrated, cast-iron "ball" variety, a lethal globe filled with explosive black powder and thrown, as most grenades would be, with the straight-arm motion of a cricketeer. They used it to clear their way across the raised tracks. Now they could begin to push forward to the village. They reached its outlying buildings. Belgian units counterattacked, driving the Germans back across the embankment and capturing 200 of them.

It was a different story up the line at Ramscappelle. Once again, the Germans hurled a profusion of grenades, soon to become the favorite weapon of close-quarters trench fighting. They got across the tracks and hauled machine guns over them. At this point, the backside of the embankment had no fire bays and traverses; the Germans were able to set up enfilade fire in both directions, cleaning up pockets of resistance. Men of the 5th Reserve Division dashed a quarter of a mile along a cobblestone road to the village church, which had a bell tower that offered a commanding view of the surrounding flatlands. They also captured a windmill and lugged heavy machine guns up the stairs, installing them in the high window openings. They hid more machine guns in houses, making frontal counterattacks all but impossible. Except for some lingering resistance in outlying buildings, which Franco-Belgian defenders clung to, Ramscappelle had fallen. The way to the French frontier and Dunkirk was opening.

A FEW MINUTES BEFORE SIX that morning, a major in the German 6th Reserve Division, opposite Pervyse, reported, "The water has risen markedly . . . All companies are standing with their feet in water and ground water is being encountered at the depth of a single spade. It is impossible for the battalion to attack." Less than three hours had passed since Geeraert, Umé, and their tiny crew had closed the North Vaart gates, blocking the seawater that had flowed in during the night. Now German officers ordered their troops outside Ramscappelle to secure whatever shelter they could and prepare to attack. The luckier of them discovered faint rises that were still above the level of the water and began to dig jumping-off trenches. In the end, their effort mattered little. "All the ditches and trenches around us were totally full of water," a *Kriegsfreiwilliger* wrote later.

Results by midmorning were mixed: setbacks balanced minor triumphs for the Germans. The III Reserve Corps could claim ownership of large segments of the embankment between Ramscappelle and Pervyse, but its accomplishment was empty if, first, reinforcements could not reach it, and second, then move forward in force. An attempted advance by the 6th Reserve Division had run into water thigh–deep that forced a retreat to firmer ground "to avoid the risk of drowning."

The Germans did have another go at Pervyse, and this time were successful. General Major von Jakobi, commander of the 11th Brigade, personally assembled assault groups that had fought their way across the embankment. Frenchmen from the 42nd Division brought them to a halt about 150 feet from the village. The Germans rose up for a final dash and, thrusting bayonets and swinging rifle butts, swept across the main square—the same place where, in the midst of a barrage, General Grossetti had installed himself on his famous camp chair. "At 10:00," Bernard scribbled in his journal, "we are given the order to retake Pervyse, which the Germans have penetrated. Therefore they have passed the railroad tracks." The German stay in Pervyse was brief: they didn't have the men to hold it, and the water rising to their rear threatened to cut them off.

At Falkenhayn's headquarters, in Mézières-Charleville, a captain named Otto Schwink tried to make sense of what was happening 175 miles away, and his assessment of reports coming in was grim at best. Hauptmann Schwink may have been as well informed as frontline commanders. This was one of those cases, all too numerous, in the Great War, in which the closer you were to the action the less you knew. The communications problem could work both ways. Schwink's starting point was 11:30 A.M. By then, the embankment attack may have been doomed, "owing to the constant rising of the water. . . . On the morning of the 30th the advancing troops had been up to their ankles in water; then it had gradually risen until they were now wading up to their knees, and they could scarcely drag their feet out of the clay soil . . ." Schwink's first reaction was to blame the torrential rains of recent days on the coast, and hope that, "on the approach of dry weather," the excellent system of canals "would soon drain off" the water overload. At that point, progress southward could continue.

But as reports of the rapidly disappearing landscape continued to arrive, Schwink began to suspect that man and not nature was responsible. The distant collator of disturbing news could almost have been there himself. "The rising flood soon prevented movement of wagons . . . the green meadows were covered with dirty, yellowish water, and the general

The panorama above, taken from a ruined tower in Nieuport in May 1915, shows the inundation from the Belgian side. Its brackish waters lap against the railway embankment that, after a bend (right foreground), ran without a twist or a kink before making a final veer into Dixmude. Call it a Roman Road of the Industrial Revolution. Up to

line of roads was only indicated by houses and rows of partly covered trees. It soon became evident that the enemy must have blown up the canal sluices and called the sea to his aid."

The Germans never seemed to imagine, at least in the early days of the inundation, that the source of their troubles resided in the Goose Foot, an easy march from their lines north of Nieuport. Once the Germans had secured it, they could have lifted the weir gates at normal hours, thus reversing the inundation. They never did.

Falkenhayn's reaction to these reports could not have been a happy one, and, to make matters worse, the kaiser would be showing up in Flanders the next day, October 31, obviously prepared to preside over a great victory. Everything now depended on Fabeck.

Railway to Dixmude

three miles separated the opposing lines, the widest no-man's-land of the Western Front, where a nasty clandestine war was waged over islets and tufts of dry ground that both sides turned into, forward observation posts. (Imperial War Museum First World War Panoramas Collection)

EVEN THOUGH THEY MAY HAVE caught glimpses of the blocking of the underpasses through the embankment and wondered what the work was about, many French and Belgian troops were just as surprised as the Germans. In the fields south of Ramscappelle and Pervyse, they re-formed and waited for fresh lines of attackers to emerge from village streets. None appeared. At one in the afternoon, an order came for Bernard's Chasseur battalion to probe Pervyse. "The enemy has fallen back because of the inundation." It was Bernard's first mention of the word. Albert's secret had been well kept. Bernard's battalion entered Pervyse unopposed. "The smell is putrid with so many dead animals. We find numerous German corpses and also the wounded, most of them lightly so, whom we take prisoner.

"18 h. I learn that the inundation forms a veritable lake and that the German offensive against us is definitely checked."

The inundation had taken effect not a moment too soon. You must not imagine that Geeraert and Umé released an immediate floodlike deluge on the Yser plain, an expanding torrent that rooted trees from the riverbanks, broke apart dikes in an irresistible sweep, carrying away houses and men. It was nothing so dramatic. To quote a contemporary account, the inundation was, in the beginning, "almost imperceptible, quiet, measured, a gradual advance of water that was silent, insinuating, cunning, with tiny wavelets, a gentle but all-powerful slowness, leveling under its stagnant uniformity the conquered territory. What hundreds and hundreds of years had done, a few days sufficed to undo . . ." Slowly saltwater mixed with fresh. At first the desperate agitation of freshwater fish—the trout, carp, and pike, which inhabited the canals, drainage ditches, and side streams—was the only indication that something out of the ordinary was happening. The fish dove and flipped and swam in frenzied circles. "*De visch doolt*," as the locals might put it: the fish are panicking. They sensed the salt. And, indeed, saltwater was taking over. The sea was recovering land that had once belonged to it, and the fish were the first victims.

Another sight was just as uncanny. Flemish novelist Stefan Hertmans, basing his narrative on notes left by his grandfather, a Belgian Army veteran, described how "a mass of dogs, cats, polecats, weasels, rats, and rabbits" swam across the flooding landscape, "like an otherworldly army, their snouts just above water." Starving men "had strict orders not to shoot at the fleeing animals, because that would betray our position. So we looked on as those sharp-nosed messengers from a doomed world . . . came on land, shook the water out of their pelts, and rushed past our trenches . . . bounding over the slick black fields of mud in the drab morning light."

AS THE HOURS PASSED, THE meadows turned increasingly boggy. The inundation was, in the grandiose but accurate words of a French general's account, "invincible and implacable in its slow progress. It stretched as an immense sheet of water, slightly undulating . . . It came noiselessly, filling the canals, leveling the ditches, the roads, and the shell holes. It glided, slipped, oozed everywhere. It was a silent conqueror at first scarcely visible. The water surrounded islets of rising ground, whence groups of soldiers fled drenched to the knees. It murmured patiently along the trenches, it came from the horizon and reached the horizon."

"A silent conqueror." It couldn't have been better put.

Some Germans remained high, and relatively dry, on the embankment, waiting to move forward the next morning, October 31. A substantial number still occupied parts of Ramscappelle. Others must have panicked as they felt the ground disappear under them. Soon it was all the Germans could do to retreat to the safety of the Yser right bank. Guns sank in the mud and had to be abandoned. The water hid ditches and creeks, into which men plunged over their heads; some undoubtedly drowned. From ruined farms they scrounged planks and laid them side by side over ditches to make improvised bridges. The rising water cut off others dug in before the embankment. They surrendered. The advancing water swept over the isolated wounded too weak to move; others died of exposure. The dead of three nations left their bones scattered everywhere in that submerged landscape.

In the early hours of the morning of the thirty-first, battalion commanders of the III Reserve Corps met to decide their options. There was only one: retire. Shortly after, Beseler, the victor of Antwerp, ordered a general withdrawal across the river. The historian of Reserve Infantry Regiment 48 later remarked that it was with chattering teeth that the men listened as the order to withdraw was read out. A rear guard, which kept up a patter of small-arms fire, covered remnants of the regiment as they retreated toward the river. The men marched in single file through knee-deep water, carrying weapons and ammunition as well as their wounded and the bodies of the dead. The regiment had lost 103 killed and almost 500 wounded on the Yser front, or about 20 percent of the 3,000-man force that had gone into battle two weeks earlier. There was no denying that all their sacrifice had been for nothing.

The Germans only suspected the true cause of the inundation. They made no further attempts to seize the Nieuport hydraulic system; the full force of their offensive was directed now at Ypres. Ypres may well have been granted a reprieve because of the Yser. But for Albert's decision to inundate, the town might have been taken from the rear in the next few days. What if the inundation hadn't worked? Once Beseler's divisions had broken into the open and headed for Dunkirk, they could, and would, have sent out overland probes toward the east, to meet Fabeck's coastward push. Should one succeed, so, no doubt, would the other.

The Allies, pincered, would then be faced with an unenviable dilemma. Should they try to save Dunkirk or Ypres? At this point, both might be beyond saving—even though, as German air observation revealed, the French were already far along in preparations for inundating the marshy lowlands around the port. The biggest dilemma of all might have been how to rescue the thousands now fighting for Ypres. Would Sir John French have had time to construct his armed camp at Boulogne? And even if he had, could the fugitive divisions have reached it? Forget Albert's desire to hold on to a small corner of his nation, another of the truly substantive issues the battle on the Yser would settle. That hope would probably have been trampled underfoot in the rush to retreat across a by-now meaningless border.

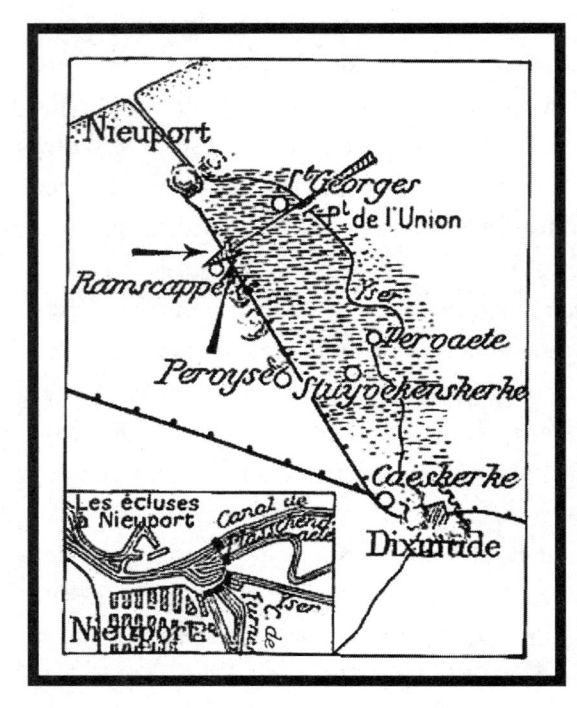

The initial inundation of the Yser River, from Nieuport to Dixmude, shown on the French Michelin Guide to the battlefields of the Yser, was almost nine miles long and three at its widest. The inundation was broken up into islands, some contested in clandestine small actions. (The inundation was later extended to the east and south.) The Nieuport floodgates appear in an inset, crossings designated in black as *les écluses*, better known locally as the Goose Foot.

A Belgian officer stands by a road disappearing into a huge man-made lagoon. The road led out of Pervyse, halfway along the embankment at a spot that the Germans had breached, sweeping into the same square where Grossetti had installed himself on his camp chair. They were about to push on when they recognized that rising waters in their rear were about to cut them off. (Imperial War Museum)

If this sounds like the stuff of fantasy, only remember: a similar evacuation happened here twenty-six years later, with the same opponents in the next continental war.

ON THE NIGHT OF OCTOBER 30–31, and the two nights following, Geeraert, Umé, and their small crew of pontoneers went back to work. By the time they were done, they had created an artificial lagoon extending from Nieuport almost to Dixmude and from the embankment to the Yser—almost nine miles long by three miles wide. At its maximum, it would be the widest separation of the two sides on the Western Front. The area underwater varied from three to ten feet in depth. There were, to be sure, sizeable patches not underwater, but they were mostly impassable marsh. What had once been an estuary of the sea had reverted to its original state.

Gunfire subsided, as did the frenzied plopping leaps of doomed freshwater fish. The land animals disappeared, and so had the Germans.

An eerie silence enveloped the new miles of stagnant ocean water returned after a millennium. When the mists rose, men standing on the embankment could look across a dead sea to the German shore—you could no longer talk about the "banks" of the Yser. Fenceposts and the tops of pollarded willows poked up, as forlorn as the gutted walls of drowned farms; an occasional burned-out church tower cast its distended, shadowy reflection over the waters. Muddy roads that disappeared into the lagoon seemed already annealed to it. Beyond, and out of reach for the duration, stood empty carts, faint waves lapping at their axles. The light caught the dull white of fish bellies, and half-starved men scooped up the first sacrifices of the inundation while they were still relatively fresh. Bodies, human and animal, floated amid a flotsam of leather helmets, knapsacks, and cartridge boxes. Bloated corpses rising to the surface marked the line of yesterday's trenches.

Belgian engineers and a determined alcoholic boatman had slammed shut an unexpected door. In a series of bloodless night operations, they had sealed for good nearly a quarter of Falkenhayn's great arc of fire. A man and a moment had come together: few of us are so fortunate. Hendrik Geeraert had allowed Albert to win the only victory he needed to win. He had kept his corner of his country.*

---

* The Belgian king, in private, was not always the Albert of Sunnybrook Farm that his public face led the Allied world to believe in. The interests of his small nation took precedence, and his stubborn refusal to be pushed around by France and Great Britain at times became an obsession. Belgium never did officially join the Allies. Albert chose instead to remain an "Associated" power and took pains not to be drawn into the sanguinary adventures of his major partners. He refused to increase the size of his army, out of a fear that the Allied generals would manage to divert the added new recruits into yet more offensive debacles.

He flirted with the notion of proclaiming Belgium neutral and leaving the war. Discrete approaches were made to the German government. Albert chose his German wife Elizabeth's brother-in-law as his go-between. Four meetings took place in Switzerland. The Germans proved heavy-handed. They insisted on "real guarantees" that Albert would abandon the Entente. Neutrality, the king soon came to see, meant becoming a German protectorate. Their negotiators flashed their chips of power too brazenly: his chief bargainer simply walked away from the table.

But, in fact, all the major powers were trying to strike deals with their opponents, in desperate secret efforts to secure some form of truce. Agreement eluded them. Hidden meetings continued through 1916. In the end they accomplished nothing. Albert, too, gave up. In the fall of 1918, it was his troops who took Dixmude, Passchendaele, Roulers, and Bruges, names that had grown too familiar.

18

The Gap

ON OCTOBER 30, OBERST—COLONEL—MARTIN VON OLDERSHAUSEN, THE deputy sector commander of the 54th Reserve Division and a freiherr (baron), called a meeting of all the regimental and battalion commanders of the division, plus their aides. Commanders like Oldershausen were no doubt aware of the events on the Yser earlier that day, as well as the ominous circumstance of newly blocked access to the Channel ports, increasing the urgency of Group Fabeck's drives on Gheluvelt and the Messines Ridge. Time would be needed to shift the better part of Beseler's divisions south, probably to make a direct thrust at Dixmude, one of the possible, but now dwindling, breakthrough opportunities.

It must have been close to midnight when they gathered in the village of Kruiseecke, captured from the British just four days earlier and now little more than a row of holed and shattered cottages along a dirt track leading to the Menin Road. Somehow Oldershausen's staff managed to find an undamaged room large enough to hold twenty to thirty officers, a space tightly packed with large men in bulky greatcoats. There must have been light enough—candles, probably—to illuminate maps tacked to walls. Cigarettes and pipes glowed in the murk. Everyone there had been leading men in battle for hours without a break and would for hours more. For both sides, extreme fatigue was the unspoken ingredient of the day that followed, and we must allow for its distortions.*

---

* The meeting described in this remarkable document is based on the eyewitness account in *Vier Jahre Westfront: Geschichte des Regiments List R.I.R. 16 (Four Years on the Western*

"Gentlemen, are we all present?" the Oberst began. "Then please pay attention! What is our current situation? . . . Good! . . . The assault on Gheluvelt will begin at dawn . . ."

There was, reports the eyewitness who recorded the scene, "noticeable movement in the back rows." The Oberst interrupted, "Do you gentlemen have something to say?"

The temporary commander of the 1st Battalion of the List Regiment, Hauptmann Franz Rubenbauer, spoke up. "Excuse me, Herr Oberst. The word 'battalions' has been mentioned. We in the center no longer have a battalion: scarcely a recognizable company." He went on, pointing out that his men had been in combat for forty-eight hours. Worse, none of them had slept for three nights. "I regard it as impossible to conduct a purely infantry assault against the strongly dug in British positions successfully unless it has been proceeded by really heavy artillery preparation."

The Oberst broke in. "Do you say impossible? There is no such thing as impossible! We are all soldiers and must accept the risk! . . . Are you saying that the Bavarians are not willing to attack?"

At this point, words grew heated. "That has nothing to do with it!" the captain replied. "But my responsibility to my troops . . ."

"You talk of responsibility?" the Oberst exclaimed. "Well, just calm down—you do not have any such responsibility! When an order is given the responsibility lies with he who gives it—and who will know how to

---

Front: The History of the List Reserve Infantry Regiment 16, by Dr. Fridolin Solleder. (It was a Bavarian custom to call new regiments by the surname of their original commander.) I have adapted this account from material in *The German Army at Ypres 1914,* by Jack Sheldon. Few works have done a more important service for the history of the Great War on the Western Front than Sheldon's pioneering series, with their translations of German memoirs, letters, diaries, regimental histories, and unpublished documents—compilations in English that never before existed. At a recent count, there are seven in print, with more presumably on the way. To this exemplary list we must add the books Sheldon has written with Nigel Cave, the editor of the Pen & Sword Battleground Europe paperbacks, including three essential volumes on the First Ypres. Only in recent years has it been adequately possible to follow the war from both sides. I would add the names of Holger H. Herwig, Hew Strachan, Dennis E. Showalter, Jörn Leonhard, Holger Afflerbach, Annika Mombauer, and Alexander Watson, among others. The list is still too short.

shoulder it. Your sole responsibility is to ensure that the order is carried out correctly!"

Oberst Julius List, commander of the Bavarian Reserve Infantry Regiment 16, stood up. List was a big man with huge shoulders: even seated, he was half a head taller than his fellow officers. At forty-nine, his distinctly bushy mustache was starting to grow gray. List cared for his men: their inexperience disturbed this consummate professional. But he was also realist enough to recognize that Bavarian authorities had scant regard for his cobbled-together voluntary regiment.

"If I may add a word," he began. "I too am of the opinion that a simple infantry attack conducted against such a cunning, intelligent and strongly dug in enemy will either fail or simply lead to bloody sacrifice of immense proportions." Like Hauptmann Rubenbauer, he was convinced that the attack could only succeed if backed by heavy artillery. It should hold back until German guns could soften up the enemy. "Otherwise, what remains of my regiment will be lost as well."

Oldershausen refused to back down. Too much was riding on the success of the next morning's drive now that the inundation had preempted their master plan.

"A delay in the attack is out of the question. Gheluvelt must fall tomorrow! Those are the orders. We have our duty to do! What will be, will be! There is no time to be lost."

The commander of the local battle group, Oberst von Bendler, now stepped forward. He pointed to a sketch of the front, with the Menin Road running through it, and in a clipped voice began to speak.

"Orders for the attack on 31 October . . ."

The meeting adjourned. You can only hope that List and Bendler, when they returned to their respective headquarters dugouts, got some rest on this, the last night of their lives.

JUST A HANDFUL OF MINUTES remained before the start of Saturday, October 31, a day that would be like no other in the war. The Germans had every reason to feel confident: the momentum of battle, as undeniable as it is indescribable, had clearly passed to them. On the other side of the line, Douglas Haig wrote that he was "full of anxiety." If he felt apprehensive, he did so with good reason. The Allied operational predicament was not an enviable one. The Yser inundation may have ended the German coastal threat but, as British military historian John Hussey points out, it "also liberated German forces for re-deployment elsewhere in the battles." Admiral Ronarc'h's French Marines still held Dixmude, but a German breakout there could open another route to Dunkirk. "The French," Hussey continues, "were gamely but unavailingly trying to carry out Foch's orders to carry the high ground north-east of Ypres." The number of men they had lost there more than canceled out the small gains they had made.

Haig's I Corps was dug in on both sides of Gheluvelt and the Menin Road that ran through the village, just four miles from Ypres. There was no polite way around it: the British were on the ropes, their wounded little army diminished dangerously in size, short not just of riflemen but of leaders at every level. If the Germans took Gheluvelt and swept over the ridge, no amount of puttying up could stop their downhill drive to Ypres. You sometimes wonder what went on in Haig's tightly shuttered mind at moments like this. Even his journals and his letters give little clue. To judge by them, imagination was not his strong suit. Order was— and, too, the ability to sidestep surprises and keep moving methodically forward. You rather suspect that he didn't allow himself more than a glancing recollection of the panicked, beaten men streaming back from Kruiseecke. Whatever, he was determined that his corps avoid a repeat of that scene.

Imagination was the commodity the German leadership needed most—imagination and nerve. Their divisions, obedient to a fault, were so close now to breaking through. Could Army Group Fabeck present Ypres to the kaiser in the next days? Intercepted messages told the British that the All Highest was somewhere out there, waiting.

The importance of the next hours cannot be overestimated. One British regimental historian called October 31 the "supremely critical day of the whole war." "The worst crisis of the whole struggle," was Liddell Hart's evaluation. "The line that stood between the British

Empire and ruin was composed of tired, haggard and unshaven men, unwashed, plastered with mud, many in little more than rags." Those words of Brig. Gen. James E. Edmonds, the British official historian, may now seem a bit over the top, but a century ago, when there still was an empire, his claim seemed perfectly sound.

The French felt less threatened, though General Dubois did call the situation of his British neighbors "altogether disturbing." He described them as approaching the day "shaken." Foch, too, was well aware of the potential for advantage-changing dislocation.

Trucks move German infantry to the front, in a photo taken in Flanders in 1914. This could have been the approach of reinforcements in the offensive by Army Group Fabeck—though much of the troop movement would have taken place at night. Mechanized transport of men had become normal, as it was not in the original summer sweep. The Germans had learned a lesson. (Windmill/Robert Hunt Library/UIG/Bridgeman Images)

October 31 was the twelfth day of the German battering ram, and there was every chance that at some contested point, an essential portion of the remaining arc from Dixmude to Armentières, which the inundation had now shortened, would come off its hinges. There seemed no bit of Salient earth that, for the defenders, did not have backs-to-the-wall potential. One big change had taken place, and it had little to do with territory acquired or relinquished, but with which of the three defending armies controlled it. Blue lines were spreading across the map, replacing much of the brown of Belgium and the red of Great Britain. On the Allied side, the First Ypres was becoming a French battle.

That French connection has too seldom been properly recognized. The First Ypres, Hussey has written, "has such resonance in British ears as the final sacrifice of the Old Army that we often forget to what extent it was a French battle." The British, he adds, "were seen as junior partners at Ypres, and unhelpful and sometimes doubtful partners at that." Even more than the Marne, this was a "coalition battle" that featured the exchange of reserves at crucial moments, inter-Allied understanding and cooperation (or at least its uncertain beginnings), and mutually dependent decision-making.

Largely overlooked in accounts of that day are what we might call the "Bookends of Battle"—savage, small encounters at either end of the line, brackets framing and supporting weightier events. They may have counted for little in an overall assessment of October 31, but they did show an unfortunate tendency of generals on both sides to throw away lives. Demonstrations deliberately designed to prevent the enemy from sending reserves to more threatened sectors were notable life-wasters: they rarely achieved their purpose. With them, the broad-front concept had reached a nadir. On the Western Front, it should be noted, German commanders tended to be even more uninspired, even more profligate, than their Allied counterparts, who usually take the blame for attritional mismanagement. At this stage in the battle, everyone was a little bit guilty. Poelcappelle was a case in point.

D'Urbal and, to a lesser extent, Foch refused to surrender their Poelcappelle obsession: its capture, they maintained, was the sure way to Passchendaele and, beyond it, Roulers. Dubois went along with them, reluctantly; he had little choice. D'Urbal was already annoyed with him for transferring troops to the British. Closer to the line, Dubois recognized how fought-out his men were and what enormous losses they had suffered. He was especially worried about the growing shortage of officers in his IX Corps. "Just yesterday," he wrote in his daily IX Corps report to d'Urbal on the night of October 31, "a battalion commander was killed, and another wounded . . .":

> In the 90th Regiment, yesterday evening, one battalion had only two officers present (one of them a reservist) . . .
> I have exhausted all my officer resources, and at the moment have only a single Lieutenant worthy of being promoted to captain.

He put in an urgent request for replacements: 55 captains and 130 lieutenants, he suggested hopefully. And then, in a footnote, he added that if he couldn't find capable infantrymen, he would even be willing to accept officers from the cavalry. Out of the mouth of an infantry general, the word "cavalry" was tainted with disdain.

IN A *POSTE DE SECOURS* at Pilckem, Dr. Nel, toiling to patch up the detritus of a raid—one of those nasty, small combats within a greater one—took a break to write in his journal: "The gloomy days that we are living through appear to be endless. Since we have been here, we have not advanced a step; the rows of enemy breastworks seem as fixed and as unbreachable as permanent walls. Numberless victims lie before them . . ."

THE GERMAN DETERMINATION TO TAKE and finally hold all of Bixschoote, nearby the canal, matched the French obsession with Poelcappelle. Two divisions of the XXIII Reserve Corps had laid siege to the village on the thirtieth, but without result; they returned to the attack on the thirty-first. Once more, their advance stalled. It was not yet 9 A.M. An order came down: try again. Casualties grew. Finally, one regiment, Reserve Infantry Regiment 211, made a lodgment in the smoking ruins. You marvel at the ardor of those men. The regiment, or its remnants, managed to hold out until the following night, November 1, when the French counterattacked and drove it out. Only one officer, a Hauptmann Brauchitsch, survived; his battalion was disbanded. RIR 211 had lost 24 officers and 674 other ranks, close to half of an already depleted regiment, a high price to pay for a diversion. That was the kind of struggle the First Ypres was becoming.

TO THE SOUTH, TWENTY-EIGHT MILES away, on the Lys end of the battle, men of both sides were having similar experiences, mixing blind courage with futility at another lethal bookend. In a little valley at the foot of Messines Ridge, the German Guard Cavalry Division (dismounted) rushed a local landmark known as Douve Farm, after the long brook that ran nearby. The Germans designed these attacks, too, to anchor the end of the line, protecting the more important actions on the ridge. (To the right of the dismounted cavalrymen, the German 26th Division was aiming for the village of Messines itself.) An officer who survived—there weren't many of them—described the frenzied scene that unfolded over a couple of miles of open fields, hedgerows, and farms with their garnish of barnyard odors. The brawl would continue throughout the day, and spill into the middle of the night. The attack on Douve Farm began with an advance of Jägers, skirmishers or scouts often affiliated with cavalry, troops in dark-green uniforms who wore shakos and not the customary spiked pickelhauben:

> The enemy met the first rush of the jaegers . . . with a hail of infantry fire . . . The assault carried on with the company commander, Count Solms, at its head [this was a distinctly aristocratic group, with not a "von"-less name among its officers] and two ensigns, Barons von Heintze and von Lattendorff, beside him. Several paces onward, both ensigns were mortally wounded. Lieutenant von Winterfeld of the machine gun company had posted his guns at a window of a house, but after a few shots the gun he was personally working burst and killed everyone around. The stubborn Englishmen [they were actually Inniskilling Fusiliers, Irishmen] would not be ousted . . . [T]he Guard jaegers pushed their advance in total disregard of heavy losses.

In the late afternoon, the horizontal rays of the sun setting behind the British trenches blinded the attackers. Dead and wounded of both sides lay scattered over the beet fields. Pedigreed young commanders seemed especially vulnerable, as the democratizing bullets of the Old Contemptibles undid centuries of class dominance. Now, German pioneers came up, to cut and blow gaps in the flimsy barbed-wire defenses of the British. In 1914, that was still a relatively easy, if hardly safe, task. Those Jägers who made it through jumped into the enemy trenches. In a free-for-all, the Germans evicted the Northern Irishmen. They would be back.

It was 8 P.M. by now, "with a nearly full moon shedding a daylight brilliance." The Jägers advanced, pushing ahead through Fusilier corpses. They took shelter in shell holes and tried to keep awake by singing folk songs, "in which all joined." For recent killers, it was a homey touch. Toward 5 A.M.—All Saints Day was dawning—the exhausted men heard a sudden loud hurrah close to their left flank. Moments later, the Irishmen were on top of them. "Only a mere handful—20 men in all—met the onslaught with the last of their cartridges." Some, led by an *Unteroffizer*— a corporal—named Wolff, "cooly picked off the enemy as though engaged in the rifle range." Once again, an official account was trying to turn a defensive sow's ear into an offensive silk purse. It couldn't be done. The language of the official report may have been redolent of triumph and bold exploits, but between the lines you read only stalemate, and more potential leaders going down. The Jägers simply ran out of men.

Could there be a more telling close-up of the suicide of a continent's elite?

YPRES LIES AT THE FOOT of a thirty-mile-long crescent-shaped ridge, an arenaceous, or sandy, outcropping on a deep clay base, the so-called Ypres Bastion. Journals and memoirs of the time share a recurring metaphor: of being stranded at the bottom of a shallow soup plate, with thousands of hostile eyes and guns fastened on you. In the language of geology, the ridge is known as a cuesta. Its outer edges fall off steeply; its inner ones subside gently into the plain from a flat, wide summit. For the Germans, the approaches to villages like Gheluvelt were short but difficult, and of course affected the character of the fighting.

The taking of Messines Ridge and a breakthrough to Kemmel was, for Fabeck, the most urgent objective. The investment of Ypres, that medieval butterfly in amber, replete with memories and monuments, would be a public-relations triumph, and Fabeck was eager to prepare the kaiser's royal way to the Cloth Hall, a trophy sumptuous enough for His Majesty. But the Monts, those stepping-stones to the Channel ports, were his true goal. Once they were in his hands, with German legions spreading across the plains they overlooked, Albert's inundation would be meaningless, just another water-filled pothole on the road back to Paris.

The height of Messines Ridge averages about 250 feet, and it might have been plucked from some downland vista in the south of England. Two villages stand at either end: Wytschaete and Messines. Before Fabeck arrived to menace them, Maj. Gen. Sir Hubert Gough and his 2nd Cavalry Division had their headquarters in Messines (population 1,400), and were responsible for the three and a half miles of ridgeline. The indefatigable Paul Maze remembered the village in its final intact days:

> It was a clean little town with a grey stone Mairie facing a wide pavé square with a few poplar trees. The charming old houses with polished brass handles on the doors were very Dutch in character. Towering behind stood a great old stone church . . . Our arrival brought the villagers a false sense of security.

The shelling of Messines grew ever more intense. Gough decided to move his headquarters to a redbrick château in the village of Kemmel, at the foot of the eponymous hill. "Often as I was on the road," Maze wrote, "I saw terrified peasants coming from distant farms wheeling their belongings away. They settled in the village of Wytschaete which, already filled with our own troops, became very much overcrowded."

Rain still fell as the night of October 30–31 began. "Gun flashes were holing the darkness everywhere," Maze wrote. All along the ridge, "an alarming tumult of musketry and machine-guns" swelled into a continuous roar. On one of his information-gathering motorcycle jaunts, Maze saw double-decker omnibuses "splashing their way through to St. Eloi packed with the London Scottish." Those sitting on top, open in those days, "were sheltering under shiny dripping mackintosh sheets." They were the first Territorial infantry to arrive on the battlefield, weekend warriors who were not supposed to serve abroad, except in times of emergency like this. Before the next day was over, they would, ready or not, be pushed into the melee on Messines Ridge.

Maj. Gen. Henry Beauvoir De Lisle's 1st Cavalry Division was now responsible for the defense of the village of Messines at the south end of the ridge, with help from the King's Own Scottish Borderers (KOSB). As the night advanced, the skies began to clear, a nearly full moon shone, and temperatures rose, the clash of cold and warm air with its heavy residue of moisture producing a layer of fog that hovered near the ground— mercifully not a thick one for once. Bursting shells mimicked the stars.

Fabeck's medium and heavy artillery had finally arrived, but too late to do more than passing damage to the thick walls of Messines before the infantry attacked: knowing that dismounted cavalry mostly held the village, he threw in an entire infantry division, the 26th, to fight with the 4,000 cavalrymen and Jägers already in action. That seemed a simple, if unsubtle, way to shorten his odds. By the night of the thirtieth/ thirty-first, the Germans lurking just beneath the ridge crest outnumbered the defenders by a ratio of 6 to 1, approximately 6,000 troops to 1,000, and probably more. Fabeck's lines were now only three or four hundred yards from the village, a not–impossible dash up an easy gradient.

Gough and De Lisle were in immediate charge; but the true rock of the ridge was the commander of the cavalry corps, Lt. Gen. Edmund Allenby. "The Bull," as this imposing figure with his capacious jaw was known, was six foot two inches tall—he was another general who towered over Sir John French—with a barrel chest and a famously furious temper. Whenever Allenby was about to make an appearance, a message in code, BBL, would go out from headquarters—"Bloody Bull's Loose." Gough, no admirer, felt that Allenby's mask of truculence concealed a personality insecure about his leadership abilities, ever afraid that he was out of his depth. Insecure he may have been, but at Messines Allenby proved himself a tenacious defender. He visited his forward units constantly and possessed (as a biographer would write) "an instinct for the 'sore spots' in his line." It didn't hurt, either, that he respected the fighting abilities of his German adversaries. "The men come on like lions," he said. But he maintained an unbroken line until French relief came. That was accomplishment enough.

A SEE-SAWING WILDNESS CHARACTERIZED THE events of the next hours. Close combat induces its own special form of hysteria. Shelling from German 8-inch howitzers countered by sniper fire from defenders dug in close to the village walls of Messines went on all night. Death or wounding were the only escapes. At 1:45 A.M. on October 31, units of the 26th Division attacked. German commanders thought that action in the dark might negate the deadly BEF rifle fire. But the rising moon provided illumination just short of daylight, as well as a multitude of targets. Indian troops still manned the southern approaches to the village, and some Germans tried to disguise themselves by donning turbans. The clumsy, racist ruse failed. Cheering and blowing horns, the 199th Grenadier Regiment stormed the southeastern street entrances to Messines. The British poured fire from loopholes and concealed trenches. Other Germans reached a trench beyond the eastern walls held by the 5th Dragoons. The dismounted cavalrymen bayoneted or shot most of them.

At 9 A.M., the 26th Division was back on the attack. Fabeck's timetable called for the capture of Messines that day, the thirty-first. Now, to prevent British reinforcements from reaching the village, Fabeck's artillery swept the ridge with shrapnel. When the mist lifted, observation balloons appeared, directing heavy artillery fire. At the same time, attackers emerged from trenches and moved ahead over broken ground, rushing across an open space one moment, crawling behind hedges and garden fences the next, searching for a hollow, a dip in the ground. Even the merest dent or shallow ditch offered momentary protection, a place to open up with screening volleys as the riflemen prepared the way for machine gunners.

Bringing the automatic weapons into the front lines was no easy task, but the results paid off. The standard Maxim Maschinengewehr 08—or, simply, MG08—had a legendary killing potential. Getting it in place was the problem. The MG08 was heavy and could be hard to assemble, especially under fire. Its water-cooled barrel weighed 49 pounds; the barrel had to be locked onto a four-legged, quadrupedal mount, or "sled," another 77 pounds, a total of 126. Four-man crews brought up each gun and its sled, hefting the disassembled component as they would a body on a stretcher. Two other men carried boxes crammed with ammunition belts as well as water cans: more pounds. A highly trained NCO commanded the Maxim crew, scanning bullet strikes with binoculars and calling for corrections.

The crews had to find places where exposure was minimal, places where they could set up their weapons and avoid being found out. Once established, the MG08s could shoot off between four hundred and five hundred rounds per minute; at a distance of up to a mile and a half, they were as accurate as a rifle. It has been said that Maxims killed more men than any weapon in history, except perhaps for the sword. The Maxims needed less than a century for that singular achievement; the sword, millennia. It was hardly a surprise that the guns came to be known as "Grim Reapers."*

THE GERMAN 125TH REGIMENT WAS the first unit to penetrate Messines. That happened at about 10 A.M., when it forced its way past a barrier on the road to Comines and pushed into the northeast corner of the village. Meanwhile, platoons probed street exits and stormed outlying houses. They did so, said one young German officer, "in the face of lacerating fire, which tore holes in their ranks." The British counterattacked, but were, he noted, "sent

---

* Lighter automatic weapons were soon devised. The MG08 was, however, ideal for stationary trench warfare, and the Germans made it a murderous fixture of the next years. It is remarkable how many of these characteristic enforcers of the Great War stalemate originated as American designs, Maxims, Hotchkisses, Lewises—and, of course, the grandfather of automatic weapons, the Gatling. Gun culture, in its many permutations, has always come naturally to the citizens of the United States.

home with bloody heads." Amid falling bricks and clouds of mortar, a house-to-house struggle began: late in the morning, German gunners dragged a field gun into a street at the north end of Messines. It proceeded to blast away at individual buildings held by Beauvoir De Lisle's 1st Cavalry Division. The Germans brought up more field and machine guns. Pioneers joined them, setting demolitions charges. The outcome, wrote one British regimental historian, "hung by a hair."

The official chronicler of the KOSB left a harrowing description of the clash within the walls of Messines:

> It was desperate, close fighting. Sometimes only 50 yards or less separated the foes. House-to-house fighting is as difficult to describe as it is to conduct . . . In that most nerve-stretching, surprising type of warfare, where death may threaten from above, below, at the side, and even from behind, the K.O.S.B. took the convent and cleaned out the houses near the church.

As Belgian soldiers mill around gawking, the flotsam of Albert's "supreme maneuver," captured Germans, trapped by the Inundation, wait to be marched off to prisoner's pens. The scene is the main square of Furnes, General Headquarters of the king's little army. Not a couple of days before, these same POWs were poised to break through to Dunkirk and the other Channel ports. (*L'Illustration*)

By 4 P.M. Messines had been sliced in two, the lines running from north to south, with the church square a no-man's-land, the British holding one side and the Germans the other. The battle ended for the day. Messines burned uncontrollably. Now action shifted to the other, and slightly larger, ridge village, Wytschaete.

By nightfall Fabeck was behind in his timetable, but the delay was not fatal. Perhaps it could be recouped in the next hours.

SIX-ODD MILES AWAY, ON THE brief but steep slopes of the cuesta below Gheluvelt, Hauptmann Franz Rubenbauer, preparing a dawn attack, had little time for sleep. The temporary commander of the 1st Battalion (Private Hitler's) of the Bavarian Reserve Regiment 16, he had taken over after Maj. Julius Graf von Zech auf Neuhofen, the aristocratic onetime governor of the West African colony of Togo, had been killed by a bullet to the head. Midnight was long past by the time the final orders for the attack reached him. About 2 A.M., just as the List Regiment was taking its place in the line, the moon disappeared behind clouds. The darkness did not become total. The nearby village of Beselare blazed, as did numberless haystacks. Rain fell—one of those intermittent squalls to which this corner of the world is prone—and then, just as quickly, the skies cleared. But the brief drenching had been so intense that trenches and parapets turned into wet, clinging, rifle-clogging clay.

Shortly before dawn, a barrage began to scour the ten and a half miles of Salient front left to the British. The German guns reduced Gheluvelt to ruins, but so far hardly touched the château. Just to the south of the Menin Road, the 16th Bavarian Reserve Regiment attacked behind only the briefest of preliminary bombardments—just what its commander, List, had openly feared. Hauptmann Rubenbauer waxed grandiose nonetheless: "Surging forward from the dense hedgerows and up the slope, the lines of infantrymen . . . worked their way in bounds, wave after wave." Fog hugged the ground, but not enough to screen the German advance; British rifles took their predictable toll. Shrapnel fell "like iron rain." The surge slowed to a trickle. Once again, the attack floundered around the windmill on the Gheluvelt ridgeline.

The day had scarcely begun, and already the Germans found themselves repulsed everywhere, taking heavy casualties. The failure of those first German infantry attacks was intolerable on high, and Deimling's XV Corps headquarters ordered a resumption of the artillery barrage, which came down not just as a downpour but a deluge. "About 8 a.m. the fog cleared and there commenced a bombardment, the like of which had never before been experienced," wrote the regimental historian of the Welch. A sergeant of the 1st Queen's, astride the Menin Road, called it "the worst we had ever had." The ground, he said, shook "as if we were in the middle of an earthquake."

FOR THE GERMANS, THAT EARLY lack of progress was about to change. Their shredded battalions, said the British *Official History,* "sprang up to charge with great enthusiasm, cheering and singing; for they had been warned that the Kaiser himself was present . . . weight of numbers told in the end." Consider that weight in the part of the line held by the Haig's 1st Division: five understrength battalions, perhaps a thousand men, faced thirteen battalions, six of them fresh, an advantage of 7 or 8 to 1.

A third of a mile south of the Menin Road, companies of the Surrey-based 1st Queen's Royal Regiment and the 2nd Battalion of the King's Royal Rifle Corps held an oblong salient, carved into the downward slope of the ridge. Next to the oblong, and shielding it, grew the carefully manicured oval of an orchard, manned by only two platoons. The Saxons of the 105th Infantry Regiment drove them out, establishing themselves amid neat rows of apple trees. Trenches were already there, and the Germans began extending them. Digging under fire, and such accurate fire, must have required enormous courage, but it allowed the Germans to enfilade the trenches of the Queen's, which were little more than shallow rifle pits. The Saxons could sweep the length of those pits with concentrated fire from the sides, a mass execution—what you might call the *t*-crossing maneuver of infantry warfare. They could have been beaters of an estate shooting party who had suddenly exposed a warren of hares. Without quite meaning to, they had found the key to the British line, and they began methodically to unlock it.

THE QUEEN'S AND THE KRRC held on until midmorning, when machine-gun fire started to come from two flanks, the orchard and the high bank of Menin Road. The survivors pulled back. The British line on both sides of the Menin Road was starting to disintegrate. Ammunition was running low; officers sent back two orderlies to request fresh supplies. A lieutenant J. D. Boyd reported seeing each of them "shot before they had run 20 yards." A regimental sergeant major named Elliott eventually appeared, carrying boxes of ammunition. Boyd described a remarkable feat of playacting:

> [Elliott] started back for battalion headquarters, zigzagging as he ran, and we saw him pitch on the road after going a few yards, and I was certain he was killed as he lay quite still without a move. Fortunately the Germans thought the same, and to our relief he suddenly got up and ran on under cover without another shot being fired; he had been hit in the arm when he fell but was otherwise all right. It was just about this time that battalion headquarters was set on fire by incendiary shells . . .

Chances for escape were becoming increasingly dicey. Boyd was ordered to take what was left of his platoon and head for the burning headquarters, a farmhouse. He could only muster three men, and the little group set out: Boyd and one other made it. Under cover of a hedgerow, he collected another eight men and made a dash for Gheluvelt Village. Glancing back, he saw German infantry swarming over the ridge: they must have found a gap somewhere. Boyd and his little party ducked behind a hedge and made their escape.

The Queen's was not the only battalion on the threshold of disintegration: by the end of the morning of the thirty-first, all in this sector faced that prospect. Having suffered catastrophic losses, the KRRC also fell back when it could no longer hold the Germans. It stationed a section of two machine guns on the Menin Road to cover its retreat. The hero this time was a lieutenant J.H.S. Dimmer. "Although the Germans constantly got within a few yards of his guns," a battalion war diary of the King's Royal Rifle Corps noted, "he held them at bay, and inflicted very heavy losses on them and eventually got back without losing either gun."*

How to describe the anarchy of those late morning hours, when the British line began to unravel? Eyewitness accounts only hint at the chaos and terror that seized the narrators. But they are the best records that we have. The writers were, for the most part, not especially imaginative— which may, in the end, give the stories they tell their greatest validity. They leave us with an extraordinary picture of men enduring stress beyond imagining.

Take the memories of October 31 that a former company commander, Captain T.B.S. Marshall of the 2nd Royal Welch, set down after the war. As soon as it was light, German aircraft had begun to fly over the British positions, spotting. Marshall's trench was on a forward slope, "absolutely exposed." About 8 A.M. the fog cleared and shelling started. It was like nothing Marshall or his men had ever before experienced:

> About 7:30 a.m. the German artillery started to bracket on my trench. About 7:45 a.m. they got their range, and proceeded to blow the trench to pieces.

Two things saved Marshall's company from complete annihilation— "for the time being." He had so few men that they weren't fatally packed

---

* There were few soldiers in the British Army quite so remarkable as Jack Dimmer. The son of a railway worker, he had enlisted in the KRRC in 1902, rising in rank as an NCO. He served as a scout in the Boer War and was commissioned a subaltern in 1908. The advancement of a commoner was unheard-of in a unit almost as elite as the Guards. He commanded Black troops in Africa. By the time the Great War started, Dimmer was a full lieutenant. His performance at Gheluvelt on October 31 earned him a Military Cross. Two weeks later, he upped the awards ante. Wounded five times, he again held off Germans with a machine gun: "The Huns fell in swathes," said one contemporary account. For this exploit, he won a Victoria Cross. By 1917, he was commanding a battalion of the Royal Berkshire Regiment. He had risen to lieutenant colonel. On March 21, 1918, in an action on the first day of the great German offensive on the Western Front, he led his men in a counterattack, riding a horse into battle. A bullet in the head killed him. Dimmer was a man who had made his mark saving lives by taking them.

in. And the German gunners "were so methodical and so accurate that the men in the traverses were able to bolt to the one that had just been shelled, and then back again and so on." Fire began to come from a copse on Marshall's left.

> We then found that the company which had dug in opposite to us was a machine gun company with shields in front of their guns, and their fire was so accurate and heavy that we soon lost a lot of men, and I found it impossible to fire over the parapet. We also found that there were only a dozen rifles that would fire, the remainder being either completely clogged up with clay or damaged by shell fire.

Some of Marshall's men attempted to gain what they thought was the safety of a sunken road, but as they ran across in the open, rifle bullets and shrapnel cut them down. It became clear that the enemy had somehow got behind the Welch, and established himself on the Gheluvelt ridge. Ammunition was running low. They held on.

Time, as it so often did that fall, was playing tricks: seconds, minutes speeded up and then stood still. Was it 9:30 A.M. or was it already 11? Lives dangled in the intervals. At the eastern end of the sunken road held by D Company of the 2nd Welch—the battalion controlled perhaps six hundred yards of the line—the company commander, Capt. Hubert Rees, tried to rally the remainder of his scattered little force. It wasn't easy. Men carried in a badly wounded lieutenant named Allan Young. Rees crawled to the end of to see whether he could retrieve any of Young's other men, "who were now in a hopeless situation." He had "a good view of their trench 50 yards off":

> There was a partially dug communication trench, only a couple of feet deep, between the end of the sunk lane and them. A number of men were trying to run across this 50 yards to the sunk lane, instead of crawling up this trench. I shouted to them to try the trench, but no voice could be heard in the uproar. About 25 men attempted the run, but not a single man got more than

halfway and they seemed to me to be all killed outright. It was useless waiting . . .

Miscommunication heightened the chaos. The commander of the 2nd Welch, Lt. Col. C. B. Morland, warned a nearby battalion, the South Wales Borderers, that the attack had forced his troops to retire. It may have been a slight retirement, but it was a retirement nonetheless. British rifles could no longer compete with German numbers. Morland sent a runner to inform the Queen's of his intention; the runner was never seen again. Did he run into Germans on the orchard? Whatever happened, word did not reach the Queen's on his right until too late. The Welch withdrawal to the top of the ridge exposed the left flank of the Queen's. Now German artillery began tearing into the windmill at the top of the ridge, the high wooden structure that had held up the advance for two days. Shattered by direct hits, it folded in a smoky roar of collapsing beams, boards, stucco, and blades. The destruction of the mill proved a turning point. The last stronghold blocking the way to the village had literally fallen. Three battalions of the German 30th Division began cautiously to probe the opening, fighting their way, building by building, along the Menin Road. The time was 11:15 A.M.

It was apparent that the Germans had opened a gap on both sides of the Menin Road. Maj. Gen. Herman Landon, commanding the 3rd Brigade of the 1st Division, rounded up a company of the 1st Gloucestershire Regiment, about 80 men, and dispatched it to plug the hole. The company encountered "terrific shell fire," which swept away more than half its number. The survivors gathered in one of the sunken lanes so characteristic of this part of rural Belgium. A Major Gardner ordered a further advance: he decided that he could not wait for reinforcements. Within a few yards he and fifteen others were dead. Those still standing gathered in yet another stretch of sunken road and tried to fight off the Germans, who now surrounded them. They swarmed over the Gloucesters, making prisoners of the few who survived.

So it went. The Germans, by now fighting in Gheluvelt itself, blocked the retreat of a diminishing number of the Queen's. This "doomed battalion" was "surrounded and shot down from front, flank, and rear, and only two officers and twelve other ranks succeeded in escaping and rejoining the 3rd Brigade." As for Captain Marshall of the 2nd Welch, whose men had run out of ammunition, it was a matter of waiting for the inevitable attack. "All the able-bodied men in 'B' Company," he later wrote, "now fixed bayonets . . . about 11:15 a.m. Two machine guns opened fire on the trench from the top of the hill behind and after they had traversed the trench, a German officer called out in English that unless the company surrendered, firing would continue. There was no choice, and Captain Marshall and 37 survivors, wounded and unwounded, out of about 120, were captured." Nonetheless Marshall's B Company had managed to block a direct advance on Gheluvelt "for several precious hours."

Hubert Rees escaped. He found his only remaining platoon crouching on the safe side of a barricade. He took momentary shelter from the shell storm behind a house. A shell "came through a wall about 10 yards away and killed a man who was passing by. Eventually I got away with about a dozen men, four of whom were carrying Young in a mackintosh sheet." Rees managed to collect forty to fifty stragglers from his battalion. Most of Gheluvelt, he discovered, had fallen by 11:30; fighting continued, though. The church, windmill, and most of the houses were in ruins; broken glass littered the streets. "Rifle fire was very heavy. I pushed on across a valley . . . through a confused mass of men, who were hopelessly disorganized and under heavy shell fire, and lost most of my scratch command in the general confusion." For the British defenders, the situation was deteriorating rapidly. "It was touch and go," a veteran remembered, "whether the line could possibly bend any further without completely breaking." He described the scene up in front as an "awful shambles."

Rees heard his name shouted. It was Colonel Morland. The battalion, he said, had been "wiped out." They climbed down into a trench; other officers joined them. "There were now eight officers standing together in the trench. . . . It was then that a shell burst in front instantly killing Captain Moore on my left and mortally wounding Colonel Morland on my right." Rees had Morland carried off on a door, but he died before he reached an aid station.

At about 5 P.M., Captain Rees was given command of the 1st Queen's. Captains were now leading battalions. Though his force totaled just 60 men and 2 officers, it was actually the remains of two battalions: the combined strength at the beginning of that morning, he estimated, "could hardly have been less than 1,200 men."

THE GERMANS HAD TAKEN GHELUVELT completely by 1 P.M. They applied themselves to widening the gap, rolling up, one by one, units to the south of the Menin Road. The North Lancashire Regiment—the Loyals— came first. The Loyals held the line next to the ill-fated Queen's. The infantry of the German 99th Regiment (30th Division), reduced by the fighting of the day to a couple thousand men, simply ran over two British companies, 250 strong. They were widely scattered in rifle pits, each of which held a couple of men. Machine-gun fire came from all sides, and German riflemen crept in from the flanks. Eighty of the Loyals surrendered; half of them were wounded.

The Germans also pushed north, reaching the Menin Road and sweeping around Gheluvelt. Capt. James Hyndson of the Loyals described how two cobbled-together companies left their trenches and, in a counterattack, pursued advanced enemy units. "The ground all around is literally alive with bursting shells, and about a score of men are struck down as they leave their trenches." The British pushed into the village, hoping to dislodge the Germans. The streets were in flames. "German shells are bursting against the houses, throwing bricks and dust in all directions." The company commander was hit and died; Hyndson took over. They reached the center of the village but, outnumbered, could penetrate no farther. Orders somehow reached them: it was time to withdraw. "Back we go. More khaki figures are left on the ground dead and dying." They made it to their original trenches and prepared to be overwhelmed.

The Germans continued to widen the gap. It was the turn of the 2nd Royal Scots Fusiliers, and then the Bedfordshires on their right: the

German onslaught had begun to envelop what was left of the unfortunate 7th Division. Last stands were the only alternative for either unit. They intended to go under in the kind of style expected of professionals.

The long day, a little more than half done, was turning into a disaster for the British.

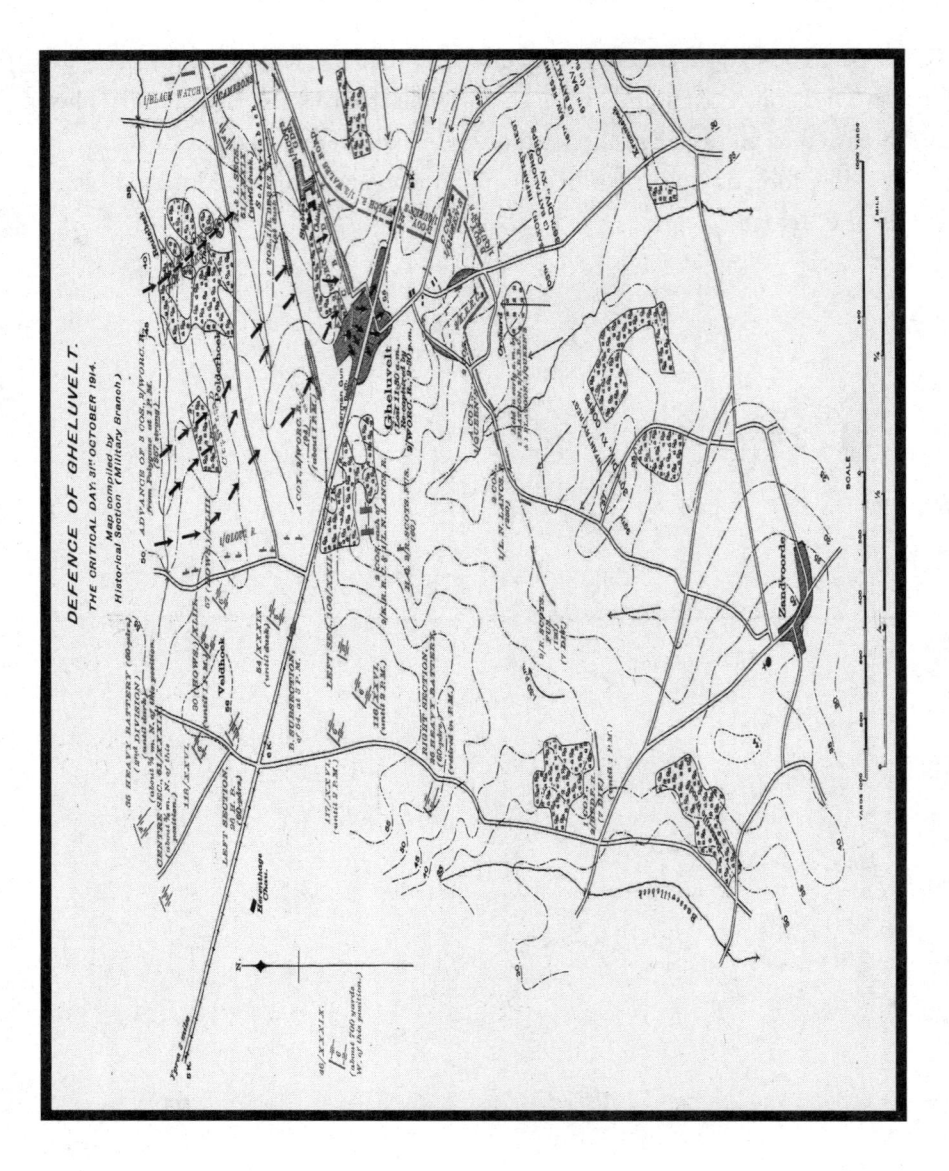

DEFENCE OF GHELUVELT.

THE CRITICAL DAY: 31ST OCTOBER 1914.

Map compiled by
Historical Section (Military Branch)

Another map from the British *Official History* records the happenings around Gheluvelt on October 31. The day began with a slow, costly, but ultimately successful German drive on both sides of the Ypres–Menin road; Gheluvelt itself fell about 11:30 A.M. The attack opened a gap of more than two miles, and British troops, many of them wounded, could be seen streaming, even running, for the safety of the rear. The Bavarian Sixteenth Reserve Regiment—Adolf Hitler's—raced across the château grounds, to take the château itself. But an exploding shell killed its commander, Julius List. Leaderless men lost direction. Then, at 1 P.M., Brigadier-General Charles FitzClarence, VC, ordered three borrowed companies, about 370 men, of the Worcestershire Regiment to counterattack. Their commander, Major E. B. Hankey, led them over a bare ridge, where German artillery caught them. Over a hundred fell in those moments, but they kept going: arrows follow their progress.

That was not the only British counterattack that afternoon. Another—not shown on this map—took place in the thick woods the British called Shrewsbury Forest, just west of the long brook (lower left), the Bassevillebeke. It was engineered by another of those mid-level officers on whom the BEF so depended, Major General Edward Bulfin, and was the last major action of a tumultuous day.

19

"Fancy Meeting You Here"

BY NOON THE GERMANS HAD OPENED A GAP JUST UNDER TWO MILES WIDE, A feat that, on the Western Front, would soon be unheard-of.

It is difficult to pinpoint when, exactly, the men holding the line first began to notice signs of an exodus for the rear. Large numbers of walking wounded, drifting back in search of aid posts, may have started it. Late in the morning, as the 1st Queen's and the 2nd KRRC began to dissolve in front of the orchard, and officer casualties mounted, they were joined by men who could walk and weren't wounded. An anonymous British soldier standing in the doorway of a Gheluvelt dressing station sensed that little time remained to escape the doomed village. "I became aware that a ghostly procession was filing down the road. They were the wounded dribbling back. Some were limping, some staggering; some hobbled with the help of a comrade's arm; I saw some even crawling. Then a few came carrying stretchers with inanimate burdens." Out in the fields men raced for their lives, dodging for cover from one peasant cottage to another amid a mounting hail of bullets. Others crumpled, struck down by dark overhead bursts of shrapnel.

The nameless soldier spotted, a few hundred yards away, gray-coated figures (mixed with a few still wearing training blue). Germans swarmed up the ridge by the hundreds, in pursuit. Men were dashing for safety, and the narrator joined them. "We ran down all those back gardens like maniacs, hurling ourselves through the hedges, with the crash of explosions on every side of us. Dimly, too, we were aware of other men running over the fields on either side of us."

He escaped to tell his tale.

A private of the Loyal North Lancashire Regiment, F. A. Bolwell, made a race for the rear that can only be described as bizarre:

> I had a run for my life that day. A chum of mine who was with us had a cock-fowl in his valise . . . He had wrung its neck but he had not quite succeeded in killing him, and, as we ran, this bird began to crow. As for myself, I had no equipment; I had run having left it in the bottom of the trench. It was quite funny as I come to think of it now—the old cock crowing as we ran, but it was really terrible at the time. We were absolutely overwhelmed . . . and had to concede nearly a thousand yards to the enemy.

Two field artillery brigades withdrew, first disassembling six guns that they would leave behind; they did the same to some 60-pounders. German shellfire chased the fugitives as explosions crept down the Menin Road toward Hooge and Haig's headquarters beyond, at the White Château, little more than a mile away from Ypres. The day was bright and observation planes were literally calling the shots.

"I was not greatly perturbed about the situation," Haig later remembered. "Of course I regarded it as serious but our troops were holding their ground as far as I then knew." He did send emissaries to check the latest developments. One was Capt. John Charteris, the head of intelligence for I Corps. A beefy, disheveled Scot who began each morning with a brandy and soda, he was not well liked. But, though inexperienced in his trade, Charteris could be sound on his day-to-day perceptions; Haig trusted his judgment. It was just after noon when Charteris returned from the front with a dismaying report:

> You cannot imagine the scene. The road was full of troops retreating, stragglers, wounded men, artillery and wagons, a horrible sight. All the time there was the noise of a terrific bombardment. It was impossible to get any clear idea of the situation. Nobody knew anything except what was happening on his immediate front and that was always the same story. The Germans were at-

tacking in overwhelming strength and our men were being driven back but fighting every inch of the way.

The bad news piled up. At about 12:30 P.M., an officer of Haig's I Corps returned from the front to report that Gheluvelt had fallen, probably about 11:30 A.M. He did add an encouraging note: men and guns were retiring in good order. There may have been confusion; there was no debacle so far. Battalions, he added, were still holding on near the Gheluvelt Château, notably elements of the 1st Queen's, the 1st South Wales Borderers, and the 1st Scots Guards. More disquieting was the word that reached Haig from the Hooge Château, where the 1st and 2nd Divisions had their joint headquarters. At 12:45 P.M. Maj. Gen. Samuel Lomax, the GOC of the 1st, spoke to the GOC of the 2nd, Charles Monro. "My line," Lomax said, "is broken." The news, relayed to Haig, "came rather as a shock."

Through the downs and ups of that day of crisis, Haig by all accounts remained calm. Perhaps he pulled at his mustache a little more than was his wont, a sure sign that he was under extreme pressure. He was not given to the violent mood swings, the palpable shows of unbuttoned emotion, of a French. Nor did he show the winning ebullience of a Foch. Let us quote at length the verdict of a later British general, Sir Anthony Farrar-Hockley. The laconic Scot was, he wrote,

> of all the commanders available in the British Expeditionary Force at that time . . . probably the officer most suited—perhaps the only one—to direct operations in front of Ypres. At times small-minded, given to criticizing faults in others of which he was himself guilty, he had nonetheless a high sense of duty, a cool head and a degree of comprehension and instinctive skill in higher tactics . . . He had now to calculate the extent to which he could hold the present corps line. There was an immense temptation to fall back.

In the situation he now faced, Haig was in his element. When it came to defensive action, he always rose to the occasion. Offense was another matter. Haig tended to overreach and underachieve. But that is not part of this story.

The British—and, for that matter, the French—had set in motion plans for a retirement that seemed, as the hours progressed, increasingly inevitable. On October 29, the first full day of the Fabeck offensive, Haig had sent out members of the I Corps Staff to explore retreat routes, especially those that avoided the potentially fatal bottleneck of Ypres. Getting across canals was a problem: north of town there were only a few bridges that would support heavy foot and vehicular traffic; south of town, and spanning the Comines Canal, almost none. The British group agreed on the digging of two lines, both of which started at Klein Zillebeke. The first, called Rice 1 after the commander of the I Corps Royal Engineers, Brig. Spring R. Rice, swung in an arc behind the front, and crossed the Menin Road above the Hooge Château. The second, Rice 2, ran closer to Ypres.

French military writers spoke disparagingly of "the English retreat." But in fact, the French were preparing two fallback lines of their own. These "successive retirement lines" (Dubois's phrase) are hardly mentioned, but late in the evening of October 30, General d'Urbal did order crews to start digging them. He also ordered the suspension of attacks by French troops in the Langemarck–Zonnebeke sector. The line closer to Ypres was to connect with Rice 2. Preparations for the retirement lines had barely started on October 31.

Haig's day began at 5:30 A.M. when he met with a French general, Moussy, who promised to contribute reinforcements. At 7:00, General d'Urbal showed up to discuss the continued digging of reserve lines and possible retirement routes. For once, he was almost pleasant. After an 8 A.M. breakfast, Haig and John Gough, Hubert's brother, "rode way beyond Hooge," Haig later noted in his diary, "and fixed upon successive positions in case of retirement being necessary." Haig decided on using the first, outer, Rice line. The two men returned to his White Château headquarters to discover that German artillery fire had hit the building; a shell splinter had killed the orderly at the front door.

The fall of Gheluvelt and the breaking of the 1st Division line convinced Haig that he could no longer delay a decision. Should he order his hard-pressed troops to stand firm, in the hope that the discipline of professionals and the persuasion of rifle fire would hold off the Germans? Or should he pull them back to Rice 1 and make a stand there? He opted for the latter. It was an alternative full of risk. Breaking cleanly away from contact with the enemy at all points would not be easy. Breaking cleanly away from contact with the enemy at all points would be easy. The British had pulled off fighting retreats at Mons and Le Cateau—battles in which he had played little or no part—but the struggle for Passchendaele Ridge was bigger and variables such as landscape more complex. Communications were the greatest problem. What if Haig's order didn't reach everyone? What if it didn't arrive in time? What if the reaction of units was piecemeal? What if the enemy was able to block the retreat?

Haig sent Brigadier Rice on horseback to carry his message to the headquarters of the 1st and 2nd Divisions, at the Hooge Château, a distance of three thousand yards. It was 2 P.M., and a ride of only fifteen minutes or so. But it was already too late. Everything had changed by then, and the order was totally out of date. The message Rice carried would never be delivered—and, in fact, there was no one to whom it could be delivered.

PUTTING THE HEADQUARTERS OF THE 1st and 2nd Divisions in one place, as Haig did, had seemed an eminently sensible idea. It would make coordination of operations easier. Haig had been using the Hooge Château, the manor house of a Baron de Vinck, a magisterial building with flat-roofed annexes at either end. An ostentatiously quaint building extending from the western annex had originally been designed to house a small artists' colony, complete with studios. Two major generals, Samuel Lomax and Charles Monro, had appropriated the many-windowed western annex with its convenient French doors. Haig had moved a mile and a half down the highway, to a bigger outpost of wealth, the tall, square White Château with its three two-story-high pillars at the entrance.

At 12:45 P.M. Major General Monro returned from the front, ready to discuss the increasingly parlous situation with Major General Lomax, GOC of the 1st Division. They had just agreed to create a new reserve for the 2nd Division by withdrawing as many men as possible from the sector that joined with the French, near Zonnebeke, halfway up the ridge. Lunch remained uneaten and was growing cold.

Neither man, nor their staffs, paid much attention to the revealing accumulation of staff cars along the drive in front of the château or the numerous horses tethered and ready to depart, carrying messengers in all directions. Once, by midday, the Germans were on top of the Gheluvelt Ridge, their advance units could clearly see the automobiles and horses gathered in front of the Hooge Château. It was obvious that the building must be a headquarters of some sort, where officers of high rank were convening. Around 1 P.M. a low-flying observation aircraft hovered over the château and confirmed suspicions. No one on the ground even bothered to take a shot at the watcher in the sky. Nor did the busy staff in the annex pay much attention; planning went on.

Then, at 1:15 P.M., a shell exploded in the garden next to the western annex. Those in the room rushed to the French doors to see what damage had been done, and whether it was just a stray shot. No one bothered to dodge behind a wall that might protect them. Monro, deliberately unconcerned, retreated to an inner room to dig out a map. A moment later, another shell, probably a 5.9, struck a windowsill and exploded. Jagged pieces of metal ripped through the room. Splinters hit, and gashed, and embedded themselves in Lomax's body. Five staff officers were killed outright, another mortally wounded. Monro and his chief of staff were knocked unconscious but were otherwise unhurt, winners of the lottery. A third shell smashed through the roof of the annex, filling the rooms with smoke, dust, and falling plaster. This time no one was hurt.

Moments after the shells hit, a 2nd Division staff officer viewed the carnage. "The killed," he later wrote, "were all instantaneously killed I judged. Trench had no sign of suffering on his face. Little trace of Percival. Trench still breathing when I returned . . ." Medical officers immediately moved Lomax; within a few days he was in a sanitarium in London. He remained there until April, when he died.

For four crucial hours, it was as though the heads of two divisions and significant parts of their limbs had been severed. Haig wanted Bulfin to take over the 1st, but he was unavailable, fighting a desperate battle south of the Menin Road. Monro recovered by nightfall, but had sustained a concussion and was still woozy. H. J. S. Landon of the 3rd Brigade took over, though he could not be found until later in the afternoon. So, for crucial hours, the 1st Division had no commander. Johnnie Gough, anxious for more information, sent Charteris on horseback to the Hooge Château. "I met a medical officer of the division white as a sheet," Charteris later wrote. "He held up a tiny piece of cloth in his hand and said, 'Do you know—?' I said, 'Yes.' 'Well,' he said, 'that is all that is left of him.'"

THE GERMANS, TOO, HAD ESSENTIAL commanders who were either killed or temporarily knocked out of action at the moments when they were most needed. As at Hooge, lucky shots may have affected the outcome of the struggle that day.

At dawn, General der Infanterie Berthold von Deimling, commander of the XV Corps, met at a crossroads near Kruiseecke with another General der Infanterie, Paul von Schäfer, who headed the 54th Reserve Division. The two German divisions were working their way up both sides of the Menin Road. Oberst von Bendler, the battle-group commander, who had, the previous night, spelled out the orders for the present attack, was there, as was the XV Corps head of artillery, Oberst von Feucht. Much of what would happen that day depended on their decisions. They were more important to the conduct of the battle than Falkenhayn, who was too far distant to make immediate decisions. Did British guns on adjacent ridges spot the gathering at the crossroads? "Either by chance or design," as Jack Sheldon puts it, shells exploded near the group. Bendler and Feucht were both mortally wounded, as were their adjutants. The two generals sustained light wounds, but they still had to spend time in a nearby forward aid post, being examined and patched up. That must have distracted them for a crucial hour or so during the early part of the day.

It was not that the temporary absence of the two overly aggressive commanders spared lives. Both divisions paid a considerable price that morning as it was. Their surrogates were all too eager to carry out their assignment, the capture of Gheluvelt, and if possible push far beyond it. Recall the words of Oberst von Oldershausen to List the night before: "A delay in the attack is out of the question. Gheluvelt must fall tomorrow! Those are the orders. We have our duty to do!"

But duty could have its limits. List's exhausted 16th Bavarian Reserve Infantry Regiment was a case in point, and much of what happened to it in the next hours can be explained by the disregard commanders like Deimling had for human life. To quote the official history of the List Regiment:

> The losses grow under the violent fire that the enemy hurls towards the attackers from cannons and machine-guns. They lean and fall down on their knees among the hedges, mown down by bursts of fire—but the yawning gaps are always filled again by fresh fighters . . . Morning passes in tough, bloody stand-up fights . . . Whole rows drop while pushing forward—crash back again, break in on themselves—is it not mad to advance in this fire?—and new waves push in—repeated hour after hour . . .

The men who did the killing felt that they had no choice. A British signaller named John Palmer, who was attempting to to run out a telephone line from his gun battery to a forward observation post, remembered how, in spite of "the terrific rifle fire . . . the Germans still came on, nearer and nearer, just a slight slowing up as they stepped over the bodies of their own dead and wounded . . . It was a ghastly and sickening sight to see this slaughter, but it was their lives or ours."

On the slopes in front of Gheluvelt, Deimling's handiwork was everywhere to be seen. "The heaps of dead and wounded seemed to increase every minute," said the same signaler. "They must be very brave unless they are being forced on by the weight of numbers in the rear."

That day it became clear why Deimling's own men had come to refer to him as the Butcher of Ypres. By the end of the morning, his wounds had been bandaged and he was back in action.

THOUGH THE GERMANS HAD TORN a wide rent in the British line, they seemed unwilling to exploit their considerable advantage. Were too many of the officers who might have led them forward lying dead or wounded on the steep slopes at last mastered? When officers perished, the initiative of the men they had commanded seemed to expire with them. Common soldiers had never been taught to take over when their leaders went down. That may have been the signal defect of the too-hasty training of the German reserve units of 1914, with its emphasis on outmoded drill systems that made no allowance for individual enterprise, especially that of experienced NCOs. With no one prepared to assume firm leadership at the battalion, company, and platoon levels, the urge to take calculated risks that passes for military nerve threatened to dissipate at the very moment when it was most needed.

By 11:30 A.M. the Germans had taken most of Gheluvelt; skirmishers were beginning to emerge from the western limits of the town. The early hours of the afternoon would be critical. Falkenhayn and his generals had not just a battle but perhaps the outcome of the war in their grasp. The Germans had the momentum. They had reached a point where the way to Ypres was mainly downhill and ran through mostly open country. They had the weight of numbers—and a beckoning gap at least two miles wide to throw them into. An opening so broad, or so thinly held by the defense, would not again present itself until the spring of 1918.

So far in those first hours, the intangible breaks of battle had gone the way of the Germans. The British seemed on the verge of disintegrating. The line held by their 1st Division was, in the words of its own commander, "broken." Trying to lead the remains of his company to a safer position, Capt. Hubert Rees of the Welch said, "If the Germans had pushed home their attack during the afternoon, there was nothing to stop them." Capt. James Hyndson of the 1st Loyal North Lancashire Regiment, or Loyals, also in retreat, echoed that sentiment. "We have literally no reserves should the Germans attempt another breakthrough." Why they hesitated has to be a mystery of military history, one of those big questions whose solution may lie in the sum of many small answers.

In only one place did a regiment-sized unit, the 105 Saxon, attempt to follow the British in the direction of Hooge, less than two miles away, half the distance to Ypres. But it kept to the Menin Road, never spreading out to take advantage of the enemy disarray on both sides. It overlooked the main secondary opportunity that a concentrated breakout can confer on an attacker: the ability to explode, fountainlike, in various directions once the original breach has been made.

In front of the Saxons were the remnants of the 1st Loyal North Lancashires, as well as a scattering of other British units. After their unsuccessful attempt just before noon to retake Gheluvelt, an order to withdraw reached the Loyals. Pursued by German infantry, and German shells, to which were added "nerve-racking machine gun and rifle fire," the Loyals retired through the fields on either side of the Menin Road. Before they reached Hooge, Captain Hyndson reported, staff officers stopped "the general backwards movement" and turned it around, the Loyals and the surviving residue of other battalions advancing along the road. The Gloucestershire regimental history relates how "the Gloucesters . . . built a barricade across the road at the Veldhoek cross-roads, and from this position shot down dozens of Germans who were still advancing along the road to Ypres." Writing in the present tense, Hyndson picks up the story:

"After going about 400 yards, we strike the leading German infantry, and a real soldiers' battle commences. So confident are they that they have broken through that they come on in massed formation, without taking any precautions, and we soon make holes in their ranks. In one instance I notice German mounted officers leading troops forward in formation of fours"—a march pattern reserved for the parade ground. "Calling on the men nearest to me to fire at this splendid target," Hyndson wrote, "we very soon shot down the officer, horse, and a great number of men." A killing frenzy seized the British. "As each body of Germans is destroyed, we surge forward and take on the next, shooting and charging alternately, bayoneting the survivors until by sheer exhaustion and losses we come to a standstill." The bayoneting part may have come from a mirage-like blurring of memory, when Hyndson came to write his memoir in the early 1930s; the exhaustion that came from too much killing was real enough, unforgettable. Was the lethal spree a payback for the dead and dying khaki figures they had left behind at midday or the release of a vindictive torrent of subconscious fury, a soldiers' grim reckoning with an impersonal enemy? The man you killed couldn't kill you.

ONE DEATH THAT AFTERNOON STANDS out. Julius List is an overlooked figure. His time was too short and his cobbled-together regiment, or by now its remnants, too second-rate to merit more than cursory attention—except, that is, for the presence of *Kriegsfreiwilliger* Hitler. List was a huge, beefy, broad-shouldered forty-nine-year-old, whose utterances could be given over to bluster and exaggeration. He had actually claimed in a dispatch that Bavarian RIR 16's first exposure to fire had been a tactical success, a triumph of the will, and not an experience that had seen privates like Hitler crawling backward to get out of harm's way. List did also look out for his men. His battered regiment hadn't known him that long, but it respected him. His men worried that he took too many risks. Indeed, once he was gone, the regiment lost the focus it so badly needed at this moment of its greatest test.

Events now swirled around the Gheluvelt Château, which for one afternoon became the most important place in Europe. It was a compact, many-windowed building three stories high, with bricks painted white. At each end stood towers capped by steep roofs that gave them the look of witches' hats. Close by were unpainted brick stables with stepped gables in the Dutch manner, a building almost as substantial as the main one. The château and its long, narrow, orderly grounds, the domain of a Monsieur Peerebone, seemed ready-made to be a way station on an irresistible German advance.

List led two battalions of his regiment north from the smoldering village. The 1st Battalion, Hitler's, came up on the Menin Road to occupy a former British trench at the town end of the château park, a relatively safe position. Between 1:30 and 2 P.M.—establishing precise times is difficult—the 2nd and 3rd Battalions entered the park and set out for the château, with List in the lead. A shell burst in front of him. He died instantly. Hauptmann Rubenbauer, waiting to go forward, picked up the story:

Suddenly a runner came pushing up and tumbled breathlessly into the trench, throwing himself exhausted at our feet. "The regimental commander has been killed." "What are you saying—The Oberst?" "Dead—over there by the hedge in the grounds of the château—during tonight's assault—right in the front line!"

Ignoring the danger, Rubenbauer dashed across the open park to see List's corpse. "He lay there in the grounds of the château, his white face set and determined . . . Covered in a blood soaked coat, he was laid to rest for all eternity at the foot of a severed tree stump, upon which hung his field cap."*

The importance of the Gheluvelt Château had not yet begun to manifest itself. In another hour, though, maybe less, it would.

EVEN AS UNIT AFTER BRITISH unit collapsed, holdouts still remained. A quarter of a mile north of the Menin Road, the Germans managed to budge but not overwhelm the 1st South Wales Borderers and, to their left, the 1st Scots Guards. Except for reaping a substantial late-season harvest of slain Germans, the two battalions knew how desperate their situation was. They could only look on as units to the south fell apart. Troops of the German 54th Reserve Division then "swarmed upon the battered trenches to which the remnants" of one company, C, "were clinging." The company commander, a major, the Borderers regimental history notes, "went down fighting to the last." The Germans drove C's few survivors, together with some men from B Company, back into, and across, the château grounds. They reached a wood and found a light railway cutting that overlooked the complex of local affluence. Though there were Germans on either side of them, they made it across the lawn and disappeared into the trees before anyone noticed and started shooting. It

---

* List's body remained at some distance to the south of the château, in the place where it had been buried in 1914. After the war, his sizeable skeleton was dug up and reburied in the huge common grave at the Langemarck German Military Cemetery, which it shares with the bones of 24,916 others.

was now between 1 and 2 P.M., the interval during which the shell killed Oberst List.

The remaining Borderers and the Scots Guards, dug in on the eastern grounds of the château, began to make trouble for the Germans. On the left, A Company held firm. A sergeant major named Hicks cajoled retreating men into joining A Company. Lt. Col. Burleigh Leach, the commander of the Borderers, dispatched a party to take over an unoccupied mound seventy yards southeast of the château. His men sprayed fire on any Germans who attempted to cross the château grounds. Meanwhile, Leach had made his way to the railway cutting where the survivors of B and C Companies had gathered and, to throw the Germans off balance, ordered a counterattack. In the words of the Borderers regimental history, "It seemed to catch the Germans by surprise: many were shot or bayoneted, others bolted, throwing away rifles and equipment as they fled." Fire from the mound accounted for more of the List-less fugitives. They left the ground littered with bodies and pieces of equipment, helmets, shakos, and caps.

But British casualties had been so heavy and his own frontline trenches were so badly battered that Leach decided not to advance any farther. Worried that the Germans might at any moment renew their attack, the colonel sent a lieutenant named Ramsden to scout out conditions in Gheluvelt. Presently Ramsden returned, to report that the enemy who roamed Gheluvelt in large numbers seemed disorganized and more concerned with finding water than with pushing on. That meant that the British still had time. But how much was another question. Leach decided to dig in, establishing a perimeter in the sheltering stand of trees to the south of the château.

Almost until the end, the 1st Scots Guards had held on to their battalion headquarters in the stables of the château. They were situated at the edge of a manicured swath of woodland that extended along the western edge of the grounds. It took as many as fifteen or twenty minutes for the Germans to pull themselves together after Leach's counterattack. That was a stroke of luck that probably wouldn't last much longer; another, even more unbelievable, was that the phones in the battalion headquarters worked. The position was too exposed for runners to get through.

A Morse code message came in, which was translated and shown to a nearby Scots Guard officer: Brig. Charles FitzClarence, who now commanded the 1st (Guards) Brigade, was on the other end. FitzClarence was calling from his command dugout near Polygon Wood and the village of Polderhoek. He ordered the Scots Guards and the Borderers to hold their position. Leach was in the building, and FitzClarence's order was relayed to him. Though the colonel feared that the Germans might surround the two battalions, he decided that, for the moment, the wisest choice was to remain where he was, to wait for the counterattack FitzClarence was apparently preparing. It was just before two o'clock.

LESS THAN A HANDFUL OF men that afternoon could be called genuine deciders. One, perhaps the most forgotten, has to be the British brigadier Charles FitzClarence. The GOC of the 1st (Guards) Brigade was, in the fall of 1914, forty-nine, a robust six foot two, never less than an imposing physical presence. Behind his standard officer's mustache, a bit thicker than usual, he had quietly handsome features, with a thin face, inquisitive eyes, and a mouth that had a trace, but not a disfiguring one, of hardness to it. His men seemed to have feared and admired him in equal parts. "The Demon," as he was known, believed in rigorous training and drilled them relentlessly in the handling of the rifle and the machine gun. They performed superbly in maneuvers. He was not an intellectual, and some superiors questioned his fitness for staff duties. "He is not at his best when he is behind a desk," one evaluation noted. FitzClarence preferred the irregular surfaces of the outdoors to the neat and polished ones of headquarters.

Combat was his element. At the beginning of the Boer War, he commanded a unit of mounted infantry that freed an armored train under attack. Leading a night raid, he dispatched four Boers with his sword. His fighting career in South Africa ended when a bullet tore through both legs. He earned a Victoria Cross, mostly because of the close-quarters brawl in the dark. Back in England, FitzClarence rose steadily, making a mark as a tactical innovator. On assignment in Ireland, he missed the early weeks of the Great War; at the end of September, he took over com-

mand of the elite Guards brigade on the Aisne. He immediately organized the first trench raid by a British unit.

From the first, FitzClarence seemed to have a sure instinct for the
way trench warfare should be fought. He displayed a knack for making
quick decisions. He scrounged for the right implements of a form of
combat that was as new as it was old: rifle grenades, extra sandbags, steel
plates pierced with loopholes to protect sentries from snipers. Noting
that the farmhouses ordinarily used as headquarters attracted shellfire,
he instead oversaw the building of command dugouts, which he surrounded with trenches and obstacles, making them difficult to overrun.
FitzClarence's present headquarters hewed to that model, a capacious,
trench-ringed dugout close by a farmhouse on the edge of a stand of timber the British called Glencourse Wood. Guards officers slept in the
building at night but vacated it during the day when German shelling
made the place too dangerous. It had a good view of Gheluvelt. The
Demon earned a new nickname, "G.O.C. of Menin Road"—and, indeed,
it was this most-pressured sector that he now defended.

By the morning of the thirty-first, British commanders were seriously considering what to do if the Germans broke through, an eventual-
ity that seemed ever more likely. The backup defensive lines were one
possibility, but, as we have seen, they were hardly started. Haig and his
two division commanders also contemplated sending the 2nd Division,
the less banged-up of the two major British Salient formations, to attack
from the northern flank. The prospect was an uncertain one. Desirable as
the results can be, pressure from the flanks is never easy to pull off, especially with troops who are already on the edge of collapse. The sight of
stragglers streaming past his dugout made FitzClarence uneasy; he
emerged and mounted his horse. FitzClarence and his staff captain, Andrew Thorne, spent much of the morning inspecting the crumbling front
of the 1st (Guards) Brigade. He considered abandoning Gheluvelt altogether and retreating half a mile west to Polderhoek Wood, but quickly
rejected the idea. As he pointed out to Thorne, such a retreat might only
open the floodgates to the Germans. He saw one alternative: an immediate counterattack. With their enemy in such visible distress, this was the
last response the Germans would expect.

It would be as much a gamble as a surprise. Only one reinforcement battalion was available in the area, the 2nd Worcestershires Regiment. General Monro of the 2nd Division had moved them to Polygon Wood, and into reserve, on October 30. It was a welcome respite. "Ten days of battle," the regimental history of the Worcesters commented, "had left all ranks haggard, unshaven and unwashed; their uniforms had been soaked with the mud of the Langemarck trenches and torn by the branches of Polygon Wood: many had lost their puttees or their caps." They were nothing if not fought out, but they were available and close by.

By now October 31 had turned calm and clear. The rain had stopped hours earlier. For the men of the Worcestershire Regiment, this was supposed to be a time to relax and recover. They sat in Polygon Wood "listening to the ever-increasing bombardment and watching the German shrapnel bursting in black puffs of smoke above the tree-tops."

Generals Lomax and Monro had informed FitzClarence that he could call on the Worcesters in an emergency. This surely was one, and no time to argue the fine points of interdivisional command. Around noon, FitzClarence dispatched a messenger to the nearby Polygon Wood: Could the commander of the 2nd Worcesters, Major E. B. Hankey—the same Hankey who had so distinguished himself at Polygon Wood on October 23—send an officer to take orders? The officer soon returned. The Worcesters were to prepare themselves for a counterattack; one company was to head out in advance, to cover the Menin Road.

At 12:45 P.M., A Company of the Worcesters, 120 men, set off with their officers and a guide for the embankment above the light railway; there it fanned out. It was ordered to fire on any German who attempted to pass beyond the houses at the western end of Gheluvelt. The principal responsibility of A Company was to prevent a concentrated breakthrough along the road.

At 1 P.M. FitzClarence summoned Hankey from Polygon Wood to his dugout headquarters in Glencourse Wood. The brigadier ordered him "to advance without delay and deliver a counter-attack with the utmost vigor against the enemy . . . and to re-establish our line there." Recognizing that Hankey was not familiar with the immediate area, FitzClarence gave him as thorough a briefing as could be fitted into twenty minutes. He

Major E. B. Hankey of the Worcester-shires was one of those exceptional mid-level officers whom no good army can do without. His initiative had already stopped the Germans at Polygon Wood. Now his Second Battalion would be called on to perform a mission even more risky and unexpected. (Mercian Regiment Museum)

spread out maps. He pointed out the Gheluvelt Church, its steeple rising above the smoke of the burning village. They could see it when they stood on the roof of his headquarters dugout. But the view of Hankey's goal, the château, was blocked by the next ridgeline. Were the grounds of the château by now overrun with German troops? Had the Borderers and the Scots Guards surrendered? These were the vital details that maps couldn't tell and the silent units at the front didn't. Hankey would have to take his chances. FitzClarence emphasized, wrote the regimental historian of the Worcesters, "that the situation was desperate and that speed was essential."

Some days later, Hankey jotted notes on two foolscap sheets. Though brief as a telegraphic message, they communicated the drama and urgency of the situation as more elaborate words could not. They read almost like a stream-of-consciousness description of the event unfolding: you have to think that these notes come close to what had gone through his mind. Hankey was as spare in language as he was in looks:

Definite orders. Thorne to guide. Packs to be left—speed essential. Wire cutting.

1:45 p.m.

I sent off Haskett Smith & Sgt & 8 scouts to cut wire etc . . .

Hankey had to be sure that any obstacles that might slow or block his attack were removed.

The men lined up for extra ammunition and fixed their bayonets. Then, at 2 P.M., they moved off in file, three companies numbering 8 officers and 370 men. Hankey and Thorne led. Hankey described how, after leaving his force hidden amid the trees at the southwest corner of Polygon Wood, he and Thorne went on "to reconnoitre and found A Coy (depressed—in the air—heavy fire—casualties . . .)." The anxiety of isolation must have assailed the diminishing number of riflemen, out there alone for almost two hours and beginning to wonder whether relief would ever come. They could see khaki-clad figures bolting up the Menin Road and across adjoining fields for the protection of a woods just beyond the burning village; too many of the hurrying men collapsed and lay still long before they reached safety. The rout down there was general enough to

An artist named Gilbert Holiday drew the moment when the 2nd Worcestershires spilled over the last concealing groundswell, through a fierce curtain of German shellfire, and down toward the Gheluvelt Château. The artist based his sketch on accounts by survivors. Hankey, unseen here, carried a hunting horn as a means of directing his men; other officers wielded sticks or swords as batons. (Mercian Regiment Museum)

hint at widespread panic: would they be left behind? But A Company had at least done what it had been left to do: its rapid rifle fire had apparently kept the Germans from advancing beyond the last straggle of Gheluvelt buildings.

Convinced that A Company would hold, the two officers went back to their men, "through nasty fire and found them glad to see me alive & Thorne left. Deafening noise—retreating men . . ." The Worcesters set off, crossing a little stream, the Reutelbeek, and filing up a bare ridge, where they fanned out, advancing now in two long lines. All the while wounded men and fleeing strays passed through their ranks, some warning that it was impossible to go on, "that it was murder etc. to attempt it." The regimental history of the Worcestershires reported that "in every direction German shells were bursting. British batteries could be seen limbering up and moving to the rear. Everywhere there were signs of retreat. The Worcesters alone were moving towards the enemy."

As they approached the crest of the ridge, the Worcesters could glimpse the château for the first time, still a thousand yards distant. German high-explosive and shrapnel shells were bursting along the crest in rapid and methodical succession. The downward slope was totally open, short rank grass and stubble underfoot. The companies broke into a steady double—a jog, almost—the officers with their swords drawn, the men with bayonets fixed. The swords served less as weapons than as the guiding batons of orchestra conductors. "No cheering," Hankey wrote, "learnt our lesson." He carried a hunting horn. Men fell, the regimental history said, "at every step." More than a hundred were killed or wounded. The rest kept on. They scrambled across the light railway, wriggled through hedges and under wire fences. They outran the German artillery fire, still plastering the hillside behind them.

The Worcesters reached the château grounds. A band of trees and the wall shielded their approach. The Germans on the other side of the wall and railing did not seem to recognize that a counterattack was about to sweep over them. They had other, more pressing, concerns, from exploring the outbuildings to mopping up British units still resisting. Some were, in the words of the *Official History*, "enjoying the repose of victory, searching for water and looting, and in no expectation of such an onslaught." Hankey, who had just negotiated a wall—he had "filtered over" it on a stile—spoke of the "curious sight of Bosche in flower beds and conservatory and rabbit shooting . . ." For the most part, the Germans were newly formed units from the 244th and 245th Reserve Regiments, in addition to the 16th Bavarian Reserve Regiment. They outnumbered the British—there were as many as 1,200 of them—but, to professional soldiers like the Worcesters, their lack of discipline seemed to be an indication that they were, by this time, mostly unofficered. As General Farrar-Hockley wrote, "The majority were in that dangerous state of relaxation to be found when unexperienced troops have taken a first objective under unseasoned leaders. Alertness declines; euphoria follows relief from fear."

The British fanned out, shooting and stabbing. They hunted the fleeing enemy, who cowered in hedgerows or tried to make a run for it across open lawns. Hankey's notes captured some of the wildness of that scene:

> . . . got into sunken road. Splendid shooting towards copse . . . shooting 10 yards!

> Time taken from start to establishment. 2–3p.m . . .

> Bosche frightened to death—2 prisoners.

> H. Smith & Sgt wounded & Killed: shelling & burning.

As they headed in the direction of Gheluvelt, Hankey and his men encountered Colonel Burleigh Leach of the South Wales Borderers, an old army friend. Almost surrounded, the Borderers and a few Scots Guards had been holding out in trenches along the southwest wall. "My God, fancy meeting you here," Hankey said.

"Thank God you have come," Leach replied.

FACED WITH THE WORCESTERS' ONSLAUGHT, the German forces ran. Was one of the fugitives *Kriegsfreiwilliger* Adolf Hitler? His 1st Battalion of the 16th Bavarian Reserve Regiment was, to be sure, hunkered down in a trench just outside the park, closer to the village, where it would have missed the worst of the panic at the château. But he and his companions may have been caught up in the race to safety. At that point in his life, he had a tendency to follow the leader, especially when survival was at stake. The stampede carried over into the village—which, at that moment, neither side could claim. Jack Sheldon cites the regimental history of Re-

serve Infantry Regiment 247 of the 54th Reserve Division, a unit that had, in a single day, lost most of its officers. It describes the situation Hitler would have stumbled into:

> The village itself was in an utterly indescribable, chaotic state. The thunder of the guns and the chattering of the rifles was continuous. Then, amidst it all, came the shout, "The British have forced their way back in!" Only with difficulty could the commanders bring the situation back under control . . . The streets were filled with rubble and everywhere shells and shrapnel crashed down. For the time being there could be no question of a

The 2nd Worcesters swarm victoriously across the grounds of Gheluvelt Château in this painting by J. P. Beadle. In the center, gesturing with his right hand while grasping a sword with his left, is a Captain E. L. Bowring, a hero of the midafternoon reversal of fortune, who would win a Distinguished Service Order (DSO), Britain's second-highest military honor—though only officers were then eligible. In the middle ground (right), Major Hankey grasps the hand of an old Army friend, Colonel H. E. Burleigh Leach of the South Wales Borderers, whose men had spent most of the day trapped in trenches behind the château. "My God," Hankey said. "Fancy meeting you here." The brick building (left rear) housed the stables where British officers with a telephone had hidden, yards away from Germans wandering through, and around, the main house. (Mercian Regiment Museum [Worcestershire])

further advance; the formations were hopelessly intermingled, so the officers did not have a firm grip on their own men and in any case, there was an increase in enemy artillery fire and the exhaustion of the men was too great.

How did the *Kriegsfreiwilliger* confront this lethal confusion? Did he panic and run with the rest? We shall never know. Though he spoke readily and often about his Great War experiences, the future Führer never mentioned Gheluvelt—or that afternoon. Few intervals should have been more memorable. Was he ashamed? Did his possibly graceless behavior under pressure not square with the image he later wanted to convey, or the self-aggrandizing myth of the model soldier he would one day create for himself? What if Hitler had been cut down in flight, or captured? History would have been deprived of one of its true monsters. We hardly need elaborate on the calamity that a single bullet might have denied the world.

This is not the place to dissect the rise of one of the truly demonic figures of recent times, merely to observe what may have been the moments of creation of that persona. Whether or not the Great War "made" Adolf Hitler, as several excellent historians maintain, it did become the defining experience of his life, and one that altered its direction. Aside from his possibly being swept up in the mass panic at Gheluvelt— circumstantial evidence is all that we have to go on—his war record was honorable but not especially meritworthy. Still, it marked the first time this twenty-five-year-old failed postcard artist had come close to what must have been his own standard of success. As a runner, he took risks; he had to. He was wounded once and gassed once. He won two Iron Crosses, one of them a first-class award for bravery. He lasted four years on the Western Front, an achievement in itself.

Hitler described himself as a "passionate soldier"; his army companions tended to shun him. If he had a talent, it was to stay alive. He had an almost preternatural ability to handle sudden change, to sense danger around the next traverse of a trench; he was a natural survivor who came to pride himself on his many near misses. Though he had no need to invent a history, he did so anyway, shamelessly. As Thomas Weber, who has written with such authority about Hitler's Great War, comments, "He erased, as he saw fit, his real war experience and replaced it with one that suited his political needs." The truth was never good enough for the man who would become "the most powerful right-wing dictator of the twentieth century."

For better or worse, Adolf Hitler was a dreamer, and perhaps the end of October 1914 was the period in time when he came to believe that those dreams, dark and violent and barely formed as they may have been, might actually come true.

THE STRUGGLE FOR GHELUVELT SWAYED back and forth through the last part of the afternoon. "Accounts say GHELUVELT in our hands," Hankey noted. "Might say it was NO MAN'S LAND—burning and shells." (That may perhaps be the first recorded mention of the phrase in the Great War—unless Hankey added it at a later date.) He ordered A Company, the one that had helped stop the German advance beyond Gheluvelt, to probe the village. "It was not possible permanently to occupy the centre of the village, for it was being bombarded by both the German and the British artillery," the regimental historian wrote. "On all sides houses were burning, roofs falling and walls collapsing. The stubborn Saxons still held some small posts in the scattered houses on the south-eastern outskirts. Nevertheless the enemy's main force had been driven out, and the peril of a collapse of the British defense about the Menin Road had been averted."

FitzClarence's borrowed troops had plugged the most threatened stretch of the gap.

On horseback, he had watched Hankey's attack unfold from the ridge above the château, then galloped off toward 1st Division headquarters to announce that the line had held. Along the way he ran into Haig and his party; they had already heard the good news—and must have told him the bad, about the Hooge disaster. After a brief conference, he returned to his dugout command post at Glencourse Wood.

At about 6 P.M. FitzClarence sent out orders to withdraw from Gheluvelt, pulling back six hundred yards from the ridgeline to a new village position on the Menin Road, Veldhoek. There, trenches could be dug on the rear-facing slope, where they could not be observed by German artillery. The retirement began. "One by one, at intervals of ten minutes," the Worcestershire regimental history wrote, "the companies withdrew from their positions":

> In the darkness they assembled under cover and then tramped back along the Menin Road to Veldhoek. The withdrawal was not realized by the enemy, and was carried out without interference . . .

The Germans made no attempt in what remained of the day to recapture Gheluvelt. Elsewhere the German advance petered out; the gap continued to narrow. "The reason for the enemy's inaction," wrote the regimental historian of the Worcesters, "is not clear. It is possible that the very boldness of the counter-attack may have given the impression that the Battalion was but the first wave of a stronger force, and possibly the enemy may have stood on the defensive to meet an imagined attack." It seems evident that command confusion, or, simply, lack of command, with a sudden collapse of will, must have afflicted the Germans. Perhaps the young troops, their best leaders already lost, refused to budge. "Perhaps," the historian speculated, "some commander of importance was disabled or some vital line of communication severed." We know the first had in fact happened; the other was all but inevitable in that war. When you find a breakdown in communications, you are just as likely to find a collective failure of nerve. They can be interchangeable.

In the event, key operational documents of that day no longer exist. The questions are legion. We can only speculate on the answers.

AFTER FOCH LEFT IN THE early hours of October 31, Sir John French went back to bed. But he was able to fit in only a couple of hours of sleep. After dawn, aides woke him. Alarming reports were coming in: the Germans were everywhere on the attack, and it seemed a matter of time before the line broke at some point and Fayolle's secret fear came true.

It was just after nine when French and two aides got into his high-roofed chauffeured automobile and set off for a daylong series of urgent staff conferences, slowed up by his passage through a landscape that seemed everywhere to be in retreat. He saw Allenby and Hubert Gough first, who briefed him about the situation on Messines Ridge. Though their relationship was chilly to the point of dislike, that morning they were acting in rare concert. Allenby's cavalry corps had been doing a credible job of holding off an entire German infantry corps for ten days along a seven-mile front—"a record feat for cavalry," Sir John French said, in a rare moment of generosity. Allenby's defense of the ridge mostly forgotten, was a shining moment, one of the few, in the sack of British cavalry on the Western Front. Allenby would lose the high ground and its villages in the end but would prevent worse from happening.

French's next destination, Haig's headquarters at the White Château, proved more difficult to reach. As his car made its stuttering way through Ypres, Sir John found panic sweeping the town. In one of the few memorable passages of his memoir, *1914*, he described his harrowing passage:

> . . . there were manifest signs of unusual excitement, and some shells were already falling on the place. It is wonderful with what rapidity the contagion of panic spreads through a civilian population. I saw loaded vehicles leaving the town, and people were gathered in groups about the streets chattering like monkeys or rushing hither and thither with frightened faces.

To pass through the town, a distance of little more than half a mile, ordinarily took no more than ten or fifteen minutes. French's automobile had to push its way against a tide of men and motor vehicles moving against him. The car finally arrived at the eastern exit in the Vauban walls, the Menin gate, where a guard, stationed there to prevent anyone from leaving and heading in the direction of Gheluvelt, stopped it. More precious minutes were lost while Sir John's ADCs satisfied the military policeman about the identity of the man in the back seat. The guard waved him on.

"The road traffic, mostly headed in the opposite direction, began to assume a most anxious and threatening appearance. It looked as if the whole of the I Corps was about to fall back in confusion on Ypres." He claimed he saw heavy howitzers moving west "at a trot—always a most significant feature of a retreat." Given the confusion on the Menin Road, it was an unlikely one. How could howitzers maintain a trot when "ammunition and other wagons blocked the road almost as far as the eye could see"? When "crowds of wounded came limping along as fast as they could go, all headed for Ypres"? Shells were screaming overhead and bursting with reverberating explosions in the adjacent fields.

"This spectacle filled me with misgiving and alarm."

His car could make little headway against the flash flood of retreat. French and his two ADCs had to walk the last hundred yards to the White Château.

It was now about 2 P.M. when French appeared. No one was expecting him. He found Haig and Johnnie Gough seated at a long table, on which a chandelier, loosened by the concussion of a shell, had just fallen and shattered. White-faced, the two men had attempted to pick up where they had left off, studying maps—or at least trying to. Haig outlined for French the catalog of recent disasters: the near-obliteration of the two divisional staffs at Hooge, the overwhelming of I Corps. "They have broken us right in and are pouring through the gap," Haig told French. They discussed withdrawing to the Rice Line (or Lines). Haig asked for reinforcements. French replied that his well of reserves had run dry. He had nothing but words of moral encouragement to offer.

In his memoir, French looked back on those cruel minutes. It was the Little Field Marshal at his most depressed. "To me, indeed, it seemed as though our line was at last broken."

> If this were the case, the immense numerical superiority of the enemy would render retreat a very difficult operation . . . Our only hope now seemed to be to make a stand on the line Ypres–Messines; but it was a great question whether this would be possible in face of a close and determined pursuit. Personally I felt as if the last barrier between the Germans and The Channel seaboard was broken down, and I viewed the situation with utmost gravity.

It was a dramatic half hour, the worst I ever spent in a life full of vicissitudes such as mine has been.

French took leave of Haig and started his walk back to his staff car. He had one hope remaining—to find Foch and more secure reinforcements from the French. It was now about 2:30 P.M.

Haig was preparing to take a ride of inspection to the front, something he had intended to do before French's arrival. He was standing on the steps of the White Château, waiting with a party of his staff for their mounts, when the unexpected happened. About an hour earlier, Haig had dispatched his chief engineer, Rice, to find out what was really going on at the front. The brigadier dashed off on his horse. Now, some sixty minutes later, he came galloping back, in the words of Charteris, "as red as a turkey-cock and sweating like a pig." Rice reported the success of the FitzClarence/Hankey counterattack, and the retaking of Gheluvelt and its château. Haig pulled at his mustache and supposedly commented that he "hoped it was not another false report." But he sent off his ADC, a Lieutenant Straker, to tell Sir John French the news. Straker, running, caught up with French just as he was getting into his car. French, too, was dubious. He drove off in search of Foch, who was, he thought, at Cassel, nineteen miles west of Ypres and at least an hour's drive away.

SOME MINUTES LATER, HAIG, HIS chief of staff, Johnnie Gough, and a select group of staff officers mounted horses and headed east on the Menin Road. It was probably a few minutes before 3 P.M. No event of that day has aroused more contention than Haig's famous (or infamous) ride. Military historians have made a meal of it, if only because Haig would become, in little more than a year, the supreme commander of the British armies on the Western Front, no longer the BEF, and one of the most controversial figures of the Great War. Everything he would do, or had done, would pass under the microscope of political and historical scrutiny.

The questions multiply, the pejoratives pile up. Was the ride staged? Was it an image-building publicity stunt? Was it more useful in burnishing Haig's reputation than in influencing the outcome of the battle? Was the sight of shined boots and immaculately turned-out officers on horseback designed to boost the morale of shattered, ragged, and grimy infantry in retreat, men in a state of near panic? What was, in fact, the true purpose of Haig's ride? Did the ride, as another historian has bizarrely claimed, even happen? At this remove, such questions, except the last, defy answers. You can't escape feeling that the whole controversy is less about the ride than the rider—the man who would preside over the Somme and Passchendaele, as well as the reverses and victories of 1918.

Haig himself saw the purpose of his mission as a simple one. In his diary, written that night, the explanation couldn't be plainer: "I got on my horse and rode forward to see if I could do anything to organize stragglers and push them forward to check enemy." Rice, who had tagged along with the party, cited another purpose. "Sir DH and staff . . . rode up the Menin Road beyond the Hooge Château where we established a sort of advanced HQ." Presently Capper of the 7th Division, Byng of the 3rd Cavalry Division, Langdon, who had temporarily replaced the wounded Lomax as GOC of the 1st Division, Monro of the 2nd Division (still groggy but now recovering from the shock of the blast), and Fitz-Clarence joined him. Though we have no records from the meeting, FitzClarence must have verified the recapture of the village of Gheluvelt and the château. At the same time Haig's generals must have warned that the battle was by no means won or survival a sure thing. As he also wrote in his diary: "Troops very exhausted and 2 Brigadiers assure me that if enemy makes a push at any point, they doubt them being able to hold on."

That important gathering was reason enough for Haig's ride, especially given the ever-present communications problem, which too often only personal contact could solve. As for bolstering morale, too few soldiers would have seen him to make much of an impression—or a difference. The dangerous pressures of the day outweighed considerations of ambition or image building. Haig had other things to worry about.

Certain reservations about the wisdom of the excursion do, however, make sense. As military historian Nikolas Gardner has pointed out, Haig "effectively removed himself and much of his staff from control of his corps at a pivotal moment in the battle. Before embarking on the ride, the I Corps commander apparently made no arrangements to ensure his timely reception of important messages." Officers carrying crucial dispatches had to wander along the Menin Road trying to find him. He put himself and his staff in harm's way at a time when German artillery had recently ripped apart his divisional command structure.

The rest of the story can be quickly told. Haig and his party rode on to Veldhoek, a village close to the front, and then doubled back to Zillebeke, where he met with the French general Moussy, who had been fighting along the canal. It was almost dark. He returned to the White Château, to find that the gap between the 1st and the 7th Divisions had closed. He had completed his circuit and no one was the worse for it.

At 7 P.M. Haig and a colleague were driven into Ypres for a meal. Despite the evacuation panic and the shelling, there were restaurants still open.

BY MIDAFTERNOON, MILITARY LUCK—THE gift of seizing opportunities the instant they present themselves, if not of anticipating them—had begun to turn in favor of the Allies.

Sir John French, however, continued to have doubts about the good news he had heard at Haig's headquarters. Had the success at Gheluvelt really happened? A cloud of gloom seemed to follow him as he headed west. Ypres was once again an impossible bottleneck. Two miles beyond town, French was passing through a village called Vlamertinge when a French officer waved down his car. He was a Major Jamet, the liaison man with Haig's I Corps. This was the "providential piece of luck" that Foch had spoken about in his memoirs. Jamet told French that Foch was at that moment in the Vlamertinge hôtel de ville, conferring with Generals d'Urbal and Dubois. They were, in fact, discussing what to do about the supposed BEF rout. Working with Haig and his generals, Jamet had seen the beginnings of an apparent disaster with his own eyes. He led the field marshal inside.

Of his meeting with the French generals, Sir John remarked, "We all went thoroughly into the situation." French and Foch discussed how best to make use of French reinforcements. That, according to Sir John's memoir, was it.

Foch, fortunately, left a more detailed account—at least three, in fact. His biographer Liddell Hart gave a version of his plea to Sir John French that is too good to resist quoting. "Marshal, your lines are pierced. You have no troops available. You are finished." And now came the Foch of legend: "You must advance. If you retreat voluntarily, you will be swept up like straws in the gale. Loss of Flanders, of Belgium, of Calais. Your army thrown into the sea. The Kaiser wishes to enter Ypres. He shall not enter."

Here was the most eloquent of military poets speaking—and you have to think of Foch in that light.

A more candid version of French's visit, and of the hot exchange that took place in the village town hall, appears in Foch's *Journées*, the day-by-day record he kept, and one that is as yet unpublished. We have a feeling here of what really happened, of words actually spoken, not the tidied-up version of Foch's unfinished memoirs. The misapprehensions, misunderstandings, the rush to fallible judgments have not been conveniently discarded. It seems clear that Sir John mentioned nothing of the retaking of Gheluvelt or of the disaster at the Hooge Château. To quote Professor Roy A. Prete's translation at length:

> The Marshal himself arrives. He paints the blackest picture of the situation. . . . The English I Corps is in a state of complete disorganization and disorder. . . . Nothing more can be done. The Marshal is going to order a retreat.

There were indications, writes John Hussey, that Sir John was ready to withdraw west of Ypres. That would have been as good as admitting that the battle was lost. Words may have been spoken that afternoon that were never recorded. If French was indeed contemplating a retreat beyond Ypres, we can hardly wonder that the exchange between the two commanders grew vehement. Now it was Foch's turn to speak. Though outranked by French, he refused to go along with the retreat order the field marshal was apparently proposing.*

> I oppose it with all the strength in my power . . . by the force of my arguments. The order absolutely forbidding retreat under any condition must be maintained; we must hold at any price. Any movement to the rear would be the signal for a thrust forward by the enemy which would sweep us away definitively and would remove all possibility of establishing a second line. The [I] Corps must hold at any price, at least until evening.

Holding on, said French, was out of the question.

> The Marshal becomes furious, declares that it is absolutely impossible . . . that his only recourse is to go and get himself killed with the I Corps if I maintain my way of thinking . . .
>   I reply that he must not get himself killed, but maintain his orders and his troops. That is the only way to save the current situation. Any other decision would compromise it for a long time. It would be a disaster of the greatest consequences.

The two men refused to budge. Sir John's intransigence was puzzling. Events were beginning to look up for the Allies. The field marshal already knew about Hankey's exploits at Gheluvelt—or had his pessimistic side taken over, leading him to doubt that it had actually happened? Not that many hours before, Foch had promised reinforcements at their middle-of-the-night meeting, reinforcements that were, even now, beginning to take their place in the line. Dubois, who was present with d'Urbal,

---

* According to John Hussey, the historian Louis Madelin, who was attached to the French Army during the Great War, wrote in 1917, in his *La Melee des Flandres,* that Sir John "clearly envisaged a withdrawal to the west of Ypres." In 1920, he added— "irritatingly," Hussey comments—that "I have seen the record of the dialogue word for word, in an authentic document—discretion stops me from quoting it." "A Hard Day at First Ypres," 87.

confirmed that men from his IX Corps were showing up alongside Haig's battalions, and that more would arrive by dawn. Foch, relentless, picked up his argument: retreat was out of the question.

> The Marshal's face is red as a rooster's comb; he again declares that it is impossible. I fully maintain my point of view, my firm decision to continue the action whatever it costs, to sustain the English I Corps with every available force, which will engage in the midst of fleeing English troops . . . Tomorrow, [when] I again have other reinforcements, I will resume the attack.

French finally surrendered. "Overpowered, but not convinced, he resigns himself not to order a retreat." Foch then dictated an order, which stated that the I Corps would hold fast and give no ground. The British 2nd Division would keep in close touch with Dubois's IX Corps. "The lateness of the day makes this organization feasible. It is useless to fall back, dangerous to do so in broad daylight."

Foch handed the paper to French, who wrote on the back, "Execute what General Foch has written." Then he sat down and scribbled a note to Haig. "It is of the utmost importance to hold the ground you now are on. It is useless for one to say this because I know you will do it if it is humanly possible. I will see if it is possible to send you any more support myself when I reach headquarters. I will then finally arrange with Foch what our future role is to be."

Two ADCs took the order and the brief note and carried them back to the White Château. They were waiting for Haig when he returned from his ride.

You might say that it was at 3 P.M. on October 31, the hour at which Foch's "instructions" were timed to go into effect, that the French general took charge of the Battle of Ypres. Foch now ran the operation. He had won the right to lead, Prete has written, "not by any act of state but by the sheer weight of personality."

———

THAT AFTERNOON, WHICH WOULD SO alter European history, was the tale of two counterattacks. The first, which we have detailed, has become a legend in British military history. The second, all but forgotten, equally deserves to be. It, too, not only saved the day for the Western Allies but also ensured a reversal of advantage in the battle. The episodes share another trait in common: They sound as though they were made up. They were not.

Joffre (left) and Foch stroll arm in arm. By now head of the French armies of the North, Foch had risen in three months to become the second most important man in the Army. When all seemed ready to give way at Ypres, Foch took charge. It was his battle to lose or win. (*L'Illustration*)

The counterstroke by FitzClarence and Hankey has a certain natural glamour, perhaps because it was played out against a backdrop of a château and its manicured grounds. The command post of Edward Bulfin, the source of what one historian has called "an audacious psychological ruse," was, on the other hand, hidden in the middle of a forest. A visitor described coming along a trail to find "some French and British orderlies in the wood, holding officer's horses, and on reaching them discovered that they were outside the Brigade Headquarters, which consisted of a large dugout or 'funk-hole.' In it were about seven officers, among them General Bulfin." The wood was still known by its Flemish name, Groenenburg, though the British would change that to Shrewsbury Forest, a nostalgic designation that stuck throughout the war. A thick mixture of beech, oak, and pine, with a tangle of underbrush, Shrewsbury was as close to deep woods as you can find in the Ypres area.

Bulfin we have met before. He was an Irishman and a Catholic, and his father had been Lord Mayor of Dublin. Bulfin had served with distinction as a colonial warrior, and was fifty-two when the Great War began. He commanded a brigade on the Aisne highlands and had masterminded the recapture of Kortekeer Cabaret. That exploit earned him a battlefield promotion to major general. October 31 found him leading a cobbled-together group of understrength battalions known as "Bulfin's Force." He was Haig's immediate choice to take over the 1st Division when Samuel Lomax was mortally wounded; but, in the middle of a desperate fight to the southwest of Gheluvelt, Bulfin was unavailable.

It was at Shrewsbury Forest that, in the hours after Hankey's counterattack, the British line was most in danger of coming apart. If the Germans could punch through here, they had every opportunity to reach the Menin Road from below, cross it, and cut off before dark what was left of the 7th Division and a sizeable portion of Haig's I Corps as well. At that point they could have made a turn and poured down the Menin to Ypres. The long last day of October was far from over.

The predictable German shell storm had started at dawn and rose in fury as the day advanced. Observation balloons appeared, to call down accurate fire. "Several shells a minute broke all along the line and men going down everywhere," Bulfin wrote in his diary. "No cover. Simply

Hell." Men were blown to pieces and no trace left. At 12:25 P.M. the German infantry emerged from trenches and moved in waves toward the trees. For all their numbers, something wasn't right. "It was fortunate for us," said the regimental history of the Grenadier Guards, who were fighting close to Bulfin's Force, "that the attack, wonderfully brave as the Germans were, was apparently quite disjointed and unorganized. No officers could be leading the men, who advanced in dense masses to within three hundred yards of the trenches and were simply mown down by the fire of the Grenadiers." Later that day, British troops up and down the line reported German dead lying "in heaps" at the edge of the forest. Those impromptu piles of eternity were turning up in the most unlikely places.

Close to 2 P.M. an officer from the 22nd Brigade of the 7th Division, holding out on the ridge to Bulfin's left, rushed into the general's dugout: the 7th, he said, was on the verge of giving way. Capper, its GOC, was talking desperate measures. He had alerted his battalion commanders that a general retirement might take place at 1500 hours, 3 P.M. He would occupy a new line running from Klein Zillebeke north across the Menin Road to Frezenberg—roughly the Rice Line that Haig had inspected in the morning, not more than an intermittent hen scratching. If the Germans followed a British retreat too closely, that retreat could be a move full of danger.

BULFIN LOOKED UP AT THE ridge to his left, and what he saw dismayed him. "Germans in long lines" were "coming over the top of the ridge held by the 7th Division. . . . Streams of Germans in unending numbers kept pouring over the ridge. As far as I could see to my north, there were endless glinting spikes of German helmets. The roar of guns and rifles was incessant." Bulfin ordered three battalions to withdraw into the woods, to conform with the uncertain line of the 7th Division: he didn't want to be outflanked and taken from the rear. As Bulfin left his dugout headquarters and headed back, Germans opened fire with small arms on the general and his scurrying staff. "My orderly carrying my coat was killed."

The Germans crashed down the slope through the undergrowth, crossed a long brook called the Bassevillebeek, and disappeared into the trees. Amid heavy smoke, sudden ambushes, and a woodscape packed with obstacles, their unit cohesion completely broke down. A young soldier named Fritz Grieshammer, fighting with Infantry Regiment 172 of the 39th Division, described the plight of men lost in the labyrinth of Shrewsbury Forest: "We stumbled over many fallen trees," he remembered, "then arrived at an open area. . . . Somebody collapsed immediately, shot through the stomach from a flank." The noise of battle made it all but impossible to tell where the British gunfire originated. "One of us was ordered to take a message to the rear. He . . . took what he thought was cover behind a tree and glanced at the enemy. There was a shot and he fell down moaning." The maze defied initiative. "An oberleutenant was determined to lead us forward. He jumped out of the trench and fell to the ground, hit by three bullets in the upper thigh, stomach, and foot. . . . We continued, leaderless, reaching a shot up wood at the cost of further casualties."

"It was complete chaos," Grieshammer admitted. "I could not locate anyone."

Bulfin must have sensed the mounting disorganization of the Germans, as the force of their attack dissipated amid the brush–choked woodland. "Bulfin's Force" was hardly in better shape. If he was to restore his crumbling front, he had to take advantage of this brief opportunity. He was running short of men, officers especially. As one of them remarked, "If we wanted any more men, we had better go across and see if the Germans could lend us some."

Bulfin elected to counterattack. As he was making his hurried plans, a member of the I Corps staff appeared on horseback. Haig had sent Lt. Col. Hugh Jeudwine, his chief of operations, or GSO-1, to find out what Bulfin's situation was. Jeudwine was a man as renowned for his courage as for his unpopularity among his peers: they found him ruthless beyond the call. He was also one of the unacknowledged heroes of that afternoon. Bulfin sent Jeudwine to alert the 2nd Gordon Highlanders that he needed them for his attack. They were about three-quarters of a mile back, digging trenches. Bulfin expected that Jeudwine would find some 200 men, but the Gordons had been badly mauled that morning, and Jeudwine could locate only 84, including the proverbial clerks and cooks. That number would have to do. The commander of the Gordons was a man described as "their giant Adjutant," Capt. John R. Stansfeld. Well over six feet tall and huge in physique, he had been the heavyweight boxing champion of the army and navy in 1903. Striding down a trench, he was never without a pipe or a cigarette.

Jeudwine left Bulfin's plan of attack with Stansfeld and continued on to the White Château, where he rounded up, and sent forward, a scattering of reinforcements, stopped to brief Bulfin's right-hand neighbor, Lord Cavan, and then headed back to report to Bulfin. He nearly didn't make it. Once he ran into a party of Germans, and only escaped because he knew the woodland trails in the area and where to dodge for safety. (A company of the Royal Sussex Regiment, posted in reserve, ran into the same Germans and wiped them out.) Jeudwine, meanwhile, decided to take a more direct route, galloping between the lines. He arrived with bullet holes in his hat and clothing. Had he not survived his remarkable circuit, the chances were, at the very least, that the timing of Bulfin's counterstroke would have been thrown off and its results nullified. An attractive figure Jeudwine may not have been, but his ride deserves as much notice as Haig's more famous, but far less hazardous, equine exploit that same afternoon.

The blind woods played into Bulfin's scheme. They hid the advance of the Gordons and disguised the small number of the attackers. Stansfeld yelled out the battalion war cry:

"Where are we, boys?"

"Here we are, Sir."

"Then give it to them," he shouted, and led the line forward.

When they were some three hundred yards behind the British firing line, the Gordons started to cheer. In his diary, Bulfin described how "I ordered the first line to open a one minute rapid fire when they heard the cheering." Two understrength battalions of the 1st Northamptonshire Regiment and the 2nd Royal Sussex "broke into one great roar and crackle"—in the words of the *Official History*—"of rapid independent fire." It was a "mad minute" of rifle fire, eighteen shots per minute. "To the Germans it must have seemed as if dozens of machine-guns had suddenly been brought against them; and as they begun to waver, the two battalions, with the Highlanders, were up and into them with the bayonet." On the right, the Oxfordshires joined in, as did the dismounted cavalry of the Royal Dragoons, which Jeudwine had led down from the White Château. "Not only was the front covered by the counter-attack cleared, but its effects extended northwards to the Germans attacking the 7th Division. Decimated units of the 7th joined the pursuit."

Major General Edward Bulfin organized a second improvised attack in the woods southwest of Gheluvelt, a wild, undermanned affair that turned another German threat into a rout. Haig wanted to build on its success; Bulfin urged him not to. He had an instinct rare among Western Front commanders: he knew when to stop. (Imperial War Museum)

Bulfin's force charged down rides, burst through thickets. "No prisoners were taken," he noted, "but hundreds of Germans were lying bayoneted [*sic*] all through the wood or shot by our people . . . We had almost got back to our old line." Capt. Harry Dillon of the Oxfordshires was more graphic: where blood was spilled in notable quantities that season, you were likely to find him. His men, he wrote to his family, "came on some fifty of the grey swine, went straight in and annihilated them. We were very quickly into the next lot and in a few minutes we were shouting, bayoneting and annihilating everything we came across." By the time darkness intervened, the afternoon had turned into a debacle for the Germans.

Haig, who overestimated the short-term success of Bulfin's operation—the long-term one was another matter—ordered the attack to resume the next day, November 1. Bulfin recognized that to continue was to risk losing everything—and more. "We were only clinging to the ground by our eyelids," he wrote, using what seems a popular phrase those days, and getting away with it. Though he had hardly slept for days, he mounted his horse and headed for the White Château. He burst in on Haig's chief of staff, Johnnie Gough, who was already in bed: "I told him that he must cancel the order, that if we were able to hold our line tomorrow it was as much as we could do, but to advance was madness and we would lose all the ground and Ypres in the bargain. He said all right." The order was canceled.

The next morning Bulfin himself became a casualty, knocked out by an exploding shell. Surgeons "took a lot of metal from my head." Bulfin became one of the 3,642 officer casualties the BEF suffered between August and November 1914. He never did get to lead the 1st Division.

THE KAISER WAS INDEED IN the neighborhood, although he was kept away from danger. No general in his right mind wanted Wilhelm in a place where he might come under fire. Was he convinced that, before much more time had passed, he would be presiding over a ceremony of triumph on the Grande Place in Ypres, in front of a newly German Cloth Hall—an edifice that still seemed worth sparing as long as the symbolic promise of such a grand occasion remained? That had been one of the principal reasons for his journey.

The night of October 31 found the kaiser dining at Linselles, that village below the border where Fabeck had his headquarters. Rupprecht had set up his temporary battle headquarters in a nearby château; the kaiser was staying with him. Falkenhayn joined the two for dinner. Over the meal, according to Rupprecht's journal, they discussed an Austro-Hungarian request for German cavalry. Falkenhayn worried about the dilution of German strength on the Western Front. The decision could wait. They had a postmortem debate about the siege of Armentières. Falkenhayn felt that the evacuation of the city had been unnecessary. Rupprecht disagreed: holding the higher ground closer to Lille was more important. He was particularly annoyed that Falkenhayn was criticizing him in front of the kaiser. They discussed a display of captured French cavalry and trench armor. All were impressed that a single German bullet had pierced a breastplate. Not a word, apparently, was said about the events of the afternoon.

An armor-piercing bullet might influence how a war was fought, but not whether it could be won. That afternoon had raised bigger issues. Was this a war still worth fighting? Had Ypres become a dead end? It seems likely that Falkenhayn was already asking himself such questions. The prospect of reaching, and winning, the Channel ports, so bright three days earlier, had abruptly begun to dim. Lossberg, who was in Linselles but wasn't present at the dinner, had been watching situation reports all day: he was ready to concede that an "advance in the general direction of Ypres was now unlikely to succeed." Did the men at that table recognize that they had been party to a reverse of Marne-like proportions, one that ratified the earlier Central Powers calamity and went beyond it? Failure had become an option.

The kaiser was not a leader noted for his patience. He waited another two days for the Allied sky to fall. It didn't, and he returned to Mézières and sawing wood in his red shirt.

20

The Kaiser's Battle

I HAVE CHARACTERIZED THE INABILITY OF THE GERMANS TO BREAK THROUGH the shattered British line on the afternoon of October 31 as a mystery. Twice they were on the verge of doing so; twice they flinched, stopped by unexpected attacks cobbled together at the last moment. The first, and most familiar, instance occurred at Gheluvelt between noon and one (Paris time). They seemed ready to push down the Menin Road, driving the British back to unprepared "prepared" positions. At the middle of the day, those scant trenches were all that stood between the Germans and Ypres.

On November 1, the day following the crisis, Corp. John F. Lucy of the Royal Irish Rifles ended a long day's march at a feeble scratch that crossed the Menin Road just east of Hooge. Haig's "prepared" line was not a reassuring sight. "The trenches were very roughly dug, and had wide, sloping walls, giving very poor cover from shrapnel. . . . There was a thin fence of barbed wire all along the front, hurriedly and haphazardly erected, and the shallow trenches were not connected."

Earlier that evening Lucy and the bare bones of a relief battalion, hastily scraped together, had marched through Ypres. He described it as "a pleasant town, busy, with lighted shops." The inhabitants, "including some nuns," the Irishman noted, "greeted us cheerfully, and did not pay very much attention to a couple shells which swished overhead." No one seemed upset by the struggle that had drawn so close. A state of denial still persisted. The wholesale exodus of what remained of the population of Ypres, and its abrupt transformation into a ghost town, could wait a few days longer. When Lucy and his companions marched through the bustling town, no one could have recognized the tectonic shift, not of continental plates but of the advantage of nations, that had just taken place on the battlefield.

The second opportunity for a rupture in the Allied line, less well known but with the more threatening potential, was the encounter in Shrewsbury Forest. Coming up from the south, the Germans might have reached the Menin Road and then made a turn full of possible consequence. They might have used the highway as a springboard to leap westward the next morning. That would have compelled an instant Allied withdrawal from the town: no one wanted to risk being trapped in a place like Ypres and being slowly crushed under the remorseless weight of artillery. Once an attack could penetrate and expand, it had the opportunity to create a gap that was genuinely wide and deep, unstoppable.

But that penetration attack never happened.

The Germans had an opportunity for a balance-changing decision in their grasp. They might have erased their midafternoon setback at Gheluvelt. They even seemed ready to turn the inundation of the Yser to their advantage. Albert's watery gambit may have slammed the door shut on the shortest route to the Channel ports, but it also freed two much-needed divisions for redeployment elsewhere on the Ypres battlefield. Dixmude was one likely opening that still remained, and the Germans were determined to exploit it. What, then, had gone wrong? Why, and how, in the space of a few hours in a single afternoon had they fumbled away openings so full of promise?

There were certainly matter-of-fact reasons for the German failure that afternoon. There were intangible ones as well, more difficult to account for. You can single out a prevailing mood, but how do you quantify or assign it a credible weight? "Turning points do often originate . . . below the historians' radars," writes one of our finest practitioners of the trade, John Lewis Gaddis. "That only imagination evokes them doesn't diminish their significance, for what documents could show a great army losing its confidence overnight?"

Exactly. Informed speculation is the task of the historian, and one of the most reasonable explanations of the command dynamics of October 31 comes from a British writer, John Hussey. Though he devotes most of his attention to the Allied side, that does not disqualify his elegant and succinct findings. "It was the Germans," he writes, "whose nerve gave on that day." The concept of nerve, in the sense of audacity framed by cool reason, is as intangible as you can find, one that I have written about and shall return to. Moltke the Younger lost his nerve on the Marne, as did his army commanders and most of the *généraux limogés* whom Joffre dismissed in 1914.

As losses of nerve go, October 31 was not an extreme example, but it represented a breakdown nevertheless. Perhaps men had been pushed too far beyond their limits in the ten days leading up to it, or lacked the training necessary to exceed those limits, that extra inner push that familiarity with the war-making trade can produce. Doing so does not come naturally. Eccentric or unusual reactions have to become automatic; the extraordinary, ordinary. The German common soldier was discouraged from assuming initiative—initiative of the sort too often missing on a day when so many officers were falling. That had to, and would, change, especially as the ranks filled up with educated youth from the middle class, some of whom became officers. In 1914, the German Army did have a knack for taking big risks: daring long shots, though, were the exclusive privilege of the highest military orders. Generals could take risks; majors and captains might; sergeants and lance corporals couldn't, at least not at that point in the war. How else to explain the Schlieffen Plan, the greatest risk of all, or Falkenhayn's calculated risk to use hastily trained reservists as frontline attack troops? Both came from above. Class and rank ruled; the common man still obeyed. No wonder Ludendorff aspired to the "von" that birth had denied him.

The tangible reasons for the German hesitation to push forward were important, too, and could mix with the intangible. Once again, a lack of substantiating documents clouds the picture. What could have been crucial orders no longer exist. We will never know whether divisional or corps commanders tried to get the attack moving forward again. Were they even aware of the gap? How much information vital to the historical record went up in the smoke of the April 1945 RAF air raid outside Berlin that destroyed the greater part of the German World War I military archives?

The breakdown must have started with communication failures: in few wars have commanders handled so many men for such extended periods and been more in the dark. Officers close to the line might appreciate weaknesses immediately in front of them, but it takes divisional or corps intelligence to collate and comprehend the information coming in, and detect that an unusual situation, such as the gap at Gheluvelt, exists. In the Great War, that sort of information rarely arrived soon enough. The top German commanders—Falkenhayn, Rupprecht, Fabeck, and chiefs of staff like Lossberg—were too far away, at Linselles in this case, ten miles at least, to make a difference. Worse, key divisional officers had been wounded, and were unavailable at the moments when they were most needed. (A German shell also dispatched two British division heads, but at least Haig had the instinct to mount his horse and ride forward.) Nothing encourages a command failure of nerve quite so much as a communication breakdown. Information didn't arrive; orders were not sent. That afternoon, as troops milling around the Gheluvelt Château waited to be told what to do, they casually looted, mourned the colonel of the regiment just killed by a stray shell, stretched out on the lawns of the château, or admired its manicured gardens and the last flowers of autumn. That order to stiffen up and advance never came.

The Germans at Gheluvelt not only had the advantage of numbers and freshness but also approached the British—in this respect at least—in experience. Of the three divisions attacking here, two were veteran units imported for the occasion. Both the 30th and 39th Divisions had fought on the Aisne heights and had held their own against Franchet d'Espèrey's revitalized Fifth Army. But time and perhaps too much experience had taken off a certain edge. The two regular army divisions may have been through a fair amount of combat, but that could be a detriment. Too much time spent in the relative safety of trenches had an unfortunate side effect: it dampened initiative, not to say enthusiasm, in the open, a reluctance to take chances that would manifest itself throughout the war.

The third division in the Gheluvelt attack, the 54th Reserve, south

Germans, to which Hitler's regiment had been temporarily assigned, followed the predictable pattern of conduct for new troops. What it boasted in spirit, it surrendered in experience. It took heavy losses, unnecessarily so. Also, such reserve formations lacked the training so requisite for maneuvers of exploitation. Though it was the single reserve division involved in the Gheluvelt confrontation, the 54th Reserve had been placed in a key position, just north of the Menin Road, and would absorb the brunt of the counterattack by Hankey's Worcesters.

All the combatants suffered from a growing shortage of officers, a deficit in command, the Germans as much as anyone—more, perhaps, if you take into consideration the generally inferior quality of leadership in the reserve divisions. Their rigid order of attack only made that shortage more acute as the day progressed. Officers at either end of advancing assault lines were conspicuous, the more so because of their aristocratic height, well-tailored uniforms, mustaches, and pistols or lifted swords. So was the occasional, but unmistakable, rider on horseback. What could he have been thinking? Riflemen and machine gunners waiting in shallow trenches or rifle pits found obvious officers natural, and easy, targets. Struggles for mere landmarks, places that, in the greater scheme of things, didn't matter, took a further toll of men capable of directing advances that were operationally significant, of making decisions to take objectives of more consequence than a random woodlot, a windmill, or an estate stable.

The tactics of rigid discipline had once again let the German Army down. Fatigue, too, played its part, as men who had been under fire for twelve or thirteen hours without respite, half a day or more, were expected to fight on. So did a deterioration of morale and unit spirit, a willingness to die. Already the losses the Germans had taken throughout the morning had dimmed the ardor of dawn. The attackers became overcautious. They had opened a wide front; they could not manage to break through a narrow one. Caution turned to disorganization and panic. Men ran. One of them may have been Adolf Hitler.

All these interpretations matter. But are they the entire story of October 31, 1914? Much remains unexplained about that afternoon, and always will.

———

THE GERMANS WEREN'T DONE YET.

The center of action now shifted back to Messines Ridge, this time to its other village of consequence, Wytschaete. The 6th Bavarian Reserve Division of Army Group Fabeck attacked at 1 A.M. on Sunday, November 1, All Saints Day. That unlikely hour was chosen because, it was hoped, darkness would negate the accuracy of British rifle fire. But, in fact, burning buildings and the full moon bathed the landscape in a rifle-friendly radiance. A military band played martial music to inspire the attackers. The rattle of musketry spread through the night with a crackling sound, Paul Maze wrote, "like a wood on fire."

He and his motorbike bumped and skidded through the fitful darkness on a scouting mission for Hubert Gough. He had asked Maze to bring back information that might help him decide where, exactly, to move his outnumbered battalions clinging to the ridge. Maze hid his motorbike in a field and ran up the main street toward the square. Shells were bursting everywhere. He had to jump up on a low cemetery wall to get out of the way of men with glinting bayonets rushing to confront Bavarians who had gotten into British trenches somewhere up ahead. Maze, too, could hear the blare and thump of a military band, "playing their men into the battle with the 'Wacht am Rhein.'" He thought at first that he was imagining things. He wasn't.

"The row was infernal. Flashes from unsuspected places were the only indication of people's whereabouts." Everything was confusion. At one point in the shadowy chaos of that brawl in the dark, the raw Bavarian troops started to fire at their own people, once again mistaking temporary shakos for British billed caps.

AMONG THE BRITISH TROOPS TAKING their place on Messines Ridge were the London Scottish, the first Territorial inftantry regiment to join the Ypres fighting. During the morning of the thirty-first, 750 men, former part-time soldiers, Scots who lived in London, had filled a gap in the line south of Wytschaete. Their kilts and gaiters must have been still damp from the drenching of the previous night. "The day was clear and the enemy must have had a fine view of us," a Pvt. Eric Wilkins remembered. "They just waited until we got nicely out into the field, when they suddenly trained machine guns, rifles and artillery on to us." Digging in the daylight was out of the question, and the Londoners could only lie down, stay low, and accept inevitably heavy casualties. Some did find cover of a sort. One NCO remembered diving into a drainage ditch beside a road, where he nestled

> against the bank with my feet in water, sweating with terror, and the shells shrieking over me, and bursting close behind. It's like being tied down on the railroad track with the express coming at you; and when they burst the universe falls in on top of you. Mostly they burst four at a time and then a lull. Presently we get wise to this, and when the lull comes, we mount our entrenching tools, and dig feverishly into the bank. I look at my watch. Three hours till dark.

They waited for the curtain of night to drop. Everyone, those who had survived, could dig now.

The German attacks began and continued into the early hours of the morning. The bands struck up their urgent anthems. The Germans threw masses of men at the Londoners, with odds approaching 3 to 1. In the village of Wytschaete itself, those odds probably reached 12 to 1.*

Except for one hindering circumstance, it was Langemarck redux. The British rifles were defective, and, unless loaded bullet by single bullet, they would jam. Wilkins again:

> An officer ordered us to cease fire and wait till the Germans got quite close to us. . . . Then the order came to fire and we simply

---

* Sometime after darkness fell, a burst of shrapnel shattered the ankle of a private named Ronald Colman. A former clerk in the City of London, Colman had also begun to appear on the stage professionally. The wounded man managed to crawl downhill to an aid post; the following spring the Army mustered him out: for the rest of his life, he would walk with a slight limp. Colman would eventually take his mustached good looks and his cultured accent to Hollywood, where he became a major star and winner of an Academy Award. Ronald Colman's war had lasted barely an hour.

poured lead into them. One could not very well miss them for they were just in front, in a great black mass. They seemed to be all talking to each other as hard as they could plainly hear their officers urging them on from behind.

That autumn would have more than its share of bizarre essences, but none was so poignantly surreal as that of doomed men hesitating, to chatter at the brink.

In the end, though, as the *Official History* put it, "weight of numbers told, as ever in night fighting." The Germans continued to throw masses of men at the ridgetop defenses of the British and French. The commander of the London Scottish, Lt. Col. G. A. Malcolm, decided that his men had two choices: retire or be wiped out. They retired.

The Londoners may have stopped the Bavarian attacks, but at a griev-

Maze took this photo of the roll call the day after the battle on Messines Ridge of the London Scottish Battalion, one of the first Territorial outfits, part-time soldiers, to reach the Western Front. It is a haunting picture of men whose worn faces indelibly reflect the strain of battle. (Imperial War Museum/Paul Maze Collection)

ous cost—394 officers and men were casualties, or about 40 percent of those who had gone into action the morning before. The French 32nd Division, which inherited the line, claimed to have counted 3,500 Bavarian corpses, a number that seems extreme. Take it more as a metaphor for massacre than as an accurate body count.

The Germans had taken Wytschaete by the morning of All Saints Day; by the early afternoon the French 32nd Division, one of the units in Foch's taxis of Flanders operation, retook it. Meanwhile the British pulled out of Messines with barely a shot fired. The Germans, no doubt relieved that their adversaries had made such a quick and painless exit, did not bother to follow.

A MEASURE OF THE TURMOIL of those hours at Wytschaete, and one of the few moments of relief in the sanguinary tale of Bavarian Reserve Infantry Regiment 17—it lost 30 percent of its men in those few hours—was the exploit of a Pvt. Johann Zott. Of its 3rd Company, embroiled in house-to-house fighting, he alone survived; a shell splinter had gashed his knapsack, but he was otherwise unhurt. As he began to dodge and grope his way through the ruins of the village, Zott heard English voices. He had the presence of mind to stop and relieve a British corpse of its cap and overcoat; a few steps farther on he bumped into a British firing line, behind which he could make out parked ammunition wagons and field kitchens. Zott made a show of feeding the horses, and even joined Gough's cavalrymen for a cup of coffee. A former seaman, he knew some English expressions and, most useful of all, swearwords, though not enough to maintain much of a conversation. Did he recognize the risk he was taking? Had he been caught in his disguise, he could have been shot as a spy.

Then Private Zott had an inspiration. As the sun rose, he drove a wagon piled with ammunition boxes to the firing line and began to unload them. While British soldiers were carrying off the boxes, he jumped on a lead horse and galloped through a break in the trenches for his own lines. Everyone, British and German alike, began to fire in his direction. He made it to a hollow and stopped. He exchanged his British overcoat for a German one, also scrounged from a corpse. (There were plenty of them lying around that morning.) Zott loaded a wounded Bavarian officer and three wounded soldiers into the wagon and resumed his journey. The officer died, but he was able to deliver the men to safety. His exploit earned him an Iron Cross Second Class.

Heroes must have been legion that season.

WHILE THE 32ND DIVISION PUSHED back at Wytschaete, French and British generals and political leaders were gathering the same afternoon in Dunkirk. For the first time in weeks, the French port was secure, thanks to the Yser inundation. Joffre was there, as were the president of France, Raymond Poincaré, and the minister of war, Alexandre Millerand. Though the meeting commenced at 4 P.M., Foch, coping with the manifold perils of the Ypres struggle, and France's growing part in it, didn't appear until 6:30 P.M., just as the assemblage was sitting down for dinner. The chief representative for Great Britain was Lord Kitchener, who came with the French ambassador to his country, Paul Cambon. Sir John French, who may have sensed trouble, with good reason, pleaded that he had a battle to fight. He did send his military secretary, a headquarters nonentity named Brig. Gen. "Billy" Lambton, to deliver a report on the situation of the British Army. In view of the stature of the others, his last-minute substitution must have seemed like a deliberate snub.

Everything about Lord Kitchener spoke of dominance: his six-two height, his intense blue eyes, his famously thick sweep of mustache, his brilliantined hair, tightly parted down the middle, his bemedaled dark-blue field marshal's uniform. He was in a dour mood, greeting the late-arriving Foch with a discouraged observation, "Well, so we are beaten!"

"I answered," Foch later wrote, "that we were not."

The main reason for the meeting was to deal with problems of reinforcement and munitions. The French promised to add an additional corps immediately, with 200,000 regulars to follow by November 15. The discussion turned to Kitchener's New Armies, the volunteers who had signed up by the thousands since Great Britain declared war on August 4.

Kitchener guaranteed a million men for the Western Front in eighteen months. For Foch at this moment, less would be more. "We do not ask for so much, but we would like it sooner and without delay."

Kitchener cautioned the assemblage that he needed time to produce reinforcements in significant numbers. To send partially trained troops into battle would amount to murder. The example of the German reserve divisions at Ypres was no doubt on many minds. He repeated his assertion that the war would be a long one. Three years was still his estimate. He was also convinced that a German invasion of England was possible. That was why he had held back the 8th Division. The near destruction of the 7th Division had left him with no choice but to release the extra men. The 8th Division would land at Le Havre by the end of the week.

Then the secretary of state for war abruptly changed the subject. He announced that he intended to fire Sir John French. His choice to replace him was Sir Ian Hamilton, Johnnie as his intimates called him. He assumed that he had Joffre's backing. After Sir John had made his proposal for digging an entrenched camp at Boulogne, Joffre, dismayed and angered, had requested that Kitchener recall French.

This afternoon, though, Joffre surprised Kitchener by coming to the defense of French. Eleven days had made all the difference. Joffre now said that he worked "well and cordially" with Sir John. He pointed out that this would be the worst time possible for a change in command, especially when morale and not much else was holding the BEF together. Poincaré backed Joffre. He explained why in his journal. "Today, under the influence of Foch, Joffre changed his mind. Foch has acquired," he added, "a certain ascendency over French, he has established a constant liaison between the two armies." As for Hamilton, Kitchener would, before many months had passed, put him in command of the Gallipoli enterprise, which he led with a notable lack of distinction. He would be relieved. There is no reason to believe that he would have performed any better on the Western Front.

Though Foch and Sir Henry Wilson did their best to buck up Sir John's sagging spirits, his insecurity only continued to fester. His distrust of Kitchener, his biographer Richard Holmes wrote, "came close to attaining the proportions of real paranoia." It drove him into the camp of

Joffre and Foch. But his distrust of France and Frenchmen remained embedded in his suspicious mind. The weathercock took another unexpected spin. On November 14, he would write to Kitchener (of all people) of his general sentiments about his allies. "One always has to remember the class the French Generals usually come from." Down deep, for Englishmen of Sir John's background, birth was the inevitable clincher.

Would he never forget Lanrezac and that half hour of mutual miscomprehension at Rethel?

FOR THE NEXT WEEK, ACTION was as constant as it was inconclusive. The day after the Dunkirk meeting, the Germans retook Wytschaete. The French 32nd Division decided its smoldering ruins weren't worth the cost in lives, and withdrew. On November 5, one of the last lovely mornings of the brief and erratic Flanders autumn, Foch remarked to d'Urbal that the Belgian front was losing its importance. Now that the Germans had started to dig themselves in, opportunities for rapid advances were diminishing. He believed that the drive to take the Channel ports had come to an end, and he was not mistaken. As Lossberg wrote, "all of the command echelons up to OHL recognized that any operational success in Flanders was no longer possible." Still OHL refused to give up its obsession with Ypres.

The general impression in the various Entente headquarters was that the worst had passed—though the broad implication of the afternoon of October 31 would never fully register on either side. It seemed a tactical victory only, of little beyond local significance. Commanders like Foch and French did suspect, however, that the Germans were preparing to ship some divisions to the Eastern Front. There, on the plains of the Polish salient—that thumb sticking in Berlin's eye—the Russians had spent much of October making life hard for the Germans and the Austrians. Even that early in the war, the Austrians seemed forever on the point of collapse. Time and again over the next four years, their German allies would have to come to their rescue, draining men and materiel from the Western Front, too often at the least opportune moment. And time and again, Schlieffen and Moltke's great gamble, a two-front war, would prove beyond the human means and physical resources of their nation. That fatal drain was already taking place in the first days of November. In the railyards of Roulers and Lille OHL was loading worn-out infantry, cavalrymen, and their jaded mounts in boxcars and dispatching them to the Eastern Front.

There, the new, but hardly fresh, arrivals would find a different sort of war. The Eastern Front was not four hundred seventy tightly packed miles long but almost a thousand, close to twice the length of the Western but held by fewer men. Typically, 1,500 Russians might garrison outposts scattered across a mile of front; on the Western the number could be 5,000 Frenchmen. Trenches did exist, but not the continuous lines of the Western Front. The space between the opposing lines was not a hundred yards but three to four thousand, a wide divide that was anything but a no-man's-land. Peasants went on farming. Cavalry still mattered, and maneuver was not just possible but was the rule. Armies retreated long distances and then advanced and retreated more long distances. In years to come, Churchill would point out the basic difference between the two fronts: "In the West the armies were too big for the country; in the East the country was too big for the armies." Ponder that and its ramifications. Oxford historian C.R.M.F. Cruttwell characterized the Russians as "an ill-equipped army with infinite elbow-room." But for all the dispersion of forces, the losses remained as heavy or heavier—proof that open warfare can be even more deadly than the siege variety taking hold in the west.

In Flanders, meanwhile, the Allied generals in charge momentarily caught their collective breaths. The developing situation of the first days of November convinced them that the Germans had given up on taking Ypres or Calais. Violent small attacks might still take place, Sir John told Kitchener in his nightly telegram of November 3, but they would be made only for the purpose of covering a large-scale retirement. Did that, or something more immediately menacing, account for the unremitting pressure that the enemy maintained?

THE SYSTEMATIC REDUCTION OF YPRES, which had begun with the brief shelling of October 28, gradually intensified. Haig's restaurant dinner the evening after Gheluvelt must have been one of the last served. The town, a dangerous place now, began to empty out. On November 4, Fr. Camille Delaere, the curé of the Church of Saint Jacques, summed up the events of the day in his journal: "The exodus of inhabitants continues. . . . The great shells continue to rain down. A cow and a horse in its stable were killed at the farm of Nestor Boudry. Oscar Seghers was killed, also a woman." Delaere was one of the priests and nuns, religious people, who stayed behind to take care of the living—and, increasingly, to minister to the dying and to preside over the burials of the dead. Some, like Delaere, Dame Columban, and a local woman, Sister Marguerite, were indefatigable record keepers and keen observers, cloistered people momentarily broken free whose goodness only enhanced the adventure of a lifetime.

On November 6, a German shell killed two children, mortally wounded another, and so badly mangled one of the hands of their father that it had to be amputated. The operation was hastily improvised at 2:30 in the morning, and was performed on a table in a classroom of a school for domestic science—what we would call home economics. Sister Marguerite, ordinarily a teacher in a local school, described how the nun assisting the surgeon fainted; she had to take over her duties. The surgeon was making his final cut when a shell burst in the garden outside, smashing a hole in the classroom wall and showering the medical team with shards of glass and flying stones. The surgeon and the nun emerged from a cloud of smoke and plaster dust, "the two of us pale with fright. He was still holding his surgical knife in his hand and me, the severed hand in mine." For a moment, all was confusion. "Ta, ta, ta," said the surgeon. "It's nothing. Continue our work."

Father Delaere noted, that same November 6, "Today the bombardment has never stopped. People don't dare go in the streets." The following night, a Saturday, was worse. Now the Germans were using incendiary shells, along with the usual diet of shrapnel and high explosives. The incendiaries set fires everywhere in the center of town. Delaere and an associate priest ventured out, "under the falling shrapnel," to see where they could pitch in. Whole streets were burning; they heard house beams crashing down. "More than once in the course of our journey . . . insupportable heat blistered our faces. There was no water, no manpower to help to put out the fires and the shells went on whistling down. The very sky was on fire."

LESS THAN THREE DAYS LATER, the Germans did indeed launch an attack, and a violent one, suspiciously so. With Ypres so close, it seemed beyond cover-up. In the early morning of November 6, they took advantage of darkness, a thick fog, and a noise-concealing bombardment to dig saps whose heads almost touched the French trenches on either side of the Comines Canal. With military bands playing, they rushed, and over-whelmed, the defenders—who, in one case, were taken "by an inexplicable panic," and left a gap of about a mile. Counterattacks plugged it, but not before the Germans had battered their way through a small forest that the British would call "Battle Wood." French corpses littered its leafy floor. The Germans came close to the village of St. Eloi and the mound of spoil left by railroad excavators called Hill 60—only three thousand yards, or less than two miles, from Ypres.

The Germans now shelled Ypres without cease, though for the moment their artillery spared the Cloth Hall. Hardly 1,800 civilians and refugees remained. The last shops and restaurants shut down. Corps and divisional headquarters moved to chateâus in safer, outlying villages. Fires burned everywhere. Soldiers headed for the front now tramped through the ruins of a dangerous ghost town.

On November 7, a day of cold, dense fog, a harbinger of winter, the British intercepted a wireless message that said that the entire German II Corps, an elite unit, was on the march, bound for the Salient. Elements of new German divisions appeared in the line; intelligence confirmed their presence. "The Allied officers who realized what these indications might portend," the *Official History* said, "and understood the German predilection for exploiting weak spots, had just cause to consider the situation a serious one."

For the British and French, the trouble was that there were almost too many weak spots to count. But the same could be said now of their opponents.

By the beginning of November, German goals had, in fact, narrowed. General headquarters, OHL, as Falkenhayn admitted in his memoirs, "could not conceal from itself that a further thorough-going success was no longer to be obtained." Alternatives were debated. Should a breakthrough be attempted "against a portion of the enemy's front on which he had weakened himself for the sake of the defense of Flanders"?

Until the last reasonable moment, Falkenhayn resisted pressure to switch the principal German effort to the east. He gave up the hope of winning a "decisive" battle in Flanders. He now admitted that, for the foreseeable future, the Channel ports were beyond Germany's reach. He would settle for a lesser result that he didn't consider lesser: the capture of Ypres—which was, he felt, "the central point of the enemy's defensive position." Though it would be a local victory, it was one bound to reverberate along the Western Front and, more important, at home. Once Ypres had fallen, he could turn his entire attention to the east.

At his Mézières headquarters, Falkenhayn informed the kaiser of his intentions. Unless he could force a genuine breakout to Ypres, and he had his doubts, his Flanders offensive had reached a dead end. "The barbed wire cannot be crossed," he told the All Highest on the eighth. According to Falkenhayn's biographer, Holger Afflerbach, the kaiser asked that he try one more time; Falkenhayn accommodated him, but with a caveat. The moment Ypres fell, he would call off the final attack. A cheerless gloom must have attended the interview. Ever the pessimist, Falkenhayn had come to feel that Germany "could no longer reckon on any great success in the west."

YOU CAN REGARD THE GREAT Flanders battle as a linked tale of châteaus: they form a kind of subtext. We now come to one of the last, and architecturally least distinguished, the Château de Woumen. It rose on the right bank of the Yser Canal, a mile south of Dixmude. A Baron Gustave de Coninck de Meriken, son of a prominent noble family, had built it in the mid-1860s. High, narrow, and heavy-set, his château was a mostly brick structure edged with white stone and capped with an unmatched mixture of mansard and rounded roofs that came to a point, those witches' hats that also dominated the Gheluvelt Château. Its signal feature was a round white tower at one end. Woumen was less redolent of good taste than of new money. As ungainly as it was, the château had an undeniable romantic background. The baron had fallen in love with, and married, one of his housemaids. She was still alive in October 1914, when the war forced her to flee, a few steps ahead of the occupying Germans.

The kaiser's accidental tourists arrived at the Château de Woumen on the evening of October 20, and immediately began to turn it into a fortress. They piled sandbags and thick timbers around the lower floor, knocked loopholes in its walls, and stationed machine guns on each of its three floors. They had honeycombed the surrounding park and farm with deep trenches and machine-gun emplacements protected by barbed wire.

General Grossetti and his 42nd Division marched into Dixmude on November 1, joining Bonarc'h and his marines. The man who had commanded French forces on the Yser front and who had now extended his command to Dixmude was determined to go over to the offensive, building on the momentum of his celebrated defense of Pervyse. He sent thrusts in the direction of neighboring villages and targeted the Château de Woumen. Ronarc'h expressed open reluctance to join in, seeing little to gain and much to lose in the way of irreplaceable manpower. He also suspected that an attack on Dixmude was imminent and wanted to prepare for it. For the Germans, a breakthrough here might be a last chance to reach Dunkirk. Grossetti, his superior in rank—he led a division, Ronarc'h was a mere brigade commander—overruled the admiral; he did not take the threat to Dixmude seriously. They continued to argue; Ronarc'h gave in. Already their relations had gotten off to any icy and contentious start.

Grossetti, consumed by his own legend, was unable to separate himself from his celebrated folding camp chair. The bearded general installed his large body in the middle of a crossroads, hands resting on the handle of a cane. Ronarc'h remarked that the general couldn't have picked a worse spot for a command post. He had no view of the attacks, and the position was too far removed from the action to transmit quick decisions or alteration of plans: he was, in fact, on the wrong side of the Yser, to the west of the little stream. The château was on the opposite bank. Grossetti refused to hear him out. The attacks would go forward; he would not move his chair.

Two battalions tried to take the village of Eessen that first day, November 2. They advanced two hundred yards in an eastward direction and went to ground. Meanwhile, as bugles announced their advance, Ronarc'h's marines and a battalion of light infantry from the 42nd Division moved down the road toward the château, but ran into daunting machine-gun fire and could not move forward. Then, overnight, sappers constructed and laid down passerelles—floating footbridges—from bank to bank of the canalized Yser. It seemed a more direct way to reach the château. Once again, though, attacks went nowhere. The following day, November 4, the French suffered another setback. Units became lost in a thick fog. Grossetti shouted himself hoarse trying to cheer them forward. He repeatedly ordered bugles to sound charges. Attacking companies fired on one another: 15 men, including a company captain, were killed or wounded—a small number by Western Front standards, but even in a petite size, a fiasco is a fiasco. Grosetti didn't regard his failed attacks as such. After sending men back into the murk a final time, the general turned to Ronarc'h. In a paternal tone, he said, "You see, this isn't difficult, but you just need to know how to do it." A hard rain began to fall.

A soaked Grossetti decided to return to his headquarters and headed for his chauffeured automobile, which was waiting near the bridge to Dixmude. The driver saw him coming, started the motor, and turned on the headlights. The general heaved his large body into the back seat. Before the car had gone only a short distance, a marine patrol, flashing bayonets, halted it. Didn't the driver know that Admiral Ronarc'h had ordered that no headlights be switched on this close to the front line? The marines were probably, Ronarc'h wrote, "lacking politeness." They began to strike the headlights with the butts of their guns; others demanded that the driver step down from the car. Attracted by the noise, a Lieutenant Colonel Frèrejean, the commander of a battalion of Senegalese troops, dashed up. He pulled the rear door open and brandished his revolver at the figure in the back seat. "Naturally, this gesture causes the general to lose control," Ronarc'h recalled, "and leads to a violent altercation that would have ended badly for Frèrejean if the chauffeur hadn't prudently decided to turn off the headlights and sped away, at the risk of going into the ditch." He and his fuming passenger escaped.

Along the road to Eessen, the men of Grossetti's division continued to flounder in the mud, with big losses and little result. They did reach the farm and the park of the Château de Woumen, which became the scene of innumerable clashes amid the trenches and barbed wire disfiguring once-manicured lawns and artificial deer parks. Now corpses lay scattered amid the shattered trunks of fallen shade trees and collapsed barns. They littered the lawns around the château, which had indeed proved a natural fortress. Undeterred by his failure to take the White Tower—the 42nd Division got no closer than a few yards—Grossetti talked about a night attack. Then orders came from Foch. He promoted Grossetti, a favorite, to command the XVI Corps, holding the line opposite Wytschaete. The Woumen operation sputtered to an inconclusive close, and was soon swallowed by the German attack on Dixmude that Ronarc'h had predicted. He must not have been sorry to see Grossetti go. "Certainly," he wrote, "the general must have had a very bad impression of our sector." Understatement was always a Ronarc'hian virtue.

ONCE AGAIN, THE GERMANS WENT back on the offensive. Their immediate goal this time was the elimination of the Dixmude bridgehead—that to be followed by a flank attack that would push westward behind the inundation. Perhaps there was still one more opportunity to reach Dunkirk, and from an unexpected direction.

On November 8, German artillery began its predictably systematic pasting of Dixmude. The shelling of the town and the trenches that surrounded it was directed by a sausage balloon, increasingly a familiar sight, and by the sharp-nosed observation biplanes called aviatiks. For the defenders, existence, of necessity, became subterranean. Men took shelter in vaults and cellars that remained untouched under the crushed buildings.

South of Dixmude, marines dug in behind the walls of the local cemetery. The journalist Charles Le Goffic, who spoke to many who had endured the siege, told how "shrapnel and *marmites* [heavy trench mortar shells] were smashing the tombstones, decapitating the crosses, breaking up the iron grilles, the crowns of *immortelles,* and the coffins themselves. The Flemish subsoil is so permeable that coffins are not sunk more than a couple of feet below the surface, so that their occupants were strewn about in a frightful way. Several marines were wounded by splinters of bone from these mobilized corpses."

AT DAYBREAK THE MORNING OF the tenth, heavy shelling resumed. Across the Yser, the spreading crash of the bombardment woke Ronarc'h, who was soon up and giving orders. It was clear that a general attack was imminent. Flames from burning buildings of the town lit up the somber dawn. One German division, the 43rd, and parts of another, the 4th Ersatz, took their places in forward trenches—the estimate by the British *Official History* of twenty battalions, even understrength ones, seems ex-

The French Marine Fusiliers make a stand on the left bank of the Yser on November 10, holding off an attempt by the German 43rd Reserve Division to cross. The marines would dynamite the flour mill, the tall structure rising in the background. The marine commander, Rear Admiral Ronarc'h, let the Germans have what remained of Dixmude—"This corpse of a town," *L'Illustration* called it—but refused to budge from the opposite bank. That night he sent a message to French headquarters: "The Germans have taken the town. I hold the Yser." (*L'Illustration*)

travagant. Certainly the Germans outnumbered the Allies, a mixture of French marines, Belgians, and Senegalese, fewer than 3,000 men, not more than one-third of the German force.

About 12:30 P.M., early in a gray mid-autumn afternoon, a phone call alerted Ronarc'h that the German assault had begun; some of their troops had already reached the inner town. A high railroad embankment passed through the center of Dixmude, and the Germans established themselves along it, scouring the streets below with rifle and machine-gun fire. The Germans probed for weak spots; they found several and poured through. But not everyone gave way. Marines who had sat out the bombardment in cellars emerged to fight from holed roofs or heaps of rubble. The first of the defenders to bend and break were the Belgians, holding the center of the line around the railroad station. The company commander had fallen, mortally wounded. Leaderless men dropped their rifles and fled in the direction of the bridge across the Yser. But a lieutenant gathered survivors, including wounded men, and they threw up improvised barricades, slowing the progress of the attackers. It was hard to tell who was fighting whom: a cloud of smoke and dust cut visibility to a few yards.

Ronarc'h decided that he needed to be closer to the action. He climbed into in his car and ordered his driver to head in the direction of the gunfire. On more than one occasion they had to wait for a curtainwall of shells to lift. Finally, he proceeded on foot to a command post near the river. Even there he could learn little of the true situation in town: phone connections had long since been severed. On his way, he asked the artillerymen of a .75 battery why they had stopped firing. They answered that they had run out of shells and that no more were available.

Ronarc'h finally reached the bridge over the Yser. He had never seen such confusion: fugitives streamed across, panic-stricken. Many had thrown away their equipment; some were walking wounded. Stretcher bearers tried to push through, carrying their muddy, blood-caked burdens. Doctors performed on-the-spot triage, sending only those whose lives seemed savable to waiting ambulances. Dead and dying men lay behind the river footpath. Shells exploded without cease, their fragments whistling in all directions. Ronarc'h pushed forward, hailing the first officer he met and ordering him to erect a barricade at the town end of the bridge; he was to allow only the wounded to pass and to turn back all who were trying to flee. Another officer brandishing a revolver ordered men without rifles to strip the dead of their weapons and return to the brawl.

The German columns continued to stream into the town through the ever-more-numerous breaches in its defenses, spreading out block by block. The general commanding Reserve Infantry Regiment 201 perished in the melee. All Dixmude was by now a battlefield. The railroad station became a rallying point for defenders. Some of the so-called chocolate soldiers refused to surrender. "We showed them no mercy," a *Kriegsfreiwilliger* from the 43rd Reserve Division remembered. He and his comrades were young men with scores to settle. "We broke down the door and our bayonets had plenty of bloody work to do." Black troops were not just enemies but were regarded as savages, less than human—and they were by now leaderless, their white officers mostly dead. But a mixture of Belgian soldiers, Senegalese riflemen, and French marines did withdraw successfully, fighting from ruin to ruin or slipping away along the railroad embankment to the river, which most managed to cross.

Ronarc'h made a decision on the spot. Instead of risking what remained of his brigade in a counterattack, he would concentrate on holding the left bank of the little river. He ordered the dynamiting of the high, squat flour mill on the town side, thus depriving the Germans of the best potential vantage point in the area. He would soon blow up the railroad bridge and the main bridge into town. "Dixmude has been a hell for us," he said. "It must become one for the Germans."

The fighting went on for several hours. A surprising number of defenders managed in one way or another to reach safety. The remnants of the three northernmost marine companies, almost 500 men, made their way through half-inundated polders. Sometimes they plunged up to their waists in shell holes filled with icy water. They supported wounded, dozens of them. At last they found themselves at the river. A stray shell ignited a haystack, lighting up the immediate area; machine guns chattered, searching for targets. The river was full of floating debris, animal carcasses, and human corpses. The men waited for the flames to die down, then dashed across a passerelle to the opposite bank. It had taken more than five hours to go five hundred yards.

French artillery scoured Dixmude, Germany's mutilated prize. The calculated explosions began. That night Ronarc'h sent a message to headquarters. "The Germans have taken the town," it read. "I hold the Yser."

The cost had been high. With reinforcements, just over 9,000 men had served at Dixmude between mid-October and the tenth of November. Of those, about 4,000 were casualties, including at least 1,000 killed. This sort of carnage appalled Ronarc'h: he hoped that France would never again become involved in a conflagration like this one. "It would only mean," he wrote, "that humanity is truly mad."

That feeling, so deeply seeded in the man, did not prevent Ronarc'h and his marines from blocking the last opening to Dunkirk.

THE BATTLE THE NEXT DAY, November 11, named after Nonne Bosschen—Nun's Wood or Nun's Copse—never should have been fought. It was less the dramatic empire-saving culmination that so many historians have portrayed than an anticlimax that did little more than reaffirm what had been decided the final day of October.

Falkenhayn had already abandoned his grand design—the breakthrough to the Channel ports—at the beginning of the month. There are indications that the high casualties he had so far suffered, and that had hardly diminished in recent days, had affected him deeply. Even the German *Official History*, Foley has written, "speaks of the General Staff Chief experiencing an 'inner change' and his close staff attested to the emotional blow caused by the high German casualties." The taking of Ypres would vindicate his efforts to some measure. But was its fall still possible, or worth the inevitable cost? At Mézières, as we have noted, the kaiser persuaded Falkenhayn to make a final try, urging him to bring in elite Guard regiments from other parts of the Western Front. Falkenhayn agreed, but with misgivings. For the final toss of the Flanders dice, he ordered two brigades to be detached from divisions in Artois. The composite assemblage of Guard regiments, brought together for this occasion only, had no number, just the temporary designation Winckler's Guard

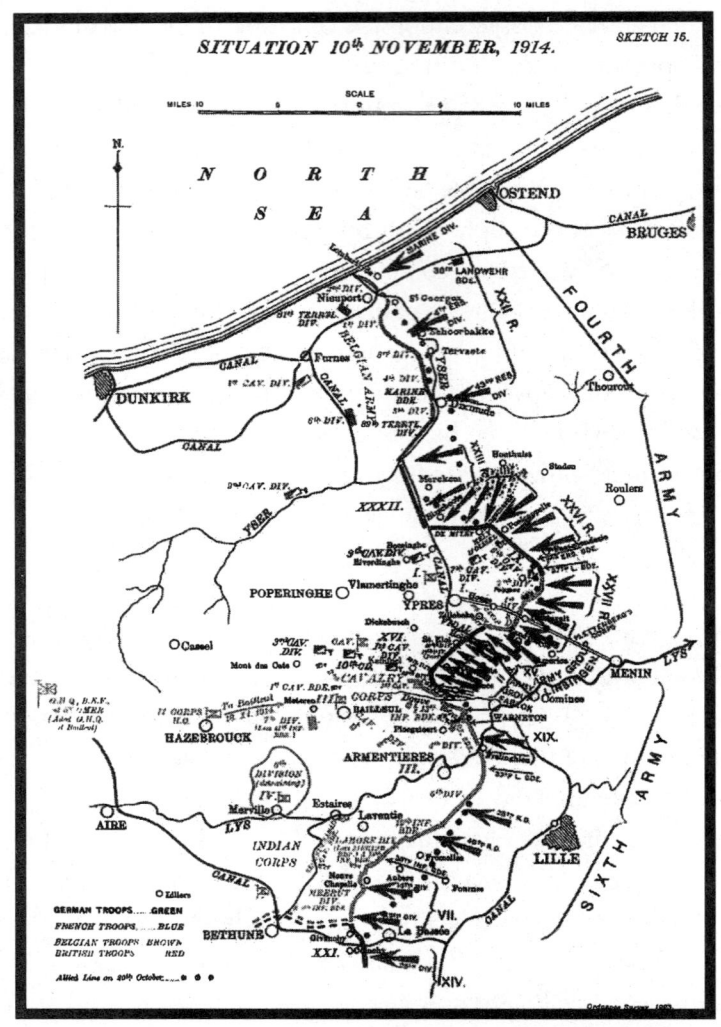

In this map, the reader can see where Falkenhayn's great Flanders offensive jumped off on October 20, 1914—marked by an irregular string of black dots. But more noteworthy is the solid line indicating the situation three weeks later, on November 10, which demonstrates how little, relatively, had changed—or, in a different accounting, how much. For Germany, it was an exercise in monstrous frustration. Door after door had closed. The Inundation had stopped the Germans on a front full of promise, the Yser. They had finally secured another elusive prize, Dixmude. But they could not push beyond the ruins they had created. They had reached the Yser Canal north of Boesinghe, but had to be content with trading shots with the French across its waters. They now held Gheluvelt, and Fabeck had pushed the Allies off Messines Ridge. The Sixth Army of Rupprecht had advanced, and then bogged down in the dismal low country south of Armentières. The Germans had nowhere come close to the Channel ports. Whether or not they could still reach Ypres itself would be decided in a final convulsion the following day, November 11, a prophetic date.

Division, after their commander, Generalleutnant Arnold von Winckler. Standard units in the German Army came from individual regions of Germany, but Guardsmen were recruited from all parts of the nation. They had to be of good physique; their minimum height was five foot six. (That the Guards were tall men meant that they had to dig deeper trenches—which, thanks to the generally high water table in Flanders, promptly filled up.) Their training in special barracks in Potsdam was exacting. Yet they were, like every other German soldier, drilled in close-order attack formations, the same ones that had led to the mass slaughter of undertrained reserve formations.

The Guards began to find their way into the line on the ninth of November: OHL anticipated that one concentrated blow would see them through the thinly held barrier of woods and bring them to the walls of Ypres, four tantalizing miles away. The Guards units boasted to the troops they were replacing that they would reach the town the following day.

As Jack Sheldon has written, the attack plan, hastily drawn up, "carried within it the seeds of its own failure." The front, especially the area facing the Menin Road, west of Gheluvelt, was wishfully wide, and packed. Twelve and a half divisions attacked along a nine-mile line, from Messines Ridge to Reutel, opposite Polygon Wood. They were split between not one but two army groups, the first, and westernmost, led by Fabeck and the second, created for the occasion, by Gen. Alexander von Linsingen, a man with a canister-shaped head and a perpetual scowl. His II Corps, which had fought with Kluck's First Army, was regarded as one of Germany's best fighting units. Again, a broad front seduced Falkenhayn. Despite the presence of the elite Guard Regiments, there was little strength in depth: a potential breakthrough didn't guarantee a concentrated thrust. Little time had been set aside for reconnaissance. Gunners had only the vaguest sense of where the Allies had located their batteries—or, for that matter, the positions of the infantry, concealed in the several woods. And throughout November 11, a cold, heavy rain would fall, making forward progress over partially flooded trenches more difficult and unpleasant. There is little glory in a drenched death.

The assumption of German staff planners was that once those elite formations broke through that woodland barrier, nothing could stop their progress to Ypres. That proved their most fatal error. Days of nonstop combat and constant shelling had turned the woods into an impenetrable tangle, and a mud trap as well. The cloying stench of unburied dead was inescapable. "At this time," said the regimental history of the 2nd Munsters, an Irish battalion, "about a quarter of the trees had been blown down by artillery fire, and these . . . made movement very difficult." Great fir trees "came crashing down in dozens," often burying or crushing the men sheltered under them. Continuous trenches could not be dug; the defenders fought from rifle pits in groups of two or three. Tree roots prevented the excavation of anything more than shallow holes. Snipers' bullets smacked into the trunks above, or into unfortunates below. Lateral communication was impossible. Food had to be thrown from pit to pit. Attacks could be heard long before they could be seen. "Loud words of command and shrill whistles were heard continually, and as the enemy approached, in the occasional pauses of the artillery fire they could be heard singing 'Die Wacht am Rhein.' "*

To attack in these woods, as the German waves did repeatedly, was filled with peril for defender and attacker alike. After nightfall on November 10, pioneers pushed saps forward toward the tree line that was the first German objective, to cut the time needed to reach it. Other engineers, armed with grenades and wire cutters—though barbed wire was as yet only an intermittent hold-up—prepared to accompany the assault regiments. NCOs wielding pistols stood behind the attacking troops, "to goad forward anybody who was hanging back," said a Major Schering, a Grenadier Guards battalion commander. The opening barrage began abruptly and lasted for two and a half hours; it was the heaviest in the long battle so far. Men could not resist putting their heads above the parapet to watch. Some were killed for their curiosity.

Then, at 9 A.M. exactly, the assault troops clambered over the parapets or headed out through the saps, passing over a flat jumble of hedges, small farmhouses, copses, and empty fields of dead stubble, harvested

---

* Singing attacks—or what appeared to be ones—are recorded into November. The clear purpose was, in this case, to maintain some semblance of cohesion and unit communication amid a confusion of trees.

just before the armies arrived. The Guardsmen had to pick their way around unburied, decomposing corpses. Rain had alternated with sleet all morning. They crossed a landscape, Schering said, which "appeared to have been turned over by rabbits."

The Guardsmen approached the edge of the woods in long, tight, patient, disciplined lines, moving at a quick walk, their rifles at the secure, tucked under their arms. The 1st Foot Guards, attacking a mile or so north of the Menin Road, wore not spiked pickelhauben, but mitres, high pointed hats with peaks in front and back, held with a strap under the chin, which lent events a vaguely ecclesiastic tone. Others followed the main road as it disappeared into the woods. The British, who had withdrawn from the front line when the shell storm began, returned. As the Guardsmen plunged through the trees, the air was full of bursting shells; dangerously sharp wood splinters flew like darts in all directions. Rifle bullets zipped between the trees. Attackers keeled over and dropped in long rows. After a moment, the attack, forced to a standstill, gained new strength and momentum as another wave came on to replace the disinte-

The Prussian Guards in their mitre-like headgear had the look of a religious order and, indeed, they were the elite of the elite, to be used on special battle occasions only, such as the breakout to Ypres on November 11, 1914, was supposed to be. Here, the Guard parades in front of the kaiser (right), in a white-plumed hat. (Alamy)

grating one. The Guardsmen disappeared into the smoke and mist that enveloped the woods, their deliberately silent passage swallowed by the rising din.

THE FRONT HAD SHRUNK APPRECIABLY in the past two weeks, which in practice now meant that the last major Flanders encounter would be even more concentrated than it had already been—though not, to use a worsened word, necessarily more decisive. The entire three-week-long struggle would eventually come to be known as the First Ypres, though nobody in 1914 would have given it that title. To do so would have implied that there were more Ypres in the future and that a long war was setting in, a prospect that all concerned still denied.

For the Allies, the first dicey moment of November 11 occurred around the Comines Canal. Around noon, the German 30th Division, a formation battle-tested on the Aisne highlands, pushed a French brigade back to a slight eminence caused by a railroad spoil bank. What made Hill 60 (after its height in meters) so desirable was its commanding view of Ypres, just three thousand yards away, less than two miles—"perilously near," said the *Official History*. Why the Germans did not make a more intensified effort to punch through here has never been satisfactorily explained: in no other place did they come as close to attaining Falkenhayn's revised goal, the victory that might have justified the Flanders convergence.

Once again, the equal distribution of forces, too equal, the broad-front concept stretched beyond its limit, had failed him. The French held. So did the cobbled-together force of Lord Cavan, the wounded Bulfin's successor, in the thick woods just to the east. Though outnumbered 2 to 1, Cavan had the advantage of defending a woodland labyrinth. One of his units, the London Scottish, removed from their hellish baptism on Messines Ridge, found that they had leapt from one frying pan to another fire. Germans, mainly from the 39th Division, which had also served on the Aisne, poured from trenches just a hundred yards away, across a clearing. A gap opened. As Farrar-Hockley wrote: "For 20 minutes, Briton and German stalked each other at a range of yards until the London Scottish worked around the intruders and opened fire steadily." Another gap had shut.

As the battle approached the Menin Road, it grew in intensity. This was where the elite Guard regiments joined the attack, the ones that were supposed to turn the tide, to carry the Germans into Ypres at last. The imperial propaganda machine could do the rest.

BELOW THE MENIN ROAD, THE Germans ran into immediate difficulties. For the 4th Guard Grenadier Regiment, the transition from bombardment to attack failed to go off on schedule. Despite orders to the contrary, the artillery did not stop firing. The timetable error cost all hope of surprise, and the Grenadiers suffered for it. Ravaged by shrapnel and rifle fire, their successive lines were broken and rebroken, until they fell back to the shelter of their own trenches. The Lincolnshires kept the Grenadiers pinned down for much of the day. The Grenadiers made a final effort at 4 P.M., but not a German came close to the British trenches. The *Official History* could easily characterize the daylong assault by the Grenadiers as well as by the Pomeranians and West Prussians of the 4th Division as "Never dangerous."

North of the main road, however, weight of numbers appeared to turn the battle in favor of the Guardsmen.

The Menin was a thoroughfare of châteaux, not grand ones like the marble pile of Hollebeke, but substantial houses nonetheless, a sort of outpost line of Walloon wealth and privilege, with stables, ornamental gardens, and woodlands stocked with pheasants. Those woods became the site of obscure struggles amid the leafless trees of the late autumn, deer parks strewn with corpses. Guards regiments collided blindly with dug-in defenders. Swarming through the trees, the Germans broke through the thin, ragged lines; the British sealed them, somehow. The German Grenadiers killed or wounded commanding officers. The British replaced them, somehow. In the woods of the château of Herenthage, what remained of a battalion of Royal Fusiliers was led by the only officers still standing, not a major but two subalterns. Except for the occupation of one short stretch of trench, the Germans gained nothing there.

Meanwhile, north of the Menin Road (which disappeared into the trees for more than a mile), the advantage swung back and forth. The British had learned some defensive lessons from their trench misadventures at places like Kruiseecke. As much as possible they now kept away from exposed forward lines. As soon as the heavy bombardment began that morning, they withdrew most of their men, leaving only a token force dug in on the front. They were a suicide detachment: why not say it? Almost without warning, lines of German Fusiliers appeared out of the mist, and were on top of the Allied defenders. They had no chance to scamper back to safety. The Fusiliers pushed on into the Veldhoek woods and advanced some five hundred yards through tangles of small oak, chestnut, and rhododendron bushes. They had reached the château itself when, near the stable, they ran up against a French-held strongpoint—trenches behind hedges laced with barbed wire. A small battle broke out. It was one of those Great War essences: hundreds fighting and dying in a dispute over a stable. British artillery fire prevented reinforcements from reaching the Fusiliers, by now trapped in the thick undergrowth. "The Fusilier Battalion," said the *Official History*, "gradually became a disorganized crowd and finally was practically annihilated." It lost 15 officers and 500 other ranks.

For the Allies so far, on the right and right center of the line, November 11 had gone well. The woods had defied the German advantage in numbers. But as that line took a curve northward, dangerous spaces were opening up. Even stubborn, clever defense, and the presence of one of the best fighting generals on the field, Charles FitzClarence, could not prevent a near disaster at midmorning. The Germans had four fresh Guards regiments north of the Menin Road, probably around 8,000 men, against three understrength Scottish Guards battalions, no more than 800. It was now that numbers would begin to make a difference.

A mile of open fields separated the road from the next sizeable forest patch, a big one, Polygon Wood. Only a couple of woodland groves intervened. Overlooking this opening was the German-held village of Reutel, built on a groundswell. The Reutel ridge was just thirty feet higher than the flatland below, but those thirty feet made it an artilleryman's dream. German guns pounded FitzClarence's shrinking (and already shrunken) battalions. When the shelling had started, most of the men of his 1st (Guards) Brigade had withdrawn to support trenches or to places where the ground provided natural cover. Only the Scots Guards, perhaps 200 men, remained up front.

Guardsmen were fighting Guardsmen, big men taking on one another, though it was hardly an equal battle. FitzClarence had attempted to right the numerical imbalance by setting up a series of strongpoints. One, later known as Black Watch Corner, lay hidden in a depression untouched by artillery fire and consisted of a trench inside a square of hedges surrounding a cottage garden: a few strands of barbed wire intertwined amid the branches had converted the hedges into a "strong point." This was the first of its defensive kind on the Western Front. By the end of the war, such wired-in localities would become a notable anchoring feature of defensive lines and zones. Beyond Black Watch Corner, a Liverpool-based unit, the 1st King's, held a mile of front along the southern edge of Polygon Wood—just 6 officers and 450 men. The men hunkered down in a series of rifle pits, one each for two men, five to ten yards apart. Behind what passed for a front line was a continuous, but unoccupied, trench. This the Germans shelled by mistake. They would soon come to regret the British troops their error had spared.

SHORTLY BEFORE 9 A.M. A German reconnaissance aircraft flew over the sector held by FitzClarence's brigade. A layer of freezing fog hid the British dispositions, and the observers had little in the way of threatening activity to report: it was safe to proceed. The barrage lifted soon after. The Prussian (as they liked to style themselves) Guardsmen left their trenches and advanced silently. The Scots Guardsmen did not see the disciplined lines of the 3rd Foot Guard approaching until they were only fifty yards from the forward trenches. They came on at a jog trot, the officers with swords conspicuously drawn—how could you fail to identify them?—and the men with their rifles under their arms. They crossed those first trenches without firing, dispatching the few defenders they encountered with bayonet thrusts. Some Scots Guardsmen attempted to run for positions in the rear; men of the Cameron Highlanders followed them. A Cameron officer, Craig Brown, "shouted to them to turn & open fire, but I might as well have shouted to the wind." The clatter of gunfire drowned out his warning command.

This time men who had distinguished themselves twelve days earlier at Gheluvelt Château were practically wiped out, but not, said their regimental history, before they "did great execution of the enemy." FitzClarence's artillerymen poured shells into the advancing lines of the 1st Foot Guards. They were able to prevent the Prussians from bringing up reinforcements. A gap of open fields a half mile wide remained, and the 1st Foot Guardsmen continued to enter it, but in diminishing numbers.

For the Prussians, optimism and plans too hastily formed began to unravel. The 3rd Foot Regiment, on the right side of the gap, was preparing to make a westward turn around Nonne Bosschen; Ypres seemed its next logical destination, and an attainable one. Once the Guard regiments reached open country, so close now, the town was a routine fighting march away, a day or so at most. But first, annoying, unexpected, and increasingly deadly rifle fire from Polygon Wood had to be dealt with. The commanders of the 3rd Foot had every reason to assume that the 54th Reserve Division, supposedly driving west from Reutel, had attacked, and neutralized, Polygon. The 54th Reserve had, in fact, never left its trenches; it managed a scattering of rifle fire, and little more. The non-performance of the division seemed to indicate a contagion of nerve failure. By November 11, these inexperienced troops had been through too much in too short a time. Winckler's Guards Division would have to go it alone.

Meanwhile the 3rd Foot had turned toward Polygon Wood to silence the rifle fire. From their pits, the men of the 1st King's Regiment shot without letup. No Germans burst through the mist. The King's prepared to start firing again. Nothing happened. "As the light improved, the men of the King's from their holes could see that what they first thought was a second attack was in reality a continuous wall of German dead and wounded, lying several deep twenty-five to seventy yards away in a turnip field."

The eleventh of November was turning against the Germans. The Guards had just sustained a second massacre, at least as bad as that of the

4th Guard Grenadiers below the Menin Road. Both must have happened within a morning hour of each other. The survivors of the 3rd Foot Guards, groping westward for the reassuring gap, blundered into one of FitzClarence's strongpoints, Black Watch Corner. Dug in behind the wired hedge were forty riflemen of the Black Watch, who forced the fugitive Guardsmen to divide. As they passed on either side, rifle fire hit them from the flank, and then from the rear; the Guardsmen broke up into a number of small parties, no longer a single threatening combat unit.

Meanwhile several hundred of the 1st Foot and 3rd Foot Regiments had passed through the gap and reached the triangle-shaped Nonne Bosschen. The British offered no resistance, and as many as 900 Guardsmen gathered in the little woods. They came under fire from a scattering of gun batteries in the fields in front of them and stopped. Most of their officers had by then been killed or wounded: initiative without leadership was something training had never urged on them. Had this directionless throng kept going, it would have discovered that there was no one, nothing, beyond those batteries out in the fields. The Germans had run up against the last British line of resistance.

It was by now probably late morning, noon at best. The attack of the Prussian Guard was as good as over.

There is a story many times told, but apparently true: A wounded Prussian Guard officer was brought back to an outpost headquarters to be interrogated. It seemed, though, that he was the one doing the questioning. "Where are your reserves?" he asked his Guardsmen counterpart. Without a word, the British officer gestured to the sparse line of guns in the fields beyond. The German refused to believe him. "What is there behind?" he asked. "Divisional headquarters," his captor answered. "God Almighty," the officer exclaimed in German.

The rest was anticlimax: close to 3 P.M. two companies of the Oxfordshires, attacking from the northwest, plunged into Nonne Bosschen. Can we be surprised that Capt. Harry Dillon led the attack? As always, he seemed to be in the place where the blood ran thickest. The Oxfordshires moved quickly, as quickly as deep and clinging mud would allow. They drove the Prussian Guardsmen before them. Some turned and ran, even before the attack reached them: they were shot down. Others surrendered in droves. In a metaphor that could only have come from the pen of a habitual upper-class weekender, a British officer compared the fleeing Prussian Guard to pheasants bolting skyward from a forest, in front of beaters, first an odd bird, then two or three, followed by a numberless rush. For the kaiser's finest, what finale could have been more humbling?

It wasn't Germans who stopped the Oxfordshires but French artillery, whose spotters, not believing that their allies could advance so fast or so far, assumed that the distant movement which they observed in Nonne Bosschen had to be German. The French guns were four thousand yards, almost three miles, to the north of the action in the wood; it took an hour to get a message to the IX Corps batteries to cease fire. Darkness brought heavy rain and hail, freezing the antagonists in their tracks. Their adventure in the low timber had cost the Oxfordshires just 5 killed and 22 wounded. Other British units fighting that day in the same sector did not get off so easily, as Ian F. W. Beckett points out. "Of the 1 Scots Guards only battalion headquarters and thirty-nine men escaped; in the Black Watch, only one of the officers was left; of the Cameron Highlanders, half the effectives were entirely wiped out." The three Scots battalions that formed the 1st (Guards) Brigade could only muster about 300 survivors. The German losses are harder to come by, depending mainly on anecdotal evidence. We know that the 1st Foot Guard Regiment alone reported 10 officers and 310 men killed on that single day. The entire Guards Division had 2,134 casualties between November 11 and 19; most of those would have come on the first day, the day of Nonne Bosschen.

The German misfortune at Nonne Bosschen—or, for that matter in the entire month-long Flanders encounter—should not surprise. Nonne Bosschen never should have happened. The wonder of that day was not that the Germans failed but that they came so close to success. The Allies were indeed (to recall Rawlinson's phrase that so offended Sir John French) "hanging on by our eyelids." But the kaiser had insisted that Falkenhayn try one more toss of the dice, and he would not be denied. He even offered the temporary use of some of the best soldiers in the world, in the futile pursuit of a public-relations coup, the taking of what was by then probably untakeable, Ypres. Sawing logs for firewood at Mézières, he must have found it easy to put the cost of wasted valor out of mind—or the lesson which that day had reinforced: in war, it is always wise to expect the unexpected, even to count on it. No man was fonder of playing soldier than the kaiser, but this was not one of those war games that Schlieffen always let the All Highest win.

Did not Nonne Bosschen represent the ultimate failure of waiting for an order from above that never arrived? Where was individual initiative? The generals gathered at Linselles, ten-odd miles away, knew nothing of the scant line, a fragile drumhead, of artillery remaining in the fields between Nonne Bosschen and Ypres. That was the story not just of November 11 but of the entire battle for Flanders. Time and again the Germans had opportunities for exploitation that they failed to exploit, beginning with their unexpected arrival at Menin in mid-October, a brilliant maneuver that hit an unexpected wall and couldn't overcome it. The fault lay not with the men who fought the battles but with those who led them, the decision-makers who seemed forever gripped by hesitation. What if the Guards had been used on October 31 at Gheluvelt rather than the reservists who did fight along the Menin Road—and then paused, directionless? What if, on the Yser front, the artillery Albrecht devoted to the reduction of Dixmude had been given to the siege master Beseler to concentrate on the railway embankment and Belgian and French centers of resistance such as Pervyse or Ramscapelle? Or if the attack along the Comines Canal on November 6, which left a wide and inviting gap in the French line, turned into a serious thrust toward Ypres, rather than the local demonstration it became?

The failure-of-nerve explanation looms ever larger, especially on the part of the German commanders. Military historians have long been fond of declaring that November 11, 1914, was the "critical" day of the battle for Flanders; it was, in fact, not that critical. Germany had already lost the war nearly two weeks earlier, lost it in the sense that the nation and its armies could no longer win the great struggle that they had initiated.

History is stingy with second chances.

THE STORY OF WHAT CAME to be known—by the British, at least—as the Battle of Nonne Bosschen had a final episode. It involved one of the genuine heroes of the fight for Ypres, Brig. Charles FitzClarence, VC.

The energy of FitzClarence amazes. He probably had slept little in the past couple of nights, and yet, long past midnight as November 12 began, he still had scores to settle. Now, "the man who saved Calais" (as he was already being called) was determined to retake trenches that his outnumbered men had lost to Winckler's Guards Division in the first hour of the attack. With the favorable change in the battlefield situation, that earlier setback clearly bothered him, a loose end that had to be tied. FitzClarence was not the sort to leave business unfinished. Those lost trenches had to be taken back. A rigorous (but not obsessive) regard for detail is the mark of a good leader; so, too, can be an inscrutable simplicity of purpose. FitzClarence seemed destined for greater things.

"I must say I did not like it a bit," said Wilfrid Smith, the lieutenant

Brigadier-General Charles FitzClarence, VC—he had won the Victoria Cross in the Boer War—conceived the counterstroke at Gheluvelt, and was already being hailed as "the man who saved Calais" when a stray bullet cut him down in a night attack. He braved shellfire to show Belgian military authorities how to flood a landscape they could no longer defend. (Imperial War Museum/Bond of Sacrifice— First World War Portraits Collection)

colonel commanding the 2nd Grenadier Guards. "We none of us knew exactly where the trenches were"—the column was somewhere out in the fields between Polygon Wood and the Menin Road—"nor had we seen the country by daylight. The men were dead-tired, it was pouring with rain and the mud was awful. . . . You could not see your hand in front of your face."

It was now about 3 A.M. "Ma" Jeffreys took up the story: "As Fitz-Clarence himself was apparently the only man who knew where the trench was, he proposed to lead the column and put us in a position to start." Jeffreys, too, had his doubts. "It seemed a mad plan, we thought!"

FitzClarence marched at the head of the Irish Guards, who had joined the Grenadiers. They were, Jeffreys remarked, "very shakey." The column came into open fields.

When we had gone two or three hundred yards a man in the rear section of fours of the Irish Guards suddenly turned around, let off his rifle in the air, and started to run back. I caught him by the collar and kicked his backside harder than I've ever kicked anyone before and pushed him back towards his place. But the moment I let go he made a dash for the hedge on the right and dived head-first through. I caught him by one leg and one of our men got him by the other, but we had to let go as he bolted into the darkness on the other side.

The commotion attracted unfortunate attention; shots were fired in front. FitzClarence halted and went forward to investigate. "Suddenly, without warning," said another account, "the moon peeped out from behind a drifting wrack of clouds and shone down full on the long column moving silently across the fields." There were more shots. "The first intimation which those in the rear of the Battalion had of the happenings at the head was the appearance of a man carrying the General's red-bound cap. Close behind came a little group of men bearing in their arms the dead body of Charles FitzClarence. A bullet had caught him in the forehead." Smith and Jeffreys detailed a sergeant and two men to bring in

FitzClarence's body. It was not an easy task; he was six-two and a big man; the mud was sticky and ankle-deep. The Guards commanders called off the attack.

Somewhere along the way to Polygon Wood, the bearers lost Fitz-Clarence's body. Did it weigh too much? Was the risk of carrying it with the enemy so close too great? Were the men too tired to care? The answer was swallowed by the fatigue and confusion of that stormy darkness.*

* All that remains of Charles FitzClarence, VC, is his name, engraved at the top of Panel 3 of the Menin Gate Memorial to the Missing of Ypres. He is one of 54,896 who have no known grave. The overflow, 34,888 names, appears on the panels of the Tyne Cot Cemetery on the ridge of Passchendaele. Farmers and construction workers still unearth skeletons, some even identifiable by the disks tied around wrist bones, the dog tags of another war—if, that is, the random but efficient havoc of German shellfire had left bones to hang disks on.

21

The Invention of No-Man's-Land

NOVEMBER 12—DECEMBER 31, 1914

IN THE GREAT WAR, NO ONE KNEW WHEN TO STOP. THE FLANDERS STRUGGLE that we now call the First Battle of Ypres, Nikolas Gardner writes, "effectively drew to a close on the 12th." (The "Second" wouldn't come until the spring of 1915, and the "Third" began in midsummer 1917.)* But the attacks continued, and so did the killing. The biggest losers of 1914, the Germans, seemed especially reluctant to call it a season, even as they pulled six divisions out of Flanders and sent them on trains to the Eastern Front. "We left Flanders," Lossberg wrote, "feeling that we had put everything into accomplishing an impossible mission." The French, who weren't usually that realistic, officially ended the battle on November 13. The British didn't call it off until November 30.

The Germans kept up sporadic attacks, as did the French. It was hard to fathom what came of these adventures. Too often it was a case of punch and counterpunch. On November 18, the Germans did take what remained standing of one of those meaningless Western Front epitomes, the stable of the Herenthage Château. Or consider the following account by General Dubois of a series of daily attacks that ran without letup from November 14 to 17 along the north face of the Salient: one of several along the length of the Western Front that Joffre ordered in mid-December:

* You might also add a "Fourth," when, in April 1918, the British gave up the gains of 1917 and retreated to a mile of the Grande Place, or what was left of it; the Germans finally took Mount Kemmel. Count the September breakthrough of the Allies, when they poured over Passchendaele Ridge and did not stop going until the war ended, as the "Fifth" Ypres.

Progress was slow. Brought to a standstill in a number of places by German gunfire, stopped on others by strong points, the troops could only advance step by step. . . . The struggle continued, the gains arduous and hard-earned, without let-up for four days. The final gain was minimal.

Trenches were lost; trenches reoccupied; the line hardly seemed to budge. A patrol, emboldened by silence, would arrive at the most recent scene of carnage, and would find it stuffed with corpses. The enemy, except for a couple of badly wounded men left behind, had disappeared. He would surely be back, and the process would begin all over again. The normal procedure was for the patrol to toss the dead bodies to both sides, front and rear, and cover them with the earth they shoveled out while deepening the trench. But not infrequently the steady rains uncovered the bodies, and sights and smells became so unpleasant that the patrol had to abandon the trench. A French corporal from Minervois named Louis Barthas described what was left behind. "A signpost at its entrance bore this lugubrious inscription: 'Tranchée de la Mort' [Trench of Death]. In truth, there were only dead men there."*

The French generals devised a name for this new form of combat: *la guerre d'usure,* "the war of wearing down." The question was, which side was worn down the most? Those involved in the actions were certain of the answer. One survivor described such attacks as "unpardonable," recalling "the mud, the rain, and the veritable jelly of corpses."

Everyone was so tired, so empty of imagination.

———

* That may have been a designation many times repeated, and with good reason. Today, only one such remains, on the south bank of the Yser, a couple of miles west of Dixmude, across the water from the spot where a French bullet may have ended Peter Kollwitz's brief life and the oil tanks had gone up in flame. These concrete sandbags, low dugout openings, and traverses were constructed by Belgian NATO troops, with time on their hands; today, that quarter mile is a local tourist attraction. Mention of this defensive stretch of line appears in the early 1915 journals of Arsène Bernard. It is called, though, not "Trenchée de la Mort," but "Le Boyau de la Mort"—roughly, "Communication Trench to Eternity" or, to give it a fanciful twist, "Stairway to Heaven."

BY MID-NOVEMBER, FALKENHAYN, EVER THE realist, had concluded that a victory in the west was beyond achieving. As Robert T. Foley writes, "The Ypres offensive had demonstrated" to him "clearly and forcefully the difficulties of attempting a 'decisive' battle under the conditions of 1914." Did he, in his pessimistic heart, believe that not just the Western Front campaign but the war itself was lost—or, at best, hopelessly stalemated? He was certainly convinced by then that Germany was not strong enough to beat all its enemies simultaneously in a two-front war—and Italy, once one of the Central Powers, was beginning to make threatening noises. Would a third front soon be added to Falkenhayn's worrisome juggle? By the late spring of 1915, it was.

He asked the chancellor, Bethmann Hollweg, Foley writes, "to find a diplomatic solution to Germany's strategic situation." His idea was to achieve a negotiated settlement with one of Germany's enemies, and then deal in turn with the other two, by means either political or military. It was, as Foley writes, "a radical step," an admission that the European hegemony that Germany sought would have to be secured through means other than purely armed ones. Germany had rolled the bones that Schlieffen and Moltke had bequeathed it; the great gamble had come up short.

The November 18 meeting between Bethmann Hollweg and Falkenhayn at the latter's Charleville-Mézières headquarters must have been a strained and uneasy confrontation. We have a good idea of what was said: soon after, the chancellor sent a detailed memorandum to Arthur Zimmermann, the under state secretary for foreign affairs. Falkenhayn's message, said Bethmann, was not promising:

> As long as Russia, France and England stay together it is impossible for us to defeat our opponents in such a way that we can make a decent peace. On the contrary we would run the risk of slowly exhausting ourselves. Either Russia or France must be detached. If we can succeed in causing Russia to make peace—and in first line this is what we should try to do—then we will be able to defeat France and England so decisively that we could dictate the peace. . . . It is, however, to be expected with certainty that if

Russia should make peace, France would also sing a different tune. Then, if England were not completely acquiescent we would wear her down, starving her out by means of a blockade based in Belgium, even though some months would be necessary to do so.

Falkenhayn reserved a particular hatred for Great Britain, and one that went almost beyond reason, especially that early in the war. In August 1914, he had noted in his journal, "Without the defeat of England this war will be lost for us." A coming to terms with Russia would free Germany to wage war to the bitter end with its "archenemy," its "most dangerous opponent." A negotiated peace between the two nations was out of the question.

The general staff chief believed that the "psychological moment for contact with Russia would be at hand if General Hindenburg should succeed in defeating the Russians in the battles now taking place." Those Eastern Front battles focused on Warsaw; the Germans, who at first had been forced into retreat, were beginning to stop, and push the Russians back.

There are indications that the chancellor at first agreed in principle with Falkenhayn's separate-peace proposal—with one difference, but an important one. He rejected the general's suggestion of "sending Russia an invitation." The feelers should come from Russia. Bethmann's "political experience," wrote German historian Fritz Fischer, "told him that the consequences at home and abroad would be disastrous if it became known that Germany was making a peace offer." Public reaction always trumps morality.

Soon doubters and naysayers began to surface; Bethmann wavered. At the end of the month, the bluff, jovial Zimmermann, regarded as the "strong man" in the Foreign Ministry, issued a negative memorandum. His main reason for rejecting Falkenhayn's proposal was, he said, his consideration for Germany's two main allies, Austria-Hungary and Turkey. They would surely regard peace overtures to Russia as a betrayal. Zimmermann had an unfortunate reputation for a looseness of lip, but no matter. The damage was done.

Then, on December 6, Bethmann traveled east to Posen, where Generalfeldmarschall Paul von Hindenburg and Generalleutnant Erich Ludendorff's headquarters, the so-called Ober Ost, was located. They made no effort to hide their distaste for the separate-peace proposal. To them, a negotiated settlement would have amounted to a humiliating defeat. They maintained that Russia should be defeated, not at the conference table but on the battlefield: for the foreseeable future, moreover, the emphasis of the war should be shifted to the east. Once Russia capitulated, Germany could turn westward again, but not before. The tough, unbending pair won Bethmann over. In the weeks that followed, the debate over a separate peace became entangled with an effort to get rid of Falkenhayn, led by Hindenburg, Ludendorff, and, most important of all, Bethmann Hollweg. Zimmermann supported Bethmann, arguing that Russia was more dangerous than England.

Falkenhayn survived for another year and a half. The separate-peace proposal did not. By giving in to the hardline easterners, Bethmann made certain that the war would continue. In his switch of positions, he may quite possibly have signed the death warrants for 8 million, mostly men, the number of lives wasted by both sides over the next four years.

The same statesmen and soldiers who, in midsummer, had worried what would happen to them if they didn't back the war, now worried about what would happen if they tried to pull out of it. They had the will to keep the war going but not the will to stop it.

The war would continue, unhindered now. It had taken on a life of its own. The moment, charged with symbolic indifference, had come. Nothing would be the same after it.

NOVEMBER 22 WAS THE DAY when the first German shells struck the Ypres Cloth Hall and, behind it, the Cathedral of St. Martin. Sister Marguerite observed the progress of destruction. "By 9, the Hall was under fire. The first shell fell on the tower, the third on the clock. At about 11 o'clock the carillon collapsed and the Hall was ablaze. It was a horrible spectacle. In a moment the building is a great sea of flame. The St. Martin's Church

On November 22 1914, the Germans began the systematic destruction of the most notable structure in Ypres, the megabuilding called the Cloth Hall. To them, once the town was out of their reach and served no propaganda purpose, the Cloth Hall was just another military target that had to be leveled, along with rest of the town. Here, *L'Illustration* recorded shelling that day of the central tower. (*L'Illustration*)

also went up." By 3 P.M. that Sunday afternoon, the two venerable buildings, cheek by ornate medieval jowl, were beyond saving. The tall main belfry of the Cloth Hall was encased in scaffolding that optimistic workers had not seen fit to remove, even as the battle raged. Ypres had become something of an attraction and the townspeople continued to look forward to the next summer. The shells that had already sheared off the carillon, with its bells that could be heard for miles, now knocked to the pavement the four spirelike corner turrets, gutted the tower, and left unsightly holes on either side of it. The wooden scaffolding added fuel to the flames. The bombardment continued until the evening of November 23. Seven centuries were no match for modern artillery.

Until now the Germans had tried to concentrate their fire on obvious military targets such as known headquarters, soldiers' housing, road junctions, or the railroad station. But those limited intentions had clearly gotten out of hand. Entire sections of Ypres were already in ruin. In the words of a French communiqué, "This magnificent old city was condemned to death on the day when the Emperor was forced renounce the hope of making an entry into it." The words may have been propaganda, but there was a bit of truth in them.

Once the Allies had finally thwarted the drive for Ypres on November 11, the German expectation of new power wielded against a backdrop of Old World practical opulence vanished. When the Germans turned their steel wrath on the Cloth Hall, the Nieuwerck, St. Martin's, and the other revered churches of Ypres, they offered a ready explanation: the Allies were using the spires and towers for observation. "German life," said a semiofficial account with an exculpatory flourish, "is more precious than the finest Gothic architecture."

A secondary purpose came into play, and one that should not be underestimated. Destruction of cultural monuments is, as historian D. C. Watt wrote, "a kind of amputation, a self-mutilation not so much of limbs as of memory and the imagination . . . cultural destruction is a particularly symbolic transgression." He was writing about World War II, but he might have been describing Louvain or Ypres. Premeditated cultural destruction is an instrument of terror, an attack on an enemy's will. How better to undermine the spirit of a nation, its capacity to survive, than to tear down a distinctive scaffolding of culture, carefully constructed over centuries?

Professor Watt's observation is a valid one, but only to a point; much can be written off to accident as well, or collateral damage. Confusing effects with causes can be risky, though understandable. People, as a novelist has recently maintained, "don't like randomness. Randomness is too absurd. They want someone to blame." Blame is comforting. But in the case of the shelling of the Cloth Hall, we have no record of an order having gone out, or of a named perpetrator. Why not a loose cannon like the kaiser-worshipping Berthold von Deimling, who might seem an ideal culprit? (On November 5, guns, apparently belonging to his XV Corps, did drop a couple of shells on the Cloth Hall, an event that Rupprecht called, in his diary, "regrettable"; Falkenhayn also disapproved.) It seems unlikely that a mere corps commander could be responsible for what amounted to a matter of policy. Such a decision could only come from OHL itself. And if OHL had done, surely it would have notified the headquarters of the Fourth and Sixth Armies. Someone would have talked, if not then but in the years after the war. Nobody did.

Both sides faced an acute shell shortage, and that, too, was a determining fact. A deliberate targeting of nonessential buildings such as the Cloth Hall or the Cathedral of St. Martin's, also hit on November 22, would have been deemed a waste of valuable, and for the moment irreplaceable, ammunition. The streams of infantry, cavalry, and supply vehicles, motorized or horse-drawn, passing back and forth along streets on either side of those buildings, were another matter. The Taubes that hovered over the town could see those ceaseless lines, which did not pause for darkness. They could make the difference in this battle and had to be disrupted. But artillery in 1914 was not a weapon of precision. The shells that holed the roof of the Cloth Hall and brought down its turrets, that set fire to the scaffolding around the tower, were probably accidents, shots that had missed their intended human targets. War, and war alone, was to blame.

Ypres rapidly became a ghost town, under fire for four years. One June day in 1915, the American novelist Edith Wharton, a carefully shepherded official visitor who had already contemplated some cooled-down and relatively safe hot spots on the Western Front, passed through. Accompanied by military guides, she strolled toward the Grande Place: "We had seen no emptiness like this. Not a human being was on the streets. Endless lines of houses looked down on us from vacant windows. Our footsteps echoed like the tramp of a crowd, our lowered voices seemed to shout. . . . Ypres has been bombarded to death, and the outer walls of its houses are still standing, so that it presents the distant semblance of a living city, while nearby it is seen as a disemboweled corpse."

The party had just reached the square when the German cannonade began. It had become a regular feature of the brutalized city's daily life, with a "roar" that "seemed to build a roof of iron over the glorious ruins of Ypres." They were forced to beat a hasty, but dignified, retreat.

VICTORS CAN AFFORD TO BE precise.

Between August 23, 1914, and the end of the year, the British sustained 89,846 casualties. At Ypres alone, the figure was 58,155, including 7,960 dead. Almost 30,000 had been wounded; around 18,000 were missing.* The original British Army had practically ceased to exist; even with replacements, it numbered around 20,000 fighting men on November 10, the day before the Prussian Guard attacked. The loss of officers at Ypres had been particularly cruel: about 1,000 were dead or prisoners of war, removed from the war for good. The 1915 edition of *Debrette's Peerage,* Allan Mallinson notes, "was delayed for many months until the editions had been able to revise the entries for almost every blue-blooded family in the kingdom." Because they were automatically elevated to command positions, members of the aristocracy of both sides suffered disproportion-

---

* "Missing" is a tricky word, and can have a variety of meanings, both benign and sinister. A missing man could be, best case, an unreported prisoner of war, or someone temporarily separated from his unit in the confusion of an attack or gone AWOL. Lost soldiers from shattered attacks often wandered around rear areas looking for what remained of their units. The military police would return those unfortunates temporarily shaken loose. Just as likely, however, the missing were men whose bodies were never found. They might have been hit by a shell and vaporized, drowned in mud, or suffocated under sand and not unearthed in time. Skeletons still turn up in the fields around Ypres. Missing men were too often dead men, never counted as such, mourned but not officially commemorated—those "intolerably nameless names" (Siegfried Sassoon's phrase) relegated to memorial walls or to a bone jumble in a head-high marble box (the French way). The Germans favored low-walled rectangles a couple of thousand feet square, eternity at rush hour.

ately from shot and shell. Consider all the "vons," dismounted cavalrymen, who "went west" in the beet fields around Douve Farm at the end of October.

In October and November of 1914, the months of Flanders, the French lost a total of 104,000 for the entire Western Front. Estimates for the Ypres–Yser campaign hover between 50,000 and 85,000. Given the constant French attacks, the higher number seems more probable.

As for the Belgians, King Albert's biographer Emile Cammaert is succinct:

> The Belgian losses can easily be estimated in comparing the effectives of the Divisions before and immediately after the battle [of the Yser]. They dropped from 52,683 men on October 18th, to 34,161 on October 30th; during those twelve days the army lost a third of its effectives in dead, wounded and missing.

That amounts to 18,522, or about 1,500 per day.*

Nobody, not even the Germans themselves, can agree on their casualty figures in the battle for Flanders. As Falkenhayn's broad-front offensive unfolded, Dixmude or Mount Kemmel or the route to Dunkirk along the dunes were objectives as important as Ypres. Only as an afterthought did that venerable town become the main prize of the autumn. The disparities in casualty estimates are a reflection not just of the complexity and scope of the drama but of the size of the German disaster, which authorities did their best to conceal from the public at home.

Historians, and some of the best, estimate that the Germans lost around 80,000 men. The casualty total in the German official history was 103,500, while its official British counterpart upped that figure to 134,315. Even the lower total stuns. What accounts for a discrepancy so wide— a gaping difference of more than 50,000? The easiest answer is that many historians consider just the German losses in the area of the Salient; in

---

* There are no figures for French casualties on the Yser. As for the Germans, they were certainly equal to those of the Belgian Army and probably, Jack Sheldon estimates, much higher. They were continually on the attack, after all, not the prescription for holding down losses.

the matter of casualties, the two official histories extend their reach to the entire distance between the North Sea and La Bassée Canal, a fifty-odd-mile area split by the River Lys.* That accounts for the German designation, the Battle of Flanders. Sir James Edmonds and more recently Ian Beckett put the number of Germans killed at more than 19,600, or about equal to the number of British troops killed on the first day of the Somme, in 1916. That is purely an estimate: the actual figure may be, and probably is, considerably higher. I repeat: we will never know.

On the night of April 14, 1945, in the last major raid on Europe of any consequence by the Royal Air Force, 500 Lancasters bombed Potsdam and destroyed the Imperial German Archives in the process. The entire history of Prussia, not just its Great War records, went up in flame. The raid was, writes Nigel Cave, one of the consummate authorities on the Western Front in the Great War, "a completely pointless attack that achieved nothing of military value, but took with it all the evidence that would have enabled mature consideration of the war to be conducted subsequently." It was a loss to history that can never be retrieved.

The complications and unremitting pressure of battle intensified the difficulty of compiling accurate casualty counts. Tallying up was hardly a primary consideration: counts only became important later on. At the beginning of the war, record-keeping was notoriously sloppy, and not just for the Germans. Once the battle for Flanders was joined, those records became not just sloppy but impossible to keep. In the German Army, for example, it was the *Feldwebels*, the first sergeants, who were charged with counting casualties, but there were so many of them killed or wounded that no one was left to perform the function. In reserve units, certain old soldiers were appointed, but they were often too shocked, too overwhelmed by the magnitude of the losses, to do the job. German casualty counters didn't even bother to include the lightly wounded in their figuring. Numbers were only collected every two weeks; what records that do exist are filled with gaps, missing days, even entire weeks.

---

* Except for brief narrative asides, necessary scene enhancers, the *Official History* rarely ventures north of the Yser Canal at Bixschoote, exclusively French and Belgian sectors.

Meanwhile the German commanders became experts at obfuscation. They failed to release the casualty totals for the Marne and Ypres. They even hid from the public the firing of the chief of the general staff, Helmuth von Moltke, until late in the fall. OHL feared that home front morale would crack if it revealed the true details of German reverses, or the problems of command. They were shameless in their efforts to cover up. Not until 1915 did the generals come to recognize that the home front remained an unexpected source of strength, and would be throughout the war. It never did crack. They should have known better.

Only later in the war did numbers become significant. The Salient battles did produce myths important to the propaganda effort. "From the German side," to quote Foley, "the so-called '*kindermord bei Ypren,*'" or "slaughter of the innocents at Ypres," quickly entered the "the social and cultural consciousness." The myth—and myth it mostly was—became a convenient means, both during and after the war, to rally support and to demonstrate the unity of the nation. Historians have derided and dismantled the notion of the singers in the mist—though, as I have pointed out elsewhere, there was something to it.

For Great Britain, too, the month of Flanders was an "iconic" experience. "The old British Army," the *Official History* says, "was gone past recall." But it had not "fallen in vain." The resistance of what the kaiser referred to as "General French's contemptible little Army," the rifle-wielding "Old Contemptibles" who held off an enemy superior in number and inflicted a disproportionate ratio of casualties, is part of another myth. Once again, the casualty count mattered. "For the British," Foley writes, "the defense of the 'immortal salient' of Ypres had to be worth the high cost."

We should consider one more estimate of loss. I recognize that it is dicey to compare statistics between armies in combat, but the losses of France, Britain, and Belgium were about equal to, and perhaps exceeded, those of the Germans, even allowing for German undercounting, or non-counting. A combined total of around 300,000 casualties was not unreasonable for the Flanders part of the Killing Season—basically a three-week stretch.

"IN NOVEMBER 1914 THE WAR of stagnation had already begun," said one British regimental historian. The quickened "pace of felt time"—George Steiner's phrase—that had defined the previous three months had experienced, in a matter of days, a "brutal deceleration" of upheaval and expectation. Time itself had slowed down. Mud was the appropriate symbol of this new world of war—mud and water. One couldn't exist without the other, and these final two months of 1914 were, even for waterlogged Flanders, the wettest in memory.

"Rain, rain, rain," noted a diarist of the Royal Welch near Armentières on December 4. "The winter floods had come. . . . The parapet fell in right and left; the ditch-trench ran with a rapid current, and had to be abandoned by day."

Mud swallowed attacks. "Suffering heavy casualties in their endeavor to cross the 250 yards of ground, deep in mud, which intervened between our line and the German trenches, they were brought to a standstill within fifty yards of the enemy's position. Here, they remained pinned to such cover as they could find." Men got stuck in the mud and had to be dug out, or they drowned in it. A trench poet of the Royal Scots Fusiliers tried to make light of their predicament:

All that's left of Bill, who took a snooze,
Is just a bayonet rising from the ooze.

Humor couldn't drive away the hardships of the men at the front—*le feu*, the French called it, the fire. In one regiment of French *tirailleurs*—riflemen—200 were sent to the hospital, suffering from frostbite; not a few had to submit to foot amputations. Men came out of the line barely recognizable as soldiers. "It would be difficult to give an idea of the state our men," a Dr. Veaux wrote. "Uniforms are in rags, dirty, soaked, torn, and lacking buttons. . . . More than one head spouts a visored schoolboy cap in place of a kepi; more than one man wears a woman's blouse found in an abandoned house. Faces are filthy, beards unkempt and covered with mud, features emaciated, hair disheveled . . . rifles rusted from twenty days of combat in the rain. Not to worry. These are admirable soldiers."

The French were indeed admirable soldiers; they had fought hard under the most severe conditions, and now they were taking over from their allies. By the end of the month the undermanned British Army held just twenty-one miles of the Western Front, from the foot of Messines Ridge, opposite Wytschaete, south to the La Bassée Canal, at Givenchy. The Salient was now entirely French and would remain so until late winter.

ON NOVEMBER 17, ALBRECHT, THE commander of the Fourth Army, ordered his troops to construct a good line of trenches and erect wire entanglements. It was a sure signal that the defense was about to take over—and that the battle was, indeed, lost. "Position warfare"—*Stellungskrieg*—the dread of German military planners, had swept over the Western Front like the freeze that already enveloped it. That, the events at Ypres had confirmed. The original confrontation in mid-October had begun as an attempt, in Foley's words, "to restore mobility to the battlefield." No failure of the Germans was more glaring. To quote:

> With no vulnerable flank to envelop, the Germans now faced a situation which they were doctrinally ill-equipped to face. German training before the war had heavily emphasized a "war of movement" (*bewegangskrieg*) that sought to exploit enemy weaknesses. Although the Russo-Japanese War and the Balkan Wars had demonstrated the likelihood and the nature of positional warfare, German manuals stressed that field positions were a temporary expedient, and Germans had only trained to conduct breakthroughs on a limited scale. They were unprepared to conduct breakthrough operations necessary on the scale now demanded by the position warfare that had engulfed the entire Western Front.

These words are key to understanding what ultimately went wrong for the Germans in the Flanders battle. Position warfare and a two-front war were now the unpleasant reality that Germany faced. Its planners had hoped to avoid both, and certainly to delay the two-front dilemma. Germany, in the person of Falkenhayn, accepted the change without enthusiasm. *Le feu* had already become a way of life. Now it was taking root in Flanders, the last bastionless bastion. Both sides were digging not just practically unbroken belts of facing trenches, great extended siege works, but also ever-widening systems, consisting of several connected lines.

As Falkenhayn wrote in 1919, two years before his death, "The transition to trench warfare was not effected by the independent decision of the Chief of the General Staff, but under the stern pressure of necessity." A defensive war is rarely a winning war. You have the suspicion that, as the Killing Season came to an end, the cynical realist knew that Germany had lost. By the time he tried to stop the fighting, it was already too late. The war had assumed a life of its own.*

WE NOW COME TO AN episode that has become one of the narrative standbys of the Great War, the Christmas Truce of 1914. A milestone on a trail that eventually led nowhere, it has received so much attention of late that it has practically become an historical cliché. And yet, even a passing mention belongs in these pages. The northern extreme of the truce was just below the village of Messines, some six miles from Ypres, where Cheshires killed a pig and, according to their regimental history, "cooked it in No Man's Land and shared it with the Boche." Though manifestations of fraternization spread the length of the Western Front, the most notable occurred in Flanders, in fields recently fought over. You have to

---

* Falkenhayn, with the backing of the kaiser, withstood the challenge to his leadership, led by Hindenburg, Ludendorff, and Bethmann Hollweg, early in the winter of 1914–15. Though Germany would emphasize the Eastern Front throughout 1915, Falkenhayn remained a Westerner at heart. It would be his undoing. Once he championed Verdun in 1916, only to see the "Meuse Mill" become a corpse factory for both sides, the team of Hindenburg and Ludendorff could at last preside over his ouster.

Saxon regimental troops and members of the Fifth London Rifle Brigade celebrate Christmas in Ploegsteert Wood on the Franco–Belgian border. The famous truce did happen and was probably more widespread than authorities on both sides let on. But in the end the truce accomplished little more than giving weary men rest and diversion, a few moments to swap beer, plum pudding, cigars, and copies of *Punch* with the enemy, as well as a chance to bury the dead lying between the lines. (Imperial War Museum)

regard this spontaneous outpouring as a consequence of, and reaction to, the horror and strain of the vast Flanders Battle.*

The images of the truce are familiar. On Christmas Eve, pine trees, with candles blazing, appear on the parapets of German trenches. All up and down the line, there are cries of "Don't shoot!" Signs are hoisted: "YOU NO FIGHT, WE NO FIGHT." Singing begins: "*Stille Nacht, Heilige Nacht*" (Silent night, holy night). French and British soldiers join Ger-

---

* Partly because those in command frowned on fraternization, you find little mention of it in official records. But reading documents such as the World War I notebooks of the French corporal Louis Barthas, one of the essential narratives of the Western Front experience, you come to recognize that the phenomenon was more widespread than we have long believed. The English-language version of the Barthas account is called *Poilu*, published by the Yale University Press and translated by Edward M. Strauss.

mans in caroling (mixed with the strains of "Home, sweet Home"). Regimental bands play national anthems.

Christmas Day dawns. Bodies are gathered from the area still known as *Vorfeld* ("the space in front") or *La Zone Neûtre* ("the neutral zone"), and British chaplains or (in one case) a German divinity student conduct joint services. Soldiers from both sides clamber from their trenches to meet what everyone will soon call no-man's-land (*"Niemandsland," "Le Nomansland," "La terre à personne"*). They exchange food, wine, tobacco, and gifts. A copy of *Punch* is worth a handful of German cigars. A juggler performs. A barber sets up shop. Barrels of German beer are rolled out and traded for British bully beef—corned beef—and plum pudding. Rifles, too, are exchanged. There are times when, even as enemies meet in brief amity, they can see neighbors, in trenches a few hundred yards away, busily engaged in trying to kill one another.

Was a football match played between Germans and British? It may or may not have happened. Saxons, it was said, took on Lancashire Fusiliers and beat them 3 to 2. On a disputed call by a referee, naturally. The winning goal scorer was supposedly offside.

The Christmas Truce ended, sooner than later, as it was bound to do. Weather and Red Tabs signaled its demise and impossibility. On December 27, the day after Boxing Day, the skies opened, and another Flemish soaker swept in. The ground unfroze and turned to deep mud. Two days later, a storm of tropical proportions followed, complete with thunder and lightning that slashed across the sky. Gale force winds drove the rain in sheets. The moment seemed right for a crackdown. Orders from the headquarters of Allied and German armies prohibited fraternization. Any approach to the enemy would be considered treason, with the appropriate penalty.

Peace from below had fared no better than peace from above.

AFTER GHELUVELT, HITLER HAD BEEN made a *Gefreiter,* lance corporal. It was a promotion, but technically it still left him a private, without the power to command other soldiers. He never, in his next four years on the Western Front, attained full corporal, a rank to which various writers have elevated him. Hitler spent most of his army career as a dispatch runner and was still learning his perilous trade when he arrived at the Messines Ridge trenches early in December.

By then, the Germans held the entire ridge; the British and French, to the west, had dug themselves in at the bottom of the hill. Archibald Wavell, later a field marshal, but then a staff officer, felt that it was his job to visit his own trenches. He was appalled by what he found:

> The trenches were a single line of very poor construction, badly sited, undrained, with very little wire to protect them. In the rain they became knee-deep in mud, and I once found the whole garrison of a trench sitting on a parapet, preferring the risk of enemy bullets to the mud in the trench. It was partly the fault of the Command and staff for not adjusting the trench line to the ground, partly lack of material and tools, and partly laziness. We started a brigade factory for making appliances to improve the trenches, duck-boards, mud scoops, revetting material, etc.

On the ridge above, conditions were not much better. As a soldier of the List Regiment named Albert Weisgerber told his wife:

> We are now rotated out of the trenches every three days as the troops would not be able to endure staying there any longer. They stand up to their knees in muck and water. The men build themselves hollows like cavemen, but the rain presses against the walls at night and everything falls in on itself. Some of the soldiers have been killed this way. The water is disgusting. . . . The rain of bullets is more tolerable.*

* At the end of 1914, Albert Weisgerber has to be reckoned the most notable member of the List Regiment. An influential painter and illustrator, his work can be seen as an attempt to bridge the considerable gap between Impressionism and Expressionism, a neat trick that he sometimes pulled off. He was a friend of Paul Klee, Wassily Kandinsky, and Henri Matisse. He was, in other words, the artist Hitler would never be. A British bullet cut him down the next spring. Weisgerber was a conspicuous loss to the German artistic community.

The Lists (as the regiment was still called) did not have to spend Christmas in trench squalor but were relieved by the 17th Bavarian Reserve Regiment and bivouacked in Messines itself, in the ruins of the village. "Messines is a village of 2,400 inhabitants," Hitler wrote, "or rather it was a village, for nothing is left of it except an enormous heap of rubble." Was this the interval when the former Viennese postcard artist did a watercolor of the gutted vaults and towers of the medieval monastery of Messines? It looks like a sketch for a postcard. Three companies of the List gathered around a Christmas tree in one of the great monastic rooms that had recently housed orphans. They sang "Silent Night," opened presents donated by businesses and the common folk of Munich, and drank beer—all except Hitler, who was a teetotaler. Did he join in the celebration? Probably, but only as a matter of show: he never hid his dislike of religion and its main events. That dislike extended to his feelings about the truce. He refused to participate. A fellow dispatch runner later remembered, "When everyone was talking about the Christmas 1914 fraternization with the Englishmen, Hitler revealed himself to be its bitterest opponent."

On Boxing Day, the twenty-sixth, the regiment returned to the line. Some of its men set up a Christmas tree on a parapet, lit candles, and rang bells attached to its branches, inviting the British garrison opposite to join them. Khaki figures, many clad in sheepskin vests and balaclavas, soon appeared in the open. Did the prudish Hitler witness the frolic between the lines that then took place? If so, Europe's ticking time bomb signaled his disgust with silence. "There was no shooting," the indefatigable Weisgerber wrote, "and instead all the soldiers came out of trenches and danced together." A British infantryman accompanied the martial merry-makers on a harmonica.

"It is a strange war," Weisgerber said.

DURING THAT FIRST CHRISTMAS OF the war, a Scots Guard Lieutenant, Sir Edward Hulse, wrote a letter home describing an impromptu hunt by men of the two sides:

Just after we had finished "Auld Lang Syne" an old hare started up, and seeing many of us about in unwonted spot, did not know which way to go. I gave one loud "view-hallow," and one and all, British and Germans, rushed about giving chase, slipping up on the frozen plough, falling about, and after a hot two minutes we killed in the open, a German and one of our fellows falling together heavily upon the completely baffled hare. Shortly afterwards we saw four more hares, and killed one again; both were good heavy weight, and had evidently been out between the two rows of trenches for the last two months, well-fed on the cabbage patches, etc., many of which are untouched on the "No Man's Land." The enemy kept one and we kept the other.

No-man's-land. That Hulse used the phrase is clear evidence that by Christmas 1914 it had already seeped into the soldiers' idiom. Major Hankey, in fact, used the phrase in his staccato account of the events of October 31. It seems to have spread as swiftly as the trenches themselves. How, and when, did the term no-man's-land originate? Did it arise spontaneously? Or did an individual coin it? And, if the latter was the case, who was the inventor?

The phrase does have fairly ancient roots. No-man's-land in medieval England was a bit of waste, or unowned, land. It was also a plot of ground lying outside the North Wall of London, where executions had once taken place—just to the north of the present Marble Arch and Speaker's Corner. At that point the term seemed to disappear from the language. The late historian Malcolm Brown traced its reappearance, in the military sense in which we have come to use it.

In 1908, a short story called "The Point of View" was published in the Edinburgh-based *Blackwood's Magazine*. The story may seem ordinary by our standards, but the author was not. His name was Ernest (later Major General Sir Ernest) Dunlop Swinton, and he was an officer and military thinker who had considerable influence in the British Army, especially his comments on operations and tactics. His martial cautionary tales, cast as fiction, were widely read by military men, at least those who took time off from horseback riding to dip into printed matter. Swinton's story appeared in a collection called *The Green Curve,* under the pseudonym "Ole Luk-Oie," apparently (Brown said) a Danish phrase meaning "Shut Eye."

"The Point of View" is set in a future war much like the one that would break out six years later. I quote from what is for us the key passage, which describes the view from a deserted zigzag trench:

> As soon as the light faded altogether from the sky, the yellow flames of different conflagrations glowed more crimson, and the great white eyes of searchlights shone forth, their wandering beams lighting up now this, now that horror. Here and there in that wilderness of dead bodies—the dreadful *"No-Man's-Land"* [italics mine] between the opposing lines—deserted guns showed up singly or in groups . . .

"The dreadful 'No-Man's-Land' between the opposing lines." As Brown writes, "a seed was planted." Fast-forward to the fall of 1914. Though the French had denied the new battlefields of the Western Front to all civilian correspondents, they were willing to accept a qualified officer. Winston Churchill proposed Swinton. Swinton responded with a series of syndicated dispatches signed simply, "Eye-Witness present with General Headquarters." If the writing and the details observed seem a bit blander than what Swinton ordinarily produced, Kitchener and his platitudinous censor's pen must take the blame.

Is it a stretch to imagine Swinton using the phrase "no-man's-land" in conversations at Sir John French's Saint Omer headquarters or in tours of the trenches? Is it a stretch, too, to imagine officers who had read "The Point of View" remembering the phrase? Swinton himself would use "no-man's-land" in a dispatch that was syndicated throughout the British Isles just after Christmas. Many may have read it over breakfast tea on Boxing Day. Another mention came in his description of British trenches below Ypres. The "Eye-Witness" had been conducting his many readers on a tour through a trench system already well developed. Suddenly he could go no farther. In a dispatch that is so vividly written that it may not have been tampered with, Swinton painted an image of terminal stagnation and death:

> Seamed with dug-outs, barrows, trenches, and excavations of every kind, . . . it is bounded on the front by a long discontinuous irregular line fringed with barbed wire and broken by saps wriggling still more to the front. This is the Ultima Thule.

> We have arrived.

> Beyond, of width varying according to the nature of the fighting and of the ground, is neutral territory, the no-man's-land between the hostile forces. It is strewn with the dead of both sides, some lying, others caught and propped in the sagging wire, where they may have been for days, still others half buried in craters or destroyed parapets. When darkness falls, with infinite caution, an occasional patrol or solitary sniper may explore this gruesome area. . . . On the other side of this zone of the unburied dead bristles a similar fringe of wire and a long succession of low mounds and parapets—the position of the enemy. And woe betide the man who in daylight puts up his head carelessly to take a long glance at it.

Could there be a better description of no-man's-land than this first one to name it in the Great War? The phrase, by now deeply embedded in the language, would outlast that war. It will outlast us all.

No-man's-land had become the barrier that men would spend years trying, without success, to breach. The tank (another word coined by Swinton) was one answer, but fell short of its mission, in that war at least. No one had planned for no-man's-land. A spontaneous creation, it had grown into the ash heap of siege craft, an impenetrable membrane of lethal indifference, the province of rats, midnight wiring parties, snipers, and the dead. It defied armies. Not that many weeks earlier, time had seemed to run riot. Now as the year dwindled to a close, no-man's-land had developed into an ultimate metaphor for time stopped, time frozen, a muddy ending without beginning or middle. The collision of armies on the Western Front had come to that.

At Ypres in 1914, loss of nerve cost the Germans a war. Pride kept them going.

Sur une route du Nord.

Too soon, the truces were over, the war returned, and men like these French troops in Flanders, drawn by the illustrator Georges Scott, were marching back to the trenches in a cold rain that never seemed to let up. What had happened to the hopes of summer? It was winter now. The dreams were gone.
(*L'Illustration*)

EPILOGUE: NOVEMBER 17–18, 1914

NEAR KLEIN ZILLEBEKE, BELGIUM

Photographed from the French wire, a German corpse dissolves into the earth in a grassy interval of no-man's-land. (*L'Illustration*)

CAPT. SIR MORGAN CROFTON GAINED HIS TITLE THE OLD–FASHIONED WAY: THE brother who was the Fifth Baronet of Mohill, Ireland, died of disease, and he became the Sixth. He inherited estates in Ireland and Hampshire. A cavalryman, he had been badly wounded in the Boer War. He now belonged to the 2nd Life Guards. An expensive divorce forced him to leave the army early in 1914 and try to turn a profit from his numerous acres. The war intervened, and he was called back in October. Crofton seems to have been a decent soldier. What distinguished him was a certain gift for observation. He kept a diary, summing up his military experiences: "Bored in billets, terrified in trenches."

Crofton crossed the Channel at the beginning of November and reached Ypres on the fourteenth. The kaiser's November 11 attack had just failed. Hostilities were allowed to simmer for the winter. It was by now early evening but already inky black when Crofton led a column of horsemen into town. They filed through dark and deserted streets, "fitful flashes of our torch" revealing "gaunt walls and debris." In a matter of days, the busy hub of Flanders had become an empty husk. "There was something very eerie in our procession along the pavé streets, which re-echoed to our horses feet. It was indeed a City of the Dead."

They left Ypres by the Menin Gate and "embarked on the long road leading to the Trenches." The guns on both sides rarely let up. "From time to time a shell sailed over the road, and burst with a resounding roar in an adjacent field." French star shells lit up the sky. "The road was one stupendous procession of horses and guns and wagons." Crofton's troop finally found the mingy peasant farm where they were to be billeted.

Three days passed before Crofton spent his first night in the trenches, near the village of Klein Zillebeke, south of Ypres. It was by then Tuesday, November 17. At the entrance to a communication trench leading to the front line, the cavalrymen dismounted, left their horses, and took off their spurs. They were walkers now, foot soldiers. "A terrific musketry fire is going on all around." That afternoon the Germans had attacked. Three times they had rushed forward, three times the British had driven them back. Stretcher bearers were still bringing out casualties. Nearby, Crofton spotted ten dead British soldiers, "laid in a line." Movement was difficult: the trenches were only five feet deep and a yard wide. Two more corpses blocked his forward progress and had to be removed. "It was horrible, for the Corpses were dragged and pushed along like sacks of potatoes, any-how, to get them clear of the Trench, the oncoming men cursing and fall-ing over them." The night was "bitterly cold, but very clear, and the stars shone like electric lamps." "The men huddled together for warmth." "About 20 yards out beyond our trenches we heard wounded Germans . . . calling out in a plaintive and mournful manner. They were like Banshees. Then one by one the cries ceased presumably as the men died."

Around 5 A.M., it became light enough "to see a bit of where we were." Crofton peered out through a peephole. He counted about forty German bodies lying in front of their stretch of trench. "Some were hanging on the barbed wire entanglements where they had been shot down." The barbed wire was a recent addition, and in places sappers had only been able to attach a single strand to posts. Bodies were hanging off that single strand too. Some of the dead "lay like heaps of old clothes, others were on their knees with their heads resting on the ground on their foreheads, as if they were trying to stand on their heads. No one, apparently, had made it all the way across No Man's Land and into the British trenches. A Sapper Officer in my section of the Trench who had witnessed the attack yesterday afternoon said that it was very halfhearted and that they had run forward, as if expecting to be killed."

"We signed on to die," a veteran of the Great War, my own father, once told me. Western civilization, and the assured way of life it represented, seemed bent on committing suicide, in the most publicly grotesque sort of way.

The future was out there, hanging on the new barbed wire.

ACKNOWLEDGMENTS

My fascination with the First World War began with my father and the stories he would tell about it. In the spring of 1917, he had taken a leave of absence from Harvard and joined the American Field Service. He would spend six months in France on the Western Front, all of them in the sector known as the Chemin des Dames.*

A quarter century later, we were in the middle of another world war. My father, hard of hearing and overage by now, had no part in this one. He was a writer. We lived in a small and isolated community in western Connecticut, where people still mainly made their living from dairy farms. In those years, you rarely saw a young man, unless he was wearing a uniform. The men I knew were all older. The First World War was their war. A large stone stood across from the town hall, with a bronze plaque fixed to it listing the names of those who had served in that war. I remember seeing two or three stars by those names, men who had died in France. That earlier war had left its scars, even in this small New England village, but nothing like the lists of the fallen you see on monuments in the U.K. or in France. There you find not just a scattering of stars but separate clusters of names, ones that in many cases outnumber the survivors.

My father sometimes talked about that war, his war. Unlike Krebs, the main character in Hemingway's story "Soldier's Home," he hadn't been so closely involved in horror and violence that he refused to talk about what he had seen and felt. His had been mainly a spectator's war.

* "The Ladies' Road." I explain its meaning in Chapter 5, "Testimony of the Spade."

He had discovered, when he arrived, that there were already too many Americans driving ambulances; my father became a reserve driver and loader for camions that carried artillery shells. He would describe to me the sight of endless columns of men and guns marching through the village where the young Americans were quartered, sometimes for days at a time. He worked in the flatlands on either side of the Aisne River, on its north bank underneath heights that the Germans mainly occupied—that same strategic ridge that both sides had competed to reach in 1914. I would listen, engrossed, as he described barrages bursting in a widening line of smoke along the ridge above. That was as close as he came to real action. Or he would recall alfresco lunches of baguettes and cheese, while an occasional German shell, big as a boxcar, would pass overhead, to thunder into some unseen target a mile or two away. All this was thrilling stuff for an eight-year-old, even if my father was probably as safe as if he had viewed the hurtling object from a tower in a switching yard.

It was a single momentary sighting many years later that set me off again. Late one afternoon early in the fall of 1969, I was driving from Paris to London. Somewhere in the countryside close to Montdidier—the German offensives of 1918 had reached this far—I spotted a steep-sloping hillside pasture that was curiously polka-dotted with rounded scoops in the earth, at that hour already shrouded in shadow. They could be only one thing: ancient shell holes.

I knew I would be back, if not here, then someplace like it. The next summer, I suggested to a magazine an article on a return to the battlefields of the First World War and was given the assignment. I was living in London then. My landlord was a retired soldier, Colonel Gundry-White—I always addressed him as "Colonel." He had spent nearly six months on the Somme in 1916 with the Norfolk Regiment. One night he came up to my flat and he talked about his time there. In *The History of the Norfolk Regiment 1914–1918*, I found references to him. He took part in the disaster of July 1, but the following day we are told that "Lieutenant Gundry-White's bombers drove off a German machine gun which had been causing loss. . . ." Late in September, we find him at another hot spot, the Schwaben redoubt. A German counterattack "across the open" was "practically annihilated by Lieutenant Gundry-

White with Lewis gun and rifle fire." The only reason he survived, he said, was his expertise in a specialized aspect of trench combat. He was sent back to England to be an instructor in the use of the grenade—or bomb, as it was called.

I decided to focus on the Somme. I spent a week there, investigating trenches still discernible in the woods and mine craters ninety feet deep, as well as places where people like Robert Graves and Siegfried Sassoon had viewed the battle unfolding. I had never before seen cemeteries so large or so numerous—"the silent cities" someone once called them. The article appeared, but my curiosity about the Great War remained.

It took a decade or more before I was able to revisit that part of the world. I spent an entire summer wandering with my wife and our two small daughters from Nieuport Bains on the North Sea to that odd ex-crescence on the Swiss border with France known as the Bec de Canard—the Duck's Bill. The distance at the end of 1914 had frozen at 470 miles; we must have traveled a couple of thousand. There were times when I would leave my family where we were staying and explore. Or I would follow paths into a forest carrying a small child on my back, to discover a bunker, its concrete green with moss and darkened with mold, its deep forward apertures, machine-gunless now, staring out at the trees with empty menace. I would poke along trenches still more than a head high, happen upon stands of original barbed wire, and slide down slanting shafts hacked through rock a century ago, while my French guide warned me to watch out for the rusting .75 shell that lay at the bottom: *"Très dangereux!"*

We spent several days in the area where my father had served, renting a three-room house in a village called Craonne. Our landlord was a friendly farmer, who seemed not to mind my hesitancy with spoken French. One afternoon he showed me a pair of chests filled with battle-field ephemera he had unearthed in the years he owned and tilled the land: nose cones of high explosive shells, shrapnel pellets, rusting French and German helmets, cartridge casings, half a pocket comb, canteens recognizable from their pointed spouts, wineskins in metal. I spent hours wandering through woods, climbing mounds still ringed with trenches, or coming upon tunnel entrances that I knew were too risky to enter. The poet Apollinaire spent time here. I found claypits (more tunnels) that might have been the ones in which a lesser poet, Alan Seeger, serving in the French Foreign Legion, sought refuge from bombardments in 1915. I looked for the sixteenth century Château de Soupir, the subject of one of the first published poems my father wrote:

> *The trenches run diagonally*
> *Across the gardens and the lawns,*
> *and jagged wire from tree to tree.*
> *The lake is desolate of swans.*
> *In tortured immobility*
> *The deities of stone and bronze*
> *abide each new catastrophe.*

All that remains of the original structure are two gates, the high iron bars of the entrance, and an impressive stone back entrance rising, unattended by walls, in the middle of a field of maize—what an American like me would call a cornfield.

Can I have had a more important inheritance from my father than his vision of that war, reverberations of memory that have become as endless as those columns of marching men he described to me so many years ago?

My father also turned me on to the American Civil War. Sometimes it seemed that the only subject we could talk about with ease was military history. We once spent a week touring major battle sites. It was the idea of the writer Hamilton Basso, a family friend, who came from New Orleans: We often talked about the war. He thought I should understand both sides and suggested that I go see for myself. He wrote me a check for $100, a fortune seventy years ago; my father chipped in. We took along a large canvas bag weighed down with books. Every night we would read up on what we would see the next day. In the wilderness in northern Virginia we came on trenches that had been dug almost nine decades earlier. To see little Round Top is to understand that the outcome of the whole battle may have depended on possession of that slight eminence: from its summit, artillery could have ripped apart the Union line. That trip may have earned me my first job after college. I applied to the now-defunct magazine of popular history, *American Heritage.* The editor-in-chief was the writer then considered the preeminent Civil War historian, Bruce Catton. He was among those who interviewed me for an opening and was impressed by my knowledge of the war; I was hired.

The 1950s were a heyday for military history. By the time of the Vietnam War, a decade later, the subject had gone out of fashion, totally; everyone I knew seemed ready to join a protest march. The magazine I worked for, *The Reporter,* a liberal-leaning news magazine, went under largely because of its support for the war. I found myself working as a book editor. I once proposed publishing an excellent manuscript on an episode in the American Revolution. "Forget it," the editor-in-chief told me. "Military history sells worse than poetry."

That eventually changed. The endless Vietnam War had to end. In time, readers even began to turn again to books on military history. Late in the 1980s two men inaugurated a magazine devoted to the subject. The late Byron Hollinshead and Elihu Rose hired me to make their idea, *MHQ: The Quarterly Journal of Military History,* a reality. The thrill (and terror) of starting a magazine, even a small-circulation specialty one, is indescribable. Everything from working with a designer—I had a good one, Marleen Adlerblum—to figure the look of our creation, to choosing a typeface, hiring a staff, commissioning enough articles to fill a first issue (I didn't have time to worry about a second), to writing a lead editorial that tried to define what I was hoping to accomplish before I really knew myself. I composed it one Sunday afternoon in August at the table of my un–air-conditioned kitchen, shirtless and drenched in sweat.

I edited *MHQ* for a decade. I had no choice but to become a reasonably competent authority on the history of arms—yes, arms and the man and, increasingly now, the woman. It was the best job I have ever had, and I loved it. I will always thank By and Elly for putting their trust in me.

Elly was our chief backer, a real estate giant of New York City, who was also an adjunct professor of military history at NYU, one of those rare individuals whose enthusiasm is constant and catching. He accompanied at least one of the tours I led to the Western Front. In Reims, we had a day off, rented a car, and headed for a fortress in the Maginot Line called Hackenberg, not knowing what we would find. When they built the line in the 1930s, the French were determined not to repeat the mistakes embedded in the construction of their Great War forts: there can be no better examples than the death traps our tour would investigate the next day in Verdun. We found ourselves in electric trolleys headed into the deep insides of a high hill, poking around dormitories and giant kitchens, and even into a dentist's office and a great chamber full of bedframes, the hospital. With the addition of several hundred mattresses, sheets, and blankets, it was practically ready for the business of war. We had happened upon the fortress during the one day of the month when it was open to the public. Talk about magic afternoons.

Seeing places where history has been made had long since become a minor passion, part hobby, part obsession. It can be a building such as Monticello or Samuel Johnson's house in London; it can be a battlefield, be it Saratoga, Antietam, Masada (with its imposing Roman siege ramp still in place), or, of course, Ypres, cradled by a low but insurmountable fishhook-shaped plateau. How can you hope to hope to write about a place and describe what happened there with any degree of accuracy and perception if you have never seen it?

Sometimes the thrill of discovery can come from locating a place where a notable historical moment happened. In Europe, often as not, you usually find such sites by the side of a road. Imagination helps, as do a supply of accurate maps and a few decent memoirs. I once spent ten days with two retired men of finance, Gurnee Hart and the late Philip Swan, who wanted to retrace the routes of the German First and Second Armies in August and September 1914, the far right of the Schlieffen/Moltke swing into France. We started at Liège and ended at the marshes of St. Gond. For me, the high point of our tour came one mid-morning when, driving south from Chateau-Thierry, I abruptly announced that we should stop the car. We had passed through a fair-sized stand of timber and, amid wheat fields now, were headed down a hill south of a village called Villiers-Ste. George. This was empty country. The only building in sight was a grain elevator rising on the eastern horizon. What was so special about this place in the middle of nowhere? Here, on the night of September 6–7, a Lieutenant Chorus, of the German 12th Grenadier Regiment, had sneaked with a patrol of scouts through the woods behind us and come on columns of French troops moving in disorderly retreat through recently harvested wheatfields. I read to my companions from the remarkable memoir *The Advance from Mons 1914* by Chorus's commander, Captain Walter Bloem. "Neither Chorus nor I guessed at that moment that he and his patrol had penetrated farther into France than any other German soldier."

MANY PEOPLE HAVE HELPED ME with this book, and several have played major roles in its shaping, perhaps unwittingly. I must begin with Bruce I. Gudmundsson (major, USMC, ret.), my friend and longtime contributor to *MHQ*. Bruce taught for years at the Marine Corps University in Quantico, Virginia: I think of him as a tactical historian, a rare but important designation, for it tells how wars on the ground are really fought. He is a linguist and a fine writer. It was Bruce Gudmundsson who sent me translations of pre–World War I German training manuals, documents that gave me a clue as to why Germany suffered such horrendous losses in 1914. I learned from him how effective, and ineffective, shrapnel could be, and how machine guns operated. It was Bruce who helped me figure out, as early as 1996, why Hitler may have panicked at Gheluvelt. Why mince words? I could not have written this book, at least not in the form it took, without his help. Whatever errors or misjudgments I have made are mine, and mine alone. That is also true of my ultimate conclusions, some of which, I'm sure, Bruce would not share.

At a time when I was floundering in a project, a journey along the Western Front, that seemed to be going west—a favorite euphemism for dying in the Great War—my agent, the late Carl Brandt, suggested that I reduce the scope of my book. I replied with an idea: the fall of 1914. He liked the idea. I felt suddenly freed. I had narrowed my story from four years to four months. At the same time that I did so, I found that, as if denying some sacred law of historical physics, my view of the war had expanded. In a single afternoon, Germany had thrown away its best chance to win. I recognize that what I say here is not the accepted view: no matter. If nothing else, it's time to shake up our thinking about the Great War. The inspiration for the redirection of my mission I owe to

Carl. My old friend from prep school and college, and my longtime agent, is, alas, no longer with us. I have been fortunate, though, in the agent Carl willed me, Henry Thayer, a person gifted with Carl's sure radar-like sense of what's right, when to act, and what direction to take.

Another individual rates special thanks, my great friend of half a century—we met in Majorca, and now we both live in Newport, Rhode Island—the writer John de St. Jorre. John and I regularly spend an evening drinking whiskey and listening to jazz, both shared passions. One night more than a year ago, I asked him for a favor: would he look at my manuscript? He did, and as a former soldier in the British Army, set me straight on certain military terms and distinctions. He wished I had written more about how the people of Ypres had experienced the developing siege by the Germans. He was right, and I did. John suggested other changes, good ones all, which I need not go into here, except to say that I made them. Can there be a greater gift from one writer to another?

Geoffrey Parker is another person who deserves special mention. He has to be considered one of the world's foremost historians; he is also a friend. His output is astounding. His books mainly describe the western way of war and how it developed in the sixteenth and seventeenth centuries, especially in Spain and the region we now describe as the Low Countries. Two are especially notable and influential. The first is *The Military Revolution: Military Innovation and the Rise of the West, 1500–1800*—the period we now call Early Modern. More to the point these days is *Global Crisis: War, Climate Change and Catastrophe in the Seventeenth Century.* Parker gives example after example of the way climate change affected history of that time over the entire world, the implication being that the situation is far worse now. It's one of the major works of history in recent years. I had the good fortune to co-edit a book with Geoffrey: *The Reader's Companion to Military History,* a one-volume encyclopedia on the subject. No one has taught me more about the historian's craft.

So many others have helped, in ways large and small. Nigel Cave, the editor of Pen & Sword's Battleground Europe series and one of the genuine authorities on the Great War, has many times answered my questions. The three books he wrote with Jack Sheldon on Ypres in 1914—Cave handled the Allies and Sheldon the Germans—are matchless sources.

Though I have never met him, I owe an enormous debt to Jack Sheldon for his own books—at last count there were seven about the German Army on the Western Front. His translations of contemporary texts from German sources, none of which have been available until recently, have presented a war that few of us knew existed, the war as German soldiers experienced it. Sheldon, along with fine military historians such as Robert A. Doughty, Holger H. Herwig, Hew Strachan, Annika Mombauer, William Philpott, Holger Afflerbach, Dennis E. Showalter, Nick Lloyd, and Alexander Watson, have begun to give us the fresh reinterpretations so needed.

To this growing list I shall add Tom Gudmestad. An emergency medical technician by profession, he tries to go to the Western Front at least once a year. Few people (except for Nigel Cave) can know every last nook and underground cranny of the Western Front quite as thoroughly as Tom does. I once traveled to Seattle and spent an evening and two days at his home there. He must have thought me a pest, but I came away with information I could not have secured otherwise. Roderick Suddaby, the Keeper of Documents at the Imperial War Museum, has to be one of the pleasantest people I've ever dealt with, and some years ago I was lucky to spend ten days researching at the IWM. Dr. Peter Liddle, founder of the Liddle Collection at the University of Leeds, has amassed over a long career a corpus of individual experience documents of the two world wars that can only be described as extraordinary. The Liddle Collection is, quite simply, a British national treasure.

There are many others who have helped along the way. Jean-Pierre Verney, one of France's foremost authorities on the war, once spent three days with me, showing me trenches, tunnels, and woods full of unexploded shells (they have since been cleaned up). Here was a hidden topography of war that I could have encountered in no other way. A large part of his collection of Great War artifacts and memorabilia can now be seen in a new museum at Meaux, on the Marne. I feel no hesitancy about consulting my neighbor and friend Peter Zwack (brig. gen. USA, ret.), the former head of military intelligence in Afghanistan and military attaché to Moscow, on military matters. I often consult Robert L. O'Connell about weaponry, or Holger H. Herwig and Bruce Gudmundson about the

German Army. Edward M. Strauss, my friend and former publisher of *MHQ*, later did the fine translation, *Poilu*, by the barrel-maker and some-time corporal Louis Barthas, a book I consider to be the best running account of the Great War. No day-by day record that I know of better chronicles the lives (and deaths) of the ordinary French soldier. Robert A. Doughty (brig. gen. USA, ret.) wrote for me. Better yet, he wrote a book that can only be called magisterial, *Pyrrhic Victory: French Strategy and Operations in the Great War*. Two writers, Victor Davis Hanson and Barry Strauss, both authorities on ancient warfare, have deepened my understanding of the conduct of men in battle.

Others have helped me in various, but important ways: Theodore R. Cook, Victor Davis Hanson, John A. Lynn, Allan R. Millett, Geoffrey Norman, Douglas Porch, Ronald H. Spector, Tim Travers, and Geoffrey C. Ward.

Too many of those to whom I owe thanks are no longer with us, but their absence should not deny them the recognition they deserve. The late Rose E. B. Coombs, MBE, wrote the pioneering guidebook to the Western Front, *Before Endeavours Fade*. Twice I spent entire days with her and came away with my head fairly spinning with fresh knowledge and lists of sites I might otherwise have overlooked. It was the writer Frederic V. Grunfeld who persuaded me to live in Europe, and when I went to the Somme that first time, I traveled in style, in the Morgan sports car he lent me. Later he gave me a book that is still a favorite memoir, Paul Maze's *A Frenchman in Khaki*. In Ypres—or Ieper, as the Flemish call it—I linked with Tony R. DeBruyne, who guided me personally, as well as acting as guest guide on tours I led, to the major sites of the Salient. Nobody was more charged with anecdotes or arcane knowledge about Ypres than Tony. Another Tony, Tony Spagnoly, was a dedicated amateur historian, who would regularly keep me posted on fresh discoveries on the Western Front. Malcolm Brown took me behind the scenes at the IWM to view works of art too rarely seen; he also wrote one of the best articles I published at *MHQ*, on no-man's-land. A Belgian professor of military history, Henri Bernard, patiently answered my questions and sent me a copy of his book, *L'An 14 et La Campagne des Illusions*, which included large portions of the diary his father, Major Arsène Bernard, kept during the first months of the war. The major commanded a battalion of chasseurs, from Liège to Antwerp to the Yser. Jan Morris, that consummate prose stylist and world traveler, wrote for me and encouraged this project. The late David Kahn, one of the great authorities on codes and codebreaking, taught me the importance of intelligence, as well as the unanticipated ways it could go wrong. Thomas Fleming and I shared a common fascination about that war. He inspired many excellent ideas; I hope I did the same for him. I lived in Connecticut for several years. There, I had no friend closer than the writer George Feifer. He had lived for years in Russia when it was still the Soviet Union. The experience resulted in several books. He branched out to write a superlative account of the Battle of Okinawa and another (which I edited) on Commodore Peary in Japan. Once you've read that, you will never doubt why our two nations would become enemies.

Calling out these names only makes me recognize the extraordinary talents we've lost. John Lukacs, a telephone acquaintance, provided me with insights that might never have occurred to me otherwise. E. B. Sledge, was the author of *With the Old Breed*, a memoir of two Pacific Island hellholes, Peleliu and Okinawa. His book has nothing to do with the Great War but everything with the experience of combat. We only had phone conversations, but they were inevitably long ones. Our relationship was always formal: he always called me "Mr. Cowley" and, in turn, I always called hm "Professor Sledge." (He taught ornithology at a small Alabama college.) How else do you address a man who has written one of the best American war memoirs, up there with U.S. Grant and Hervey Allen's *Toward the Flame*, which is about the First World War. I edited one marvelous book by David Fromkin, *A Peace to End All Peace*, about the Near East after the Great War; it was another of David's books, *Europe's Last Summer*, that led me to Helmuth von Moltke the Younger, the man who, as it were, pulled the switch. I had the good fortune to know, consult, and publish John Keegan, Alistair Horne, Stephen E. Ambrose, David McCullough, Dennis E. Showalter, Williamson (Wick) Murray, Carlo W. D'Este, Otto Friederich, and Stanley Weintraub while they were still alive. I should also mention Rod Paschall (Col., USA, ret.), the distinguished career military man who succeeded me as editor of *MHQ*.

The list of inevitable mortalities swells. Why should I be surprised? As I write this, I am just about a month away from turning ninety. There are names, though, that I hate to write. Thaddeus Holt, a former Deputy Undersecretary of the Army and one of the group that founded MHQ, became a great friend and frequent contributor: conversations that began in New York City had a way of ending at his summer house in Kent, CT. Samuel Hynes, who had been a dive-bomber pilot in the Pacific and, later, head of the English Department at Princeton, also wrote for me. A couple of times a year I would take off from work to spend a day talking with him. Sam was another of the people who, when my book seemed to be going nowhere, counseled me to rethink it and keep writing. I did. The novelist Caleb Carr also had a firm and deep, if contrarian, knowledge of military history, which he taught for several years at Bard. Caleb repeatedly counseled me always to question the easiest, the most popular, or the safest answer. It is advice that I have done my best to follow. Ted Morgan I had known for fifty years at least. When he came into my office late in the sixties, he was still going by his French name, Sanche de Gramont. I published two of his autobiographical books, *On Becoming American* and *My Battle of Algiers*, which, among many other things, talked about his name change. A few years ago, I told him about the section of my book that was about Louis-Ferdinand Céline's wounding at Ypres, Ted replied that he had once interviewed the French novelist-doctor in Paris. "I wasn't much of a doctor," Céline said, "but I was *raisonnable.*"

Four armies fought on the Western Front in those last five months of 1914; all four are represented in this book. Elizabeth Venant handled most of the long translations of French and Belgian writers, with some additional contributions by Ed Strauss and me. Some of the translations from German were done by Anthony Hollingsworth, Tania Inowlocki, Bruce Gudmundsson, and another friend of many years, Ernst Rothe. But the majority of German eyewitness accounts are taken from various books by Jack Sheldon. Thanks to him, the study of the Great War on the Western Front will never be the same.

I regard any attempt to deal with, and explain, technical matters as virtually a function of the translation process, and so it is with the mysteries of hydrology. Though I had written about the decision of the Belgian

King Albert to inundate a large remaining stretch of his country, much of the present account depends on a remarkably useful book, *In Flanders Flooded Fields,* by Paul van Pul, a hydraulic engineer turned historian. Think of him as an expert's expert. His book contains details and technical knowledge to be found nowhere else, information that helped me amend and correct the sources available to me thirty-odd years ago. But that, as you might say in this case, is water over the dam.

I would be remiss if I didn't thank Random House: this will be my third book under its imprint. Think of me as a prodigal son. I was an editor there for seven years. Jonathan Jao and Will Murphy brought me back as a consultant and Jonathan signed up *The Killing Season.* Mika Kasuga took over from him and helped me to reduce my elephantine original manuscript. In spite of all the years I had spent as an editor, I discovered, to my chagrin, that I didn't know how to write a book of my own. A book is more than just a long magazine article. Responding to Mika's cuts, as well as her many questions, I forced myself to do a near-total rewrite. I had a genuine book at last. Mika moved on, but passed me to a truly able editor, Molly Turpin. No one has better understood what I have tried to achieve or my determination to focus on a period of the war that has received too little attention, one that may be the most important of all.

Several people have admirably backed Molly. Her assistant, Monica Brown, has been obliging beyond the call. Rachelle Mandik has proved a careful and incisive copy editor. Ted Allen has shepherded me through the final stages of this book. And, as a longtime magazine editor, I know the importance of an imaginative picture researcher. Carol Poticny is one of the best, a person who, time and again, came up with images I never knew existed.

I want to thank my family especially. They have been patient beyond belief, no one more so than my wife of forty-seven years, Didi Lorillard. I adore her: I can't put it any other way. I feel a father's love for my four daughters from two marriages, each different, each accomplished in their separate ways. They were children when I first explored the possibility of a book. Had all of them been born yet? I can't remember. It was that long ago.

Now they are adults, with careers and children of their own.

This book has been years in the making. Or as another pal from my Majorca days, the journalist and author Lawrence Malkin—whom, alas, I must add to that lengthening list of departed—said, when I told him that I had finally finished *The Killing Season*, "What took you so long?"

These pages are the best, the only, answer I can give.

I WANT TO MAKE ONE final point. I may have cited many names in these pages of acknowledgment, but the overarching views I have expressed in these pages are mine, and mine alone. Where other historians deserve credit, I have tried to give it to them. I have also tried to be open about my disagreements. For example, no better account of the Battle of the Marne exists than Holger H. Herwig's *The Marne 1914*. It should remain the standard book on the subject for years to come. But I no longer feel that the Marne deserves the primacy of confrontation that it has long been accorded. That changes my admiration for Professor Herwig's book not a single whit. To pick a second example, I find that Holger Afflerbach's *On a Knife Edge: How Germany Lost the First World War* is an exceptional study, surely one of the best books on the subject. Afflerbach locates the moment of Germany's disintegration as coming in the summer of 1918. I would maintain, however, that the Great War was not as close-run as he does. We have both attempted to lift the argument from its marble box, like those you see in French shrines to the missing of La Grande Guerre, to make sense of the jumble of factual bones inside. Disagreements with such a fine historian are what keep the study of the past vital. It is high time to reconsider what John Keegan called "an unnecessary conflict." It was. Though more than a century has passed since the signing of the Armistice, we are still paying the monstrous price that the Great War exacted.

Robert Cowley
Armistice Day, 2024

NOTES

INTRODUCTION

xiii   **in the first four months** James McRandle and James Quirk, "Blood Test Revisited," *The Journal of Military History* 70, no. 3 (July 2006), 676 and 679 (Tables 2 and 4).

xiii   **"The enormous losses in August and September"** Alan Kramer, *Dynamic of Destruction,* Oxford University Press, Oxford, U.K., 2007, 34–35.

xiii   **On a single day** Jean-Michel Steg, *22 Août 1914* Fayard, Paris, 2013), 9, 23; Hew Strachan, *The First World War: To Arms,* I, Oxford University Press, Oxford, U.K., 2001, 230; Jean-Claude Delhez, *La Bataille des Frontières,* Economica, Paris, 2013, 170 (Delhez reduces the figure to 26,000).

xiii   **roughly one Frenchman killed** I have taken the month-by-month estimates for 1914 from a chart prepared by the French Ministry of Defense, which appears in Steg, *22 Août 1914,* 248, Table 2. Also see www.grande-guerre-1418.com—and then bring up *Récapitulatif approximatif du nombre de morts par mois et par année.* The deaths in the five months of 1914 exceed those in the five worst months of 1915, another *année terrible;* 90, 300.

     All French and German casualty figures for the last five months of 1914 are, as I have stated elsewhere, approximations. If given a choice, my temptation for the early period of the war is always to accept the higher estimate.

xiii   **Let us take the number of Germans killed** McRandle and Quirk, "The Blood Test Revisited," 682, Table 6. Compare with Winston S. Churchill, *The World Crisis* (single volume condensed version), Charles Scribner's Sons, New York, 1992, Appendix, Table III.

xiv   **"The casualties of the First World War"** George Steiner, *In Bluebeard's Castle,* Yale University Press, New Haven, CT, 1971, 32.

xiv   **"as many as 29.3 percent of those men"** Kramer, *Dynamic of Destruction,* 41.

xiv   **"We cannot think about the crises"** Steiner, *In Bluebeard's Castle,* 32–33.

xiv **"It is possible to calculate"** Alexandre Lafon, "War Losses (France)," *International Encyclopedia of the First World War* (Online–October 8, 2014).

xvi **4 million** Erich von Falkenhayn, *General Headquarters*, The Battery Press, Nashville, TN, Appendix, 295.

xvi **"into poorly charted and largely unknown territory"** Robert T. Foley, *German Strategy and the Path to Verdun*, Cambridge University Press, Cambridge, 2005, 84.

xvii **"ground to be defended with fewer troops"** Strachan, *To Arms*, 261.

xvii **"literally quickened the pace"** Steiner, *In Bluebeard's Castle*, 11.

xviii **"a concrete and living reality"** Marc Bloch, *The Historian's Craft*, trans. Peter Putnam, Vintage Books, New York, 1953, 27.

PROLOGUE: AUGUST 20, 1914, NEAR CHARLEROI, BELGIUM

3 **"There was a moment in the experience"** Edward Spears, *Liaison 1914*, Cassell, London, 1930, 1968, 105.

3 **"an outsider in both countries"** Max Egremont, *Under Two Flags: The Life of Major General Sir Edward Spears*, Weidenfeld & Nicolson, London, 1997, xii.

4 **"how great armies could possibly fight"** Spears, *Liaison 1914*, 106.

5 **"still and wonderfully peaceful"** Spears, *Liaison 1914*, 106–107.

1. "THE VIRTUOSITY OF SHEER AUDACITY"

6 **"No strategic plan goes with any certainty"** Jack Snyder, *The Ideology of the Offensive*, Cornell University Press, Ithaca and London, 1984, 135.

7 **"the neutrality of Luxembourg"** Robert T. Foley, ed. and trans., *Alfred von Schlieffen's Military Writings*, Frank Cass, London and Portland, OR, 2003, 165. (Except where noted, all the translations of Schlieffen come from Foley's version of the *Military Writings*.)

8 **"It can be assumed"** Foley, *Military Writings*, 167.

9 **"If one allows them to proceed"** Foley, *Military Writings*, 172.

9 **"If you march into France"** Herbert Rosinki, *The German Army*, Pall Mall Press, London, 1966, 129.

9 **"apt to be professionals"** Gordon A. Craig, Introduction to Rosinki's *The German Army*, 8–9.

9 **"An unimportant obstacle"** Walter Goerlitz, *History of the German General Staff*, trans. Brian Battershaw, Frederick A. Praeger, New York, 1953, 129.

10 **"a gambler's belief in the virtuosity of sheer audacity"** B. H. Liddell Hart, "Foreword," in Gerhard Ritter, *The Schlieffen Plan*, trans. Andrew and Eva Wilson, Frederick A. Praeger, New York, 1958, 4.

11 **"detach a sufficient number of corps"** Foley, *Military Writings*, 169.

12 **"I lack the power of rapid decision"** Otto Friedrich, *Blood and Iron*, HarperCollins, New York, 1995, 227.

14 **"the windpipe that enables us"** Annika Mombauer, *Helmuth von Moltke and the Origins of the First World War*, Cambridge University Press, Cambridge, 2001, 94.

15 "securing our eastern provinces" Annika Mombauer, "The Moltke Plan," in *The Schlieffen Plan*, eds. Hans Ehlert et al., University Press of Kentucky, Lexington, KY, 2014, 51.

16 "It will be adviseable" Ritter, *The Schlieffen Plan*, 175.

16 "It must come to a fight" Barbara W. Tuchman, *The Guns of August*, The Macmillan Company, New York, 1962, 25.

17 "a bulky, slow-moving, loosely-built man" Edward Spears, *Liaison 1914*, 19–20.

17 "a perfectly good stationmaster" André Bourachot, *Marshal Joffre*, trans. Andrew Uffindell, Pen & Sword Military, Barnsley, South Yorkshire, U.K., 2014, 9.

17 "the modern Delphic Oracle" B. H. Liddell Hart, *Reputations Ten Years After*, Little, Brown, and Company, Boston, 1928, 13.

17 "In less than a quarter of an hour" Joseph Jacques Césaire Joffre, *My March to Timbuctoo*, Chatto & Windus, London, 1915, 70–71.

19 "more power over the French Army" Robert A. Doughty, "French Strategy in 1914: Joffre's Own," *Journal of Military History* 67, no. 2 (April 2003), 429.

19 "Only the offensive yields positive results" Robert A. Doughty, *Pyrrhic Victory*, The Belknap Press of Harvard University Press, Cambridge, MA, and London, 2005, 26.

19 "An energetic commander-in-chief" Doughty, *Pyrrhic Victory*, 27.

20 "our officers were not prepared" Joseph Jacques Césaire Joffre, *The Personal Memoirs of Joffre*, trans. T. Bentley Mott, Harper & Brothers, New York and London, 1932, I, 33.

21 "dangerous to disclose in advance" Joffre, *Personal Memoirs*, I, 106.

22 general alliance to be secret Luigi Albertini, *The Origins of the War of 1914*, 1, Enigma Books, New York, 1952, 2005, 73–7.

22 "The realities of war" Joffre, *Personal Memoirs*, I, 59.

23 "Joffre, waving his pudgy hand" Stefan Schmidt, "French Plan XVII," in Hans Ehlert et al., *The Schlieffen Plan*, 227.

23 "It is at the very heart of Germany" Joffre, *Personal Memoirs*, I, 23.

23 Russia placed 1.2 million men Sean McMeekin, *The Russian Origins of the First World War*, Harvard University Press, Cambridge, MA and London, 2011 80.

23 "the metaphor which best describes" McMeekin, *Russian Origins*, 79.

24 the treaty of cooperation that came to be known as the Entente Cordiale Samuel R. Williamson Jr., *The Politics of Grand Strategy*, The Ashfield Press, London and Atlantic Highlands, NJ, 1969, 1990, 1–2.

24 "Britain in 1914" John Terraine, *Mons*, The Macmillan Company, New York, 1960, 16.

25 "the ugliest man in the British Army" B. H. Liddell Hart, *Foch—The Man of Orleans*, Little, Brown, and Company, 1932, 50.

26 "Always a glutton for exercise" C. E. Callwell, *Field-Marshal Sir Henry Wilson*, Charles Scribner's Sons, New York, 1927, I, 51.

26 "the topography of a funny little country" Samuel R. Williamson, *The Politics of Grand Strategy*, xiii.

26 "with a cordiality" Liddell Hart, *Man of Orleans*, 50.

26 "His appreciation of the German move" Liddell Hart, *Man of Orleans*, 51, and Callwell, *Field-Marshal Sir Henry Wilson*, I, 78.

27 **"What would you say was the smallest"** Liddell Hart, *Man of Orleans,*
51, and Callwell, *Field-Marshal Sir Henry Wilson,* I, 78–79.

27 **"It was agreed"** Margaret MacMillan, *The War That Ended Peace,*
Random House, New York, 2013, 457.

27 **"l'Armée W"** Liddell Hart, *Man of Orleans,* 144 (note 2).

29 **"Enormous preparations for war"** Callwell, *Field-Marshal Sir Henry
Wilson,* I, 135.

29 **he was five feet six inches tall** George H. Cassar, *The Tragedy of Sir
John French,* University of Delaware Press, Newark, DE, and Associated
University Presses, London and Toronto, 1985, 20.

30 **"ruddy-faced"** Spears, *Liaison 1914,* 73–74.

30 **"He graced the house parties"** Richard Holmes, *The Little Field
Marshal,* Weidenfeld & Nicolson, London, 1981, 168.

30 **"a natural soldier"** Winston S. Churchill, *Great Contemporaries,* eds.
James W. Miller et al., ISI Books, Wilmington, DE, 2012, 84.

30 **"perhaps the most distinguished"** Cassar, *Tragedy of Sir John French,*
291.

30 **that day in February 1900** Vivid accounts of the cavalry charge that
relieved Kimberley appear in Archibald Wavell, *Allenby,* Oxford University Press, New York, 1941, 82–84; Holmes, *Little Field Marshal,* 89–93;
Cassar, *Tragedy of Sir John French,* 48–50; Adam Hochschild, *To End All
War,* Houghton Mifflin Harcourt, Boston and New York, 2011, 24–26;
and Thomas Packenham, *The Boer War,* Random House, New York, 1979,
343–346.

30 **"'E's a daisy"** Holmes, *Little Field Marshal,* 81.

31 **"The sphere of action"** John French, "Preface," in Friedrich von
Bernhardi, *Cavalry,* George H. Doran Company, New York, 1914, 15.

31 **"could be a good friend"** Holmes, *Little Field Marshal,* 93.

31 **Haig gave him the loan** John Terraine, *Douglas Haig: The Educated
Soldier,* Cassell, London, 1963, 2005, 55; Gary Sheffield, *The Chief,*
Aurum Press Limited, London, 2011, 39; Holmes, *Little Field Marshal,*
51. The amount of the loan is sometimes given as £2,500, sometimes as
£2,000.

32 **"rapidly becoming the sole & governing"** Keith Jeffrey, *Field Marshal
Sir Henry Wilson: A Political Soldier,* Oxford University Press, Oxford
and New York, 2006, 119.

32 **"The future"** Churchill, *Great Contemporaries,* 83.

33 **"My impression of French"** Churchill, *Great Contemporaries,* 84.

33 **"I was to command it"** Sir John French, *1914,* Leonaur, Driffield, East
Yorkshire, U.K., 2009, 12.

34 **"In my own heart"** Douglas Haig, *Douglas Haig: War Diaries and Letters
1914–1918,* eds. Gary Sheffield and John Bourne, Weidenfeld & Nicolson,
London, 2005, 56.

2. THE MAN WHO WILLED A WAR

35 **"Preventive war"** Bismark's remark, quoted in Margaret MacMillan,
The War That Ended Peace, 560.

35 **"would destroy the culture"** Annika Mombauer, *Helmuth von Moltke
and the Origins of the First World War,* 202.

36 **"On questions of motive"** Mombauer, *Helmuth von Moltke*, 6 (note).

37 **"I consider a war unavoidable"** Mombauer, *Helmuth von Moltke*, 140.

37 **Churchill attended a special meeting** Winston S. Churchill, *The World Crisis* (abridged edition), 38.

37 **Did Moltke give away his intentions** Mombauer, *Helmuth von Moltke*, 165–167; Émile Cammaerts, *Albert of Belgium: Defender of Right*, The Macmillan Company, New York, 1935, 134–136; Émile Joseph Galet, *Albert King of the Belgians in the Great War*, trans. Ernest Swinton, Houghton Mifflin Company, Boston and New York, 1931, 23–24.

37 **"to lead the march on Paris"** Barbara W. Tuchman, *The Guns of August*, 106.

38 **"his view of how soon"** Franz Graf Conrad von Hötzendorf, *Aus Meiner Dienstzeit* (*My Years of Service*), III, trans. Bruce I. Gudmundsson, Rikola, Vienna, 1921–1923, 673.

39 **"Today we are still a match"** Mombauer, *Helmuth von Moltke*, 172; Otto Friedrich, *Blood and Iron*, 236.

40 **"Tone-deaf to nuances"** T. G. Otte, *July Crisis*, Cambridge University Press, Cambridge, 2014, 71.

40 **the infamous "blank check"** Useful accounts appear in Otte, *July Crisis*, 82–90; Fritz Fischer, *Germany's Aims in the First World War*, W. W. Norton & Company, New York, 1967, 51–57; Sean McMeekin, *July 1914: Countdown to War*, Basic Books, New York, 2013, 98–100; Christopher Clark, *The Sleepwalkers*, HarperCollins, New York, 2013, 412–415; Samuel R. Williamson Jr. and Russel Van Wyck, *July 1914: Soldiers, Statesmen, and the Coming of the Great War*, Bedford/St. Martin's, Boston and New York, 2003, 98–100; Luigi Albertini, *The Origins of the War of 1914*, Enigma Books, New York, 2005, II, 140–150; MacMillan, *War That Ended Peace*, 556–559; and David Fromkin, *Europe's Last Summer*, Alfred A. Knopf, New York, 2004, 156–161.

40 **"Certainly in no circumstances"** Williamson and Van Wyck, *July 1914*, 99.

41 **"The blank check would determine"** Otte, *July Crisis*, 81.

41 **"Should Belgium oppose the German troops"** Léon van der Essen, *The Invasion and the War in Belgium*, T. Fisher Unwin Ltd., London, 1917, 27.

42 **"His Majesty . . . claims, . . . as he says, that the ball that is rolling can no longer be stopped"** Mombauer, *Helmuth von Moltke*, 199.

42 **"Germany could not afford to wait"** Mombauer, *Helmuth von Moltke*, 203.

42 **"Late in the evening an argument"** Otte, *July Crisis*, 405.

43 **"overworked day and night"** Mombauer, *Helmuth von Moltke*, 197.

43 **"a sort of confidence trick"** Fromkin, *Europe's Last Summer*, 291, 303–305.

44 **a call to a corps commander** George Malcolm Thomson, *The Twelve Days*, G. P. Putnam's Sons, New York, 1964, 135–136.

45 **"Who rules in Berlin"** Holger H. Herwig, *The First World War: Germany and Austria-Hungary 1914–1918*, Arnold/Hodder Headline Group, 1997, 28; Mombauer, *Helmuth von Moltke*, 205.

45 **"there was only one topic"** Philipp Scheidemann, *Memoirs* (1929), quoted in Williamson and Van Wyck, *July 1914*, 107–108.

45 **wearing an eagle helmet** Thomson, *Twelve Days*, 152.

45 **"his face bathed in perspiration"** McMeekin, *Countdown to War*, 341.

45 **a telegram from Prince Lichnowsky** Mombauer, *Helmuth von Moltke*, 219–220; Otte, *July Crisis*, 476–478.

46 **"Well, now we simply march"** Otte, *July Crisis*, 476–477. For slightly different translations, see Mombauer, *Helmuth von Moltke*, 219–220, 222.

46 **"a mass of disorderly armed men"** Otte, *July Crisis*, 477; and Mombauer, *Helmuth von Moltke*, 220.

46 **"Your uncle would have given"** Mombauer, *Helmuth von Moltke*, 222; Otte, *July Crisis*, 477; and McMeekin, *July 1914*, 343.

47 **"I want to wage war"** Otte, *July Crisis*, 479.

47 **"He was dark red in the face"** Mombauer, *Helmuth von Moltke*, 222.

47 **"no positive English proposal"** Otte, *July Crisis*, 480.

47 **"I THINK THERE MUST BE SOME MISUNDERSTANDING"** McMeekin, *July 1914*, 348.

48 **"Now do as you please"** Mombauer, *Helmuth von Moltke*, 224.

3. "THE STRENGTH OF DESPAIR"

52 **"Boredom"** Émile Cammaerts, *Albert of Belgium*, 391.

52 **"He would have discovered a pretext"** Cammaerts, *Albert of Belgium*, 373.

53 **their 117,000-man field army** Hew Strachan, *The First World War: Volume I: To Arms*, 210; Luigi Albertini, *The Origins of the War of 1914*, III, 460, *note 2*.

53 **It took the German ultimatum** Albertini, *Origins of the War of 1914*, III, 452–469.

53 **An extraordinary council of war** Albertini, *Origins of the War of 1914*, III, 510–511.

54 **an accounting of the call to arms** Holger H. Herwig, *The First World War: Germany and Austria-Hungary 1914–18*, 75.

54 **proved to be an inept tactician** Terence Zuber, *Ten Days in August: The Siege of Liège 1914*, Spellmount/The History Press, Brimscombe Port Stroud, Gloucestershire, U.K., 2014, 185.

54 **"He placed commanders at the heads"** Joe and Janet Robinson and Randall Gilbert, *Handstreich:* privately printed, Coppell, TX, 2021, Appendix A, 131–2.

54 **"We've been washed"** Zuber, *Ten Days in August*, 96–97.

55 **German casualties on the night of August 5–6** Zuber, *Ten Days in August*, 250.

55 **"It is critical that we use"** Herwig, *First World War*, 35.

55 **Too soon Moltke's coup de main** Strachan, *To Arms*, 210–212; John Keegan, *The First World War*, Alfred A. Knopf, New York, 1999, 77–78, 86–87; Tuchman, *Guns of August*, 163–176, 191–193; *Germany's Western Front: Translations from Der Weltkrieg, the German Official History of the Great War, 1914*, Part I, eds. Mark Osbourne Humphries and John Maker, trans. William J. Kesselbach, Wilfred Laurier University Press, Waterloo, Ontario, Canada 2013, 96–107; Zuber, *Ten Days in August*. Terence Zuber's book is the most thorough account of the siege. Chapter 6, "The German Artillery Takes Liège," 199–252, is especially

illuminating. Zuber makes a convincing case that the giant tubes that Keegan and Tuchman describe so vividly played only a small role in the siege.

56   **"in stark contrast"** Zuber, *Ten Days in August*, 252.

56   **What infantry couldn't finish off, artillery did** Zuber, *Ten Days in August*, 234, 236, 242, 250, 252.

58   **Kluck's First Army streamed through**, Alexander von Kluck, *The March on Paris 1914*, Edward Arnold, London, 1920, 19.

58   **"Dark, dull and gloomy"** Sir John French, *1914*, Leonaur/Oakpost, London, 2009, 38–9.

59   **Sir John French went to Paris** Richard Holmes, *The Little Field Marshal*, 205; *The Personal Memoirs of Joffre, I*, 161; Edward L. Spear, *Liaison 1914*, 45; John Terraine, *Mons*, The Macmillan Company, New York, 205, 52; Sir John French, *1914*, 41–2.

59   **French had always had trouble with languages** Holmes, *The Little Field Marshal*, 205; Winston S. Churchill, *Great Contemporaries*, 85–6.

59   **"The best commander"** French, *1914*, 42.

60   **adding about 70,000 men** Spears, *Liaison 1914*, 45, FN, 474–7; Tuchman, *The Guns of August*, 255.

60   **"Very spic and span"** Spears, *Liaison 1914*, 73.

60   **"Well, here you are"** General [Victor] Huguet, *Britain in the War*, Cassell and Company Ltd, London, 1928, 51.

60   **"A big, flabby man"** Spears, *Liaison 1914*, 46–7.

61   **neither of whom could speak the other's language** Spears, *Liaison 1914*, 73–80. This is the classic account. Major-General Sir C.E. Callwell, Wilson's official biographer, dismisses the meeting and its importance, noting that it did not pass off altogether satisfactorily, neither of the two distinguished commanders apparently forming a high opinion of the other." In a footnote he adds,"Lanrezac knew no English, and Sir John's French was not of a kind readily intelligible to a Frenchman." Callwell, *Field-Marshal Sir Henry Wilson*, I, 164.

61   **"I judged that it was useless to insist"** Charles Louis Marie Lanrezac, *Le Plan de Campagne Français*, Payot & Cie, Paris, 1920, 91.

61   **"Mon Général, est-ce que"** Spears, *Liaison 1914*, 75.

62   **"with the usual compliments"** C.E. Callwell, *Field-Marshal Sir Henry Wilson, I*, 164 (FN).

63   **"The fight in the wood had cost"** Karl Deuringer, *The First Battle of the First World War: Alsace-Lorraine*, Translated and Edited by Terence Zuber, The History Press, Stroud, Gloucestershire, UK, 2014, 93,98, 100.

63   **"A sorry spectacle"** Général H. Colin, *Le Gars Du 26*e, Payot, Paris, 1932, 55. For a succinct discussion of Morhange and encounters nearby on August 20, 1914, see also Jonathan Bott, *Haig's enemy*, Oxford University Press, Oxford, 2018, 23–4. The "Enemy" was Crown Prince Rupprecht of Bavaria.

64   **"A great forest of small trees"** Sewell Tyng, *The Campaign of the Marne*, Westholme, Yardley, PA, 2007, 79.

65   **"It was in fact not one battle"** Tyng, *The Campaign of the Marne*, 81.

66   **"Suddenly deprived of their artillery support"** Tyng, *The Campaign of the Marne*, 83.

66   **"Dazed by the thunderclaps"** Jean Galtier-Boissière, *En Rase Campagne 1914*, Berger-Levault, Paris, 1917, 48.

67   **"The battle is lost"** Paul Lintier, *Ma Pièce*, Plon-Nourrit et Cie, Paris, 1916, 81.

67   **"Wave after wave of bayonet charges,"** Robert A. Doughty, *Pyrrhic Victory*, 67; Simon J. House, *Lost Opportunity: The Battle of the Ardennes 22 August 1914*, Helion & Company Ltd., Warwick, UK, 2017, 131.

67   **"To the effectiveness"** Terence Zuber, *Ardennes 1914: The Battle of the Frontiers*, History Press, Port Stroud, Gloucestershire, UK, 2013, 123.

67   **3,200 men** House, *Lost Opportunity*,131–2. Compare that 88 percent with the casualty rate at Bertrix, 82 percent. See Bruce I. Gudmundsson, "Unexpected Encounter at Bertrix," in *The Great War*, edited by Robert Cowley, Random House, New York, 2003, 35.

68   **"Between them lost 11,153"** Doughty, *Pyrrhic Victory*, 67.

68   **"A burst from a German machine gun"** Zuber, *Ardennes 1914*, 114.

68   **"At one stage the general looked at me"** House, *Lost Opportunity*, 134. Other speculations about the last hours of General Raffenel can be found in Jean-Claude Delhez, *La Bataille des Frontières*, Economica, Paris, 2013, 84 and Jean-Michel Steg, *22 Aout 1914*, Fayard, Paris, 2013, 49–50.

68   **"Three generals, 2,600 men"** Colonel E. Valarché, *La Bataille des Frontières*, Editions Berger-Levrault, Paris, 1932, 142.

68   **wrapped the colors** Steg, *22 Août 1914*, 55.

69   **"All corps engaged today"** Tyng, *The Campaign of the Marne*, 89.

69   **"One must face the facts"** Joffre to Adolphe Messimy, War Minister, August 24, 1914. *Armées Français, Tome II*, No. 2, *Annex* 149; Spears, *Liaison 1914*,192; Elizabeth Greenhalgh, *The French Army and the First World War*, Cambridge University Press, Cambridge, 2014, 43. I have used the Spears translation.

71   **"sending back reports"** Strachan, *To Arms*, 231.

71   **"By August 29, casualties had soared to 206,515"** Greenhalgh, *The French Army in the First World War*, "Casualties for August–November 1914," 59. Greenhalgh's figures come from the French Official History, *Les Armées Français dans la Grande Guerre*, called here, *Armées Français*. Strachan relies on somewhat revised figures, but to avoid confusion, I have chosen to go along with *Les Armées Français*.

71   **the average daily peacetime death rate** Henri Contamine, *La Victoire de la Marne: 9 Septembre1914*, Gallimard, Paris, 1970, 120.

72   **"Now . . . let's get on with our work"** B.H. Liddell Hart, *Foch: The Man of Orleans*, The Atlantic Monthly Press, Boston,1932, 118.

72   **"France was able to make up for its losses"** Strachan, *To Arms*, 230–1. I can hardly deny Strachan's reasoning, but consistency dictates my staying with the figures in *Les Armées Français*.

73   **"First weigh the cost and then dare"** William J. Astore and Dennis E. Showalter, *Hindenburg*, Potomac Books, Inc., Dulles, VA., 2005, 15.

73   **"Few victories in history"** C.R.M.F. Cruttwell, *A History of the Great War 1914–1918*, Oxford University Press, Oxford, 1934, 47.

74   **"all hopes of dramatic change"** Robert A. Doughty, *Pyrrhic Victory*, 84.

74   **nearly three-quarters of its annual ore output** Niall Ferguson, *The Pity of War*, Basic Books, New York, 1999, 96.

75   **"What do you want?"** Leonard V. Smith, Stéphane Audoin-Rouzeau, Annette Becker, *France and the Great War 1914–1918*, Sections written in French translated by Helen McPhail, Cambridge University Press, Cambridge, UK, 2003, 35.

76   **"Adding another 6,000–7,000"** Damien Baldwin, Emmanuel Saint-Fuscian, *Charleroi: 21–23 Août 1914*, Tallandier, Paris, 2012, 117; Contamine, *La Victoire de la Marne*, 118.

76   **"A dirty-looking factory town"** John F. Lucy, *There's a Devil in the Drum*, The Naval & Military Press, Uckfield, East Sussex, UK, 1993, 109.

77   **"Kluck could have outflanked the British"** Cyril Falls, *The First World War*, Pen & Sword, Barnsley, South Yorkshire, UK, 1960, 2014, 28.

78   **"Might very well have taken"** Dennis E. Showalter, Joseph P. Robinson and Janet A. Robinson, *The German Failure in Belgium, August 1914*, McFarland & Company, Inc., Jefferson, NC, 2019, 184.

78   **"Four, and eventually six"** John Terraine, *Mons*, the Macmillan company, New York, 1960, 105.

78   **"Wherever I looked"** Walter Bloem, *The Advance from Mons*, Translated by G.C. Wynne, Helion & Company Ltd, Solihull, West Midlands, UK, 2011, 43.

79   **"Soon all that remained"** John F. Lucy, *There's a Devil in the Drum*, 115.

79   **British casualties** Jack Horsfall and Nigel Cave, *Mons 1914*, Pen & Sword, Barnsley, South Yorkshire, UK, 2014, 129–30; John Terraine, *Mons*, 104–5; David Lomas, *Mons 1914*, Praeger, London and Westport, CT, 1995, 55; David Ascoli, *The Mons Star*, Berlinn, Edinburgh, 2001, 73,84. A good summation of the Mons casualties debate appears in Spencer Jones, *The Great Retreat of 1914*, Sharpe Books, North Haven, CT, 2018, 39–40.

79   **"To retire without consulting them"** Spears, *Liaison 1914*, 171.

81   **"On the whole, the deployment ran like clockwork"** Mark Osborne Humphries and John Maker, Editors, *Germany's Western Front: 1914, Part 1* (Translation of the German Official History of World War I, *Der Weltkrieg*), Wilfred Laurier University Press, Waterloo, Ontario, 2013, 122.

82   **"replied in French"** Captain G.C. Wynne, *Landrecies to Cambrai: Case Studies of German Offensive and Defensive Operations on the Western Front 1914–1918*, Helion & Company, Ltd., Solihull, West Midlands, UK, 2011, 11.

82   **"We must sell our lives dearly"** J.P. Harris, *Douglas Haig and the First World War*, Cambridge University Press, Cambridge, UK, 2000, 75.

83   not **"Haig's finest hour"** Harris, *Douglas Haig and the First World War*, 76.

83   **"Demanded that Joffre allocate"** Joffre, *The Personal Memoirs of Joffre, I*, 192.

83   **"The menace of governmental interference"** Joffre, *The Personal Memoirs of Joffre, I*, 195.

84   **"The windows and shutters were closed"** Spears, *Liaison 1914*, 228.

84   **"I expected to find the same calm officer"** Joffre, *The Personal Memoirs of Joffre, I*, 195.

85 **"Coolness" and "lack of cordiality"** General [Victor] Huguet, *Britain and the War*, Translated by Captain H. Cotton Minchin, 67.

85 **"My general, what is your plan?"** Charles Louis Marie Lanrezac, *Le Plan de Campagne Français*, 209.

85 **"The scene *needs no commentary*"** Lanrezac, *Le Plan de Campagne Français*, 209–10.

85 **"I gathered that he was by no means satisfied"** Sir John French, *1914*, 79.

86 **"I carried away with me a serious impression"** Joffre, *The Personal Memoirs of Joffre*, I, 196–7.

87 **"[O]ne of the most splendid feats"** Terraine' *Mons*, 143.

89 **"H.W. had no time to put on his leggings"** Callwell, *Field-Marshal Sir Henry Wilson*, I, 169.

89 **"Troops fighting Douglas Haig cannot fight you."** Callwell, *Field-Marshal Sir Henry Wilson*, I, 169.

89 **"Yours is the first cheerful voice"** Callwell, *Field-Marshal Sir Henry Wilson*, I, 169; *OH 1914*, I, 142.

90 **"A free hand"** Richard Holmes, *The Little Field Marshal*, 222; Horace Smith-Dorrien, *Smith-Dorrien: Isandlwhana to the Great War* (Originally titled *Memories of Forty-eight Years' Service*), Leonaur/Oakpost, Ltd, London, 2009, 448; George H. Cassar, *The Tragedy of Sir John French*, University of Delaware Press, Newark, DE, 120.

90 **"They were entrenching as well as they could"** J.L. Jack (Edited by John Terraine), *General Jack's Diary 1914–1918*, 36.

90 **"For God's sake men"** Lucy, *There's a Devil in the Drum*, 141–2.

91 a **"hurricane of shrapnel"** *OH, 1914*, I, 173.

91 **"We stayed there all day under"** Nigel Cave and Jack Sheldon, *Le Cateau*, Battleground Europe Series, Pen & Sword Miliary, Barnsley, South Yorkshire, UK,2008, 62.

91 **"blotted out"** J.L. Jack (Edited by John Terraine), *General Jack's Diary 1914–1918*, 36.

92 **"Our artillery with superb courage"** J.L. Jack (Edited by John Terraine), *General Jack's Diary 1914–1918*, 37.

92 **Thirty-eight guns** *OH, 1914*, I, 191.

92 **"There could not be greater activity"** Cave and Sheldon, *Le Cateau*, 52–3.

93 **"The trickle of wounded,"** J.L. Jack (Edited by John Terraine), *General Jack's Diary 1914–1918*, 35.

93 **"I was told"** J.L. Jack, *General Jack's Diary 1914–1918*, 37.

93 **"the closest the BEF would ever come"** Nick Lloyd, *The Western Front*, W. W. Norton & Company, 2021, 33.

94 **"Transport, guns, and Infantry"** Arthur Herbert Hossey and Major D.S. Inman, *The Fifth Division in the Great War*, Nisbet & Co. Ltd, London, 1921, 16.

94 **"It looked to be the break-up of an army"** F. Loraine Petre, *The History of the Norfolk Regiment 1685–1918, Vol. II*, Naval & Military Press LTD, Uckfield, East Sussex, UK, 2015.

94 **"One could barely see the infantry"** Jerry Murland, *Retreat and Rearguard 1914*, Pen & Sword Military Ltd, Barnsley, South Yorkshire, UK 2011, 76.

95 **Estimates of German casualities** Sir John French put BEF losses at 14,000 (*1914*, Leonaur, London, 2009, 76); he said that the battle came close to being "a stupendous repetition of Sedan." Was he attempting to cover for his own faintheartedness during the next two weeks? Some would say that he was the person who deserved to be court-martialed. French's casualty estimate was almost twice the official British count of 7,812, many of whom were taken prisoner. Cave and Sheldon find even that total to be on the high side. They have, after a careful examination, arrived at approximately 5,000, which seems more reasonable (Nigel Cave and Jack Sheldon, LeCateau, Pen & Sword Military, 2008, 9).

95n **According to that capable** Spencer Jones, *The Great Retreat of 1914*, Sharpe Books, North Haven, CT, 2018, 66–7.

96 **"The British had narrowly escaped"** *Germany's Western Front, Part 1, 1914*, (Translation of the German Official History of World War I, *Der Weltkrieg*).

97 **"Order–Counter-order–Disorder,"** *Germany's Western Front, Part 1, 1914*, (Translation of the German Official History of World War I, *Der Weltkrieg*).

98 **"Do you want me to remove you"** Charles Louis Marie Lanrezac, *Le Plan de Campagne Français*, trans. Elizabeth Venant, Payot, Paris, 1920, 225.

99 **"understandably livid"** Gary Sheffield, *The Chief: Douglas Haig and the British Army*, Aurum Press Limited, London, 2011, 2012, 80.

99 **Joffre sat all morning in Lanrezac's office** Lanrezac, *Le Plan de Campagne Français*, 235–239.

99 **"Far-sighted he was, and clever, too, too clever perhaps"** Spears, *Liaison 1914*, 269.

100 **"This swinging of units"** John Terraine, *The Western Front* ("The Battle of Guise"), Pen & Sword, Barnsley, South Yorkshire, UK, 2014. 129–130.

100 **a Napoleonic demonstration** Terraine, *Western Front*, 130.

100 **"You are used up"** Joseph Jacques Césaire Joffre, *The Personal Memoirs of Joffre*, I, 238.

102 **Kitchener boarded a fast destroyer** Trevor Royle, *The Kitchener Enigma*, Michael Joseph, London, 1985, 309–310; Richard Holmes, *The Little Field Marshal*, 233.

4. THE ANTWERP DIVERSION

103 **"The troops could not bivouac"** Émile Galet, *Albert, King of the Belgians in the Great War*, trans. Ernest Swinton, 74.

103 **a decidedly nineteenth-century look** Jonathan North, *An Illustrated Encyclopedia of Uniforms of World War I*, Lorenz Books/Anness Publishing, Ltd., Wigston, Leicestershire, U.K., 2011, 172–174.

104 **only 102 machine guns** Leon van der Essen, *The Invasion and the War in Belgium*, 46.

105 **One patrol . . . reached a village called Haelen** van der Essen, *Invasion and the War in Belgium*, 107–114; Galet, *Albert, King of the Belgians*, 98–100; *L'Illustration*, No. 3730, *22 Aout 1914*, Paris, 151–154.

106   **Colonel Adelbert told Albert's generals** Émile Cammaerts, *Albert of Belgium*, 157–158; Galet, *Albert, King of the Belgians*, 106, 122–125; Barbara Tuchman, *The Guns of August*, 190.

106   **The messages that flooded** Galet, *Albert, King of the Belgians*, 112, 330 (Annexe VIII).

107   **"The military consequences"** Galet, *Albert, King of the Belgians*, 122, 124.

108   **"The retreat of the Army"** Galet, *Albert, King of the Belgians*, 133.

108   **this patent act of insubordination** Galet, *Albert, King of the Belgians*, 135.

109   **"could not move forward"** C.R.M.F. Cruttwell, *A History of the Great War*, Oxford at the Clarendon Press, Oxford, U.K., 1934, 94.

109   **"scratch force"** John Keegan, *The First World War*, 127.

110   **"The infantry did not deploy fully"** Galet, *Albert, King of the Belgians*, 142–143.

110   **We will never know exactly** Excellent descriptions abound of the torchings and killings that began on the night of August 25, 1914. None may be better known than Barbara W. Tuchman's chapter "The Flames of Louvain" in *Guns of August*, 310–324. A model longer analysis appears in John Horne and Alan Kramer, *German Atrocities 1914*, Yale University Press, New Haven and London, 2001, 94–139. Kramer, in his important book *Dynamics of Destruction: Culture and Mass Killing in the First World War*, 19–24 (Oxford Universtiy Press, Oxford, 2007), is also excellent on the subject. Larry Zuckerman's *The Rape of Belgium* (New York University Press, New York and London, 2004) has an arresting discussion of Louvain, as well as of the German obsession with franc-tireurs. A special nod must be directed to Richard Harding Davis's Louvain dispatch, which took up the front page of the *New-York Tribune* on August 31, 1914.

111   **"Every non-uniformed person"** Horne and Kramer, *German Atrocities*, 95.

113   **"The slightest unfamiliar noise"** Horne and Kramer, *German Atrocities*, 117.

115   **"When you come before the enemy"** There are numerous accounts, but none to my mind is better than the version in Christopher Clark, *Kaiser Wilhelm II*, Pearson Education Ltd., Harlow, Essex, U.K., 2000 169–170.

115   **"Its object"** Galet, *Albert, King of the Belgians*, 178.

117   **"Every now and then a soldier"** E. Alexander Powell, *Fighting in Flanders*, Charles Scribner's Sons, New York, 1914, 164–165.

117   **Albert's regulars were down** Galet, *Albert, King of the Belgians*, 187.

118   **to eradicate the Antwerp menace** See brief life of Gen. Hans von Beseler in J. M. Bourne, *Who's Who in World War I*, Routledge, London and New York, 2001, 24; Gilbert, *Challenge of War*, 104–105; James E. Edmonds, ed., *Military Operations, France and Belgium 1914*, II, 32–133 (henceforth to be called either British *Official History*, or its abbreviation, OH). Originally published in 1925 by Macmillan and Co., Ltd., London. The present publishers of the *Official History* are the Imperial War Museum, London, and The Battery Press, Inc., Nashville, TN.

119   **"What a spectacular evening"** Henri Bernard, *L'An 14*, La Renais-

sance du livre, Brussels, Belgium, 1983, 127. Much of Bernard's book is based on the diary kept by the author's father, Maj. Arsène Bernard, whose descriptions of the siege of Antwerp are memorable: see in particular 120, 121, 127, 128, and 131.

120 **He came without being asked** Gilbert, *Challenge of War*, 107–108. See the accounts of Henry Stephens, 108–109, and Gino Calza Bedola, 115, which Gilbert quotes.

121 **"The war, for the English"** Bernard, *L'An 14*, 123.

121 **"Homeric laugh"** Gilbert, *Challenge of War*, 113.

121 **"without water bottles"** Cruttwell, *History of the Great War*, 95–96 (note 2). See also Sir Frederick Ponsonby, *The Grenadier Guards in the Great War*, I, Macmillan and Co., Ltd., London, 1920, 85.

122 **"Everyone cheered"** Douglas Jerrold, *The Royal Naval Division*, Naval and Military Press, Uckfield, U.K., 2009, 25.

122 **"The men of the 1st and 2nd"** *Official History 1914*, II, 63.

122 **none of these last reinforcements** *Official History 1914*, II, 51 and 497–498 (Appendix 8).

123 **the Germans had fired 297 shells** Bernard, *L'An 14*, 129.

123 **"The most powerful fortified position"** Bernard, *L'An 14*, 141.

123 **"The moment when a battle"** Robin Prior and Trevor Wilson, *Command on the Western Front*, Blackwell, Oxford, U.K., and Cambridge, MA, 1992, 9.

124 **"The road"** Galet, *Albert, King of the Belgians*, 226.

124 **"Then it's over"** *Official History 1914*, II, 57.

125 **"It was a still starlit night"** *Official History 1914*, II, 59.

125 **"Beyond the river"** *Official History 1914*, II, 60–63.

126 **"Confusion also reigned"** Jerrold, *Royal Naval Division*, 34–37.

127 **"the Antwerp Blunder"** Gilbert, *Challenge of War*, singles out some of those critics, including David Lloyd George (quoted by his secretary/mistress), 132, and Sir David Beatty, 133–134.

127 **They blamed him for the capture and internment** Jerrold, Royal Naval Division, 39.

127 **"Only one man"** Gilbert, *The Challenge of War*, 125.

5. TESTIMONY OF THE SPADE

128 **"a blend of military headquarters"** Annika Mombauer, *Helmuth von Moltke*, 232 (note 23).

129 **"We have neither gas nor electric lights"** Holger H. Herwig, *The Marne, 1914*, 171.

129 **"Communications remained the Achilles' heel"** Herwig, *The Marne*, 171.

129 **patrols rode into Écouen** Martin Gilbert, *The First World War*, Henry Holt and Company, New York, 1994, 68.

129 **"Impressed on Moltke"** B. H. Liddell Hart, *Reputations Ten Years After*, Little, Brown, and Company, Boston, 1928, 51.

129 **"If one allows them"** Robert T. Foley, ed. and trans., *Alfred von Schlieffen's Military Writings*, 172.

130 **"it was furious improvisation"** Martin van Creveld, *Supplying War*, Cambridge University Press, Cambridge, 1977, 140.

131 "The retreat was ordered" Liddell Hart, *Reputations,* 50.

131 "a sick, broken man" Herwig, *The Marne,* 285–286; Mombauer, *Helmuth von Moltke,* 265; Jonathan Bott, *Haig's Enemy,* Oxford University Press, Oxford, 2018, 29. Bott gives a slightly different translation but its substance is the same.

132 "All the German armies" Sewell Tyng, *The Campaign of the Marne,* Westholme, Yardley, PA, 2007, 328.

132 "slammed his fist" Herwig, *The Marne,* 301.

132 "in good time" *Official History 1914,* II, 426.

132 "It was the hardest decision" Mombauer, *Helmuth von Moltke,* 257.

132 "Our general staff has totally" Herwig, *The Marne,* 286; Robert T. Foley, *German Strategy and the Path to Verdun,* 84.

132 "I saw many men cry" Herwig, *The Marne,* 302.

132 "This could not be" Herwig, *The Marne,* 303.

132 "and scarcely recognized them" Capt. Walter Bloem, *The Advance from Mons,* Award Books/Tandem Books, New York and London, 1967, 183.

133 "Big crisis in the evening" Mombauer, *Helmuth von Moltke,* 267.

133 "I refuse to do this" Herwig, *The Marne,* 301–302; Mombauer, *Helmuth von Moltke,* 267–269.

133 "It is dreadful to be condemned" Mombauer, *Helmuth von Moltke,* 281.

133 "It did not seem fitting" Erich von Falkenhayn, *General Headquarters, 1914–1916,* The Battery Press, Nashville, TN, 2000, 1–2. (Originally published 1919.)

134 The Austrian representative to OHL Liddell Hart, *Reputations,* 53–54.

134 "By German reckoning" Cyril Falls, *The First World War,* Pen & Sword Military, Barnsley, South Yorkshire, U.K., 1960, 2014, 52.

135 "If cultural progress signifies" Robert A. Asprey, *The German High Command at War,* Quill/William Morrow, New York, 1991, 111.

135 "Aloof, reserved, notoriously ambitious" Liddell Hart, *Reputations,* 53–54.

135 "The mood in the general staff" Laird M. Easton, ed. and trans., *Journey to the Abyss: The Diaries of Count Harry Kessler, 1880–1918,* Alfred A. Knopf, New York, 2011, 715.

136 "the unconditional trust" Fritz von Lossberg, *Lossberg's War: The World War I Memoirs of a German Chief of Staff,* University Press of Kentucky, Lexington, KY, 2017, 124.

136 "If we don't lose the war" Asprey, *German High Command,* 130.

136 "The technique of field entrenchment" Liddell Hart, *Reputations,* 57.

137 Trenches were hardly a new phenomenon in 1914 See Robert Cowley, "The Unreal City," *MHQ: The Quarterly Journal of Military History* 6, no. 2 (Winter 1994), 8–21.

137 archaeologists found evidence "Outer 'Wall' of Troy Now Appears to Be a Ditch," *The New York Times,* Tuesday, September 28, 1993, C5; Barry M. Strauss, *The Trojan War,* Simon and Schuster Paperbacks, New York, 2006, 2007, 81–82.

137 the so-called Great Wall of the Dutch Republic Geoffrey Parker, *The*

Military Revolution, Cambridge University Press, Cambridge and New York, 1988, 39.

137   **"mole's work"** Parker, *Military Revolution,* 37.

138   **Torres Vedras** Ian V. Hogg, *Fortress,* St. Martin's Press, New York, 1977, 73.

139   **"King of Spades"** Shelby Foote, *The Civil War,* I, Random House, New York, 1986, 131.

139   **one-third of** Gerald F. Linderman, *Embattled Courage: The Experience of Combat in the Civil War,* The Free Press, New York, 1989, 145.

139   **"Spades were trumps"** Linderman, *Embattled Courage,* 143.

139   **"siege warfare in the field"** *Official History 1914,* I, 431.

140   **a "crawl"** Falls, *First World War,* 49.

140   **"I thought our movements very slow"** John Terraine, *Douglas Haig: The Educated Soldier,* 91–92.

140   **"a sense of lost opportunity"** J. P. Harris, *Douglas Haig and the First World War,* Cambridge University Press, Cambridge, 2008, 2009, 88.

141   **"an immense fortress"** Douglas W. Johnson, *Battlefields of the World War,* Oxford University Press, Oxford and New York, 1921, 291–292.

142   **"The prospects of a break-through"** *Official History 1914,* I, 384.

143   **played a leading role** *Official History 1914,* I, 232, and 393–394, summarizes Johann von Zwehl's personal account (only published in Germany), *Maubeuge, Aisne, Verdun.*

143   **Westphalians from the industrial cities** Alistair Horne, *The Price of Glory,* Penguin Books, New York, 1912, 1964, 1993, 58.

144   **"he would have left the way clear"** *Official History 1914,* I, 393.

144   **"the crisis . . . was, for the Germans"** *Official History 1914,* I, 394.

144   **"remarkable even for a modern battlefield"** *Official History 1914,* I, 394.

145   **"Everywhere on the ridge"** F. Loraine Petre, Wilfred Ewart, and Major General Sir Cecil Lowther, *The Scots Guards in the Great War,* John Murray, London, 1925 and reprint, the Naval & Military Press, Uckfield, U.K., 2002, 15.

145   **"I was with a party"** David Ascoli, *The Mons Star,* Birlinn, Edinburgh, 2001, 170.

146   **"gradually dribbled back"** *Official History 1914,* I, 401.

146   **"We came to the conclusion"** J. M. Craster, *"Fifteen Rounds a Minute": The Grenadiers at War,* Macmillan, London, 1976, 87.

146   **Haig's I Corps had lost** *Official History 1914,* I, Appendix 46, 569; Terraine, *Educated Soldier,* 93.

146   **In each German infantry company** *Handbook of the German Army, 1912 (Amended to August 1914),* The Imperial War Museum, London/in association with The Battery Press, Nashville, TN and Articles of War, Ltd., 2002, 102, 320–321.

146   **"The fighting on 14 September"** Harris, *Douglas Haig and the First World War,* 90.

147   **Operation Order No. 26** *Official History 1914,* I, Appendix 46, 569.

147   **"proved to be the official notification"** *Official History 1914,* I, 430.

147   **"were not yet ends in themselves"** Hew Strachan, *The First World War, Vol. I, To Arms,* 261.

147   **just over three hundred miles** (Distance converted from kilometer

estimate) Henry Contamine, *La Victoire de la Marne,* Gallimard, Paris, 1970, 289–290.

148   **a recent biography . . . sets the date of the commencement of trench warfare** Jonathan Boff, *Haig's Enemy,* 26.

148   **"There was plenty of work"** Paul Kendell, *Aisne 1914,* Spellmount: The History Press, Stroud, Gloucestershire, U.K., 2012, 344.

148   **"Every man had to dig"** Malcolm Brown, The Imperial War Museum Book of *1914,* Sidgwick & Jackson, London, 2004, 140.

149   **"little more than shallow furrows"** Rudyard Kipling, *The Irish Guards in the Great War: The First Battalion,* Sarpedon, New York, 1997, 44.

149   **"I got six"** Sir Thomas O. Marden, *The History of the Welch Regiment 1914–1918,* Naval & Military Press, Uckfield, East Sussex, U.K., 2015, 310.

149   **"Our front is now well covered"** Reginald Berkely, *The History of the Rifle Brigade,* I, The Naval & Military Press, Uckfield, East Sussex, U.K., 2007, 27; Kendell, *Aisne 1914,* 330.

150   **"a new place on earth"** Kendell, *Aisne 1914,* 343.

150   **"was covered with unburied bodies"** Sir Frederick Ponsonby, *The Grenadier Guards in the Great War of 1914–1918,* I, 77.

150   **"the weather became hot"** Kendell, *Aisne 1914,* 344.

151   **"an unmistakably modern phenomenon"** Paddy Griffith, *Battle Tactics of the Western Front,* Yale University Press, New Haven & London, 1994, 108.

151   **"At the beginning"** *Official History 1914,* I, 433.

152   **"would seem to have been the most outstanding"** Terraine, *Educated Soldier,* 94–95.

153   **"The high-explosive shell"** *Official History 1914,* I, 437.

153   **"made holes big enough"** Ponsonby, *Grenadier Guards,* I, 72.

153   **"Our own high explosive"** Terraine, *Educated Soldier,* 95.

154   **"'I believe he likes it'"** Walter Raleigh, *The War in the Air,* I, Naval & Military Press, in association with The Imperial War Museum, 1922, 2020, 339.

154   **"4.2 p.m."** Raleigh, *War in the Air,* I, 344.

155   **first British aviator wounded** Raleigh, *War in the Air,* I, 344.

155   **daily wastage from shellfire** *Official History 1914,* I, 439.

155   **"I had an awful night"** Kendell, *Aisne 1914,* 314.

156   **September 20 began** *Official History 1914,* I, 446–449; Everhard Wyrall, *The West Yorkshire Regiment in the War 1914–1918,* I, Naval & Military Press, Uckfield, East Sussex, U.K., 2016, 11–12; H. C. Wylly, *The 1st and 2nd Battalions: The Sherwood Foresters in the Great War,* Naval & Military Press, Uckfield, East Sussex, U.K., 2004, 97–98.

156   **"The whole affair was a mystery"** Wyrall, *West Yorkshire Regiment,* I, 12.

157   **"tried to entrench themselves"** *Official History 1914,* I, 448.

157   **"Altogether the 20th September"** *Official History 1914,* I, 449.

157   **The time had come to stop** Quoted in *Official History 1914,* I, 450 (FN).

158   **a costly one for both sides** Kendell, *Aisne 1914,* 349.

158   **"I think the battle"** Brown, *1914,* 140.

6. RACE TO THE SEA

159 **"A race it was"** John Keegan, *The First World War*, Alfred A. Knopf, New York, 1999, 127.

160 **"It still seemed possible"** General Erich von Falkenhayn, *General Headquarters*, 13.

160 **"For against a force"** Trevor Wilson, *The Myriad Faces of War*, Polity Press, Cambridge, 1986, 102.

161 **"had been prevented by the superiority"** Falkenhayn, *General Headquarters*, 27.

161 **"If Joffre had a secret weapon"** Robert A. Doughty, *Pyrrhic Victory*, 99.

162 **"twenty-four hours and an army corps"** B. H. Liddell Hart, *Reputations Ten Years After*, 29.

162 LES ALLEMANDS SONT À NOYON C.R.M.F. Cruttwell, *A History of the Great War*, 111.

164 **"Except for sleeping together"** Doughty, *Pyrrhic Victory*, 28.

164 **possessed a distinct character** Sources for the descriptions of open warfare on the Somme, September–October 1914, include: Jean Ratinaud, *La Course à la Mer*, Fayard, Paris, 1967; Général Barthélemy E. Palat (Pierre Lehautcourt), *La Grande Guerre sur la Front Occidental*, VII, (*La Course à la Mer*) Librairie Chapelot, Paris, 1921; Jack Sheldon, *The German Army on the Somme, 1914–1916*, Pen & Sword Military, Barnsley, South Yorkshire, U.K., 2005; Ralph J. Whitehead, *The Other Side of the Wire*, I, Helion & Company Ltd., Solihull, West Midlands, U.K., 2009; Jonathan Boff, *Haig's Enemy: Crown Prince Rupprecht and Germany's War on the Western Front*; M. von Posseck, *The German Cavalry 1914 in Belgium and France*, Naval & Military Press, Uckfield, East Sussex, 2007; William Philpott, *Three Armies on the Somme*, Alfred A. Knopf, New York, 2010; Général Henri Colin, *Le Gars du 26e*, Payot, Paris, 1932; and Captain Ferdinand Belmont, *A Crusader in France*, E. P. Dutton & Company, New York, 1917.

166 **"With lances couched"** Poseck, *German Cavalry 1914*, 168.

166 **"Despite enemy attempts"** Sheldon, *German Army on the Somme*, 28.

166 **"Where on earth"** Sheldon, *German Army on the Somme*, 20.

167 **"The battles in Lorraine"** Sheldon, *German Army on the Somme*, 20.

167 **"We are nose to nose"** Colin, *Le Gars du 26e*, 134, 139, 143.

167 **"I went forward across the battlefield"** Sheldon, *German Army on the Somme*, 36.

168 **turning villages into fortresses** Whitehead, *Other Side of the Wire*, I, 84.

168 **"We are in a continuous line"** Maréchal Fayolle, *Cahiers Secret de la Grande Guerre*, ed. Henry Contamine, trans. Elizabeth Venant, Plon, Paris, 1964, 40–41.

169 **"All movements are made at night"** Ferdinand Belmont, *A Crusader of France: The Letters of Captain Ferdinand Belmont*, E. P. Dutton & Company, New York, 1917, 96.

169 **"a small active man"** Douglas Haig, *Douglas Haig: War Diaries and Letters*, eds. Gary Sheffield and John Bourne, Weidenfeld & Nicolson, London, 2005, 104.

169   **the struggle for Arras** If this encounter, medium in size but intense in nature, is undeservedly overlooked, it is because accounts of it are relatively scarce. Jack Sheldon's *The German Army at Vimy Ridge 1914–1917* (Pen & Sword Military, Barnsley, South Yorkshire, U.K., 2008) and Boff's *Haig's Enemy* present the view from the German side. The French accounts are fuller: *La Division Barbot* (Librairie Hachette et cie, Paris, 1919) by Capitaine Humbert, contains potent color; *La Grande Guerre sur le Front Occidental. La Course à la Mer* by Général Palat offers a useful sweeping account, as does the more recent *La Course à Mer* by Jean Ratinaud. As for the subsequent 1914 struggle for Vimy Ridge, there is no matching Sheldon's book; Palat and Ratinaud are also helpful. Since the British did not participate in the "race" until the end, their historians have pretty much left it alone, though Peter Hart's *Fire and Movement*, Oxford University Press, Oxford, 2015, is excellent on the late British role.

171   **just 3,000 remained standing** Humbert, *La Division Barbot*, 22. At this point the Germans didn't even try to estimate.

171   **"This wavering is deplorable"** Fayolle, *Cahiers Secrets*, 42.

171   **"Thus we sink deeper"** Holger H. Herwig, "Eyeball to Eyeball with the Enemy," *MHQ: The Quarterly Journal of Military History* (Winter 2009), 88.

172   **"shell shock"** Anthony Babington, *Shell-Shock*, Leo Cooper, London, 1997, 43–44.

173   **"a mere pocket handkerchief"** B. H. Liddell Hart, *Foch: The Man of Orleans*, 22.

174   **"enshrined"** Liddell Hart, *Reputations*, 153.

174   **"To charge"** General Ferdinand Foch, *The Principles of War*, trans. J. de Morinni, The H. K. Fly Company, New York, 1918, 366.

174   **"numbers could be nullified"** Liddell Hart, *Man of Orleans*, 31.

174   **"The art of war"** Foch, *Principles of War*, 14.

174   **"The goal of the military art"** Jean Autin, *Foch ou le triomphe de la volonté*, Librairie Académique Perrin, Paris, 61.

174   **"A lost battle"** Liddell Hart, *Man of Orleans*, 26.

174   **"One goes forward"** Liddell Hart, *Reputations*, 166.

175   **"Le perroquet, animal subtil"** E. L. Spears, *Prelude to Victory*, Jonathan Cape, London, 1939, 56.

175   **"Je me f—"** Elizabeth Greenhalgh, *Foch in Command*, Cambridge University Press, Cambridge and New York, 2011, 60.

176   **"The question of the (non-)arrival"** Greenhalgh, *Foch in Command*, 17–18. Greenhalgh speculates that a member of Foch's staff received the message, pocketed it, and, in the heat and confusion of the surprise German attack, failed to show it to his boss.

176   **"for an important command"** Greenhalgh, *Foch in Command*, 21.

176   **"to break through and split"** Greenhalgh, *Foch in Command*, 41.

177   **"It was evident"** Ferdinand Foch, *The Memoirs of Marshal Foch*, Doubleday, Doran and Company, Garden City, NY, 1931, 73.

177   **"The first days I was beaten"** Liddell Hart, *Man of Orleans*, 113.

178   **"Green hillsides dotted"** Holger H. Herwig, *The Marne, 1914*, 258.

178   **"the attack directed against"** Liddell Hart, *Man of Orleans*, 108. This report, sent by Foch to Joffre on the evening of September 8, was

certainly the root of Foch's celebrated non-quote. That it varies from source to source can be explained by differing translations of the chimeric words. I have based mine on an early history, Palat's *La Grande Guerre*, VI, 257 (note). Palat's account was originally printed in 1917, and reprinted, with updates, in 1920. Greenhalgh, that admirably hard-headed Australian military historian, dismisses Foch's alleged words as "rather silly." And so they are.

178   **"You say you cannot hold on"** Liddell Hart, *Man of Orleans*, 112.

178   **"Audace réfléchie"** Greenhalgh, *Foch in Command*, 36.

180   **"It was difficult . . . to pass"** Foch, *Memoirs*, 87.

180   **"through villages disfigured"** Foch, *Memoirs*, 114.

180   **In the next fifty-seven hours** Cyril Falls, *Marshal Foch*, Blackie & Son Limited, London and Glasgow, 1931, 77; Liddell Hart, *Man of Orleans*, 122.

180   **"You are speaking to a wall"** Greenhalgh, *Foch in Command*, 48.

181   **"Maud'huy, I embrace you"** Liddell Hart, *Man of Orleans*, 122.

181   **"Fight to the last man"** *Official History 1914*, I, 461 (note).

182   **"We had to win"** Greenhalgh, *Foch in Command*, 40.

182   **The capital city of Flanders** See the Wikipedia entry for Lille; Greenhalgh, *Foch in Command*, 53.

182   **a ludicrous foul-up** The two best accounts are in French: Ratinaud, *La Course à la Mer*, 205–210, and Palat, *La Grande Guerre*, VII, 319–321.

182   **"A terrible street battle"** Herbert Sulzbach, *With the German Guns*, trans. Richard Thonger, Leo Cooper Ltd., London, 1973, 31–33.

185   **"Strangely, the trams are running"** Sulzbach, *With the German Guns*, 33.

185   **a forced march** Greenhalgh, *Foch in Command*, 55; *Official History 1914*, II, 73.

185   **"You could see a huge fiery glow"** Sulzbach, *With the German Guns*, 34–35.

185   **The bombardment went on** Ratinaud, *La Course à la Mer*, 204–205, 210.

186 ·   **"In unbelievably scruffy condition"** Sulzbach, *With the German Guns*, 35.

187   **"succeeded in averting"** Martin Gilbert, *Winston S. Churchill: The Challenge of War 1914–1916*, 81.

187   **"to disengage us"** Richard Holmes, *The Little Field Marshal*, 242; Joseph Jacques Césaire Joffre, *The Personal Memoirs of Joffre*, 300.

188   **"irrefutable"** Joffre, *Personal Memoirs*, 300.

188   **"The movement contemplated"** Joffre, *Personal Memoirs*, 302.

188   **"the almost complete interruption"** Joffre, *Personal Memoirs*, 303–304.

188   **"The French filed in"** Everard Wyrall, *The History of the Second Division*, I, Thomas Nelson and Sons, Ltd., London, Edinburgh, and New York, 1921 (Reprinted by the University of Michigan Libarary, Ann Arbor, MI), 105.

189   **A German wireless message** *Official History 1914*, I, 464.

190   **"the sound of heavy gunfire"** J. M. Craster, *"Fifteen Rounds a Minute": The Grenadiers at War, August to December 1914*, 106.

7. ACCIDENTAL TOURISTS

192   "to obstruct England's Channel traffic" General Erich von Falken-hayn, *General Headquarters 1914–1916*, 27–28.

193   "There was no longer time" Falkenhayn, *General Headquarters*, 30.

193   "One cavalry regiment after another" Herbert Sulzbach, *With the German Guns*, 32.

195   "It was impossible to see" M. von Poseck, *The German Cavalry: 1914 in Belgium and France*, 199–201.

196   said to possess four thousand looms Michelin et Cie, *Ypres and the Battles of Ypres*, Michelin & Cie, Clermont-Ferrand, France, 1920, 69–71.

197   "when God had made" Douglas W. Johnson, *Battlefields of the World War*, 7.

198   "the whistle of shells" Lyn MacDonald, *1914*, Atheneum, New York, 1988, 348–349.

198   Two stone lions Ian F. W. Beckett, *Ypres: The First Battle, 1914*, Pearson/Longman, Harlow, U.K., 2004, 2006, 31. (The pagination is slightly different in the paperback edition, used here.)

198   a levy of 70,000 francs Beckett, *The First Battle*, 31.

198   From Madame Heursel's jewelry store MacDonald, *1914*, 349.

198   "The railway station" Dame M. Columban ("D.M.C."), *The Irish Nuns at Ypres*, Smith, Elder & Co., London, 1915, 6–9.

200   "A marvelous evening mood" Jack Sheldon, *The German Army at Ypres 1914*, Pen & Sword Military, Barnsley, South Yorkshire, U.K., 2010, 17–19.

200   "Twenty or so cavalrymen" MacDonald, *1914*, 349.

200   Stolberg-Rossla and his band Poseck, *German Cavalry*, 201.

200   "a complete though thin line" *Official History 1914*, II, 77.

201   "little better than a morass" *Official History 1914*, II, 79.

201   Mont des Cats *Official History 1914*, II, 95–96.

201   gave his gold pocket watch F. C. Hitchcock, *"Stand To": A Diary of the Trenches*, The Naval & Military Press, Uckfield, East Sussex, U.K., 2006, 276 (note 2).

202   "accurately located" Poseck, *German Cavalry*, 206.

202   On October 10 . . . a meeting *Ypres: The First Battle, 1914*, by Ian F. W. Beckett, 28, offers a credible reconstruction of the meeting; Émile Galet, *Albert King of the Belgians in the Great War*, trans. Ernest Swinton, 248–249, is also valuable, especially since Galet was a witness; Émile Cammaerts, *Albert of Belgium: Defender of Right*, 183–189, provides detail about the collision of demands; and Henri Bernard, *L'An 14 et La Campagne des Illusions*, 150–151, is useful in its description of Albert's flirtation with sending of his army to France—and his final decision to make a stand on the Yser.

203   "the Belgian Army is not in a condition to fight" Galet, *Albert King of the Belgians*, 251.

203   "It might suit the Allies" Galet, *Albert King of the Belgians*, 255.

204   "formed a veritable natural entrenched camp" Galet, *Albert King of the Belgians*, 256.

204　**"The Yser, merely the largest"** C.R.M.F. Cruttwell, *A History of the Great War*, 100.

205　**the first British troops to arrive** Descriptions of the arrival of Allied troops in Ypres are found in Raoul Nel, *Boesinghe, ou, Les Combats de la 87e Division Territoriale sur L'Yser*, Impr. Bretonnes, Rennes, France, 1922, 35–36; Columban, *Irish Nuns at Ypres*, 15; MacDonald, *1914*, 355–357; *Official History 1914*, II, 67; and C. T. Atkinson, *The Seventh Division 1914–1918*, The Naval & Military Press, Uckfield, East Sussex, U.K., 2011, 16, 20.

205　**"engaged in chalking the doors"** *Official History 1914*, II, 67.

206　**"The country people"** Atkinson, *Seventh Division*, 20.

207　**"gazing at the triangle"** Charles Le Goffic, *The Epic of Dixmude*, trans. Florence Simmonds, J. B. Lippincott, Philadelphia, 1916, 58–59.

208　**units of Albert's army** Hew Strachan, *The First World War, Vol. I: To Arms*, 275; Bernard, *L'An 14*, 149; Galet, *Albert King of the Belgians*, 264.

208　**"We had reached our limit"** Galet, *Albert King of the Belgians*, 267.

208　**"Situation very bad"** Bernard, *L'An 14*, 151.

208　**the king met with Foch** Galet, *Albert King of the Belgians*, 267.

209　**"The line of the Yser"** Bernard, *L'An 14*, 153.

209　**the first sound of cannon fire** Bernard, *L'An 14*, 163.

8. OCTOBER SURPRISE

211　**"Joffre was not a general"** B. H. Liddell Hart, *Reputations Ten Years After*, 39.

211　**"Did not an unfortunate spirit exist?"** André Bourachot, *Marshal Joffre*, 189.

213　**"It did not lie in his power"** Joseph Jacques Césaire Joffre, *The Personal Memoirs of Joffre*, I, 152.

213　**"In 1914 generals received"** Bourachot, *Marshal Joffre*, 181.

214　**the first *limogé*** Joffre, *Personal Memoirs*, I, 143–144, 149, 152, and 156; Barbara W. Tuchman, *The Guns of August*, 186–187.

214　**"as soon as I saw him"** Joffre, *Personal Memoirs*, I, 206–207.

215　**"His excited way of talking"** Joffre, *Personal Memoirs*, I, 220–221.

215　**Joffre dispatched 96 officers** Bourachot, *Marshal Joffre*, 183, 210 (notes 2 and 5).

215　**Messimy's demand** Joffre, *Personal Memoirs*, I, 151–152 and 184–185; Bourachot, *Marshal Joffre*, 182. The minister of war twice recommended the extreme penalty for officers convicted of cowardice under fire.

215　**"I have decided"** Bourachot, *Marshal Joffre*, 210 (note 2).

216　**Mangin gained fame** Louis-Eugène Mangin, *Le Général Mangin*, Éditions Fernand Lanore, Paris, 1986, 150–151.

217　**"Whatever you do"** J. M. Bourne, *Who's Who in World War I*, 193.

217　**"I am afraid of being afraid"** Maréchal Fayolle, *Cahiers Secrets de la Grande Guerre*, 13.

217　**"a symptomatic trembling"** Bourachot, *Marshal Joffre*, 186. Though Bourachot identifies him only as "General B—, the commander of the French 70th Reserve Division," that was the same division Fayolle took charge of the day after Bizard was *limogé*.

217 **"I am going into the campaign"** Fayolle, *Cahiers Secrets*, 19.

217 **blamed the British** Roy A. Prete, *Strategy and Command: The Anglo-French Coalition on the Western Front, 1914*, McGill-Queen's University Press, Montreal, 2009, 154–160.

217 **"retake Lille without striking a blow"** Prete, *Strategy and Command*, 159.

218 **"The floods of the Lys"** Douglas W. Johnson, *Battlefields of the World War*, 26–28.

220 **"dismal country to work over"** *Official History 1914*, II, 79.

220 **"a series of British misadventures"** *Official History 1914*, II, 78–81; Anthony Farrar-Hockley, *Death of an Army*, William Morrow and Company, New York, 1968, 46–50; Edward Gleichen, *Infantry Brigade: 1914*, Leonaur Ltd., London, 2001, 110–111.

221 **They were able to force their way** *Official History 1914*, II, 81–87; Albert Herbert Hussey, *The Fifth Division in the Great War*, Nisbet & Co. Ltd., London, 1921, 38; Farrar-Hockley, *Death of an Army*, University of Michigan Library (Reprint), Ann Arbor, MI, 2012, 51–54.

221 **"They attacked all day"** Letter from a lieutenant in the 1st Duke of Cornwall's Light Infantry Regiment, October 15, 1914, The Liddle Collection, The Library of the University of Leeds.

221 **"high-water mark"** *Official History 1914*, II, 85.

222 **"We must push, push, push"** C. E. Callwell, *Field-Marshal Sir Henry Wilson*, I, 182.

223 **just short of 200,000 men** Alex Watson, " 'For Kaiser and Reich': The Identity and Fate of the German Volunteers, 1914–1918," *War in History*, 12 no. 1, 2005, 66 (note 88).

223 **"the danger of an effective encirclement"** General Erich von Falkenhayn, *General Headquarters 1914–1916*, 29.

224 **"in thick masses"** Watson, " 'For Kaiser and Reich,' 65; Jack Sheldon, *The German Army at Ypres 1914*, 8.

224 **"The new Fourth Army is to advance"** Sheldon, *German Army at Ypres*, 53, 55.

224 **"to obstruct England's Channel traffic"** Falkenhayn, *General Headquarters*, 27–28.

224 **"The prize to be won"** Falkenhayn, *General Headquarters*, 28.

225 **"joined hands"** *Official History 1914*, II, 67, 99.

226 **"the most completely ignorant general"** J. M. Bourne, *Who's Who in World War I*, 239.

226 **The Battle of Meteren** *Official History 1914*, II, 96–97; John Ashby, *Seek Glory, Now Keep Glory* (The Royal Warwickshire Regiment), Helion and Company, Solihull, West Midlands, U.K., 2000, 112–116.

227 **One of the wounded** Alan Moorehead, *Montgomery, A Biography*, Hamish Hamilton, London, 1946, 56ff.

228 **"We were loaded up with gifts"** Farrar-Hockley, *Death of an Army*, 66–67.

229 **"certain large new formations"** *Official History 1914*, II, 119.

229 **"the formidable enemy movement"** Walter Raleigh, *The War in the Air*, I, 347.

230 **marching along four parallel paved roads** Dennis E. Showalter, *Instrument of War: The German Army 1914–1918*, Osprey, Oxford, 2016,

49–50, 84–87; Farrar-Hockley, *Death of an Army*, 76, 78; *Official History 1914*, II, 121–122.

232 **But for the accident of an imprecise word** *Official History 1914*, II, 115–116; C. T. Atkinson, *The Seventh Division*, 23, (note 3); Ian F. W. Beckett, *Ypres 1914: The First Battle*, 76–77.

233 **"Owing to nothing"** Callwell, *Field-Marshal Sir Henry Wilson*, I, 183.

233 **"tenacious peasants continued"** Dudley Ward, *Regimental Records of the Royal Welch Fusiliers*, Naval & Military Press, Uckfield, East Sussex, U.K., 2005, 74.

234 **"For a little while"** Farrar-Hockley, *Death of an Army*, 79–80.

235 **"In front of us the fires"** Raoul Nel, *Boesinghe, ou, Les Combats de la 87e Division Territoriale sur l'Yser*, trans. Elizabeth Venant, 45, 48, Diary entries for October 19 and 20, 1914.

236 **"backward in advancing"** Atkinson, *The Seventh Division*, 22.

236 **"the enemy's strength on the front"** In a diary entry for October 19, 1914, Haig recorded Sir John French's order. From *Douglas Haig: War Diaries and Letters 1914–1918*, eds. Gary Sheffield and John Bourne, 73; *Official History 1914*, II, 137, gives a slightly different reading, but it amounts to the same message. I'll go with the always reliable (and later) Sheffield and Bourne version.

236 **"Bruges for all practical purposes"** Callwell, *Field-Marshal Sir Henry Wilson*, I, 184.

237 **"We can apparently get no further"** Billy Congreve, *Armageddon Road: A VC's Diary*, ed. Terry Norman, William Kimber, London, 1982, 53, diary entry for October 19.

238 **"bearing their homely London labels"** James Lochhead Jack, *General Jack's Diary: 1914–1918*, ed. John Terraine, Eyre & Spottiswoode, London, 1964, 66 (October 20).

238 **"were in our thoughts"** Captain J. C. Dunn, *The War the Infantry Knew*, Abacus, London, 1994, 74.

238 **"a thunder of gun-fire"** H. FitzM. Stacke, *The Worcestershire Regiment in the Great War*, G. T. Cheshire & Sons, Ltd., Kidderminster, Worcestershire, U.K., 1929, 26.

238 **The disaster at Le Pilly** Farrar-Hockley, *Death of an Army*, 81–83.

9. THE SALIENT

246 **That advantage disappeared once night fell** *Official History 1914*, II, 138–141; H. C. Wylly, *History of the Sherwood Foresters Nottinghamshire and Derbyshire Regiment in the Great War*, 102–105; Everard Wyrall, *The First Yorkshire in the War 1914–1918*, I, 21–23; Herbert Sulzbach, *With the German Guns*, 37.

247 **"We all pull forward"** Sulzbach, *With the German Guns*, 37 (October 21).

248 **"Little did we think"** Frank Richards, *Old Soldiers Never Die*, Naval & Military Press, Uckfield, East Sussex, U.K., 2001, 34.

248 **"Almost for the first time"** Sir Frederick Ponsonby, *The Grenadier Guards in the Great War of 1914–1918*, I, 109.

249 **the 7th Division's eight-mile front** C. T. Atkinson, *The Seventh Division*, 41.

249 "Effective assistance" Atkinson, *Seventh Division*, 32–33.

251 "All had a look of terror" Ponsonby, *Grenadier Guards in the Great War*, I, 104.

251 "There is not a soul left" J. M. Craster, *"Fifteen Rounds a Minute": The Grenadier Guards at War*, 112.

251 noted in a heavy ledger The baker Van den Bulke's ledger can be seen in the Zonnebeke Streeksmuseum. Courtesy Aleks Deseyne.

251 "Crowds of people in the streets" Craster, *"Fifteen Rounds a Minute,"* 108.

252 "Outside, the noise grew ever louder" Dame M. Columban, *The Irish Nuns at Ypres*, 35–36.

253 "The Commander-in-Chief intends" Army Operation Order No. 39, in *Official History 1914*, II, 514 (Appendix 28).

253 "All went satisfactorily" Callwell, *Field-Marshal Sir Henry Wilson*, I, 184.

254 "had to cross a stretch of country" G. C. Wynne, trans., *Ypres 1914: An Official Account Published by Order of the German General Staff*, The Battery Press, Nashville, TN, in association with The Imperial War Museum, London, and Articles of War, Ltd., Skokie, IL, 1919, 1994, 33–34.

255 "Sniping prevented the counting" *Official History 1914*, II, 150; Anthony Farrar-Hockley, *Death of an Army*, 91; Jack Sheldon, *The German Army at Ypres 1914*, 39–40, 44, 48.

256 "I shall expect to learn" Anthony Farrar-Hockley, *Goughie*, Hart-Davis, MacGibbon, Ltd., London, 1975, 140.

257 "I passed a dull day" Sheldon, *GermanArmy at Ypres 1914*, 45.

257 "gradually congealed" Marquess of Anglesey, *A History of the British Cavalry, 1816–1919*, VII, Leo Cooper, London, 1996, 209.

257 "The corps staff had drawn" Farrar-Hockley, *Death of an Army*, 92.

258 "As fast as we shot them down" David Ascoli, *The Mons Star*, 211–212.

259 "The enemy came on" Atkinson, *Seventh Division*, 36–37.

259 "a hare started up" Rudyard Kipling, *The Irish Guards in the Great War: The First Battalion*, 53.

259 "The guns were run up" *Official History 1914*, II, 156.

260 population 7,438 but emptying fast *OH 1914*, II, 157.

260 "officers and men tumbled" Wyrall, *Second Division*, 113. For Oxford and Bucks casualties, see *OH 1914*, II, 158.

261 "a busy day for doctors" Everard Wyrall, *The History of the Second Division*, 114.

261 "slowly but steadily" R. M. Grazebrook, *The Gloucestershire Regiment: War Narratives, 1914–1915*, Naval & Military Press, Uckfield, East Sussex, U.K., 2009, 37.

261 "one unending roar" G. C. Wynne, trans., *Ypres 1914: The First Battle*, 94.

261 "To die by daylight" R. G. Vliet, *Water and Stone*, Random House, New York, 1980, 55–56.

262 "On the left of D Company" Everard Wyrall, *The Gloucestershire Regiment in the War, 1914–1918*, Naval & Military Press, Uckfield, East Sussex, U.K., 2003, 67.

262 **"it was indispensable"** *OH 1914*, II (quoting from "Review Militaire Générale," 1921, 5), 161.

263 **"The whole sky to the east"** Craster, *"Fifteen Rounds a Minute"* 109.

263 **"Coldstream and not Coldstreams"** Ponsonby, *The Grenadier Guards in the Great War*, I, 145.

264 **"He was full of confidence"** Craster, *"Fifteen Rounds a Minute"* 111.

264 **Battles Nomenclature Committee** See the long footnote in the *OH 1914*, II, 125–126.

266 **"there was a feeling of anxiety"** Sheldon, *German Army at Ypres 1914*, 99.

266 **"The Feldgrauen lay piled"** Sheldon, *German Army at Ypres 1914*, 99.

266 **"There was no order"** Sheldon, *German Army at Ypres 1914*, 101.

267 **"I am delighted that today"** Jack Sheldon and Nigel Cave, *Ypres 1914: Langemarck*, Pen & Sword Military, Barnsley, South Yorkshire, U.K., 2014, 71.

267 **"all my worst forebodings"** Sir John French, *1914*, Leonaur, London, 2009, 193.

268 **"that in view of the unexpected reinforcements"** Wyrall, *History of the Second Division*, 116.

268 **"it would have had the same result"** Ian F. W. Beckett, *The Making of the First World War*, 2.

269 **"The Germans nearer meant greater danger"** Dame M. Columban, *Irish Nuns at Ypres*, 50–51.

269 **"Our life, by this time"** Dame M. Columban, *Irish Nuns at Ypres*, 53.

269 **"It was not their last card"** John Terraine, *Douglas Haig: The Educated Soldier*, 105.

10. SHOULDER TO SHOULDER

270 **to forge a rough statistical portrait** Alex Watson, "'For Kaiser and Reich': The Identity and Fate of the German Volunteers, 1914–1918," *War in History*, 12, No. 1 (2005), 44–74; Watson would incorporate that paper into the chapter, "Mobilizing the People," in his *Ring of Steel*, Basic Books, New York, 2014. Also, the early chapters of two other works already cited are invaluable in the characterizing of the German volunteer: *Instrument of War: The German Army 1914–18*, by Dennis E. Showalter, and *The First World War: Germany and Austria Hungary 1914–1918*, by Holger H. Herwig.

270 **The greatest number belonged** Watson, "'For Kaiser and Reich,'" 56.

271 **"At the proper distance"** Anonymous, translated for the General Staff, U.S. Army by Francis J. Behr, Coast Artillery Corps, "Drill Regulations for the Infantry, German Army 1906," 44.

272 **no more than one-third to a quarter of 1 percent** John Ellis, *Eye-Deep in Hell: Trench Warfare in World War I*, Pantheon Books, New York, 1976, 78–79; Denis Winter, *Death's Men*, Penguin Books, New York, 1979, 39–40; T. J. Mitchell and G. M. Smith, *Medical Services*, The Imperial War Museum, London and The Battery Press, Nashville, TN, 1931, 1997.

273 **"absolute and unthinking"** Stephen D. Jackman, "Shoulder to Shoulder: Close Control and 'Old Prussian Drill' in German Offensive

Infantry Tactics, 1871–1914," *The Journal of Military History* 68, no. 1 (January 2004), 82.

273 **"Love of life"** Jackman, "Shoulder to Shoulder," 82.

273 **Apparently some did not** The source for the footnote is R. M. Grazebrook, *The Gloucestershire Regiment: War Narratives, 1914–1915*, 39.

273 **"For enthusiasm"** Jackman, "Shoulder to Shoulder," 95.

273 **"the treatment of the mostly educated"** Watson, " 'For Kaiser and Reich,' " 68.

274 **"The unwillingness of the German Army"** Bruce I. Gudmundsson, *Stormtroop Tactics: Innovation in the German Army, 1914–1918*, Praeger, New York, Westport, CT and London, 1989, 19.

274 **"to keep his entire company in sight"** Gudmundsson, *Stormtroop Tactics*, 8.

274 **"a dispersed attack"** Jackman, "Shoulder to Shoulder," 100.

275 **Experimenters at the Spandau Marksmanship School** Jackman, "Shoulder to Shoulder," 85.

275 **"Riflemen, trained to fire"** Gudmundsson, *Stormtroop Tactics*, 20–21.

276 **"a shrieking hell"** Letter from Lt. J. D. Cunningham, 2nd Battalion Argyll and Sutherland Highlanders, undated, Liddle Collection, Brotherton Library, University of Leeds, U.K. Quotation cited in a letter from Peter Liddle to the author, October 26, 1997.

276 **"two, three or even four hundred yards"** *OH, 1914*, II, 175–176. The detail about the scarcity of barbed wire comes from Anthony Farrar-Hockley, *Goughie: The Life of General Sir Hubert Gough*, 138.

276 **"It was only at night"** *OH, 1914*, II, 176.

277 **"The enemy's fire"** C. T. Atkinson, *The Seventh Division*, 43.

277 **"The German masses staggered"** *OH, 1914*, II, 178.

278 **"I am wounded somewhere"** H. C. Wylly, *The Green Howards*, The Naval & Military Press, Uckfield, East Sussex, U.K., 2007, 45.

279 **"We made some progress, but the majority were hit"** Jack Sheldon, *The German Army at Ypres 1914*, 121.

279 **"most trying"** H. FitzM. Stacke, *The Worcestershire Regiment in the Great War*, 29.

280 **The Territorials marched out** Dr. Raoul Nel, *Boesinghe*, trans. Edward M. Strauss, 53; Anthony Farrar-Hockley, *Death of an Army*, 93; *OH, 1914*, II, 174; F. Loraine Petre et al., *The Scots Guards in the Great War*, John Murray, London, 1925/Naval & Military Press, Uckfield, East Sussex, U.K., 2002, 48.

280 **"This time, captain, we'll get them"** Nel, *Boesinghe*, 54.

280 **A Scots Guard lieutenant** Nel, *Boesinghe*, 55; F. Loraine Petre et al., *Scots Guards in the Great War*, 48.

281 **"Bullets and shrapnel are now whistling"** Nel, *Boesinghe*, 55.

281 **"At the Boesinghe railway bridge"** Nel, *Boesinghe*, 55.

281 **"The room is packed"** Nel, *Boesinghe*, 56.

281 **"You could be a virgin in horror"** Louis-Ferdinand Céline, *Journey to the End of the Night*, trans. Ralph Manheim, New Directions, New York, 1983, 9.

282 **"a particularly fine feat"** Grazebrook, *Gloucestershire Regiment: War Narratives*, 40.

282 **"The windows of the mill . . . became quite untenable"** Regimental

Committee, *Historical Records of the Queen's Own Cameron Highland-ers*, III, quoted in Sheldon and Cave, *Langemarck*, 83–87; *OH, 1914*, II, 180–181; Tony Spagnoly and Ted Smith, *Salient Points Two*, Leo Cooper, Barnsley, South Yorkshire, U.K., 1998.

283 **"by acting offensively"** *Les Armées Français dans la Grande Guerre*, I, Pt. III, 321; *Official History, 1914*, II, 183; Farrar-Hockley, *Death of an Army*, 96–97.

283 **"had expressed his astonishment"** Émile Galet, *Albert, King of the Belgians in the Great War*, trans. Ernest Swinton, 279–280; Émile Cammaerts, *Albert of Belgium: Defender of Right*, 193–194.

283 **"A major counter-attack by the Allies"** Farrar-Hockley, *Death of an Army*, 97.

284 **"A message came to say"** Craster, *"Fifteen Rounds a Minute"* 112.

284 **"He seemed to have no Headquarters"** Craster, *"Fifteen Rounds a Minute"* 112–113.

284 *"Allons, Allons, mes enfants"* Craster, *"Fifteen Rounds a Minute"* 113.

285 **"to make a plan and insist"** Farrar-Hockley, *Death of an Army*, 98.

286 **"We are now close to the 'Bosche'"** J.G.W. Hyndson, *From Mons to the First Battle of Ypres*, Privately Printed, Wyman & Sons Ltd., London, Reading and Fakenham, 1932, 78–79.

286 **"Suddenly the glorious sight"** Hyndson, *From Mons*, 81.

287 **When the British entered the tavern** Sheldon and Cave, *Langemarck*, 109–119; *OH, 1914*, II, 186; Farrar-Hockley, *Death of an Army*, 103; H. C. Wylly, *History of the Queen's Royal (West Surrey) Regiment in the Great War*, Naval & Military Press, Uckfield, 2006, 21; Hyndson, *From Mons*, 78–81.

288 **"The leading Germans got"** The attack of October 22, as reported by Lt. Col. H. R. Davies of the 2nd Ox and Bucks in Sheldon and Cave, *Langemarck*, 76.

289 **"The night came on"** Captain Henry Montifort Dillon of the 2nd Oxfordshire and Buckinghamshire Light Infantry on defending against the German mass attack of October 23. Dillon's letter to his sister, written the following day, has been often quoted, and with good reason. It is one of the key documents of the Great War. The letter was originally published first in a local newspaper, and later in *The Oxfordshire and Buckinghamshire Light Infantry Chronicle, 1914–1915*, vol. 24, 186–188. Since that is not easy to come by, I have relied on the versions reprinted in Sheldon and Cave, *Langemarck*, 102–105, and Peter Hart, *Fire and Movement: The British Expeditionary Force and the Campaign of 1914*, Oxford University Press, Oxford and New York, 2015, 287–288. Both are invaluable sources.

Confusion has arisen from the fact that there were *two* attacks by German reserve formations on the battalion Dillon belonged to, at the same time, 5:30 P.M., on successive evenings, October 22 and 23. The first attack was smaller, but still full of menace; the second was the one Dillon described in the letter to his sister. It definitely took place on the 23rd. Some writers have also misidentified the attacking division: it was the 51st Reserve Division, XXVI Reserve Corps, based in Poelcappelle, not the 46th Reserve, XXIII Reserve Corps, pushing down from the Houthulst Forest. *The British Official History, 1914*, II, 179 and 188, or the accompanying map case, should clear up any mix-up. I cannot recommend the

Battleground Europe series that Cave edits too highly. For me, the three Sheldon and Cave volumes on the 1914 combats around Ypres were beyond useful.

290 **740 corpses** *OH 1914*, II, 188.

11. SINGERS IN THE MIST

292 **bravery and tenacity** Anon., G. C. Wynne, trans., *Ypres 1914: An Official Account Published by Order of the German General Staff*, 37–38 (note 1); Jack Sheldon, *The German Army at Ypres 1914*, 124–125; R. M. Grazebrook, *The Gloucestershire Regiment, War Narratives 1914–1915*, 41–42.

292 **"Mentally and spiritually"** Sheldon, *German Army at Ypres*, 122.

292 **"The men are all burnt out"** Alex Watson, " 'For Kaiser and Reich': The Identity and Fate of the German Volunteers, 1914–1918," *War in History* 12, no. 1 (2005), 70.

292 **no satisfactory way to estimate German casualties** Conversation with Dennis E. Showalter, November 10, 1994. Showalter is one of the foremost authorities on the German Army and author of *Instrument of War: The German Army 1914–1918*. Sheldon's *The German Army at Ypres 1914* details the whittling away in less than a week of a single unit involved, Reserve Regiment 215, 123. Everard Wyrall, *The Gloucestershire Regiment in the War*, 70, and Thomas O. Marden, *The History of the Welch Regiment 1914–1918*, Naval & Military Press, Uckfield, 2015, 314, describe the carnage that the Germans left behind.

293 **"For the future . . . we only knew"** Dame M. Columban, *The Irish Nuns at Ypres*, 28–29.

294 **"almost certainly unreliable"** Watson, " 'For Kaiser and Reich,' " 66.

294 **The most widespread explanation** Anthony Babington, *Shell-Shock: A History of the Changing Attitudes to War Neurosis*, Leo Cooper, London, 1997, 43–44, 56.

294 **The first British troops** "Aftershock," by Robert S. Worth, *The New York Times Magazine*, June 12, 2016, 23–33.

295 **"After 1914 one seldom saw"** Marden, *History of the Welch Regiment*, 314 (note 1).

295 **the combined population** Erich von Falkenhayn, *General Headquarters 1914–1916*, 295 (Appendix B).

296 **the first officer to direct his men to sing** Sheldon, *German Army at Ypres 1914*, 125.

296 **the phenomenon of the singing attacks** The basic ingredients of the legend were brought together in such works from the early 1930s as Joseph Magnus Wehner, *Langemarck: Ein Vermächtnis* (*Langemarck: A Legacy*) Tsd, Munich, 1936, and Hermann Thimmermann (Fred Hildenbrand) *Der Sturm auf Langemarck* (*The Storm at Langemarck*), Knorr & Hirtz, Munich, 1933. See also Robert Cowley, "The Massacre of the Innocents," *MHQ: The Quarterly Journal of Military History* (Spring 1998), and Reinhard Dithmar, ed., *Der Langemarck Mythos*, Luchterhand, Berlin, 1992.

297 **"the name sounds like a heroic legend"** Thimmermann, *Der Sturm auf Langemarck*, 7.

297 **"West of Langemarck"** Quoted in Wynne, *Ypres 1914*, 109–110.

298   **"Then a crackling and a roaring"** Adolf Hitler, *Mein Kampf* (*My Struggle*), trans. Ralph Manheim, Houghton Mifflin/Mariner Books, Boston, New York, 1929, 164–165.

301   **first military experiments with the field telephone** Brian N. Hall, "Technological Adaptation in a Global Conflict," *The Journal of Military History* 78, no. 7, (January 2014), 42–48; see also the Wikipedia article on the military history of the field telephone.

301   **Hauptmann Dehgen, sword in hand** Sheldon, *The German Army at Ypres 1914*, 148.

301   **the Scots Fusiliers and the 2nd Wiltshires were in trouble** *OH 1914*, II, 196–197; Anthony Farrar-Hockley, *Death of an Army*, 112; C. T. Atkinson, *The Seventh Division*, 53–54.

303   **"To avoid shooting our own men"** Henry FitzM. Stacke, *The Worcestershire Regiment in the Great War*, 30.

304   **"sat or stood about helplessly"** *OH 1914*, II, 199.

304   **"At one point a party"** Stacke, *Worcestershire Regiment*, 31.

305   **"ready-made wire entanglements"** Atkinson, *The Seventh Division*, 52.

305   **"We have advanced barely two hundred paces"** Hans Schroeder, *An Airman Remembers*, trans. Claud W. Sykes, Aviation Book Club, London, 1935, 46–47.

305   **"The next few moments are terrible"** Schroeder, *An Airman Remembers*, 49.

306   **"All the paths"** From a contemporary account by Corp. A. G. Chambers, the Liddle Collection, Leeds University Library (Brotherton Library), University of Leeds, U.K. Letter from Peter H. Liddle, Keeper of Peter Liddle's 1914–1918 Personal Experience Archives, to the author, October 26, 1997.

306   **"a nightmare of a wood"** Stacke, *Worcestershire Regiment*, 31 (note C).

306   **That morning** Sheldon, *German Army at Ypres 1914*, 150–151.

306   **Fighting went on all day** Général Barthélemy E. Palat (Pierre Lehautcourt), *La grande Guerre sur le Front Occidental, VIII, La Ruée vers Calais* (The race to Calais), Librairie Chapelot, Paris, 1922, 120–121.

307   **Just six yards** Everard Wyrall, *The History of the Second Division, 1914–1918*, I, 124.

12. THE RIVER REDOUBT

308   **"Dixmude can hardly be seen"** Anthony Farrar-Hockley, *Death of an Army*, Naval & Military Press, Uckfield, East Sussex, U.K., 2009, 93.

309   **"the race for the sea may be said"** Julian S. Corbett, *Naval Operations*, I, 213, 215.

309   **"reaped a dreadful harvest"** Jack Sheldon, *The German Army at Ypres 1914*, 61.

310   **"The nearer we approached the river"** Sheldon, *German Army at Ypres 1914*, 68–69.

311   **"like ardent furnaces"** Max Deauville (Maurice Dewez), *Jusqu'à l Yser*, trans. Elizabeth Venant, Calmann-Lévy, Éditeurs, Paris, 1917, 135.

312   **"I do trust you realize"** Martin Gilbert, *Winston S. Churchill, Volume III 1914–16, The Challenge of War*, 136.

313   **"To wait for the weather"** Corbett, *Naval Operations*, I, 217.

313   **"The bombardment becomes"** Paul van Pul, *In Flanders Flooded Fields,* Pen & Sword Military, Barnsley, South Yorkshire, U.K., 2006, 110–111.

313   **"The material effect"** *OH 1914,* II, 118.

313   **"to lead the life of cave dwellers"** Corbett, *Naval Operations,* I, 233 (note 1).

314   **"there was one flank they could not turn"** Corbett, *Naval Operations,* I, 233.

314   **"could hardly have stayed"** C.R.M.F. Cruttwell, *The Role of British Strategy in the Great War,* Cambridge University Press, London, 1936, 30.

315   **he did not come from a typical background** See Robert Cowley, "The Mourning Parents," *MHQ: The Quarterly Journal of Military History* 3, no. 1 (Autumn 1990), 30–39, republished in Robert Cowley, ed. *The Great War,* Random House, New York, 2003, 473–488; Jay Winter, *Sites of Memory, Sites of Mourning,* Cambridge University Press, Cambridge, 1995, 2014, 108, 110–111.

316   **"Back of the individual life"** Kaethe Kollwitz, quoted in Winter, *Sites of Memory,* 110.

316   **"Deep in our hearts"** Thomas Mann, *Reflections of a Nonpolitical Man,* "Thoughts in Wartime," trans. Cosina Mattner and Mark Lilla, New York Review Books, New York, 2021, 496.

316   **"I sat on my bed and cried"** Hans Kollwitz, ed., *The Diary and Letters of Kaethe Kollwitz,* trans. Richard and Clara Winston, Northwestern University Press, Evanston, IL, 1955, 1988, 93.

316   **Germany seemed fixated on the notion of sacrifice** Robert Weldon Whalen, *Bitter Wounds: German Victims of the Great War, 1914–1939,* Cornell University Press, Ithaca and London, 1984, 24–26.

318   **"this great friend of humanity"** J. Pinguet, *Trois Étapes de la Brigade des Marins,* Perrinet Cie, Paris, 1918, 143.

318   **"At dawn the regiment buried him"** Hans Kollwitz, ed., *The Diary and Letters of Kaethe Kollwitz,* trans. Richard and Clara Winston, 143.

319   **A Berlin friend told them** *Diary and Letters of Kaethe Kollwitz,* 144.

319   **More than 80 percent** George L. Mosse, *Fallen Soldiers: Reshaping the Memory of the World Wars,* Oxford University Press, Oxford and New York, 1990, 71.

320   **"First he fell in battle"** Cowley, "The Mourning Parents," *The Great War,* 478.

320   **"I walk in half-darkness"** Whalen, *The Great War,* 478.

320   **Occasionally a cow would suddenly collapse** Deauville, *Jusqu'à L'Yser,* 128.

320   **"The water is very bad"** From the diary of a dead German officer, quoted in Pierre Ronarc'h, *Souvenirs de la Guerre,* I, trans. Robert Cowley, Payot & Cie, Paris, 1921, 100.

321   **"The wounded come one by one"** Deauville, *Jusqu'à L'Yser,* 130.

322   **"In what bitter disappointment"** *Kriegsfreiwilliger* Albert Buchalsky, quoted in Philipp Witkop, ed., *German Students' War Letters,* trans. A. F. Wedd, Pine St. Books, Philadelphia, 2002, 13.

323   **"it will be necessary to consider"** *Les Armées Françaises dans La Grande Guerre,* I, 326. (Henceforth to be called *Armées Français.*)

324   "horsy-looking little man" Sir Tom Bridges, *Alarms and Excursions: Reminiscences of a Soldier*, Longman's Green and Co, London, New York, and Toronto, 1938, 116.

324   "The weather was abominable" Bridges, *Alarms and Excursions*, 115–116.

324   "You held out for eight days" Van Pul, *In Flanders Flooded Fields*, 144.

324   "If one only had a band" Bridges, *Alarms and Excursions*, 87–88.

326   his signature folding camp chair Farrar-Hockley, *Death of an Army*, 117; Général Palat, *La Ruée vers Calais*, 73–74.

326   "I have no idea where the enemy is" Ronarc'h, *Souvenirs*, 100; Léon van der Essen, *The Invasion & the War in Belgium from Liège to the Yser*, 336.

327   "So, under those conditions" Van Pul, *In Flanders Flooded Fields*, 158.

327   He protested to Foch Henri Bernard, *L'An 14 et la Campagne des Illusions*, 179–180.

327   "the key to the door" Général R. Normand, "Tactique de Fortification de Vauban," *Revue du Génie Militaire*, Tome XIV (1er Septembre 1929), 142.

329   Pieter Ghewy made an early pitch Van Pul, *In Flanders Flooded Fields*, 114.

331   There was a water supervisor, Charles Cogge Van Pul, *In Flanders Flooded Fields*, 158–164.

332   Albert immediately ordered the necessary work Émile Galet, *Albert King of the Belgians in the Great War*, 288.

333   How close the Belgians were to disintegrating Brécard to d'Urbal, October 26, 1914, and Foch to GQG, same day, *Armées Français*, Vol. 4, Book 1, 337.

334   The embankment must hold Albert's General Order, October 26, 1914, *Armées Français*, Vol. 4, Book 1, 337.

334   "German tactics" Galet, *Albert King of the Belgians*, 289.

335   "Shortly afterward the Germans started" Charles Cogge's account, quoted in Van Pul, *In Flanders Flooded Fields*, 170–171.

338   "A few reliable battalions" Bridges, *Alarms and Excursions*, 118.

338   "Notwithstanding our lack of success" Galet, *Albert King of the Belgians*, 290.

339   The inundation attempt had failed Van Pul, *In Flanders Flooded Fields*, 190–191.

340   "The line isn't long" Deauville, *Jusqu'à L'Yser*, 148.

13. THE GREAT FEAR

341   a population of scarcely 4,000 Léon Bocquet and Ernest Hosten, *L'Agonie de Dixmude*, Librarie Jules Tallandier, Paris, 1916, 5.

343   a flag officer Jean Norton Cru, *Témoins*, "Les Etincelles," Paris, 1929, 236.

344   The original strength Jean Mabire, *La Bataille de L'Yser*, Fayard, Paris, 1979, 342.

344   "Under the present circumstances" Foch to Ronarc'h, October 16, 1914, Anthony Farrar-Hockley, *Death of an Army*, 72.

344   "the wisdom of laying off" Farrar-Hockley, *Death of an Army*, 72.

344 **"Up until then we had not heard"** Jack Sheldon, *The German Army at Ypres 1914*, 180.

345 **"in a particularly disagreeable manner"** Jean Pinguet, *Trois Étapes de la Brigade des Marins*, 122.

345 **Maussion de Condé stood up amid the sugar beets** Maibre, *La Bataille de L'Yser*, 134. Charles Le Goffic, *The Epic of Dixmude*, vividly describes the fight for Beerst, based on eyewitness accounts, 61–67.

346 **Ronarc'h was not pleased** Pierre Ronarc'h, *Souvenirs de la Guerre*, I, 71–72.

346 **"and they are heralded by a creaking sound"** Le Goffic, *Epic of Dixmude*, 73.

347 **"An honest bullet"** John Horne and Alan Kramer, *German Atrocities 1914: A History of Denial*, 96.

348 **The record of unprovoked killings** Statistics of German franc-tireur executions in Belgian Flanders (including the shooting of two eight-year-old girls) and deportations of civilians can be found in Horne and Kramer, *German Atrocities 1914*, 74–78.

349 **When "an assembly, an army"** Georges Lefebvre, *The Great Fear of 1789*, trans. Joan White, Vintage Books, New York, 1973, 50.

350 **"Deliberately confining himself to German sources"** Horne and Kramer, *German Atrocities 1914*, 89–90.

350 **"the trauma of German soldiers"** Horne and Kramer, *German Atrocities 1914*, 90.

350 **"The sheer speed necessitated"** Horne and Kramer, *German Atrocities 1914*, 117.

351 **In West Flanders, there were eight incidents** Horne and Kramer, *German Atrocities 1914*, 73.

351 **a growing toll** Horne and Kramer, *German Atrocities 1914*, 430.

352 **The first German shells** Ronarc'h, *Souvenirs*, I, 68–102; Général Palat (Pierre Lehautcourt), *La Ruée vers Calais (15 Octobre—13 Décembre 1914)*, 47–51, 59–64, 72–78; Sheldon, *German Army at Ypres 1914*, 183–194; Bocquet and Hosten, *L'Agonie de Dixmude*, 135–150, 174–188; Le Goffic, *Epic of Dixmude*, 42–116.

352 **twenty to thirty explosions per minute** Palat, *La Ruée vers Calais*, 73.

353 **Around 8 A.M. on October 21** Ronarc'h, *Souvenirs*, I, 76.

353 **"the most horrible scene"** Bocquet and Hosten, *L'Agonie de Dixmude*, 143, trans. by Robert Cowley.

353 **"There was a stench of burning flesh"** Bocquet and Hosten, *L'Agonie de Dixmude*, 149.

354 **"a continuous marching past"** Ronarc'h, *Souvenirs*, I, 79.

355 **"lacerating fire"** *Kriegsfreiwilliger* Karl Classow, quoted in Sheldon, *German Army at Ypres 1914*, 187–188.

356 **"After all we had only been soldiers"** Sheldon, *German Army at Ypres 1914*, 191.

356 **"Our wounded lay out to our front"** Sheldon, *German Army at Ypres 1914*, 192.

357 **"We profit from it"** Ronarc'h, *Souvenirs*, I, 80.

357 **"These attacks, which are ineffectual"** Ronarc'h, *Souvenirs*, I, 83.

358 **"very diminished in strength"** Ronarc'h, *Souvenirs*, I, 90.

358 **"They only wanted to relieve us"** Claude Prieur (Charles Poisson), *De Dixmude à Nieuport*, Perrin et Cie, Paris, 1916, 59–60.

358 **"The range was good"** Prieur, *De Dixmude à Nieuport*, 60.

359 **"I sense how much"** Prieur, *De Dixmude à Nieuport*, 60.

359 **"A frenzy of extermination"** Bocquet and Hosten, *L'Agonie de Dixmude*, 147.

360 **Led by the major, the detachment surged** Maibre, *La Bataille de L'Yser*, 216–219; Sheldon, *German Army at Ypres 1914*, 202–204.

360 **"Now it made no difference"** Sheldon, *German Army at Ypres 1914*, 205.

361 **About sixty men** Le Goffic, *Epic of Dixmude*, 99–109.

362 **They shot Jeanniot** Le Goffic, *Epic of Dixmude*, 108, 115.

363 **"I asked him to point out"** Ronarc'h, *Souvenirs*, 99–102.

363 **a field notebook** Ronarc'h, *Souvenirs*, 99–102; Léon van der Essen, *The Invasion & the War in Belgium from Liège to the Yser*, 336, 338, 342–343.

14. "HANGING ON BY OUR EYELIDS"

366 **"a line to the sea"** Sir John French, *1914*, Leonaur, Driffield, East Yorkshire, U.K., 2009, 200.

366 **"quite incapable of making"** George H. Cassar, *The Tragedy of Sir John French*, 168.

367 **"In my inmost heart"** French, *1914*, 185.

367 **"evil genius"** Sir James Edmonds, *The Memoirs of Sir James Edmonds*, ed. Ian F. W. Beckett, Tom Donovan Editions, Brighton, U.K., 2013, 256.

367 **"Although Ypres as a city"** French, *1914*, 210.

368 **"practically won"** *OH 1914*, II, 235.

368 **"It was a wild evening"** Cyril Falls, *The Royal Irish Rifles (Now the Royal Ulster Rifles) in the Great War*, The Naval & Military Press, Uckfield, East Sussex, U.K., 2009, 18.

368 **"a wild fury of rush"** Falls, *Royal Irish Rifles*, 18; a concise account of the operations around Armentières, October 22–November 2, 1914, appears in the *OH 1914*, II, 225–231.

369 **a rate of 150 an hour** That was the calculation of a Second Lieutenant Chatfield of the Border Regiment, who no doubt kept count to distract himself from the terror of an all-day bombardment. From H. C. Wylly, *The Border Regiment in the Great War*, The Naval & Military Press, Uckfield, East Sussex, U.K., 2006, 8.

369 **"Although I looked for a great addition"** French, *1914*, 193.

369 **"had closed his eyes"** Cassar, *Tragedy of Sir John French*, 163.

371 **"It was impossible to leave"** Wylly, *Border Regiment in the Great War*, 8.

371 **one every seven yards** Nikolas Gardner, *Trial by Fire*, Praeger, Westport, CT and London, 2003, 156.

372 **"very cold to me"** Robin Prior and Trevor Wilson, *Command on the Western Front: The Military Career of Sir Henry Rawlinson*, 13.

372 **"disappointed"** Gardner, *Trial by Fire*, 156.

372 **no division in Flanders suffered more casualties** *OH 1914*, II, 466.

373 **"His steely blue eyes"** Christopher D'Arcy Baker-Carr, *From Chauffeur to Brigadier*, Leonaur, Driffield, East Yorkshire, U.K., 2014, 50–51.

373   **"What! Nobody on the Staff"** John Charteris, *At G.H.Q.*, Cassell and Company, Ltd., London, 1931, 58.

373   **"too full of nerves"** Richard Olsen, " 'An Inspirational Warrior: Major-General Sir Thompson Capper' " in Spencer Jones, ed., *Stemming the Tide*, Helion, Solihull, West Midlands, U.K., 2013, 203.

373   **"No one but Capper himself"** Gardner, *Trial by Fire*, 152.

374   **"I do not understand"** Gardner, *Trial by Fire*, 152. A slightly different version of French's message to Rawlinson appears in Richard Holmes, *The Little Field Marshal*, 243. The documentary basis of the Gardner seems more solid than Holmes, whose main source is Sir John's memoir, *1914*.

375   **"just as well that the I Corps"** Gardner, *Trial by Fire*, 159.

375   **the shattering losses the 7th had suffered** *OH 1914*, II, 201.

375   **"most of our troubles and losses"** Prior and Wilson, *Command on the Western Front*, 13.

375   **"We are only hanging on"** Prior and Wilson, *Command on the Western Front*, 13; Ian F. W. Beckett, *Ypres 1914*, 121.

376   **a letter of apology** Prior and Wilson, *Command on the Western Front*, 13–14; Beckett, *Ypres 1914*, 121–122.

376   **Operations Order No. 40** *OH 1914*, II, Appendix 33, 520.

376   **"He [Rawlinson] is not really wanted"** Gardner, *Trial by Fire*, 165.

378   **"sheets of lead"** C. T. Atkinson, *The Seventh Division*, 58.

378   **"every night, under cover"** H. C. Wylly, *The Green Howards in the Great War*, 46 (footnote).

378   **"Never have I been through"** F. Loraine Petre, Wilfred Ewart, and Cecil Lowther, *The Scots Guards in the Great War*, 41.

379   **buried alive** Sir Frederick Ponsonby, *The Grenadier Guards in the Great War*, I, 118;, Anthony Farrar-Hockley, *Death of an Army*, 122–123.

379   **"Then we noticed"** Petre, Ewart, and Lowther, *The Scots Guards in the Great War*, 42.

380   **"The exact sequences of events"** Atkinson, *Seventh Division*, 59.

380   **the drumming of the rain** Petre, Ewart, and Lowther, *Scots Guards in the Great War*, 42–45; *OH 1914*, II, 239–240; Atkinson, *Seventh Division*, 59–61.

381   **"an estaminet in the village"** *Ypres 1914*, 118–120. Ian F. W. Beckett quotes from the war reminiscences of the Hon. St. Vincent Broke de Saumarez, which can be found in the Liddle Collection at the Leeds University Brotherton Library in the U.K. Saumarez was wounded in December 1914. See Petre, Ewart, and Lowther, *Scots Guards in the Great War*, 62–63.

381   **"that difficulty"** Petre, Ewart, and Lowther, *Scots Guards in the Great War*, 44.

382   **"counted over 120 shell bursts"** Petre, Ewart, and Lowther, *Scots Guards in the Great War*, 44.

383   **"the Englishmen began to leave"** M. von Poseck, *The German Cavalry 1914 in Belgium and France*, 212–213.

383   **"At last . . . the Germans were on them"** Petre, Ewart, and Lowther, *Scots Guards*, 45.

384   **"part of 20th Inf"** Gardner, *Trial by Fire*, 164.

384 "rode out about 3 p.m." Douglas Haig, *Douglas Haig: War Diaries and Letters*, eds. Gary Sheffield and John Bourne, 75.

384 "It was sad to see fine troops" Haig, *War Diaries*, 75 (note 36).

384 "some confusion and much shelling" Gardner, *Trial by Fire*, 164.

385 The Germans themselves The best sources are Jack Sheldon, *The German Army at Ypres 1914*, 152–156, and Poseck, *German Cavalry 1914*, 212–213.

385 "paved with German dead" Atkinson, *Seventh Division*, 63 (note 3).

385 casualties were shattering Atkinson, *Seventh Division*, 63, 78; Ernest W. Hamilton, *The First Seven Divisions*, E. P. Dutton and Company, New York, 1916, 232; *OH 1914*, II, 248.

386 nightly drumbeat of optimism *OH 1914*, II, 252; Cassar, *Tragedy of Sir John French*, 168.

386 Kitchener that day dispatched officers *OH 1914*, II, 252.

386 lines of men wearing red kepis Jonathan North, *Uniforms of World War I*, 90–91.

386 uncomfortable 1893-model knapsacks Jean Echenoz, *1914*, 41–42. This may be a novel, but it contains details that I have to accept as real and likely to be overlooked in formal historical accounts. Beggars for the human trivia of the past can't always be choosy.

387 "I don't think that the warriors" Louis Barthas, *Poilu: The World War I Notebooks of Corporal Louis Barthas, Barrelmaker*, trans. Edward M. Strauss, Yale University Press, New Haven & London, 2014, 47.

387 "At the stage we have arrived at" Gen. Victor d'Urbal's Special Order to Gen. Pierre Dubois, October 23, 1914. Quoted in Général A. Dubois, *Deux Ans de Commandement*, Book II, Henri Charles-Lavauzelle, Paris, 1921, 26. A somewhat different translation appears in the *OH 1914*, II, 192.

387 "There must be decision" *OH 1914*, II, 193. Foch's full telephone message to Dubois is reproduced in *Armées Français*, I, Pt. 4, *Annexes* IV, 3296 (24 Octobre 1914).

388 the weapon was wildly overrated John Ellis, *Eye-Deep in Hell*, Pantheon Books, New York, 1976, 78–79; *OH, Medical Services*. See Table 15—Percentage of wounds caused by different weapons, Imperial War Museum, London/The Battery Press, Nashville, TN, 1931, 1997, 40.

389 "No man in this war" Ellis, *Eye-Deep in Hell*, 78.

389 genius named Hiram Maxim The best book on the inventor Hiram Maxim and his equally resourceful brother Hudson, an explosives expert, is *Blood Brothers* by Iain McCallum (Chatham Publishing, London, 1999). Arresting information on the weapon in the First World War appears in such books as John Ellis, *The Social History of the Machine Gun* (Pantheon Books, New York, 1975); Robert Bruce, *Machine Guns of World War I* (Windrow & Greene, London, 1997); and Mark Adkin, *The Western Front Companion* (Stackpole Books, Mechanicsburg, PA, 2013). I am especially indebted to Bruce I. Gudmundsson of the U.S. Marine Corps, an incomparable authority on the history of tactics. Much of the information about the machine gun, including the quotes from German officers, comes from *The Tactical Notebook* of November 1992, Vol. II, published by the Institute of Tactical Education, P.O. Box 125, Quantico, VA, 22134.

389 **"feeding, firing, extracting"** McCallum, *Blood Brothers*, 46.

390 **"The machine guns in use"** Charles Carrington, *Soldier from the Wars Returning*, David McKay Company, Inc., New York, 1965, 25.

391 **Foch floated a coded proposal** *Armées Françaises*, I, Book 4, Pt. 3, 334–335.

392 **"Poelcappelle must be carried"** Dubois, *Deux Ans de Commandement*, Book 2, 36.

15. ONE DAY

395 **"there was no longer time"** Erich von Falkenhayn, *General Headquarters 1914–1916*, 30.

395 **"it could expect to force"** Falkenhayn, *General Headquarters*, 28–29.

398 **"daringly searched a house"** "Lieutenant H. H. Price Maurice Victor Donald of Battenberg, KCVO," Masonic Great War Project, August 29, 2016. (From the Wikipedia article on Prince Maurice of Battenberg.)

398 **"a terrific shell and rifle fire"** Everard Wyrall, *The History of the Second Division, 1914–1918*, 130; Tony Spagnoly and Ted Smith, *Salient Points: Cameos of the Western Front*, Leo Cooper, London, 1995, 34–41.

399 **"The guns were making such a noise"** Captain W. Dyer, quoted in the entry for Prince Maurice of Battenberg under lordmountbattenofburma .com. See also Old Wellington lodge No. 3404.

399 **"The hour is late"** Anthony Farrar-Hockley, *Death of an Army*, 128.

399 **"THE JOLLY PRINCE"** Front page of *The Daily Sketch*, October 29, 1914.

400 **"In the morning I set out"** Pierre Petit, *Souvenirs de Guerre*, diary entry for October 27, 1914, trans. Robert Cowley, Académie Européenne du Livre, Nanterre, 1989, 46.

400 **"a mad desire to dash"** Petit, *Souvenirs de Guerre*, 45.

401 **"You're not leaving me"** Petit, *Souvenirs de Guerre*, 45.

402 **"I routed thirteen Germans out"** Petit, *Souvenirs de Guerre*, 46.

403 **Italy was testing powered flight** John H. Morrow Jr., *The Great War in the Air*, Smithsonian Institution Press, Washington, DC, and London, 1993, 25; Lee Kennett, *The First Air War*, The Free Press, New York, 1991, 17–18, 35; "Italo-Turkish War of 1911–12," Wikipedia; James D. Crabtree, *On Air Defense*, Praeger, Westport, CT, 1994, 9.

404 **"looking quite normal"** Arthur Gould Lee, *No Parachute: A Fighter Pilot in World War I*, Harper & Row, New York and Evanston, 1968, 15.

405 **"no heater, no oxygen"** Lee, *No Parachute*, 47.

405 **A Taube needed fifteen minutes** Climbing rates based on figures in Morrow, *The Great War in the Air*, 73.

405 **"The wind . . . was the heaviest trial"** Walter Raleigh, *The War in the Air: Being the Story of the Part Played in the Great War by the Royal Air Force*, I, Naval & Military Press/The Imperial War Museum, Uckfield, East Sussex, U.K./London, 2020, 312.

405 **"Aerial observers . . . could detect"** Morrow, *The Great War in the Air*, 86.

405 **"There . . . is that wretched bird"** Morrow, *The Great War in the Air*, 87.

406 **"The deadly and effective method"** Raleigh, *The War in the Air*, I, 350–351.

406 **"Aviation is fine as sport"** Morrow, *The Great War in the Air,* 35.

407 **"The observer's seat"** John Connell, *Wavell: Scholar and Soldier,* Collins, London, 1964, 95.

408 **"could only watch them"** Raleigh, *The War in the Air,* I, 348.

409 **"mistaken for German"** (see "Ma" Jeffreys's diary entry for Tuesday, 27 October 1914.) J. M. Craster, *"Fifteen Rounds a Minute": The Grenadiers at War,* 118.

410 **"Either I will command the army"** Crown Prince Rupprecht, journal entry for October 27, 1914, in *Mein Kriegstagebuch,* I, E. S. Mittler & Sohn, Berlin, 1929, 232–234, trans. Anthony Hollingsworth. Most of the account of the October 27 meeting is based on Rupprecht's journals.

411 **"on account of his tough nature"** Rupprecht, *Kriegstagebuch,* I, 233.

412 **German numbers in both men and artillery** *OH 1914,* II, 254–256, 258–259; Jonathan Boff, *Haig's Enemy,* Oxford University Press, Oxford, 2018, 45–46; Fritz von Lossberg, *Lossberg's War: The World War I Memoirs of a German Chief of Staff,* eds. and trans. David T. Zabecki and Dieter J. Biedekarken, 90–94; Ian F. W. Beckett, *Ypres 1914,* 123; Jack Sheldon, *The German Army at Ypres 1914,* 230.

412 **"After lengthy negotiations"** Rupprecht, *Mein Kriegstagebuch,* I, 233.

413 **"Nobody thought much about it"** Général A. Dubois, *Deux Ans de Commandement sur le front de France,* Tome II, 44.

413 **"vigorous and incessant action"** D'Urbal, quoted in Général A. Dubois, *Deux Ans de Commandement sur le Front de France,* 42.

415 **"a long tunnel full of mists"** Patrick McCarthy, *Céline: A Biography,* A Richard Seaver Book/The Viking Press, New York, 1975, 13.

415 **"Soon we'd be at the heart"** Louis-Ferdinand Céline, *Journey to the End of the Night,* trans. Ralph Manheim, A New Directions Book, New York, 1983, 26.

415 **"Down the road"** Céline, *Journey to the End of the Night,* 7, 9.

416 **"I had had enough"** Céline, *Journey to the End of the Night,* 13.

417 **"Morale is pretty much"** Frédéric Vitoux, *Céline: A Biography,* trans. Jesse Browner, Paragon House, New York, 1992, 69.

417 **"I never have seen"** Vitoux, *Céline: A Biography,* 71.

418 **"We got back on our nags"** Vitoux, *Céline: A Biography,* 74.

418 **"the bullet that hit him"** Letter from Fernand Destouches to his brother Charles, quoted in Céline, *Lettres,* Gallimard, Paris, 2009, 120; Vitoux, *Céline: A Biography,* 75; Tom Quinn, *The Traumatic Memory of the Great War, 1914–1918, in Louis-Ferdinand Céline's Voyage au Bout de la Nuit,* Edwinn Mellen Press, Lewiston, NY, 2005, 114.

419 **"Your son was wounded"** Letter from Captain A. Schneider to Fernand Destouches, October 28, 1914, quoted in Vitoux, *Céline: A Biography,* 75. A shorter version appears in Céline, *Lettres,* 119.

419 **"the last coward on earth"** Céline, *Journey to the End of the Night,* 9.

420 **"At such times he wanted"** Vitoux, *Céline: A Biography,* 78.

420 **"a black voracious void?"** Céline, *Journey to the End of the Night,* 32

420 **His later life bore the marks** For recent research on combat-related injury to the brain, see Robert F. Worth, "Aftershock," *New York Times Magazine,* June 6, 2016, 28–33. Much has since been, and continues to be, discovered.

420 **"one of the loneliest figures"** McCarthy, *Céline,* 7.

421   **"When you have no imagination"** Céline, *Journey to the End of the Night*, 14.

421   **"I've never stopped sleeping"** Louis-Ferdinand Céline, *Guerre*, ed. Pascal Fouché, Gallimard, Paris, 2022, 25–26; Alice Kaplan, "The Master of Blame," *The New York Review of Books*, July 21, 2022, 22.

422   **"Once again, men are dispatched"** The entries that follow are all for October 27, 1914, from Raoul Nel, *Boesinghe, ou, Les Combats de la 87e Division Territoriale sur l'Yser*, trans. Elizabeth Venant, 73.

422   **"decimated"** Nel, *Boesinghe*, 65–66.

422   **"So where are you going?"** Nel, *Boesinghe*, 73.

423   **"He is visibly happy"** Nel, *Boesinghe*, 74.

423   **"The number of stretcher bearers"** Nel, *Boesinghe*, 74.

423   **"We go silently"** Nel, *Boesinghe*, 74.

424   **"How long will this nightmare last?"** Nel, *Boesinghe*, 75.

424   **The failure of the Spanish Lock operation** Paul van Pul, *In Flanders Flooded Fields*, 194–196.

426   **"It was all fire"** Charles Cogge, from his memoir in Flemish, translated and quoted by Paul van Pul, *In Flanders Flooded Fields*, 201.

427   **"that people whose antagonism"** Crown Prince Rupprecht's proclamation, quoted in John F. Williams, *Corporal Hitler and the Great War 1914–1918*, Frank Cass, London and New York, 2005, 49.

427   **"a shambles"** Thomas Weber, *Hitler's First War*, Oxford University Press, Oxford, 2010, 32–33.

427   **the appearance of the marchers** Weber, *Hitler's First War*, 19; North, *Uniforms of World War I*, 214.

428   **"I couldn't sleep"** Adolf Hitler, letter to a Munich acquaintance, February 5, 1915, quoted in Weber, *Hitler's First War*, 27.

429   **"company provided the troops with ropes"** Weber, *Hitler's First War*, 27.

16. THE BARGEMAN'S SOLUTION

433   **"a very good soldier overall"** Fritz von Lossberg, *Lossberg's War*, eds. and trans. David T. Zabecki and Dieter J. Biedekarken, 17–18.

434   **notably stingy with promotions** Email to the author on December 17, 2014 from Holger H. Herwig, author of *The First World War: Germany and Austria-Hungary 1914–1918* and *The Marne 1914*.

435   **"We were convinced that our attack"** Lossberg, *Lossberg's War*, 92–93.

438   **the last major cultural monuments** See Alan Kramer, *The Dynamic of Destruction: Culture and Mass Killing in the First World War*. Also, though its subject is the coming of the Second World War, I recommend D. C. Watt, *How War Came*, Pantheon, New York, 1989, 5–8.

438   **"Offered the enticing prospect"** Gary Sheffield, *The Chief: Douglas Haig and the British Army*, Aurum, London, 2011, 2012, 90.

438n   **"on a clear day"** Douglas W. Johnson, *Battlefields of the World War*, 37–38.

440   **"This breakthrough"** *OH 1914*, II, 282; Martin Gilbert, *The First World War: A Complete History*, Henry Holt and Company, New York, 1994, 96.

443   **Brussels had carelessly sent** *OH 1914*, II, 256; Anthony Farrar-Hockley, *Death of an Army*, 128; Ian F. W. Beckett, *Ypres: The First Battle, 1914*, 146.

443   **a wireless set specially modified** Farrar-Hockley, *Death of an Army*, 128 (note).

443   **"Telephone equipment of all kinds"** Spencer Jones, "'The Demon': Brigadier-General Charles FitzClarence V.C.," in Spencer Jones, ed., *Stemming the Tide*, 253.

444   **"The hand telephone attachments"** Brian N. Hall, "Technological Adaptation in a Global Conflict," *The Journal of Military History* 78, no. 1 (January 2014), 44.

444   **"Visual signaling"** Hall, "Technological Adaptation," 40.

444   **"The absence of suitable"** Hall, "Technological Adaptation," 39–40.

444   **"the general air of uncertainty"** Hall, "Technological Adaptation," 40.

445   **"After infantry had gone"** Gary Sheffield, *Forgotten Victory*, Review/ Headline Book Publishing, London, 2002, 121.

445   **"The era of the Great War"** Gary Sheffield, *Forgotten Victory*, 120.

445   **"We heard"** Dame M. Columban, *The Irish Nuns at Ypres*, 39.

446   **"a happy accident"** Dubois, *Deux Ans de Commandement*, 44.

446   **"A sharp movement"** Farrar-Hockley, *Death of an Army*, 132, 134.

447   **unsatisfactory for defense** *OH 1914*, II, 264.

447   **"letting off myriads"** J.G.W. Hyndson, *From Mons to the First Battle of Ypres*, 88.

449   **"a great enemy of full glasses"** Paul van Pul, *In Flanders Flooded Fields*, 79.

449   **"now seemed to regard"** Julian S. Corbett, *Naval Operations*, I, 232–234.

450   **"The artillery alone"** *Armées Françaises*, I, Annexes, Book 4, 231–232, Brécard to d'Urbal et Foch, 3451 and 3452.

451   **"a mishmash of nets"** Van Pul, *In Flanders Flooded Fields*, 211.

453   **"Terrific shelling which begins"** Hyndson, *From Mons*, 88.

453   **"there was wire"** *OH 1914*, II, 264.

454   **"God knows how many"** F. Loraine Petre, Wilfred Ewart, and Cecil Lowther, *Scots Guards in the Great War*, 50.

454   **the loss of the crossroads** Everard Wyrall, *The Gloucestershire Regiment in the War*, 72; Farrar-Hockley, *Death of an Army*, 135.

454   **"a tremendous storm"** C. T. Atkinson, *The Seventh Division*, 74.

455   **a perfect example of the lottery of war** H. C. Wylly, *The Border Regiment in the Great War*, 10.

455   **"The problem was how"** Sir Frederick Ponsonby, *The Grenadier Guards in the Great War 1914–1918*, I, 125–126.

456   **"volunteered to bring in their commander"** Everard Wyrall, *The Gloucestershire Regiment*, 74.

456   **"From our position"** Craster, *"Fifteen Rounds a Minute"* 119.

457   **That one gun had killed 15** Jack Sheldon, *The German Army at Ypres 1914*, 160.

457   **"a last awakening"** Hans Mend, quoted in John F. Williams, *Corporal Hitler and the Great War 1914–19*, 58.

457 **Gewehr 98s** See the useful essay on Great War rifles and bayonets, in Mark Adkin, *The Western Front Companion*, 172–174.

457 **"We can barely see anything"** Thomas Weber, *Hitler's First War*, 42.

458 **"It was terrifying"** Weber, *Hitler's First War*, 43.

458 **"The 'List' men poured"** August Haugg, quoted in Sheldon, *The German Army at Ypres 1914*, 162–163.

459 **"Why aren't the Bavarians"** Sheldon, *German Army at Ypres 1914*, 163.

459 **"advancing in rather a dense line"** Sir Thomas O. Marden, *The History of the Welch Regiment 1914–1918*, Part II, 316.

460 **"Do not like the situation at all"** E. S. Bulfin, quoted in Beckett, *First Battle*, 151.

460 **began to tot up its losses** See various regimental histories (*Gloucestershire*, 75; *Black Watch*, I, 19; *Coldstream Guards*, I, 220; *Grenadier Guards*, I, Naval & Military Press, Uckfield, East Sussex, U.K., 2003, 179–180). Also *OH 1914*, II, 268.

461 **"Without question October 29th"** Atkinson, *The Seventh Division 1914–1918*, 79.

461 **"The enemy was apparently quite unaware"** Ponsonby, *Grenadier Guards in the Great War*, I, 128–129.

462 **"each time"** Van Pul, *In Flanders Flooded Fields*, 215.

463 **"We were sitting there"** Van Pul, *In Flanders Flooded Fields*, 216.

17. DEAD SEA

465 **Germans now outnumbered the Cavalry Corps** Sir Stuart Hare, *The Annals of the King's Royal Rifle Corps*, V, *The Great War*, John Murray, London, 1932/Naval & Military Press, Uckfield, East Sussex, 2002, 57.

466 **"a queer long cry"** Anthony Farrar-Hockley, *Goughie: The Life of General Sir Hubert Gough*, 143.

466 **"Operations will continue"** *OH 1914*, II, Appendix 38, 522.

466 **"Orders as to the resumption of the offensive"** *OH 1914*, II, 279.

467 **"had lacked any depth"** Lossberg, *Lossberg's War*, 90.

469 **"Is it reasonable to suppose"** George Steiner, *In Bluebeard's Castle*, 23.

469 **"itch for chaos"** Steiner, *In Bluebeard's Castle*, 11.

469 **"What turned professional"** Steiner, *In Bluebeard's Castle*, 31.

472 **"did terrible execution"** C. T. Atkinson, *The Seventh Division*, 82.

472 **"We had very little ammunition"** Anthony Farrar-Hockley, *Death of an Army*, 143.

473 **"raking their trenches"** *OH 1914*, II, 288.

473 **"About 8 a.m. the shelling increased"** C. H. Dudley Ward, *Regimental Records of the Royal Welch Fusiliers*, III, *France and Flanders*, The Naval & Military Press, Uckfield, East Sussex, U.K., 2005, 94–95.

473 **Of some 400** *OH 1914*, II, 289; Farrar-Hockley, *Death of an Army*, 143; Ward, *Regimental Records of the Royal Welch Fusiliers*, III, 95.

474 **"the deadly accuracy of a few snipers"** H. C. Wylly, *The Green Howards in the Great War*, 47.

474 **"possibly they could not conceive"** *OH 1914*, II, 301.

475 **"Found cavalry had retired early"** Bulfin journal entry for October 30, quoted in chapter, "'A Tower of Strength': Brigadier-General Edward Bulfin," from Spencer Jones, ed., *Stemming the Tide*, 230.

476   **"We had a splendid French general"** John Charteris, *At G.H.Q.*, 52.

476   **"Business went on as usual"** C. D. Baker-Carr, *From Chauffeur to Brigadier*, 51.

476   **Nel described the trip** Raoul Nel, *Boesinghe*, 79, 75.

477   **"blow after blow"** Jack Sheldon, *The German Army at Ypres 1914*, 236–237.

479   **"A lovely drive"** Paul Maze, *A Frenchman in Khaki*, William Heinemann, Ltd., London, 1934, 85–86.

481   **"This is the last picture"** Roy Jenkins, *Churchill: A Biography*, Plume/Penguin Putnam Inc., New York, 2002, 546.

481   **"strong hostile counter-attacks"** G. C. Wynne, trans., *Ypres 1914: An Official Account Published by Order of the German General Staff*, 68.

482   **"Bronzed Indian troops"** Sheldon, *German Army at Ypres 1914*, 236.

482   **"were an awful nuisance"** Peter Hart, *Fire and Movement*, 304–305 (note).

483   **Khudadad played dead** Gordon Corrigan, *Sepoys in the Trenches*, Spellmount, Staplehurst, Kent, U.K., 1999, 60.

485   **"That night there was strange"** Sheldon, *German Army at Ypres 1914*, 233.

485   **a late-night serenade** Farrar-Hockley, *Death of an Army*, 145.

485   **"Generally speaking"** Ferdinand Foch, *The Memoirs of Marshal Foch*, trans. T. Bentley Mott, 155.

486   **"to get information on the spot"** Foch, *Memoirs*, 155.

486   **"As is their custom"** Roy A. Prete, *Strategy and Command*, McGill-Queen's University Press, Montreal & Kingston, 2009, 164; B. H. Liddell Hart, *Foch—Man of Orleans*, 138; Foch, *Memoirs*, 155.

486   **"Ypres and all her communications"** Prete, *Strategy and Command*, 164.

487   **"establish himself firmly"** Foch, *Memoirs*, 155.

487   **"It is of historical note"** Liddell Hart, *Man of Orleans*, 144 (note).

488   **"When Sir John retired to bed"** Richard Holmes, *The Little Field Marshal*, 250.

488   **"from one sleeve"** Maxime Weygand, *Mémoires*, I, Flammarion, Paris, 1953, 215–216, quoted in Prete, *Strategy and Command*, 86 (note), 252.

488   **"studied the situation together"** Foch, *Memoirs*, 155–156.

488   **"I see Wilson"** Prete, *Strategy and Command*, 164.

489   **"We are all in for it"** Liddell Hart, *Man of Orleans*, 138.

491   **"as the determining factor"** Julian S. Corbett, *Naval Operations*, I, 232.

491   **"the incident"** Corbett, *Naval Operations*, I, 234.

492   **"The enemy has flooded"** Sheldon, *German Army at Ypres 1914*, 81.

493   **"woken by hell-like cannon fire"** Henri Bernard, *L'An 14 et la Campagne des Illusions*, 185.

493   **seldom used until now** Anthony Saunders, *Weapons of the Trench War 1914–1918*, Sutton Publishing, Stroud, Gloucestershire, U.K., 1999, 1, 8; Ian Hogg, *Grenades and Mortars*, Ballantine Books, New York, 1974, 14.

494   **"The water has risen markedly"** Sheldon, *German Army at Ypres 1914*, 82.

494   **"All the ditches and trenches"** Sheldon, *German Army at Ypres 1914*, 83.

495   "At 10:00" Bernard, *L'An 14 et la Campagne des Illusions*, 185.

495   "owing to the constant rising" Van Pul, *In Flanders Flooded Fields*, 221–222.

498   "almost imperceptible" Léon Bocquet and Ernest Hosten, *L'Agonie de Dixmude*, trans. Elizabeth Venant, 214–216.

498   "a mass of dogs" Stefan Hertmans, *War & Turpentine*, trans. from the Dutch by David McKay, Pantheon, New York, 2016, 173.

498   "invincible and implacable" Émile Cammaerts, *Albert of Belgium: Defender of Right*, 197–198.

499   with chattering teeth Sheldon, *German Army at Ypres 1914*, 88–89.

499   The regiment had lost Sheldon, *German Army at Ypres 1914*, 89.

18. THE GAP

504   "Gentlemen, are we all present?" An adaptation from Dr. Fridolin Sollider, *Vier Jahre Westfront (Four Years on the Western Front): The History of the List Reserve Regiment 16*, quoted in Jack Sheldon, *The German Army at Ypres 1914*, 167–168.

506   "full of anxiety" John Terraine, *Douglas Haig: The Educated Soldier*, 112.

506   "also liberated German forces" John Hussey, "A Hard Day at First Ypres—The Allied Generals and Their Problems: 31st October 1914," *The British Army Review* 107 (1994), 75.

506   "The French" Hussey, "A Hard Day at First Ypres," 75.

506   "supremely critical day" Stair Gillon, *The K.O.S.B. in the Great War*, Thomas Nelson, London, 1930/Naval & Military Press, Uckfield, East Sussex, U.K., 2009, 52.

506   "The worst crisis" B. H. Liddell Hart, *Foch—The Man of Orleans*, 138.

506   "The line that stood between" *OH 1914*, II, 304.

507   "altogether disturbing" Général A. Dubois, *Deux Ans de Commandement sur le Front de France*, II, 53.

508   "has such resonance" Hussey, "A Hard Day at First Ypres," 75.

509   "Just yesterday" *French Official History*, I, Annexes, Book 4, 414 (3674, 31 Octobre 1914).

509   "The gloomy days" Raoul Nel, *Boesinghe*, 80.

510   a high price to pay Jack Sheldon and Nigel Cave, *Ypres 1914: Langemarck*, 127.

510   "The enemy met the first rush" M. von Poseck, *The German Cavalry 1914 in Belgium and France*, 215–217.

511   In the language of geology Douglas W. Johnson, *Battlefields of the World War*, 12–13.

512   "It was a clean little town" Paul Maze, *A Frenchman in Khaki*, 80–81.

512   "Often as I was on the road" Maze, *Frenchman in Khaki*, 81.

512   "Gun flashes were holing the darkness" Maze, *Frenchman in Khaki*, 86–87.

513   he threw in an entire infantry division Anthony Farrar-Hockley, *Goughie*, 143; Archibald Wavell, *Allenby*, Oxford University Press, New York, 1941, 148; *OH 1914*, II, 307.

513   "Bloody Bull's Loose" Lawrence James, *Imperial Warrior*, Lume Books, London, 1993, 2021, 116.

514 **"an instinct for the 'sore spots'"** Wavell, *Allenby*, 149.

514 **"The men come on like lions"** Wavell, *Allenby*, 149.

515 **The MG08 was heavy** Robert Bruce, *Machine Guns of World War I*, 12–31. (Essential information is scattered throughout a long essay on the MG08.)

515 **"in the face of lacerating fire"** Sheldon, *German Army at Ypres 1914*, 242.

516 **"hung by a hair"** Gillon, *K.O.S.B. In the Great War*, 52.

516 **"It was desperate, close fighting"** Gillon, *K.O.S.B. in the Great War*, 52–53.

517 **"Surging forward from the dense hedgerows"** Sheldon, *German Army at Ypres 1914*, 171.

518 **"About 8 a.m. the fog cleared"** Sir Thomas O. Marden, *The History of the Welch Regiment 1914–1918*, 320.

518 **"the worst we had ever had"** Anthony Farrar-Hockley, *Death of an Army*, 151.

518 **"sprang up to charge"** *OH 1914*, II, 316.

519 **"shot before they had run 20 yards"** H. C. Wylly, *History of the Queen's Royal (West Surrey) Regiment in the Great War*, Naval & Military Press, Uckfield, East Sussex, U.K., 2006, 24–25.

519 **"Although the Germans constantly got"** Sir Steuart Hare, *The Annals of the King's Royal Rifle Corps*, V, *The Great War*, 58.

520 **"About 7:30 a.m."** Marden, *History of the Welch Regiment*, 320.

521 **"who were now in a hopeless situation"** An excerpt from a record of the First Battle of Ypres by Captain H. C. Rees, Welch Regiment, Imperial War Museum transcript memoir, 2006-04-20; Peter Hart, *Fire and Movement*, 309–310.

522 **"terrific shell fire"** Everard Wyrall, *The Gloucestershire Regiment in the War*, 79 (Account based on R. M. Grazebrook, *War Narratives 1914– 1915*, 48).

523 **"'B' Company . . . now fixed bayonets"** Marden, *History of the Welch Regiment*, 321.

524 **"The ground all around"** J.G.W. Hyndson, *From Mons to the First Battle of Ypres*, 93.

19. "FANCY MEETING YOU HERE"

528 **"I became aware"** E. B. Hankey, "A Survivor's Story," Courtesy of Mercian Regimental Archives, Worcester, U.K.

529 **"I had a run for my life"** F. A. Bolwell, *With a Reservist in France*, George Routledge & Sons, Ltd., London, 1916, 89.

529 **"I was not greatly perturbed"** John Hussey, "A Hard Day at First Ypres—The Allied Generals and Their Problems: 31st October 1914," *The British Army Review* 107 (1994), 81.

529 **"You cannot imagine the scene"** John Charteris, *At G.H.Q.*, 52.

530 **"My line"** Hussey, "A Hard Day at First Ypres," 77; Nigel Cave and Jack Sheldon, *Ypres 1914: The Menin Road*, 88.

530 **"came rather as a shock"** Hussey, "A Hard Day at First Ypres," 81.

530 **"of all the commanders available"** Anthony Farrar-Hockley, *Death of an Army*, 160.

531 **"rode way beyond Hooge"** Hussey, "A Hard Day at First Ypres," 81.

533 **the revealing accumulation of staff cars** Frank Davies and Graham Maddocks, *Bloody Red Tabs*, Leo Cooper, London, 1995/Pen & Sword Military, Barnsley, South Yorkshire, U.K., 2014, 29.

533 **"The killed"** Ian F. W. Beckett, *Ypres: The First Battle, 1914*, 173.

534 **"I met a medical officer"** Charteris, *At G.H.Q.*, 53.

534 **"Either by chance or design"** Jack Sheldon, *The German Army at Ypres 1914*, 173.

535 **"The losses grow under the violent fire"** John F. Williams, *Corporal Hitler and the Great War 1914–1918: The List Regiment*, 61.

535 **"The terrific rifle fire"** Signaler John Palmer, in Peter Hart, *Fire and Movement*, 314, 315.

536 **"If the Germans had pushed home their attack"** An extract from a manuscript record of the First Battle of Ypres, by Captain H. C. Rees, The Welch Regiment, 2006-04-20, 6, in the Imperial War Museum.

536 **"We have literally no reserves"** J.G.W. Hyndson, *From Mons to the First Battle of Ypres*, 96.

537 **"nerve-racking machine gun and rifle fire"** Hyndson, *From Mons*, 94.

537 **"The Gloucesters . . . built a barricade"** Everard Wyrall, *The Gloucestershire Regiment in the War*, by 80.

537 **"After going about 400 yards"** Hyndson, *From Mons*, 95.

538 **the domain of a Monsieur Peerebone** Recollection of Chaplain Major Edmund Kennedy, from "Iron Europe 1914–1918," greatwars-gamburd.blogspot.com/2008/09.

539 **"Suddenly a runner came"** Sheldon, *German Army at Ypres 1914*, 172.

539 **the bones of 24,916 others** Rose E. B. Coombs, *Before Endeavours Fade, After the Battle*, London, 1976, 2001 (ed. and revised by Karel Margry), 37.

539 **"swarmed upon the battered trenches"** C. T. Atkinson, *The History of the South Wales Borderers 1914–1918*, 46–47.

540 **"It seemed to catch the Germans by surprise"** Atkinson, *History of the South Wales Borderers*, 47.

541 **Brig. Charles FitzClarence was on the other end** Much of the biographical commentary on FitzClarence in this, and in the following chapter, is based on several sources. The first, almost contemporary, account appeared in the venerable Edinburgh journal *Blackwood's Magazine*, Vol. 202, August 1917: "Gheluvelt, 1914: The Man Who Turned the Tide," by "X," 209–221; J. M. Craster's *"Fifteen Rounds a Minute"* a collection of journal entries and letters by Grenadier Guards officers, notably George Darrell ("Ma") Jeffreys, in the fall of 1914, is, quite simply, indispensable. FitzClarence was one of them. The most complete telling of his life is " 'The Demon': Brigadier-General Charles FitzClarence V.C.," by Spencer Jones, a chapter in Spencer Jones, ed., *Stemming the Tide*. Useful information about FitzClarence can also be found in Ian F. W. Beckett, *Ypres: The First Battle, 1914;* Nigel Cave and Jack Sheldon, *Ypres 1914: The Menin Road;* and Robert Cowley, "The What Ifs of 1914," in Robert Cowley, ed., *What If?*, G. P. Putnam's Sons, New York, 1999.

541 **"He is not at his best"** Jones, *Stemming the Tide*, 246.

542 **"G.O.C. of Menin Road"** Jones, *Stemming the Tide*, 254.

543   "Ten days of battle" H. Fitz-M Stacke, *The Worcestershire Regiment in the Great War,* G. T. Cheshire & Sons, Ltd., Kidderminster, U.K., 1929, 32.

543   "to advance without delay" Jones, *Stemming the Tide,* 254.

544   "the situation was desperate" Stacke, *The Worcestershire Regiment,* 33.

544   "Definite orders" Transcript of notes E. B. Hankey, DSO, quoted in internet entry, "The Battle of Gheluvelt: Saturday, October 31, 1914," courtesy of Mercian Regimental Archives, Worcester, U.K.

546   "that it was murder etc." Jones, *Stemming the Tide,* 259.

546   "in every direction German shells" Stacke, *The Worcestershire Regiment,* 33.

546   "No cheering" Transcript of notes by Maj. E. B. Hankey, Mercian Regimental Archives.

546   "enjoying the repose of victory" *OH 1914,* II, 329.

547   "curious sight of Bosche" Transcript of notes by Maj. E. B. Hankey, Mercian Regimental Archives.

547   They outnumbered the British Beckett, *The First Battle,* 182.

547   "The majority were in that dangerous state" Farrar-Hockley, *Death of an Army,* 158.

547   "got into sunken road" Transcript of notes by Maj. E. B. Hankey, Mercian Regimental Archives.

547   "My God, fancy meeting you here" Stacke, *The Worcestershire Regiment,* 34.

549   "The village itself was" Sheldon, *German Army at Ypres 1914,* 174.

550   "passionate soldier" Volker Ullrich, *Hitler: Ascent 1889–1939,* trans. Jefferson Chase, Alfred A. Knopf, New York, 2016, 58.

551   "He erased, as he saw fit" Thomas Weber, *Hitler's First War,* 345.

551   "the most powerful right-wing dictator" Weber, *Hitler's First War,* 347.

551   "Accounts say GHELUVELT in our hands" Transcript of notes by Maj. E. B. Hankey, Mercian Regimental Archives.

551   "It was not possible permanently to occupy" Stacke, *The Worcestershire Regiment,* 34.

552   "One by one, at intervals of ten minutes" Stacke, *The Worcestershire Regiment,* 35.

552   "The reason for the enemy's inaction" Stacke, *The Worcestershire Regiment,* 34.

553   "a record feat for cavalry" Jones, *Stemming the Tide,* 187.

553   "there were manifest signs" Sir John French, *1914,* 209.

553   "The road traffic" French, *1914,* 210.

554   No one was expecting him John Hussey, "A Hard Day at First Ypres— The Allied Generals and their Problems: 31st October 1914," *The British Army Review* 107 (1994), 83–84; Beckett, *The First Battle, 1914,* 177–78; J. P. Harris, *Douglas Haig and the First World War,* 101, 103.

554   "To me, indeed" French, *1914,* 213.

555   "as red as a turkey-cock" John Charteris, *At G.H.Q.,* 53; Harris, *Douglas Haig and the First World War,* 103; Beckett, *The First Battle, 1914,* 178.

555   "hoped it was not another false report" Harris, *Douglas Haig and the First World War,* 103.

556 **as another historian has bizarrely claimed** Denis Winter, *Haig's Command*, 36–37.

556 **"I got on my horse and rode forward"** Douglas Haig, *Douglas Haig: War Diaries and Letters 1914–1918*, eds. Gary Sheffield and John Bourne, 76; Gary Sheffield, *The Chief*, 94; Jones, *Stemming the Tide*, 129; Nikolas Gardner, *Trial by Fire*, 220–221; Beckett, *The First Battle, 1914*, 178–179; Hussey, "A Hard Day at First Ypres," 85; John Terraine, *Douglas Haig: The Educated Soldier*, 115.

556 **"Troops very exhausted"** Haig, *War Diaries and Letters 1914–1918*, 76.

556 **"effectively removed himself"** Gardner, *Trial by Fire*, 220.

557 **"providential piece of luck"** Ferdinand Foch, *The Memoirs of Marshal Foch*, trans. T. Bentley Mott, 156.

557 **"We all went thoroughly"** French, *1914*, 215.

558 **"Marshal, your lines are pierced"** B. H. Liddell Hart, *Foch—The Man of Orleans*, 140.

558 **"The Marshal himself arrives"** Roy A. Prete, *Strategy and Command: The Anglo-French Coalition on the Western Front, 1914*, 165–166.

560 **"Overpowered, but not convinced"** Prete, *Strategy and Command*, 166.

560 **"The lateness of the day"** Hussey, "A Hard Day at First Ypres," 87.

560 **"Execute what General Foch has written"** Prete, *Strategy and Command*, 166.

560 **"It is of the utmost importance"** Hussey, "A Hard Day at First Ypres," 87.

560 **"not by any act of state"** Prete, *Strategy and Command*, 166.

562 **"an audacious psychological ruse"** Michael Stephen LoCicero, "'A Tower of Strength': Brigadier-General Edward Bulfin," in Jones, *Stemming the Tide*, 230.

562 **"some French and British orderlies"** Jones, *Stemming the Tide*, 230–231, footnote 105.

562 **"Several shells a minute"** Jones, *Stemming the Tide*, 231.

563 **"It was fortunate for us"** Sir Frederick Ponsonby, *The Grenadier Guards in the Great War of 1914–1918*, I, 133.

563 **"Germans in long lines"** Jones, *Stemming the Tide*, 231.

564 **"We stumbled over many fallen trees"** Nigel Cave and Jack Sheldon, *Ypres 1914: Messines*, Pen & Sword Military, Battleground Europe Series, Barnsley, South Yorkshire, U.K., 2015, 188.

564 **"If we wanted any more men"** Beckett, *The First Battle, 1914*, 185.

565 **"Where are we, boys?"** From notices in the *Craven Herald* (North Yorkshire, U.K.), February 19, 1915. See also web entries for John R. E. Stansfeld, officer in the Gordon Highlanders, World War I—especially the Wikipedia and Soldier's Record articles.

565 **"I ordered the first line"** Jones, *Stemming the Tide*, 233.

565 **"broke into one great roar"** *OH 1914*, II, 337.

566 **"No prisoners were taken"** Bulfin Diary, October 31, 1914, quoted in Jones, *Stemming the Tide*, 233.

566 **"came on some fifty of the grey swine"** Letter of November 4, 1914, from Captain Harry Dillon, Imperial War Museum. Quoted in Jones, *Stemming the Tide*, 233.

567 **"We were only clinging"** Jones, *Stemming the Tide*, 234.

567 **"I told him that he must"** Bulfin Diary, 31 October–1 November 1914, in Jones, *Stemming the Tide*, 234; Sheffield, *The Chief*, 95.

567 **"took a lot of metal"** Jones, *Stemming the Tide*, 238.

567 **one of the 3,642 officer casualties** *OH 1914*, II, 467.

567 **the kaiser dining at Linselles** Crown Prince Rupprecht, October 31, 1914, journal entry, *Mein Kriegstagebuch*, I, 238–239.

568 **"advance in the general direction"** Fritz von Lossberg, *Lossberg's War*, 95.

20. THE KAISER'S BATTLE

569 **"The trenches were very roughly dug"** John F. Lucy, *There's a Devil in the Drum*, 269.

569 **"a pleasant town, busy"** Lucy, *Devil in the Drum*, 268–269.

570 **"Turning points do often originate"** John Lewis Gaddis, *On Grand Strategy*, Penguin Press, New York, 2018, 199.

571 **"It was the Germans whose nerve gave"** John Hussey, "A Hard Day at First Ypres—The Allied Generals and Their Problems: 31st October 1914," 88.

572 **The breakdown must have started** I would refer the interested reader to a pair of outstanding examinations of the problem, Brian N. Hall, "Technological Adaptation in a Global Conflict," *The Journal of Military History* 78, no. 1 (January 2014), 37–71 (especially 37–48); and Gary Sheffield's brief but lucid discussion of communications difficulties in the Great War in *Forgotten Victory*, Review, London, 2002, 120–123.

574 **"like a wood on fire"** Paul Maze, *A Frenchman in Khaki*, 88–89.

575 **"The day was clear"** Pvt. Eric Wilkins, quoted in Mark Lloyd, *The London Scottish in the Great War*, Leo Cooper/Pen & Sword, Barnsley, South Yorkshire, U.K., 2001, 40–41.

575 **"against the bank"** Lloyd, *London Scottish in the Great War*, 39.

575 **"An officer ordered us to cease fire"** *The London Scottish in the Great War*, 42.

575*n* **Ronald Coleman's war** Anthony Spagnoly and Ted Smith, *Salient Points*, 100 (note 5).

576 **"weight of numbers told"** *OH 1914*, II, 350.

577 **a metaphor for massacre** Lloyd, *London Scottish in the Great War*, 43, 45.

577 **the exploit of a Pvt. Johann Zott** Jack Sheldon, *The German Army at Ypres 1914*, 252–253.

578 **"Well, so we are beaten!"** Ferdinand Foch, *The Memoirs of Marshal Foch*, trans. T. Bentley Mott, 162; Ian F. W. Beckett, *Ypres: The First Battle, 1914*, 190.

579 **"We do not ask for so much"** Roy A. Prete, *Strategy and Command: The Anglo-French Coalition on the Western Front, 1914*, 176.

579 **"Today, under the influence"** Prete, *Strategy and Command*, 173.

579 **As for Hamilton** C. E. Callwell, *Field-Marshal Sir Henry Wilson*, I, 186–187; Richard Holmes, *The Little Field Marshal*, 254.

579 **"came close to attaining"** Holmes, *The Little Field Marshal*, 254.

580 **"One always has to remember"** Trevor Royle, *The Kitchener Enigma*, Michael Joseph, London, 1985, 307.

580   losing its importance *OH 1914*, II, 381.

580   "all of the command echelons" Fritz von Lossberg, *Lossberg's War*, 97.

581   a different sort of war Norman Stone, *World War I: A Brief History*, Basic Books, New York, 2009, 57–58.

581   "In the West the armies were too big" Winston S. Churchill, *The Unknown War*, Charles Scribner's Sons, New York, 1931, 76.

581   "an ill-equipped army" C.R.M.F. Cruttwell, *A History of the Great War 1914–1918*, 85.

581   But for all the dispersion of forces Consider that in the opening campaign of August–September 1914 in Galicia, the Austro-Hungarians suffered losses of 400,000 and the Russians, 250,000. That was open warfare. Such huge casualty figures remained fairly constant throughout the war on the eastern front. Norman Stone, *The Eastern Front*, Penguin, New York, 1998, 91.

581   Violent small attacks *OH 1914*, II, 378.

581   in his nightly telegram *OH 1914*, II, 381.

582   "The exodus of inhabitants continues" Lyn MacDonald, *1914*, Attreneum, New York, 1988, 409.

582   "the two of us pale with fright" Sister Marguerite, quoted in Sir Alexander B. W. Kennedy, *Ypres to Verdun*, Country Life / Charles Scribner's Sons, London & New York, 1921, 8.

582   "Today the bombardment" MacDonald, *1914*, 410.

582   "under the falling shrapnel" MacDonald, *1914*, 411.

583   In the early morning of November 6 Général A. Dubois, *Deux Ans de Commandement sur le Front de France*, II, 84–86; Beckett, *The First Battle 1914*, 207.

583   "by an inexplicable panic" Barthelémy-Edmond Palat (Pierre Lehaut-court), *La Grande Guerre sur le Front Occidental*, VIII, *La Ruée vers Calais*, 282.

583   Hardly 1,800 civilians and refugees remained *OH 1914*, II, 386.

583   "The Allied officers who realized" *OH 1914*, II, 409.

584   "could not conceal" Erich von Falkenhayn, *General Headquarters 1914–1916*, 33–34.

584   "the central point" Robert T. Foley, *German Strategy and the Path to Verdun*, Cambridge University Press, Cambridge, 2005, 103.

584   "The barbed wire cannot be crossed" Foley, *German Strategy*, 103; Holger Afflerbach, *Falkenhayn: Politiches Denken und Handlen im Kaiser-reich*, trans. Ernst Rothe, R. Oldenbourg Verlag Muenchen, 1994, 196.

584   "could no longer reckon" Foley, *German Strategy*, 103. A slightly different translation appears in Falkenhayn, *General Headquarters*, 33–34.

585   consumed by his own legend Jean Mabire, *La Bataille de L'Yser; Les Fusiliers Marins à Dixmude*, 255–256.

586   "You see, this isn't difficult" Pierre Ronarc'h, *Souvenirs de la Guerre*, I, trans. Elizabeth Venant, 112.

586   headed for his chauffeured automobile Ronarc'h, *Souvenirs de la Guerre*, I, 114–115; Mabire, *La Bataille de L'Yser*, 271–272.

587   "Certainly . . . the general" Ronarc'h, *Souvenirs de la Guerre*, I, 116.

587   "shrapnel and *marmites*" Charles Le Goffic, *The Epic of Dixmude*, trans. Florence Simmonds, 146–147.

590 **"We showed them no mercy"** Sheldon, *German Army at Ypres 1914,* 220.

590 **"Dixmude has been a hell"** Ronarc'h, *Souvenirs de la Guerre,* 125.

591 **"The Germans have taken the town"** Ronarc'h, *Souvenirs de la Guerre,* 124.

591 **"It would only mean"** Ronarc'h, *Souvenirs de la Guerre,* I, 329.

I want to add a note about the siege of Dixmude, an overlooked, if not completely forgotten, episode of the autumn of 1914, the market town Thermopylae of the Great War. Only two relatively recent accounts exist; one of them is forty years old and only appeared in France. A chapter on Dixmude in Jack Sheldon's *The German Army at Ypres 1914* is the best new telling, and one that at last views the struggle from the German side: pages 216–220 are devoted to the final convulsion of November 10. Jean Mabire's *La Bataille de L'Yser: Les Fusiliers Marines à Dixmude* contains useful information and important leads, but the author's reliance on interpolated dialogue is not only annoying but also rules out his book as a serious historical text. I do, however, owe M. Mabire an enormous debt. One afternoon in the summer of 1981, I came upon his book in a bookstore in Arras and bought it, a lucky accident that made me aware that there had even been a siege of Dixmude. (That same afternoon I also came on a copy of the journals of Louis Barthas, barrel maker, one of the memorable books of the war, which had at that point only appeared in France. Years later I showed it on to my friend and colleague Edward M. Strauss, who translated it, with memorable results. The result was *Poilu,* which Yale University Press published. Some afternoon.)

Two accounts, both published in Paris during 1916, are now more than a century old, but since both depend on eyewitness testimony, they are automatically valuable. Charles Le Goffic's *The Epic of Dixmude* was translated into English and contains information to be found nowhere else. Léon Bocquet and Ernest Hosten's *L'Agonie de Dixmude* provides a useful supplement. Two Marine Fusilier journals, published at the time, are sharply observed and vivid: *Trois étapes de la Brigade des Marins: La Marne, Gond, et Dixmude,* by Jean Pinguet (Perrin et Cie, Paris, 1918) and *De Dixmude à Nieuport,* by Claude Prieur (Perrin et Cie, Paris, 1916). But the most informative book of all is Rear Admiral Pierre Ronarc'h's own account, *Souvenirs de la Guerre* (*Memories of the War*), I, Payot & Cie, Paris, 1921. His book may devote a brief space only to the fall of Dixmude—pages 122–134—but those pages proved to be the backbone of my description of the town's final day. The excerpts from the recollections of the remarkable rear admiral that are scattered through this book were ably translated by Elizabeth Venant.

591 **"speaks of the General Staff Chief"** Robert T. Foley, "East or West? Erich von Falkenhayn and German Strategy, 1914–15," in Matthew Hughes and Matthew Seligmann, eds., *Leadership in Conflict 1914–1918,* Leo Cooper/Pen & Sword, Barnsley, South Yorkshire, U.K., 2000, 119.

591 **The taking of Ypres** Afflerbach, *Falkenhayn,* 195–197.

593 **to be of good physique** Beckett, *The First Battle, 1914,* 206.

593 **"carried within it the seeds"** Sheldon, *German Army at Ypres 1914,* 341.

594   **"about a quarter of the trees"** H. S. Jervis, *The 2nd Munsters in France,* The Naval & Military Press, Uckfield, East Sussex, U.K., 2015, 9–10.

594   **"to goad forward"** Sheldon, *German Army at Ypres 1914,* 342.

595   **"appeared to have been turned over"** Sheldon, *German Army at Ypres 1914,* 344.

596   **"perilously near"** *OH 1914,* II, 423.

596   **"For 20 minutes, Briton and German"** Anthony Farrar-Hockley, *Death of an Army,* 175–176.

597   **"Never dangerous"** *OH 1914,* II, 427.

598   **"The Fusilier Battalion"** *OH 1914,* II, 431. In addition to the inescapable *Official History* account of the struggle for Herenthage and Veldhoek Woods, I have also consulted a number of British regimental histories, including H. C. O'Neill, *The Royal Fusiliers in the Great War* (William Heinemann, London, 1922); James J. Fisher, *A History of the Duke of Wellington's West Riding Regiment*; and C. R. Simpson, *A History of the Lincolnshire Regiment, 1914–1918* (The Medici Society, London, 1931). For the German side of the story, two books are indispensable: Jack Sheldon, *The German Army at Ypres 1914,* 342–348, and Nigel Cave and Jack Sheldon, *Ypres 1914: The Menin Road.*

599   **Black Watch Corner** *OH 1914,* II, 438; A. G. Wauchope, *A History of the Black Watch [Royal Highlanders] in the Great War, 1914–1918,* The Medici Society, London, 1925, 22; Cave and Sheldon, *Menin Road,* 127–128.

600   **"shouted to them to turn"** Beckett, *The First Battle, 1914,* 215.

600   **"did great execution"** Petre, Ewart, and Lowther, *Scots Guards in the Great War,* 54.

600   **around Nonne Bosschen** An excellent compact account of the battle appears in Cave and Sheldon, *Menin Road,* 113–136 (chapter 5).

600   **"As the light improved"** *OH 1914,* II, 435.

601   **forty riflemen of the Black Watch** Wauchope, *History of the Black Watch,* 23.

601   **There is a story many times told** Various versions of this tale, which almost seems like fiction, have appeared over the years, and I am inclined to believe it. To cite some of the books: Beckett, *First Battle, 1914,* 216–217; Cyril Falls, *The First World War,* Pen & Sword Military, Barnsley, South Yorkshire, U.K., 1960, 2014, 62; and a breezily popular account in Tim Carew, *Wipers,* Coronet Books/Hodder and Stoughton, 1974, 185. Even the British *Official History* has a rendition (*OH 1914,* II, 439)— though in a footnote, to be sure. It is also the earliest, and is based on a memoir now in the document collection of the Imperial War Museum in London.

602   **pheasants bolting skyward** *OH 1914,* II, 441 (note 1).

602   **Other British units fighting** *OH 1914,* II, 443. German casualty figures, harder to come by, hint at high losses. See Beckett, *The First Battle, 1914,* 218.

604   **one of the genuine heroes** An excellent and thoroughly researched biographical portrait of FitzClarence can be found in Spencer Jones: "The Demon," in Jones, ed., *Stemming the Tide,* 240–262.

604   **"I must say I did not like it"** J. M. Craster, *"Fifteen Rounds a Minute": The Grenadiers at War,* 151.

605   **"As FitzClarence himself was apparently"** Craster, *"Fifteen Rounds a Minute"* 137–138.

605   **"Suddenly, without warning"** X, "Gheluvelt, 1914: The Man Who Turned the Tide," *Blackwood's Magazine,* Vol. 202 (August 1917), 220–221.

605   **"The first intimation"** X, "Gheluvelt, 1914," 220–221.

606   **All that remains of Charles FitzClarence** The footnote is based on Rose E. B. Coombs, *Before Endeavours Fade,* 29, 40, 46.

21. THE INVENTION OF NO-MAN'S-LAND

607   **"effectively drew to a close"** Nikolas Gardner, *Trial by Fire,* 227.

607   **"We left Flanders"** Fritz von Lossberg, *Lossberg's War,* 103.

608   **"Progress was slow"** Général A. Dubois, *Deux Ans de Commandement sur Le Front de France, 1914–1916,* Book II, 138, my translation.

608   **toss the dead bodies** Louis Barthas, *Poilu: The World War I Notebooks of Corporal Louis Barthas, Barrelmaker, 1914–1918,* trans. Edward M. Strauss, Yale University Press, New Haven & London, 2014, 33.

608   **"Unpardonable"** Jean Bernier, *La Percée,* Agone, Paris, 2014, 39.

609   **"The Ypres offensive had demonstrated"** Robert T. Foley, *German Strategy and the Path to Verdun: Erich von Falkenhayn and the Development of Attrition,* 104.

609   **"to find a diplomatic solution"** Foley, *German Strategy,* 106.

609   **"As long as Russia"** Foley, *German Strategy,* 106.

611   **"Without the defeat of England"** Robert T. Foley, "East or West? Erich von Falkenhayn and German Strategy, 1914–15," in Matthew Hughes and Matthew Seligmann, eds., *Leadership in Conflict 1914–1918,* 121, Herwig, *The First World War,* 116.

611   **"psychological moment"** Foley, *German Strategy,* 107.

611   **"sending Russia an invitation"** Fritz Fischer, *Germany's War Aims in the First World War,* W. W. Norton & Company, New York, 1967, 185–187.

612   **"By 9, the Hall was under fire"** Ian F. W. Beckett, *Ypres: The First Battle, 1914,* 224–225.

613   **"This magnificent old city"** Anonymous (Ernest Dunlop Swinton), *A French communiqué quoted in Eye-Witness Narrative of the War: From the Marne to Neuve Chappelle, September 1914 to March 1915,* Edward Arnold, London, 1915, 14–15.

613   **"German life"** *Ypres, 1914: An Official Account Published by Order of the German General Staff,* trans. G. C. Wynne, 14–15.

613   **"a kind of amputation"** D. C. Watt, quoted in Alan Kramer, *Dynamics of Destruction,* 1–2.

614   **"don't like randomness"** David Diop, *At Night All Blood Is Black,* trans. Anna Moschovakis, Farrar, Straus and Giroux, New York, 2020, 37–38.

614   **deliberate targeting of nonessential buildings** When I asked Nigel Cave and Jack Sheldon for their opinion, Cave relayed an email exchange they had just had about my question, on July 31, 2022. It's a position hard to refute, and I have summarized it above. The target was more the columns marching along streets on either side of the buildings, to and

from the Grande Place, than it was buildings themselves. I might give more weight to the sanctioning of destruction of cultural monuments after the fact, advanced by the Irish historian Alan Kramer.

614 **"We had seen no emptiness like this"** Edith Wharton, *Fighting France*, Charles Scribner's Sons, New York, 1918, 151–154.

615 **89,846 casualties** *OH 1914*, II, 466–467.

615 **"was delayed for many months"** Allan Mallinson, *1914: Fight the Good Fight*, 426.

615 **"intolerably nameless names"** Siegfried Sassoon, "On Passing the Menin Gate."

616 **the French lost a total** The estimates for French losses, while shocking, are probably undercountings. Here I rely on Winston S. Churchill, *The World Crisis* (abridged edition), Appendix I, Table II, "Pertes Des Armées Français" (Charles Scribner's Sons/Macmillan, New York, 1931), and Beckett, *The First Battle, 1914*, 226.

616 **"The Belgian losses"** I have relied on Émile Cammaerts, *Albert of Belgium: Defender of Right*, 200, and on extensive information supplied me in a letter from Major Luc de Vos of the École Royale Militaire in Brussels, in March 1984, when I was researching an article on the inundation of the Yser.

616 **Historians, and some of the best** Hew Strachan, *The First World War*, I, *To Arms*, 278; Dennis E. Showalter, *Instrument of War*, 92; and Max Hastings, *Catastrophe 1914* (Alfred A. Knopf, New York, 2013) all put the total German losses at 80,000.

616 **the German official history** The casualty figures come from the official histories of Great Britain and Germany (Volumes 5 and 6 of *Der Weltkrieg*). Dr. Foley cited them in a talk delivered to the Defence Studies Department of King's College, London on September 24, 2014: "The First Battle of Ypres and the Problem of Counting Casualties." (http:// defenceindepth.co/2014/09/23/the-first-battle-of-ypres-and-problem -of-counting-casualties/) Also see Beckett, *The First Battle, 1914*, and Max Hastings, *Catastrophe 1914*, 495, both of whom go withg the 80,000 figure.

617 **"a completely pointless attack"** Email to the author from Nigel Cave, July 29, 2022.

617 **notoriously sloppy** Phone interview with Professor Dennis E. Showalter, November 10, 1994. See also Robert T. Foley, "The First Battle of Ypres and the Problem of Counting Casualties," a paper delivered before the Defense Studies Department, King's College, London, 3.

618 **"From the German side"** Foley, "Problem of Counting Casualties," 2.

618 **"The old British Army"** *OH 1914*, II, 465.

618 **"For the British"** Foley, "Problem of Counting Casualties," 2.

619 **"In November 1914 the war of stagnation"** Sir Frederick Ponsonby (Baron Sysonby), *The Grenadier Guards in the Great War of 1914–1918*, I, 187.

619 **"pace of felt time"** George Steiner, *In Bluebeard's Castle*, 11.

619 **"brutal deceleration"** Steiner, *In Bluebeard's Castle*, 17.

619 **"Rain, rain, rain"** J. C. Dunn, ed., *The War the Infantry Knew 1914–1919*, 97.

619   **"Suffering heavy casualties in their endeavor"** H. R. Sandilands, *The Fifth in the Great War,* D. W. Grigg and Son, Dover, U.K., 1938, 67.

619   *"All that's left of Bill"* These lines by Lt. Col. A.M.H. Forbes are quoted in the John Buchan, *History of the Royal Scots Fusiliers 1678–1918,* Naval & Military Press/Imperial War Museum, Uckfield, East Sussex, U.K./London, 2015, 311.

619   **"It would be difficult to give an idea"** Général Palat (Pierre Lehaut-court), *La Ruée vers Calais (15 Octobre 13—Decembre 1914), Tome VIII de La Grande Guerre sur le Front Occidental,* 333, translation mine.

620   **"With no vulnerable flank"** Foley, "East or West?" 118–119.

621   **"The transition to trench warfare"** Erich von Falkenhayn, *General Headquarters 1914–1916,* 40.

621   **"cooked it in No Man's Land"** Malcolm Brown and Shirley Seaton, *Christmas Truce: The Western Front December 1914,* Secker & Warburg, London, 1984, 116.

622   **"YOU NO FIGHT"** Stanley Weintraub, *Silent Night: The Story of the World War I Christmas Truce,* The Free Press, New York, 2001, 25.

623   **Was a football match played** Both *Christmas Truce* and *Silent Night* go into the possibility that matches were played. If they were, they were spur-of-the-moment encounters. Some accounts have the Germans scoring winning goals. They were inevitably offsides—of course.

624   **"The trenches were a single line"** John Connell, *Wavell, Scholar and Soldier,* 103.

624   **"We are now rotated out"** Thomas Weber, *Hitler's First War,* 55.

625   **"Messines is a village of"** Weber, *Hitler's First War,* 51.

625   **"When everyone was talking"** Weber, *Hitler's First War,* 63.

625   **"There was no shooting"** Weber, *Hitler's First War,* 61.

626   **"Just after we had finished"** F. Loraine Petre, Wilfred Ewart, and Cecil Lowther, *Scots Guards in the Great War 1914–1918,* 67.

627   **"As soon as the light"** Ole Luk-Oie (E. D. Swinton), short story, "Point of View," in *The Green Curve and Other Stories,* Doubleday, Page & Company, 1914, 243.

627   **"a seed was planted"** Malcolm Brown, "No Man's Land," *MHQ: The Quarterly Journal of Military History* 8, no. 4 (Summer 1996), 33.

628   **"Seamed with dug-outs"** Ernest Dunlop Swinton, *Eye-Witness's Narrative of the War: From the Marne to Neuve Chappelle, September, 1914—March, 1915,* 166–167.

EPILOGUE: NOVEMBER 17–18, 1914, NEAR KLEIN ZILLEBEKE, BELGIUM

632   **"Bored in billets"** Gavin Roynon, "Introduction," in *Massacre of the Innocents: The Crofton Diaries, Ypres 1914–1915,* ed. Gavin Royon, Sutton Publishing, Stroud, Gloucestershire, U.K., 2004, xxi.

632   **"Fitful flashes of our torch"** Roynon, *Massacre of the Innocents,* 19.

632   **"A terrific musketry fire"** Roynon, *Massacre of the Innocents,* 27–29.

633   **"Some were hanging on"** Roynon, *Massacre of the Innocents,* 30.

633   **"We signed on to die"** The speaker was my father, Malcolm Cowley. In 1917, he left college to join the American Field Service. He spent six months in France on the Chemin des Dames front. He returned to the

United States and enlisted in the American Army. He was about to finish training when the war ended. As for the quote, he said those words to me many times: I can give no specific date, although the occasion I especially remember was during a car trip we took to his birthplace, Belsano, PA, in July 1984. Call it a valedictory excursion, a time for summing up. I shall let my father have the last words in this book. He was the person, after all, who started me on my journey to no-man's-land.

INDEX

ABOUT THE AUTHOR

ROBERT COWLEY is an authority on American and European military history whose writing spans the Civil War to World War II. He has held several senior positions in book and magazine publishing and is the founding editor of the award-winning *MHQ: The Quarterly Journal of Military History*. Cowley has also written and edited three collections of essays in counterfactual history known as *What If?* As part of his research he has traveled the entire length of the Western Front, from the North Sea to the Swiss border. He and his wife live in Newport, Rhode Island.

ABOUT THE TYPE

This book was set in Ehrhardt, a typeface based on the original design of Nicholas Kis, a seventeenth-century Hungarian type designer. Ehrhardt was first released in 1937 by the Monotype Corporation of London.